DATE DUE

THE FIRST AMENDMENT

AND

THE FOURTH ESTATE

THE LAW OF MASS MEDIA

By

T. BARTON CARTER

Assistant Professor of Mass Communication
College of Communication
Boston University

MARC A. FRANKLIN

Frederick I. Richman Professor of Law
Stanford University

JAY B. WRIGHT

Professor of Journalism
S.I. Newhouse School of Public Communications
Syracuse University

THIRD EDITION

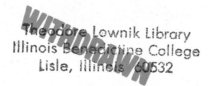
Mineola, New York
THE FOUNDATION PRESS, INC.
1985

COPYRIGHT © 1977, 1981 THE FOUNDATION PRESS, INC.
COPYRIGHT © 1985 By THE FOUNDATION PRESS, INC.
All rights reserved
Printed in the United States of America

Library of Congress Cataloging in Publication Data

ISBN 0–88277–240–6

C., F. & W.First Amend.3rd Ed. FP

For Eleonore, Ruth, and Yolanda

*

*   *   *

Burke said that there were Three Estates in Parliament; but, in the Reporters' Gallery yonder, there sat a *Fourth Estate* more important far than they all. It is not a figure of speech, or witty saying; it is a literal fact,—very momentous to us in these times.

THOMAS CARLYLE in
On Heroes and Hero-Worship (1841)
(Marble edition, 1897, p. 219)

*   *   *

*

PREFACE TO THE THIRD EDITION

The preface to this book's first edition stated its primary purposes to be "to clarify the major legal doctrines that affect mass media, to explain their origins and asserted justifications, and to evaluate their soundness. In these efforts we focus upon the language of the Supreme Court of the United States, whose interpretations of the First Amendment provide the essential starting point."

These goals have remained at the core of subsequent editions. Students are well able to read Supreme Court opinions and they must do so in order to understand the thought processes of the Justices who are making First Amendment law. Future participants in the world of journalism, broadcasting, advertising, or any related field, must know more than the words of the First Amendment, some "rules" developed by the Court, and a few glorious, but out-of-context, quotations from famous cases.

Much has happened in the four years since the publication of the second edition. The Court has continued to address several important media cases each year; the Federal Communications Commission is continuing its efforts toward undoing much of the regulation that has surrounded broadcasting; and the scientific world has continued to develop and improve a variety of technologies that may revolutionize the world and law of communications in coming years.

The basic organization of the second edition has been continued, though with a few important changes. First, the book has been divided into seventeen chapters, replacing the earlier organization that relied upon seven chapters. We believe that this move will make it easier for students to cope with the increasing content of media law.

The most important organizational changes from the second edition include bringing together the several forms of invasion of privacy; joining the problems of concentrated ownership of print and broadcast media; and addressing in one place issues of access to the media that affect both the print and broadcast worlds. These latter changes will allow students to focus more sharply on key differences between the print and broadcast worlds, but will also allow the subject matter to be separated if the instructor wishes to do so.

Chapter XVII on Cable and New Technologies offers students a substantial, but not overpowering, view of the world that is on the horizon if not yet in our homes and offices.

Perhaps the major point to be made about this new edition is that two new co-editors have come aboard. In the first edition, I was joined by my wife, Ruth Franklin, who has had extensive journalism experience. Robert Trager, who was an experienced teacher of, and writer on, media law, assisted on the second edition. The First Amendment and the Fourth Estate has sufficiently established itself in the world of media law education to warrant the step of developing a team of co-editors that will work together to see the book through future revisions.

Barton Carter and Jay Wright bring to this book energy and talent that have served well as we prepared this third edition. We all agree with the philosophy that emphasizes reading the decisions, not only the language, of the Supreme Court. We have had extensive experience teaching earlier editions of this book to graduate students as well as to undergraduates. These shared experiences have played a major part in determining the organizational structure and substantive coverage reflected in this edition.

In some collaborative efforts each editor is identified as being responsible for a particular part of the material. The way this edition has evolved, each editor has taken a major role in reviewing everything that has found its way into print—as well as what has not.

Despite the various changes in this edition, the core of the book has remained true to the goal of earlier editions: "Students read major Supreme Court opinions to learn how judges analyze difficult media law questions, to learn how to be critical of judicial performance, and to be able to understand the basics of the legal process."

MARC A. FRANKLIN

Stanford
March, 1985

ACKNOWLEDGEMENTS

Thanks are due the authors and copyright holders who permitted excerpts from the following works to be included in this book:

American Law Institute. Restatement (Second) of Torts, copyright 1977 by the American Law Institute; reprinted with the permission of the American Law Institute;

Blasi, Vince, "The Newsman's Privilege: An Empirical Study," Michigan Law Review, Vol. 70 (1971);

Godofsky, Stanley, "Protection of the Press from Prior Restraint and Harassment Under Libel Laws," University of Miami Law Review, Vol. 29 (1975);

Henkin, Louis, "The Right to Know and the Duty to Withhold: The Case of the Pentagon Papers," University of Pennsylvania Law Review, Vol. 120 (1971). Reprinted by permission of the publisher and Fred B. Rothman & Company;

Owen, B.M., Beebe, J.H., and Manning, W.G., Jr., Television Economics, Lexington, Mass.: Lexington Books, D.C. Heath and Company, 1974. Reprinted by permission of the publisher;

Paul, Dan, "Why a Shield Law?," University of Miami Law Review, Vol. 29 (1975).

*

SUMMARY OF CONTENTS

SUMMARY OF CONTENTS

APPENDICES

*

TABLE OF CONTENTS

TABLE OF CONTENTS

*

TABLE OF CASES

The principal cases are in italic type. Cases cited or discussed are in roman type. References are to Pages. Cases cited to the United States Supreme Court will be found under both plaintiff and defendant.

---

*

THE FIRST AMENDMENT

AND

THE FOURTH ESTATE

THE LAW OF MASS MEDIA

*

Chapter I

INTRODUCTION: THE AMERICAN
LEGAL SYSTEM

For most communications students, the study of the law of freedom of expression is just one part of a full professional curriculum. While some students in communications schools may decide to go on to law school and then to practice law, the vast majority will be users or consumers of law. It is primarily for the latter that this book is intended. Presumably, an intelligent professional in any aspect of communications should know enough about the law to make some on-the-spot judgments (sometimes under deadline pressure), should know enough to alert a superior when a potential legal problem is spotted, and should know—particularly after reaching management level—when to seek the advice of an attorney. With some experience, the consumer of legal advice learns how to take the attorney's advice. Some attorneys are much more cautious than others, and they will tend to give advice discouraging journalists who are clients from broadcasting or publishing materials that might lead to a law suit; other attorneys, particularly those who represent major media, may be much more daring and may say to a media client, "Publish or broadcast what you need to as journalists. If there's a suit, we'll worry about that then."

Newcomers are sometimes surprised to discover how uncertain the law seems to be. Many questions have never been anticipated by legislators nor been answered by the courts. Sometimes in two similar cases in different parts of the country, different courts have reached opposite conclusions. Bright attorneys disagree when they predict the outcomes of cases. Judges—even the nine justices of the Supreme Court of the United States—frequently disagree with one another and arrive at split decisions based on 5–4 or 6–3 votes. Newcomers to the law may be surprised to find, after they have read the opinion of the majority of the court and agreed with it, that they think they also agree with points made in the dissenting opinion. It should not be quite so surprising that frequently there are good arguments on *both* sides of a dispute that has reached the Supreme Court.

Textbooks like this one give heavy emphasis to opinions of the Supreme Court, because those opinions influence the application of the law in the courts below and they influence out-of-court decisions made on a much less formal basis. It should be recognized, however, that a case that reaches the Supreme Court is an unusual case rather than a typical one. If, for example, we were to examine one thousand instances in which the media had published or broadcast something erroneous about individuals, we would probably find that

1

most of the resulting "disputes" were resolved by the media's re-tracting the erroneous statements or by the unhappy individuals' being advised that they did not have a libel case because they really had suffered no reputational harm as a result of the error, or by the individuals' deciding that they did not have the time, inclination, or money to file a lawsuit. Even if 100 of those disputes resulted in lawsuits, the odds would still favor an out-of-court settlement or a decision by a trial court without getting into the appellate courts. If a single one of those 100 lawsuits reached the Supreme Court it would be surprising.

If Supreme Court cases are so relatively rare, one might ask, why not study the "ordinary" cases instead? The answer, of course, is that the way journalists and attorneys assess their chances of winning or losing a suit, and thereby decide whether to pursue it in court or to settle, is by applying the principles from decisions in the major cases.

In this Chapter we look not just at Supreme Court cases but at a variety of sources of law in America and at the way legal cases proceed.

A. THE SOURCES OF LAW IN AMERICA

Law has always been an important force in American life—and courts have always been at the center of our legal system. All state constitutions created state court systems. The United States Constitution established the Supreme Court of the United States and empowered Congress to create lower federal courts. Many critical national questions have been addressed and resolved in court, from sedition questions after the Revolutionary War to the treatment of blacks after the Civil War, from school desegregation beginning in the 1950's to questions of Presidential behavior in office in the 1970's. Hindsight shows that not all judicial decisions over 200 years have been correct, nor have they all been popular. But the overall respect Americans have for the legal system, even when they may disagree with particular decisions or dislike particular judges, has allowed the country to solve most major problems without violent upheavals.

In general terms, the law is a system of rules of conduct that individuals and institutions are expected to follow, rules given force by a community's decision to punish those who violate them. In the United States, laws and sanctions for disobeying them come from four major sources: Constitutions, statutes, administrative decisions, and the judge-made law called the common law.

Constitutions. Although much of our legal system was borrowed from Great Britain, that country has no written constitution. This important form of law was developed in the United States. Not only is there a federal constitution, but each state has one. These documents decree governmental organization, describe the duties and responsibilities of governmental branches and officials, and frequently specify certain individual rights, such as freedom of expression.

Constitutions are written to allow flexibility as social conditions change. As new questions arise courts must interpret whether the document permits or requires certain conduct. For instance, the First Amendment to the United States Constitution reads in part: "Congress shall make no law . . . abridging the freedom of speech, or of the press . . .." As simple as this seems, our study of mass media law will show the complexity of these words.

Statutes. Another source of law is the array of statutes passed by Congress, state legislatures, and city and county governments. The law we inherited from Great Britain generally served as basic authority in the early days of the United States. After that, statutes adopted by legislative bodies began to be more important than the judicially-developed law. Today, statutes are the dominant form of lawmaking. Much judicial time is spent interpreting these laws and deciding how they apply to specific situations. Statutes are general in scope and prospective in operation.

Today, all criminal laws in this country are statutory. Crimes must be described carefully so that people know precisely what is forbidden. Case law would rarely provide sufficient guidance. Obscenity, copyright, and broadcasting are examples of areas in which statutes affect mass communications law.

Administrative Regulations and Decisions. Today, much law comes from decisions of administrative agencies. These were first developed by Congress as a way of bringing expertise to bear on areas under the legislature's responsibility. The first administrative agency was the Interstate Commerce Commission, but today such agencies are numerous. The Federal Communications Commission, the Federal Trade Commission, and the Copyright Royalty Tribunal, all of which affect mass communications law, are just a few of the federal agencies. Administrative agencies also exist on the state and city levels. Much more law is created by these agencies through their delegated lawmaking powers than by all the courts in the country.

Common Law. The term "common law" is sometimes used to distinguish the Anglo-American legal system from the "civil law" systems of continental Europe. More commonly, the term refers to those areas of law in which no statutes exist and, thus, in which courts are expected to chart their own decisional course without legislative direction. The product of this process, law based on cases alone, is called common law. It is the ever growing result of specific but principled decisions in individual disputes rather than a written body of prospective general rules set down by a legislature.

The common law came from England, where the term first was used to distinguish law made by the King's courts from that made by ecclesiastical courts. But if the law were made by courts, not following a written statute, could not each court—each judge—decide similar cases in different ways? Not only would this cause consternation among citizens who would not know how to act, but judges might totally reconsider whole areas of law as each case arose. The concept of *stare decisis* emerged from these concerns. This is the doctrine of precedent under which judges refer to previous decisions involving basically similar legal issues and facts in order to decide the case at hand. It is then possible to look at previous cases and decisions to see how a court is likely to decide future cases. However, courts are not strictly bound by *stare decisis*. They can "distinguish" a current case from previous cases and refuse to follow the guidance of the past if they find the facts sufficiently different. Or, in an unusual situation, a court can overrule precedents and explicitly embark on a new approach to the legal area. In general, though, judges work within the boundaries of *stare decisis*.

Although the common law was dominant at the time of the Revolution, the increasing complexity of our society and other factors have brought legislation in almost all areas—and a consequent reduction in the role of the common law. It still retains importance for us, however, in the areas of defamation and privacy.

Hierarchy. There is a hierarchy among these four sources of law. Within a state the state constitution is dominant. If a question is not answered in the constitution, an appropriate statute, as interpreted by the courts, will be the final word. But a statute in conflict with the constitution will be struck down by the courts.

Within the spheres of their statutory authority, administrative agency rulings have the force of a statute and will be upheld by courts unless the ruling violates the constitution, the agency has violated its own rules in making the decision, or the ruling is arbitrary and capricious.

When no constitution, statute, or administrative agency ruling controls, courts will apply common law principles to decide a dispute.

Federalism. The hierarchy just discussed applies within a single state. But the federal structure of the United States creates a second hierarchy of legal sources that must be explored. When the United States Constitution was written, most space was devoted to creating the three branches of government—Legislature in Article I, Executive in Article II, and Judiciary in Article III. Those articles dealt only with how the federal government should conduct its internal affairs. In this respect, the federal government's structure resembled that of a state government.

But the nature of federalism required that some attention be paid to the relationship between the existing state governments and the new federal government. This was addressed in Article VI, Section 2, the Supremacy Clause, which provides that

This Constitution, and the Laws of the United States which shall be made in pursuance thereof . . . shall be the supreme Law of the Land; and the Judges in every State shall be bound thereby, any Thing in the Constitution or Laws of any State to the Contrary notwithstanding.

In cases of conflict, then, the Constitution of the United States and statutes properly passed by Congress (and rulings of federal administrative agencies) are superior to conflicting laws adopted by a state. Thus, a ruling of the Federal Communications Commission has a higher place in our legal hierarchy than a conflicting provision of a state constitution.

This aspect of federalism becomes very important because many of our cases involve claims that state laws are invalid because they conflict with some federally protected right. Notice also that state court judges are obligated to declare state laws invalid if they conflict with federal provisions.

Finally, notice how important the courts are at every stage of the legal system. Although courts act only to resolve specific disputes that the parties cannot settle, the judicial power permeates every layer of the two hierarchies. When a constitutional provision is relied upon by one of the parties to the dispute, the court must interpret its meaning and its application to the dispute before it. When one party relies upon a statute, the court may have to interpret it—and may also have to decide whether it is consistent with the state's constitution. When an administrative ruling is involved in the dispute, the court must decide whether the agency acted constitutionally, acted within its statutory authority, followed its own rules, and acted without being arbitrary or capricious. When none of these sources appears to have a bearing on the litigation, the court turns to common-law decisionmaking.

When federalism is involved, state and federal courts are obligated to assure that in cases of conflict proper scope is given to the federal provisions in resolving the case before them.

An Introduction to Litigation

The judicial system must deal with several kinds of controversies. What they all have in common is that one party (a person, group or government) claims its rights or, in the case of government, its laws, are being violated by a second party. The controversies we consider in this book have arisen primarily in three contexts.

One is the criminal case in which a government seeks to punish a party, perhaps a reporter, for illegal behavior. The defense may claim that the legal rule allegedly violated is invalid because it conflicts with the First Amendment. The court must decide whether the statute in question is constitutional.

The second form of litigation also arises from the passage of a statute. Here, however, those restricted by the statute do not wait to be prosecuted for a violation of the statute, but instead initiate a suit to have the statute or regulation declared unconstitutional. The court is asked to render a "declaratory judgment" that it would be unconstitutional for the government to enforce the statute against the complaining parties. Another way to test a statute's constitutionality without risking criminal prosecution is to seek an injunction to prohibit state officials from enforcing the statute—again on the ground that to do so would violate the constitutional rights of the plaintiff.

The third type of case involves "tort" litigation between two private parties for harm that one has caused the other. Examples include auto accidents and injuries caused by defective products. A tort action is usually brought for damages for alleged violation of a common law duty. We shall be concerned mainly with tort actions for damages for defamation and for invasion of privacy. In these cases it is possible for the defendant to argue that if the state court finds the defendant liable and orders it to pay damages to plaintiff, the action of the court would be "state action" that would infringe the defendant's constitutional right to freedom of expression.

Note that all three situations raise the question of whether a government's action, be it legislation or a court order, violates a party's constitutional right to be free from government interference.

We will encounter a fourth type of legal conflict, the administrative proceeding, when we discuss advertising and broadcasting. A party who wishes to acquire a license to broadcast, for example, must apply to the Federal Communications Commission.

Finally, we will also consider "injunctions"—court orders not to do something. Violations of injunctions can lead to one's being held in contempt of court.

The courtroom drama that comes to mind in terms of litigation actually occurs primarily in criminal cases, where facts are disputed: can the victim accurately identify the defendant or is the jury persuaded by the defendant's alibi witnesses? In conventional criminal cases, the parties agree on the legal rules but they disagree about the facts—and a trial is needed to determine the facts governed by these rules.

In most of the cases in this book, and most First Amendment cases generally, the crucial questions that will determine the outcome do not depend on disputed facts. Rather, the parties usually disagree over what legal rule applies to an accepted set of facts. Such a dispute raises legal questions to be resolved by a judge, often with no need for a trial.

The dispute will be brought in one of two court systems—state or federal. Before the United States Constitution was adopted, each state had its own court system—with trial and appellate courts. These systems survived. As a result of the adoption of the United States Constitution, and early action of Congress, a second court system—the federal system—was created.

When one party sues another party in the same state, under state libel law for example, the trial will take place in a state court. When the parties are individuals or corporations in different states, questions beyond our present concerns arise about whether the litigation will take place in a state or federal court. Regardless, the trial will provide the opportunity for the presentation of evidence, including testimony by witnesses. Usually a jury would hear the case, but in some instances the trial judge will decide the case alone.

At the conclusion of the trial, either or both of the parties may believe that errors were made in the trial—either errors in procedure or errors in substantive law. If they choose to appeal to a higher (appellate) court, they will submit a transcript of the trial proceedings and a *brief*, a document explaining the alleged errors to the appellate court. Depending on the system, the appellate court may or may not have to take the case for review; although one is entitled to one's "day in court," one is not necessarily entitled to a "second day."

Depending on the size of the state and the complexity of the state system, state verdicts might be appealed to one or more levels of appellate courts before reaching the highest court in the state— typically, but not always, called the supreme court. In the federal system, decisions from the trial court, called the U.S. District Court, are appealed to the Court of Appeals and then to the Supreme Court of the United States.

The Supreme Court performs two distinct roles. As the final appellate court for litigants who have lost cases in lower federal courts, it is at the apex of the federal system of courts. Second, states and state courts have obligations imposed upon them by the United States Constitution. Some are explicit prohibitions, such as those in Article I, Section 10, that no state may adopt an ex post facto law or coin its own currency. Other limitations are imposed by the Supremacy Clause of Article VI, Section 2, which declares that when federal and state law conflict, the federal law is supreme—and the judges of the state courts are required to recognize that supremacy. The Supreme Court of the United States has the power to review the actions of state courts to assure that states are complying with federal obligations.

Many of the cases we consider have come to the Supreme Court from the state courts. The losing party has usually claimed that the decision of the state courts has incorrectly interpreted the First Amendment—which applies to the states because of the Fourteenth Amendment, as explained shortly. Although state courts may render decisions interpreting the First and Fourteenth Amendments, the

Supreme Court is the *final* authority on the meaning of the United States Constitution.

In the first part of this book, our primary concern is with the First Amendment. If a case poses an important question involving the First Amendment or some other part of the United States Constitution, it can wind up in the Supreme Court whether it starts in the state courts or in the federal courts. Since broadcasting is totally the concern of federal law, the second part of the book stresses federal courts and a federal administrative agency, the Federal Communications Commission.

In most instances the Supreme Court has been given discretion by Congress to choose what cases it will hear, and of the many thousands of cases that are brought each year, the Court accepts only some 200 for hearing and decision. To seek review by the Supreme Court the litigant who lost the case in the lower court files what is called a "petition for certiorari" stating the nature of the dispute, the decision below, and the reasons why the Court should review this case. Since a case usually reaches the Supreme Court only after several lower courts, state or federal, have considered it, it rarely suffices for the petitioner to allege that the judges below made a mistake—a better reason is necessary. A serious claim that a state law violates the First Amendment is such a reason.

After the petition for certiorari is filed, the party who won below will usually file a memorandum trying to persuade the Court either that the case is not important, that there is no conflict with other decisions, or that the decision is clearly correct in light of previous Supreme Court cases. In deciding whether or not to grant a petition for certiorari, all the justices will meet in conference and vote. The Court follows the so-called "rule of four" under which, if four justices believe the case should be heard, the petition for certiorari will be granted.

If the Supreme Court decides not to hear the case, it will usually not state its reasons and will issue an order that says simply "The petition for certiorari is denied." In this book that procedure is indicated when "certiorari denied" is part of the citation. Although this outcome favors the party that won in the lower court, the legal effect is different from having the Supreme Court listen to the case on the merits and decide to affirm the decision of the lower court. When the Supreme Court denies certiorari all that is clear is that the Court did not think the case worthy of full consideration. This does not mean that the Court believes that the case was correctly decided below. It may mean only that the Court does not think the issue is important enough to justify further attention.

When the Supreme Court decides it will listen to a case, it will generally issue an order "granting" the petition for certiorari and directing the parties to file formal briefs arguing the merits of the controversy. The losing party below, the petitioner, prepares a brief, trying to persuade the Court to decide the case on the merits in petitioner's favor. The respondent's brief seeks to persuade the Court to affirm the result reached by the lower court.

The Court will schedule oral arguments at which the attorneys representing both parties have a limited period of time before the justices of the Court to make the best arguments they can for their clients and to answer questions posed by the justices. Because new evidence is not presented at the appellate level, and witnesses are not heard, the parties to the case need not even be present. In a sense, the discussion is about whether errors have been made in the trial court below, and it is not necessary to hear from the witnesses. The witnesses' testimony and other evidence is already reflected in the transcripts of the case filed with the Court, so the oral argument should, as the name suggests, focus on the attempts to persuade the justices as to the outcome of the case.

Following the oral arguments in the case, the justices meet privately to discuss the case and to indicate how they expect to vote. In the Supreme Court, if the Chief Justice is a member of the majority, he may assign the writing of the majority opinion to himself or to any of the other justices in the majority. Similarly, the senior justice among the dissenters may assign the dissenting opinion. When the Chief Justice is dissenting, the senior justice among the majority assigns the majority opinion. Drafts of opinions, written by the justices and their clerks, are circulated privately among the justices. Agreement is reached where possible, but each of the justices reserves the right to publish his own opinion if he chooses. In the Pentagon Papers case, to use a most unusual example, all nine justices wrote opinions.

A single opinion that has the support of a majority of the participating justices is denominated an "opinion of the Court." As such it becomes binding on the Court, establishing a precedent for subsequent decisions (unless later overruled by the Court itself). Sometimes six of the nine justices may vote to affirm a lower court decision, but four will do it for one reason and two will do it for a different reason. In such a case, the opinion written by the four justices is a "plurality" opinion, but not a majority opinion. Such an opinion is entitled to substantially less precedential value than an opinion of the Court. The first line of the reported decision will indicate the nature of the opinion—a named justice either delivers the "opinion of the Court" or announces "the judgment of the Court and an opinion joined by" up to three other justices. The "judgment of the Court" means the bare result, such as affirmance or reversal. The reasons for the judgment are found in the opinions.

B. READING THE LAW

Supreme Court decisions are not, obviously, written for readers who are totally unfamiliar with legal language. Typically, they refer to, or *cite,* earlier cases which you may or may not have read. Not surprisingly, some of the justices are better writers than others. The meaning of some paragraphs may be perfectly clear, but some confuse even the best of lawyers and require subsequent cases to resolve the confusion. Although reading Supreme Court decisions may seem difficult at first, it usually becomes easier as you become more familiar with the language and gradually develop some background in reading the law.

As you read the cases, note the names. When the losing party in the lower court files a petition for certiorari, the petitioner's name comes first in the title of the case. The initial plaintiff thus may later become the *respondent* and be listed second in the title in the Supreme Court. A few other appellate courts follow the practice of putting the losing party's name first. As you read the appellate cases in this book, do not assume that the party named first in the title was the original plaintiff.

On a related point, every title of a case is followed by a group of numbers and abbreviations called a "citation." This tells which volumes in the law library contain the full report of the opinions in the case. For example, the citation to Branzburg v. Hayes, 408 U.S. 665 (1972), means that the case can be found in volume 408 of the United States Reports at page 665, and likewise volume and page for the other systems of court reporting. Current decisions of the United States Court of Appeals are found in the Federal Reporter Second Series (F.2d). Decisions of the United States District Courts are found in the Federal Supplement (F.Supp.). State decisions usually have two citations: one to a state reporter and one to a private service that groups state decisions in regional volumes. Thus, in Barber v. Time, Inc., 348 Mo. 1199, 159 S.W. 291 (1942), the first reference is to volume 348 of the official Missouri reports at page 1199, and the second is to volume 159 of the Southwestern Reporter at page 291, where the Missouri case will also be found.

The foregoing discussion of litigation and the role of the Supreme Court, vital to an understanding of what follows, has necessarily been general and abstract. As we turn to actual cases you should review this information if some aspect of a case puzzles you. Any unusual matters will be discussed in the introduction to the case or in the notes that follow the opinions.

Some of the terms used in the text, particularly the Latin ones, may be unfamiliar to you at first. While there are a variety of legal dictionaries published, some in paperback, you will probably find most of the terms defined in any good collegiate dictionary. As you see them used in the cases, they will become part of your legal vocabulary.

Chapter II

INTRODUCTION TO FREEDOM OF EXPRESSION

A. ANTECEDENTS

1. THE ENGLISH BACKGROUND

In England, repression of ideas antithetical to the government was in operation by the 13th century. In 1275 and again in 1379 Parliament made it criminal to speak against the state. Later known as "seditious libel," words that questioned the crown in any way were punished by the King's Council sitting in the "starred chamber." Ecclesiastical laws forbidding heresy already existed, thus making it dangerous to say anything in opposition to the Church or the state. ⁹

With the advent of printing, around 1500, the government became even more concerned about statements that questioned the secular powers. To prevent the wider dissemination that the printing press made possible, the Crown established a system of censorship, similar to one already used by the Church, for all publications. This repression lasted until almost 1700.

The core of the censorship system was licensing. In the Elizabethan era, the system was overseen by agencies of the Queen. The Stationers Company, established in 1556, gave to a select group of London printers a monopoly over all printing in the country. Its members had the exclusive right to print certain categories of books, such as Bibles and spellers, and could search other printers' offices to look for "illegal" materials. Since all printed matter was to be registered with the Stationers Company, complete prepublication review was possible.

Violators of the licensing system were tried by the infamous Court of the Star Chamber, which became notorious for its secret proceedings and severe punishments. For example, William Prynn's book, Histrio-Mastix, published without permission, said only whores acted in plays. The book appeared six weeks before Queen Elizabeth appeared briefly on stage, but Prynn was convicted of ridiculing the Queen. He was sentenced to a fine and life imprisonment, to be pilloried, and to have his ears docked.

Bonding was also a part of the licensing system, forcing printers not part of the Stationers Company to post a large sum of money, a bond, before being granted a license to print. Publishing anything in opposition to the Church or crown meant forfeiture of the bond.

But an unlicensed publication meant more; it could lead to charges of criminal libel. This crime was divided into four categories: (1) blasphemous libel involved heretical statements opposing the

11

Church; (2) obscene or immoral libel dealt with unpermitted literary subject matter; (3) private libel involved offending words directed to private individuals, which also could lead to civil action (suing the publisher for monetary damages to assuage the harm to the offended person's reputation); (4) seditious libel was criticism of the crown. Frederick Siebert in Freedom of the Press in England 1476–1776 (1952) said that "convictions for seditious libel ran into hundreds" in the 17th and 18th centuries in Great Britain.

In trials for seditious libel, the jury decided whether the defendant had published the material and whether it carried the meaning charged by the government. But judges decided whether the words were published with malice and had a "bad tendency" to damage the government, usually the two crucial points. The defendant could not plead the truth of the words as a defense; indeed, truth made the offense more severe, since truthful charges would increase the public's disrespect for the crown.

This approach to criminal libel persisted even after the licensing system disappeared in 1695, making it still unsafe to criticize the government or the Church.

Until 1688, even members of Parliament were occasionally imprisoned for discussing forbidden subjects. Parliament had long struggled with the King to assure freedom of speech for its Speaker, and this was gradually extended to all members. The privilege to initiate discussion on any subject was recognized in 1649, and later the House of Lords declared that seditious words uttered in Parliament could not be punished in court. Full freedom of speech and debate, including the right to criticize the crown, had been assured in Parliament well before the American Revolution. See F. Siebert, Freedom of the Press in England 1476–1776, 100–02, 112–16 (1952).

In addition to criminal prosecutions for libel, the English government found taxation to be an effective way to control the press. The purpose of the Stamp Act of 1711 and later laws was to reduce the circulation of newspapers. This was done by forcing publishers to raise their sale price to cover the cost of the tax, which applied not only to newspapers, but to advertisements, pamphlets, and paper as well. Initially, it was effective, with half the country's newspapers going out of business in the first year of the Act. But loopholes in the law soon were found, and supporters of the government, who felt compelled not to evade the tax, became the ones most seriously hurt.

It was possible for Great Britain to have the Stamp Act, licensing, the Star Chamber, and bonding and still contend that freedom of the press existed. Sir William Blackstone, the most famous compiler of the common law, wrote in the late 1760's:

> [w]here blasphemous, immoral, treasonable, schismatical, seditious, or scandalous libels are punished by the English law . . . the liberty of the press, properly understood, is by no means infringed or violated. The liberty of the press is indeed essential

to the nature of a free state; but this consists in laying no previous restraints upon publications, and not in freedom from censure for criminal matter when published. Every freeman has an undoubted right to lay what sentiments he pleases before the public: to forbid this is to destroy the freedom of the press: but if he publishes what is improper, mischievous, or illegal, he must take the consequences of his own temerity . . . . [T]o punish (as the law does at present) any dangerous or offensive writings . . . is necessary for the preservation of peace and good order, of government and religion, the only solid foundations of civil liberty. Thus the will of individuals is still left free; the abuse only of that free-will is the object of legal punishment. Neither is any restraint hereby laid upon freedom of thought or enquiry: liberty of private sentiment is still left; the disseminating, or making public, of bad sentiments, destructive of the ends of society, is the crime which society corrects.

W. Blackstone, 4 Commentaries on the Laws of England 151–52 (1765–69).

Blackstone is central to this analysis because he was a major influence on English and American legal thinking in the period when our Constitution was taking shape. His definition of freedom of the press as the absence of "previous restraints upon publications," and the distinction between liberty thus defined, and licentiousness, for which punishment was considered legitimate, made clear that freedom of expression meant, as a minimum, rejection of prior restraint; uncertainty remains as to the legitimacy of subsequent punishment for seditious libel, and as to what types of expression constitute punishable "licentiousness."

2. THE COLONIAL EXPERIENCE

Those who drafted and adopted the United States Constitution and the Bill of Rights were well aware of this background of repression in Great Britain. They also knew of, and had experienced, similar restrictions on freedom of expression imposed by Britain on the colonies.

The first laws passed by Parliament levying taxes on newspapers applied only to British newspapers and were intended to be repressive. According to C. Miller in The Supreme Court and the Uses of History 76–79 (1969), the Stamp Act of 1765 was directed specifically against the colonies and was meant to offset "the expense of defending, protecting and securing" the colonies, including the high cost of conducting the Seven Years' War just ended. In fact, the Act served more to anger colonists than to raise revenue. Many communities did not have the stamps, which were supposed to be affixed to every copy of a newspaper distributed, and many printers in other communities simply ignored the law. But the colonists saw the Act as "taxation without representation" and rebelled against it.

Prior to that, however, laws that applied to the press in England during the 17th and 18th centuries were also applied to the emerging colonial press, and the licensing of presses in the colonies closely paralleled the English practice. The colonies saw printers jailed and their books burned for publishing without permission. In 1662, Massachusetts appointed censors. When Benjamin Harris printed the first edition of *Publick Occurrences* in 1690, it became the last edition of that newspaper; he had not gained prior approval. The colonies' second newspaper, the *Boston News-Letter*, published by John Campbell beginning in 1704, clearly informed its readers that it was printed with authority.

After Parliament abolished licensing at the end of the 17th century, the colonial governors managed to retain it for several years more. Its decline in the colonies began in the early 1720's when James Franklin, Ben's brother, ignored an order to have his *New England Courant* licensed. He was briefly punished and once substituted his brother's name as publisher, but his refusal to obey the order brought licensing to a halt. In both England and the colonies, however, after the end of licensing, there was still the threat of punishment after the fact for matters the authorities deemed licentious. Contempt of the legislative branch was a real risk and prosecutions for seditious libel occurred.

In 1721, the colonies first discovered the ardent views of "Cato" on Freedom of Speech in Benjamin Franklin's *Pennsylvania Gazette*. Cato was the pseudonym of two Whig journalists whose essays in London newspapers became very popular and were widely reprinted in the colonies. Cato described free speech as "the Right of every Man, as far as by it he does not hurt or control the Right of another; And this is the only Check which it ought to suffer, the only Bounds it ought to know." Free speech and free government thrived together, or they failed together: "in those wretched Countries where a Man cannot call his Tongue his own he can scarce call any Thing else his own," and "Freedom of Speech is ever the Symptom as well as the Effect of good Government." In Reflections upon Libelling, Cato favored the fullest freedom of expression but conceded that extreme libels might be punished, if they were false. These essays are reprinted in L. Levy, Freedom of the Press from Zenger to Jefferson 10–24 (1966).

These letters also appeared in another journal that criticized the administration. In addition to reprinting Cato's letters, the *New York Weekly Journal* published several anonymous essays that echoed these sentiments: ". . . Liberty of the Press . . . is a Curb, a Bridle, a Terror, a Shame, and Restraint to evil Ministers; and it may be the only Punishment, especially for a Time. But when did Calumnies and Lyes ever destroy the Character of one good Minister? . . . Truth will always prevail over Falsehood." Levy, supra, at 29.

In 1734, John Peter Zenger, who printed the *Weekly Journal,* was charged with seditious libel by the Governor General of New York, whom Zenger had criticized. Since the grand jury refused to indict, the prosecution was begun by the filing of an information—an accusation of a crime made by a public officer rather than by an indictment by a grand jury. Zenger, unable to post the high bail imposed, spent almost a year in jail awaiting trial. By the traditional common law standards he was surely guilty because he had published the articles in question and the law did not recognize truth as a defense. Since 1670, the judge no longer had the power to coerce juries into following his instructions by imprisonment or by levying fines to ensure compliance. Jurors who decided cases "against the manifest evidence" could not be punished. This gave jurors the power to nullify disliked legal rules by refusing to follow the judge's instructions. Zenger's lawyer, Andrew Hamilton, convinced the jury that the only question in the case involved the liberty to write the truth and the jury, despite the judge's instructions, acquitted Zenger. Although the verdict set no precedent (because a jury verdict is not a legal ruling), it did signal a change in the political climate.

In the years preceding the Revolutionary War, freedom of expression faced another challenge—not from the government, but from rival political factions. Patriot newspapers were staunch supporters of separation from England. The Patriots argued that freedom of the press was a natural, God-given right, and they exercised it vigorously during the Partisan Press period. But they would not extend the same right to Tory newspapers, published by those who opposed revolution and separation. Tories were threatened with violence and destruction of their printing equipment by mobs who wanted only the Patriot side to be heard.

American journalism underwent changes after the Revolutionary War. Many Colonial newspapers stopped publishing, but a number of new papers were started. During the period before and after the Revolution, papers could be started with ease, though not all were able to survive financially. More than 60 new papers were started in the mid-1780's, and by the 1790's about 450 newspapers were begun. Pre-war papers were adjuncts of print shops, being amalgams of information the printer came by, including vitriolic pro- or anti-English diatribes. Since little new equipment was necessary, it was relatively simple for a print shop owner to publish a newspaper. After the war, newspapers were arms of political parties rather than products of printers. They were run by editors who would slant the contents as they wished. This was one feature that remained from the pre-war period—partisanship in the press. But instead of being Patriot versus Tory, it became Federalist versus Republican.

The two major political parties had a number of supportive newspapers, but each also had a flagship. Federalists established the *Gazette of the United States* in New York City as their leading political organ, the first issue being published in 1789 and edited by John Fenno. Two years later, after the split between Hamilton and Jefferson, the Republicans established the *National Gazette* in Philadelphia under editor Philip Freneau. Freneau was passionately partisan, hitting hard at Federalists, frequently through satire, and widening the Hamilton-Jefferson schism. See F. Mott, *American Journalism* 113–14, 122–26 (3d ed. 1962).

After the successful American revolution the governments of the former colonies sought to come together to form a nation. Their internal structures were similar, reflecting common antecedents, but no overarching government controlled relations among these new political entities. Even before the war was ended the colonies had attempted to form a national government under the Articles of Confederation, devised in 1783. This document allowed the states to retain much power, leaving little for the central government. The Articles contained no mention of freedom of expression or conscience, but many argued such a clause was not necessary. Since the federal government had no power to interfere with citizens, there was no need to forbid it from exercising power it did not have. Additionally, most states had some form of a bill of rights in their state constitutions.

It soon became clear that a stronger national union was needed. A central government could provide security against foreign attack and could ease the movement of goods and persons among the former colonies. The new Constitution, formulated at the Constitutional Convention of 1787, created the national government with three branches.

Except for such incidental provisions as the prohibitions on ex post facto laws contained in Article I, Sections 9 and 10, little attention was given to protecting individual citizens against government. Some states in their own constitutions had protected citizens against state government action, but the federal Constitution was not primarily concerned with that problem. This omission led some critics to oppose ratification because the new government might itself threaten the freedom of citizens of the new country.

While the records of the Constitutional Convention are sketchy, it is known that discussion of a bill of rights did not take place until the last few days of the meeting. That short-lived debate was inconclusive. The Constitution was promulgated without a bill of rights and sent to the states for ratification.

During ratification debates, according to historian Leonard Levy, "[m]any of the principal advocates of a Bill of Rights had only a nebulous idea of what it ought to contain. Freedom of the press was everywhere a grand topic for declamation, but the insistent demand for its protection on parchment was not accompanied by a reasoned analysis of what it meant, how far it extended, and under what circumstances it might be limited. . . . Nor do the newspapers, pamphlets, or debates of the state ratifying conventions offer illumination." See L. Levy, Legacy of Suppression: Freedom of Speech and Press in Early American History (1960).

Even though 13 states ratified the Constitution, five expressed concern that a bill of rights had been omitted.

As a result of this dissatisfaction, James Madison introduced a set of amendments to the Constitution when the First Congress met. The House of Representatives approved an amendment that protected freedom of speech and press from infringement "by any state." The Senate struck the provision limiting the powers of the states and the final version provided that "Congress shall make no law . . . abridging the freedom of speech, or of the press. . . . " This was the third of 12 amendments submitted to the states for ratification. When the first two failed, this became the First Amendment to the United States Constitution.

Although it was later argued that the Bill of Rights was intended to protect citizens against invasions by the state as well as the federal government, this was rejected in Barron v. Baltimore, 7 Peters (32 U.S.) 243 (1833) when the Supreme Court decided that the Bill of Rights applied solely against the federal government. Constraints on the states were those specified in Article I, Section 10 and in such other provisions as the Supremacy Clause. It was only after the Civil War, when states were placed under the additional restraints of the Thirteenth, Fourteenth, and Fifteenth Amendments, that they came under a federal requirement to accord freedom of speech and press. As a result, what Congress may not do because of the First Amendment, a state may not do because of the Fourteenth Amendment. This development is discussed at p. 33, infra. The Constitution restrains only governments, not private individuals, from interfering with the exercise of freedom of expression.

According to Levy (at p. 236):

> No one can say for certain what the Framers had in mind. . . . It is not even certain that the Framers themselves knew what they had in mind; that is, at the time of the drafting and ratification of the First Amendment, few among them if any at all clearly understood what they meant by the free speech-and-press clause, and it is perhaps doubtful that those few agreed except in a generalized way and equally doubtful that they represented a consensus. . . .

In Free Speech in the United States (1941), Prof. Chafee, acknowledging that very little was said about the meaning of freedom of speech, reviewed some contemporary statements that suggest that in the years before the First Amendment "freedom of speech was conceived as giving a wide and genuine protection for all sorts of discussion of public matters." He argued that "such a widely recognized right must mean something," and that merely reaffirming the freedom of the press from previous censorship would have been pointless. During the 18th century, besides the narrow legal meaning of liberty of the press, there existed "a definite popular meaning: the right of unrestricted discussion of public affairs," and Chafee thought the framers were aware of basic differences between Great Britain and the former colonies.*

B. BASES FOR FREEDOM OF COMMUNICATION

Although Leonard Levy, in his Legacy of Suppression (1960), contended that no clear understanding lay behind adoption of the First Amendment, a number of latter-day reasons have emerged to support freedom of expression. These may be seen as important to individuals and to society, and to a new conception of the purpose of the mass media.

1. FOR INDIVIDUALS

A concept of "natural law" was actively discussed for two centuries before the Constitution was adopted. In attempting to reconcile government's role with individual rights, certain personal freedoms were seen as inviolable. They were "natural rights" of individuals, rights that official persons or bodies had no power to affect. Among these rights was freedom of expression.

This concept derived in large part from the 17th century English philosopher John Locke, who contended that government's purpose was to use its power to protect life, liberty, and property, natural rights to which each individual was entitled. Locke's views influenced the language of the First Amendment with the notion of free speech as a natural right, and the Fifth Amendment ("No person shall . . . be deprived of life, liberty, or property, without due process of law. . . .").

Locke discussed the origin of society in terms of a social contract. He believed the pre-social status was one of freedom. Private property was recognized, but no security existed. To achieve security, people surrendered a certain amount of freedom to establish a government. But the government rested on the consent of the governed, who would control the government rather than vice versa. A government that encroached on an individual's rights should be abolished or changed.

Several commentators believe that even with this Lockean philosophy to draw on, the framers had no clear concept of the First

---

* One aspect of freedom of expression that was retained was the complete parliamentary privilege for legislators. The scope of the legislator's free expression is found in Article I, Section 6 of the United States Constitution, providing that "for any Speech or Debate in either House, [Senators and Representatives] shall not be questioned in any other Place." This has been taken to mean that such speech may not form the basis for criminal or civil liability. A comparable provision is contained in virtually every state constitution to protect members of the state legislatures. These are collected in Tenney v. Brandhove, 341 U.S. 367 n. 5 (1951).

Amendment's purpose.   Recall Levy's statement that during the ratification controversy "[m]any of the principal advocates of a Bill of Rights had only a nebulous idea of what it ought to contain." Professor Lillian BeVier, however, in The First Amendment and Political Speech: An Inquiry into the Substance and Limits of Principle, 30 Stan.L.Rev. 299, 307 (1978), suggested this may have been deliberate:

> If history suggests that the framers had no specific meaning in mind . . . it also permits the conclusion that no particular meanings were deliberately foreclosed, except perhaps a meaning that would permit prior licensing restraints.   Thus, the framers may have intended the very vagueness of the text [of the First Amendment] to delegate to future generations the task of evolving a precise meaning.

No matter what the framers might have had in mind, however, they could not have foreseen the many changes in media technology and society generally.   Thus, more expansive views of freedom of communication became necessary.

Professor Thomas I. Emerson, in The System of Freedom of Expression 6–9 (1970), asserted that "the system of freedom of expression in a democratic society" is based on four premises:

> (1) freedom of expression facilitates self-fulfillment,

> (2) it is an essential tool for advancing knowledge and discovering truth,

> (3) it is a way to achieve a more stable and adaptable community, and

> (4) it permits individuals to be involved in the democratic decision-making process.

Perhaps the most powerful judicial statement of the justifications for free expression is that of Justice Brandeis, concurring, in Whitney v. California, 274 U.S. 357, 375–77 (1927):

> Those who won our independence believed that the final end of the State was to make men free to develop their faculties; and that in its government the deliberative forces should prevail over the arbitrary.   They valued liberty both as an end and as a means.   They believed liberty to be the secret of happiness and courage to be the secret of liberty.   They believed that freedom to think as you will and speak as you think are means indispensable to the discovery and spread of political truth; that without free speech and assembly discussion would be futile; that with them, discussion affords ordinarily adequate protection against the dissemination of noxious doctrine; that the greatest menace to freedom is an inert people; that public discussion is a political duty; and that this should be a fundamental principle of the American government.   They recognized the risks to which all human institutions are subject.   But they knew that order cannot

be secured merely through fear of punishment for its infraction; that it is hazardous to discourage thought, hope and imagination; that fear breeds repression; that repression breeds hate; that hate menaces stable government; that the path of safety lies in the opportunity to discuss freely supposed grievances and proposed remedies; and that the fitting remedy for evil counsels is good ones. Believing in the power of reason as applied through public discussion, they eschewed silence coerced by law—the argument of force in its worst form. Recognizing the occasional tyrannies of governing majorities, they amended the Constitution so that free speech and assembly should be guaranteed.

Each of these explanations has been used, to a greater or lesser extent, by the Supreme Court to justify the high value placed on freedom of speech in our constitutional scheme of government. Each may justify different notions of the breadth and depth of the First Amendment freedom and each may apply with peculiar force in particular contexts.

These fundamental justifications for protecting speech tend to divide into two main groups: those that stress the values to the individual and those that stress the values to the society of freedom of speech. The emphasis on the individual, contained in what are variously called the self-fulfillment or self-realization models, is on the importance of expression as a route to individual development and fulfillment.

Large press organizations have little basis for asserting that their expressive activities contribute to their own self-fulfillment. Smaller press operations can more plausibly assert such a claim to the extent that they are the "alter-egos" of an individual publisher or editor.

The notion of self-fulfillment involves an individual's attempt to fully achieve his or her potential. Restrictions on beliefs or forms of expression inhibit this process and are "an affront to the dignity" of an individual, said Emerson. Without the individual's freedom to search for truth and to discuss questions of right or wrong, society becomes a "despotic" commander and places a person in "the arbitrary control of others." Also, a person has a right to be involved in the decisions that affect that person.

Emerson asserted that the individual's right to freedom of expression is independent of society's needs. That is, free communication may or may not enhance society's goals. Regardless, it is "a good in itself"—almost a natural right. Society's objectives must be achieved through other methods, such as counter-expression and "the regulation of conduct which is not expression."

Recall that the first point in Justice Brandeis's statement asserted the "final end of the State was to make men free to develop their faculties." In addition, from a less lofty side, it may be argued that the "safety valve" argument that both Emerson and Brandeis identify plays a role in the self-fulfillment side in the sense that "blowing off steam"—even if no other person receives the message—may help individuals to develop their potentials most fully.

The line between speech and conduct is crucially important to theorists who rely on self-fulfillment as the basis of the First Amendment, for without such a line the rationale spreads so far as to become unworkable. After all, virtually everything we do arguably contributes to our self-fulfillment. Yet no one argues that the First Amendment protects those who seek self-fulfillment by traveling at 80 miles per hour on the freeways or, more graphically, by committing murder or arson. Unfortunately, the speech-conduct line, though crucial, has proven difficult to maintain. Several theorists ask: if self-fulfillment is the rationale, what makes speech peculiarly self-fulfilling in contradistinction to all the other ways one may seek to realize that goal?

Despite these theoretical difficulties, the self-fulfillment rationale remains a powerful theme in First Amendment doctrine. Many continue to believe that there is something special about speech that justifies more protection than what we would accord to conduct. Indeed, some recent theorists have built their First Amendment analyses entirely from a focus on the individual. In some cases, the social goals are viewed as sub-values that may derive from the achievement of the primary goal of individual self-fulfillment. See the discussions in Baker, Scope of First Amendment Freedom of Speech, 25 UCLA L.Rev. 964 (1978) and Redish, The Value of Free Speech, 130 U.Pa.L.Rev. 591 (1982). Their approach is challenged in Schauer, Must Speech Be Special?, 78 Nw.U.L.Rev. 1284 (1983), with both Baker and Redish responding in comments after that article.

2. FOR SOCIETY

Just as the self-fulfillment justification is necessarily tied to individuals, the other reasons offered for protection are society-centered. Neither disputing nor relying upon the assertion that we as individuals profit from freedom of speech, these bases explain why we as a people are the better for the First Amendment freedoms. Here, categorizing the speaker as "press" or "individual" may be irrelevant. Under the social justifications, the important matter may be the role of the audience rather than the speaker. We turn now to further considerations of each social justification.

---

a. *Marketplace of Ideas*

The seminal view that freedom of expression enhances the social good came from John Milton's Areopagitica in 1644. Milton, an English poet and essayist, wanted a divorce and wrote an essay he hoped would lower the strict legal barriers prohibiting it. He was chastized for publishing without a license, and wrote Areopagitica to induce Parliament to allow unlicensed printing. Milton argued that licensing was unworkable and an affront to those who had views to express. But more, he said, it was harmful to society, since people are better able to function as citizens if they are knowledgeable and exposed to different points of view. Attempting to assuage official fears that the Crown's views would be overwhelmed if unlicensed printing were allowed, Milton wrote: "And though all the winds of doctrine were let loose to play upon the earth, so Truth be in the field, we do injuriously by licensing and prohibiting to misdoubt her strength. Let her and Falsehood grapple; who ever knew Truth put to the worse, in a free and open encounter?"

Milton, however, was not ready to give freedom of expression to everyone on every subject. As a Puritan, he would not allow free discussion of Catholicism or atheism. In the context of his time, though, Milton's view was a major shift away from the stringent censorship that prevailed.

Perhaps Milton's most enduring contribution to the philosophy of freedom of expression was his statement that unrestricted debate would lead to the discovery of truth. Writing in England some 50 years later, John Locke retained some of this faith that truth would prevail. In "A Letter Concerning Toleration" (1689), he wrote:

> [T]ruth certainly would do well enough if she were once left to shift for herself. She seldom has received, and I fear never will receive, much assistance from the power of great men, to whom she is but rarely known and more rarely welcome. She is not taught by laws, nor has she any need of force to procure her entrance into the minds of men. Errors indeed prevail by the assistance of foreign and borrowed succors. But if truth makes not her way into the understanding by her own light, she will be but the weaker for any borrowed force violence can add to her.

Locke's regard for freedom of expression arose out of a skepticism about the state or any individual as a source of guidance in seeking truth, and he shared Milton's view that governmental restrictions on freedom of inquiry would increase the likelihood of error. He condemned those "places where care is taken to propagate the truth without knowledge." Like Milton, Locke opposed prior restraints, and in 1694, he joined the opposition that finally obtained the abolition of the Licensing Order. Yet also like Milton, Locke did not question the common law punishment for expression after publication, and advocated the suppression of "opinions contrary to human society or to those moral rules which are necessary to the preservation of civil society."

By 1776 the pendulum had swung still further away from government restriction of expression, on both sides of the Atlantic. In England, Jeremy Bentham in his "Fragment on Government" was waging war against Blackstone. He wrote that one of the differences between a free and a despotic government was "the security with which malcontents may communicate their sentiments, concert their plans, and practise every mode of opposition short of actual revolt, before the executive power can be legally justified in disturbing them."

English philosopher and economist John Stuart Mill, who wrote 200 years after Milton, believed more in full and free discussion than did Milton. Mill thought that society could function well only with such freedom. He saw freedom of thought, discussion, and investigation as "goods in their own right" but, more importantly, society benefits from an exchange of ideas. People could trade their false notions for true ones, but only if they could hear the true ones. Such open discussion would necessarily mean that false as well as true ideas would be expressed.

Mill, in On Liberty, contended that government could not "prescribe opinions" or "determine what doctrines or what arguments" people should hear. Not even if the government and the populace were at one on an issue should coercion regarding freedom of expression be allowed:

> The power itself is illegitimate. The best government has no more title to it than the worst. It is as noxious, or more noxious, when exerted in accordance with public opinion, than when in opposition to it. If all mankind minus one were of one opinion, and only one person were of the contrary opinion, mankind would be no more justified in silencing that one person, than he, if he had the power, would be justified in silencing mankind. . . . [T]he peculiar evil of silencing the expression of an opinion is, that it is robbing the human race: posterity as well as the existing generation; those who dissent from the opinion, still more than those who hold it. If the opinion is right, they are deprived of the opportunity of exchanging error for truth; if wrong, they lose, what is almost as great a benefit, the clearer perception and livelier impression of truth, produced by its collision with error.
>
>   . . .
>
> [T]he dictum that truth always triumphs over persecution is one of those pleasant falsehoods which men repeat after one another till they pass into common-places, but which all experience refutes. History teems with instances of truth put down by persecution. If not suppressed forever, it may be thrown back for centuries. . . . It is a piece of idle sentimentality that truth, merely as truth, has any inherent power denied to error of prevailing against the dungeon and the stake.

The concept of the marketplace of ideas, first enunciated by Milton and later developed by Mill, was recognized in American law by Justice Oliver Wendell Holmes. In Abrams v. United States, 250 U.S. 616 (1919), Abrams and others were accused of publishing pamphlets that criticized President Wilson's sending of troops to help counter the Russian revolution. The pamphlets also advocated a strike against munitions plants. A majority of the Supreme Court ruled that publishing such pamphlets during war time was not protected by the First Amendment. In dissent, Justice Holmes, joined by Justice Louis Brandeis, argued that the pamphlets did not attack the form of the United States government, and thus did not violate the sedition statute as charged. More generally, Holmes wrote:

> Persecution for the expression of opinions seems to me perfectly logical. If you have no doubt of your premises or your power and want a certain result with all your heart you naturally express your wishes in law and sweep away all opposition. To allow opposition by speech seems to indicate that you think the speech impotent, as when a man says that he has squared the circle, or that you do not care whole-heartedly for the result, or that you doubt either your power or your premises. But when men have realized that time has upset many fighting faiths, they may come to believe even more than they believe the very foundations of their own conduct that the ultimate good desired is better reached by free trade in ideas—that the best test of truth is the power of the thought to get itself accepted in the competition of the market, and that truth is the only ground upon which their wishes safely can be carried out. That at any rate is the theory of our Constitution. It is an experiment, as all life is an experiment.

A similar sentiment was voiced by Judge Learned Hand in an antitrust case in which the government was attempting to stop restrictive practices of the Associated Press. He observed that one of the most "vital of all general interests" was "the dissemination of news from as many different sources, and with as many different facets and colors as is possible. That interest is closely akin to, if indeed it is not the same as, the interest protected by the First Amendment; it presupposes that right conclusions are more likely to be gathered out of a multitude of tongues, than through any kind of authoritative selection. To many this is, and always will be, folly; but we have staked upon it our all." United States v. Associated Press, 52 F.Supp. 362 (S.D.N.Y.1943), affirmed 326 U.S. 1 (1944).

The marketplace of ideas approach has been criticized from several sides. In a Marxist attack, American philosopher Herbert Marcuse disagrees with the basic premise of the marketplace notion, that rational beings engage in a free interchange of opinions and information. People are not rational because government and mass media manipulate them—each for its own purposes, he says. In an essay entitled "Repressive Tolerance" in A Critique of Pure Tolerance (1965), he starts from the premise that "the people must be capable of deliberating and choosing on the basis of knowledge." He is appalled by the blandness of the newspaper layout that intermingles advertisements and disasters and trivia, and the broadcaster's reporting of the momentous and the mundane in the same monotone: "It offends against humanity and truth by being calm where one should be enraged, by refraining from accusation where accusation is in the facts themselves." More than that, "in endlessly dragging debates over the media, the stupid opinion is treated with the same respect as the intelligent one, the misinformed may talk as long as the informed and propaganda rides along with education, truth with falsehood."

The "concentration of economic and political power" allows "effective dissent" to be blocked where it could freely emerge, and the "monopolistic media" prejudice "right and wrong, true and false . . . wherever they affect the vital interests of the society." The situation is so dangerous that Marcuse recommends "suspension of the right of free speech and free assembly" so, that "spurious objectivity" is replaced by "intolerance against movements from the Right, and toleration of movements from the Left."

In effect, Marcuse is advocating the silencing of certain views in order to achieve true freedom, a view that has been heard, in various forms, since Plato's Republic: "[T]he only poetry that should be allowed in a state is hymns to the gods and paeans in praise of good men; once you go beyond that and admit the sweet lyric or epic muse, pleasure and pain become your rulers instead of law and the rational principles commonly accepted as best."

Another group adopted a quite different approach. In the mid-1940's the Commission on Freedom of the Press was organized to study the press in America. Funded primarily by Time, Inc., and Encyclopedia Britannica, Inc., and chaired by Robert M. Hutchins, the Commission was composed of philosophers, historians, law professors, and others. No media professionals were included on the panel, but some were called to share their views with Commission members. The Commission found that press freedom was not seriously threatened in mid-20th century America. The press had, however, despite the enforcement of antitrust laws, become increasingly concentrated in the hands of fewer individuals. Media owners, in fact, were reasonably free from government interference, but the First Amendment had little direct application to most people.

The Commission argued that publishers and broadcasters should be more socially responsible, treating each media outlet not as a personal soapbox, but as a means of disseminating a wide range of viewpoints. It suggested that the government finance new communications outlets and that an independent government agency oversee the press's performance in A Free and Responsible Press (1947). Such recommendations were not well received by the press, which attacked the ideas in editorials and opinion columns.

The Commission, then, encouraged altering the existing marketplace of ideas into a subsidized and more regulated one in which a number of views could be disseminated through the limited number of outlets that concentration of media ownership had caused. This social responsibility approach is explored in Siebert, et al., Four Theories of the Press (1956).

Philosopher and Professor William Ernest Hocking, a member of the Commission, expanded on the group's work. He noted that protecting the press when it is composed of many units protects the consumer, who will have access to a wide range of offerings. But when the number of sources shrinks, the consumer is left defenseless under traditional views of the First Amendment.

Hocking believed the public had a "right" as well as a need to have its news. Particularly since "the citizen's *political* duty is at stake, the right to have an adequate service of news becomes a *public responsibility* as well." The press thus becomes "clothed with a public interest" and must therefore be "adequate"—a term Hocking acknowledged to be "an indefinite standard." Adequacy, however, does imply giving the public a breadth of news coverage and viewpoints. To accomplish this, Hocking suggested comparing the press to privately owned public utilities or to private schools, which must meet certain government-established standards. Although government should not intrude on press activities, it should "regulate the conditions under which those activities take place, so that the public interest is better served." He defined this to mean the "best service to the most people," to be accomplished by a "continuous survey of press performance" by an independent agency, with the government supplementing the private press by issuing information on its own. W. Hocking, Freedom of the Press 161–90 (1947).

Another Commission member, Professor Zechariah Chafee, Jr., stated that the press could not play its proper part in society in the "mere absence of governmental restrictions." Rather, "affirmative action by the government or others" would be needed. Chafee started with Justice Holmes's formulation, "The best test of truth is the power of the thought to get itself accepted in the competition of the market." Abrams v. United States, 250 U.S. 616, 630 (1919). But how, Chafee asked, could views compete in a market constricted because of a lack of media outlets? He answered that "a free market requires regulation, just as a free market for goods needs law against monopoly. . . . The government can lay down the rules of the game which will promote rather than restrict free speech." Such laws might require "essential facilities accessible to all," methods to assure that communication channels remain open, and measures directed at particular communication industries "intended to promote freedom, improve content, or otherwise make them perform their proper function in a free society." Z. Chafee, 2 Government and Mass Communications 471 ff. (1947).

More recently, law professor Jerome A. Barron adopted the same approach. He believes the marketplace is an antiquated concept that no longer works because of changes in the media and society since 1791. It is difficult for a person to begin a newspaper because of the prohibitive cost or to begin a broadcast service because of limits in spectrum allocation. Barron finds censorship by media because they limit the views they disseminate and permit few new or unpopular ideas to be heard widely. Barron concluded that those who do not control media should be able to express their views through the mass media. "At the very minimum," Barron wrote, "the creation of two remedies is essential—(1) a nondiscriminating right to purchase editorial advertisements in daily newspapers, and (2) a right of reply for public figures and public officers defamed in newspapers." J. Barron, Freedom of the Press for Whom? 6 (1973). See also, Barron, Access to the Press—a New First Amendment Right, 80 Harv.L.Rev. 1641 (1967).

We shall consider legal responses to the Commission and to Barron later.

b. Safety Valve

When a government permits freedom of expression it not only allows society to be exposed to a wide range of ideas, it also brings about a stable and adaptable community, according to Professor Thomas Emerson. See T. Emerson, The System of Freedom of Expression 11–14 (1970). Substituting force for logic, which is what happens when freedom of expression is suppressed, makes it impossible to come to rational decisions. In addition, coercion is ineffective in changing thoughts and beliefs. Instead, stifling expression breeds discontent that focuses not on the issues being suppressed, but on the act of suppression itself.

Thus, limiting freedom of expression leads to an inflexible and stultified society, one that cannot adapt to new circumstances because new ideas have not been allowed to flourish. Any tendency of a society to lose its vitality and become rigid is exacerbated when its members cannot exchange ideas freely. Innovative approaches to old problems and to methods of coping with new concerns will not develop unless dissent and opposition are allowed to exist. If opposition is driven underground, open confrontation may emerge between the government and the opposition, including the use of physical force.

Emerson's argument, then, is that freedom of expression will not cause society to become fragmented, to divide into opposing camps. Rather, suppression of communication will do that. Freedom of speech and press will allow dissidents to express their ideas "in a release of energy, a lessening of frustration and a channeling of resistance into courses consistent with law and order."

When people have had an opportunity to convince others of their ideas and have been rejected, the dissidents are more likely to accept the majority view. So long as they think they have not had a chance to persuade others, the minority will continue to believe their cause would be accepted if only heard. When certain they have been treated fairly, however, and have not won over others, they are less likely to use force, and others in society are less likely to view force as a legitimate alternative.

Recall Justice Brandeis's emphasis on the importance of this justification.

c. Self-governance

A third reason that freedom of communication is valuable in a democratic society is that such a society is based on self-governance, on an informed citizenry that will intelligently elect representatives. James Madison believed that the people, not the government, were sovereign, and that the purpose of freedom of speech was to allow citizens to govern themselves in a free society. But in 1798, less than a decade after adoption of the First Amendment, Federalists in Congress passed the Sedition Act, which specified a fine and imprisonment for anyone who "shall write, print, utter or publish . . . any false, scandalous and malicious writing . . . against the government of the United States, or either house of the Congress . . . or the President . . . with intent to defame . . . or to excite against them . . . the hatred of the good people of the United States. . . ." Passed over Republican objections, the law prompted about 25 arrests and 10 convictions over the next three years. Thomas Jefferson and Madison objected to the legislation, Madison introducing resolutions into the Virginia legislature that called the Sedition Act unconstitutional.

In his draft of the Virginia resolutions, Madison argued that in the British form of government Parliament was omnipotent and the apparent threat was the Crown. "In the United States, the case is altogether different. The people, not the government, possess the absolute sovereignty. The legislature, no less than the executive, is under limitations of power." Thus the Constitution secures the people against invasions by both branches: "This security of the freedom of the press requires, that it should be exempt, not only from previous restraint by the executive, as in Great Britain, but from legislative restraint also; and this exemption, to be effectual, must be an exemption not only from the previous inspection of licensers, but from the subsequent penalty of laws." The Virginia Report of 1799, 225–227 (J. Randolph ed. 1850). Madison also observed that

> Whether it has, in any case, happened that the proceedings of either, or all of those branches, evince such a violation of duty as to justify a contempt, a disrepute or hatred among the people,

can only be determined by a free examination thereof, and a free communication among the people thereon.

    . . .

> Let it be recollected, lastly, that the right of electing the members of the government, constitutes more particularly the essence of a free and responsible government. The value and efficacy of this right, depends on the knowledge of the comparative merits and demerits of the candidates for public trust; and on the equal freedom, consequently, of examining and discussing these merits and demerits of the candidates respectively.

Madison's rationale for freedom of expression represents a significant departure from the English thinking of that period, and is a more far-reaching conception of that freedom than Madison had expressed previously.

In the late 1940's, Professor Alexander Meiklejohn agreed that self-governance is the most important concern of the First Amendment. He advocated distinguishing between two kinds of expression. Speech concerning the self-governing process was "political speech" and deserved absolute protection from government interference. Speech that was nonpolitical in character, "private speech," was protected only by the due process clause of the Fifth Amendment, which permits the government some leeway for regulation.

Meiklejohn drew this distinction between political and private speech because he believed the central purpose of the First Amendment is to give citizens the greatest opportunity to discuss and hear about society's problems, the very information one must have to function in a self-governing society.

Meiklejohn's emphasis on the self-governing focus of the First Amendment led him to reject more individualistic and subjective justifications for free speech. In Free Speech and Its Relation to Self-Government at 65–66 (1948) he said:

> Shall we, then, as practitioners of freedom, listen to ideas which, being opposed to our own, might destroy confidence in our form of government? Shall we give a hearing to those who hate and despise freedom, to those who, if they had the power, would destroy our institutions? Certainly, yes! Our action must be guided, not by their principles, but by ours. We listen, not because they desire to speak, but because we need to hear. If there are arguments against our theory of government, our policies in war or in peace, we the citizens, the rulers, must hear and consider them for ourselves. That is the way of public safety. It is the program of self-government.

Also, in The First Amendment Is An Absolute, 1961 Supreme Court Review, 245, 263, he stated:

> I have never been able to share the Miltonian faith that in a fair fight between truth and error, truth is sure to win. . . . In

my view, "the people need free speech" because they have decided, in adopting, maintaining, and interpreting their Constitution, to govern themselves rather than to be governed by others.

Meiklejohn's emphasis on self-government might have suggested that the First Amendment would protect only what we conventionally regard as political speech. His vagueness on this point in his 1948 edition was criticized by Chafee, who was concerned about what types of speech were being relegated to the Fifth Amendment's protection. Chafee observed that "there are public aspects to practically every subject." The citizen gains understanding from many sources: "He can get help from poems and plays and novels. No matter if Shakespeare and Whitehead do seem very far away from the issues of the next election." If Meiklejohn intended this broad view of the First Amendment, then Chafee wondered how there could be any limitations in such traditionally regulated areas as obscenity and libel. If, however, Meiklejohn were to place scholarship and the arts in the category of private speech, Chafee would regard it as "shocking to deprive these vital matters of the protection of the inspiring words of the First Amendment." Book Review, 62 Harv.L. Rev. 891, 900 (1949).

In his 1961 article, Meiklejohn resolved this question in favor of the broad view of the First Amendment:

Second, there are many forms of thought and expression within the range of human communications from which the voter derives the knowledge, intelligence, sensitivity to human values: the capacity for sane and objective judgment which, so far as possible, a ballot should express. These, too, must suffer no abridgment of their freedom. I list four of them below.

1. Education, in all its phases, is the attempt to so inform and cultivate the mind and will of a citizen that he shall have the wisdom, the independence, and, therefore, the dignity of a governing citizen. Freedom of education is, thus, as we all recognize, a basic postulate in the planning of a free society.

2. The achievements of philosophy and the sciences in creating knowledge and understanding of men and their world must be made available, without abridgment, to every citizen.

3. Literature and the arts must be protected by the First Amendment. They lead the way toward sensitive and informed appreciation and response to the values out of which the riches of the general welfare are created.

4. Public discussions of public issues, together with the spreading of information and opinion bearing on those issues, must have a freedom unabridged by our agents. Though they govern us, we, in a deeper sense, govern them. Over our governing, they have no power. Over their governing we have sovereign power.

His inclusion of literature and the arts within the categorical protection of the First Amendment led Meiklejohn to rule out prosecutions even for obscenity. He regretted that "Our dominant mood is not the courage of people who dare to think. It is the timidity of those who fear and hate whenever conventions are questioned." Can this breadth be reconciled with Meiklejohn's earlier view that "a merchant advertising his wares [and] a paid lobbyist fighting for the advantage of his client" are covered only by the limited protection of the Fifth Amendment?

As to libel, Meiklejohn argued that the libel of a private person "if it has no relation to the business of governing" could lead to liability, but criticism of candidates or government officials should be protected. Yet, "vituperation which fixes attention on the defects of an opponent's character or intelligence and thereby distracts attention from the question of policy under discussion may be forbidden as a deadly enemy of peaceable assembly."

Chafee's detailed review of Meiklejohn's 1948 volume praised its political wisdom but regretted that Meiklejohn, a philosopher, had attempted to read his political ideas into the Constitution. Chafee thought Meiklejohn's claim "of a firmly established purpose to make all political discussion immune" was negated by actions for civil and criminal libels in state courts after the Revolution, and asserted that although the framers "had no very clear idea as to what they meant" in the First Amendment, they intended the amendment to give speech "all the protection they desired, and had no idea of supplementing it by the Fifth Amendment." Book Review, 62 Harv.L.Rev. 891, 897–98 (1949). In his 1961 article, Meiklejohn acknowledged the lack of historical support but argued that the constitutional principle of self-government was capable of development and changing consequences as its implications became understood.

Chafee also claimed that Meiklejohn's constitutional approach would be unworkable in practice because "few judges" would grant protection to certain types of inciting speech clearly within the realm of "public discussion." Also, the line between public and private speech might well be elusive.

Others have suggested different versions of the role of political speech in terms of the First Amendment. After reviewing several justifications for protecting speech in his Neutral Principles and Some First Amendment Problems, 47 Indiana L.J. 1, 23–35 (1971), Robert Bork suggested that the only acceptable basis for protecting speech more than other activities is the importance of the "discovery and spread of political truth" facilitated by the unique ability of speech to deal "explicitly and specifically and directly with politics and government." But this difference "exists only with respect to one kind of speech: explicitly and predominantly political speech. This seems to me the only form of speech that a principled judge can

prefer to other claimed freedoms. All other forms of speech raise
only issues of human gratification. . . ."

Professor Lillian BeVier agreed that the First Amendment "in
principle protects only 'political' speech—speech that participates in
the process of representative democracy. . . ." But she said
Bork's view is too narrow, that the need to "protect political speech
fully in practice may justify the Court's extending first amendment
protection to categories of speech other than the strictly political."
This extra tier of protection is defensible because of the difficulty in
predicting how the Court will later draw the line between political
and non-political speech. Rather than sacrificing some of the political
to exclude all non-political, the Court should give more protection to
the latter to ensure protecting the former. BeVier, The First Amendment and Political Speech: An Inquiry Into the Substance and Limits
of Principle, 30 Stan.L.Rev. 299 (1978).

In commenting on the Chafee and Meiklejohn approaches to the
First Amendment, Professor Alexander Bickel observed:

> Now, the interest in truth of which Chafee spoke is not inconsis-
> tent with the First Amendment's protection of demonstrable
> falsehood for, as I have indicated, men may be deterred from
> speaking what they believe to be true because they fear that it
> will be found to be false, or that the proof of its truth will be too
> expensive. Moreover, the individual interest that Chafee men-
> tioned has its truth-seeking aspect. Yet the First Amendment
> does not operate solely or even chiefly to foster the quest for
> truth, unless we take the view that truth is entirely a product of
> the marketplace and is definable as the perceptions of the majori-
> ty of men, and not otherwise. The social interest that the First
> Amendment vindicates is rather, as Alexander Meiklejohn and
> Robert Bork have emphasized, the interest in the successful
> operation of the political process, so that the country may better
> be able to adopt the course of action that conforms to the wishes
> of the greatest number, whether or not it is wise or is founded in
> truth.

Professor Bickel then concluded that discussion and exchange of
views were "crucial to our politics. . . . It would follow, then,
that the First Amendment should protect and indeed encourage
speech so long as it serves to make the political process work,
seeking to achieve objectives through the political process by persuading a majority of voters; but *not* when it amounts to an effort to
supplant, disrupt, or coerce the process, as by overthrowing the
government, by rioting, or by other forms of violence, and also *not*
when it constitutes a breach of an otherwise valid law, a violation of
majority decisions embodied in law." A. Bickel, The Morality of
Consent 62–63 (1976).

From a different direction, Professor Vince Blasi suggested that
Meiklejohn's emphasis on self-governance may be unrealistic in light

of our traditionally low participation in elections and political discussions. (Blasi noted that the framers did not intend that a large majority of the population would participate in political decisions.) Rather, Blasi would stress that the press needs extensive protection because it is the only continuing and well-funded organization in the private sector that can "check" official misbehavior by extensive investigation and reporting. Government corruption is a serious problem and, as government grows, the problem gets more serious, as does the difficulty of discovering the misbehavior. The "central premise of the checking value is that abuse of government is an especially serious evil—more serious than the abuse of private power, even by institutions such as large corporations which can affect the lives of millions of people."

The checking value allows citizens to follow their private pursuits while the press serves as a "watchdog" over government. Most investigative reporting, brought to the public's attention during the Watergate affair, emphasizes the "checking value" more than the self-governance rationale. Blasi, The Checking Value in First Amendment Theory, 1977 American Bar Foundation Research Journal 521.

C. THE FIRST AMENDMENT AND THE INSTITUTIONAL PRESS

"Congress shall make no law . . . abridging the freedom of speech, or of the press . . .."

The lack of a broad consensus concerning the philosophical underpinnings of the majestic words of the First Amendment does not mean that the courts and legislatures of the United States are released from the obligation to obey the Amendment's dictates. To the contrary, our Nation's lawmaking bodies have clearly acknowledged that the Amendment represents a constitutional bar to government action in numerous situations.

An appreciable and important fraction of these situations involve the institution of "the press" and these specific applications of First Amendment doctrine are the core of this book. The remainder of this Chapter sketches those elements of general First Amendment doctrine that apply most directly to the press. Some aspects of the First Amendment that do not primarily involve the press are presented in passing. Students interested in a more comprehensive exposition of First Amendment doctrine might consult M. Nimmer, Nimmer on Freedom of Speech (1984).

1. Restriction on Government Power

Though on its face the First Amendment appears to bind only the Congress, it is well established today that the prohibitions of the First Amendment extend to all branches of both the federal and state governments by way of the "due process" clause of the Fourteenth

Amendment. The First Amendment guarantees, the Supreme Court has held, are a fundamental element of the "liberty" protected by the Fourteenth Amendment. Gitlow v. New York, 268 U.S. 652 (1925).

This liberty is protected against encroachments of state governments to the exact same extent that the First Amendment itself protects the freedoms of speech and press from the federal government. Lawyers and judges have developed the shorthand expression "incorporation" to express this idea. Since the First Amendment has been "incorporated" into the Fourteenth Amendment, its prohibitions are no less specific by virtue of such incorporation. This means that branches of the state governments are bound, to the same extent as the federal government, to respect the guarantees of the First Amendment.

Despite the considerable expansion of the field of operation of the First Amendment as a result of the incorporation doctrine, it is important to remember that the First Amendment is a bar only to abridgments by government. Private parties are free to "abridge" another's exercise of the speech and press clauses at will so long as they do not violate some other valid law in the process. For example, it is established that a right to distribute printed material is part and parcel of the First Amendment freedoms and the government is prohibited from interfering with such distribution. Lovell v. Griffin, 303 U.S. 444 (1938). On the other hand, the private owner of property may prohibit such a distribution from taking place on *his* property without running afoul of the First Amendment. See PruneYard Shopping Center v. Robins, 447 U.S. 74 (1980).

2. THE PROTECTED SPHERE

a. *Speech v. Conduct*

More difficult than determining who is prohibited from interfering with protected expression is determining what forms of expressive activity fall within the protected category. Perhaps the most basic line between the protected and the unprotected is suggested by the distinction between "speech" and "conduct." Presumptively, at least, all oral and written communication falls within the protected sphere while non-verbal conduct remains outside the domain of the First Amendment. Difficulties abound when verbal and non-verbal elements are mixed into a single expressive activity, such as labor picketing, protest marches, or the wearing of armbands. See Tinker v. Des Moines Independent School District, 393 U.S. 503 (1969), regarding armbands.

The speech-conduct dichotomy does not, however, pose a serious problem in determining the First Amendment rights of "the institutional press." Virtually all expressive conduct by the news media is verbal in nature, either oral or written. As a first approximation, then, all mass media expression is protected as "speech."

b.　Non-protected Speech

Though speech *generally* is a protected activity, the Supreme Court has long placed certain categories of words outside the First Amendment's protection. In 1942, the Court asserted, in Chaplinsky v. New Hampshire, 315 U.S. 568 (1942), that certain classes of expression might be subject to legal sanctions. Chaplinsky had been arrested for calling a town marshal a "God-damned racketeer and a damned Fascist." The Supreme Court characterized the expression as "fighting words . . . likely to cause violence." The words were not protected expression because they invited a violent response by the person to whom they were directed. The Court then observed that other types of speech were similarly outside the protection of the First Amendment:

> There are certain well-defined and narrowly limited classes of speech, the prevention and punishment of which have never been thought to raise any Constitutional problem. These include the lewd and obscene, the profane, the libelous, and the insulting or "fighting" words—those which by their very utterance inflict injury or tend to incite an immediate breach of the peace. It has been well observed that such utterances are no essential part of any exposition of ideas, and are of such slight social value as a step to truth that any benefit that may be derived from them is clearly outweighed by the social interest in order and morality.

Libel and obscenity are matters that frequently involve the mass media. Obscenity remains a category of unprotected speech. Most libels, however, excluding only those uttered with "actual malice," have been removed from the unprotected category by decisions since *Chaplinsky* and now receive varying degrees of First Amendment protection. We consider libel in Chapter III, and obscenity in Chapters VII and XVI.

In addition to the *Chaplinsky* categories, several other types of verbal expression are not considered to be constitutionally protected speech. The knowing lie, for instance, has never been protected. For this reason criminal statutes punishing perjury, and the common law civil actions for fraud raise no constitutional issue under the First Amendment. More recently, child pornography has been removed from the protected sphere even if it is not legally "obscene." This development is discussed in Chapter VII.

c.　Distribution

Freedom of speech and press have been held to imply more than the freedom only to speak and write. The First Amendment guarantees include the right to disseminate the words produced after creating them. In a milestone case, a city ordinance in Griffin, Georgia, prescribed criminal penalties for distributing printed material without permission. The Court found the ordinance was overly broad because it included all "literature," making no distinction between that which the First Amendment does and does not protect. Also, the ordinance gave the city manager unbridled censorship powers since he was given no criteria for decision and was not obligated to explain why he refused permission to distribute. Lovell v. Griffin, 303 U.S. 444 (1938).

Distribution by Mail. Historically, one of the principal means of circulation of magazines, and to a lesser extent newspapers, has been through the United States mail. Since the creation of the Post Office, periodicals have received the benefit of rates lower than those for letters. The lower rates were designed "to encourage the dissemination of news and of current literature of educational value."

Note that the First Amendment does not enter into the question of whether to establish subsidies for media. It has not been argued that the Constitution *requires* Congress to subsidize the media. Rather, this is a question for Congress to decide—at least so long as Congress does not discriminate for or against certain periodicals because of their editorial positions or because of political favoritism.

In the Classification Act of 1879, Congress created the four classes of mail that still exist, and established eligibility requirements for second-class mail that are virtually unchanged today: publication in unbound form at regular intervals at least four times a year, issued from a known office of publication and "originated and published for the dissemination of information of a public character, or devoted to literature, the sciences, arts, or some special industry."

The limitations on postal authority control over second-class mails have been developed through interpretation of these criteria. The discretion of postal officials reached its outermost limits in Milwaukee Social Democratic Publishing Co. v. Burleson, 255 U.S. 407 (1921). The Postmaster General had revoked the second-class privileges of the *Milwaukee Leader*, a left-wing newspaper critical of United States involvement in World War I. The second-class privilege was available only to "mailable" matter, and the Court found authorization for the ban in the Espionage Act of 1917, which provided that any newspaper that published false statements intended to promote the success of the enemies of the United States was "nonmailable." Furthermore, the Court reasoned that once an unspecified number of issues of a newspaper had revealed its "nonmailable" character, it was a "reasonable presumption" that future issues would be nonmailable, thus justifying the indefinite revocation.

Justice Brandeis, dissenting, argued that the nonmailability provisions gave the Postmaster General authority only to exclude from the mails specific issues that he found to be nonmailable and he could not close the mails to future issues of the same publication or future mail tendered by a particular person. To allow more would be to attribute to Congress the desire to create a "universal censor of publication" because "a denial of the use of the mail would be for most publications tantamount to a denial of the right of circulation."

Finally, in Hannegan v. Esquire, Inc., 327 U.S. 146 (1946), the Court in effect adopted Justice Brandeis's views and drastically restricted the discretion of the Postmaster General, who had revoked the second-class privileges of *Esquire Magazine.* He had expressly stipulated that he was not finding the magazine to be obscene and thus "nonmailable" under the obscenity provisions. Instead, he argued that the "public character" eligibility requirement gave him the power to exclude publications that, though not "obscene in a technical sense," are "morally improper and not for the public welfare and the public good." The Court concluded that such a view would "grant the Postmaster General a power of censorship. Such a power is so abhorrent to our traditions that a purpose to grant it should not easily be inferred." By narrowing the sweep of the statute, the Court did not have to deal with the constitutional issue.

d. Gathering

The "right to gather" information from willing private sources began to take shape in 1972 with two cases. In Kleindienst v. Mandel, 408 U.S. 753 (1972), American scholars sought to invite Mandel, a Belgian Marxist economist, to attend conferences and to speak at several American universities. Congress had barred visas for aliens who advocated "the economic, international, and governmental doctrines of world communism or the establishment in the United States of a totalitarian dictatorship." Such an alien might be admitted temporarily if the Attorney General approved a recommendation to that effect from the Department of State. A recommendation was made for Mandel but, based on information about Mandel's behavior on a previous trip to the United States, the Attorney General refused to approve the visa application. Mandel and the scholars sued. After concluding that Mandel, as an alien, had no constitutional right of entry, the Court turned to the rights claimed by the scholars:

> The Government . . . suggests that the First Amendment is inapplicable because [the scholars] have free access to Mandel's ideas through his books and speeches, and because "technological developments," such as tapes or telephone hookups, readily supplant his physical presence. This argument overlooks what may be particular qualities inherent in sustained, face-to-face debate, discussion and questioning. . . . We are loath to hold on this record that existence of other alternatives extinguishes altogether any constitutional interest on the part of the [scholars] in this particular form of access.

The Court, however, concluded that this interest was overcome by the government's longstanding power to make rules for excluding aliens.

Three dissenters argued that since the government was prevented from encumbering the entry of books and pamphlets, there was no basis for excluding Mandel unless it could be shown that he posed "an actual threat to the country." They relied on Lamont v. Postmaster General, 381 U.S. 301 (1965), in which the Court held unconstitutional a statute permitting the government to require the addressee of unrequested "communist political propaganda" to request in writing that the post office deliver such matter.

The second case to provide some indirect support for protection of gathering was Branzburg v. Hayes, 408 U.S. 665 (1972). Although the Court held that the reporters had no First Amendment right to refuse to testify before a grand jury, the majority acknowledged that the Court was not suggesting "that news gathering does not qualify for First Amendment protection; without some protection for seeking out the news, freedom of the press could be eviscerated." The protection of the confidentiality of reporters' sources is considered in detail in Chapter X.

e. *Refusal to Speak*

Most freedom of communication questions concern whether the government can prevent a person from, or punish a person for, speaking. The other side of that coin is whether individuals can be forced to speak against their will. The Supreme Court confronted this issue in West Virginia State Board of Education v. Barnette, 319 U.S. 624 (1943), in which it held that public school children could not be compelled to participate in a flag salute exercise. The Court said forcing someone to express a view, such as respect for the flag, was as offensive to the First Amendment as forbidding a person to do so.

The right not to speak, though infrequently asserted by mass media, continues to represent an important element of First Amendment protections. For example, in Miami Herald v. Tornillo, 418 U.S. 241 (1974), a case examined in Chapter XIII, the Court held that a state statute compelling the *Herald* to print a political candidate's reply to a *Herald* attack violated the *Herald's* First Amendment right to freely exercise editorial judgment concerning the contents of its publication. The *Herald*, in effect, had a First Amendment right not to print Tornillo's reply. As the Court made clear in *Tornillo:*

> "[A] compulsion exerted by government on a newspaper to print that which it would not otherwise print . . . is unconstitutional. A responsible press is an undoubtedly desirable goal, but press responsibility is not mandated by the Constitution and like many other virtues it cannot be legislated." Id. at 284.

Despite arguments that an individual should at least be able to purchase advertising time or space in the media to disseminate a message, courts have held that a private newspaper may reject advertising for any reason, or no reason, so long as its motive or effect is not anticompetitive. See Chapter XIII.

The situation applicable to broadcasters is much less clear. The courts have concluded that the airwaves represent a scarce public resource and that this permits government to require broadcasters to grant others access to the microphone in some situations. These obligations are discussed in detail in Chapters XIII through XVII.

3.　ABRIDGMENT DEFINED

Determining whether the press is engaged in protected speech represents only half the question in evaluating whether a constitutional issue has been raised under the First Amendment. Courts must also determine whether an abridgment has taken place.

a.　*Prior Restraints*

Recall from p. 12, that in the traditional, Blackstonian, view, prior restraints represented the quintessential, indeed exclusive, abridgments of speech. "Prior restraint" meant that rather than punishing the publisher by criminal or civil sanctions for what was published, the government barred the publication from occurring in the first place. This is, of course, the essence of censorship. In English history, the censor was an administrative official, who administered the licensing system we have already considered.

Although it might have been argued that only administrative or executive branch behavior could constitute a prior restraint, it has become clear in this country that judicial orders that bar publications are also analyzed as prior restraints. Nonetheless, court orders imposing prior restraints are thought somewhat less objectionable than similar administrative action because of a perception that administrators may cut procedural corners and otherwise be unfair in executing their obligations. Even so, some administrative prior restraints are permitted even today. The most obvious example is that the Supreme Court has permitted states to license motion pictures. Under such a system, it is a crime to exhibit a film that has not been approved in advance, even if the film is totally unobjectionable on any ground. This type of licensing system was upheld in Freedman v. Maryland, 380 U.S. 51 (1980), so long as the administrative decision was subject to swift judicial review.

The deep-rooted antagonism to prior restraint is seen in the Supreme Court's decision in Near v. Minnesota, 283 U.S. 697 (1931), the first case in which the Court invalidated a state law because it violated the First and Fourteenth Amendments to the United States Constitution. More specifically, *Near* established the Court's initial approach to the question of prior restraint. *Near* involved a Minnesota statute allowing officials to stop publication of "malicious, scandalous, and defamatory" newspapers and periodicals. Once stopped, publication could be resumed only on order of a judge, who would have to approve the content before allowing continued printing. The county attorney brought an action to stop publication of *The Saturday Press,* printed in Minneapolis. The complaint said the *Press* had accused certain government officials of being involved in bootlegging and gambling which according to the *Press,* were controlled by a "Jewish gangster." The state courts "perpetually enjoined" the defendants from publishing *The Saturday Press.*

The Supreme Court of the United States reversed the state court, saying the case involved "questions of grave importance." Chief Justice Charles Evans Hughes, writing for the 5–4 majority, noted that Blackstone's observation that "[t]he liberty of the press . . . consists in laying no *previous* restraints upon publications . . ." was too broad. Although prior restraint is presumed to be unconstitutional, "the protection . . . is not absolutely unlimited." The Court then suggested some areas in which such restraints might be upheld:

> No one would question but that a government might prevent actual obstruction to its recruiting service or the publication of sailing dates of transports or the number and location of troops. On similar grounds, the primary requirements of decency may be enforced against obscene publications. The security of the community life may be protected against incitements to acts of violence and the overthrow by force of orderly government. The constitutional guaranty of free speech does not "protect a man from an injunction against uttering words that may have all the effect of force." [ ]

Since the defendant's charges in the Near case did not come within any of these categories, prior restraint was impermissible.

Prior restraint may present special problems when invoked against student publications in public high schools and colleges. If the high school principal were a town's mayor and the student newspaper were the local daily, prior restraint would be permissible only if one of the *Near* or similar exceptions existed. Public school officials represent the state just as a mayor does. But does the special context of a high school or college allow school officials more leeway under the First and Fourteenth Amendments than is allowed a mayor?

Tinker v. Des Moines Independent School District, 393 U.S. 503 (1969), established that public school students' First Amendment rights could be limited only if their exercise would cause material and substantial interference with school operations or if there is a "colli[sion] with the rights of others."

The question of prior restraint on the public high school campus has never been decided by the Supreme Court, and the lower courts have not yet evolved a common approach.

b. Subsequent Sanctions

Though perhaps less compelling from a historical point of view, it is quite clear that sanctions imposed after publication may be like prior restraints, in that they may prevent would-be speakers and writers from publishing protected speech. Such sanctions, whether they are penal in nature, such as imprisonment or fines, or civil damage awards, or the denial of some privilege, generally raise precisely the same issues as prior restraints on publication.

In Smith v. Daily Mail Publishing Co., 443 U.S. 97 (1979), the Supreme Court was faced with a statute that made it a crime for a newspaper to publish a juvenile offender's name unless the paper had obtained the prior written approval of a court. The paper argued that the prior approval requirement acted in "operation and effect" like a licensing scheme. As such, the paper argued that the statute carries "a 'heavy presumption' against its constitutional validity," quoting earlier cases. The Court responded by avoiding the question:

> The resolution of this case does not turn on whether the statutory grant of authority to the juvenile judge to permit publication of the juvenile's name is, in and of itself, a prior restraint. First Amendment protection reaches beyond prior restraints. . . .
>
> Whether we view the statute as a prior restraint or as a penal sanction . . . is not dispositive because even the latter action requires the highest form of state interest to sustain its validity. Prior restraints have been accorded the most exacting scrutiny in previous cases. [ ] However, even when a state attempts to punish publication after the event it must nevertheless demonstrate that its punitive action was necessary to further the state interests asserted. [ ] Since we conclude that this statute cannot satisfy the constitutional standards defined in *Landmark Communications, Inc.*, we need not decide whether, as argued by [the newspaper], it operated as a prior restraint.

This case suggests that much of the distinction traditionally drawn between prior restraints and other forms of inhibitions on the activities of the press may be vanishing. As we shall see throughout this book, the criteria that the Court uses in reviewing challenged state actions are usually quite rigorous no matter what the form of the state inhibition.

c. Neutral Regulation

On the other hand, the great proportion of government regulation of the press has never been considered to be abridgment so long as it is neutrally applied despite the considerable costs such regulation may exact from the press. Thus, for example, one may not publish a newspaper without obeying local building codes, the income tax laws and other tax statutes, the antitrust laws, the Occupational Safety and Health Act, legislation dealing with labor relations or any of the myriad other bodies of general regulatory law administered by local, state and federal governments.

Since the government apparently is not attempting to suppress a particular point of view or a particular speaker with these general regulations, we might call them "non-speech" measures. If the government is attempting to prevent certain speech, we might call that an "anti-speech" regulation.

Courts have recognized that states have the power, generally called the "police power," to make and enforce regulations relating to the public health, safety, morals, and general welfare. Under the police powers, municipalities have imposed restrictions on the time, place, and manner of exercising freedom of expression. Generally, courts have upheld this type of regulation if it is nondiscriminatory (applying to all, not just some), not based on content, and reasonable (a regulation allowing everyone to distribute leaflets only at midnight would not be reasonable).

In Cox v. New Hampshire, 312 U.S. 569 (1941), the Supreme Court upheld an ordinance requiring licenses for parades through city streets. The licenses were granted on time, place, and manner considerations. The Court said the ordinance served the community's legitimate interest in regulating traffic by, for instance, not allowing parades during rush hours and avoiding simultaneous parades. Since there was no indication that licenses were denied on a discriminatory basis, the ordinance was upheld.

Note that these categories do not involve the question of what point of view the speaker has expressed on a subject. Indeed, the Court frequently has asserted that government must not encourage or hinder speech based on whether officials like the views being expressed. For instance, a city cannot allow peaceful picketing by union members while prohibiting all other peaceful picketing. Such an ordinance in Chicago, which allowed demonstrations near school buildings only if labor matters were involved, was invalidated by the Court. Chicago Police Department v. Mosley, 408 U.S. 92 (1972). The Court said:

> [U]nder . . . the First Amendment . . ., government may not grant the use of a forum to people whose views it finds acceptable, but deny use to those wishing to express less favored or more controversial views. And it may not select which issues are worth discussing or debating in public facilities. There is an equality of status in the field of ideas, and government must afford all points of view an equal opportunity to be heard. Once a forum is opened up to assembly or speaking by some groups, government may not prohibit others from assembling or speaking on the basis of what they intend to say. Selecting exclusions

from a public forum may not be based on content alone, and may not be justified by reference to content alone.

This ringing statement has presented problems in application in certain areas, as we shall see in Chapter XVI. *Mosley* can be seen as an attempt to carefully distinguish between non-speech and anti-speech regulation. Where a non-speech regulation is challenged, it will be upheld if it is found to have a rational relationship to a legitimate state interest. But state efforts to control the content of speech must meet much more rigorous criteria, as we discuss in the next section.

D. APPLYING THE FIRST AMENDMENT

An "abridgment" of protected speech is not, despite the apparently unqualified language of the First Amendment, necessarily unconstitutional.

1. BALANCING

Most frequently, the Supreme Court has used a "balancing test" to determine the propriety of a restraint on freedom of expression. The test involves weighing two interests—the government's concern about protecting a particular interest, such as national security or individual reputation, and the individual's and society's interests in expression.

Professor Chafee, an early advocate of balancing, expressed the virtues of that approach in his Free Speech in the United States (1941) at 31 as follows:

> Or to put the matter another way, it is useless to define free speech by talk about rights. The agitator asserts his constitutional right to speak, the government asserts its constitutional right to wage war. The result is a deadlock. . . . To find the boundary line of any right, we must get behind rules of law to human facts. In our problem, we must regard the desires and needs of the individual human being who wants to speak and those of the great group of human beings among whom he speaks. That is, in technical language, there are individual interests and social interests, which must be balanced against each other, if they conflict, in order to determine which interest shall be sacrificed under the circumstances and which shall be protected and become the foundation of a legal right. It must never be forgotten that the balancing cannot be properly done unless all the interests involved are adequately ascertained, and the great evil of all this talk about rights is that each side is so busy denying the other's claim to rights that it entirely overlooks the human desires and needs behind that claim.

Most freedom of expression cases are decided by balancing interests. The Supreme Court, without always explaining its approach, will use one of two variations of the balancing test. Focusing on the interests at stake in the individual case is commonly characterized as "ad hoc" balancing: the specific interests applicable to the facts of the particular case are considered crucial. The court attempts to identify the state's interest in limiting or preventing the speech in question and the would-be speaker's and society's interests in having the speech permitted. Balancing on a case-by-case basis involves such case-specific factors that it is often difficult to predict what weight a resolution reached on one set of facts will be accorded in a subsequent case with somewhat different facts.

At other times, a more general process, called "definitional" or "categorical" balancing, is used. Here the interests analyzed transcend the merits of a particular case. Rather than asking, for example, whether the value of speech in a particular case outweighs the arguments for proscribing it, the Court might generalize and consider the values of that category of speech, or that category of speaker, and develop a more general analysis. This approach makes it easier to predict outcomes because of the explicitly generalized character of the decision.

2. PREFERRED POSITION

A basic tenet of constitutional law calls upon courts to presume that enactments of legislative bodies are constitutional. If the legislation has a rational basis, courts will generally hold it constitutional. In United States v. Carolene Products Co., 304 U.S. 144 (1938), involving the validity of a federal economic regulation, Justice Stone, writing for the majority, restated this generally accepted view of deference to legislatures. But in one of the Court's most famous footnotes, Justice Stone wrote:

> There may be narrower scope for operation of the presumption of constitutionality when legislation appears on its face to be within a specific prohibition of the Constitution, such as those of the first ten amendments, which are deemed equally specific when held to be embraced within the Fourteenth. . . .

> It is unnecessary to consider now whether legislation which restricts those political processes which can ordinarily be expected to bring about repeal of undesirable legislation, is to be subjected to more exacting scrutiny under the general prohibitions of the Fourteenth Amendment than are most other types of legislation. . . .

Justice Stone was suggesting that legislation that inhibits political freedoms, such as freedom of communication, must survive more "exacting judicial scrutiny" than other legislative acts. Instead of having a presumption of constitutionality, such legislation might be presumed to inhibit a basic freedom and the government might have to show an overriding need for it, not simply a rational basis. As a result of some cases that built on this footnote, freedom of communication became a "preferred freedom," one that courts would not allow the legislature to restrict without a compelling state interest.

Professor Nimmer, in his book "Freedom of Speech," explained the modern method of valuing free speech and press in the balancing process:

The First Amendment command that freedom of speech may not be abridged, although not viewed with a literal absolutism, at the very least means "that any significant restriction of First Amendment freedom carries a heavy burden of justification." For a period Supreme Court opinions frequently referred to First Amendment freedoms as occupying "a preferred position." Although this particular phraseology proved somewhat controversial, and has fallen into disuse, there can be no doubt that the implication it suggests for the weighing process remains an important part of First Amendment jurisprudence. Insofar as the conflicting speech and anti-speech interests may be said to be of equal weight, the speech interest must prevail by reason of the constitutional commitment to this value. But, of course, in the real world neither legal nor sociological calibrations are so precise as to justify the conclusion that conflicting interests are ever of exactly equal weight. Rather, "the preference for freedom" suggests an approach, not a formula, whereby doubtful balancing questions are resolved in favor of the speech interest. There is nevertheless a balancing, and the speech interest does not always win.

3. CLEAR AND PRESENT DANGER

Most of the remainder of this book will focus on how the balance between speech and anti-speech interests is struck in a wide variety of issues affecting mass media. In defamation, for example, speech interests are balanced against the individual's interest in reputation. In other cases, speech interests must be balanced against privacy interests, property interests, security interests, public safety and morals, and even countervailing speech interests, to name only a few. The balance struck in each situation differs as the countervailing interests vary in weight and as the value of the speech interest itself changes in various contexts. Even in the *same* context the balancing process often yields varying results over time as the hierarchy of values and weights accorded various interests change.

One important example of the balancing process is the evolution of the "clear and present danger" test originally framed by Justice Oliver Wendell Holmes in an important series of cases arising out of the Espionage Act of 1917. These cases represent the struggle of the courts to accommodate the federal government's interest in maintaining the integrity of its effort to wage war with dissenters' free speech rights. The Espionage Act banned attempts to cause insubordination in the armed forces or to obstruct military recruiting or to conspire to achieve these results. Most of these cases, which confronted the Court from 1919 until the mid-1920's, involved radical speakers who opposed the war effort and criticized the political and economic structure of the country.

Based on his marketplace of ideas approach, Holmes saw the clear and present danger test as least intrusive on freedom of expression in a society in which absolute freedom was impractical. In Schenck v. United States, 249 U.S. 47 (1919), Justice Holmes said that expression could be punished when "the words used are used in such circumstances and are of such a nature as to create a clear and present danger that they will bring about the substantive evils that Congress has a right to prevent. It is a question of proximity and degree."

Schenck involved a prosecution under the Espionage Act for publishing a leaflet that interfered with recruiting by urging young men to violate the draft law. Holmes, writing for the majority, found that the leaflet could be closely connected with violations of the Conscription Act (proximity) and that this was a serious danger to the country's security (degree).

Abrams v. United States, 250 U.S. 616 (1919), involved pamphlets calling for a strike of munitions workers. The Supreme Court upheld the convictions. This time Justice Holmes and Brandeis dissented, saying:

> . . . I think that we should be eternally vigilant against attempts to check the expression of opinions that we loathe and believe to be fraught with death, unless they so imminently threaten immediate interference with the lawful and pressing purposes of the law that an immediate check is required to save the country. I wholly disagree with the argument of the Government that the First Amendment left the common law as to seditious libel in force. History seems to me against the notion. I had conceived that the United States through many years had shown its repentance for the Sedition Act of 1798 [ ], by repaying fines that it imposed. Only the emergency that makes it immediately dangerous to leave the correction of evil counsels to time warrants making any exception to the sweeping command, "Congress shall make no law . . . abridging the freedom of speech." Of course I am speaking only of expressions of opinion and exhortations, which were all that were uttered here, but I regret that I cannot put into more impressive words my belief that in their conviction upon this indictment the defendants were deprived of their rights under the Constitution of the United States.

It was uncertain what test the majority was using during this period. After some movement toward clear and present danger, the Court confronted a case involving a state statute that explicitly proscribed certain language.

The case, Gitlow v. New York, 268 U.S. 652 (1925), involved a prosecution under a New York criminal statute that barred advocating overthrow of the government by violence. The majority upheld the conviction:

> By enacting the present statute the State has determined, through its legislative body, that utterances advocating the overthrow of organized government by force, violence and unlawful means, are so inimical to the general welfare and involve such danger of substantive evil that they may be penalized in the exercise of its police power. That determination must be given great weight. Every presumption is to be indulged in favor of the validity of the statute. . . . The State cannot reasonably be required to measure the danger from every such utterance in the nice balance of a jeweler's scale. A single revolutionary spark may kindle a fire that, smouldering for a time, may burst into a sweeping and destructive conflagration. It cannot be said that the State is acting arbitrarily or unreasonably when in the exercise of its judgment as to the measures necessary to protect the public peace and safety, it seeks to extinguish the spark without waiting until it has enkindled the flame or blazed into the conflagration. It cannot reasonably be required to defer the adoption of measures for its own peace and safety until the revolutionary utterances lead to actual disturbances of the public peace or imminent and immediate danger of its own destruction; but it may, in the exercise of its judgment, suppress the threatened danger in its incipiency. . . .
>
> . . .
>
> In other words, when the legislative body has determined generally, in the constitutional exercise of its discretion, that utterances of a certain kind involve such danger of substantive evil that they may be punished, the question whether any specific utterance coming within the prohibited class is likely, in and of itself, to bring about the substantive evil, is not open to consideration. It is sufficient that the statute itself be constitutional and that the use of the language comes within its prohibition.
>
> . . . In such cases it has been held that the general provisions of the statute may be constitutionally applied to the specific utterance of the defendant if its natural tendency and probable effect was to bring about the substantive evil which the legislative body might prevent. . . .

Justice Holmes, with whom Justice Brandeis joined, dissented in an opinion that rejected a "natural tendency" test:

> . . . I think that the criterion sanctioned by the full Court in Schenck v. United States, 249 U.S. 47, 52, applies. "The question in every case is whether the words used are used in such circumstances and are of such a nature as to create a clear and present danger that they will bring about the substantive

evils that [the State] has a right to prevent." It is true that in my opinion this criterion was departed from in Abrams v. United States, 250 U.S. 616, but the convictions that I expressed in that case are too deep for it to be possible for me as yet to believe that it and Schaefer v. United States, 251 U.S. 466, have settled the law. If what I think the correct test is applied, it is manifest that there was no present danger of an attempt to overthrow the government by force on the part of the admittedly small minority who shared the defendant's views. It is said that this manifesto was more than a theory, that it was an incitement. Every idea is an incitement. It offers itself for belief and if believed it is acted on unless some other belief outweighs it or some failure of energy stifles the movement at its birth. The only difference between the expression of an opinion and an incitement in the narrower sense is the speaker's enthusiasm for the result. Eloquence may set fire to reason. But whatever may be thought of the redundant discourse before us it had no chance of starting a present conflagration. If in the long run the beliefs expressed in proletarian dictatorship are destined to be accepted by the dominant forces of the community, the only meaning of free speech is that they should be given their chance and have their way.

Justice Brandeis, in a separate opinion joined by Justice Holmes, had occasion to expand upon their thinking two years later in Whitney v. California, 274 U.S. 357 (1927) (another case in which the majority had rejected the clear and present danger approach):

Fear of serious injury cannot alone justify suppression of free speech and assembly. Men feared witches and burnt women. It is the function of speech to free men from the bondage of irrational fears. To justify suppression of free speech there must be reasonable ground to fear that serious evil will result if free speech is practiced. There must be reasonable ground to believe that the danger apprehended is imminent. There must be reasonable ground to believe that the evil to be prevented is a serious one. Every denunciation of existing law tends in some measure to increase the probability that there will be violation of it. . . . In order to support a finding of clear and present danger it must be shown either that immediate serious violence was to be expected or was advocated, or that the past conduct furnished reason to believe that such advocacy was then contemplated.

. . . If there be time to expose through discussion the falsehood and fallacies, to avert the evil by the processes of education, the remedy to be applied is more speech, not enforced silence. Only an emergency can justify repression. Such must be the rule if authority is to be reconciled with freedom. Such, in my opinion, is the command of the Constitution. It is therefore always open to Americans to challenge a law abridging free speech and assembly by showing that there was no emergency justifying it.

Moreover, even imminent danger cannot justify resort to prohibition of these functions essential to effective democracy, unless the evil apprehended is relatively serious. Prohibition of free speech and assembly is a measure so stringent that it would be inappropriate as the means for averting a relatively trivial harm to society. A police measure may be unconstitutional merely because the remedy, although effective as means of protection, is unduly harsh or oppressive. Thus, a State might, in the exercise of its police power, make any trespass upon the land of another a crime, regardless of the results or of the intent or purpose of the trespasser. It might, also, punish an attempt, a conspiracy, or an incitement to commit the trespass. But it is hardly conceivable that this Court would hold constitutional a statute which punished as a felony the mere voluntary assembly with a society formed to teach that pedestrians had the moral right to cross unenclosed, unposted, waste lands and to advocate their doing so, even if there was imminent danger that advocacy would lead to a trespass. The fact that speech is likely to result in some violence or in destruction of property is not enough to justify its suppression. There must be the probability of serious injury to the State. Among free men, the deterrents ordinarily to be applied to prevent crime are education and punishment for violations of the law, not abridgment of the rights of free speech and assembly.

The Court had no occasion to return to these discussions for some time. Ironically, the return occurred in a case in which the plurality of the Court recognized that the Holmes-Brandeis position had evolved to become a majority view—but the plurality then refused to apply it to its case. This curious case was Dennis v. United States, 341 U.S. 494 (1951), involving prosecution of 11 leading members of the Communist Party for conspiring to advocate the forcible overthrow of the government of the United States. The plurality observed that "Although no case subsequent to *Whitney* and *Gitlow* has expressly overruled the majority opinions in those cases, there is little doubt that subsequent opinions have inclined toward the Holmes-Brandeis rationale."

At the same time, however, the plurality noted that each case confronting Justices Holmes and Brandeis involved "a comparatively isolated event, bearing little relation in their minds to any substantial threat to the safety of the community. . . . They were not confronted with any situation comparable to the instant one—the development of an apparatus designed and dedicated to the overthrow of the Government, in the context of world crisis after crisis."

The Court adopted the test framed by Judge Learned Hand in the lower court: "In each case [courts] must ask whether the gravity of the 'evil,' discounted by its improbability, justifies such invasion of free speech as is necessary to avoid the danger." That statement "takes into consideration those factors which we deem relevant, and relates their significances. More we cannot expect from words."

The plurality found that the requisite danger existed. The formation of a "highly organized conspiracy, with rigidly disciplined members subject to call when the leaders, these petitioners, felt the time had come for action, coupled with the inflammable nature of world conditions, similar uprisings in other countries, and the touch-and-go nature of our relations with countries with whom petitioners were in the very least ideologically attuned, convince us that their convictions were justified on this score . . . . If the ingredients of the reaction are present, we cannot bind the Government to wait until the catalyst is added."

In 1957, the Court limited the impact of the Smith Act, which had made it illegal to advocate overthrowing the government by force or violence. In Yates v. United States, 354 U.S. 298 (1957), the Court reversed five convictions under the Act and ordered new trials for the other nine defendants. Justice John M. Harlan for the Court said that *Dennis* allowed restricting only "advocacy found to be directed to 'action for the accomplishment of forcible overthrow.'" This required a direct relationship between speech and action that the government found it difficult to prove.

The status of clear and present danger after *Dennis* and *Yates* remained unclear until Brandenburg v. Ohio, 395 U.S. 444 (1969), involving prosecution of a Ku Klux Klan member for advocating racial and religious bigotry. The criminal syndicalism statute under which Ohio proceeded bore close similarities to the statute in *Whitney*. "But *Whitney* has been thoroughly discredited by later decisions. See [*Dennis*]. These later decisions have fashioned the principle that the constitutional guarantees of free speech and free press do not permit a State to forbid or proscribe advocacy of the use of force or of law violation except where such advocacy is directed to inciting or producing imminent lawless action and is likely to incite or produce such action."

Since the statute permitted punishment of advocacy with no requirement of a showing that imminent lawless action was likely to follow, the convictions could not stand. *Whitney* was overruled.

Brandenburg was reinforced in Hess v. Indiana, 414 U.S. 105 (1973). The defendant was arrested during an antiwar demonstration on a college campus for shouting, "We'll take the fucking street later (or again)." His subsequent conviction was overturned by the Supreme Court. "At best, [the] statement could be taken as counsel for present moderation; at worst, it amounted to nothing more than advocacy of illegal action at some indefinite future time." Since there was no showing that the words "were intended to produce, and likely to produce, *imminent* disorder, those words could not be punished by the State on the ground that they had a 'tendency to lead to violence.' "

Despite the extended period during which the clear and present danger test has been discussed in the Supreme Court, its importance and utility must not be overstated. As one observer has noted, although "it has uses in the area of seditious speech where it arose, it is not a broad-spectrum sovereign remedy for such other complaints as defamation, obscenity, and invasions of. privacy, where the complex of interests at stake requires closer diagnosis and more refined treatment." Freund, The Great Disorder of Speech, 44 American Scholar 541, 544–45 (1975). Elsewhere the same observer has noted that even where it is applicable, the test is not self-applying: "No matter how rapidly we utter the phrase . . . or how closely we hyphenate the words, they are not a substitute for the weighing of values." P. Freund, The Supreme Court of the United States 44 (1961).

4. THE LITERALIST INTERPRETATION OF THE FIRST AMENDMENT

Some have argued that the First Amendment allows no room for interpretation because its language is absolute: "Congress shall make no law . . . abridging the freedom of speech, or of the press law . . .." They have concluded that the federal government "is without any power whatever under the Constitution to put any type of burden on speech and expression of ideas of any kind." Ginzburg v. United States, 383 U.S. 463, 476 (1966) (Black, J., dissenting). He strongly criticized the balancing approach to First Amendment questions because the test could be used to justify a judge's predilections. But Justice Black did not believe that action should be protected to the same extent.

Justice Black's distinction between speech and action provided the escape hatch for his absolutist view. For instance, he would not have required states to allow public high school students to wear black arm bands to protest the Vietnam war. Tinker v. Des Moines Independent School District, 393 U.S. 503, 515 (1969) (Black, J., dissenting). He called the behavior "action," not speech, and thus not protected by the First Amendment.

In his book, The System of Freedom of Expression 17 (1970), Professor Thomas Emerson drew a similar distinction, believing, with Justice Black, that expression should be absolutely protected by the First Amendment:

> "Expression" must be freely allowed and encouraged. "Action" can be controlled, subject to other constitutional requirements, but not by controlling expression. . . . The character of the system [of freedom of expression] can flourish, and the goals of the system can be realized, only if expression receives full protection under the First Amendment. . . . The govern-

ment may protect or advance other social interests through regulation of action, but not by suppressing expression.

Recall Meiklejohn, too, believed in an absolute approach to the First Amendment—but only for "political speech." As with Justice Black and Emerson, his distinction narrows the types of expression to be afforded absolute protection, leaving to the courts the problem of defining "political speech" and differentiating it from unprotected or less protected expression.

E. "OR OF THE PRESS"

Until this point we have used the terms "freedom of speech" and "freedom of the press" interchangeably. Some have argued, however, that the speech and press guarantees have independent and distinct significance. Are there some types of activity protected under the press clause that are not protected under the speech clause? Or, are there some activities that, though they constitute protected speech, lay outside the press guarantee?

1. THE SPEECH CLAUSE V. THE PRESS CLAUSE?

The most prominent proponent of the theory that the press clause is of greater scope than the speech clause is Justice Potter Stewart, who contended that the press clause, in contradistinction to the speech guarantee, was a *structural* provision of the Constitution. Stewart relied heavily on the notion that the institutional press has a special role in our constitutional scheme as an additional check on the power of government officials. Because of this special role, he asserted that the institutional press in certain situations had rights of access and immunities growing out of the press clause to which the general citizenry could not lay claim.

Justice Stewart reiterated this view in a case in which the Court overturned the conviction of a newspaper publisher for violating a statute that made it a crime to divulge information about investigations of judicial conduct being conducted by a state board. Concurring in the judgment, Justice Stewart saw an important governmental interest in protecting the quality of its judiciary. He would have allowed the statute to be applied against individuals but would not allow the state to punish a newspaper for printing the same information. Landmark Communications, Inc. v. Virginia, 435 U.S. 829, 848–49 (1978) (Stewart, J., concurring) We return to this case in Chapter VI.

Chief Justice Burger rejected this analysis. Concurring in First National Bank of Boston v. Bellotti, 435 U.S. 765 (1978), he contended that the speech and press clauses of the First Amendment complement each other, but the latter does not give the "institutional press" a special status. First, the framers did not contemplate special privileges for the press, according to the Chief Justice. That does not mean the press clause is redundant. Rather, it is meant to focus "specifically on the liberty to disseminate expression broadly," while the speech clause is to protect "the liberty to express ideas and beliefs." The press clause, "although complementary to and a natural extension of Speech Clause liberty, merited special mention simply because it had been more often the object of official restraints." Thus, he saw "no difference between the right of those who seek to disseminate ideas by way of newspaper and those who give lectures or speeches."

Second, the Chief Justice foresaw difficulty in defining what was and was not included in the "institutional press" if it were to be accorded special status. Including some entities while excluding others would be "reminiscent of the abhorred licensing system" of England, which the First Amendment was meant, in part, to prevent. He noted that the Court had not, in related matters, allowed officials "to distinguish the protected from the unprotected on the basis of such variables as content of expression, frequency or fervor of expression, or ownership of the technological means of dissemination."

To date the issue of special protections for the press has been carefully left open by the Supreme Court in a number of areas. It remains unclear, for example, whether the constitutional rules protecting defendants in defamation actions apply equally to media and non-media defendants. In Chapter XI, the question resurfaces in the Houchins and Pell cases in connection with the press assertion of a right of access to prisons to gather information.

Regardless of how the issue of special protection is resolved, it is true as a practical matter that certain First Amendment issues arise in connection with the institutional press, while others are generally raised in the context of individual speech. Be careful to distinguish cases in which the press is asserting a special press right from cases in which the press is claiming a protection that, though it belongs to all, is unlikely to be asserted by non-media individuals and institutions. This might occur, for example, in cases in which reporters seek access to obscure sources of information, not because they are reporters, but because they are trying to run down stories, while the rest of us are busy doing things other than trying to gather information. The cluster of First Amendment claims asserted primarily by the institutional press are the focus of this book.

Among the issues most frequently associated with the institutional press are gathering information, the protection of confidential sources, and question of broadcast regulation. In the chapters that follow, students should determine whether the issues raised are of particular importance to the institutionalized press and, if so, whether that fact has an impact upon how the Supreme Court balances the interests at stake.

2. SPECIAL SPEECH ISSUES

Just as some aspects of First Amendment doctrine are usually associated with the press, other elements almost always involve individuals rather than the press. Though less central to our concern with the mass media, these non-press aspects of the First Amendment are important historically and intellectually, and help complete the overall picture. Indeed, the very roots of modern First Amendment law are to be found in the cases discussed above that articulate the clear and present danger test. Recall that these tended to involve individual, not press, defendants. A few other areas of non-press First Amendment Law deserve brief mention here before we begin our extended consideration of the issue of most concern to mass media.

a. *"Symbolic Speech"*

The Supreme Court has held that some limited types of nonverbal expressive conduct are entitled to protection under the First Amendment. Examples of such "symbolic speech" include wearing an armband or displaying an American flag upside down in protest. Since the print and broadcast media are virtually always engaged in what most consider the clearest case of verbal expression, they, unlike individuals, have had little cause to assert their claim to symbolic speech rights.

The most commonly used analysis of restrictions on symbolic speech was developed in United States v. O'Brien, 391 U.S. 367 (1968):

> This Court has held that when "speech" and "nonspeech" elements are combined in the same course of conduct, a sufficiently important governmental interest in regulating the nonspeech element can justify incidental limitations on First Amendment freedoms. . . . [W]e think it clear that a governmental regulation is sufficiently justified if it is within the constitutional power of the Government; if it furthers an important or substantial governmental interest; if the governmental interest is unrelated to the suppression of free expression; and if the incidental restriction on alleged First Amendment freedoms is no greater than is essential to the furtherance of that interest.

In *O'Brien* itself the Court upheld a criminal statute punishing the deliberate mutilation of draft cards, a common form of protest against the Vietnam war in the 1960's. For cases going each way under this analysis, see Tinker v. Des Moines Community School District, 393 U.S. 503 (1969) (wearing of protest armbands in school protected); Spence v. Washington, 418 U.S. 405 (1974) (displaying a defaced American flag as a symbol of protest against the Vietnam war protected); Clark v. Community for Creative Non-Violence, 468 U.S. ___ (1984) (sleeping in public park to protest plight of homeless not protected).

b. Hostile Audience

The hostile audience issue arises when a speaker on a platform or on a street corner angers the crowd to such an extent that a breach of the peace is threatened. The question arises when the police, instead of controlling the crowd, order the speaker to stop speaking. This is sometimes said to raise the question of the "heckler's veto." Again, the issue does not involve mass media because speaker and hostile audience must confront one another for the problem to occur—and this is uniquely a speech situation.

In Feiner v. New York, 340 U.S. 315 (1951), police ordered a speaker on a soap box to stop his talk because members of the audience were threatening to attack him. When the speaker refused, he was arrested. The Court said that since disorder was threatened, the policeman's order was lawful and the speaker could be punished for disobeying it. In dissent, Justice Black said those breaking the law should be arrested, not the speaker.

In subsequent cases, the Court appears to be granting greater protection to the expressive activity. See Edwards v. South Carolina, 372 U.S. 229 (1963) (187 black students in a march could not be convicted of breach of the peace for failing to obey an order to disperse, since the Court's majority found no threatened violence from the large crowd of onlookers) and Gregory v. Chicago, 394 U.S. 111 (1969) (peaceful marchers in a demonstration could not be convicted of disorderly conduct for failure to disperse when crowd became unruly). See also Village of Skokie v. National Socialist Party, 69 Ill. 2d 605, 14 Ill.Dec. 890, 373 N.E.2d 21 (1978).

c. The Public Forum

The media have little need to use the public forum since each publisher or broadcaster is itself a forum for expressive activity. Individuals, however, have long claimed the right to speak in places where there is a chance for them to be seen and heard, usually on public property. The Supreme Court first explicitly recognized the right to speak in a public forum in Hague v. CIO, 307 U.S. 496 (1939):

> [T]he . . . streets and parks . . . have immemorially been held in trust for the use of the public and, time out of mind, have been used for purposes of assembling, communicating thoughts between citizens, and discussing public questions. Such use of the streets and public places has, from ancient times, been a part of the privileges, immunities, rights and liberties of citizens.

But the right is not absolute. While public streets and parks and some other public places, such as state capitol grounds and airport areas, are available for use to express ideas and opinions, the city's police powers permit certain regulations. The main consideration is that the activity not interfere with the primary purposes of the building or facility in question. Some other areas that are "public" in some senses are not public forums for expressive activities, such as jails, military bases, and the reading room of the Library of Congress.

3. THE CAPTIVE AUDIENCE

As we have seen, the role of the audience may be relevant to arguments that implicate the First Amendment. Those justifications for freedom of expression that relied heavily upon the role of speech in the governance of the community or in the marketplace of ideas necessarily made some assumptions about the willingness of the audience to receive the message or at least messages of that type. Those justifications that are based on ideas of self-expression or self-fulfillment, with no audience implications, may nevertheless involve speech that is intended to, or does, reach an audience.

We now consider the implications for freedom of speech when the proposed audience does not wish to receive the message but lacks the freedom audiences usually have to avoid the message.

The issue may arise in media or nonmedia situations. It usually arises in the context of time, place, and manner regulations that seek to reduce noise, protect privacy, or to protect audiences that are unable to avoid messages. What follows is a brief introduction to a subject that can arise in many contexts and that involves many variables. Note that some of the cases discussed below, involve government efforts to protect audiences from specific kinds of speech. These attempts, as we have seen, raise much more serious questions than attempts that are not based on content. The subject of captive audiences is discussed at length in M. Nimmer, Nimmer on Freedom of Speech § 1.02[F][2] (1984).

Perhaps the most obvious case for protecting a captive audience arises when an ordinance seeks, without regard to the content of the message, to prevent sound trucks from blaring their messages in residential neighborhoods. The most apparent justification for such an ordinance would be that when persons are in their homes they should not have to endure noise that cannot be readily and easily silenced. The Supreme Court has upheld efforts to achieve this kind of result. Kovacs v. Cooper, 336 U.S. 77 (1949) (upholding ban on "loud and raucous" sound trucks). This result can be justified by stressing the special interest that persons have in the solitude of their homes or the particular difficulty of avoiding this kind of communication.

In Rowan v. Post Office, 397 U.S. 728 (1970), the Court upheld a statute allowing a homeowner who had received advertisements in the mail that the "addressee in his sole discretion believes to be erotically arousing or sexually provocative" to instruct the Post Office to order the mailer to send no more mail to the addressee. The majority relied on the sanctity of the home and rejected the claim that the homeowner had an adequate remedy in simply throwing out unwanted material. To require homeowners to receive and then discard the material would be to "license a form of trespass and would make hardly more sense than to say that a radio or television viewer may not twist the dial to cut off an offensive or boring communication and thus bar its entering his home."

In Bolger v. Youngs Drug Products Corp., 463 U.S. 60 (1983), the Court overturned a statute that had barred the mailing of unsolicited advertisements for contraceptives. Here, the homeowner's ability to send the mail on a "short, though regular, journey from mail box to trash can . . . is an acceptable burden, at least so far as the Constitution is concerned." One distinction from *Rowan* was that here the burden was on the sender not to mail its message to anyone who had not affirmatively requested it.

Outside the home, the Supreme Court has tended to protect those who would speak—at least where the audience can relatively easily avoid the communication. In Cohen v. California, 403 U.S. 15 (1971), the Court overturned a conviction for wearing, in a Los Angeles courthouse, a jacket with the message "Fuck the Draft." The words were not obscene because the message was not "erotic."

The state argued that, even so, the message could not be thrust upon unwilling or unsuspecting audiences, especially of women and children. The Court rejected the argument, 5–4. The majority asserted that government's ability to protect an audience from hearing a message was "dependent upon a showing that substantial privacy interests are being invaded in an essentially intolerable manner. Any broader view of this authority would effectively empower a majority to silence dissidents simply as a matter of personal predilections."

The state could not meet the required standard here because those who confronted the jacket "could effectively avoid further bombardment of their sensibilities simply by averting their eyes." Although the claim to a "recognizable privacy interest" was greater when "walking through a courthouse corridor than, for example, strolling through Central Park, surely it is nothing like the interest in being free from unwanted expression in the confines of one's own home."

The majority also concluded that the state had "no right to cleanse public debate to the point where it is grammatically palatable to the most squeamish among us. Yet no readily ascertainable general principle exists for stopping short of that result were we to affirm the judgment below."

The majority also recognized that "words are often chosen as much for their emotive as their cognitive force. We cannot sanction the view that the Constitution, while solicitous of the cognitive content of individual speech, has little or no regard for that emotive function which, practically speaking, may often be the more important element of the overall message sought to be communicated."

The Court reached a similar result in a case involving an ordinance forbidding the showing of nudity on screens of outdoor movie theatres that were visible from public streets. Erznoznik v. Jacksonville, 422 U.S. 205 (1975). The screen of a drive-in movie theatre "is not 'so obtrusive as to make it impossible for an unwilling individual to avoid exposure to it.'"

See Chapter VII for additional discussion of indecency and obscenity.

But an individual outside the home is not necessarily able to avoid undesired communications. In Public Utilities Commission v. Pollak, 343 U.S. 451 (1952), the majority upheld the right of a municipal transit company to play radio news, music, and commercials over the loudspeaker systems on its buses, on the ground that the expectations of privacy were quite different when one ventured out of the house. Justice Douglas dissented: "One who tunes in on an offensive program at home can turn it off or tune in another station as he wishes. One who hears disquieting or unpleasant programs in public places, such as restaurants, can get up and leave. But the man on the streetcar has no choice but to sit and listen, or perhaps to sit and try not to listen."

In Lehman v. City of Shaker Heights, 418 U.S. 298 (1974), the Court upheld an ordinance banning political advertising in the city's transit vehicles. Five justices based their votes in whole or in part on the captive audience notion: "There is no difference when the message is visual not auricular [as was the case in *Pollak*]. In each the viewer or listener is captive." The passengers could not simply avert their eyes because "the degree of captivity makes it impractical for the unwilling viewer . . . to avoid exposure." (The case was complicated by the fact that nonpolitical advertising was permitted.)

Finally, should it matter that a large majority of the captive audience affirmatively wishes to hear the message? Professor Nimmer suggests that "there is something abhorrent in requiring even a few persons to be subjected to such a force-feeding of speech." M. Nimmer, Nimmer on Freedom of Speech § 1.02[F][2][e] (1984).

Many of these issues came together in FCC v. Pacifica Foundation, 438 U.S. 726 (1978), in which, during the middle of a weekday, a radio station broadcast a program containing some words that might offend some listeners. The case is reprinted and the issue is discussed in detail in Chapter XVI.

Chapter III

DEFAMATION

In this Chapter and several that follow we will consider the range of legal arguments for prohibiting certain communications because of their substantive content. In each case we will consider, among other points, the justifications offered for restriction and the value of the communication. The justifications are as diverse as the situations to which they are applied. Arguments for limiting speech and press to protect privacy are unlikely to resemble the arguments based on national security.

Even if the speech is determined to be subject to governmental control, there is the further question of what types of sanctions may be imposed. Among the array are criminal prosecutions, civil damage remedies, and bans on speech imposed by administrative techniques or by court injunction. Again, particular sanctions are used for specific kinds of speech. Even when speech is found to be defamatory, for example, it is regulated after the fact and is not enjoined. On the other hand, speech held to invade privacy has been barred from publication. In sum, the sanctions available are as diverse as the justifications offered to restrict the speech in the first place.

We begin our survey of restraints on communication with a justification based on the state's interest in granting redress to persons whose reputations have been hurt by false statements. We start with defamation law in part because it is one of the earliest legal actions available against publishers and broadcasters and in part because even today it is still the most common type of legal danger that can befall publishers and broadcasters. It is certainly the most extensively litigated area of media law.

Harm to reputation is one of the earliest injuries recognized by virtually every legal system. Early societies were undoubtedly concerned that the failure to provide legal recourse to those whose reputations had been impugned would lead to breaches of the peace. Although that concern has eased as civilization has advanced, states may still be concerned about the potential for violence. Beyond that, however, traditional values emphasize the importance of an individual's good name. Whatever the justifications, the action for defamation has long had a place in the common law.

English law has redressed and punished attacks on reputation since the feudal days. After the Norman conquest, defamations were treated as a form of sin by ecclesiastical courts whose penalties were ecclesiastical in nature. During the 16th century, the common law courts began to assert jurisdiction in defamation cases and ordered that damages be paid to the plaintiff. As noted in Chapter II, during this period the authorities began using the law of defamation to punish political criticism of the government and its officials. These attacks were referred to as seditious libel.

Although it is doubtful that the English law of seditious libel was transplanted in this country, it seems clear that the tort law that provided damage remedies to individuals did cross the Atlantic. After independence, defamation law continued to be enforced. The First Amendment's statement that "Congress shall make no law . . . abridging the freedom of speech, or of the press . . ." had no apparent impact upon defamation law until quite recently. Since defamation law was a creature of state law—the power to regulate defamation law was not delegated to Congress—the First Amendment had no immediate effect on the states' administration of that law.

Even after it became clear that the First Amendment applied to the states through the Fourteenth Amendment, these provisions were thought inapplicable to false statements that adversely affected an individual's reputation. The Supreme Court did not tie defamation and the First Amendment together until the seminal case of New York Times Co. v. Sullivan, decided in 1964. That case not only brought major change to the law of defamation, but also provided a philosophy that has led to many other recent developments in mass media law. We shall consider the impact of this case on defamation law shortly.

Before we can appreciate the significance of the constitutional developments, however, we must understand the common-law world of defamation. The constitutional developments have not created a totally new legal area; rather they have altered some of the pre-existing state rules and left the remaining ones in place. States remain free to protect reputation in whatever manner they see fit so long as they do so consistently with the First Amendment.

A second reason for inquiring into state law is that state law itself has a significant number of protections for those who are sued for defamation. It is often possible for a defendant to win a defamation case under the state's traditional rules without ever having to rely upon the protection of the First Amendment.

Why might a defendant who could win a case under First Amendment principles try to win that case under state rules? There are several practical explanations. Perhaps the major one is that, as a matter of procedure, the state defenses may permit a defendant to win the case earlier in the litigation (such as on a motion to dismiss, rather than on a motion for summary judgment or perhaps only after a trial is held). It is often faster and cheaper for a media defendant to succeed on state law grounds than to rely exclusively on the more glorious but perhaps less expeditious ground of the First and Fourteenth Amendments.

A quick example demonstrates this point. In most states, if a statement has two possible meanings, one of which would be defamatory and one of which would not be defamatory, the jury decides how recipients of that statement understood it. Illinois, however, has a special "innocent construction" rule providing that if a statement has one innocent meaning the defendant wins the case immediately. The plaintiff cannot argue that the defendant "really meant" the defamatory version. The case is simply over. This rule has permitted defendants in Illinois to win an overwhelming percentage of their defamation cases and to win them quickly without having to rely on federal constitutional defenses.

The point is that we must understand the basic operation of traditional state defamation law as well as the Constitution. We turn first to the state law and then to the impact of constitutional law.

A. THE STATE LAW OF DEFAMATION

1. THE REPUTATION ELEMENT

a. *Definition*

The essence of the action for defamation is the claim that defendant has uttered a false statement that has harmed the plaintiff's reputation. Historically, some states required that the defendant's statement expose the plaintiff to hatred, ridicule, contempt, scorn, or shame, or words to that effect. The modern view is that a statement is defamatory if it harms the plaintiff's reputation by lowering him in the estimation of the community or by deterring others from associating or dealing with him. It is easy to think of statements that will fit such a very broad definition. It obviously covers charges that plaintiff committed a crime, that he was inept in his chosen trade or profession, or that he was a member of a group or a political party that was in disrepute in the community. It is enough that the published statement be of the sort that would lead a segment of the community to think less of the plaintiff.

That segment need not be large. In one case, for example, the plaintiff, an expert on Palestinian art and customs, was falsely stated to have written an article for the Sunday newspaper on that subject. The article would have impressed virtually all the newspaper's regular readers. Unfortunately, the article had several errors that would embarrass the author among fellow experts. The court ruled that the relevant community in that case was the small group of experts on the subject—and that a jury could find that those experts would have thought less of plaintiff as a scholar after hearing that she had written such an article. Ben-Oliel v. Press Publishing Co., 251 N.Y. 250, 167 N.E. 432 (1929).

Most cases have involved charges of volitional behavior by plaintiff—committing a crime, lacking skill, or writing an article. The broad sweep of the definition, however, extends to accusations that the plaintiff was of illegitimate birth, had been raped, or was in dire financial straits. Even though the plaintiff cannot be blamed for a condition, the courts have nonetheless bowed to reality and recognized that these kinds of charges may in fact cause others to shun, or refrain from associating with, the plaintiff. Judges "take the world as we find it" even if the segment of the community that thinks less of the plaintiff can be characterized as "wrong-thinking"—as they would be in the illegitimacy and rape examples.

At the same time, there is a limit to that principle. Consider, for example, a false charge that the mob's gunman missed his target. Were the gunman to sue and assert that his reputation had been tarnished among the underworld, it is unlikely that a court would entertain the charge. Is it appropriate to redress a claim based on an audience segment that is criminal rather than simply wrong thinking?

b. Corporations

Until now, the discussion has been directed to the question of protecting the reputation of a human being. Not infrequently, however, defamatory statements are made about corporations. It is generally held that corporations also have reputations that they may vindicate through actions for defamation. Generally the corporation must be attacked in a way that affects its credit or profit-making ability if it is a corporation organized for profit. For example, in one case a corporate plaintiff's restaurant was asserted to be a good place "to meet a connection" to buy cocaine. The corporation was allowed to bring suit because such a charge might well adversely affect the restaurant's patronage. See El Meson Espanol v. NYM Corp., 521 F.2d 737 (2d Cir.1975).

A non-profit corporation may also be defamed if the charge is one that tends to interfere with its ability to obtain financial support from the public. A corporation that relies on public donations may be able to sue for defamation if the charge would interfere with its ability to obtain such funds.

Some governmental activities are undertaken by corporations specially organized for particular purposes. Such corporations are not usually permitted to bring defamation actions. The reason is that to permit such law suits would come perilously close to reviving the action for seditious libel that, as you recall, was used in England by the government against its critics. As one court has observed, "no court of last resort in this country has ever held, or even suggested, that prosecutions for libel on government have any place in the American system of jurisprudence." City of Chicago v. Tribune Co., 307 Ill. 595, 601, 139 N.E. 86, 88 (1923). This issue reemerges later in the New York Times case.

When a business sues, questions arise as to whether the business is more like an individual who is a public figure or like an individual who is a private figure—a distinction discussed in Gertz v. Robert Welch, Inc., 418 U.S. 323 (1974), at p. 99, infra. In Bank of Oregon v. Independent News, 298 Or. 434, 693 P.2d 35 (1985), for example, an Oregon bank and its president were held to be private figures because they had not established "general fame or notoriety" in the community or exhibited "pervasive involvement in the affairs of society."

c. Ambiguity

As noted earlier, statements are often ambiguous. In such cases the prevailing rule is to have the judge decide whether any of the statement's possible meanings can reasonably be understood to have a defamatory impact. If the judge decides that at least one of the possible meanings would be defamatory, it then becomes a function of the jury to decide the meaning that was in fact conveyed. In a famous example involving Horace Greeley and James Fenimore Cooper, Greeley had written in the *New York Tribune* that he was not worried about a suit that Cooper had previously filed against him because "Mr. Cooper will have to bring his action to trial somewhere. He will not like to bring it in New York, for we are known here, nor in Otsego, for he is known there." Cooper sued again—this time for defamation. Greeley contended that the statement meant only "that a prophet has no honor in his own country. The point of the article is the intimation that the plaintiff would prefer a trial where the prejudice and rivalries which assail every man at home could not reach him." Cooper alleged that the statement meant that he was in bad repute in Otsego. The court held that a jury should decide which of the two meanings was understood by readers of the article. Cooper v. Greeley, 1 Denio 347 (N.Y.1845).

It should be noted here that the Supreme Court in one discussion of ambiguous statements resolved the question itself. The case arose from a tumultuous city council meeting involving the plaintiff, who was a local real estate developer, in a negotiation with the city council. Members of the audience characterized the plaintiff's bargaining position as "blackmail." The defendant newspaper accurately reported the meeting and included the blackmail charges—sometimes without quotation marks. The state courts granted plaintiff a judgment against the newspaper.

Justice Stewart, in part of a longer opinion, observed that "as a matter of constitutional law, the word 'blackmail' in these circumstances was not" defamatory:

> It is simply impossible to believe that a reader who reached the word "blackmail" in either article would not have understood exactly what was meant; it was Bresler's public and wholly legal negotiating proposals that were being criticized. No reader could have thought that either the speakers at the meeting or the

newspaper articles reporting their words were charging Bressler with the commission of a criminal offense. On the contrary, even the most careless reader must have perceived that the word was no more than rhetorical hyperbole . . ..

Justice White dissented. He could not "join the majority claim of superior insight with respect to how the word 'blackmail' would be understood by the ordinary reader in Greenbelt, Maryland." Greenbelt Cooperative Publishing Association v. Bresler, 398 U.S. 6 (1970).

Sometimes the words themselves may be absolutely clear but their use may present problems. For example, former Senator George Smathers of Florida was once reported to have made the following statement to some of his rural audiences while campaigning in the Democratic primary for United States Senator against the incumbent, Claude Pepper: "Are you aware that Claude Pepper is known all over Washington as a shameless extrovert? Not only that, but this man is reliably reported to practice nepotism with his sister-in-law, and he has a sister, who was once a thespian in wicked New York. Worst of all, it is an established fact that Mr. Pepper, before his marriage, practiced celibacy." See R. Sherrill, Gothic Politics in the Deep South 150 (1968). Smathers denies making the statement and has offered a reward to anyone who can prove he had ever made it. See The New York Times, Feb. 24, 1983, at p. 10. (How can one ever disprove allegations that he once made a statement?)

Had Smathers made the statement, would it be possible for a court to find a statement defamatory when the words, given their only acceptable dictionary meanings, are not likely to lower plaintiff's esteem in the community? Would it be extremely dangerous for free speech to allow a court to decide that, even though the words themselves are not defamatory, the speaker should be punished for trying to get an uneducated audience to think that the words were defamatory? Should the legal system be able to do something in this case?

Verbal ambiguities aside, the meaning of a statement may be altered by punctuation, paragraphing, and typography. Thus, in Wildstein v. New York Post Corp., 40 Misc.2d 586, 243 N.Y.S.2d 386, affirmed without opinion 24 A.D.2d 559, 261 N.Y.S.2d 254 (1965), the defendant wrote that the plaintiff was one of "several women described as 'associated' with" a slain executive. The judge observed that if the word "associated" had not been in quotation marks the statement would not have been defamatory; the quotation marks implied a euphemistic use of the word, suggesting an illicit relationship between plaintiff and the deceased. The actual paragraphing of the story may also be crucial in determining meaning.

Another problem arises when part of an article has a defamatory impact but another part of the article negates that impact. The headline may be defamatory although the article is not; the lead paragraph alone may be defamatory but the article as a whole may be harmless; and one sentence may be defamatory but the whole paragraph may be harmless. Gambuzza v. Time, Inc., 18 A.D.2d 351, 239 N.Y.S.2d 466 (1963), involved a two-page spread of 12 photographs in a magazine article, each with a three-line legend beneath it. The story involved reports of the activities of a convicted spy. One photograph of plaintiff was captioned "HIS ADMIRER. Frank Gambuzza, a radio dealer who sold Abel some parts for a wireless receiver, praised the Russian for his electronic know-how." Plaintiff alleged that the first two words suggested sympathy for Abel and his cause. The majority noted that sometimes headlines might be read separately from the article and judged by their own words because "a person passing a newsstand . . . may be able to catch a glimpse of a headline without the opportunity or desire to read the accompanying article or may skim through the paper jumping from headline to headline." But this was not such a case because the caption was so close to the text that they had to be read together: "the article must be considered as a whole and its meaning gleaned not from isolated portions thereof but rather from the entire article. . . ." Two dissenters emphasized that the critical words in the caption were in bold capital type and thus should be considered separately from the rest of the article.

In Kunst v. New York World Telegram Corp., 28 A.D.2d 662, 280 N.Y.S.2d 798 (1967), the lead paragraph and a photograph caption conveyed a defamatory implication that was negated by a statement that a "persistent and careful reader would discover near the end of the reasonably lengthy article." The majority upheld the complaint, stressing that the writing must be "construed, not with the high degree of precision expected of and used by lawyers and judges, but as it would be read and understood by an ordinary member of the public to whom it is directed." A dissenter responded, "It is true this appears near the end of the article, but the article is to be taken as a whole and read in its entirety." He relied on *Gambuzza.*

A statement may be defamatory even though the thrust of the accusation is not clear from the words used. In this type of indirect defamation case, the plaintiff's complaint must show the court how the statement defames him. The description of how plaintiff does this involves the use of three technical words. If the plaintiff himself is not directly named he must show by "colloquium" that the statement was "of and concerning" him. If it is still not clear how the plaintiff has been defamed, he must plead extrinsic facts that would permit a defamatory meaning to be applied to defendant's words. This allegation of extrinsic facts is called the "inducement." Finally we have "innuendo." Where the statement is not clearly defamatory on its face it is the function of the innuendo to assert the meaning that plaintiff attaches to the passage and any additions by colloquium and inducement. The innuendo is not a fact but is the plaintiff's assertion of how the passage would be understood by those who heard the defendant's words and knew the additional unstated facts.

An example may help clarify the matter. Let us assume defendant says, "The man who lives in the house two doors east of my house was the only person in the Smith home between 7:00 p.m. and 8:00 p.m. last night." If the plaintiff thinks that this statement is defamatory of him and wishes to sue, his pleading must establish how he has been defamed. For colloquium he might allege, "I am the only man who lives in the house two doors east of the speaker's house." This ties the plaintiff to the statement but does not clarify its defamatory nature. The defamation is clarified if the plaintiff alleges as inducement that the Smith house was burglarized between 7:00 and 8:00 p.m. that night. The plaintiff will then assert that the innuendo is that he is being charged by defendant with the crime of burglary.

d. *"Of and Concerning Plaintiff"*

In order for a defamatory statement to adversely affect the plaintiff, the reader must connect that statement with the plaintiff. The plaintiff must show that the statement objected to was "of and concerning" him. Sometimes this is a problem because of the ambiguity of the statement or because the plaintiff is only indirectly identified. In those cases our discussion about ambiguous statements will help resolve the case. If readers could plausibly believe that the plaintiff was referred to then a jury will decide whether the statement was in fact so understood.

e. *Groups*

Another aspect of this problem involves statements that attack large groups of people. In such cases is it possible for an individual member of that group to assert that the statement hurt his personal reputation? At the extreme, an attack on all lawyers in the United States or on all clergymen would be held to be such a general broadside that no individual lawyer or clergyman could sue. The same would be true of broadside attacks on racial, religious or ethnic groups.

At the other extreme it is generally accepted that a charge made against a small group may defame all members of that group. For example, a newspaper article may assert that "the officers" of a corporation have embezzled funds. There are only four officers of the corporation. Each of them may be found to have been defamed. Even if the statement had said "one of the officers of the corporation" had embezzled funds, the group is small enough so that all four officials are put under a shadow and can sue.

As the group grows larger the impact of the statement may depend on the number accused. In a recent case, a defamatory charge was made against one unidentified member of a 21-member police force. All 21 sued. The court dismissed the case. It feared that allowing the action would permit a suit by an entire baseball team over a report that one member was disciplined for brawling. Such a result "would chill communication to the marrow." But suppose the charge had been against "all but one" of the members of that police force. Such a statement may reflect on each member of the force though the same charge made against only one of the 21 might not. Arcand v. Evening Call Publishing Co., 567 F.2d 1163 (1st Cir.1977).

One case presented three aspects of this problem. Two authors, in a book about Dallas, stated that "some" department store models were "call girls . . .. The salesgirls are good, too—pretty and often much cheaper . . .." And "most of the [male] sales staff are fairies, too."

Suits were filed by all nine models, 15 of the 25 salesmen, and 30 of the 382 saleswomen. The defendants did not challenge the right of the nine models to sue. (Would it have mattered if only three had sued?) The other two groups were challenged as being too large.

The case for "the salesgirls" was dismissed. The result would be the same even if the authors had explicitly referred to "all"—and even if all 382 had sued. The judge could find no case allowing a group of 382 to sue. He cited cases rejecting suits when the statements attacked all officials of a state-wide union or all the taxicab drivers in Washington, D.C.

On the other hand, the salesmen's case was not dismissed. It was close to others involving members of a posse, or the 12 doctors on a hospital's residential staff. Would the result have been the same if the authors had referred to "some" or "a few" of the men? Neiman-Marcus v. Lait, 13 F.R.D. 311 (S.D.N.Y.1952).

Is the reasoning behind these cases that attacks on a large group don't hurt any particular member of the group? Is it that such broad accusations are not taken seriously by hearers or readers? Is it that the legal system would find it administratively difficult to handle a damage action brought by 382 plaintiffs, even though they might deserve some compensation?

Even though all states deny damage actions to large groups, a few have attempted to use criminal statutes to prevent or punish such charges against racial or ethnic groups. We consider this at p. 125, infra.

f. Opinions—A Special Problem

At common law there was much confusion about whether opinion, as distinguished from fact, could be the basis for a defamation action. Since a strongly expressed unfavorable opinion could easily lower a person's reputation in the eyes of others, the courts usually held that such a statement could form the basis of a defamation action even though it could not be found to be true or false. Occasionally, the courts held that although truth was a defense to defamation, that did not mean that a statement could be defamatory only if it could be shown to be false. The impossibility of proving a certain type of statement to be true did not mean that it was not actionable. Instead, courts held that those sued for publishing defamatory opinions might invoke the defense of fair comment—the privilege of stating opinions that they actually held and did not express solely for the purpose of hurting the object of the attack.

Much of this confusion is disappearing, largely as a result of a passage from Gertz v. Robert Welch, Inc., 418 U.S. 323 (1974), reprinted at p. 95, infra: "Under the First Amendment there is no such thing as a false idea. However pernicious an opinion may seem, we depend for its correction not on the conscience of judges and juries but on the competition of other ideas." 418 U.S. at 339–40. The American Law Institute, a private but prestigious group that publishes summaries of the law, seized upon the opportunity to clarify this area of law. Restatement, Second, Torts § 566 (1977) declares:

> A defamatory communication may consist of a statement in the form of an opinion, but a statement of this nature is actionable only if it implies the allegation of undisclosed defamatory facts as the basis for the opinion.

In short, if the opinion is based on unstated facts that are known to the speaker and the recipients, there can be no liability for defamation. If the opinion is accompanied by stated facts, there may be liability for the facts under the usual rules, but there can be no liability for the opinion as such. Whether the stated opinion implies the existence of "undisclosed defamatory facts" becomes the crucial issue.

Thus, if A and B are walking on the street discussing someone known only to A, and A says "I think W is an alcoholic," that conveys the idea that A knows facts that he has not stated—and the statement can be sued upon. Compare the following statement by A: "My friend W takes two martinis at lunch every day. I think he is an alcoholic." Since the basis for the opinion is apparently fully stated, the opinion itself cannot form the basis for a defamation action. If A and B are discussing a mutual friend, X, and both know an equal amount about X, then A's statement "I think X is an alcoholic" would be protected because the unstated underlying facts are known to both parties. Finally, if as A and B are walking down the street they see a stranger stagger out of a tavern and reel across their path, A's statement "I think that man is an alcoholic" could not give rise to a suit because it is based on facts that both A and B know equally.

The states have moved sharply to clarify their own law without waiting for further prodding from the Supreme Court. In Rinaldi v. Holt, Rinehart & Winston, Inc., 42 N.Y.2d 369, 397 N.Y.S.2d 943, 366 N.E.2d 1299, certiorari denied 434 U.S. 969 (1977), an author had strongly attacked a judge's decisions and competence. The court relied on the *Gertz* dictum: "The expression of opinion, even in the form of pejorative rhetoric, relating to fitness for judicial office or to performance while in judicial office, is safeguarded. . . . Plaintiff may not recover from defendants for simply expressing their opinion of his judicial performance, no matter how unreasonable, extreme or erroneous these opinions might be." In his writing, the author "set forth the basis for his belief that plaintiff is incompetent and should be removed. Based upon the facts stated and public debate provoked by the statements, each reader may draw his own conclusions as to whether Newfield's views should be supported or challenged." The court did note that a charge that the judge was "probably corrupt" was not protected as opinion: "The ordinary and average reader would likely understand the use of these words, in the context of the entire article, as meaning that plaintiff had committed illegal and unethical actions."

See also The Sierra Breeze v. Superior Court, 86 Cal.App.3d 102, 149 Cal.Rptr. 914 (1978), holding that a charge that a public official voted to "squander property tax funds for Tahoe airport" was a statement of opinion.

In cases arising from statements during political campaigns, the courts have concluded that much commentary must have been understood by the electorate as opinion. One letter to the editor accused the plaintiff of "contrived public opinion polls, unfounded statements, emphatic denials, committees no one ever heard of, attacks on straw men and a lot of slick, big-time expensive political public relations." It also charged him with an "amateurish job of chicanery."

The court concluded that "distasteful as this letter may have been to Block, it sounds remarkably similar to the usual and ordinary kind of political rhetoric which is all too often composed of equal parts of bombast, hyperbole, and billingsgate." The reader could only conclude that Block was being accused of "being a city slicker who is trying to bamboozle the good citizens of Palm Springs with the old snake-oil routine . . .. As such it is a statement of opinion, not fact." Desert Sun Publishing Co. v. Superior Court, 97 Cal.App. 3d 49, 158 Cal.Rptr. 519 (1979).

In Hotchner v. Castillo-Puche, 551 F.2d 910 (2d Cir.), certiorari denied 434 U.S. 834 (1977), the action arose out of the claim in defendant's book that plaintiff had not been as close a friend of Ernest Hemingway as plaintiff had earlier suggested in his own writings. Although many of the unflattering phrases are opinions, the court, after quoting *Gertz*, observed that liability

. . . may attach, however, when a negative characterization of a person is coupled with a clear but false implication that the author is privy to facts about the person that are unknown to the reader. If an author represents that he has private, first-hand

knowledge which substantiates the opinions he expresses, the
expression of opinion becomes as damaging as an assertion of
fact. In this case, the jury could have found that, contrary to the
impression of intimacy conveyed by his book, Castillo-Puche's
actual contact with and first-hand knowledge about Hotchner
was virtually nil.

The *Hotchner* court also seized on the point that pure opinions
cannot be proven to be true or false and concluded that an "assertion
that cannot be proved false cannot be held libellous."

In Ollman v. Evans, 713 F.2d 838 (D.C.Cir.1983), a University of
Maryland political science professor who had been nominated to head
the University's Department of Politics and Government sued nation-
ally-syndicated columnists Evans and Novack after their column
characterized him as an "outspoken proponent of political Marxism."
The column quoted Professor Bertell Ollman's writings and asked,
"What is the true measurement of Ollman's scholarship? Does he
intend to use the classroom for indoctrination? Will he indeed be
followed by other Marxist professors? Could the department in time
be closed to non-Marxists, following the tendency at several English
universities?"

The professor sued for defamation, and the defendants sought
summary judgment on the ground that the statements were all
statements of opinion. The federal district court's granting of summary judgment was reversed on appeal, raising anew the difficult
question of separating opinion from assertions of fact.

g. Vagueness

Recently, some courts have found language too imprecise to
form the basis of a defamation action. An accusation that William F.
Buckley, Jr. was a "fellow traveler" of fascist causes was too
"loosely definable" and too "variously interpretable" to be actionable
as a defamation. The court suggested that there might be a difference between that vague charge and a more specific charge that
plaintiff was a member of a particular party or group that subscribed
to that type of belief. Buckley v. Littell, 539 F.2d 882 (2d Cir.1976),
certiorari denied 429 U.S. 1062 (1977).

Similarly, a charge that a police union's collective bargaining
efforts involved the "inroad of communism" was held too vague to
support a suit. National Association of Government Employees, Inc.
v. Central Broadcasting Corp., 379 Mass. 220, 396 N.E.2d 996 (1979).
The court thought it clear from the context and words used that no
hearer in the community after even brief reflection would understand
the speaker to be charging plaintiff with complicity in the "horrors
distinctive of a totalitarian regime."

2. Libel and Slander—The Damage Question

So far we have been discussing the general subject of "defamation." It becomes necessary to introduce the subcategories of libel and slander. Historically, slanders were oral defamations and were handled by the common-law courts; libels were written defamations that, because of the development of printing, became a major concern of the crown. After the end of the days of the Star Chamber, oral and written defamations were redressed by the common-law courts. Those courts, however, preserved some distinctions between the two that have survived to our day.

The critical distinction relates to what types of damages a plaintiff must show in order to be allowed to bring an action for defamation. Two types of damages are central to this discussion. "Special damages" are specific identifiable losses that the plaintiff can prove he has sustained and can trace to the defendant's defamatory statement. "General damages" are damages to reputation that the plaintiff is presumed, without any proof, to have sustained as a result of the defendant's statement. The jury is permitted to speculate on the extent of injury based on the words used, the medium used, and the predicted response of the community.

The common law courts have treated libel as substantially more serious than slander. The distinction arose when relatively few people could read and the written word was awesome and thus more credible. A writing may be given more weight because it requires more thought and planning than a spontaneous oral utterance. Futhermore, the writing is more lasting and is likely to reach a larger audience than most, if not all, slanders. Thus, libels as a class were more likely to cause harm than slanders and courts declared that plaintiffs in libel cases were able to recover general damages without any showing of special damages. Therefore, a plaintiff proceeding under libel has always been at least as well off as, and often better off than, a plaintiff suing for slander for precisely the same words.

If an action is for slander, plaintiff must prove "special damages" unless the defamatory thrust fits into at least one of four categories. These categories are: the imputation of a serious crime involving moral turpitude; imputation of an existing loathsome disease; a charge that attacks the plaintiff's competence or honesty in his business, trade or profession; or a charge of unchastity in a woman. Such a spoken charge is called "slander per se" and permits an action enabling plaintiff to claim general damages to his or her reputation without proving actual pecuniary harm. Here the jury may conclude that publication of the charge caused substantial harm in the community, and can measure damages according to the number and identity of those who learned of the charge, and their presumed reaction based on the seriousness and credibility of the charge. If a plaintiff can also establish special damages, these could be recovered in addition to the general damages presumed.

If the slander is not within the four categories, then an action must be supported by proof of special damages. These must be pecuniary in nature—such as the loss of employment, the collapse of an advantageous business deal, or some other identifiable economic harm. Special damages have proven remarkably difficult to establish in many cases. If they are required and established, the plaintiff may also recover his general reputational damages.

Two developments have blurred the line between libel and slander. First, the courts began to distinguish between two types of libels: those clear on their face, called libel *per se*, to which courts applied the traditional general damage rules, and others, called libel *per quod*, in which the reader had to know one or more unstated facts in order to understand the defamatory thrust of the writing. Some courts began to hold that the plaintiff must prove special damages in libel *per quod* cases unless the words used, if spoken, would have fit into one of the four categories of slanders for which special damages were not required. As a result, in some states plaintiffs now must prove special damages in defamation cases. For example, such slanders as calling someone a gambler, a dirty liar, a bedwetter and the like generally would not fit within one of the four categories of slander *per se* and the plaintiff would have to show special damages before he could win a slander case.

If these words were written, traditional libel rules would allow the plaintiff to recover general damages even if he could show no special damages. But if the libel did not say "X is a gambler" but instead said "X spends his evenings at 123 Hay Road," the situation would be different. Specifying what goes on at that address can show the defamatory nature of the statement, but resorting to facts outside the statement means that the libel is not clear on its face. Some states require the plaintiff to prove special damages for such a libel since the words, if spoken, would not fit into one of the four categories of slander *per se*.

The second blurring has resulted from the development of new modes of communication. Until this century, it was a fair bet that a written defamation would reach more people than an oral one. But with the development of radio and then of television the odds have shifted. In analyzing new technology should we stick to the traditional oral-written line or should we develop an approach that treats all modes of mass communication as libel and other modes of communication as slander? In a few states, legislation has resolved the matter. For example, California provides that broadcasting is slander. On the other hand, an English statute calls it libel. In the states that are resolving the question by common law, the tendency has been to treat broadcasting as libel.

The resulting libel-slander rules have sometimes permitted a plaintiff to recover enormous amounts in general damages and have at other times barred a plaintiff from recovering anything whatever because special damages were required but could not be proven although serious general harm seemed likely.

In addition to the critical distinction between general and special damages, two other classifications loom large in defamation law: nominal damages and punitive damages. Although nominal damages are unimportant in most tort actions, they may be central in defamation cases. The award of a symbolic amount such as six cents usually shows that the jury found the attack to be false but also found the words not to have hurt, either because the speaker was not credible or the plaintiff's strong reputation blunted the harm (or his reputation was so low nothing could really hurt it). For an example, see the suit by Quentin Reynolds against the Hearst Corporation and one of its columnists, upholding a jury award of $1 in compensatory damages and $175,000 in punitive damages against the various defendants. Reynolds v. Pegler, 223 F.2d 429 (2d Cir.), certiorari denied 350 U.S. 846 (1955) (Black, J. dissenting).

A few states declare that punitive damages, which are to punish defendants for serious misbehavior, are never recoverable. Most states allow them in appropriate cases.

As we shall see shortly, the Supreme Court in Gertz v. Robert Welch, Inc., introduced some constitutional constraints on the availability of certain types of common law damages.

3. THE BASIS FOR LIABILITY—THE TROUBLE SPOT

Before one person is liable in tort law for hurting another, commonly, but not universally, some "fault" must be ascribed to the actor's conduct. For example, a plaintiff cannot win an automobile accident case simply by showing that the defendant's car hit the plaintiff. Instead, plaintiff must show that the defendant driver was "at fault" in his behavior. (It is, of course, different in so-called "no-fault" states, which emphasize the harm to plaintiff rather than the fault of the defendant.)

In defamation, the common law long took the view that fault played no part in the tort. In other words, historically, the plaintiff had only to show that the defendant's statement hurt the plaintiff's reputation and prove whatever damages were required by the libel-slander rules. It was irrelevant that the defendant did not realize that its statement could hurt plaintiff, or anyone.

Thus, newspapers lost cases in which they published a birth announcement that was a hoax—the couple had been married only three months. Those who read the article and who knew the fact of plaintiff's recent marriage would have given the story a meaning the newspaper never intended. Even if the newspaper had tried unsuccessfully to check the story but failed to learn about the hoax, it would not have mattered. The common law asserted that defendants in defamation cases were subject to "strict liability" or a liability that was not based on fault. The peril to free speech is readily apparent today. But the response in earlier times was that the remedy was accuracy and refusal to write about things that were not known first hand.

As we shall see, this troubling aspect of the common law has become the focus of constitutional developments.

Traditionally, the plaintiff's action for defamation has been easy to establish. The plaintiff had to prove the publication to a third person of a statement of and concerning plaintiff that injured his reputation, and then had to meet whatever damage showing was required under the relevant libel-slander rules. These elements shown, it was up to the defendant to present a defense.

4. Common Law Defenses

Several common law libel defenses are typically recognized in state law. They include truth, the absolute privilege accorded participants in certain official proceedings, the qualified privilege accorded to those who quote accurately from such proceedings, and the qualified privilege of criticism, sometimes called "fair comment." These defenses were used by libel defendants under strict liability prior to the New York Times v. Sullivan decision. We will discuss them first and then look at the important constitutional defense of absence of malice in a separate section.

a. Truth

The most obvious defense, but one rarely used, is to prove the essential truth of the defamatory statement. Most states recognize truth as a complete defense regardless of the speaker's motives. Because the action is intended to compensate those whose reputations are damaged incorrectly, if the defendant has spoken the truth the reputational harm is deemed to provide no basis for an action. A minority of states have required the truth to have been spoken with "good motives" or for "justifiable ends" or both, but in the wake of *Sullivan* and its progeny, such requirements may not last.

The defendant need not prove literal truth but must establish the "sting" of his charge. Thus, if the defendant has charged the plaintiff with stealing $25,000 from a bank, truth will be established even if the actual amount was only $12,000. If the defendant cannot prove any theft whatever but can prove that the plaintiff is a bigamist, this information will not support his defense of truth, but it may help mitigate damages to show that the plaintiff's reputation is already in low esteem for other reasons and thus he has suffered less harm than might otherwise have occurred.

Truth is little used as a defense, though it would enable a decisive confrontation, because the defense may be very expensive to establish.   A defendant relying on truth almost always bears the legal costs of a full-dress trial as well as the sometimes major expense of investigating the matter and gathering enough evidence to ensure the outcome.   Particularly when the charge involved is vague and does not allege specific events, the defense of truth may be very costly—and risky.

We shall see, however, that new constitutional developments affect the defense of truth.   It is likely that anyone suing a publisher or broadcaster must bear the burden of proving that the defamatory statement is false—rather than forcing the publisher or broadcaster to prove it is true.

b. State Privileges

Not only were there disadvantages to the defense of truth, there were attractive alternatives.   Over the centuries the law of defamation has developed several privileges to protect those who utter defamations.   Some privileges are "absolute" in the sense that if the occasion gives rise to an absolute privilege, there will be no liability even if the speaker deliberately lied about the plaintiff.   The most significant example is the federal and state constitutional privilege afforded legislators who may not be sued for defamation for any statement made during debate.   High executive officials, judges and participants in judicial proceedings also have an absolute privilege to speak freely on matters relevant to their obligations.   No matter how such a speaker abuses the privilege by lying, no tort liability will flow.   See Barr v. Matteo, 360 U.S. 564 (1959).   The only circumstance that gives absolute privilege to the media occurs when broadcasters are required to grant equal opportunity to all candidates for the same office.   If a candidate commits defamation the broadcaster is not liable for the defamation.   See Farmers Educational & Cooperative Union of America v. WDAY, Inc., 360 U.S. 525 (1959), discussed in Chapter XV.

The much more common type of privilege is "conditional" or "qualified."   The defendant who has such a privilege will prevail in an action for defamation unless the plaintiff can show that the speaker "abused" the privilege.   The plaintiff shows abuse by proving that the defendant did not honestly believe what he said or that defendant published more information or published it more widely than was justified by the occasion that provided the privilege.

Most common law privileges serve individuals and do not specifically affect media—with two important exceptions.   The first involves the privilege to make fair and accurate reports of governmental proceedings.   Under general defamation law, one who repeats another's statement is responsible for the truth of what he repeats.   Thus, if X states that "Y told me that Z is a murderer," and Z sues X for defamation, X will be treated as the publisher who is responsible for his own statement. In order to prevail on the defense of truth, X must prove that Z is in fact a murderer—it is not enough for X to prove that in fact Y told him that Z was a murderer. The general reason underlying this view is the reluctance to protect gossip.

It was not long, however, before the courts and the legislatures began to realize that sometimes speakers should be encouraged to repeat others' statements. The federal and state constitutions had already provided that members of the legislative branch could quote others in debate with absolute protection against legal sanctions.

The major example of the value of repetition was found in the reporting of how government was functioning and what government officials were saying. Thus, observers were to be encouraged to report what legislators said on the floor or in committee as well as events in court. It would put reporters in a hopeless situation to be able to safely report only the truthful statements of government officials or of witnesses at a trial. As a result of these considerations, a privilege developed, sometimes called the privilege of "record libel," under which reports of what occurs in governmental proceedings are privileged even if some of those quoted have spoken falsely—so long as the report is accurate or a fair summary of what transpired.

The second major common law privilege of value to the media was the privilege of fair comment upon matters of public interest.

Apparently this privilege entered English law in 1808 in Carr v. Hood, 1 Camp. 355, 170 Eng.Rep. 983. The defendant was charged with ridiculing the plaintiff author's talent so severely that sales of his book were discouraged and his reputation was destroyed. The plaintiff's attorney conceded that his client had exposed himself to literary criticism by making the book public, but insisted that the criticism should be "fair and liberal" and seek to enlighten the public about the book rather than to injure the author. The judge noted that ridicule may be an appropriate tool of criticism, but that criticism unrelated to the author as such would not be privileged. He urged that any "attempt against free and liberal criticism" should be resisted "at the threshold." The result was a rule that criticism, regardless of its merit, was privileged if it was made honestly, with honesty measured by the accuracy of the critic's descriptive observations. If a critic describing a literary, musical or artistic endeavor gave the "facts" accurately and fairly, his honest conclusions would be privileged as "fair comment."

American law recognized this privilege, and when it was applied in cases of literary and artistic criticism it caused little confusion. Problems raised by such comment are discussed in the classic Cherry v. Des Moines Leader, 114 Iowa 298, 86 N.W. 323 (1901) in which a reviewer scathingly described a performance by the Cherry Sisters. But at the turn of the century cases arose in which the privilege of fair comment was claimed with regard to other matters of public interest, including the conduct of politicians. This was not the privilege of reporting what certain public officials were doing in their official capacity. Rather the privilege claimed would permit citizens to criticize and argue about the conduct of their officials, and these cases presented the problem of distinguishing between facts and opinion. In the literary criticism area the application of the privilege could depend upon the accuracy of the "facts" because they were usually readily apparent. When dealing with politics, however, the "facts" were often elusive. This new problem created a judicial split.

Most state courts decided that in order for criticism of government officials and others to be privileged, the facts upon which the comments were based had to be true. A minority of courts, including Coleman v. MacLennan, 78 Kan. 711, 98 P. 281 (1908), disagreed. They decided that facts relating to matters of public interest may not form the basis for a defamation case even if the facts are incorrect, so long as the speaker honestly believed them to be true.

It was from this disagreement among the states that the constitutional developments sprang.

B. CONSTITUTIONAL PRIVILEGE

So long as state law controlled, publishers and broadcasters could try to persuade state courts and legislatures to alter the defamation rules. As we have seen, their success varied among the states. Early efforts to gain further protection in defamation cases by invoking federal constitutional law to limit state power did not fare well.

In Near v. Minnesota, 283 U.S. 697 (1931), the case that perhaps first reinforced the protection of the press in this country, the majority observed, "But it is recognized that punishment for the abuse of the liberty accorded to the press is essential to the protection of the public, and that the common-law rules that subject the libeler to responsibility for the public offense, as well as for the private injury, are not abolished by the protection extended in our Constitution."

Recall the passage in Chaplinsky v. New Hampshire, p. 35, supra:

> There are certain well-defined and narrowly limited classes of speech, the prevention and punishment of which have never been thought to raise any Constitutional problem. These include the lewd and obscene, the profane, the libelous, and the insulting or "fighting" words—those which by their very utterance inflict injury or tend to incite an immediate breach of the peace. It has been well observed that such utterances are no essential part of any exposition of ideas, and are of such slight social value as a step to truth that any benefit that may be derived from them is clearly outweighed by the social interest in order and morality.

This language was often quoted approvingly. Justice Frankfurter, writing for a 5–4 majority in Beauharnais v. Illinois, 343 U.S. 250 (1952), to sustain a state criminal libel law, relied on *Chaplinsky* for the proposition that libelous utterances were not "within the area of constitutionally protected speech."

This sequence set the stage for the following case from Alabama, a state that had long followed the majority rule that there was no privilege for incorrect facts, even in stories of public importance.

NEW YORK TIMES CO. v. SULLIVAN

(Together with Abernathy v. Sullivan)

Supreme Court of the United States, 1964.
376 U.S. 254, 84 S.Ct. 710, 11 L.Ed.2d 686.

[This action was based on a full-page advertisement in *The New York Times* on behalf of several individuals and groups protesting a "wave of terror" against blacks involved in non-violent demonstrations in the South. Plaintiff, one of three elected commissioners of Montgomery, the capital of Alabama, was in charge of the police department. When he demanded a retraction, as state law required, *The Times* instead responded that it failed to see how he was defamed. He then filed suit against *The Times* and four clergymen whose names appeared as sponsors—although they denied having authorized this—in the ad. Plaintiff alleged that the third and the sixth paragraphs of the advertisement libelled him:

"In Montgomery, Alabama, after students sang 'My Country, 'Tis of Thee' on the State Capitol steps, their leaders were expelled from school, and truckloads of police armed with shotguns and tear-gas ringed the Alabama State College Campus. When the entire student body protested to state authorities by refusing to re-register, their dining hall was padlocked in an attempt to starve them into submission."

. . .

"Again and again the Southern violators have answered Dr. King's peaceful protests with intimidation and violence. They have bombed his home almost killing his wife and child. They have assaulted his person. They have arrested him seven times—for 'speeding,' 'loitering' and similar 'offenses.' And now they have charged him with 'perjury'—a *felony* under which they could imprison him for *ten years*. . . ."

Plaintiff claimed that he was libelled in the third paragraph by the reference to the police, since his responsibilities included supervision of the Montgomery police. He asserted that the paragraph could be read as charging the police with ringing the campus and seeking to starve the students by padlocking the dining hall. As to the sixth paragraph, he contended that the word "they" referred to his department since arrests are usually made by the police and the paragraph could be read as accusing him of committing the acts charged. Several witnesses testified that they read the statements as referring to plaintiff in his capacity as commissioner.

The defendants admitted several inaccuracies in these two paragraphs: the students sang "The Star Spangled Banner", not "My Country, 'Tis of Thee"; nine students were expelled, not for leading the demonstration, but for demanding service at a lunch counter in the county courthouse; the dining hall was never padlocked; police at no time ringed the campus though they were deployed nearby in large numbers; they were not called to the campus in connection with the demonstration; Dr. King had been arrested only four times; and officers disputed his account of the alleged assault. Plaintiff proved that he had not been commissioner when three of the four arrests occurred and that he had nothing to do with procuring the perjury indictment.

The trial judge charged that the statements were libel per se, that the jury should decide whether they were made "of and concerning" the plaintiff, and, if so, general damages were to be presumed. Although noting that punitive damages required more than carelessness, he refused to charge that they required a finding of actual intent to harm or "gross negligence and recklessness." He also refused to order the jury to separate its award of general and punitive damages. The jury returned a verdict for $500,000—the full amount demanded. The Alabama Supreme Court affirmed, holding that malice could be found in several aspects of *The Times*'s conduct.]

MR. JUSTICE BRENNAN delivered the opinion of the Court.

.   .   .

I.

We may dispose at the outset of two grounds asserted to insulate the judgment of the Alabama courts from constitutional scrutiny. The first is the proposition relied on by the State Supreme Court— that "The Fourteenth Amendment is directed against State action and not private action." That proposition has no application to this case. Although this is a civil lawsuit between private parties, the Alabama courts have applied a state rule of law which petitioners claim to impose invalid restrictions on their constitutional freedoms of speech and press. It matters not that that law has been applied in a civil action and that it is common law only, though supplemented by statute. [ ] The test is not the form in which state power has been applied but, whatever the form, whether such power has in fact been exercised. [ ]

The second contention is that the constitutional guarantees of freedom of speech and of the press are inapplicable here, at least so far as the Times is concerned, because the allegedly libelous statements were published as part of a paid, "commercial" advertisement. The argument [was rejected.]

II.

Under Alabama law as applied in this case, a publication is "libelous per se" if the words "tend to injure a person . . . in his reputation" or to "bring [him] into public contempt"; the trial court stated that the standard was met if the words are such as to "injure him in his public office, or impute misconduct to him in his office, or want of official integrity, or want of fidelity to a public trust . . . ." The jury must find that the words were published "of and concerning" the plaintiff, but where the plaintiff is a public official his place in the governmental hierarchy is sufficient evidence to support a finding that his reputation has been affected by statements that reflect upon the agency of which he is in charge. Once "libel per se" has been established, the defendant has no defense as to stated facts unless he can persuade the jury that they were true in all their particulars. [ ] His privilege of "fair comment" for expressions of opinion depends on the truth of the facts upon which the comment is based. [ ] Unless he can discharge the burden of proving truth, general damages are presumed, and may be awarded without proof of pecuniary injury. A showing of actual malice is apparently a prerequisite to recovery of punitive damages, and the defendant may in any event forestall a punitive award by a retraction meeting the statutory requirements. Good motives and belief in truth do not negate an inference of malice, but are relevant only in mitigation of punitive damages if the jury chooses to accord them weight. [ ]

The question before us is whether this rule of liability, as applied to an action brought by a public official against critics of his official conduct, abridges the freedom of speech and of the press that is guaranteed by the First and Fourteenth Amendments.

Respondent relies heavily, as did the Alabama courts, on statements of this Court to the effect that the Constitution does not protect libelous publications. Those statements do not foreclose our inquiry here. None of the cases sustained the use of libel laws to impose sanctions upon expression critical of the official conduct of public officials. . . . In deciding the question now, we are compelled by neither precedent nor policy to give any more weight to the epithet "libel" than we have to other "mere labels" of state law. NAACP v. Button, 371 U.S. 415, 429 (1963). Like insurrection, contempt, advocacy of unlawful acts, breach of the peace, obscenity, solicitation of legal business, and the various other formulae for the repression of expression that have been challenged in this Court, libel can claim no talismanic immunity from constitutional limitations. It must be measured by standards that satisfy the First Amendment.

The general proposition that freedom of expression upon public questions is secured by the First Amendment has long been settled by our decisions. . . . Mr. Justice Brandeis, in his concurring opinion in Whitney v. California, 274 U.S. 357, 375–376 (1927), gave the principle its classic formulation:

> "Those who won our independence believed . . . that public discussion is a political duty; and that this should be a fundamental principle of the American government. . . . Believing in the power of reason as applied through public discussion, they eschewed silence coerced by law—the argument of force in its worst form. Recognizing the occasional tyrannies of governing majorities, they amended the Constitution so that free speech and assembly should be guaranteed."

Thus we consider this case against the background of a profound national commitment to the principle that debate on public issues should be uninhibited, robust, and wide-open, and that it may well include vehement, caustic, and sometimes unpleasantly sharp attacks on government and public officials. See Terminiello v. Chicago, 337 U.S. 1, 4 (1949); De Jonge v. Oregon, 299 U.S. 353, 365 (1937). The present advertisement, as an expression of grievance and protest on one of the major public issues of our time, would seem clearly to qualify for the constitutional protection. The question is whether it forfeits that protection by the falsity of some of its factual statements and by its alleged defamation of respondent.

Authoritative interpretations of the First Amendment guarantees have consistently refused to recognize an exception for any test of truth—whether administered by judges, juries, or administrative officials—and especially one that puts the burden of proving truth on the speaker. Cf. Speiser v. Randall, 357 U.S. 513, 525–526 (1958). The constitutional protection does not turn upon "the truth, popularity, or social utility of the ideas and beliefs which are offered." NAACP v. Button, 371 U.S. 415, 445 (1963). As Madison said, "Some degree of abuse is inseparable from the proper use of every thing; and in no instance is this more true than in that of the press." 4 Elliot's Debates on the Federal Constitution (1876) p. 571. In Cantwell v. Connecticut, 310 U.S. 296, 310 (1940), the Court declared:

> "In the realm of religious faith, and in that of political belief, sharp differences arise. In both fields the tenets of one man may seem the rankest error to his neighbor. To persuade others to his own point of view, the pleader, as we know, at times, resorts to exaggeration, to vilification of men who have been, or are, prominent in church or state, and even to false statement. But the people of this nation have ordained in the light of history, that, in spite of the probability of excesses and abuses, these liberties are, in the long view, essential to enlightened opinion and right conduct on the part of the citizens of a democracy."

That erroneous statement is inevitable in free debate, and that it must be protected if the freedoms of expression are to have the "breathing space" that they "need . . . to survive," NAACP v. Button, 371 U.S. 415, 433 (1963), was also recognized by the Court of Appeals for the District of Columbia Circuit in Sweeney v. Patterson, 76 U.S.App.D.C. 23, 24, 128 F.2d 457, 458, certiorari denied, 317 U.S. 678 (1942). Judge Edgerton spoke for a unanimous court which affirmed the dismissal of a Congressman's libel suit based upon a newspaper article charging him with anti-Semitism in opposing a judicial appointment. He said:

> "Cases which impose liability for erroneous reports of the political conduct of officials reflect the obsolete doctrine that the governed must not criticize their governors. . . . The interest of the public here outweighs the interest of appellant or any other individual. The protection of the public requires not merely discussion, but information. Political conduct and views which some respectable people approve, and others condemn, are constantly imputed to Congressmen. Errors of fact, particularly in regard to a man's mental states and processes, are inevitable. . . . Whatever is added to the field of libel is taken from the field of free debate." [13]

Injury to official reputation affords no more warrant for repressing speech that would otherwise be free than does factual error. Where judicial officers are involved, this Court has held that concern for the dignity and reputation of the courts does not justify the punishment as criminal contempt of criticism of the judge or his decision. Bridges v. California, 314 U.S. 252 (1941). This is true even though the utterance contains "half-truths" and "misinformation." Pennekamp v. Florida, 328 U.S. 331, 342, 343, n. 5, 345 (1946). . . . Criticism of their official conduct does not lose its constitutional protection merely because it is effective criticism and hence diminishes their official reputations.

If neither factual error nor defamatory content suffices to remove the constitutional shield from criticism of official conduct, the combination of the two elements is no less inadequate. This is the lesson to be drawn from the great controversy over the Sedition Act of 1798, 1 Stat. 596, which first crystallized a national awareness of the central meaning of the First Amendment. . . .

Although the Sedition Act was never tested in this Court,[16] the attack upon its validity has carried the day in the court of history. Fines levied in its prosecution were repaid by Act of Congress on the

---

13. See also Mill, On Liberty (Oxford: Blackwell, 1947), at 47:

". . . [T]o argue sophistically, to suppress facts or arguments, to misstate the elements of the case, or misrepresent the opposite opinion . . . all this, even to the most aggravated degree, is so continually done in perfect good faith, by persons who are not considered, and in many other respects may not deserve to be considered, ignorant or incompetent, that it is rarely possible, on adequate grounds, conscientiously to stamp the misrepresentation as morally culpable; and still less could law presume to interfere with this kind of controversial misconduct."

16. The Act expired by its terms in 1801.

ground that it was unconstitutional. . . . The invalidity of the Act has also been assumed by Justices of this Court. [   ] These views reflect a broad consensus that the Act, because of the restraint it imposed upon criticism of government and public officials, was inconsistent with the First Amendment.

There is no force in respondent's argument that the constitutional limitations implicit in the history of the Sedition Act apply only to Congress and not to the States. It is true that the First Amendment was originally addressed only to action by the Federal Government, and that Jefferson, for one, while denying the power of Congress "to control the freedom of the press," recognized such a power in the States. [   ] But this distinction was eliminated with the adoption of the Fourteenth Amendment and the application to the States of the First Amendment's restrictions. [   ]

What a State may not constitutionally bring about by means of a criminal statute is likewise beyond the reach of its civil law of libel. The fear of damage awards under a rule such as that invoked by the Alabama courts here may be markedly more inhibiting than the fear of prosecution under a criminal statute. [   ] Alabama, for example, has a criminal libel law which subjects to prosecution "any person who speaks, writes, or prints of and concerning another any accusation falsely and maliciously importing the commission by such person of a felony, or any other indictable offense involving moral turpitude, and which allows as punishment upon conviction a fine not exceeding $500 and a prison sentence of six months. [   ] Presumably a person charged with violation of this statute enjoys ordinary criminal-law safeguards such as the requirements of an indictment and of proof beyond a reasonable doubt. These safeguards are not available to the defendant in a civil action. . . . And since there is no double-jeopardy limitation applicable to civil lawsuits, this is not the only judgment that may be awarded against petitioners for the same publication.[18] Whether or not a newspaper can survive a succession of such judgments, the pall of fear and timidity imposed upon those who would give voice to public criticism is an atmosphere in which the First Amendment freedoms cannot survive. Plainly the Alabama law of civil libel is "a form of regulation that creates hazards to protected freedoms markedly greater than those that attend reliance upon the criminal law." Bantam Books, Inc. v. Sullivan, 372 U.S. 58, 70 (1963).

The state rule of law is not saved by its allowance of the defense of truth. . . . Allowance of the defense of truth, with the burden of proving it on the defendant, does not mean that only false speech

18. The Times states that four other libel suits based on the advertisement have been filed against it by others who have served as Montgomery City Commissioners and by the Governor of Alabama; that another $500,000 verdict has been awarded in the only one of these cases that has yet gone to trial; and that the damages sought in the other three total $2,000,000.

will be deterred.[19] Even courts accepting this defense as an adequate safeguard have recognized the difficulties of adducing legal proofs that the alleged libel was true in all its factual particulars. See, e.g., Post Publishing Co. v. Hallam, 59 F. 530, 540 (C.A. 6th Cir.1893); see also Noel, Defamation of Public Officers and Candidates, 49 Col.L. Rev. 875, 892 (1949). Under such a rule, would-be critics of official conduct may be deterred from voicing their criticism, even though it is believed to be true and even though it is in fact true, because of doubt whether it can be proved in court or fear of the expense of having to do so. They tend to make only statements which "steer far wider of the unlawful zone." Speiser v. Randall, supra, 357 U.S., at 526. The rule thus dampens the vigor and limits the variety of public debate. It is inconsistent with the First and Fourteenth Amendments.

The constitutional guarantees require, we think, a federal rule that prohibits a public official from recovering damages for a defamatory falsehood relating to his official conduct unless he proves that the statement was made with "actual malice"—that is, with knowledge that it was false or with reckless disregard of whether it was false or not. An oft-cited statement of a like rule, which has been adopted by a number of state courts, is found in the Kansas case of Coleman v. MacLennan, 78 Kan. 711, 98 P. 281 (1908). . . .

Such a privilege for criticism of official conduct is appropriately analogous to the protection accorded a public official when *he* is sued for libel by a private citizen. In Barr v. Matteo, 360 U.S. 564, 575 (1959), this Court held the utterance of a federal official to be absolutely privileged if made "within the outer perimeter" of his duties. The States accord the same immunity to statements of their highest officers, although some differentiate their lesser officials and qualify the privilege they enjoy. But all hold that all officials are protected unless actual malice can be proved. The reason for the official privilege is said to be that the threat of damage suits would otherwise "inhibit the fearless, vigorous, and effective administration of policies of government" and "dampen the ardor of all but the most resolute, or the most irresponsible, in the unflinching discharge of their duties." Barr v. Matteo, supra, 360 U.S., at 571. Analogous considerations support the privilege for the citizen-critic of government. It is as much his duty to criticize as it is the official's duty to administer. . . .

We conclude that such a privilege is required by the First and Fourteenth Amendments.

19. Even a false statement may be deemed to make a valuable contribution to public debate, since it brings about "the clearer perception and livelier impression of truth, produced by its colli-sion with error." Mill, On Liberty (Oxford: Blackwell, 1947), at 15; see also Milton, Areopagitica, in Prose Works (Yale, 1959), Vol. II, at 561.

III.

We hold today that the Constitution delimits a State's power to award damages for libel in actions brought by public officials against critics of their official conduct. Since this is such an action, the rule requiring proof of actual malice is applicable. While Alabama law apparently requires proof of actual malice for an award of punitive damages, where general damages are concerned malice is "presumed." Such a presumption is inconsistent with the federal rule. . . . Since the trial judge did not instruct the jury to differentiate between general and punitive damages, it may be that the verdict was wholly an award of one or the other. But it is impossible to know, in view of the general verdict returned. Because of this uncertainty, the judgment must be reversed and the case remanded.
[ ]

Since respondent may seek a new trial, we deem that considerations of effective judicial administration require us to review the evidence in the present record to determine whether it could constitutionally support a judgment for respondent. . . .

Applying these standards, we consider that the proof presented to show actual malice, lacks the convincing clarity which the constitutional standard demands, and hence that it would not constitutionally sustain the judgment for respondent under the proper rule of law. The case of the individual petitioners requires little discussion. Even assuming that they could constitutionally be found to have authorized the use of their names on the advertisement, there was no evidence whatever that they were aware of any erroneous statements or were in any way reckless in that regard. The judgment against them is thus without constitutional support.

As to the Times, we similarly conclude that the facts do not support a finding of actual malice. . . .

. . .

We also think the evidence was constitutionally defective in another respect: it was incapable of supporting the jury's finding that the allegedly libelous statements were made "of and concerning" respondent. Respondent relies on the words of the advertisement and the testimony of six witnesses to establish a connection between it and himself. . . . There was no reference to respondent in the advertisement, either by name or official position. A number of the allegedly libelous statements—the charges that the dining hall was padlocked and that Dr. King's home was bombed, his person assaulted, and a perjury prosecution instituted against him—did not even concern the police; despite the ingenuity of the arguments which would attach this significance to the word "They," it is plain that these statements could not reasonably be read as accusing respondent of personal involvement in the acts in question. The statements upon which respondent principally relies as referring to him are the two allegations that did concern the police or police functions: that "truckloads of police . . . ringed the Alabama State College Campus" after the demonstration on the State Capitol steps, and that Dr. King had been "arrested . . . seven times." These statements were false only in that the police had been "deployed near" the campus but had not actually "ringed" it and had not gone there in connection with the State Capitol demonstration, and in that Dr. King had been arrested only four times. The ruling that these discrepancies between what was true and what was asserted were sufficient to injure respondent's reputation may itself raise constitutional problems, but we need not consider them here. Although the statements may be taken as referring to the police, they did not on their face make even an oblique reference to respondent as an individual. Support for the asserted reference must, therefore, be sought in the testimony of respondent's witnesses. But none of them suggested any basis for the belief that respondent himself was attacked in the advertisement beyond the bare fact that he was in overall charge of the Police Department and thus bore official responsibility for police conduct; to the extent that some of the witnesses thought respondent to have been charged with ordering or approving the conduct or otherwise being personally involved in it, they based this notion not on any statements in the advertisement, and not on any evidence that he had in fact been so involved, but solely on the unsupported assumption that, because of his official position, he must have been. This reliance on the bare fact of respondent's official position was made explicit by the Supreme Court of Alabama. . . .

This proposition has disquieting implications for criticism of governmental conduct. For good reason, "no court of last resort in this country has ever held, or even suggested, that prosecutions for libel on government have any place in the American system of jurisprudence." City of Chicago v. Tribune Co., 307 Ill. 595, 601, 139 N.E. 86, 88 (1923). The present proposition would sidestep this obstacle by transmuting criticism of government, however impersonal it may seem on its face, into personal criticism, and hence potential libel, of the officials of whom the government is composed. There is no legal alchemy by which a State may thus create the cause of action that would otherwise be denied for a publication which, as respondent himself said of the advertisement, "reflects not only on me but on the other Commissioners and the community." Raising as it does the possibility that a good-faith critic of government will be penalized for his criticism, the proposition relied on by the Alabama courts strikes at the very center of the constitutionally protected area of free expression.[30] We hold that such a proposition may not

---

30. Insofar as the proposition means only that the statements about police conduct libeled respondent by implicitly criticizing his ability to run the Police Department, recovery is also precluded in this case by the doctrine of fair comment. See American Law Institute, Restatement of Torts (1938), § 607. Since the Fourteenth Amendment requires recognition of the conditional privilege for honest misstatements of fact, it follows that a defense of fair comment must be af-

constitutionally be utilized to establish that an otherwise impersonal attack on governmental operations was a libel of an official responsible for those operations. Since it was relied on exclusively here, and there was no other evidence to connect the statements with respondent, the evidence was constitutionally insufficient to support a finding that the statements referred to respondent.

The judgment of the Supreme Court of Alabama is reversed and the case is remanded to that court for further proceedings not inconsistent with this opinion.

Reversed and remanded.

MR. JUSTICE BLACK, with whom MR. JUSTICE DOUGLAS joins, concurring.

I concur in reversing this half-million-dollar judgment against the New York Times Company and the four individual defendants. In reversing the Court holds that "the Constitution delimits a State's power to award damages for libel in actions brought by public officials against critics of their official conduct." I base my vote to reverse on the belief that the First and Fourteenth Amendments not merely "delimit" a State's power to award damages to "public officials against critics of their official conduct" but completely prohibit a State from exercising such a power. The Court goes on to hold that a State can subject such critics to damages if "actual malice" can be proved against them. "Malice," even as defined by the Court, is an elusive, abstract concept, hard to prove and hard to disprove. The requirement that malice be proved provides at best an evanescent protection for the right critically to discuss public affairs and certainly does not measure up to the sturdy safeguard embodied in the First Amendment. Unlike the Court, therefore, I vote to reverse exclusively on the ground that the Times and the individual defendants had an absolute unconditional constitutional right to publish in the Times advertisement their criticisms of the Montgomery agencies and officials. . . .

The half-million-dollar verdict does give dramatic proof, however, that state libel laws threaten the very existence of an American press virile enough to publish unpopular views on public affairs and bold enough to criticize the conduct of public officials. . . . In fact, briefs before us show that in Alabama there are now pending eleven libel suits by local and state officials against the Times seeking $5,600,000 and five such suits against the Columbia Broadcasting System seeking $1,700,000. Moreover, this technique for harassing and punishing a free press—now that it has been shown to be possible—is by no means limited to cases with racial overtones; it can be used in other fields where public feelings may make local as well as out-of-state newspapers easy prey for libel verdict seekers.

forded for honest expression of opinion based upon privileged, as well as true, statements of fact. Both defenses are of course defeasible if the public official proves actual malice, as was not done here.

In my opinion the Federal Constitution has dealt with this deadly danger to the press in the only way possible without leaving the free press open to destruction—by granting the press an absolute immunity for criticism of the way public officials do their public duty. Compare Barr v. Matteo, 360 U.S. 564 (1959). Stopgap measures like those the Court adopts are in my judgment not enough. This record certainly does not indicate that any different verdict would have been rendered here whatever the Court had charged the jury about "malice," "truth," "good motives," "justifiable ends," or any other legal formulas which in theory would protect the press. Nor does the record indicate that any of these legalistic words would have caused the courts below to set aside or to reduce the half-million-dollar verdict in any amount.

. . .

We would, I think, more faithfully interpret the First Amendment by holding that at the very least it leaves the people and the press free to criticize officials and discuss public affairs with impunity. . . . An unconditional right to say what one pleases about public affairs is what I consider to be the minimum guarantee of the First Amendment.[6]

I regret that the Court has stopped short of this holding indispensable to preserve our free press from destruction.

MR. JUSTICE GOLDBERG, with whom MR. JUSTICE DOUGLAS joins, concurring in the result.

. . .

In my view, the First and Fourteenth Amendments to the Constitution afford to the citizen and to the press an absolute, unconditional privilege to criticize official conduct despite the harm which may flow from excesses and abuses. . . .

. . .

. . . It may be urged that deliberately and maliciously false statements have no conceivable value as free speech. That argument, however, is not responsive to the real issue presented by this case, which is whether that freedom of speech which all agree is constitutionally protected can be effectively safeguarded by a rule allowing the imposition of liability upon a jury's evaluation of the speaker's state of mind. If individual citizens may be held liable in damages for strong words, which a jury finds false and maliciously motivated, there can be little doubt that public debate and advocacy will be constrained. And if newspapers, publishing advertisements dealing with public issues, thereby risk liability, there can also be little doubt that the ability of minority groups to secure publication of their views on public affairs and to seek support for their causes will be greatly diminished. . . .

6. Cf. Meiklejohn, Free Speech and Its Relation to Self-Government (1948).

. . .

This is not to say that the Constitution protects defamatory statements directed against the private conduct of a public official or private citizen. Freedom of press and of speech insures that government will respond to the will of the people and that changes may be obtained by peaceful means. Purely private defamation has little to do with the political ends of a self-governing society. The imposition of liability for private defamation does not abridge the freedom of public speech or any other freedom protected by the First Amendment.[4] . . .

. . .

If the government official should be immune from libel actions so that his ardor to serve the public will not be dampened and "fearless, vigorous, and effective administration of policies of government" not be inhibited, Barr v. Matteo, supra, at 571, then the citizen and the press should likewise be immune from libel actions for their criticism of official conduct. . . .

The conclusion that the Constitution affords the citizen and the press an absolute privilege for criticism of official conduct does not leave the public official without defenses against unsubstantiated opinions or deliberate misstatements. "Under our system of government, counterargument and education are the weapons available to expose these matters, not abridgment . . . of free speech. . . ." Wood v. Georgia, 370 U.S. 375, 389 (1962). The public official certainly has equal if not greater access than most private citizens to media of communication. . . .

. . .

Notes and Questions

1. What is the justification for the majority position?

2. The majority twice observes that deliberate falsity is used in argument. Why is such behavior not protected here?

3. Do you consider either of the concurring opinions preferable to the majority approach? Would it be desirable to enable a public official to have a jury assess the truth of charges against him— without seeking damages?

4. Commenting after the *Times* case, Professor Kalven speculated on the case's future:

> The closing question, of course, is whether the treatment of seditious libel as the key concept for development of appropriate constitutional doctrine will prove germinal. It is not easy to

---

4. In most cases, as in the case at bar, there will be little difficulty in distinguishing defamatory speech relating to private conduct from that relating to official conduct. I recognize, of course, that there will be a gray area. The difficulties of applying a public-private standard are, however, certainly of a different genre from those attending the differentiation between a malicious and nonmalicious state of mind. . . .

predict what the Court will see in the *Times* opinion as the years roll by. It may regard the opinion as covering simply one pocket of cases, those dealing with libel of public officials, and not destructive of the earlier notions that are inconsistent only with the larger reading of the Court's action. But the invitation to follow a dialectic progression from public official to government policy to public policy to matters in the public domain, like art, seems to me to be overwhelming. If the Court accepts the invitation, it will slowly work out for itself the theory of free speech that Alexander Meiklejohn has been offering us for some fifteen years now.

Kalven, The New York Times Case: A Note on "The Central Meaning of the First Amendment," 1964 Sup.Ct.Rev. 191, 221. Does his prediction seem sound? Keep it in mind as we consider the cases decided since *Times*.

5. The majority in the New York Times case did not explicitly condemn the concurring approaches. A few months later, in Garrison v. Louisiana, 379 U.S. 64 (1964), the Court, in an opinion by Justice Brennan, extended the *Times* rule to cases of criminal libel and also held that truth must be a defense in cases brought by public officials. The majority explained its refusal to protect deliberate falsity:

> Although honest utterance, even if inaccurate, may further the fruitful exercise of the right of free speech, it does not follow that the lie, knowingly and deliberately published about a public official, should enjoy a like immunity. At the time the First Amendment was adopted, as today, there were those unscrupulous enough and skillful enough to use the deliberate or reckless falsehood as an effective political tool to unseat the public servant or even topple an administration. [ ] That speech is used as a tool for political ends does not automatically bring it under the protective mantle of the Constitution. For the use of the known lie as a tool is at once at odds with the premises of democratic government and with the orderly manner in which economic, social, or political change is to be effected. Calculated falsehood falls into that class of utterances which "are no essential part of any exposition of ideas, and are of such slight social value as a step to truth that any benefit that may be derived from them is clearly outweighed by the social interest in order and morality. . . ." Chaplinsky v. New Hampshire, 315 U.S. 568, 572 (1942). Hence the knowingly false statement and the false statement made with reckless disregard of the truth, do not enjoy constitutional protection.

6. The next major case was Rosenblatt v. Baer, 383 U.S. 75 (1966). Plaintiff Baer had been hired by the three elected county commissioners to be Supervisor of a public recreation facility owned by Belknap County, New Hampshire. Defendant, in his weekly newspaper col-

umn, noted that a year after plaintiff's discharge the facility was doing much better financially. The column could be understood as charging either inefficiency or dishonesty. In reversing plaintiff's state court judgment, the Supreme Court said that the vague language could be read as an attack on government—and that Baer could not sue unless he showed that he had been singled out for attack. Justice Brennan's majority opinion then held that Baer was a "public official" under the *Times* rule and that the trial judge's charge did not give the jury the correct "malice" standard. It said that, "It is clear . . . that the 'public official' designation applies at the very least to those among the hierarchy of government employees who have, or appear to the public to have, substantial responsibility for or control over the conduct of governmental affairs."

7. The Supreme Court next considered two cases together, Curtis Pub. Co. v. Butts, and Associated Press v. Walker, 388 U.S. 130 (1967). In *Butts* the defendant magazine had accused the plaintiff athletic director of disclosing his game plan to an opposing coach before their game. Although he was on the staff of a state university Butts was paid by a private alumni organization. In *Walker*, the defendant news service reported that the plaintiff, a former United States Army general who resigned to engage in political activity, had personally led students in an attack on federal marshals who were enforcing a desegregation order at the University of Mississippi.

In both cases, lower courts had affirmed substantial jury awards against the defendants and had refused to apply the *Times* doctrine on the ground that public officials were not involved. The Supreme Court divided several ways on several issues, affirming *Butts*, 5–4, and reversing *Walker*, 9–0. Chief Justice Warren wrote the pivotal opinion in which he concluded that both men were "public figures" and that the standard developed in *New York Times* should apply to "public figures" as well:

> To me, differentiation between "public figures" and "public officials" and adoption of separate standards of proof for each has no basis in law, logic, or First Amendment policy. Increasingly in this country, the distinctions between governmental and private sectors are blurred. Since the depression of the 1930's and World War II there has been a rapid fusion of economic and political power, a merging of science, industry, and government, and a high degree of interaction between the intellectual, governmental, and business worlds. Depression, war, international tensions, national and international markets, and the surging growth of science and technology have precipitated national and international problems that demand national and international solutions. While these trends and events have occasioned a consolidation of governmental power, power has also become much more organized in what we have commonly considered to

be the private sector. In many situations, policy determinations which traditionally were channeled through formal political institutions are now originated and implemented through a complex array of boards, committees, commissions, corporations, and associations, some only loosely connected with the Government. This blending of positions and power has also occurred in the case of individuals so that many who do not hold public office at the moment are nevertheless intimately involved in the resolution of important public questions or, by reason of their fame, shape events in areas of concern to society at large.

Viewed in this context then, it is plain that although they are not subject to the restraints of the political process, "public figures," like "public officials," often play an influential role in ordering society. And surely as a class these "public figures" have as ready access as "public officials" to mass media of communication, both to influence policy and to counter criticism of their views and activities. Our citizenry has a legitimate and substantial interest in the conduct of such persons, and freedom of the press to engage in uninhibited debate about their involvement in public issues and events is as crucial as it is in the case of "public officials." The fact that they are not amenable to the restraints of the political process only underscores the legitimate and substantial nature of the interest, since it means that public opinion may be the only instrument by which society can attempt to influence their conduct.

He found that on the merits the standard had not been met in *Walker.* In *Butts* he found that defendant's counsel had deliberately waived the *Times* doctrine and he also found evidence establishing reckless behavior. He thus voted to reverse *Walker* and affirm *Butts.*

Justice Harlan, joined by Justices Clark, Stewart and Fortas, argued that the *Times* standard should not apply to public figures because criticism of government was not involved:

We consider and would hold that a "public figure" who is not a public official may also recover damages for a defamatory falsehood whose substance makes substantial danger to reputation apparent, on a showing of highly unreasonable conduct constituting an extreme departure from the standards of investigation and reporting ordinarily adhered to by responsible publishers. . . .

Applying that standard Justice Harlan concluded that Walker had failed to establish a case, but that Butts had shown that the Saturday Evening Post ignored elementary precautions in preparing a potentially damaging story. Together with the Chief Justice's vote, there were five votes to affirm *Butts.*

Justices Brennan and White agreed with the Chief Justice in *Walker* but found no waiver in *Butts* and would have reversed both cases. They agreed with the Chief Justice that *Butts* had presented enough evidence to come within the *Times* standard but thought that errors in the charge required a new trial.

Justices Black and Douglas adhered to their position, urged that the *Times* rule be abandoned, and voted to reverse both cases.

8. In St. Amant v. Thompson, 390 U.S. 727 (1968), the defendant, a candidate for public office, read on television a series of statements he had received from Mr. Albin, a member of a Teamsters' Union local. The statements, made under oath, falsely implied that the plaintiff, a deputy sheriff, had taken bribes. The defendant had not checked the facts stated by Albin, nor had he investigated Albin's reputation for veracity. The state court ruled that these failures to inquire further sufficed to meet the required standard of reckless disregard for the truth. The Supreme Court reversed and concluded that the standard of "reckless disregard" had not been met. It recognized that the term could receive no single "infallible definition" and that its outer limits would have to be developed in "case-to-case adjudication, as is true with so many legal standards for judging concrete cases, whether the standard is provided by the Constitution, statutes or case law." There "must be sufficient evidence to permit the conclusion that the defendant in fact entertained serious doubts as to the truth of his publication" in order for recklessness to be found. Anticipating the charge that this position would encourage publishers not to verify their assertions, Justice White, for the Court stated:

> The defendant in a defamation action brought by a public official cannot, however, automatically insure a favorable verdict by testifying that he published with a belief that the statements were true. The finder of fact must determine whether the publication was indeed made in good faith. Professions of good faith will be unlikely to prove persuasive, for example, where a story is fabricated by the defendant, is a product of his imagination, or is based wholly on an unverified anonymous telephone call. Nor will they be likely to prevail when the publisher's allegations are so inherently improbable that only a reckless man would have put them in circulation. Likewise, recklessness may be found where there are obvious reasons to doubt the veracity of the informant or the accuracy of his reports.

Justice Fortas dissented on the ground that the failure to make "a good-faith check" of the statement was sufficient to establish "reckless disregard." How would the Court's test apply to an extreme partisan who would readily believe anything derogatory about his opponent?

9. Next the Court decided three cases as a group. Two of them involved false charges made about a candidate for office. The Court unanimously extended the *Times* rationale to candidates because "it can hardly be doubted that the constitutional guarantee has its fullest

and most urgent application precisely to the conduct of campaigns for political office." Monitor Patriot Co. v. Roy, 401 U.S. 265 (1971) and Ocala Star-Banner Co. v. Damron, 401 U.S. 295 (1971). In *Roy*, the charge related to criminal activity that allegedly took place many years earlier. The Court decided that the *Times* rule should include "anything which might touch on an official's fitness for office" when a candidate's behavior is being discussed. "The principal activity of a candidate in our political system . . . consists in putting before the voters every conceivable aspect of his public and private life that he thinks may lead the electorate to gain a good impression of him. A candidate who, for example, seeks to further his cause through the prominent display of his wife and children can hardly argue that his qualities as a husband or father remain of 'purely private' concern." The Court concluded that a "charge of criminal conduct, no matter how remote in time or place, can never be irrelevant to an official's or a candidate's fitness for office" for purposes of applying the *Times* rule.

In *Damron*, the candidate was said to have been charged with a crime, when in fact his brother was the one charged. Again, the *Times* rule applied.

In the third case, Time, Inc. v. Pape, 401 U.S. 279 (1971), a report by the Civil Rights Commission included some unverified complaints of police brutality as examples of the types of complaints being received. *Time* reported the release of the volume and quoted one of the complaints without indicating that it had not been verified. The police named in that complaint sued *Time*. The *Times* rule admittedly applied and the question was whether the facts would permit a jury to find the requisite malice. The Court chose a very narrow ground that stressed the difficulties of reporting what someone has said as opposed to what someone has done. Here the Commission's own words might have been read to suggest that the complaints were probably valid and thus *Time* may have accurately captured the sense of the Commission's report, even though it excluded the word "alleged." Even if the story was inaccurate, the Court held as a matter of law that there was no basis for finding deliberate or reckless falsity.

10. A plurality of the Court took the next step in Rosenbloom v. Metromedia, Inc., 403 U.S. 29 (1971), involving a broadcaster's charge that a magazine distributor sold obscene material and was arrested in a police raid. Justice Brennan, joined by Chief Justice Burger and Justice Blackmun, held that the *Times* standard should be extended to "all discussion and communication involving matters of public or general concern, without regard to whether the persons involved are famous or anonymous." The arrest and the distributor's subsequent claims against the police were thought to fit this category and the *Times* standard was applied. In reaching that position Justice Brennan concluded that the focus on the plaintiff's status begun in the

Times case bore "little relationship either to the values protected by the First Amendment or to the nature of our society. . . . Thus, the idea that certain 'public' figures have voluntarily exposed their entire lives to public inspection, while private individuals have kept theirs carefully shrouded from public view is, at best, a legal fiction." Discussion of a matter of public concern must be protected even when it involves an unknown person. If the states fear that private citizens will be unable to respond to adverse publicity, "the solution lies in the direction of ensuring their ability to respond, rather than in stifling public discussion of matters of public concern," a reference to possible use of the right of reply. 403 U.S. at 47.

Is this a rejection of the philosophy of the *Times* case? Is it persuasive?

Justice White concurred on the narrow ground that the press is privileged to report "upon the official actions of public servants in full detail." Justice Black provided the fifth vote against liability for the reasons stated in his earlier opinions. Justices Harlan, Stewart and Marshall dissented on various grounds but they agreed that the private plaintiff should be required to prove no more than negligence in this case. Justice Douglas did not participate.

Because there was no majority opinion from the Court in *Rosenbloom,* the case provided little guidance for future defamation cases. Three years later, in Gertz v. Robert Welch, Inc., the Court handed down a major libel decision, considered by many to be the most important since *Sullivan.* As you will see, *Gertz* attempts to clarify the difference between public and private figure libel plaintiffs. It also lifts from many private figure plaintiffs—depending on the state in which they sue—the burden of proving "actual malice" to collect compensatory damages.

GERTZ v. ROBERT WELCH, INC.

Supreme Court of the United States, 1974.
418 U.S. 323, 94 S.Ct. 2997, 41 L.Ed.2d 789.

[Plaintiff, an attorney, was retained to represent the family of a youth killed by Nuccio, a Chicago policeman. In that capacity, plaintiff attended the coroner's inquest and filed an action for damages but played no part in a criminal proceeding in which Nuccio was convicted of second degree murder. Respondent publishes *American Opinion,* a monthly outlet for the views of the John Birch Society. As part of its efforts to alert the public to an alleged nationwide conspiracy to discredit local police, the magazine's editor engaged a regular contributor to write about the Nuccio episode. The article that appeared charged a frame-up against Nuccio and portrayed plaintiff as a "major architect" of the plot. It also falsely asserted that he had a long police record, was an official of the Marxist

League for Industrial Democracy, and was a "Leninist" and a "Communist-fronter." The editor made no effort to verify the story.

Gertz filed an action for libel in District Court because of diversity of citizenship. The trial judge first ruled that Gertz was not a public official or public figure and that under Illinois law there was no defense. The jury awarded $50,000. On further reflection, the judge decided that since a matter of public concern was being discussed, the *Times* rule should apply and he granted the defendant judgment notwithstanding the jury's verdict. He thus anticipated the plurality's approach in Rosenbloom v. Metromedia, Inc. The court of appeals, relying on the intervening decision in *Rosenbloom*, affirmed because of the absence of "clear and convincing" evidence of "actual malice." Gertz appealed.]

MR. JUSTICE POWELL delivered the opinion of the Court.

. . .

II

The principal issue in this case is whether a newspaper or broadcaster that publishes defamatory falsehoods about an individual who is neither a public official nor a public figure may claim a constitutional privilege against liability for the injury inflicted by those statements. The Court considered this question on the rather different set of facts presented in Rosenbloom v. Metromedia, Inc., 403 U.S. 29 (1971). Rosenbloom, a distributor of nudist magazines, was arrested for selling allegedly obscene material while making a delivery to a retail dealer. The police obtained a warrant and seized his entire inventory of 3,000 books and magazines. He sought and obtained an injunction prohibiting further police interference with his business. He then sued a local radio station for failing to note in two of its newscasts that the 3,000 items seized were only "reportedly" or "allegedly" obscene and for broadcasting references to "the smut literature racket" and to "girlie-book peddlers" in its coverage of the court proceeding for injunctive relief. He obtained a judgment against the radio station, but the Court of Appeals for the Third Circuit held the *New York Times* privilege applicable to the broadcast and reversed. 415 F.2d 892 (1969).

This Court affirmed the decision below, but no majority could agree on a controlling rationale. The eight Justices who participated in *Rosenbloom* announced their views in five separate opinions, none of which commanded more than three votes. The several statements not only reveal disagreement about the appropriate result in that case, they also reflect divergent traditions of thought about the general problem of reconciling the law of defamation with the First Amendment. One approach has been to extend the *New York Times* test to an expanding variety of situations. Another has been to vary the level of constitutional privilege for defamatory falsehood with the status of the person defamed. And a third view would grant to the press and broadcast media absolute immunity from liability for defamation. To place our holding in the proper context, we preface our discussion of this case with a review of the several *Rosenbloom* opinions and their antecedents.

. . .

In his opinion for the plurality in Rosenbloom v. Metromedia, Inc., 403 U.S. 29 (1971), Mr. Justice BRENNAN took the *New York Times* privilege one step further. He concluded that its protection should extend to defamatory falsehoods relating to private persons if the statements concerned matters of general or public interest.

. . .

. . .

In *Rosenbloom* Mr. Justice Harlan . . . acquiesced in the application of the privilege to defamation of public figures but argued that a different rule should obtain where defamatory falsehood harmed a private individual. He noted that a private person has less likelihood "of securing access to channels of communication sufficient to rebut falsehoods concerning him" than do public officials and public figures, 403 U.S., at 70, and has not voluntarily placed himself in the public spotlight. Mr. Justice Harlan concluded that the States could constitutionally allow private individuals to recover damages for defamation on the basis of any standard of care except liability without fault.

. . . The principal point of disagreement among the three dissenters concerned punitive damages. Whereas Mr. Justice Harlan thought that the States could allow punitive damages in amounts bearing "a reasonable and purposeful relationship to the actual harm done . . . ," id., at 75, Mr. Justice Marshall concluded that the size and unpredictability of jury awards of exemplary damages unnecessarily exacerbated the problems of media self-censorship and that such damages should therefore be forbidden.

III

We begin with the common ground. Under the First Amendment there is no such thing as a false idea. However pernicious an opinion may seem, we depend for its correction not on the conscience of judges and juries but on the competition of other ideas. But there is no constitutional value in false statements of fact. Neither the intentional lie nor the careless error materially advances society's interest in "uninhibited, robust, and wide-open" debate on public issues. . . .

Although the erroneous statement of fact is not worthy of constitutional protection, it is nevertheless inevitable in free debate. . . . And punishment of error runs the risk of inducing a cautious and restrictive exercise of the constitutionally guaranteed freedoms of speech and press. Our decisions recognize that a rule of strict liability that compels a publisher or broadcaster to guarantee the accuracy of his factual assertions may lead to intolerable self-censorship. Allowing the media to avoid liability only by proving the truth of all injurious statements does not accord adequate protection to First Amendment liberties. . . . The First Amendment requires that we protect some falsehood in order to protect speech that matters.

The need to avoid self-censorship by the news media is, however, not the only societal value at issue. If it were, this Court would have embraced long ago the view that publishers and broadcasters enjoy an unconditional and indefeasible immunity from liability for defamation. . . .

The legitimate state interest underlying the law of libel is the compensation of individuals for the harm inflicted on them by defamatory falsehood. We would not lightly require the State to abandon this purpose, for, as Mr. Justice Stewart has reminded us, the individual's right to the protection of his own good name

> "reflects no more than our basic concept of the essential dignity and worth of every human being—a concept at the root of any decent system of ordered liberty. The protection of private personality, like the protection of life itself, is left primarily to the individual States under the Ninth and Tenth Amendments. But this does not mean that the right is entitled to any less recognition by this Court as a basic of our constitutional system." Rosenblatt v. Baer, 383 U.S. 75, 92 (1966) (concurring opinion).

Some tension necessarily exists between the need for a vigorous and uninhibited press and the legitimate interest in redressing wrongful injury. . . .

The *New York Times* standard defines the level of constitutional protection appropriate to the context of defamation of a public person. Those who, by reason of the notoriety of their achievements or the vigor and success with which they seek the public's attention, are properly classed as public figures and those who hold governmental office may recover for injury to reputation only on clear and convincing proof that the defamatory falsehood was made with knowledge of its falsity or with reckless disregard for the truth. This standard administers an extremely powerful antidote to the inducement to media self-censorship of the common-law rule of strict liability for libel and slander. And it exacts a correspondingly high price from the victims of defamatory falsehood. Plainly many deserving plaintiffs, including some intentionally subjected to injury, will be unable to surmount the barrier of the *New York Times* test. Despite this substantial abridgment of the state law right to compensation for wrongful hurt to one's reputation, the Court has concluded that the protection of the *New York Times* privilege should be available to publishers and broadcasters of defamatory falsehood

concerning public officials and public figures. [ ] We think that
these decisions are correct, but we do not find their holdings justified
solely by reference to the interest of the press and broadcast media in
immunity from liability.   Rather, we believe that the *New York
Times* rule states an accommodation between this concern and the
limited state interest present in the context of libel actions brought
by public persons.   For the reasons stated below, we conclude that
the state interest in compensating injury to the reputation of private
individuals requires that a different rule should obtain with respect to
them.

Theoretically, of course, the balance between the needs of the
press and the individual's claim to compensation for wrongful injury
might be struck on a case-by-case basis.   As Mr. Justice Harlan
hypothesized, "it might seem, purely as an abstract matter, that the
most utilitarian approach would be to scrutinize carefully every jury
verdict in every libel case, in order to ascertain whether the final
judgment leaves fully protected whatever First Amendment values
transcend the legitimate state interest in protecting the particular
plaintiff who prevailed."   Rosenbloom v. Metromedia, Inc., 403 U.S.,
at 63 (footnote omitted).   But this approach would lead to unpredictable results and uncertain expectations, and it could render our duty
to supervise the lower courts unmanageable.   Because an *ad hoc*
resolution of the competing interests at stake in each particular case
is not feasible, we must lay down broad rules of general application.
Such rules necessarily treat alike various cases involving differences
as well as similarities.   Thus it is often true that not all of the
considerations which justify adoption of a given rule will obtain in
each particular case decided under its authority.

With that caveat we have no difficulty in distinguishing among
defamation plaintiffs.   The first remedy of any victim of defamation
is self-help—using available opportunities to contradict the lie or
correct the error and thereby to minimize its adverse impact on
reputation.   Public officials and public figures usually enjoy significantly greater access to the channels of effective communication and
hence have a more realistic opportunity to counteract false statements than private individuals normally enjoy.[9]   Private individuals
are therefore more vulnerable to injury, and the state interest in
protecting them is correspondingly greater.

More important than the likelihood that private individuals will
lack effective opportunities for rebuttal, there is a compelling normative consideration underlying the distinction between public and private defamation plaintiffs.   An individual who decides to seek governmental office must accept certain necessary consequences of that

9. Of course, an opportunity for rebuttal seldom suffices to undo harm of
defamatory falsehood. Indeed, the law
of defamation is rooted in our experience
that the truth rarely catches up with a
lie. But the fact that the self-help remedy of rebuttal, standing alone, is inadequate to its task does not mean that it is
irrelevant to our inquiry.

involvement in public affairs. He runs the risk of closer public scrutiny than might otherwise be the case. And society's interest in the officers of government is not strictly limited to the formal discharge of official duties. As the Court pointed out in Garrison v. Louisiana, 379 U.S., at 77, the public's interest extends to "anything which might touch on an official's fitness for office . . .. Few personal attributes are more germane to fitness for office than dishonesty, malfeasance, or improper motivation, even though these characteristics may also affect the official's private character."

Those classed as public figures stand in a similar position. Hypothetically, it may be possible for someone to become a public figure through no purposeful action of his own, but the instances of truly involuntary public figures must be exceedingly rare. For the most part those who attain this status have assumed roles of especial prominence in the affairs of society. Some occupy positions of such persuasive power and influence that they are deemed public figures for all purposes. More commonly, those classed as public figures have thrust themselves to the forefront of particular public controversies in order to influence the resolution of the issues involved. In either event, they invite attention and comment.

Even if the foregoing generalities do not obtain in every instance, the communications media are entitled to act on the assumption that public officials and public figures have voluntarily exposed themselves to increased risk of injury from defamatory falsehood concerning them. No such assumption is justified with respect to a private individual. He has not accepted public office or assumed an "influential role in ordering society." Curtis Publishing Co. v. Butts, supra, at 164 (Warren, C.J., concurring in result). He has relinquished no part of his interest in the protection of his own good name, and consequently he has a more compelling call on the courts for redress of injury inflicted by defamatory falsehood. Thus, private individuals are not only more vulnerable to injury than public officials and public figures; they are also more deserving of recovery.

For these reasons we conclude that the States should retain substantial latitude in their efforts to enforce a legal remedy for defamatory falsehood injurious to the reputation of a private individual. The extension of the *New York Times* test proposed by the *Rosenbloom* plurality would abridge this legitimate state interest to a degree that we find unacceptable. And it would occasion the additional difficulty of forcing state and federal judges to decide on an *ad hoc* basis which publications address issues of "general or public interest" and which do not—to determine, in the words of Mr. Justice MARSHALL, "what information is relevant to self-government." Rosenbloom v. Metromedia, Inc., 403 U.S., at 79. We doubt the wisdom of committing this task to the conscience of judges. Nor does the Constitution require us to draw so thin a line between the drastic alternatives of the *New York Times* privilege and the common law of strict liability for defamatory error. The "public or general interest" test for determining the applicability of the *New York Times* standard to private defamation actions inadequately serves both of the competing values at stake. On the one hand, a private individual whose reputation is injured by defamatory falsehood that does concern an issue of public or general interest has no recourse unless he can meet the rigorous requirements of *New York Times*. This is true despite the factors that distinguish the state interest in compensating private individuals from the analogous interest involved in the context of public persons. On the other hand, a publisher or broadcaster of a defamatory error which a court deems unrelated to an issue of public or general interest may be held liable in damages even if it took every reasonable precaution to ensure the accuracy of its assertions. And liability may far exceed compensation for any actual injury to the plaintiff, for the jury may be permitted to presume damages without proof of loss and even to award punitive damages.

We hold that, so long as they do not impose liability without fault, the States may define for themselves the appropriate standard of liability for a publisher or broadcaster of defamatory falsehood injurious to a private individual. This approach provides a more equitable boundary between the competing concerns involved here. It recognizes the strength of the legitimate state interest in compensating private individuals for wrongful injury to reputation, yet shields the press and broadcast media from the rigors of strict liability for defamation. At least this conclusion obtains where, as here, the substance of the defamatory statement "makes substantial danger to reputation apparent." [11] This phrase places in perspective the conclusion we announce today. Our inquiry would involve considerations somewhat different from those discussed above if a State purported to condition civil liability on a factual misstatement whose content did not warn a reasonably prudent editor or broadcaster of its defamatory potential. Cf. Time, Inc. v. Hill, 385 U.S. 374 (1967). Such a case is not now before us, and we intimate no view as to its proper resolution.

IV

Our accommodation of the competing values at stake in defamation suits by private individuals allows the States to impose liability on the publisher or broadcaster of defamatory falsehood on a less demanding showing than that required by *New York Times*. This conclusion is not based on a belief that the considerations which prompted the adoption of the *New York Times* privilege for defamation of public officials and its extension to public figures are wholly

11. Curtis Publishing Co. v. Butts, supra, at 155.

inapplicable to the context of private individuals. Rather, we endorse this approach in recognition of the strong and legitimate state interest in compensating private individuals for injury to reputation. But this countervailing state interest extends no further than compensation for actual injury. For the reasons stated below, we hold that the States may not permit recovery of presumed or punitive damages, at least when liability is not based on a showing of knowledge of falsity or reckless disregard for the truth.

The common law of defamation is an oddity of tort law, for it allows recovery of purportedly compensatory damages without evidence of actual loss. Under the traditional rules pertaining to actions for libel, the existence of injury is presumed from the fact of publication. Juries may award substantial sums as compensation for supposed damage to reputation without any proof that such harm actually occurred. The largely uncontrolled discretion of juries to award damages where there is no loss unnecessarily compounds the potential of any system of liability for defamatory falsehood to inhibit the vigorous exercise of First Amendment freedoms. Additionally, the doctrine of presumed damages invites juries to punish unpopular opinion rather than to compensate individuals for injury sustained by the publication of a false fact. More to the point, the States have no substantial interest in securing for plaintiffs such as this petitioner gratuitous awards of money damages far in excess of any actual injury.

We would not, of course, invalidate state law simply because we doubt its wisdom, but here we are attempting to reconcile state law with a competing interest grounded in the constitutional command of the First Amendment. It is therefore appropriate to require that state remedies for defamatory falsehood reach no farther than is necessary to protect the legitimate interest involved. It is necessary to restrict defamation plaintiffs who do not prove knowledge of falsity or reckless disregard for the truth to compensation for actual injury. We need not define "actual injury," as trial courts have wide experience in framing appropriate jury instructions in tort actions. Suffice it to say that actual injury is not limited to out-of-pocket loss. Indeed, the more customary types of actual harm inflicted by defamatory falsehood include impairment of reputation and standing in the community, personal humiliation, and mental anguish and suffering. Of course, juries must be limited by appropriate instructions, and all awards must be supported by competent evidence concerning the injury, although there need be no evidence which assigns an actual dollar value to the injury.

We also find no justification for allowing awards of punitive damages against publishers and broadcasters held liable under state-defined standards of liability for defamation. In most jurisdictions jury discretion over the amounts awarded is limited only by the gentle rule that they not be excessive. Consequently, juries assess punitive damages in wholly unpredictable amounts bearing no necessary relation to the actual harm caused. And they remain free to use their discretion selectively to punish expressions of unpopular views. Like the doctrine of presumed damages, jury discretion to award punitive damages unnecessarily exacerbates the danger of media self-censorship, but, unlike the former rule, punitive damages are wholly irrelevant to the state interest that justifies a negligence standard for private defamation actions. They are not compensation for injury. Instead, they are private fines levied by civil juries to punish reprehensible conduct and to deter its future occurrence. In short, the private defamation plaintiff who establishes liability under a less demanding standard than that stated by *New York Times* may recover only such damages as are sufficient to compensate him for actual injury.

V

Notwithstanding our refusal to extend the *New York Times* privilege to defamation of private individuals, respondent contends that we should affirm the judgment below on the ground that petitioner is either a public official or a public figure. There is little basis for the former assertion. Several years prior to the present incident, petitioner had served briefly on housing committees appointed by the mayor of Chicago, but at the time of publication he had never held any remunerative governmental position. Respondent admits this but argues that petitioner's appearance at the coroner's inquest rendered him a "de facto public official." Our cases recognize no such concept. Respondent's suggestion would sweep all lawyers under the *New York Times* rule as officers of the court and distort the plain meaning of the "public official" category beyond all recognition. We decline to follow it.

Respondent's characterization of petitioner as a public figure raises a different question. That designation may rest on either of two alternative bases. In some instances an individual may achieve such pervasive fame or notoriety that he becomes a public figure for all purposes and in all contexts. More commonly, an individual voluntarily injects himself or is drawn into a particular public controversy and thereby becomes a public figure for a limited range of issues. In either case such persons assume special prominence in the resolution of public questions.

Petitioner has long been active in community and professional affairs. He has served as an officer of local civic groups and of various professional organizations, and he has published several books and articles on legal subjects. Although petitioner was consequently well known in some circles, he had achieved no general fame or notoriety in the community. None of the prospective jurors called at the trial had ever heard of petitioner prior to this litigation, and respondent offered no proof that this response was atypical of the local population. We would not lightly assume that a citizen's participation in community and professional affairs rendered him a public figure for all purposes. Absent clear evidence of general fame or notoriety in the community, and pervasive involvement in the affairs of society, an individual should not be deemed a public personality for all aspects of his life. It is preferable to reduce the public-figure question to a more meaningful context by looking to the nature and extent of an individual's participation in the particular controversy giving rise to the defamation.

In this context it is plain that petitioner was not a public figure. He played a minimal role at the coroner's inquest, and his participation related solely to his representation of a private client. He took no part in the criminal prosecution of Officer Nuccio. Moreover, he never discussed either the criminal or civil litigation with the press and was never quoted as having done so. He plainly did not thrust himself into the vortex of this public issue, nor did he engage the public's attention in an attempt to influence its outcome. We are persuaded that the trial court did not err in refusing to characterize petitioner as a public figure for the purpose of this litigation.

We therefore conclude that the *New York Times* standard is inapplicable to this case and that the trial court erred in entering judgment for respondent. Because the jury was allowed to impose liability without fault and was permitted to presume damages without proof of injury, a new trial is necessary. We reverse and remand for further proceedings in accord with this opinion.

It is so ordered.

Mr. Justice Blackmun, concurring.

[Although I joined the *Rosenbloom* plurality opinion,] I am willing to join, and do join, the Court's opinion and its judgment for two reasons:

1. By removing the spectors of presumed and punitive damages in the absence of *New York Times* malice, the Court eliminates significant and powerful motives for self-censorship that otherwise are present in the traditional libel action. By so doing, the Court leaves what should prove to be sufficient and adequate breathing space for a vigorous press. What the Court has done, I believe, will have little, if any, practical effect on the functioning of responsible journalism.

2. The Court was sadly fractionated in *Rosenbloom*. A result of that kind inevitably leads to uncertainty. I feel that it is of profound importance for the Court to come to rest in the defamation area and to have a clearly defined majority position that eliminates the unsureness engendered by *Rosenbloom's* diversity. If my vote were not needed to create a majority, I would adhere to my prior view. A definitive ruling, however, is paramount. [ ]

For these reasons, I join the opinion and the judgment of the Court.

MR. CHIEF JUSTICE BURGER, dissenting.

The doctrines of the law of defamation have had a gradual evolution primarily in the state courts. In New York Times Co. v. Sullivan, 376 U.S. 254 (1964), and its progeny this Court entered this field.

Agreement or disagreement with the law as it has evolved to this time does not alter the fact that it has been orderly development with a consistent basic rationale. In today's opinion the Court abandons the traditional thread so far as the ordinary private citizen is concerned and introduces the concept that the media will be liable for negligence in publishing defamatory statements with respect to such persons. Although I agree with much of what Mr. Justice White states, I do not read the Court's new doctrinal approach in quite the way he does. I am frank to say I do not know the parameters of a "negligence" doctrine as applied to the news media. Conceivably this new doctrine could inhibit some editors, as the dissents of Mr. Justice Douglas and Mr. Justice Brennan suggest. But I would prefer to allow this area of law to continue to evolve as it has up to now with respect to private citizens rather than embark on a new doctrinal theory which has no jurisprudential ancestry.

The petitioner here was performing a professional representative role as an advocate in the highest tradition of the law, and under that tradition the advocate is not to be invidiously identified with his client. The important public policy which underlies this tradition— the right to counsel—would be gravely jeopardized if every lawyer who takes an "unpopular" case, civil or criminal, would automatically become fair game for irresponsible reporters and editors who might, for example, describe the lawyer as a "mob mouthpiece" for representing a client with a serious prior criminal record, or as an "ambulance chaser" for representing a claimant in a personal injury action.

I would reverse the judgment of the Court of Appeals and remand for reinstatement of the verdict of the jury and the entry of an appropriate judgment on that verdict.

MR. JUSTICE DOUGLAS, dissenting.

. . .

. . . The standard announced today leaves the States free to "define for themselves the appropriate standard of liability for a publisher or broadcaster" in the circumstances of this case. This of course leaves the simple negligence standard as an option with the jury free to impose damages upon a finding that the publisher failed to act as "a reasonable man." With such continued erosion of First Amendment protection, I fear that it may well be the reasonable man who refrains from speaking.

Since in my view the First and Fourteenth Amendments prohibit the imposition of damages upon respondent for this discussion of public affairs, I would affirm the judgment below.

MR. JUSTICE BRENNAN, dissenting.

I agree with the conclusion, expressed in Part V of the Court's opinion, that, at the time of publication of respondent's article, petitioner could not properly have been viewed as either a "public official" or "public figure"; instead, respondent's article, dealing with an alleged conspiracy to discredit local police forces, concerned petitioner's purported involvement in "an event of public or general interest." . . .

. . .

Although acknowledging that First Amendment values are of no less significance when media reports concern private persons' involvement in matters of public concern, the Court refuses to provide, in such cases, the same level of constitutional protection that has been afforded the media in the context of defamation of public persons. The accommodation that this Court has established between free speech and libel laws in cases involving public officials and public figures—that defamatory falsehood be shown by clear and convincing evidence to have been published with knowledge of falsity or with reckless disregard of truth—is not apt, the Court holds, because the private individual does not have the same degree of access to the media to rebut defamatory comments as does the public person and he has not voluntarily exposed himself to public scrutiny.

While these arguments are forcefully and eloquently presented, I cannot accept them, for the reasons I stated in *Rosenbloom:*

"The *New York Times* standard was applied to libel of a public official or public figure to give effect to the [First] Amendment's function to encourage ventilation of public issues, not because the public official has any less interest in protecting his reputation than an individual in private life. While the argument that public figures need less protection because they can command media attention to counter criticism may be true for some very prominent people, even then it is the rare case where the denial overtakes the original charge. Denials, retractions, and corrections are not 'hot' news, and rarely receive the prominence of the original story. When the public official or public figure is a minor functionary, or has left the position that put him in the public eye . . ., the argument loses all of its force. In the vast majority of libels involving public officials or public figures, the ability to respond through the media will depend on the same complex factor on which the ability of a private individual depends: the unpredictable event of the media's continuing interest in the story. Thus the unproved, and highly improbable, generalization that an as yet [not fully defined] class of 'public figures' involved in matters of public concern will be better able to respond through the media than private individuals also involved in such matters seems too insubstantial a reed on which to rest a constitutional distinction." [ ]

. . .

. . . Under a reasonable-care regime, publishers and broadcasters will have to make pre-publication judgments about juror assessment of such diverse considerations as the size, operating procedures, and financial condition of the newsgathering system, as well as the relative costs and benefits of instituting less frequent and more costly reporting at a higher level of accuracy. [ ] Moreover, in contrast to proof by clear and convincing evidence required under the *Times* test, the burden of proof for reasonable care will doubtless be the preponderance of the evidence. . . .

The Court does not discount altogether the danger that jurors will punish for the expression of unpopular opinions. This probability accounts for the Court's limitation that "the States may not permit recovery of presumed or punitive damages, at least when liability is not based on a showing of knowledge of falsity or reckless disregard for the truth." [ ] But plainly a jury's latitude to impose liability for want of due care poses a far greater threat of suppressing unpopular views than does a possible recovery of presumed or punitive damages. Moreover, the Court's broad-ranging examples of "actual injury," including impairment of reputation and standing in the community, as well as personal humiliation, and mental anguish and suffering, inevitably allow a jury bent on punishing expression of unpopular views a formidable weapon for doing so. Finally, even a limitation of recovery to "actual injury"—however much it reduces the size or frequency of recoveries—will not provide the necessary elbowroom for First Amendment expression. . . .

On the other hand, the uncertainties which the media face under today's decision are largely avoided by the *Times* standard. I reject the argument that my *Rosenbloom* view improperly commits to judges the task of determining what is and what is not an issue of "general or public interest." [3] I noted in *Rosenbloom* that perform-

3. The Court, taking a novel step, would not limit application of First Amendment protection to private libels involving issues of general or public interest, but would forbid the States from imposing liability without fault in any case where the substance of the defamatory statement made substantial danger to reputation apparent. As in Rosenbloom v. Metromedia, Inc., 403 U.S. 29, 44 n. 12, 48–49, n. 17 (1971), I would leave open the question of what constitutional standard, if any, applies when defamatory falsehoods are published or broadcast concerning either a private or public person's activities not within the scope of the general or public interest.

Parenthetically, my Brother White argues that the Court's view and mine will prevent a plaintiff—unable to demonstrate some degree of fault—from vindicating his reputation by securing a judgment that the publication was false. This argument overlooks the possible enactment of statutes, not requiring proof of fault, which provide for an action for retraction or for publication of a court's determination of falsity if the plaintiff is able to demonstrate that false statements have been published concerning his activities. Cf. Note, Vindication of the Reputation of a Public Official, 80 Harv.L.Rev. 1730, 1739–1747 (1967). Although it may be that questions could be

ance of this task would not always be easy. Id., at 49 n. 17. But surely the courts, the ultimate arbiters of all disputes concerning clashes of constitutional values, would only be performing one of their traditional functions in undertaking this duty. . . .

. . .

MR. JUSTICE WHITE, dissenting.

. . .

The impact of today's decision on the traditional law of libel is immediately obvious and indisputable. No longer will the plaintiff be able to rest his case with proof of a libel defamatory on its face or proof of a slander historically actionable *per se*. In addition, he must prove some further degree of culpable conduct on the part of the publisher, such as intentional or reckless falsehood or negligence. And if he succeeds in this respect, he faces still another obstacle: recovery for loss of reputation will be conditioned upon "competent" proof of actual injury to his standing in the community. This will be true regardless of the nature of the defamation and even though it is one of those particularly reprehensible statements that have traditionally made slanderous words actionable without proof of fault by the publisher or of the damaging impact of his publication. The Court rejects the judgment of experience that some publications are so inherently capable of injury, and actual injury so difficult to prove, that the risk of falsehood should be borne by the publisher, not the victim. . . .

So too, the requirement of proving special injury to reputation before general damages may be awarded will clearly eliminate the prevailing rule, worked out over a very long period of time, that, in the case of defamations not actionable *per se*, the recovery of general damages for injury to reputation may also be had if some form of material or pecuniary loss is proved. Finally, an inflexible federal standard is imposed for the award of punitive damages. No longer will it be enough to prove ill will and an attempt to injure.

These are radical changes in the law and severe invasions of the prerogatives of the States. . . .

. . .

The central meaning of *New York Times*, and for me the First Amendment as it relates to libel laws, is that seditious libel—criticism of government and public officials—falls beyond the police power of the State. . . .

. . .

The Court evinces a deep-seated antipathy to "liability without fault." But this catch-phrase has no talismanic significance and is

raised concerning the constitutionality of such statutes, certainly nothing I have said today (and, as I read the Court's opinion, nothing said there) should be read to imply that a private plaintiff, unable to prove fault, must inevitably be denied the opportunity to secure a judgment upon the truth or falsity of statements published about him. [ ]

almost meaningless in this context where the Court appears to be addressing those libels and slanders that are defamatory on their face and where the publisher is no doubt aware from the nature of the material that it would be inherently damaging to reputation. He publishes notwithstanding, knowing that he will inflict injury. With this knowledge, he must intend to inflict that injury, his excuse being that he is privileged to do so—that he has published the truth. But as it turns out, what he has circulated to the public is a very damaging falsehood. Is he nevertheless "faultless?" Perhaps it can be said that the mistake about his defense was made in good faith, but the fact remains that it is he who launched the publication knowing that it could ruin a reputation.

In these circumstances, the law has heretofore put the risk of falsehood on the publisher where the victim is a private citizen and no grounds of special privilege are invoked. The Court would now shift this risk to the victim, even though he has done nothing to invite the calumny, is wholly innocent of fault, and is helpless to avoid his injury. I doubt that jurisprudential resistance to liability without fault is sufficient ground for employing the First Amendment to revolutionize the law of libel, and in my view, that body of legal rules poses no realistic threat to the press and its service to the public. The press today is vigorous and robust. To me, it is quite incredible to suggest that threats of libel suits from private citizens are causing the press to refrain from publishing the truth. I know of no hard facts to support that proposition, and the Court furnishes none.

The communications industry has increasingly become concentrated in a few powerful hands operating very lucrative businesses reaching across the Nation and into almost every home. Neither the industry as a whole nor its individual components are easily intimidated, and we are fortunate that they are not. Requiring them to pay for the occasional damage they do to private reputation will play no substantial part in their future performance or their existence.

In any event, if the Court's principal concern is to protect the communications industry from large libel judgments, it would appear that its new requirements with respect to general and punitive damages would be ample protection. . . .

It is difficult for me to understand why the ordinary citizen should himself carry the risk of damage and suffer the injury in order to vindicate First Amendment values by protecting the press and others from liability for circulating false information. This is particularly true because such statements serve no purpose whatsoever in furthering the public interest or the search for truth but, on the contrary, may frustrate that search and at the same time inflict great injury on the defenseless individual. The owners of the press and the stockholders of the communications enterprises can much better bear the burden. And if they cannot, the public at large

should somehow pay for what is essentially a public benefit derived
at private expense.

. . .

. . . Whether or not the course followed by the majority is
wise, and I have indicated my doubts that it is, our constitutional
scheme compels a proper respect for the role of the States in
acquitting their duty to obey the Constitution. Finding no evidence
that they have shirked this responsibility, particularly when the law
of defamation is even now in transition, I would await some demonstration of the diminution of freedom of expression before acting.

For the foregoing reasons, I would reverse the judgment of the
Court of Appeals and reinstate the jury's verdict.

Notes and Questions

1. Why did the majority adhere to the *Times* rule for public officials? Public figures? Some have argued that *Gertz* was a public
figure and that the case should have been analyzed along the lines of
Butts and *Walker*. See Pember and Teeter, Privacy and the Press
Since Time, Inc. v. Hill, 50 Wash.L.Rev. 57, 75 (1974): "Gertz was a
member of numerous boards and commissions in Illinois, had published several books on civil rights matters, had frequently been
honored by civil rights groups and had represented some rather
famous clients. . . . His publishing record belies the notion that he
was a poor, helpless, private individual who could not gain access to
the press." Would that suffice to meet the standard?

2. Why does the majority in *Gertz* prefer its approach to the
plurality's approach in *Rosenbloom?*

3. What criteria might be relevant in deciding whether a newspaper
has been at fault in publishing a false statement?

4. If a private citizen proves fault, why can he not recover traditional damages for defamation?

5. The Supreme Court has not decided finally whether libel plaintiffs may recover punitive damages.

6. The first significant application of *Gertz* occurred in Time, Inc. v.
Firestone, 424 U.S. 448 (1976), in which a magazine reported, perhaps
incorrectly, that a member of "one of America's wealthier industrial
families" had received a divorce because of his wife's adultery. The
divorce decree was probably based on either "extreme cruelty" or
"lack of domestication," but the judge was not explicit. The state
court upheld the wife's defamation award of $100,000. *Time* argued
that the "actual malice" standard should apply for two reasons.
First, it asserted that the plaintiff was a public figure, but the
majority disagreed: "Respondent did not assume any role of especial
prominence in the affairs of society, other than perhaps Palm Beach
society, and she did not thrust herself to the forefront of any
particular public controversy in order to influence the resolution of

the issues involved in it." The Court rejected the argument that because the case was of great public interest, the respondent must have been a public figure: "Dissolution of a marriage through judicial proceedings is not the sort of 'public controversy' referred to in *Gertz,* even though the marital difficulties of extremely wealthy individuals may be of interest to some portion of the reading public." Moreover, plaintiff was compelled to go to court to seek relief in a marital dispute and her involvement was not voluntary. The fact that she held "a few" press conferences during the case did not change her otherwise private status. She did not attempt to use them to influence the outcome of the trial or to thrust herself into an unrelated dispute.

The second claim was that negligent errors in the reporting of judicial proceedings should never lead to liability. Justice Rehnquist's opinion for the Court rejected the contention:

It may be that all reports of judicial proceedings contain some informational value implicating the First Amendment, but recognizing this is little different from labeling all judicial proceedings matters of "public or general interest," as that phrase was used by the plurality in *Rosenbloom.* Whatever their general validity, use of such subject matter classifications to determine the extent of constitutional protection afforded defamatory falsehoods may too often result in an improper balance between the competing interests in this area. It was our recognition and rejection of this weakness in the *Rosenbloom* test which led us in *Gertz* to eschew a subject matter test for one focusing upon the character of the defamation plaintiff. [ ] By confining inquiry to whether a plaintiff is a public officer or a public figure who might be assumed to "have voluntarily exposed themselves to increased risk of injury from defamatory falsehood," we sought a more appropriate accommodation between the public's interest in an uninhibited press and its equally compelling need for judicial redress of libelous utterances. Cf. Chaplinsky v. New Hampshire, 315 U.S. 568 (1942).

. . .

It may be argued that there is still room for application of the *New York Times* protections to more narrowly focused reports of what actually transpires in the courtroom. But even so narrowed, the suggested privilege is simply too broad. Imposing upon the law of private defamation the rather drastic limitations worked by *New York Times* cannot be justified by generalized references to the public interest in reports of judicial proceedings. The details of many, if not most, courtroom battles would add almost nothing towards advancing the uninhibited debate on public issues thought to provide principal support for the decision in *New York Times.* [ ] And while participants in some litigation may be legitimate "public figures," either generally or for the limited purpose of that litigation, the majority will more likely resemble respondent, drawn into a public forum largely against their will in order to attempt to obtain the only redress available to them or to defend themselves against actions brought by the State or by others. There appears little reason why these individuals should substantially forfeit that degree of protection which the law of defamation would otherwise afford them simply by virtue of their being drawn into a courtroom. The public interest in accurate reports of judicial proceedings is substantially protected by *Cox Broadcasting Co.*, supra. As to inaccurate and defamatory reports of facts, matters deserving no First Amendment protection, [   ], we think *Gertz* provides an adequate safeguard for the constitutionally protected interests of the press and affords it a tolerable margin for error by requiring some type of fault.

Plaintiff had withdrawn her claim for damages to reputation before trial but the Court held that the award could be sustained on proof of anxiety and concern over the impact of the adultery charge on her young son. The Court vacated the judgment for lack of consideration of fault by either the jury or any of the state courts. Justices Powell and Stewart, though joining the majority, asserted that the grounds of divorce were so unclear in this "bizarre case" that there was "substantial evidence" that *Time* was not negligent. Justice White, believing that the state courts had found negligence, would have affirmed the award. In addition, since the article had been written before *Rosenbloom* and *Gertz*, he saw no reason to require any showing of fault. Justice Brennan dissented on the ground that reports of judicial proceedings should not lead to liability unless the errors are deliberate or reckless. He observed that even those who would confine the central meaning of the First Amendment to "explicitly political speech" would extend protection to speech concerned with governmental behavior. He also thought the damage limits of *Gertz* had been "subverted" by the recovery allowed here with no showing of reputational harm. Justice Marshall, dissenting, thought that plaintiff was a public figure; he also doubted the existence of negligence. Justice Stevens took no part.

The Florida Supreme Court ordered a new trial but plaintiff dropped the case, saying that she had been vindicated.

Recall that under the common law "record libel" privilege, reports of governmental proceedings were privileged if they were fair and accurate reports of what had happened—even if the speaker being quoted had committed a defamation. Under the common law privilege, *Time*'s report, if incorrectly reporting the basis of the divorce decree, would not have been protected. For this reason *Time* had to assert a constitutional privilege.

7. In Wolston v. Reader's Digest Association, 443 U.S. 157 (1979), defendant published a book in 1974 that included plaintiff's name on a

list of "Soviet agents identified in the United States." A footnote said that the list consisted of agents "who were convicted of espionage or falsifying information or perjury and/or contempt charges following espionage indictments or who fled to the Soviet bloc to avoid prosecution."

Plaintiff had been convicted of contempt of court in 1958 for failing to appear before a grand jury investigating Soviet espionage. He was never indicted for any of the other offenses. At the time, plaintiff did not attempt to debate the propriety of his behavior. During the six weeks between his failure to appear and his sentencing, plaintiff's case was the subject of 15 stories in Washington and New York newspapers. "This flurry of publicity subsided" following the sentencing and plaintiff "succeeded for the most part in returning to the private life he had led" prior to the subpoena.

When plaintiff sued for libel, the lower courts held that in both 1958 and 1974 he was a public figure and that summary judgment was properly granted against him because he had presented no evidence of actual malice. (In the Supreme Court, plaintiff abandoned the argument that even if he was a public figure in 1958, he was no longer in 1974).

The Supreme Court reversed. For the majority, Justice Rehnquist reviewed the "self-help" and the "assumption of risk" explanations developed in *Gertz* to support the public-private distinction, and concluded that the second was the more important. He then quoted the passage from *Gertz* stating that some persons may be public figures because they "occupy positions of such persuasive power and influence that they are deemed public figures for all purposes. More commonly, those classed as public figures have thrust themselves to the forefront of particular public controversies in order to influence the resolution of the issues involved."

Justice Rehnquist concluded that plaintiff had neither "voluntarily thrust" nor "injected" himself into the forefront of the controversy surrounding the investigation of Soviet espionage in the United States. (He also noted that it was difficult to determine the relevant "public controversy" into which plaintiff was alleged to have thrust himself.)

> It would be more accurate to say that petitioner was dragged unwillingly into the controversy. The government pursued him in its investigation. Petitioner did fail to respond to a grand jury subpoena, and this failure, as well as his subsequent citation for contempt, did attract media attention. But the mere fact that petitioner voluntarily chose not to appear before the grand jury, knowing that his action might be attended by publicity, is not decisive on the question of public figure status. In *Gertz*, we held that an attorney was not a public figure even though he voluntarily associated himself with a case that was certain to receive extensive media exposure. 418 U.S., at 352. We empha-

sized that a court must focus on the "nature and extent of an individual's participation in the particular controversy giving rise to the defamation." . . .

Petitioner's failure to appear before the grand jury and citation for contempt no doubt were "newsworthy," but the simple fact that these events attracted media attention also is not conclusive of the public figure issue. A private individual is not automatically transformed into a public figure just by becoming involved in or associated with a matter that attracts public attention. To accept such reasoning would in effect reestablish the doctrine advanced by the plurality opinion in Rosenbloom v. Metromedia, Inc., 403 U.S. 29, 44 (1971), which concluded that the *New York Times* standard should extend to defamatory falsehoods relating to private persons if the statements involved matters of public or general concern. We repudiated this proposition in *Gertz* and in *Firestone*, however, and we reject it again today. A libel defendant must show more than mere newsworthiness to justify application of the demanding burden of *New York Times*. [ ]

Nor do we think that petitioner engaged the attention of the public in an attempt to influence the resolution of the issues involved. . . . He did not in any way seek to arouse public sentiment in his favor and against the investigation. Thus, this is not a case where a defendant invites a citation for contempt in order to use the contempt citation as a fulcrum to create public discussion about the methods being used in connection with an investigation or prosecution. . . . In short, we find no basis whatsoever for concluding that petitioner relinquished, to any degree, his interest in the protection of his own name.

This reasoning leads us to reject the further contention of respondents that any person who engages in criminal conduct automatically becomes a public figure for purposes of comment on a limited range of issues relating to his conviction. [ ] We declined to accept a similar argument in Time, Inc. v. Firestone.

Here Justice Rehnquist quoted the passage from *Firestone* above about protecting those drawn into a courtroom. He concluded, "We think that these observations remain sound, and that they control the disposition of this case. To hold otherwise would create an 'open season' for all who sought to defame persons convicted of a crime."

Justice Blackmun, joined by Justice Marshall, concurred in the result. He thought that the majority "seems to hold . . . that a person becomes a limited-issue public figure only if he literally or figuratively 'mounts a rostrum' to advocate a particular view. I see no need to adopt so restrictive a definition . . . on the facts before us." He would hold that even if plaintiff had acquired public figure status in 1958, "he clearly had lost that distinction" by 1974. Although plaintiff had not pressed that argument in the Supreme

Court, Justice Blackmun, noting that the lower courts had decided the point, thought it still open as a basis for decision.

He quoted the passage from *Gertz* indicating that a person may become a public figure for a limited range of issues if he "voluntarily injects himself or is drawn into a particular public controversy." (Justice Rehnquist did not refer to that passage.) Even if, in 1958, plaintiff had access to the press to rebut the charge that he was a Soviet spy, it "would strain credulity" to suggest that he could command such media interest in 1974. Also, his "conscious efforts to regain anonymity" removed any assumption of risk justification for calling him a public figure in 1974.

Justice Blackmun recognized that his view put a more difficult burden on historians than on contemporary commentators:

> This analysis implies, of course, that one may be a public figure for purposes of contemporaneous reporting of a controversial event, yet not be a public figure for purposes of historical commentary on the same occurrence. Historians, consequently, may well run a greater risk of liability for defamation. Yet this result, in my view, does no violence to First Amendment values. While historical analysis is no less vital to the marketplace of ideas than reporting current events, historians work under different conditions than do their media counterparts. A reporter trying to meet a deadline may find it totally impossible to check thoroughly the accuracy of his sources. A historian writing *sub specie aeternitatis* has both the time for reflection and the opportunity to investigate the veracity of the pronouncements he makes.

Justice Brennan dissented. He thought plaintiff a public figure for the limited purpose of comment on his connection with espionage in the 1940's and 1950's. He remained a public figure in 1974 because the issue of Soviet espionage "continues to be a legitimate topic of debate today . . .." But he found enough evidence of "actual malice" to warrant a trial under the *Times* standard.

The next case was decided on the same day as *Wolston*.

8. Hutchinson v. Proxmire, 443 U.S. 111 (1979), arose from Senator Proxmire's awarding of one of his Golden Fleece awards—made to government agencies that he believed engaged in wasteful spending. In this case he awarded it to agencies that had funded the plaintiff-scientist's research work on aggression in animals. The Senator had uttered the alleged defamation in several forums, including a speech prepared for delivery on the Senate floor; advance press releases; a newsletter sent to 100,000 people; and a television interview program. The Court first decided that in this case Article I, Section 6 of the Constitution—the so-called Speech or Debate Clause—protected only a speech delivered on the floor.

The Court then turned to the First Amendment issue. Chief Justice Burger began with the same *Gertz* passage that Justice Rehnquist had built upon in *Wolston.* Neither the fact that plaintiff had successfully applied for federal funds nor that he had access to media after Sen. Proxmire's charges, "demonstrates that Hutchinson was a public figure prior to the controversy . . .."

On this record Hutchinson's activities and public profile are much like those of countless members of his profession. His published writings reach a relatively small category of professionals concerned with research in human behavior. To the extent the subject of his published writings became a matter of controversy it was a consequence of the Golden Fleece Award. Clearly those charged with defamation cannot, by their own conduct, create their own defense by making the claimant a public figure. See Wolston v. Reader's Digest, Inc., [ ].

Hutchinson did not thrust himself or his views into public controversy to influence others. Respondents have not identified such a particular controversy; at most, they point to concern about general public expenditures. But that concern is shared by most and relates to most public expenditures; it is not sufficient to make Hutchinson a public figure. If it were, everyone who received or benefited from the myriad public grants for research could be classified as a public figure—a conclusion that our previous opinions have rejected. The "use of such subject-matter classifications to determine the extent of constitutional protection afforded defamatory falsehoods may too often result in an improper balance between the competing interests in this area." Time, Inc. v. Firestone, supra, at 456.

Moreover, Hutchinson at no time assumed any role of public prominence in the broad question of concern about expenditures. Neither his applications for federal grants nor his publications in professional journals can be said to have invited that degree of public attention and comment on his receipt of federal grants essential to meet the public figure level. The petitioner in Gertz v. Robert Welch, Inc., had published books and articles on legal issues; he had been active in local community affairs. Nevertheless, the Court concluded that his activities did not make him a public figure.

Finally, we cannot agree that Hutchinson had such access to the media that he should be classified as a public figure. Hutchinson's access was limited to responding to the announcement of the Golden Fleece Award. He did not have the regular and continuing access to the media that is one of the accoutrements of having become a public figure.

Justice Brennan was the sole dissenter. He believed that "public criticism by legislators of unnecessary governmental expenditures, whatever its form, is a legislative act shielded by the Speech or Debate Clause." He did not reach the public figure question.

Senator Proxmire subsequently made a public retraction, before television cameras, of his comments about Hutchinson.

9. The Hutchinson case provided a trio of significant footnotes. In footnote 8, the Court noted that the district court had considered Hutchinson a public official because he served as director of research at a state mental hospital. The Chief Justice observed that "The Court has not provided precise boundaries for the category of 'public official'; it cannot be thought to include all public employees, however."

In footnote 16, the Court noted that the lower courts had not decided whether the *Times* standard "can apply to an individual defendant rather than to a media defendant. . . . This Court has never decided the question; our conclusion (in this case) makes it unnecessary to do so in this case."

Commonly, every state and lower federal court that has addressed the question has concluded that the *Times* standard does apply to all defendants. There has been some division over whether the *Gertz* standard applies to nonmedia defendants.

Notice that the Court has in fact dealt with cases involving individual defendants, such as the clergymen in the New York Times case itself. However, the individual was charged with some involvement in preparing or delivering a statement over some medium of mass communication.

The lower courts had granted Senator Proxmire summary judgment on the question of "actual malice" and had suggested that early decisions in defamation cases were the rule and trials were the exception. Footnote 9 observed that considering the nuances of the "actual malice" issue, "we are constrained to express some doubt about the so-called 'rule.' The proof of 'actual malice' calls a defendant's state of mind into question [citing *New York Times*] and does not readily lend itself to summary disposition . . .. In the present posture of the case, however, the propriety of dealing with such complex issues by summary judgment is not before us." Despite speculation in 1979 that the footnote could lead to a dramatic increase in trials in such cases, it seems less significant today than it did then.

It should be noted that the protections applicable to media defendants in libel actions brought by private individuals do not necessarily apply to non-media defendants. See Greenmoss Builders, Inc. v. Dun & Bradstreet, Inc., 143 Vt. 66, 461 A.2d 414 (1983), certiorari granted ___ U.S. ___ (1983).

Differences Between the Two Proof Requirements

The distinction between public and private plaintiffs is relevant only to the question of what kind of proof the plaintiff must present in order to prevail at the trial and the nature of that recovery. The "fault" required under *Gertz* is generally thought to be the sort of conduct that must be shown in automobile accident cases, when visitors slip and fall on another's premises, or when a physician is sued for harm suffered by a patient. Briefly, in each of these situations the plaintiff must show that the defendant did not behave as a hypothetical reasonable person would have behaved under similar circumstances. Thus, in an automobile accident case, the question whether the driver was at fault, or negligent, is the same as asking whether he or she behaved as a hypothetical reasonable driver confronted with the same situation would have acted.

Translating that to the press area is not so easy because it is unclear whether a reporter or editor on a small rural daily should be expected to behave in the same manner as a reporter or editor on a large urban daily or a monthly magazine. These are some of the unresolved questions that lie ahead in applying the "fault" principle of the *Gertz* rule in private plaintiff cases.

Generally, in auto accident cases and in other civil cases, the plaintiff need only persuade the judge or jury that his version of the facts is more likely than competing versions. This is often referred to as proving your case by a "fair preponderance of the evidence" or meeting the "more likely than not" standard. Contrast this with the traditional burden of proof in criminal cases, which requires the prosecution to prove its case "beyond a reasonable doubt."

The situation changes sharply when the *Times* rule comes into play. Recall the idea of "deliberate or reckless falsity" that emerges from that case. Recall also that cases under the *Times* rule must be proven with "convincing clarity"—a standard certainly more stringent than the usual burden in civil cases.

The Court has twice had occasion to consider aspects of the *Times* standard. One such instance was in St. Amant v. Thompson, p. 93, supra, in which actual malice was defined as having prior knowledge of falsity or "entertaining serious doubts" as to the truth of the publication.

The next significant case on proving "actual malice" raised the issue of what types of questions the plaintiff could ask the media defendants during the pretrial effort to obtain evidence for the trial. The normal rule in civil cases is that any evidence that would be admissible at the trial may be obtained by "discovery" beforehand— usually either by deposition (oral testimony given by a prospective witness with only the lawyers for the sides present) or by interrogatories (written answers to written questions). This exchange of information allows the parties to know the strengths and weaknesses of their cases and avoids surprises at trial.

In Herbert v. Lando, 441 U.S. 153 (1979), the plaintiff, an admitted public figure, sued the producer and reporter of the television program "60 Minutes" and the CBS network for remarks on the program about his behavior while in military service in Vietnam. During his deposition, Lando, the producer, generally responded but he refused to answer some questions about why he made certain investigations and not others; what he concluded about the honesty of certain people he interviewed for the program; and about conversations he had with Mike Wallace, the reporter, in the preparation of the program segment. Lando contended that these thought processes and internal editorial discussions were protected from disclosure by the First Amendment. The Supreme Court disagreed.

Justice White, for the Court, began by observing that liability for defamation was "well established in the common law when the First Amendment was adopted" and the framers showed no intention of abolishing it. During the period before *New York Times*, mental processes and attitudes were often relevant on questions of conditional privilege and defendants often testified to their good faith in writing a story. "Courts have traditionally admitted any direct or indirect evidence relevant to the state of mind of the defendant and necessary to defeat a privilege" or to justify punitive damages in egregious cases.

Justice White understood the defendants to be arguing that "the defendant's reckless disregard of truth, a critical element, could not be shown by direct evidence through inquiry into the thoughts, opinions and conclusions of the publisher but could be proved only by objective evidence from which the ultimate fact could be inferred." This was a barrier of some substance "particularly when defendants themselves are prone to assert their good-faith belief in the truth of their publications, and libel plaintiffs are required to prove knowing or reckless falsehood with 'convincing clarity.' "

Justice White concluded that permitting plaintiffs "to prove their cases by direct as well as indirect evidence is consistent with the balance struck by our prior decisions." He "found it difficult to believe that error-avoiding procedures will be terminated or stifled simply because there is liability for culpable error and because the editorial process will itself be examined in the tiny percentage of instances in which error is claimed and litigation ensues."

Justice White did note that pretrial discovery techniques had led to "mushrooming litigation costs" but this was happening in all areas of litigation. Until major changes in pretrial procedures were developed for all cases, the Court would rely on "what in fact and in law are ample powers of the district judge to prevent abuse." (In this case, Lando's deposition had continued intermittently for over a year and filled nearly 3,000 pages.) Trial judges, who indirectly supervise these procedures, were reminded that discovery should be allowed only for "relevant" evidence.

Justice Powell concurred in the opinion of the Court but wrote separately to emphasize that trial judges must consider First Amendment interests as well as the private interests of plaintiffs in deciding how much pretrial discovery to allow.

Three justices dissented in separate opinions. Justice Stewart asserted that when the issue involves "actual malice" the only concern is what "was in fact published. What was *not* published has nothing to do with the case."

Justice Brennan agreed with the Court that questions about a reporter's mental processes in preparing a story were unlikely to be "chilled in the very processes of thought" if his mind could be explored in litigation. The "exceedingly generous standards" of the New York Times case were sufficient protection. He disagreed, however, with allowing discovery of editorial discussions because he feared this would hinder useful exchanges. He would have required revelation of such discussions only after the plaintiff had first proven that he had been defamed by a false statement.

Justice Marshall agreed with the Court and with Justice Brennan as to the mental processes. He would have granted editorial discussions absolute protection from ever having to be disclosed. He also wanted trial judges to control discovery more rigorously. In defamation cases, "some plaintiffs are animated by something more than a rational calculus of their chances to recovery."

This case indirectly suggests problems when a reporter is asked to identify the source of a story. That subject is discussed at length in Chapter X.

It is important to remember that Justice Powell's opinion in *Gertz* provided that states might use whatever standard they wanted to use so long as they met the minimum requirements of fault and the damage rules of *Gertz*. Thus, at the extreme, nothing in the Court's opinion would prevent a state from completely abolishing all suits for defamation. Some states have responded to *Gertz* by adopting the *Rosenbloom* approach. A few are developing their own rules, but most appear to be choosing the *Gertz* minimum standards as their own. See McCarthy, How State Courts Have Responded to *Gertz* in Setting Standards of Fault, 56 Journ.Q. 531 (1979).

A claim of absolute privilege for slanders uttered during reportorial investigation has been rejected. Davis v. Schuchat, 510 F.2d 731 (D.C.Cir.1975). An investigative reporter was trying to develop information about someone who, years earlier, had been acquitted on perjury charges. While interviewing sources the reporter asserted that the man once had been "convicted of a felony." The reporter stated that his interview technique involved "throwing a lot of thoughts out in an interview just to get a response." The court assumed that private persons and the press were equally privileged but failed to see "why a comment on a matter of public interest should be any more protected in the private sphere than it is in the public arena." A judgment against the reporter was upheld.

The Bose Case

In Bose Corp. v. Consumers Union, 466 U.S. ___ (1984), the Supreme Court held in favor of the publisher of Consumer Reports magazine in a product disparagement suit filed by the manufacturer of loudspeakers criticized in the magazine. The magazine said that Bose 901 speakers produced sounds that "tended to wander about the room" and that a violin "appeared to be 10 feet wide and a piano stretched from wall to wall."

The federal judge who presided at the trial in Boston ruled prior to the trial that the Bose Corporation, as a "public figure" plaintiff, would have to prove actual malice to win. Also to be determined at trial was the question of whether the statements in the magazine were opinion (in which case they would be privileged as "fair comment") or fact. The trial court found that the statements were indeed false statements of fact, because the sound of instruments heard through the speakers tended to wander "along the wall" between the speakers, rather than "about the room," as the magazine had stated. Finding also that the false statement was made with actual malice, the court awarded Bose $115,000 damages.

On appeal, the U.S. Court of Appeals did an independent review of the evidence presented at trial and reversed the trial court, saying that actual malice had not been proved after all. In seeking review by the Supreme Court, Bose argued that the appeals court had gone too far in reviewing the evidence—in effect virtually retrying the case. The Supreme Court held that appeals courts, when reviewing findings of actual malice in libel cases and other cases governed by New York Times v. Sullivan, must exercise their own judgment in determining whether actual malice was shown with convincing clarity. Thus, the Court of Appeals decision in favor of Consumers Union was affirmed.

A New Constitutional Privilege?

One federal case suggests the possibility of a First Amendment privilege that differs from the *Times-Gertz* variety. In the case, Edwards v. National Audubon Society, Inc., 556 F.2d 113 (2d Cir.), certiorari denied sub nom. Edwards v. New York Times Co., 434 U.S. 1002 (1977), a *Times* nature reporter was following the continuing dispute between the Audubon Society and the chemical industry over the impact of various pesticides on birds. Based in part on the fact that annual bird counts conducted by the Audubon Society showed increasing numbers, some scientists retained by industry argued that pesticides were not harmful. The Society believed that the higher numbers were due to more watchers with more skill using better observation areas.

An editorial in a Society publication asserted that whenever members heard a scientist use the bird count in an argument "you are in the presence of someone who is being paid to lie, or is parroting something he knows little about." The reporter called the Society and, the jury found, was told the names of five scientists that Society officials had in mind. The reporter then wrote a story accurately reporting the dispute and stating that a Society official had said that the scientists referred to in the editorial included five the reporter then named. In a suit by the scientists, the court held that an accurate report of this nature could not constitutionally lead to a libel judgment against the newspaper:

> At stake in this case is a fundamental principle. Succinctly stated, when a responsible, prominent organization like the National Audubon Society makes serious charges against a public figure, the First Amendment protects the accurate and disinterested reporting of those charges, regardless of the reporter's private views regarding their validity. [ ] What is newsworthy about such accusations is that they were made. We do not believe that the press may be required under the First Amendment to suppress newsworthy statements merely because it has serious doubts regarding their truth. Nor must the press take up cudgels against dubious charges in order to publish them without fear of liability for defamation. [ ] The public interest in being fully informed about controversies that often rage around sensitive issues demands that the press be afforded the freedom to report such charges without assuming responsibility for them.

> The contours of the press's right of neutral reportage are, of course, defined by the principle that gives life to it. Literal accuracy is not a prerequisite: if we are to enjoy the blessings of a robust and unintimidated press, we must provide immunity from defamation suits where the journalist believes, reasonably and in good faith, that his report accurately conveys the charges made. [ ] It is equally clear, however, that a publisher who in fact espouses or concurs in the charges made by others, or who deliberately distorts these statements to launch a personal attack of his own on a public figure, cannot rely on a privilege of neutral reportage. In such instances he assumes responsibility for the underlying accusations. [ ]

> It is clear here, that Devlin reported Audubon's charges fairly and accurately. He did not in any way espouse the Society's accusations: indeed, Devlin published the maligned scientists' outraged reactions in the same article that contained the Society's attack. The *Times* article, in short, was the exemplar of fair and dispassionate reporting of an unfortunate but newsworthy contretemps. Accordingly, we hold that it was privileged under the First Amendment.

What are the limits of the *Edwards* principle? It was distinguished in Dixson v. Newsweek, Inc., 562 F.2d 626 (10th Cir.1977), on the ground that *Edwards* involved public figures whereas Mr. Dixson was a private citizen. Are there times when the public should be informed of charges that are not made by a "responsible, prominent organization"? What is the test for whether a report of a particular charge is "newsworthy"? What level of error in the report, if any, should deprive the reporter of the privilege?

Some courts have rejected the neutral reportage defense as inconsistent with *St. Amant,* since *Edwards* would allow one who reports a story that he knows to be false or has serious doubts about, to be protected from liability.

One can only conjecture about whether the neutral reportage privilege retains much vitality. In the 1970's and 1980's, some courts adopted the standard and some flatly rejected it. An example of the former is Barry v. Time, Inc., 584 F.Supp. 1110 (N.D.Cal.1984). An example of the latter is Postill v. Booth Newspapers, Inc., 118 Mich.App. 608, 325 N.W.2d 511, 518 (1982).

Note that the record libel privilege discussed earlier is a state privilege that can be limited by state statutes and decisions. In New York, for example, the relevant statute requires "official proceedings" before a privilege comes into play—and the New York courts have not expanded that privilege. Thus, in *Edwards*, the state statute did not apply.

C.　REMEDIES FOR DEFAMATION

1.　INJUNCTIONS

Injunctions. Injunctions are generally unavailable for reasons discussed in Chafee's Government and Mass Communication 91–92 (1947): "One man's judgment is not to be trusted to determine what people can read. . . . So our law thinks it better to let the defamed plaintiff take his damages for what they are worth than to intrust a single judge (or even a jury) with the power to put a sharp check on the spread of possible truth." Furthermore, there are gradations of partial truth that are too subtle for a blanket injunction.

2.　REPLY

Reply. If the plaintiff completes the obstacle course we have described, damages are the only available remedy of any importance. The right of reply mentioned by Justice Brennan in *Rosenbloom* and *Gertz* would allow the victim of the defamation to respond in his own words in the offending publication, but states rarely require this, and such a requirement now appears to have serious constitutional problems. See Miami Herald Pub. Co. v. Tornillo, Chapter XIII. As to the role of reply in broadcasting, see Chapters XIII and XV.

3. RETRACTION

Retraction. The common law itself had some rules that tended to reduce the amount of damages recoverable in defamation. They were called "partial" defenses since they did not defeat liability but only reduced the size of the award. At common law if the defendant voluntarily retracted the statement, that fact was admissible to show that the plaintiff had not been damaged as badly as he claimed. It might also show that the defendant had not acted maliciously in the first place. Some states have enacted retraction statutes that grant further protection to mass media defendants. These apply to media only because of the requirement that the retraction be published promptly and with the same prominence as the defamation. It would be meaningless to make the retraction privilege available to media such as books and motion pictures, and the effectiveness of retraction varies even among those media that are covered in most states. It is generally thought, for example, that a retraction in the same space in a newspaper or magazine is more likely to reach the audience that read the original defamation than would most retractions over radio or television of a broadcast defamation.

The statutes vary in covering those who defame innocently, carelessly, or maliciously. What they have in common is a requirement that the prospective plaintiff demand a retraction shortly after the defamation. If the publisher complies within a similar period of time, then the plaintiff may recover only his special damages, and no general damages. If the retraction is not published within the time limit, the plaintiff may recover whatever damages the common law allowed—subject now to the damage limitations of *Gertz*.

Some "retractions," of course, result in something far less than a full withdrawal of an allegation or an apology. In General William Westmoreland's 1984 libel suit against CBS, for example, the joint statement that was part of the litigants' out-of-court settlement was subject to varied interpretations. Westmoreland's supporters tried to claim at least partial victory from CBS's statement that it never intended to suggest that the general was unpatriotic. Media advocates, on the other hand, stressed the fact that CBS stood by its original program.

D. CRIMINAL LIBEL AND GROUP LIBEL

Criminal Libel. Criminal libel is not generally available although it is part of the law in most states. California's version, which was typical, declared a libel to be "a malicious defamation" that tended to blacken the memory of the dead or of one who is alive. Malice was presumed "if no justifiable motive" was shown. Truth could be put in evidence and if the matter was "true, and was published with good motives and for justifiable ends, the party shall be acquitted." Such actions have been defended as deterring breaches of the peace—particularly when the defamed person is dead and no civil action will lie.

Criminal libel had already fallen into disuse before *Garrison*, p. 90, supra. The strictures placed on the action in that case diminished still further its usefulness. The role of the action is even more doubtful when it is used by prosecutors in behalf of famous or powerful persons who do not wish to bring a civil action themselves. This was the situation in 1976 when a state court declared the California criminal libel law unconstitutional because of its limitations on the defense of truth and its presumption of malice. Since other states have taken the same path, criminal libel no longer appears to be a serious risk to publishers.

Group Libel Statutes. The main concern in the debate over group libel has been the hazards of unrestricted hate propaganda. Curbs on group defamation have been advocated to reduce friction among racial, religious, and ethnic groups. As early as 1917 some states enacted criminal group libel laws for that purpose. The Nazi defamation of minority groups, and conspicuous racial tensions in the United States, brought renewed attention to group libel laws in the 1940's and 1950's. David Riesman's Democracy and Defamation: the Control of Group Libel, 42 Columbia L.Rev. 727 (1942), revived the debate as to the efficacy of group libel laws as a means of reducing group hatred and preventing the spread of socially disruptive attitudes.

The most common method of confronting group libel has been the enactment of criminal laws directed specifically at the problem. Such laws typically prohibit communications that are abusive or offensive toward a group or that tend to arouse hatred, contempt, or ridicule of the group. Penalties have ranged from a fine of $50 or 30 days imprisonment, to $10,000 or two years in prison.

Beauharnais v. Illinois, 343 U.S. 250 (1952), is the only Supreme Court decision to review the constitutionality of group libel legislation. The Court, 5–4, affirmed a conviction under Illinois' 1917 group libel statute. The law prohibited publications portraying "depravity, criminality, unchastity, or lack of virtue of a class of citizens, of any race, color, creed, or religion" that subjected those described to "contempt, derision, or obloquy or which is productive of breach of the peace or riots." Beauharnais, the president of an organization called the "White Circle League," had distributed leaflets calling on the Mayor and City Council to halt the "further encroachment, harassment and invasion of white people, their property, neighborhoods and persons, by the Negro." The flyer also included an application for membership in the League and a call for a million white people to unite, adding that: "If persuasion and the need to prevent the white race from becoming mongrelized by the negro will not unite us, then the aggressions . . . rapes, robberies, knives, guns and marijuana of the negro, surely will."

Justice Frankfurter's opinion for the Court treated the statute as "a form of criminal libel law" and accepted the dictum of Chaplinsky v. New Hampshire, 315 U.S. 568 (1942), that libel was one of those "well-defined and narrowly limited classes of speech, the prevention and punishment of which has never been thought to raise any constitutional problem." He traced the history of violent and destructive racial tension in Illinois and concluded that it would "deny experience" to say that the statute was without reason. He disposed of the First Amendment question in a single paragraph near the end of his opinion:

> Libelous utterances not being within the area of constitutionally protected speech, it is unnecessary, either for us or for the State courts, to consider the issue behind the phrase "clear and present danger." Certainly no one would contend that obscene speech, for example, may be punished only upon a showing of such circumstances. Libel, as we have seen, is in the same class.

Of the four dissenters, only Justices Black and Douglas addressed the First Amendment problems that the majority had cast aside by excluding the whole area of libel from First Amendment protection. Justice Black analyzed the decision as extending the scope of the law of criminal libel from "the narrowest of areas" involving "purely private feuds" to "discussions of matters of public concern." This was an invasion of the First Amendment's absolute prohibition of laws infringing the freedom of public discussion. Justice Douglas concurred in Justice Black's opinion and wrote separately to emphasize that he would have required a demonstration that the "peril of speech" was "clear and present." He agreed with Justice Black that allowing a legislature to regulate "within reasonable limits" the right of free speech was "an ominous and alarming trend." Only a half-dozen states retain group defamation statutes.

Group libel statutes also raise practical objections. Group libel prosecutions normally involve issues on which the community is sharply divided. The incidence as well as the outcome of prosecutions may thus depend on which segments of the community are represented in the office of the prosecuting attorney and on the jury. Moreover, a defendant could use the trial to promote his views and might well benefit regardless of the result: an acquittal would validate his viewpoint, while a conviction would make him a martyr whose civil liberties had been violated. These difficulties have led most commentators and many representatives of minority groups to oppose group libel legislation.

E. PRACTICAL CONSIDERATIONS FOR MEDIA DEFENDANTS

1. MEGAVERDICTS

Much has been written in the last few years about the dollar size of libel suits and about jury verdicts for millions of dollars sometimes characterized as "megaverdicts" or "monster verdicts." To some extent the media play into the hands of plaintiffs seeking publicity through multi-million dollar suits, because such amounts are the stuff of which headlines are made. Among the suits receiving extraordinary attention were actress Carol Burnett's suit against the *National Enquirer* and Army General William Westmoreland's suit against CBS. A jury awarded Carol Burnett $1,600,000 in damages. Westmoreland sued CBS for $120 million. These cases are hardly typical, but large damage awards are not imaginary either. The Libel Defense Resource Center showed average damage judgments, in thirty-four libel cases that plaintiffs won between 1982 and 1984, to be more than $2 million. What press headlines usually fail to point out is how many of these large damage awards are reversed or reduced by appellate courts. Apparently, no damage award over $500,000 has yet been paid. Most of those that claimed big headlines have subsequently been reduced. In the Carol Burnett case, for example, the original award was reduced to $200,000. With the possibility of a new trial on the damage amount, Burnett and *National Enquirer* settled out of court for an undisclosed amount rumored to be about $400,000—still only one-fourth the amount of the original award. The Westmoreland case, on the other hand, ended with no money changing hands between the litigants (but with both sides having incurred major legal expenses). Even though we have not yet seen multi-million dollar verdicts sustained by appellate courts, the publicity surrounding them may encourage libel plaintiffs to file more and larger libel suits, and there may be a chilling effect on both large media organizations, who may fear that they will be the targets of such suits because of their "deep pockets," and on smaller organizations which seldom consult their legal counsel and sometimes are afraid to publish because they fear the kinds of immobilizing libel suits they read about.

2. LIBEL INSURANCE

When a court awards damages against a media defendant in a libel suit, it is legally irrelevant whether that defendant carries libel insurance. As a practical matter, of course, it is extremely important. Media employers are often reluctant to be candid about their insurance, even with their own employees. Certainly no employer wants his employees to take unnecessary risks, and media employers typically value their reputations for accuracy so they do not want to lose libel suits even if they do carry insurance. Media libel insurance policies typically provide for a deductible amount which is paid by the insured before the insurance coverage comes into play. The higher the deductible, the lower the premiums that the employer pays for the insurance. Media employers who could afford to sustain losses of $50,000 or $100,000 on each damage award against them or who can afford the legal expenses might elect to be "self-insured" for those amounts and to carry insurance policies with the $50,000 or $100,000 deductible clause to cover them for any awards or expenses greater than those amounts. The increasing size of trial court awards for libel damages has, inevitably, led to an increase in libel insurance premiums; that increase in the premiums in turn has a negative effect on virtually every insured media organization—not just those that are sued.

3. DEFENSE COSTS

Even the media defendants who win their cases in trial or appellate courts may spend large sums of money defending themselves. In major cases some defendants have spent several million dollars defending themselves. While vindication in court may seem ideal, the cost of lawyers and the cost in terms of one's own employees' time may make it tempting to settle out of court with the plaintiff—even where there is substantial likelihood that the defendant would ultimately prevail should the case be decided by an appellate court. A media defendant who developed the reputation of settling out of court too easily could become a target for nuisance suits brought by plaintiffs who did not really expect to win but hoped defendants would buy them off by settling out of court without ever going to trial. Some major media organizations have adopted the position of never settling out of court for just that reason, but such a posture is difficult to maintain in an instance where the media organization really did publish a false statement, particularly where the plaintiff is a private figure who does not need to prove actual malice and who has real damages. Furthermore, the size of the verdicts of recent years makes the risk of going to trial all the greater and increases the temptation to settle out of court.

4. STATUTE OF LIMITATIONS AND JURISDICTION

As indicated earlier, libel statutes give plaintiffs a limited period of time in which to bring suit, often one year. Beyond a year, it might become increasingly difficult for a plaintiff to prove the harm suffered, and it might also become increasingly difficult for the defendant to offer a successful defense. The Supreme Court decision in Keeton v. Hustler Magazine, 465 U.S. ___ (1984), makes the statute of limitations a serious concern for media organizations whose publications or audiences are in more than one state. In *Keeton*, a resident of New York State brought a libel suit in New Hampshire against *Hustler Magazine*, even though the publisher was incorporated in Ohio and its principal place of business was in California. Her case had already been dismissed in Ohio as barred by the statute of limitations. New Hampshire then had a six-year limitation period. Use of New Hampshire's "long-arm statute" was unanimously upheld by the Supreme Court, because of the magazine's circulation of 10,000–15,000 copies in that state. The decision obviously has serious implications for potential media defendants, who now may have to be prepared to defend themselves in libel suits long after the period for a suit has expired under the statute of limitations in the state in which they have their headquarters.

The Court in *Keeton* held that the New Hampshire courts had sufficient basis for jurisdiction even if they applied the so-called "single publication rule"—a principle under which only one legal action can be maintained for damages resulting from any single publication, all damages suffered in all jurisdictions can be recovered in the one action, and a judgment for or against the plaintiff upon the merits of any action for damages bars any other action for damages between the same parties in all jurisdictions.

In another case decided the same day, the Supreme Court faced a different issue involving jurisdiction. In Calder v. Jones, 465 U.S. ___ (1984), the Court upheld the California courts' jurisdiction in a suit brought by actress Shirley Jones (a California resident) against a Florida corporation which publishes *The National Enquirer* and a reporter and editor for the publication. Although the reporter frequently travelled to California on business, the editor did not. The Court noted that California was the focal point of the story and that the defendants' actions were aimed at California, and that they could reasonably expect being "haled into court" in California. Merely being an employee of the magazine, however, would not be a sufficient basis for upholding jurisdiction by the California courts.

5. EVIDENCE AND WITNESSES

Attorneys representing media clients sometimes have a difficult choice to make: if they scare the journalists too much about possible libel suits, they may create their own chilling effect; but if they ignore the subject, the journalists may fall into traps that can make the defense of a libel suit more troubling. Plaintiffs who are public officials or public figures will, of course, be seeking evidence that the defendant published with knowledge of falsity or with a high degree of awareness of probable falsity. Internal memos or margin notes written on copy expressing doubts about the facts in a story can be just the kind of evidence the plaintiff will seek. Newsroom conversations about doubts—even doubts in one's own mind—may be discoverable (see discussion of Herbert v. Lando). In an age in which libel litigation is common, journalists publishing material that may damage a person's reputation would be wise to think of the story subject as a potential plaintiff and to be as sure of their facts as possible. Just as such nationally-known journalists as Dan Rather and Mike Wallace have been called to discuss their stories from the witness stand, younger journalists may have to do the same and should be unafraid to do so if they have followed accepted journalistic practices. (The latter can present interesting questions, because professional standards in journalism vary. Codes of ethics—like the code of The Society of Professional Journalists, Sigma Delta Chi, in Appendix C of this book—may be of some use. Principles such as getting at least two independent sources before publishing or broadcasting damaging information may be widely followed but still are not provably a part of a universally accepted code of conduct for the journalist. The behavior of the "prudent publisher," to use the term used by Justice Harlan in Butts v. Curtis Publishing Co., may vary with the individual journalist's concept of just what constitutes prudence.)

6. EXPERT WITNESSES

Attorneys for both plaintiffs and defendants in libel cases have in recent years sometimes put expert witnesses on the witness stands. Plaintiffs seek witnesses who will testify that the defendant departed from professional standards; defendants counter with witnesses who will testify that mistakes may happen in even the most professional news operation and that the defendant did not depart from the standards of the profession. Some witnesses have been paid quite well for the time they spent preparing to testify and testifying. Because journalists themselves are often quite reluctant to testify against fellow journalists, some plaintiffs and defendants have sought journalism professors as witnesses. The professors are divided on the ethics of testifying in such cases—some believing that it is an appropriate way to share their expertise and others believing that it is an inappropriate role for an academic. It is far from clear that the testimony of expert witnesses on either side of the case is effective. Although trial judges and jurors may think they need the advice of doctors as expert witnesses in medical malpractice suits, judges and jurors seem to feel that they can understand journalism sufficiently well without the testimony of the expert witnesses. And, as a practical matter, some attorneys say, the contradictory testimony of the witnesses on the two sides of the case tends to negate the effectiveness of either.

Chapter IV

PRIVACY

Defamation, which we discussed in the last Chapter, and invasion of privacy, which we discuss in this one, are sometimes treated together in law courses as related rights to protect one's dignity. In defamation, we balance the right of freedom of expression against the right of individuals to protect their reputations. In privacy, we balance the right of freedom of expression against the right of individuals to be let alone. Although people tend to think of privacy as a basic human right and many assume that it is constitutional, the word privacy never appears in the Constitution. Compared to defamation, privacy is a relatively new legal concept with many facets.

Concerns for privacy in the 1980's are diverse—involving such varied issues as the dissemination of personal credit information via computerized systems, electronic eavesdropping, the protection of newsrooms from police searches, release of personal information about individuals by government, and a right to know what is in one's own academic records. Some of these issues we will address elsewhere in this book, because they are related to other topics; the protection of newsrooms from police searches, for example, is dealt with in Chapter X on journalist's privilege because the "privacy" of the newsroom is directly related to the confidentiality of journalists' sources and their notes.

In this Chapter we will be concerned primarily with invasion of privacy as a tort, or civil wrong or injury. Although the recognition of privacy torts varies from state to state, scholars generally have recognized four different torts or branches of invasion of privacy. One of these relates to the newsgathering stage of the communications process; intruding on the plaintiff's physical solitude. It is akin to the tort of trespass. The other three torts or branches of invasion of privacy relate to the publication stage of the communications process. They are publication of embarrassing private (true) facts; putting the plaintiff in a false light in the public eye; and appropriation of another's name or likeness for commercial or trade purposes. One might note that of the four branches, the "false-light" tort comes the closest to the tort of defamation, because it is the only one that involves falsity. Because of the similarities between defamation and false-light invasion of privacy, some of the traditional defenses in defamation are also applicable to this branch of invasion of privacy—including truth. Truth is not, obviously, a defense for publication of embarrassing private facts, because the fact that an embarrassing publication is true may just make it all the more embarrassing. Because defenses that are applicable vary with the branch of invasion of privacy being discussed, we shall touch on defenses at several different points in this Chapter.

A. HISTORICAL DEVELOPMENT

The idea that a right of privacy from the media should be legally protected can be traced to a law review article by Louis D. Brandeis and his law partner, Samuel D. Warren, The Right to Privacy, 4 Harv.L.Rev. 193 (1890), often considered the most influential law review article ever published. The authors, reacting to the editorial practices of Boston newspapers, made clear their concerns:

> The press is overstepping in every direction the obvious bounds of propriety and of decency. Gossip is no longer the resource of the idle and of the vicious, but has become a trade, which is pursued with industry as well as effrontery. To satisfy a prurient taste the details of sexual relations are spread broadcast in the columns of the daily papers. To occupy the indolent, column upon column is filled with idle gossip, which can only be procured by intrusion upon the domestic circle. . . . When personal gossip attains the dignity of print, and crowds the space available for matters of real interest to the community, what wonder that the ignorant and thoughtless mistake its relative importance. Easy of comprehension, appealing to that weak side of human nature which is never wholly cast down by the misfortunes and frailties of our neighbors, no one can be surprised that it usurps the place of interest in brains capable of other things. Triviality destroys at once robustness of thought and delicacy of feelings. No enthusiasm can flourish, no generous impulse can survive under its blighting influence.

Working with a variety of rather remote precedents from other areas of law, the authors developed an argument that courts should recognize an action for invasion of privacy by media publication.

The theory was rejected in the first major case to consider it. In Roberson v. Rochester Folding Box Co., 171 N.Y. 538, 64 N.E. 442 (1902), the defendants, a flour company and a box company, obtained a good likeness of the plaintiff, a very pretty girl, and reproduced it on their advertising posters. Plaintiff said she was humiliated and suffered great distress. The court, 4–3, rejected a common law privacy action on grounds that suggested concern about innovating after so many centuries; an inability to see how the doctrine, once accepted, could be judicially limited to appropriate situations; and skepticism about finding liability for behavior that might actually please some potential "victims." The Warren and Brandeis article was discussed at length but the court concluded that the precedents relied upon were too remote to sustain the proposed rights.

The outcry was immediate. At its next session, the New York legislature created a statutory right of privacy (New York Civil Rights Law, §§ 50 and 51). The basic provision was that "a person, firm or corporation that uses for advertising purposes, or the purposes of trade, the name, portrait or picture of any living person without having first obtained the written consent of such person, or if a minor of his or her parent or guardian, is guilty of a misdemeanor." The other section provided for an injunction and created an action for compensatory and punitive damages. The meaning of "advertising purposes" was clear but the phrase "purposes of trade" was not self-explanatory. Eventually it came to mean that an accurate story carried as editorial (non-advertising) content was not actionable.

Other states, perhaps learning from the New York experience, slowly began to develop a common law right to privacy that was not influenced by statutory language and not limited to advertising invasions. In addition to an action for commercial use of one's name, the courts also developed actions for truthful uses of plaintiff's name that were thought to be outside the areas of legitimate public concern. The action for invasion of privacy by publication of true editorial material began to take hold during the 1920's and early 1930's.

Courts in the late 1930's became more attentive to the Supreme Court's expanding protection of expression. Operating on a common law level, they tended to expand protection for the media by taking a narrow view of what were legitimately private areas.

For the embarrassing private facts tort, the courts allowed a defense of newsworthiness to be expanded, because they were reluctant to impose normative standards of what should be newsworthy. Instead, they leaned toward a descriptive definition of newsworthiness that protected whatever editors had decided would interest their readers. By the 1960's some doubted whether the action for invasion of privacy had any remaining vitality.

It was precisely during the last part of the 1960's and the beginning of the 1970's, however, that privacy as a general social value was perceived to be threatened in different ways by the encroachment of computers, data banks, and electronic devices, as well as the media. The concept of privacy also expanded as the Supreme Court dealt with birth control, abortion, and other problems in the context of a right of privacy. This was bound to have an impact on the media aspects of privacy as well.

One result of the new thinking was to broaden the area of privacy protection.

B. THE BRANCHES OF INVASION OF PRIVACY

Because the Supreme Court has decided many fewer privacy cases than defamation cases, we will look in this section at some state court decisions, for purposes of illustration, in addition to the Supreme Court decisions.

1. PUTTING THE PLAINTIFF IN A FALSE LIGHT

As indicated earlier, the tort of putting the plaintiff in a false light in the public eye is the privacy tort closest to defamation, because both involve publication of falsity. There is a critical difference between the two, however: the publication which results in a successful defamation action is *harmful* as well as false. The publication which results in a successful false light invasion of privacy action may not be harmful in the sense of harming the plaintiff's reputation. It may be just the opposite—a publication that falsely portrays the plaintiff to be better than he is in real life (i.e., a hero) or simply *different* than he is in real life.

In one example, a group used the plaintiff's name without authorization on a petition to the governor to veto a bill. Although falsely stating that plaintiff had signed the petition would not be defamatory, the court found the situation actionable because it cast plaintiff in a false light.

The first two Supreme Court decisions involving alleged invasions of privacy by the mass media both happened to be false light cases. They were Time, Inc. v. Hill, 385 U.S. 374 (1967) and Cantrell v. Forest City Publishing Co., 419 U.S. 245 (1974).

In September, 1952, James Hill and his family were held hostage in their home for 19 hours by three escaped convicts who apparently treated them decently. The incident received extensive nationwide coverage. Thereafter the Hills moved to another state, sought seclusion and refused to make public appearances. A novel modeled in general on the event was published the following year. In 1955, *Life* magazine in a very short article announced that a play and a motion picture were being made from the novel, which they said was "inspired" by the Hill episode. The play, "a heartstopping account of how a family rose to heroism in a crisis," would enable the public to see the Hill story "re-enacted." Photographs in the magazine showed actors performing scenes from the play at the house at which the original events had occurred. The Hills claimed that the story was inaccurate because the novel and the play showed the convicts committing violence on the father and uttering a "verbal sexual insult" at the daughter.

Suit was brought under the New York statute that required plaintiff to show that the article was being used for advertising purposes or for purposes of trade. A truthful article, no matter how unpleasant for the Hills, would not have been actionable. The state courts had previously indicated that falsity would show that the article was really for the purposes of trade and not for public enlightenment. The state courts allowed recovery after lengthy litigation.

The Supreme Court, by a fragile majority, decided that the privilege to comment on matters of public interest had constitutional protection (remember that the Court extended the *Times* rule to matters of public interest in Rosenbloom v. Metromedia in 1971, and then retreated from that position in Gertz v. Robert Welch, Inc., in 1974) and could not be lost by the introduction of falsity unless actual malice could be proved. Thus, the Hill family lost.

The decision should be viewed in the context of what was happening in the court's defamation decisions in the same period. This was only three years after the Court had decided, in New York Times v. Sullivan, that public officials would be required to prove actual malice in defamation cases. By 1967 thinking, the members of the Hill family were public figures—having become so involuntarily as the result of having been part of a newsworthy event. And 1967 was the same year in which the Court extended the actual malice rule of Times v. Sullivan to public figures like Wally Butts and former Army General Edwin Walker.

One should not miss the irony that the attorney who represented the Hill family before the Supreme Court was a man with a strong sense of privacy and considerable distaste for media: then former Vice President, not-yet-President Richard M. Nixon.

It is far from clear that the Supreme Court today would reach the same decision in the Hill case. Under the criteria for determining public figure status in Gertz v. Robert Welch and subsequent cases, the members of the Hill family would surely be private figures. Prior to the single incident which brought them unwanted attention, they certainly were not widely known people likely to be classed as all-purpose public figures. Nor had they entered any public controversy with the intention of trying to influence its outcome, so they would not be classed as "vortex" public figures. Immediately after their release by the convicts they may have had an access to the media more characteristic of that enjoyed by public figures than by private figures (they reportedly turned down an opportunity to appear on the Ed Sullivan network television show), that had undoubtedly faded by the time the article in *Life* appeared. If the Hills were private figures and we were to apply post-Gertz defamation thinking to the privacy area, it would seem reasonable to say that as private figure false-light plaintiffs they should not have to prove actual malice. Depending on the state in which they sued, proof of fault, simple negligence, might suffice. For the Hill family, however, this sort of speculation becomes irrelevant as a practical matter, because their case had already been decided.

The next false-light privacy case decided by the Supreme Court was Cantrell v. Forest City Publishing Co. A reporter for *The Cleveland Plain Dealer* had written a prize-winning story about a bridge collapse that had killed 44 people, including Melvin Cantrell. Some months later the reporter returned to the Cantrell home for a follow-up on how the family coped with the disaster. Although Mrs. Cantrell was not present, her children were. The reporter's story failed to make clear that Mrs. Cantrell had been absent, and a reader presumably would have concluded just the opposite from the story, which said she "will talk neither about what happened nor about how they are doing. She wears the same mask of non-expression she wore at the funeral. She is a proud woman. Her world has changed. She says that after it happened, the people in town offered to help them out with money and they refused to take it." The family sought damages on a false-light privacy theory.

The Court, in an opinion by Justice Stewart, held that the First Amendment did not protect deliberate or reckless falsity (actual malice). He also observed that because the actual malice standard was met in this case, it was not an appropriate case in which to consider the hypothetical question of whether private figure plaintiffs like the Cantrells *had* to prove actual malice or might merely be asked to prove simple negligence. As Justice Stewart put it, it was not an appropriate occasion to "consider whether a State may constitutionally apply a more relaxed standard of liability for a publisher . . . of false statements injurious to a private individual under a false-light theory of privacy, or whether the constitutional standard announced in Time, Inc. v. Hill applies to all false-light cases." The decisions in *Gertz* and subsequent private figure defamation cases would certainly suggest that the Supreme Court might not demand proof of actual malice from private figures.

Justice Douglas was the sole dissenter in *Cantrell:* "Those who write the current news seldom have the objective, dispassionate point of view—or the time—of scientific analysts. They deal in fast-moving events and the need for 'spot reporting'. . . . [I]n such matters of public import such as the present news reporting, there must be freedom from damages lest the press be frightened into playing a more ignoble role than the Framers visualized."

Defenses. Many of the same defenses that can be used by media defendants in defamation cases might also be argued to have application in a false-light privacy case. *Truth* would be a strong defense unless the words in question were literally true but were used in such a *context* as to put the plaintiff in a false light. Qualified privilege might be offered as a defense if one had quoted accurately from a record of an official proceeding. Privileged criticism or fair comment might work as defenses if the publication alleged to put the plaintiff in a false light was actually a statement of opinion rather than a statement of fact. If the plaintiff is a public official or a public figure, absence of malice would be a strong defense. The procedural statute-of-limitations defense could be relevant to a false-light case or cases brought under any of the other privacy torts, but we will mention it only here. To a large extent, the applicability of the libel defenses in privacy cases is yet to be determined in the courts.

It might be noted here that the two most commonly mentioned defenses for invasion of privacy—newsworthiness and consent—have little or no application in false-light cases. Newsworthiness is *not* a false-light defense, because erroneous information is not newsworthy—there is no public good to be served in its dissemination. A plaintiff would be unlikely to have *formally* consented to being portrayed in a false light, as by a signed model release, but an argument might be made that a plaintiff tacitly consented to being portrayed in a false light by behaving in a way which would create an erroneous impression or by failing to protest when previously portrayed in a false light.

2. INTRUSION ON THE PLAINTIFF'S PHYSICAL SOLITUDE

As suggested earlier, intrusion on the plaintiff's physical solitude is the only one of the four branches of privacy that comes up in the context of *newsgathering* rather than in the context of publication. In the absence of any Supreme Court decision involving such an invasion of privacy by the mass media, we will look here at some cases decided in the lower courts as examples.

The major divisions of this branch of invasion of privacy reflect the type of consent problem involved. Within each subsection we consider the types of invasions that plaintiff may complain about. The most traditional are trespass (unpermitted entry) on land and theft of personal property. The claim is that the physical zone of privacy that surrounds each of us has been intruded upon—usually in an effort to obtain information that would otherwise not be available.

a. *Invasions Without Express Consent*

Trespass. For centuries, the act of intentionally entering the land of another without consent made the entrant liable for trespass. The civil damages included any actual harm done to the property and some damages for the symbolic invasion of the owner's or occupier's legal interest. If accompanied by ill will or spite or a desire to harm the owner, perhaps punitive damages as well were awarded. Comparable rules apply to a person who legally enters land but then remains on it against the wishes of the owner or occupier of the land.

In one clear case, the plaintiff alleged that his wife had committed suicide during the day; that when he returned to the house that evening he discovered that the screen over the kitchen window had been cut and that a photograph of his wife that had been on a table in the living room that morning had been taken. Although the plaintiff failed to prove that the defendant's reporters had committed the trespass, the court indicated that the only problem in the case was one of identification. The trespass and theft could not be defended even if there had been great public interest in the photograph. Metter v. Los Angeles Examiner, 35 Cal.App.2d 304, 95 P.2d 491 (1939).

In a more recent case, plaintiff land owner sued to prevent the defendant from entering plaintiff's land in search of a fragment of a pre-Revolutionary War statue of King George III. The court observed that even if the defendant's goal were solely to engage in historical and archeological research, "that fact will not justify his entering upon the property of another without permission. It is unquestioned that in today's world even archeologists must obtain permission from owners of property . . . before they can conduct their explorations." Favorite v. Miller, 176 Conn. 310, 407 A.2d 974 (1978).

Sometimes the reporter may claim that he has authority to enter the property even though the owner has not expressly consented. Two Florida cases present examples.

In Florida Publishing Co. v. Fletcher, 340 So.2d 914 (Fla.1976), the plaintiff alleged that after she had left town on a trip, a fire broke out in her house that killed her 17-year-old daughter; that after the daughter's body was removed from the floor a silhouette was revealed; that defendant newspaper's photographer took a photograph of the silhouette; and that plaintiff first learned of the tragedy by reading the story in a newspaper and seeing the accompanying photographs. In her claim for trespass, the depositions revealed that police and fire officials, as was their standard practice, invited press photographers and reporters to enter the house; that the media representatives entered through an open door without objection; and that they entered quietly and did no damage to the property. The fire marshal wanted a clear picture of the silhouette to show that the body had been on the floor before the heat of the fire damaged the room. After the official took one picture, he ran out of film and asked the newspaper photographer to take pictures for the official investigation. He did so and also made copies for his own paper, which published them.

The defendant moved for summary judgment on the trespass claim. Affidavits from various government and media sources stated that entering private property and inviting the press in this type of situation was common practice. Plaintiff filed only her own affidavit and none from media or other experts. She conceded that it was proper for the police and fire officials to enter and also admitted that no one had objected to the entry of the press. The trial judge granted summary judgment because the affidavits "attest to the fact that it is common usage, custom and practice for news media to enter private premises and homes to report on matters of public interest or a public event."

The Florida Supreme Court agreed that implied consent covered the case. Research showed that implied consent by custom and usage "do not rest upon the previous nonobjection to entry by the particular owner of the property in question but rest upon custom and practice generally." In addition to the fact that here the press entered in response to an express invitation from public officials, the court stressed that this was the first case presenting the question. "This, in itself, tends to indicate that the practice has been accepted by the general public since it is a widespread practice of longstanding." One judge dissented on jurisdictional grounds. The Supreme Court denied certiorari, 431 U.S. 930 (1977).

Compare Green Valley School Inc. v. Cowles Florida Broadcasting, Inc., 327 So.2d 810 (Fla.App.1976). State officials planned a midnight raid, under a properly issued warrant, to search the premises of a controversial local private school. The head of the party of 50 raiders invited reporters and photographers from several local media organizations to accompany the party. The defendant television station presented an extensive report of the raid on the evening news the following night, suggesting that the raid had turned up evidence of mistreatment of the students and rampant sexual misbehavior and use of drugs. The school sued the station for defamation and for trespass.

The trial judge granted summary judgment to the station on the trespass claim. The court of appeal reversed, addressing the question entirely in the following passage:

> To uphold appellees' assertion that their entry upon appellant's property at the time, manner, and circumstances as reflected by this record was as a *matter of law* sanctioned by "the request of and with the consent of the State Attorney" and with the "common usage and custom in Florida" could well bring to the citizenry of this state the hobnail boots of a Nazi stormtrooper equipped with glaring lights invading a couple's bedroom at midnight with the wife hovering in her nightgown in an attempt to shield herself from the scanning TV camera. In this jurisdiction, a law enforcement officer is not as a *matter of law* endowed with the right or authority to invite people of his choosing to invade private property and participate in a midnight raid of the premises.

On the same day that it decided *Fletcher,* the Florida Supreme Court dismissed an appeal in the Green Valley case, indicating that it found no conflict between the results in the two cases. Can they be reconciled?

As soon as we move from private residential property to premises that are usually open to the public for some purpose the questions get more difficult.

In Le Mistral v. Columbia Broadcasting System, 61 App.Div.2d 491, 402 N.Y.S.2d 815 (1978), CBS, as owner and operator of WCBS–TV in New York City, directed reporter Rich and a camera crew to visit restaurants that had been cited for health code violations. Plaintiff was on the list. The crew entered plaintiff's restaurant with cameras "rolling" and using bright lights that were necessary to get the pictures. The jury found CBS liable for trespass and awarded plaintiff $1,200 in compensatory damages and $250,000 in punitive damages. After verdict (in a passage approved on appeal), the trial judge stated:

> The instructions given to the crew, whether specific to this event or as standing operating procedure, were to avoid seeking an appointment or permission to enter any of the premises where a story was sought, but to enter unannounced catching the occupants by surprise; "with cameras rolling" in the words of CBS' principal witness, Rich. From the evidence the jury was entitled to conclude that following this procedure the defendant's employees burst into plaintiff's restaurant in noisy and obtrusive fashion and following the loud commands of the reporter, Rich, to photograph the patrons dining, turned their lights and camera upon the dining room. Consternation, the jury was informed, followed. Patrons waiting to be seated left the restaurant. Others who had finished eating, left without waiting for their checks. Still others hid their faces behind napkins or table cloths or hid themselves beneath tables. (The reluctance of the plaintiff's clientele to be video taped was never explained, and need not be. Patronizing a restaurant does not carry with it an obligation to appear on television). [The] president of the plaintiff and manager of its operations, refused to be interviewed, and as the camera continued to "roll" he pushed the protesting Miss Rich and her crew from the premises. All told, the CBS personnel were in the restaurant not more than ten minutes, perhaps as little as one minute, depending on the testimony the jury chose to credit. The jury by its verdict clearly found the defendant guilty of trespass and from the admissions of CBS' own employees they were guilty of trespass. The witness Rich sought to justify her crew's entry into the restaurant by calling it, on a number of occasions, a "place of public accommodation", but, as she acknowledges, they did not seek to avail themselves of the plaintiff's "accommodation"; they had no intention of purchasing food or drink.

The trial judge upheld the determination of liability but set aside both damage awards because he had erroneously barred a defense witness from testifying as to CBS's motive and purpose in entering the premises. On appeal, the court held that its review of the record "demonstrates an adequate basis to justify the compensatory damage award rendered by the jury and, accordingly, such award must stand." As to punitive damages, the court agreed that the judge had erred in excluding the testimony because all "circumstances immediately connected with the transaction tending to exhibit or explain the motive of the defendant are admissible." One judge thought it clear that the defendants were "not motivated by actual malice or such an intentional disregard of plaintiff's rights as would justify the imposition of punitive damages. [ ] The defendant was merely pursuing a newsworthy item in the overly aggressive but good faith manner that characterizes the operation of the news media today. . . . In this sensitive and evolving First Amendment area, I would permit this precedent-setting opinion to stand as a warning to all news gatherers that future trespasses may well be met with an award of punitive damages."

CBS, dissatisfied with the decision, sought to appeal to New York's highest court to argue that no trespass had been committed and also that, in any event, punitive damages were improper. That court refused to hear the appeal until after another trial had been held.

The case is complicated by the disruptive presence of the television cameras. If a newspaper reporter had entered the restaurant would he have been a trespasser from the moment he entered—or only from the moment he refused to leave? If, while the newspaper reporter was leaving, he continued watching the scene and making mental notes of what he saw, would that be improper? If the court is suggesting that the premises were open only to those seriously considering purchasing food or drink, why should it matter whether the entry was disruptive?

Under traditional law, the owner could prevent entry by posting a notice on the front door stating that no reporters are permitted on the premises. But today it is possible that the courts of New York would develop a special rule allowing reporters to enter "newsworthy" premises—at least so long as they are not disruptive. Further, the courts might develop some First Amendment privilege to allow reporters to enter certain types of "private" premises—at least until they are explicitly asked to leave. All of this is most unclear but does serve to advise reporters of some of the lurking perils in this area. See Watkins, Private Property vs. Reporter Rights—A Problem in Newsgathering, 54 Journ.Q. 690 (1977).

In order for the plaintiff to claim damages for trespass or theft of property, he must own or occupy the property. If the property has been abandoned—the former owner has indicated a desire to relinquish his control over it—then no civil damage action can be brought. An example of this situation may have occurred in 1975 when it was revealed that a reporter had been sifting through the garbage cans outside the house of Secretary of State Kissinger. A reporter who went on the land to reach the garbage cans, would have been a trespasser. If the cans were on the public sidewalk, the only claim would be interference with personal property—the garbage. But if, as seems likely, the property has been abandoned, no civil liability would be possible. Commenting on the episode in an editorial, Editor & Publisher (July 19, 1975 at 6) attacked the practice: "Pawing through someone else's garbage is a revolting exercise and doing it in the name of journalism makes it none the less so." Do you agree?

Invasions of Privacy. We turn now to alleged invasions of privacy that do not fit into the trespass mold. These involve issues of how far persons may use cameras or high-technology equipment to obtain information about a subject; wiretapping; and secretly recording conversations to which the person is a party.

Galella v. Onassis, 487 F.2d 986 (2d Cir.1973), involved aggressive efforts by a "paparazzo" photographer to obtain photographs of the widow and children of President Kennedy. "Paparazzi make themselves as visible to the public and obnoxious to their photographic subjects as possible to aid in the advertisement and wide sale of their works." Among his actions, Galella brought his power boat close to Mrs. Onassis as she was swimming; jumped out of bushes as she was walking past; jumped into her son's path to take a photograph of him riding his bicycle; and invaded the children's private schools. Those acts that reasonably put the subject in fear of personal safety would create tort liability under longstanding rules. But those that involved annoyance presented harder questions.

Mrs. Onassis claimed that when she went through the streets to go shopping or to visit a friend, or walked alone in Central Park she was engaged in private activities that should not be the subject of any unwanted photography. The court disagreed. Mrs. Onassis was "a public figure and thus subject to news coverage" although the First Amendment provided no "wall of immunity protecting newsmen" from liability for torts committed while gathering news. The court balanced Mrs. Onassis' concern about intrusion with the legitimate interests of photography by ordering Galella to stay 25 feet from Mrs. Onassis at all times; not to block her movement in public places; and not to do "any act foreseeably or reasonably calculated" to place Mrs. Onassis in jeopardy or frighten her. Any further restriction on his taking and selling photographs of her would be improper.

Galella was subsequently charged with criminal contempt for violating the order, but he avoided paying a $120,000 fine for contempt by agreeing not to take any more pictures of Mrs. Onassis.

In 1979, a TV camera crew trailed a man as he was trying to pay a ransom to persons who had kidnapped his wife. Despite his pleas, the crew followed the man, apparently along public ways. The episode attracted much press discussion after the FBI said the action had "put that woman's life in danger." An editorial in Editor & Publisher, July 28, 1979 at 6, asserted that although the TV crew might have considered its actions "enterprising reporting . . . it was more like sheer stupidity. . . . It is this sort of arrogance and brashness that gets media in trouble with the public."

After the woman was released, the couple sued the station for endangering the woman's life. Since no harm actually occurred in the case the suit might be difficult. Should the husband be able to sue for mental anguish he suffered as a result of the crew's actions?

Criminal liability might be possible if it is shown that the crew learned of the man's movements by making unauthorized interceptions of messages on a nonbroadcast frequency in violation of § 605 of the Communications Act. Should the law impose a sanction against reporters whose gathering efforts in fact lead to harm because kidnappers panic or get angry that their instructions apparently are not being followed?

———

Where solitude is invaded, the courts speak of the subject's reasonable expectations of privacy as the guide to available protection. Thus, one who leaves his curtains open, knowing that persons in the building across the street can look inside his apartment, can claim no reasonable expectation of privacy. But if the only vantage point from which the inside of the apartment can be seen is a hilltop two miles away, a court might well find that a reporter who set up a very powerful telescope on that hill and looked through the open window has invaded privacy.

Similarly, a person inside a dwelling can make no reasonable claim of invasion of privacy if he shouts at his spouse and is overheard by others outside. But if he speaks in a normal or hushed voice—and is overheard because a highly sensitive microphone in the next apartment or across the street has picked up the communication, a court would probably find an invasion of privacy.

Wiretapping and other forms of intercepting messages frequently have been involved in litigation. For a thorough discussion of the issue, see Middleton, "Journalists and Tape Recorders: Does Participant Monitoring Invade Privacy?" 2 Comm/Ent L.J. 287 (Winter 1979–80). Although some early cases did impose tort liability in these cases, the major development occurred when Congress passed The Omnibus Crime Control and Safe Streets Act of 1968, 18 U.S.C. §§ 2510–2520. The basic provision subjects to criminal liability "any person" who without a warrant "willfully intercepts" any "wire or oral communication." Section 2520 provides that violators are liable for compensatory and punitive damages. Some exclusions apply, but none that apply to reporters.

In one case the court awarded damages under the statute against a law enforcement officer who used an extension phone to intercept a conversation involving a prison inmate. Neither participant had consented to the monitoring. No consent was to be implied from the fact that the call was being made in a prison because no regulations informed prisoners that their calls might be monitored. (The law enforcement exceptions in the act were held inapplicable.) The court also found liability under the parallel Massachusetts statute that protected privacy of communications. Campiti v. Walonis, 611 F.2d 387 (1st Cir.1979).

Some states have statutes that are more restrictive than the federal statute. In Warden v. Kahn, 99 Cal.App.3d 805, 160 Cal.Rptr. 471 (1979), defendant made a tape recording of a telephone conversation he had with plaintiff. The court found this to violate the California statute that applied to any person who "intentionally and without the consent of all parties to a confidential communication, by means of any electronic amplifying or recording device, eavesdrops upon or records such confidential communication."

The defendant argued that interpreting the statute to bar participant recording did not protect privacy because the speaker had already shown a willingness to allow others to hear his words. The court disagreed and quoted a law review comment:

> There is a qualitative as well as a quantitative difference between secondhand repetition by the listener and simultaneous dissemination to a second auditor, whether that auditor be a tape recorder or a third party. In the former situation the speaker retains control over the extent of his immediate audience. Even though that audience may republish his words, it will be done secondhand, after the fact, probably not in entirety, and the impact will depend upon the credibility of the teller. Where electronic monitoring is involved, however, the speaker is deprived of the right to control the extent of his own firsthand dissemination. . . . In this regard participant monitoring closely resembles third-party surveillance; both practices deny the speaker a most important aspect of privacy of communication—the right to control the extent of first instance dissemination of his statements.

The court added its own sense that "we are all likely to react differently to a telephone conversation we know is being recorded, and to feel our privacy in a confidential communication to be invaded far more deeply by the potential for unauthorized dissemination of an actual transcription of our voice."

Florida has a statute that reaches participant monitoring by barring persons "not acting under color of law" from intercepting a wire or oral communication unless all parties to the communication had given their prior consent. An important lawsuit arose from a general attack on the statute by reporters who claimed that the use of concealed recording equipment was essential to investigative reporting for three reasons: it aided accuracy of reporting; persons being interviewed would not be candid if they knew they were being recorded; and the recording provided corroboration in case of suit for defamation.

The Florida Supreme Court upheld the statute's constitutionality. The statute allows "each party to a conversation to have an expectation of privacy from interception by another party to the conversation. It does not exclude any source from the press, intrude upon the activities of the news media in contacting sources, prevent the parties to the communication from consenting to the recording, or restrict the publication of any information gained from the communication. First Amendment rights do not include a constitutional right to corroborate news gathering activities when the legislature has statutorily recognized the private rights of individuals."

In response to the argument that secret recording may be the only way to get credible information about crime, the court stated that protection against intrusion might protect even a person "reasonably suspected of committing a crime." Shevin v. Sunbeam Television Corp., 351 So.2d 723 (Fla.1977).

Based on the briefs and without argument, the Supreme Court dismissed the appeal by the press for want of a substantial federal question, 435 U.S. 920 (1978). Justices Brennan, White and Blackmun thought the case should be given full consideration and voted to set the case for oral argument.

The Florida court had relied to some extent on the case of Dietemann v. Time, Inc., 449 F.2d 245 (9th Cir.1971). In that case, two reporters obtained access to plaintiff's home to find out whether he was a medical quack. While plaintiff was diagnosing the alleged ailment of one reporter, the other secretly took photographs with a hidden camera. The entire conversation was transmitted to confederates outside by means of a transmitter hidden in one reporter's purse. In this part of the case, the court concluded that California would impose liability for invasion of privacy:

> [One who invites others to his home] does not and should not be required to take the risk that what is heard and seen will be transmitted by photograph or recording, or in our modern world, in full living color and hi-fi to the public at large or to any segment of it that the visitor may select. A different rule could have a most pernicious effect upon the dignity of man and it would surely lead to guarded conversations and conduct where candor is most valued, e.g., in the case of doctors and lawyers.

The defendant claims that the First Amendment immunizes it from liability for invading plaintiff's den with a hidden camera and its concealed electronic instruments because its employees were gathering news and its instrumentalities "are indispensable tools of investigative reporting." We agree that newsgathering is an integral part of news dissemination. We strongly disagree, however, that the hidden mechanical contrivances are "indispensable tools" of newsgathering. Investigative reporting is an ancient art; its successful practice long antecedes the invention of miniature cameras and electronic devices. The First Amendment has never been construed to accord newsmen immunity from torts or crimes committed during the course of newsgathering. The First Amendment is not a license to trespass, to steal, or to intrude by electronic means into the precincts of another's home or office. It does not become such a license simply because the person subjected to the intrusion is reasonably suspected of committing a crime.

Defendant relies upon the line of cases commencing with New York Times Co. v. Sullivan, 376 U.S. 254 (1964) . . . to sustain its contentions that (1) publication of news, however tortiously gathered, insulates defendant from liability for the antecedent tort . . . .

As we previously observed, publication is not an essential element of plaintiff's cause of action. Moreover, it is not the foundation for the invocation of a privilege. Privilege concepts developed in defamation cases and to some extent in privacy actions in which publication is an essential component are not relevant in determining liability for intrusion conduct antedating publication. [ ] Nothing in *New York Times* or its progeny suggests anything to the contrary. Indeed, the Court strongly indicates that there is no First Amendment interest in protecting news media from calculated misdeeds. [ ]

b. Consent Has Been Obtained

We turn now to cases in which the reporter contends that what might otherwise be a tort is not because the plaintiff consented to the conduct in question. The basic legal principle is not in doubt. Occasionally, the cases involve such neat situations as a plaintiff who signs a written consent. Usually, the cases are more complex.

In Cassidy v. American Broadcasting Companies, 60 Ill.App.3d 831, 17 Ill.Dec. 936, 377 N.E.2d 126 (1978), an undercover policeman was sent to a massage parlor. After paying $30 he was escorted to a room to watch "de-luxe lingerie modeling." On entering the very warm room he observed camera lights. He asked, "What are we on, TV?" The model replied, "Yes, we're making a movie." As plaintiff reclined on the bed watching the model change her lingerie several times, he made suggestive remarks and advances. He then arrested the model for solicitation. The entire scene was in fact being photographed from an adjacent room by a local television station through a two-way mirror. The manager of the parlor had asked the defendant to film the episode to show that police were harassing him.

Plaintiff's suit failed because, among other reasons, the plaintiff apparently did not intend his conduct to be private because he knew that someone might be making a movie of his conduct. He testified his actions were in the line of duty as an officer and that if the model wished to sell him a completed film he would use it as evidence in his investigation. Plaintiff had no expectation of privacy.

Although plaintiff had not explicitly consented to being filmed, his conduct after being informed that a film was being made amounted to consent. But should the same rule apply if a jury could reasonably find that the model made her statement jokingly or sardonically so that a reasonable person in plaintiff's position would not have believed what she said?

The most common problems reporters face in consent cases appear to involve consents that are obtained by some type of misrepresentation. Since reporters often investigate alleged misdeeds they are unlikely to get consent to do interviews, go to certain places or record interviews if they identify themselves as reporters. In such cases, what is the role of consent?

In *Dietemann*, the reporters posed as a couple seeking medical advice from the plaintiff, who lived a quiet life and did not advertise or even have a telephone. They went to his gate and rang the bell. When plaintiff appeared, the reporters falsely said that they had been sent by a certain person and wanted to see plaintiff because the female visitor had a lump in her breast that she wanted diagnosed. Plaintiff admitted the pair to his den and made his diagnosis. On this part of the case the court observed:

> Plaintiff's den was a sphere from which he could reasonably expect to exclude eavesdropping newsmen. He invited two of defendant's employees to the den. One who invites another to his home or office takes a risk that the visitor may not be what he seems, and that the visitor may repeat all he hears and observes when he leaves.

Why does plaintiff take the risk that a visitor may not be who he claims to be, or that a visitor may repeat what he hears inside, but not take the risk that secret recordings and photographs are being made? Is it that the plaintiff does in fact intend to deal with the persons who are standing before him—whatever names they give or whatever reasons they give for coming?

Courts generally rule that consent to enter one section of land does not authorize entering any other part; and that consent to do one thing, such as reading the gas meter, does not authorize removal of the gas meter. In these cases, it is apparent that the actor has exceeded the consent. In *Dietemann*, however, the plaintiff gave consent to enter the land and come to the den—and that is precisely what the reporters did. His misunderstanding about identity did not lead him to consent to one thing but to be hit with another. (A person who wants legal protection against someone who is told a secret and then reveals it may obtain it by entering into a contract in which the recipient makes legally enforceable promises about his future behavior.)

If misrepresenting identity doesn't raise major legal problems, it does raise ethical questions that are much discussed among journalists. The matter is reviewed at length in Zimmerman, By Any Other Name . . ., Washington Journalism Review (Nov./Dec.1979) at 32.

The matter received much attention in 1979 when the Pulitzer Prize for local investigative reporting was denied to a newspaper that uncovered massive official corruption after it bought and ran a bar in Chicago under a false name. At about the same time, a reporter posed as a Congressman to obtain a seat at the signing of the Egyptian-Israeli peace treaty. The reporter said that the episode involved telling "only one lie." Editor & Publisher, June 9, 1979 at 6, responded, "But *how many lies* are too many? Are we getting back to the no-holds-barred philosophy that the story should be gotten at any cost?" Noting that the press complains loudly when someone impersonates a newsman, the editorial continued, "We believe that newsmen's impersonations of others in order to get a story [are] equally damaging to their believability and should be scrupulously avoided." Some have suggested that if reporters will lie to get a story readers may believe that they would also lie in writing the story if they thought the matter important enough.

The argument the other way, of course, stresses that uncovering crime or other misbehavior is very hard—that it would have been virtually impossible to have demonstrated the corruption in Chicago without setting up the fake business. A recent example involved a reporter who got a job as a guard at the Three Mile Island nuclear plant after the malfunctioning and then took photographs while on the job. His goal was to show how easy it was to get a job—his asserted background and references were never checked—and to show how lax security was inside the plant. Are there other ways to obtain this information? How important is it to obtain the information? Does such behavior damage the credibility of the press?

It should be noted here that although civil actions by persons deceived in these cases may not be likely, some of the cases may well involve potential criminal liability—particularly cases involving impersonation of government officials or lying to government officials.

Should different principles apply if reporters knowingly accept material improperly obtained by others? In one case, aides to a United States Senator removed numerous documents from his files, copied them, and passed the copies to columnists who knew how they had been obtained. The court held that the columnists had committed no tort:

> If we were to hold appellants liable for invasion of privacy on these facts, we would establish the proposition that one who receives information from an intruder, knowing it has been obtained by improper intrusion, is guilty of a tort. In an untried and developing area of tort law, we are not prepared to go so far. A person approached by an eavesdropper with an offer to share in the information gathered through the eavesdropping would perhaps play the nobler part should he spurn the offer and shut his ears. However, it seems to us that at this point it would place too great a strain on human weakness to hold one liable in damages who merely succumbs to temptation and listens.

Pearson v. Dodd, 410 F.2d 701 (D.C.Cir.) certiorari denied 395 U.S. 947 (1969). Should the result change if a reporter had said to the aide "I'd sure love to see your file on" a particular matter—and three days later the aide presented the file?

Defenses. As discussed above, consent (if not exceeded) can be a defense for an intrusion on physical solitude suit. Such defamation defenses as truth and absence of malice have no relevance because neither falsity nor its cause are part of an intrusion suit. It should be noted specifically that newsworthiness is *not* a defense for intrusion: the fact that a journalist wants news is no justification for violating another's rights in order to obtain it.

c. *Criminal Liability*

At several points during the foregoing discussion of civil liability, we have had occasion to touch on related criminal sanctions. In this section we draw together the likely sources of criminal liability that may confront newsgatherers.

At the outset, federal and state governments have statutes punishing such acts as the theft of government property, and the concealment or removal of official records and documents. See, e.g., 18 U.S.C. §§ 641, 2071. In addition, conspiracy to commit criminal acts is also a crime. Other statutes directly relate to property or information in specific areas, such as national security or nuclear energy. Knowingly receiving stolen property may also be criminal even though the recipient had nothing to do with the original theft.

In one prosecution, an editor was charged with receiving stolen property—a list of the names, home addresses, and telephone numbers of 80 undercover state narcotics agents. The facts surrounding the transaction were not entirely clear and the court ruled that the state had presented insufficient proof that the defendant knew that the document had been stolen (rather than temporarily removed from the office with the intention of returning it). People v. Kunkin, 9 Cal. 3d 245, 107 Cal.Rptr. 184, 507 P.2d 1392 (1973).

Other crimes involving direct harms to government may include impersonating an officer, not obeying a lawful order of a police officer, or bribing a government employee. The latter was involved when a news photographer paid a prison guard to take secret photographs of the accused killer known as "Son of Sam."

The government also uses criminal legislation to support the civil law in protecting individual property and privacy. We have seen some in operation already, such as the criminal punishment for intercepting communications whether by wiretapping or otherwise. Breaking into a home and stealing a photograph from the table would involve several criminal offenses as well as tort liability. Other protections are available. In one recent episode a publisher has been charged with extortion by allegedly threatening to write untrue stories about people in the community unless they supplied information for forthcoming stories or agreed to advertise in the paper. Editor & Publisher, June 30, 1979 at 19.

Reporters covering a demonstration at a construction site for a nuclear plant in Oklahoma were convicted of trespassing on private property. The utility, PSO, did not want extensive coverage of the marchers—as had occurred at an early demonstration. This time, PSO warned all reporters that they would be arrested if they entered the fenced property at any point not permitted by PSO. PSO then set up a viewing area that reporters might use on its otherwise closed property. It was not clear in advance whether the demonstration or any confrontation would be visible from that point.

Several reporters used the viewing area. Others followed the demonstrators and entered the land when the demonstrators went through the fence. These reporters were the ones convicted of trespass. The judge found that they knew or should have known of PSO's intent to prosecute this conduct. He ruled that newsmen had no constitutional right of access to scenes when the general public was excluded, but he also found a First Amendment right to reasonable access to the news such as is available to the public generally. (Since the property was closed, the origin of this right is not clear.) He then decided that some balancing was required. Against the interest in gathering the news, he arrayed PSO's right to be secure in its property and the police power of the state to maintain public order and enforce criminal statutes. In making his balance the judge also threw in the fact that PSO's purpose in hampering news coverage was "an ignoble one hardly compatible with the rights of a free people." He also gave some weight to the fact that when the marchers entered the land at a point not readily visible from the "viewing area," reporters in that area demanded, and were taken to, a better spot. (How could this have been known in time to the reporters who were with the marchers?)

The judge thought the balance favored the government because the restrictions did not deny access to "particularly significant news" since those in the viewing area could see almost everything. When several defendants claimed that they had to enter the land to meet "their professional obligation to report the news," the judge responded that although this might have been a matter of conscience, it was also "a deliberate violation of law." If a person commits an act of civil disobedience, he "may claim an exemption from an obligation to obey a particular law on moral or professional grounds, but that person may not claim immunity from application of sanction for committing that offense." Each was fined $25. Stahl v. State, 665 P.2d 839 (Okl.Crim.App.1983), cert. denied 464 U.S. ___ (1984).

3. PUBLICATION OF EMBARRASSING PRIVATE FACTS

Publication of embarrassing private facts (which we address in this section) and appropriation of another's name or likeness for commercial or trade purposes (which we address in the next section) are the two branches of invasion of privacy that have to do with truthful publication that interferes with someone's right to be let alone. The former is of greater importance to journalism students; the latter is of greater importance to advertising and public relations students. Redundant though it may seem, it may be helpful to think of the former as publication of embarrassing private *true* facts.

a. Categories

The cases of publication of embarrassing private facts fall into a small number of categories—those dealing with sexual matters, commission of crime, poverty, idiosyncratic qualities, and other embarrassing stories.

The important point is not whether these state cases are decided "correctly." The area is so new and unformed that the cases do not fit into a neat pattern—except that plaintiffs rarely win. The results are given in capsule form at the end of each case, without reasons, simply to satisfy curiosity—not to suggest the proper resolution. Remember that after reviewing this catalogue of litigation, we will explore approaches to this very troublesome area. The law aside, prospective reporters and editors should consider how the facts of each story should be handled.

Sexual Matters. 1. In a study of official misconduct at a county home, a newspaper reported that among the misconduct was the involuntary sterilization of a named 18-year-old young woman seven years earlier. Howard v. Des Moines Register and Tribune Co., 283 N.W.2d 289 (Iowa 1979), certiorari denied 445 U.S. 904 (1980) (case dismissed).

2. A newspaper columnist included the following item: "More education stuff: The students at the College of Alameda will be surprised to learn that their student body president, Toni Diaz, is no lady, but is in fact a man whose real name is Antonio.

"Now I realize, that in these times, such a matter is no big deal, but I suspect his female classmates in P.E. 97 may wish to make other showering arrangements." The plaintiff won a $775,000 judgment at the trial court, but it was reversed on appeal, and the parties settled the case shortly thereafter. Diaz v. Oakland Tribune, Inc., 139 Cal.App.3d 118, 188 Cal.Rptr. 762 (1983).

3. During an assassination attempt on President Ford in San Francisco, Oliver Sipple knocked the arm of the assailant as she sought to aim a second shot at the President. Sipple was the object of extensive media attention, including stories that identified him as a homosexual. Sipple, asserting that relatives who lived in the Midwest did not know of his orientation, sued the San Francisco Chronicle. The newspaper defended in part on the argument that privacy was not involved because Sipple had marched in gay parades and had

acknowledged that at least 100 to 500 people in San Francisco knew he was a homosexual. The newspaper argued that his sexual orientation was relevant to the story because, although some stereotyped gays as sissies, Sipple was an ex-marine who acted heroically. Sipple v. Chronicle Publishing, 154 Cal.App.3d 1040, 201 Cal.Rptr. 665 (1984).

4. Television cameras went to the scene of a report that a man was threatening harm to his housekeeper's sister. The crew arrived and began filming as police led the stark-naked man from the house. In a news report the following evening, plaintiff's "buttocks and genitals were visible to television viewers for a time period of approximately eight-to-nine-tenths of one second." Taylor v. KTVB Inc., 96 Idaho 202, 525 P.2d 984 (1974) (case remanded to determine defendant's reasons for using the film; settled out of court).

5. Plaintiff was kidnapped by her estranged husband and taken to an apartment. He forced her to disrobe and then beat her. Police came. Following the suicide of the husband, police hurried plaintiff from the apartment nude "save for a mere towel." Photographers on the scene took photographs and turned them over to defendant newspaper, which ran several of them. Cape Publications, Inc. v. Bridges, 423 So.2d 426 (Fla.App.1982), cert. denied 464 U.S. __ (1983) (judgment for $10,000 reversed on appeal).

6. A group of Pittsburgh Steeler fans urged a photographer from Sports Illustrated to take pictures of them. The photographer did so. From among many photographs available for use, the editors chose one that showed the plaintiff with his fly open. Neff v. Time, Inc., 406 F.Supp. 858 (W.D.Pa.1976) (case dismissed).

7. A newspaper reported the identity of a deceased rape victim. Cox Broadcasting Corp. v. Cohn, 420 U.S. 469 (1975) (case is reported at p. 158, infra).

Criminal Behavior. 8. A magazine article about truck hijacking, to prove that it was a chancy venture, reported that 11 years earlier the plaintiff and another had hijacked a truck in Kentucky, only to find that it contained four bowling pin spotting machines. The article was published in 1967, by which time plaintiff alleged that he had served his time, had become rehabilitated, and was living in California with family and friends who did not know about his past. Briscoe v. Reader's Digest Association, 1 Med.L.Rptr. 1852 (C.D.Cal.1972) (summary judgment for defendant upheld).

9. A newspaper reproduced the front page of a 1952 edition as part of its regular feature called "Page from Our Past." The page contained an article about the cattle theft trial of three brothers who asserted that the 25-year-old matter was no longer of public concern and that they had been law-abiding and hard working citizens of the community, and had ultimately received full pardons. Roshto v. Hebert, 439 So.2d 927 (La.1983). (Judgment for plaintiffs reversed on appeal.)

10. Plaintiff was arrested for drunk driving. At the police station, he was "hitting and banging on his cell door, hollering and cursing from the time of his arrest" until five hours later. A local broadcaster taped some of the noise and played excerpts from it on the radio. Holman v. Central Arkansas Broadcasting Co., 610 F.2d 542 (8th Cir.1979) (case dismissed).

Poverty. 11. A newspaper article included a front-page photograph of the plaintiff's home. The photograph was one of a series on the newspaper's hometown and its environs. The caption read, "one of Crowley's stately homes, a bit weatherworn and unkempt, stands in the shadow of a spreading oak." Jaubert v. Crowley Post-Signal, Inc., 375 So.2d 1386 (La.1979) (case dismissed).

Idiosyncrasies. 12. The New Yorker magazine did one of its extensive profiles on a man who, 27 years earlier, had been an 11-year-old child prodigy who had lectured to mathematicians. For the last 20 years, however, he had lived as unobtrusively as possible. The profile reported that the plaintiff was living in a hall bedroom in Boston's "shabby south end," that his room was untidy, that he had a curious laugh, that he collected street car transfers, and that he was interested at the moment in the lore of the Okamakammessett Indians. The article was "merciless in its dissection of intimate details of its subject's personal life" and a "ruthless exposure of a once public character who has since sought and has now been deprived of the seclusion of private life." Sidis v. F–R Publishing Corp., 113 F.2d 806 (2d Cir.), certiorari denied 311 U.S. 711 (1940) (case dismissed).

13. Sports Illustrated planned an article about a California beach reputed to be the world's most dangerous site for body surfing. Plaintiff, known as the most daring surfer at the site, was interviewed and was referred to in the story as one who extinguished cigarettes in his mouth, ate spiders and other insects, dove head first down a flight of stairs, had never learned to read, and was perceived by other surfers as "abnormal." Virgil v. Time, Inc., 527 F.2d 1122 (9th Cir.1975), certiorari denied 425 U.S. 998 (1976) (affirming denial of summary judgment). (Although plaintiff had once consented to be interviewed, he withdrew the consent when he learned the shape the story would take. The court rejected the defense of consent.)

Embarrassment or Ridicule. 14. A newspaper article reported that the basketball team at the state university was in trouble because four named players, of the eight who were returning, "are on academic probation and in danger of flunking." Bilney v. Evening Star Newspaper Co., 43 Md.App. 560, 406 A.2d 652 (1979) (case dismissed).

15. Plaintiff was a janitor who found $240,000 that had fallen from an armored car. He returned it (and received a reward of $10,000), to the scorn of his neighbors and his children's friends. When their hostile reaction was reported, he received many congratu-

latory letters and messages, including one from President Kennedy. The full story was reported in a periodical and reprinted in a college English textbook. Johnson v. Harcourt, Brace, Jovanovich, Inc., 43 Cal.App.3d 880, 118 Cal.Rptr. 370 (1974) (case dismissed).

b. Legal Analysis

As the law has been developing, the plaintiff must show that the information made public was in fact "private" and that the disclosure would be "highly offensive to a reasonable person." We look at each element in turn.

Private Information. The courts have not been very attentive to this aspect of the matter—perhaps because in most cases the information is clearly something that the plaintiff has held closely and did not want bandied about. Our examples ranged from one extreme to the other. The plaintiff in the sex-change case had not publicized the surgery. On the other hand, private facts are unlikely to exist as to the exterior of a home, when someone at a football game with his fly open poses for a professional photographer, or when someone at a police station shouts so loudly that others cannot help but hear what is said.

Between these extremes we have cases like that of Oliver Sipple, whose sexual orientation was not a secret among his friends and his immediate community, and who was willing to march in gay parades, but who wanted the information kept inside San Francisco. Although some cases should be eliminated on the ground that the information published had not been "private" at the time of the publication, most do seem to involve matters that most people would attempt to keep secret.

"Highly Offensive to a Reasonable Person." This formulation has received much more attention. Although the specific language is taken from the Restatement of Torts (Second) § 652D, similar expressions have been used in the cases during this tort's development. The single most important consideration appears to be the substance of the statement. In some cases it appears difficult to argue that the revelation would be highly offensive to a reasonable person—as in the case of the janitor who returned the money he found, even though some members of plaintiff's community criticized his behavior. It would also apply to the "weatherworn and unkempt" house. Perhaps a similar analysis would apply to the cases involving idiosyncrasies—the body surfer and the child prodigy. Even though the article about the prodigy was described as "merciless in its dissection of intimate details of its subject's personal life," perhaps what was revealed would not be highly offensive to a reasonable person. That some people may wish to keep private some of their quirks is not the same as saying that reasonable people would find the revelation of that information to be highly offensive.

It is no coincidence that the cases most commonly involve sexual topics, which are generally thought to involve the most intimate matters. Another area has involved revelations about rehabilitated criminals. As we shall see, simply showing that the revelation would be highly offensive to a reasonable person does not guarantee that the defendant will be held liable for an invasion of privacy. It is, however, an essential first step.

Note that no complex damage rules, such as exist in defamation, have emerged in privacy. The plaintiff who can successfully demonstrate an invasion of privacy will recover damages measured by the emotional harm suffered. Obviously, damages here cannot rehabilitate the plaintiff in the way that damages in defamation might pay for the reputational harm caused by the false statement.

c. *"Newsworthiness" or "Legitimate Concern" Defense*

In addition to requiring that the publicized matter be private and "highly offensive to a reasonable person," the courts demand that the matter be "not of legitimate concern to the public." Most litigation has revolved around this or similar phrases, such as claims that the article in question was "newsworthy" or that it was of "general or public concern." It should be emphasized at the outset that this requirement exists under state common law and has been applied with greater or lesser rigor in every major state case in which a privacy claim has been raised.

As noted in the introduction to this section, there was a period in which the courts seemed to treat "newsworthy" or "of legitimate concern" as descriptive terms. Any article appearing in a newspaper would meet that requirement because if an editor chose to include it, it must be newsworthy. Such an approach would soon eliminate the privacy action. More recently, the courts have shifted and now attempt to develop normative guidelines to determine when the information might be of "legitimate concern to the public."

The main distinction here is between voluntary and involuntary public figures. It should not be surprising that those who seek the public limelight should be thought to have a lesser claim to privacy protection than those brought into the glare of publicity simply because they are either the unfortunate victims of an accident or crime or are otherwise swept up in an event. But even involuntary subjects are not immune. As a comment to the Restatement puts it:

> These persons are regarded as properly subject to the public interest, and publishers are permitted to satisfy the curiosity of the public as to its heroes, leaders, villains and victims, and those who are closely associated with them. As in the case of the voluntary public figure, the authorized publicity is not limited to the event that itself arouses the public interest, and to some extent includes publicity given to facts about the individual that would otherwise be purely private.

One should note that the categorization of voluntary and involuntary public figures used in privacy law should not be confused with the distinction between public figures and private figures in post-*Gertz* libel law. In libel one assumes that one *must* be voluntary to be public; in privacy, however, one can be involuntarily drawn into the public eye.

Our examples include a variety of plaintiffs. The body surfer has voluntarily brought himself into the public eye by his prowess, his continued attendance at a particular beach, and his engaging in a particular type of activity. Sidis, who may have been a voluntary public figure at age 11 and in his teens, later sought obscurity—but the public has a legitimate concern with what happens to prodigies in later life. Is there a similar concern with criminals? Others "voluntarily" become public figures on the spur of the moment—as when Sipple knocked the arm of the President's assailant or when Johnson returned the money he found in the street. Most of our examples, however, involved involuntary public figures—those who wished to keep their sterilization or mental retardation private, and in no other way had been voluntarily in the public spotlight.

Although courts sometimes suggest that the distinction is relevant to the decision, the difference is at most a matter of degree and more often may control the question of whether the editor will choose to name the person in the story. As a practical matter, a voluntary public figure who is involved in an accident or other misfortune is much more likely to be named in any story that results from the episode than is a previously anonymous person. Those who seek the limelight risk having their names used in unwanted contexts. But this does not mean that every aspect of their lives, or that no aspects of the lives of involuntary figures, may be revealed. The Restatement seeks to draw a line in the following comment:

> Permissible publicity to information concerning either voluntary or involuntary public figures is not limited to the particular events that arouse the interest of the public. That interest, once aroused by the event, may legitimately extend, to some reasonable degree, to further information concerning the individual and to facts about him, which are not public and which, in the case of one who had not become a public figure, would be regarded as an invasion of his purely private life. Thus the life history of one accused of murder, together with such heretofore private facts as may throw some light upon what kind of person he is, his possible guilt or innocence, or his reasons for committing the crime, are a matter of legitimate public interest. . . . On the same basis the home life and daily habits of a motion picture actress may be of legitimate and reasonable interest to the public that sees her on the screen.

> The extent of the authority to make public private facts is not, however, unlimited. There may be some intimate details of her life, such as sexual relations, which even the actress is

entitled to keep to herself. In determining what is a matter of legitimate public interest, account must be taken of the customs and conventions of the community; and in the last analysis what is proper becomes a matter of the community mores. The line is to be drawn when the publicity ceases to be the giving of information to which the public is entitled, and becomes a morbid and sensational prying into private lives for its own sake, with which a reasonable member of the public, with decent standards, would say that he had no concern. The limitations, in other words, are those of common decency, having due regard to the freedom of the press and its reasonable leeway to choose what it will tell the public, but also due regard to the feelings of the individual and the harm that will be done to him by the exposure. Some reasonable proportion is also to be maintained between the event or activity that makes the individual a public figure and the private facts to which publicity is given. Revelations that may properly be made concerning a murderer or the President of the United States would not be privileged if they were to be made concerning one who is merely injured in an automobile accident.

In a study of public attitudes toward privacy, 1,500 persons were asked whether certain media stories invaded privacy. The percentage responses follow:

	Invasion of Privacy	Not an Invasion of Privacy	Not Sure
Details of an extramarital affair that a public official is having with another person	78	19	3
Names of people on welfare	71	25	4
Photograph of a well-known politician entering a pornographic book shop	70	26	4
Names of young people under 16 years old who are accused of committing crimes	51	44	5
Names of men who have been arrested for soliciting prostitutes	49	47	4
Names of doctors who have received large sums of money under Medicare and Medicaid	30	65	6
Names of people who are arrested for possessing illegal drugs	27	68	4
Contents of confidential government papers that reveal incompetence or dishonesty by public officials	21	73	6

The results of the very broad survey, taken by Louis Harris & Associates, Inc. for Sentry Insurance, were released in May, 1979, in a volume called The Dimensions of Privacy.

Are you surprised at the results? Questions about "invasion of privacy" do not tell us whether the respondents were saying that the details of a public official's extramarital affairs were always out of bounds—or that the details were particularly sensitive but might properly be reported upon if the official were to run for elective office again. Might these types of polls help juries or courts determine "community mores"?

d. *Constitutional Privilege Defense*

The Supreme Court of the United States has not been called upon frequently in this area because the state courts, operating at common law, have tended to protect the press. Because they have prevailed under state law, the media defendants rarely have needed recourse to the Supreme Court to assert constitutional rights. In *Cox*, the case of the naming of a deceased rape victim, however, the state court ruled that the plaintiffs were entitled to a judgment. The broadcaster's appeal led to the first, and still the only, Supreme Court decision in this area.

———

COX BROADCASTING CORP. v. COHN

Supreme Court of the United States, 1975.
420 U.S. 469, 95 S.Ct. 1029, 43 L.Ed.2d 328.

[Mr. Cohn's 17-year-old daughter was raped in Georgia and did not survive the occurrence. In Georgia it was a misdemeanor for "any news media or any other person to print and publish, broadcast, televise or disseminate through any other medium of public dissemination . . . the name or identity of any female who may have been raped. . . ." Ga.Code Ann. § 26–9901. Similar statutes exist in a few other states. The girl was not identified at the time. Eight months later, appellant's reporter, Wassell, also an appellant, attended a hearing for the six youths charged with the rape and murder and learned the girl's name by inspecting the indictment in the courtroom. His report naming the girl was telecast.

The Georgia Supreme Court held that the complaint stated a common law action for damages for invasion of the father's own privacy. Defendant's First Amendment argument was rejected on the ground that the statute was an authoritative declaration that Georgia considered a rape victim's name not to be a matter of public concern. The court could discern "no public interest or general concern about the identity of the victim of such a crime as will make the right to disclose the identity of the victim rise to the level of First Amendment protection."

On appeal, the Supreme Court first decided that the decision below was a "final" judgment so as to give the court jurisdiction. The Court then turned to the First Amendment issue.]

MR. JUSTICE WHITE delivered the opinion of the Court.

. . .

Georgia stoutly defends both § 26–9901 and the State's common-law privacy action challenged here. Her claims are not without force, for powerful arguments can be made and have been made, that however it may be ultimately defined, there *is* a zone of privacy surrounding every individual, a zone within which the State may protect him from intrusion by the press, with all its attendant publicity. Indeed, the central thesis of the root article by Warren and Brandeis, The Right to Privacy, 4 Harv.L.Rev. 193, 196 (1890), was that the press was overstepping its prerogatives by publishing essentially private information and that there should be a remedy for the alleged abuses.

More compellingly, the century has experienced a strong tide running in favor of the so-called right of privacy. . . .

. . . Because the gravamen of the claimed injury is the publication of information, whether true or not, the dissemination of which is embarrassing or otherwise painful to an individual, it is here that claims of privacy most directly confront the constitutional freedoms of speech and press. The face-off is apparent, and the appellants urge upon us the broad holding that the press may not be made criminally or civilly liable for publishing information that is neither false nor misleading but absolutely accurate, however damaging it may be to reputation or individual sensibilities.

. . .

. . . Rather than address the broader question whether truthful publications may ever be subjected to civil or criminal liability consistently with the First and Fourteenth Amendments, or to put it another way, whether the State may ever define and protect an area of privacy free from unwanted publicity in the press, it is appropriate to focus on the narrower interface between press and privacy that this case presents, namely, whether the State may impose sanctions on the accurate publication of the name of a rape victim obtained from public records—more specifically, from judicial records which are maintained in connection with a public prosecution and which themselves are open to public inspection. We are convinced that the State may not do so.

In the first place, in a society in which each individual has but limited time and resources with which to observe at first hand the operations of his government, he relies necessarily upon the press to bring to him in convenient form the facts of those operations. Great responsibility is accordingly placed upon the news media to report fully and accurately the proceedings of government, and official records and documents open to the public are the basic data of governmental operations. Without the information provided by the press most of us and many of our representatives would be unable to vote intelligently or to register opinions on the administration of government generally. With respect to judicial proceedings in particular, the function of the press serves to guarantee the fairness of trials and to bring to bear the beneficial effects of public scrutiny upon the administration of justice. See Sheppard v. Maxwell, 384 U.S. 333, 350 (1966).

Appellee has claimed in this litigation that the efforts of the press have infringed his right to privacy by broadcasting to the world the fact that his daughter was a rape victim. The commission of crime, prosecutions resulting from it, and judicial proceedings arising from the prosecutions, however, are without question events of legitimate concern to the public and consequently fall within the responsibility of the press to report the operations of government.

The special protected nature of accurate reports of judicial proceedings has repeatedly been recognized. This Court, in an opinion written by Mr. Justice Douglas, has said:

"A trial is a public event. What transpires in the court room is public property. If a transcript of the court proceedings had been published, we suppose none would claim that the judge could punish the publisher for contempt. And we can see no difference though the conduct of the attorneys, of the jury, or even of the judge himself, may have reflected on the court. *Those who see and hear what transpired can report it with impunity.* There is no special perquisite of the judiciary which enables it, as distinguished from other institutions of democratic government, to suppress, edit, or censor events which transpire in proceedings before it." Craig v. Harney, 331 U.S. 367, 374 (1947) (emphasis added).

.   .   .

The developing law surrounding the tort of invasion of privacy recognizes a privilege in the press to report the events of judicial proceedings. The Warren and Brandeis article, supra, noted that the proposed new right would be limited in the same manner as actions for libel and slander where such a publication was a privileged communication: "the right to privacy is not invaded by any publication made in a court of justice .   .   . and (at least in many jurisdictions) reports of any such proceedings would in some measure be accorded a like privilege."

.   .   .

Thus, even the prevailing law of invasion of privacy generally recognizes that the interests in privacy fade when the information involved already appears on the public record. The conclusion is compelling when viewed in terms of the First and Fourteenth Amendments and in light of the public interest in a vigorous press. The Georgia cause of action for invasion of privacy through public disclosure of the name of a rape victim imposes sanctions on pure expression—the content of a publication—and not conduct or a combination of speech and non-speech elements that might otherwise be open to regulation or prohibition. See United States v. O'Brien, 391 U.S. 367, 376–377 (1968). The publication of truthful information available on the public record contains none of the indicia of those limited categories of expression, such as "fighting" words, which "are no essential part of any exposition of ideas, and are of such slight social value as a step to truth that any benefit that may be derived from them is clearly outweighed by the social interest in order and morality." Chaplinsky v. New Hampshire, 315 U.S. 568, 572 (1942) (footnote omitted).

By placing the information in the public domain on official court records, the State must be presumed to have concluded that the public interest was thereby being served. Public records by their very nature are of interest to those concerned with the administration of government, and a public benefit is performed by the reporting of the true contents of the records by the media. The freedom of the press to publish that information appears to us to be of critical importance to our type of government in which the citizenry is the final judge of the proper conduct of public business. In preserving that form of government the First and Fourteenth Amendments command nothing less than that the States may not impose sanctions on the publication of truthful information contained in official court records open to public inspection.

We are reluctant to embark on a course that would make public records generally available to the media but forbid their publication if offensive to the sensibilities of the supposed reasonable man. Such a rule would make it very difficult for the media to inform citizens about the public business and yet stay within the law. The rule would invite timidity and self-censorship and very likely lead to the suppression of many items that would otherwise be published and that should be made available to the public. At the very least, the First and Fourteenth Amendments will not allow exposing the press to liability for truthfully publishing information released to the public in official court records. If there are privacy interests to be protected in judicial proceedings, the States must respond by means which avoid public documentation or other exposure of private information. Their political institutions must weigh the interests in privacy with the interests of the public to know and of the press to publish.[26] Once true information is disclosed in public court documents open to public inspection, the press cannot be sanctioned for publishing it. In this instance as in others reliance must rest upon the judgment of those who decide what to publish or broadcast. See Miami Herald Pub. Co. v. Tornillo, 418 U.S., at 258.

---

26. We mean to imply nothing about any constitutional questions which might arise from a state policy not allowing access by the public and press to various kinds of official records, such as records of juvenile court proceedings.

Appellant Wassell based his televised report upon notes taken during the court proceedings and obtained the name of the victim from the indictments handed to him at his request during a recess in the hearing. Appellee has not contended that the name was obtained in an improper fashion or that it was not on an official court document open to public inspection. Under these circumstances, the protection of freedom of the press provided by the First and Fourteenth Amendments bars the State of Georgia from making appellants' broadcast the basis of civil liability.[27]

Reversed.

MR. CHIEF JUSTICE BURGER concurs in the judgment.

MR. JUSTICE POWELL, concurring.

.   .   .

I am in entire accord with the Court's determination that the First Amendment proscribes imposition of civil liability in a privacy action predicated on the truthful publication of matters contained in open judicial records. But my impression of the role of truth in defamation actions brought by private citizens differs from the Court's. . . .

MR. JUSTICE DOUGLAS, concurring in the judgment.

I agree that the state judgment is "final," and I also agree in the reversal of the Georgia court.* On the merits, . . . there is no power on the part of government to suppress or penalize the publication of "news of the day."

MR. JUSTICE REHNQUIST, dissenting.

Because I am of the opinion that the decision which is the subject of this appeal is not a "final" judgment or decree, . . . I would dismiss this appeal for want of jurisdiction.

---

27. Appellants have contended that whether they derived the information in question from public records or instead through their own investigation, the First and Fourteenth Amendments bar any sanctions from being imposed by the State because of the publication. Because appellants have prevailed on more limited grounds, we need not address this broader challenge to the validity of § 26–9901 and of Georgia's right of action for public disclosure.

* While I join in the narrow result reached by the Court, I write separately to emphasize that I would ground that result upon a far broader proposition, namely, that the First Amendment, made applicable to the States through the Fourteenth, prohibits the use of state law "to impose damages for merely discussing public affairs . . .." [ ] In this context, of course, "public affairs" must be broadly construed—indeed, the term may be said to embrace "any matter of sufficient general interest to prompt media coverage . . .." Gertz v. Robert Welch, Inc., [ ] (Douglas, J. dissenting). By its now-familiar process of balancing and accommodating First Amendment freedoms with state or individual interests, the Court raises a specter of liability which must inevitably induce self-censorship by the media, thereby inhibiting the rough-and-tumble discourse which the First Amendment so clearly protects.

Notes and Questions

1. What issues does the majority opinion avoid deciding? Why do you think the majority took the approach it did?

2. In the Briscoe case, involving the man who hijacked the truck with the bowling pin spotters 11 years before the article was published, the court observed that "Ideally, his neighbors should recognize his present worth and forget his past life of shame. But men are not so divine as to forgive the past trespasses of others, and plaintiff therefore endeavored to reveal as little as possible of his past life." The court concluded that a remand was required. If a jury should find that plaintiff had in fact been rehabilitated, it should decide whether "identifying him as a former criminal would be highly offensive and injurious to the reasonable man," and whether defendant had published the information "with a reckless disregard for its offensiveness." This case was decided before *Cox*. Could the *Briscoe* court still reach the same conclusions now? (On remand in *Briscoe*, the defendant was granted summary judgment and the case was not appealed again.)

3. On the importance of the passage of time, consider this comment to Restatement, Second § 652D:

> The fact that there has been a lapse of time, even of considerable length, since the event that has made the plaintiff a public figure, does not of itself defeat the authority to give him publicity or to renew publicity when it has formerly been given. Past events and activities may still be of legitimate interest to the public, and a narrative reviving recollection of what has happened even many years ago may be both interesting and valuable for purposes of information and education. Such a lapse of time is, however, a factor to be considered, with other facts, in determining whether the publicity goes to unreasonable lengths in revealing facts about one who has resumed the private, lawful and unexciting life led by the great bulk of the community . . . . Again the question is to be determined upon the basis of community standards and mores. Although lapse of time may not impair the authority to give publicity to a public record, the pointing out of the present location and identity of the individual raises a quite different problem.

Is this passage consistent with the Cox case? Does it help analyze the problem of Sidis, the child prodigy? Consider *Roshto*, p. 152, supra.

4. The principal opinion in *Howard*, the involuntary sterilization case, responded to the argument that plaintiff's name was unnecessary as follows:

> Here the disclosure of plaintiff's involuntary sterilization was closely related to the subject matter of the news story. It

documented the article's theme of maladministration and patient abuses at the Jasper County Home. . . .

In the sense of serving an appropriate news function, the disclosure contributed constructively to the impact of the article. It offered a personalized frame of reference to which the reader could relate, fostering perception and understanding. Moreover, it lent specificity and credibility to the report.

In this way the disclosure served as an effective means of accomplishing the intended news function. It had positive communicative value in attracting the reader's attention to the article's subject matter and in supporting expression of the underlying theme.

Examined in the light of the first amendment, we do not believe the disclosure could reasonably be held to be devoid of news value. [   ]

Assuming, as plaintiff agrees, the newspaper had a right to print an article that documented extrastatutory involuntary sterilizations at the Jasper County Home, the editors also had a right to buttress the force of their evidence by naming names. We do not say it was necessary for them to do so, but we are certain they had a right to treat the identity of victims of involuntary sterilizations as matters of legitimate public concern. . . .

This is a far cry from embarrassing people by exposing their medical conditions or treatment when identity can add nothing to the probity of the account. [   ]

The disclosure of plaintiff's identity in this case could not reasonably be viewed as the spreading of gossip solely for its own sake. . . .

Would *Cox* reach the same result?

5. In *Deaton*, the case involving the mentally retarded school children, the court noted that its decision was not inconsistent with *Cox* because in its case "the information published was not taken from public records, but was by state law made unavailable to the public."

There is no suggestion in the case that the press stole the documents or in any way acquired them illegally. Apparently, the newspaper got the information from some leak. Since the data in question were in government files but were declared not available to the public, the rationale of the *Cox* case did not apply.

6. In Virgil v. Time, Inc., involving the body surfer, the publisher, citing *Cox*, argued in its brief that the First Amendment protected almost all true statements from liability:

A press which must depend upon a governmental determination as to what facts are of 'public interest' in order to avoid liability for their truthful publication is not free at all. . . . A constitutional rule can be fashioned which protects all the interests involved. This goal is achieved by providing a privilege for truthful publications which is defeasible only when the court concludes as a matter of law that the truthful publication complained of constitutes a clear abuse of the editor's constitutional discretion to publish and discuss subjects and facts which in his judgment are matters of public interest.

The court rejected the argument and adopted the view of the Restatement (Second) of Torts, that liability may be imposed if the matter published is "not of legitimate concern to the public." Then the court relied on a passage from the Restatement that was quoted earlier in this section—that "in the last analysis what is proper becomes a matter of the community mores."

In libel and obscenity cases juries utilize community standards and the court thought they should do so here, too, "subject to close judicial scrutiny to ensure that the jury resolutions comport with First Amendment principles." What is the difference between *Time*'s position and that adopted by the court? Is the court's view consistent with *Cox?* Over the dissents of Justices Brennan and Stewart, the Supreme Court denied certiorari in *Virgil*. 425 U.S. 998 (1976). The case was remanded for trial.

On remand, the trial judge held that the magazine was entitled to summary judgment. First, the judge concluded that the facts revealed were not "highly offensive." Even if they were, the facts were "included as a legitimate journalistic attempt to explain Virgil's extremely daring and dangerous style of body surfing at the Wedge. There is no possibility that a juror could conclude that the personal facts were included for any inherent morbid, sensational, or curiosity appeal they might have." Virgil v. Sports Illustrated, 424 F.Supp. 1286 (S.D.Cal.1976).

7. Although the courts have tended to take this area case-by-case, editors complain that such an approach breeds intolerable uncertainty. An editor must decide today what might happen in court in several years—and the standards are said to be vague. What will be found "highly offensive to a reasonable person" or to violate "community standards and mores"? Juries given these questions may punish unpopular publishers or broadcasters.

Compare this situation with that confronting an editor in the defamation area. There the editor, with advice from lawyers, must decide whether the *Times* or *Gertz* rule applies and then decide whether the publication's conduct meets that standard. And truth is always a defense. Do you see a sharp difference between the editor's position there and where the case involves privacy?

8. The 1980's have seen some embarrassing private facts cases brought under the principle of infliction of emotional distress or "outrage." An example is Hyde v. City of Columbia, 637 S.W.2d 251 (Mo.App.1982), cert. denied 459 U.S. 1226 (1983), in which the complaining witness in an abduction sued reporters, newspapers, and the

municipality after being identified in the press and then terrorized by the criminal defendant. A dismissal of the claim was reversed by the appellate court.

e. Enjoining Violations of Privacy

Many commentators have observed that damages in defamation are a more adequate remedy than in truthful invasion of privacy cases. In defamation the award of damages, especially special damages, may compensate the plaintiff for a loss of reputation that has in fact injured him financially. Even a judgment for nominal damages may have a vital symbolic function. In privacy, however, once the invasion has occurred the embarrassing truth is out and a judgment or an award of money does not resurrect a sullied reputation or undo other harm caused by the publication. Counterattack and counter-speech are not useful here.

Thus, courts have looked more seriously at alternatives in privacy suits, and have been somewhat more responsive to a plea for an injunction to prevent the utterance of the invasion in the first place. Often the plaintiff learns about the invasion only after actual publication, but in some situations prevention is feasible. Because the privacy action is so recent in origin, it lacks a long history like that of defamation during which the injunction came to be totally rejected in actions for private defamations.

The Supreme Court has had a curious record with regard to injunctions barring invasions of privacy by the media. Although three significant cases have presented the issue, the Court has yet to come to grips with it. In the first, a famous baseball player persuaded the New York courts to enjoin the publication of an unauthorized biography that contained false dialogue. Spahn v. Julian Messner, Inc., 21 N.Y.2d 124, 286 N.Y.S.2d 832, 233 N.E.2d 840 (1967). The defendants compromised and settled their dispute while it was being appealed to the Supreme Court.

The second chance came in a case involving a motion picture about conditions inside a Massachusetts institution for the criminally insane. The state court barred showing of the picture except to selected groups because of the producer's invasion of the privacy of the inmates, assertedly in violation of an agreement he signed in order to get permission to make the film. Commonwealth v. Wiseman, 356 Mass. 251, 249 N.E.2d 610 (1969). The Supreme Court denied certiorari to Wiseman, the producer, 398 U.S. 960 (1969), over the lengthy dissent of Justice Harlan, joined by Justices Douglas and Brennan:

Petitioners seek review in this Court of a decision of the Massachusetts Supreme Judicial Court enjoining the commercial distribution to general audiences of the film "Titticut Follies." Petitioners' film is a "documentary" of life in Bridgewater State

Hospital for the criminally insane. Its stark portrayal of patient-routine and treatment of the inmates is at once a scathing indictment of the inhumane conditions that prevailed at the time of the film and an undeniable infringement of the privacy of the inmates filmed, who are shown nude and engaged in acts that would unquestionably embarrass an individual of normal sensitivity. . . .

The balance between these two interests, that of the individual's privacy and the public's right to know about conditions in public institutions, is not one that is easily struck, particularly in a case like that before us where the importance of the issue is matched by the extent of the invasion of privacy. . . . A further consideration is the fact that these inmates are not only the wards of the Commonwealth of Massachusetts but are also the charges of society as a whole. It is important that conditions in public institutions should not be cloaked in secrecy, lest citizens may disclaim responsibility for the treatment that their representative government affords those in its care. At the same time it must be recognized that the individual's concern with privacy is the key to the dignity which is the promise of civilized society. [   ]

. . .

I am at a loss to understand how questions of such importance can be deemed not "certworthy." To the extent that the Commonwealth suggests that certiorari be denied because petitioners failed to comply with reasonable contract conditions imposed by the Commonwealth, that question in itself is one of significant constitutional dimension, for it is an open question as to how far a government may go in cutting off access of the media to its institutions when such access will not hinder them in performing their functions. Cf. Estes v. Texas, 381 U.S. 532 (1965); [   ]. In the case before us, however, the only asserted interest is the State's concern for the privacy of the inmates in its care, and the basis for the decision below was the predominance of that interest over that of the general public in seeing the film.

The third Supreme Court case involved a claim by a former patient trying to enjoin her analyst from publishing a book the analyst had written about the patient's treatment. Although names and other facts were changed in the book, plaintiff alleged that she and her family were easily identifiable. The state courts granted a preliminary injunction enjoining all distribution until the litigation had concluded. The defendants, including the book's publisher, sought certiorari, claiming that the injunction against publishing concededly true statements of medical and scientific importance violated the First Amendment. The Court granted certiorari, Roe v.

Doe, 417 U.S. 907 (1974), and heard oral arguments. It then decided not to decide the case by dismissing the writ of certiorari as having been "improvidently granted." 420 U.S. 307 (1975). The complication of the confidential relationship between the parties and the murky record caused by the use of Does and Roes might have dissuaded the Court from deciding the case.

The case then went to trial on the merits. The trial judge found that the plaintiff was entitled to a remedy because of defendant's violation of an implied agreement to treat the plaintiff in confidence. He awarded damages for the harm plaintiff suffered from the release of 220 copies of the book before the preliminary injunction was issued. He also permanently enjoined distribution of the remaining stock. Doe v. Roe, 93 Misc.2d 201, 400 N.Y.S.2d 668 (1977). By subsequent order, the remaining volumes were destroyed.

How might one analyze the competing interests in these invasion of privacy cases when the issue becomes one of a remedy for a true statement that is adjudged an invasion? How do these cases square with concern about prior restraint?

f. Ethical Considerations

In addition to considering how these matters are analyzed legally, a prospective journalist must also consider the more basic question of whether a reporter or an editor should include this type of material in a story. Even though the legal system may ultimately protect the overwhelming majority of the stories, that does not necessarily answer the question of how a newspaper should handle them.

Not all newspapers go as far as the law may permit. The *St. Louis Post-Dispatch* has announced that although it will continue to identify burglary victims and losses, the stories will not indicate whether any valuables were overlooked, and addresses will be given in block numbers rather than specific numbers. The paper will not identify victims of sex crimes if the report would tend to degrade the victim. Editor & Publisher, Feb. 8, 1975 at 17. What about the accused? Are these sound lines to draw?

The press itself has been notably timid in this area, perhaps uncertain about the degree to which it is protected because the courts have been generous, but vague. In an article in the April, 1975, issue of [MORE], Washington columnist Brit Hume condemned the reluctance of editors to publish stories about Congressmen who seem senile at Committee hearings, extramarital activities of Presidents and Congressmen, public drunkenness of Congressmen and similar matters. Are these equally deserving of disclosure? Would you distinguish between reporting actions or behavior apparent to any observer, and reporting information acquired surreptitiously? He quotes an editor as saying that prying into the lives of public officials "smells of Hollywood gossip." Could you draw a line between the two? One approach was to print such information only when the circumstance "affects their public performance." Hume argues that this is a poor standard because it is often very difficult to tell why a Congressman is not being effective. He cites one case in which it was thought that a Senator objected to the sexual behavior of a Congressman from his state and that the tension between them probably hurt the Congressman's effectiveness. Hume notes other problems relating to relatives of those in public office: an official's son who gets into a minor traffic accident, or the mental health of the wife or child of a possible presidential candidate.

During the 1976 political campaign, the *Detroit News* reported that the Democratic candidate for United States Senator from Michigan had had an extra-marital sexual relationship seven years earlier with a member of his Congressional staff. This was not a case in which the woman on the Congressional payroll was performing only sexual favors. Mike Royko, a newspaper columnist, argued that the newspaper should not have carried the story since there was no claim that the behavior cost the taxpayers money, that it affected his performance as a Congressman, or that the woman was intrinsically newsworthy, such as a spy. He suggested that the motive lay in the fact that the paper was supporting the Republican opponent. Should the paper have printed the story?

In one case, a newspaper had reason to know that naming CIA agents might lead to their harm or death. In another, a former double agent told a newspaper that if it named him in a forthcoming story he would commit suicide. The paper ran the name and the agent committed suicide that day. See [MORE] Feb. 1976 at 12; The Quill, May 1976 at 11.

Extensive press discussion followed the decision of a newspaper in Missoula, Montana, to report that the daughter of "one of the city's best-known families," who had dropped out of Radcliffe, had been murdered in Washington, D.C., where she was working as a prostitute. See Hart and Johnson, Fire Storm in Missoula, The Quill, May, 1979 at 19.

The issue, of course, transcends individual privacy. In "Why Scoop the Court?" Columbia Journalism Review, July-Aug. 1979 at 23, Professor David Rubin suggested that publishing leaks about forthcoming Supreme Court decisions served no legitimate purpose. In the next issue (p. 76), Tom Wicker, Associate Editor of the *New York Times*, suggested that editors should not worry about the consequences of what they publish: "Are editors to say that *some* advance stories should be published but not others? . . . Are newspapers and broadcast journalists to seek to be first with *some* news, but not with other news? If so, how is that policy to be justified? There are only two rules that can bring us anywhere near evenhandedness: First, find out what you can. Second, publish or broadcast what you know." Rubin responded that "editors and reporters are paid to make precisely the kind of judgments before which Wicker trembles . . .."

4. APPROPRIATION

The fourth branch of invasion of privacy is appropriation of another's name or likeness for commercial or trade purposes. Its major impact is on the field of advertising, since news reports have generally been held not to be "for commercial or trade purposes." But see, Zacchini v. Scripps-Howard Broadcasting, infra. As is the case with the other branches of invasion of privacy, truth is not a defense. A manufacturer who advertises that John Smith uses his product may not be able to defend himself merely by proving that John Smith does use his product, although that is important for other reasons that will be discussed in Chapter VIII.

What must be demonstrated to avoid a successful appropriation action is consent. This usually comes in the form of a written "release" since many states require that consent to appropriation be written. Indeed, it is common for advertising agencies and even news organizations to have standard release forms available for use. Many release forms are limited releases in that they restrict the uses that can be made of a particular name or likeness or the period of time during which the use will be permitted. Numerous appropriation cases have been the result of using a picture in a manner not covered by the original release.

Determining what constitutes commercial or trade purposes has not always proved easy for the courts. A New York trial court held it was not for commercial or trade purposes when a gubernatorial candidate used a murder suspect's picture in a campaign commercial. Davis v. Duryea, 99 Misc.2d 933, 417 N.Y.S.2d 624 (1979). On the other hand, a television station that telephoned a couple during the program, "Dialing for Dollars", and aired the ensuing conversation found itself liable for appropriation. Jeppson v. United Television, 580 P.2d 1087 (Utah 1978). Does the following case offer any guidance?

ZACCHINI v. SCRIPPS–HOWARD BROADCASTING CO.

Supreme Court of the United States, 1977.
433 U.S. 562, 97 S.Ct. 2849, 53 L.Ed.2d 965.

MR. JUSTICE WHITE delivered the opinion of the Court.

Petitioner, Hugo Zacchini, is an entertainer. He performs a "human cannonball" act in which he is shot from a cannon into a net some 200 feet away. Each performance occupies some 15 seconds. In August and September 1972, petitioner was engaged to perform his act on a regular basis at the Geauga County Fair in Burton, Ohio.

He performed in a fenced area, surrounded by grandstands, at the fair grounds. Members of the public attending the fair were not charged a separate admission fee to observe his act.

On August 30, a freelance reporter for Scripps-Howard Broadcasting Co., the operator of a television broadcasting station and respondent in this case, attended the fair. He carried a small movie camera. Petitioner noticed the reporter and asked him not to film the performance. The reporter did not do so on that day; but on the instructions of the producer of respondent's daily newscast, he returned the following day and videotaped the entire act. This film clip, approximately 15 seconds in length, was shown on the 11 o'clock news program that night, together with favorable commentary.[1]

Petitioner then brought this action for damages, alleging that he is "engaged in the entertainment business," that the act he performs is one "invented by his father and . . . performed only by his family for the last fifty years," that respondent "showed and commercialized the film of his act without his consent," and that such conduct was an "unlawful appropriation of plaintiff's professional property." App. 4–5. Respondent answered and moved for summary judgment, which was granted by the trial court.

. . .

. . . Insofar as the Ohio Supreme Court held that the First and Fourteenth Amendments of the United States Constitution required judgment for respondent, we reverse the judgment of that court.

. . .

Even if the judgment in favor of respondent must nevertheless be understood as ultimately resting on Ohio law, it appears that at the very least the Ohio court felt compelled by what it understood to be federal constitutional considerations to construe and apply its own law in the manner it did. In this event, we have jurisdiction and should decide the federal issue; for if the state court erred in its understanding of our cases and of the First and Fourteenth Amendments we should so declare, leaving the state court free to decide the privilege issue solely as a matter of Ohio law. [ ] If the Supreme Court of Ohio "held as it did because it felt under compulsion of federal law as enunciated by this Court so to hold, it should be relieved of that compulsion. It should be freed to decide . . . these suits according to its own local law." [ ]

. . .

1. The script of the commentary accompanying the film clip read as follows:

"This . . . now . . . is the story of a *true spectator* sport . . . the sport of human cannonballing . . . in fact, the great *Zacchini* is about the only human cannonball around, these days . . . just happens that, *where he is*, is the Great Geauga County Fair, in Burton . . . and believe me, although it's not a *long* act, it's a thriller . . . and you really need to see it *in person* . . . to appreciate it. . . ." (Emphasis in original.)

The Ohio Supreme Court relied heavily on Time, Inc. v. Hill, 385 U.S. 374 (1967), but that case does not mandate a media privilege to televise a performer's entire act without his consent. Involved in Time, Inc. v. Hill was a claim under the New York "Right of Privacy" statute that Life Magazine, in the course of reviewing a new play, had connected the play with a long-past incident involving petitioner and his family and had falsely described their experience and conduct at that time. The complaint sought damages for humiliation and suffering flowing from these nondefamatory falsehoods that allegedly invaded Hill's privacy. The Court held, however, that the opening of a new play linked to an actual incident was a matter of public interest and that Hill could not recover without showing that the Life report was knowingly false or was published with reckless disregard for the truth—the same rigorous standard that had been applied in New York Times Co. v. Sullivan [   ].

Time, Inc. v. Hill, which was hotly contested and decided by a divided Court, involved an entirely different tort from the "right of publicity" recognized by the Ohio Supreme Court. . . .

The differences between these two torts are important. First, the State's interests in providing a cause of action in each instance are different. "The interest protected" in permitting recovery for placing the plaintiff in a false light "is clearly that of reputation, with the same overtones of mental distress as in defamation." Prosser, supra, 48 Calif.L.Rev., at 400. By contrast, the State's interest in permitting a "right of publicity" is in protecting the proprietary interest of the individual in his act in part to encourage such entertainment. As we later note, the State's interest is closely analogous to the goals of patent and copyright law, focusing on the right of the individual to reap the reward of his endeavors and having little to do with protecting feelings or reputation. Second, the two torts differ in the degree to which they intrude on dissemination of information to the public. In "false light" cases the only way to protect the interests involved is to attempt to minimize publication of the damaging matter, while in "right of publicity" cases the only question is who gets to do the publishing. An entertainer such as petitioner usually has no objection to the widespread publication of his act as long as he gets the commercial benefit of such publication. Indeed, in the present case petitioner did not seek to enjoin the broadcast of his act; he simply sought compensation for the broadcast in the form of damages.

. . .

Moreover, Time, Inc. v. Hill, *New York Times*, *Metromedia*, *Gertz*, and *Firestone* all involved the reporting of events; in none of them was there an attempt to broadcast or publish an entire act for which the performer ordinarily gets paid. It is evident, and there is no claim here to the contrary, that petitioner's state-law right of publicity would not serve to prevent respondent from reporting the newsworthy facts about petitioner's act. Wherever the line in particular situations is to be drawn between media reports that are protected and those that are not, we are quite sure that the First and Fourteenth Amendments do not immunize the media when they broadcast a performer's entire act without his consent. The Constitution no more prevents a State from requiring respondent to compensate petitioner for broadcasting his act on television than it would privilege respondent to film and broadcast a copyrighted dramatic work without liability to the copyright owner, [ ], or to film and broadcast a prize fight, [ ], or a baseball game, [ ], where the promoters or the participants had other plans for publicizing the event. There are ample reasons for reaching this conclusion.

The broadcast of a film of petitioner's entire act poses a substantial threat to the economic value of that performance. As the Ohio court recognized, this act is the product of petitioner's own talents and energy, the end result of much time, effort, and expense. Much of its economic value lies in the "right of exclusive control over the publicity given to his performance"; if the public can see the act free on television, it will be less willing to pay to see it at the fair.[12] The effect of a public broadcast of the performance is similar to preventing petitioner from charging an admission fee. . . . Moreover, the broadcast of petitioner's entire performance, unlike the unauthorized use of another's name for purposes of trade or the incidental use of a name or picture by the press, goes to the heart of petitioner's ability to earn a living as an entertainer. Thus, in this case, Ohio has recognized what may be the strongest case for a "right of publicity"—involving, not the appropriation of an entertainer's reputation to enhance the attractiveness of a commercial product, but the appropriation of the very activity by which the entertainer acquired his reputation in the first place.

Of course, Ohio's decision to protect petitioner's right of publicity here rests on more than a desire to compensate the performer for the time and effort invested in his act; the protection provides an economic incentive for him to make the investment required to produce a performance of interest to the public. This same consideration underlies the patent and copyright laws long enforced by this Court. . . .

There is no doubt that entertainment, as well as news, enjoys First Amendment protection. It is also true that entertainment itself can be important news. Time, Inc. v. Hill. But it is important to note that neither the public nor respondent will be deprived of the benefit of petitioner's performance as long as his commercial stake in

12. It is possible, of course, that respondent's news broadcast increased the value of petitioner's performance by stimulating the public's interest in seeing the act live. In these circumstances, petitioner would not be able to prove damages and thus would not recover. But petitioner has alleged that the broadcast injured him to the extent of $25,000, App. 5, and we think the State should be allowed to authorize compensation of this injury if proved.

his act is appropriately recognized. Petitioner does not seek to enjoin the broadcast of his performance; he simply wants to be paid for it. Nor do we think that a state-law damages remedy against respondent would represent a species of liability without fault contrary to the letter or spirit of Gertz v. Robert Welch, Inc., [   ]. Respondent knew exactly that petitioner objected to televising his act but nevertheless displayed the entire film.

We conclude that although the State of Ohio may as a matter of its own law privilege the press in the circumstances of this case, the First and Fourteenth Amendments do not require it to do so.

Reversed.

MR. JUSTICE POWELL, with whom MR. JUSTICE BRENNAN and MR. JUSTICE MARSHALL join, dissenting.

Disclaiming any attempt to do more than decide the narrow case before us, the Court reverses the decision of the Supreme Court of Ohio based on repeated incantation of a single formula: "a performer's entire act." The holding today is summed up in one sentence:

> "Wherever the line in particular situations is to be drawn between media reports that are protected and those that are not, we are quite sure that the First and Fourteenth Amendments do not immunize the media when they broadcast a performer's entire act without his consent."

I doubt that this formula provides a standard clear enough even for resolution of this case.[1] In any event, I am not persuaded that the Court's opinion is appropriately sensitive to the First Amendment values at stake, and I therefore dissent.

Although the Court would draw no distinction, I do not view respondent's action as comparable to unauthorized commercial broadcasts of sporting events, theatrical performances, and the like where the broadcaster keeps the profits. There is no suggestion here that respondent made any such use of the film. Instead, it simply reported on what petitioner concedes to be a newsworthy event, in a way hardly surprising for a television station—by means of film coverage. The report was part of an ordinary daily news program, consuming a total of 15 seconds. It is a routine example of the press fulfilling the informing function so vital to our system.

---

1. Although the record is not explicit, it is unlikely that the "act" commenced abruptly with the explosion that launched petitioner on his way, ending with the landing in the net a few seconds later. One may assume that the actual firing was preceded by some fanfare, possibly stretching over several minutes, to heighten the audience's anticipation: introduction of the performer, description of the uniqueness and danger, last-minute checking of the apparatus, and entry into the cannon, all accompanied by suitably ominous commentary from the master of ceremonies. If this is found to be the case on remand, then respondent could not be said to have appropriated the "entire act" in its 15-second newsclip—and the Court's opinion then would afford no guidance for resolution of the case. Moreover, in future cases involving different performances, similar difficulties in determining just what constitutes the "entire act" are inevitable.

The Court's holding that the station's ordinary news report may give rise to substantial liability has disturbing implications, for the decision could lead to a degree of media self-censorship. [ ] Hereafter whenever a television news editor is unsure whether certain film footage received from a camera crew might be held to portray an "entire act," he may decline coverage—even of clearly newsworthy events—or confine the broadcast to watered-down verbal reporting, perhaps with an occasional still picture. The public is then the loser. This is hardly the kind of news reportage that the First Amendment is meant to foster. [ ]

In my view the First Amendment commands a different analytical starting point from the one selected by the Court. Rather than begin with a quantitative analysis of the performer's behavior—is this or is this not his entire act?—we should direct initial attention to the actions of the news media: what use did the station make of the film footage? When a film is used, as here, for a routine portion of a regular news program, I would hold that the First Amendment protects the station from a "right of publicity" or "appropriation" suit, absent a strong showing by the plaintiff that the news broadcast was a subterfuge or cover for private or commercial exploitation.[4]

. . . In a suit like the one before us, however, the plaintiff does not complain about the fact of exposure to the public, but rather about its timing or manner. He welcomes some publicity, but seeks to retain control over means and manner as a way to maximize for himself the monetary benefits that flow from such publication. But having made the matter public—having chosen, in essence, to make it newsworthy—he cannot, consistent with the First Amendment, complain of routine news reportage. Cf. Gertz v. Robert Welch, Inc., [ ] (clarifying the different liability standards appropriate in defamation suits, depending on whether or not the plaintiff is a public figure).

Since the film clip here was undeniably treated as news and since there is no claim that the use was subterfuge, respondent's actions were constitutionally privileged. I would affirm.

[MR. JUSTICE STEVENS dissented on the ground that he could not tell whether the Ohio Supreme Court had relied on federal constitutional issues in deciding the case. He would have remanded the case to that court "for clarification of its holding before deciding the federal constitutional issue."]

On remand, the Ohio Supreme Court took advantage of the opportunity afforded by the majority opinion and decided that nothing in the Ohio Constitution protected the behavior of the media

---

4. This case requires no detailed specification of the standards for identifying a subterfuge, since there is no claim here that respondent's news use was anything but bona fide. [ ] I would point out, however, that selling time during a news broadcast to advertisers in the customary fashion does not make for "commercial exploitation" in the sense intended here. [ ]

defendant. The case was remanded for trial. Zacchini v. Scripps-Howard Broadcasting Co., 54 Ohio St.2d 286, 376 N.E.2d 582 (1978).

Notes and Questions

1. How important is it that the majority treats the 15 seconds as the "entire act"?

2. Does this case involve an aspect of "privacy"? Does it resemble the Cox Broadcasting case in that both involved lawfully obtained information of interest or concern to the public? Can you explain why the defendant in *Cox Broadcasting* did not have to pay while the defendant in *Zacchini* did have to pay?

3. After *Zacchini*, what would happen in a case in which a street artist who survives on contributions from passersby—a mime, an accordionist, a dancer—is photographed by the local television station and shown in a story about summer diversions on the streets of the city? Is the street artist's claim as strong as Zacchini's?

Right of Publicity. The Zacchini case is an example of an offshoot of appropriation known as right of publicity. This particular right was once defined as follows:

> The distinctive aspect of the common-law right of publicity is that it recognizes the commercial value of the picture or representation of a prominent person or performer and protects his proprietary interest in the profitability of his public reputation or persona. Ali v. Playgirl, Inc., 447 F.Supp. 723 (S.D.N.Y.1978).

Unlike the traditional tort of appropriation, right of publicity is exclusively the province of well-known individuals. Also, whereas the original tort was at least partially rooted in the concept of the right to be left alone and not to be exploited for commercial or trade purposes, this new variation seems only concerned with who should reap the financial benefits. In essence it is a property right, as opposed to a personal right. Thus, Johnny Carson was able to sue a manufacturer of portable toilets that were marketed under the name, "Here's Johnny." Carson v. Here's Johnny Portable Toilets, Inc., 698 F.2d 831 (6th Cir.1983), reversing 498 F.Supp. 71 (E.D.Mich.1980). Similarly, the estate of Elvis Presley won their claim against the producers of THE BIG EL SHOW, an imitation of Presley's performances. Estate of Presley v. Russen, 513 F.Supp. 1339 (D.N.J.1981).

In some cases it is not even the true name or likeness of a person, but rather some character or role that is at issue. In Groucho Marx Productions v. Day and Night Co., 523 F.Supp. 485 (S.D.N.Y.1981), reversed on other grounds, 689 F.2d 317 (2d Cir.1982), the court held that the play, "A Day in Hollywood, a Night in the Ukraine," appropriated the Marx brothers' characters. In this context, a suit for appropriation has become a new method of protecting creative work. We will discuss another method of protecting such work in Chapter V.

Descendability. Personal rights such as those protected by defamation and invasion of privacy law terminate at death. Thus, for example, one can publish defamatory statements about deceased individuals with impunity (unless the same statement also defames people who are still alive). Because the right of publicity is a property right, a great controversy has developed as to whether it survives the death of its creator. Currently, there seem to be three distinct approaches being taken by various courts. One is that the right terminates upon death. Under this view as soon as people die, their names, likenesses and characterizations are available for anyone to use without legal liability. At the other extreme is the position that death has no effect on the right of publicity. In jurisdictions that adhere to this view, the consent of whoever owns the right of publicity in question (perhaps the individual's heirs or someone who has purchased the right) is always necessary. Finally, there is an intermediate approach that holds the right of publicity to survive death only if it was commercially exploited during the person's lifetime. With this approach the right of publicity is a property right only if the individual treated it as such.

Chapter V

COPYRIGHT

As we discussed in Chapter IV, there are several ways to protect a creative work product. Historically, this protection was first achieved through copyright law. Although many problems in copyright law involve fiction, we will stress situations in which the plaintiff attempts to protect his or her efforts that have produced material in the nonfiction sector.

A. THE NATURE OF COPYRIGHT

1. COPYRIGHT PROTECTION

The laws of copyright are among the most obvious but least condemned restraints on freedom of expression. Article I, § 8, of the Constitution of the United States gives Congress the power "to promote the progress of science and useful arts by securing for limited times to authors and inventors the exclusive right to their respective writings and discoveries . . . ." The very first Congress utilized that authority to adopt copyright legislation and it has been with us in some form ever since.

The origins of copyright are interwoven with the licensing procedures we discussed in Chapter II. One technique for controlling the printing press was to organize printers into a group that became known as the Stationers Company. The Crown granted to that company a monopoly of all printing, with the power to seek out and suppress material published by non-members who violated the monopoly. The Crown's goal was to thwart seditious libel and other objectionable material. The printers, for their part, seized on the monopoly situation to control reproduction of whatever they printed. The result was the licensed printers' right to control copies based on the censorship of the 16th and 17th centuries. When licensing was discontinued in 1695, the rights of the printers were undermined. They petitioned Parliament to adopt protections resembling what they had under the licensing schemes. In 1709 Parliament responded with the Statute of Anne, which has set the pattern for copyright legislation both in England and in this country. The Stationers Company remained but its new role was to register printed material, which would serve to protect that material against unauthorized copying.

The first Congress adopted a similar procedure: printed matter could be protected by filing a copy with the newly established copyright office, headed by the "Register of Copyrights." The types of writings protected and the period of protection have been expanded since the 1790 statute, which protected only books, maps and charts for a period of 14 years plus renewal for a second 14-year term.

In 1976, the copyright statute enacted in 1909 was replaced with new legislation that preserves the basic philosophical strands of copyright law, including the denial of copyright for federal government documents. Changes have been made in legal technicalities or to accommodate media that emerged after 1909 and did not easily fit within the old framework.[*]

The copyright statute is found in title 17 of the United States Code. Section 102 of the new legislation sets out the basic pattern of protection when it states that copyright protection subsists in "original works of authorship fixed in any tangible medium of expression, now known or later developed, from which they can be perceived, reproduced, or otherwise communicated, either directly or with the aid of a machine or device." The statute lists such categories as literary works, musical works, dramatic works, motion pictures and sound recordings as coming within "works of authorship." The section then states the other side of the coin: "In no case does copyright protection for an original work of authorship extend to any idea, procedure, process, system, method or operation, concept, principle, or discovery, regardless of the form in which it is described, explained, illustrated, or embodied in such work."

This issue arose in a case involving the explosion and crash of the German dirigible Hindenburg in New Jersey in 1937. The plaintiff author developed the theory that a crew member sabotaged the dirigible to please a Communist girlfriend. Plaintiff sued two others whose versions of the disaster developed a similar explanation. Hoehling v. Universal City Studios, Inc., 618 F.2d 972 (2d Cir.), certiorari denied 449 U.S. 841 (1980). The court began its discussion by placing copyright in its broader context:

> A grant of copyright in a published work secures for its author a limited monopoly over the expression it contains. The copyright provides a financial incentive to those who would add to the corpus of existing knowledge by creating original works. Nevertheless, the protection afforded the copyright holder has never extended to history, be it documented fact or explanatory hypothesis. The rationale for this doctrine is that the cause of knowledge is best served when history is the common property of all, and each generation remains free to draw upon the discoveries and insights of the past. Accordingly, the scope of copyright in historical accounts is narrow indeed, embracing no more than the author's original expression of particular facts and

---

[*] Under the 1909 statute, published works were protected by federal law while unpublished works were protected under state law. Under the new legislation, all protection is to be found in a single national framework. Perhaps the most vigorous political controversy concerned the relationship between broadcasters and cable television will be discussed in Chapter XVII.

theories already in the public domain. As the case before us illustrates, absent wholesale usurpation of another's expression, claims of copyright infringement where works of history are at issue are rarely successful.

The court asserted that although plaintiff had a valid copyright on his book, to prove "infringement" he had to prove that defendants had "improperly appropriated" his "expression." Although plaintiff admitted that his idea was not copyrightable he correctly argued that "his 'expression' of *his* idea is copyrightable." The court analyzed that claim as follows:

> He relies on Learned Hand's opinion in [Sheldon v. Metro-Goldwyn Pictures Corp., 81 F.2d 49 (2d Cir.), certiorari denied 298 U.S. 669, (1936)] holding that *Letty Lynton* infringed *Dishonored Lady* by copying its story of a woman who poisons her lover, and Augustus Hand's analysis in Detective Comics, Inc. v. Bruns Publications, Inc., 111 F.2d 432 (2d Cir.1940), concluding that the exploits of "Wonderman" infringed the copyright held by the creators of "Superman," the original indestructible man. Moreover, Hoehling asserts that, in both these cases, the line between "ideas" and "expression" is drawn, in the first instance, by the fact finder.

> *Sheldon* and *Detective Comics*, however, dealt with works of fiction, where the distinction between an idea and its expression is especially elusive. But, where, as here, the idea at issue is an interpretation of an historical event, our cases hold that such interpretations are not copyrightable as a matter of law. In Rosemont Enterprises, Inc. v. Random House, Inc., 366 F.2d 303 (2d Cir.1966), cert. denied, 385 U.S. 1009 (1967), we held that the defendant's biography of Howard Hughes did not infringe an earlier biography of the reclusive alleged billionaire. Although the plots of the two works were necessarily similar, there could be no infringement because of the "public benefit in encouraging the development of historical and biographical works and their public distribution." Id. at 307; accord, Oxford Book Co. v. College Entrance Book Co., 98 F.2d 688 (2d Cir.1938). To avoid a chilling effect on authors who contemplate tackling an historical issue or event, broad latitude must be granted to subsequent authors who make use of historical subject matter, including theories or plots. Learned Hand counseled in Myers v. Mail & Express Co., 36 C.O.Bull. 478, 479 (S.D.N.Y.1919), "[t]here cannot be any such thing as copyright in the order of presentation of the facts, nor, indeed, in their selection."

The court went further, however, and asserted that even some fictitious episodes may not be protectible:

> The remainder of Hoehling's claimed similarities relate to random duplications of phrases and sequences of events. For

example, all three works contain a scene in a German beer hall, in which the airship's crew engages in revelry prior to the voyage. Other claimed similarities concern common German greetings of the period, such as "Heil Hitler," or songs, such as the German National anthem. These elements, however, are merely *scenes a faire*, that is, "incidents, characters or settings which are as a practical matter indispensable, or at least standard, in the treatment of a given topic." [ ] Because it is virtually impossible to write about a particular historical era or fictional theme without employing certain "stock" or standard literary devices, we have held that *scenes a faire* are not copyrightable as a matter of law. See Reyher v. Children's Television Workshop, 533 F.2d 87, 91 (2d Cir.), cert. denied, 429 U.S. 980 (1976).

Finally, the court brought these several aspects of the case together and recognized that breaking the copyrighted work up into many little parts created a new danger:

All of Hoehling's allegations of copying, therefore, encompass material that is non-copyrightable as a matter of law, rendering summary judgment entirely appropriate. We are aware, however, that in distinguishing between themes, facts, and *scenes a faire* on the one hand, and copyrightable expression on the other, courts may lose sight of the forest for the trees. By factoring out similarities based on non-copyrightable elements, a court runs the risk of overlooking wholesale usurpation of a prior author's expression. A verbatim reproduction of another work, of course, even in the realm of nonfiction, is actionable as copyright infringement. See Wainwright Securities, Inc. v. Wall Street Transcript Corp., 558 F.2d 91 (2d Cir. 1977), cert. denied, 434 U.S. 1014 (1978). Thus, in granting or reviewing a grant of summary judgment for defendants, courts should assure themselves that the works before them are not virtually identical. In this case, it is clear that all three authors relate the story of the Hindenburg differently.

In works devoted to historical subjects, it is our view that a second author may make significant use of prior work, so long as he does not bodily appropriate the expression of another. *Rosemont Enterprises, Inc.,* supra, 366 F.2d at 310. This principle is justified by the fundamental policy undergirding the copyright laws—the encouragement of contributions to recorded knowledge. The "financial reward guaranteed to the copyright holder is but an incident of this general objective, rather than an end in itself." Berlin v. E.C. Publications, Inc., 329 F.2d 541, 543–44 (2d Cir.), cert. denied, 379 U.S. 822 (1964). Knowledge is expanded as well by granting new authors of historical works a relatively free hand to build upon the work of their predecessors.

2. OWNERSHIP

The authors of a work are the initial copyright owners unless the work is a "work made for hire." This is defined as:

(1) a work prepared by an employee within the scope of his or her employment; or

(2) a work specially ordered or commissioned for use as a contribution to a collective work, as a part of a motion picture or other audiovisual work, as a translation, as a supplementary work, as a compilation, as an instructional text, as a test, as answer material for a test, or as an atlas, if the parties expressly agree in a written instrument signed by them that the work shall be considered a work made for hire.

In the case of a "work made for hire" the original ownership belongs to the employer or person who commissioned the work. As is the case with any property right, ownership of a copyright can be left to the owner's heirs or sold.

3. DURATION

Under the 1909 Act copyright protection lasted for 28 years with the opportunity for one 28-year renewal. Under the 1976 Act it lasts for the life of the author plus 50 years. With joint authors it is 50 years from the last surviving author's death. Anonymous and pseudonymous works are protected for 75 years from publication or 100 years from creation, whichever comes first.

4. STATUTORY FORMALITIES

Under the Copyright Act of 1976, any work is protected as soon as it is "fixed in a tangible medium." However, to retain this protection certain statutory formalities must be observed. Every copy must carry notice consisting of the word copyright, copr. or ©️ plus the name of the copyright proprietor. A printed literary, musical or dramatic work, must also have the year of first publication. With maps, works of art, reproductions of works of art, drawings or plastic works of a scientific or technical character, photographs and prints or pictures, notice may consist of ©️ plus the initials, monogram, mark or symbol of proprietor.

Under the 1909 Act failure to follow the notice procedure exactly resulted in the loss of copyright protection. Under the 1976 Act omission or error in placing the notice no longer results in automatic forfeiture of the copyright. It can, however, limit the author's remedies in the event of infringement.

The other requirement for obtaining full copyright protection is to register the work with the Register of Copyrights. Registration is a prerequisite for filing a copyright infringement suit and involves filling out a form, paying a small fee and providing a few copies of the work.

5. NATURE OF COPYRIGHT PROTECTION

Section 106 states the nature of the protection extended to the copyright owner:

> Subject to sections 107 through 118, the owner of copyright under this title has the exclusive right to do and to authorize any of the following:
>
> (1) to reproduce the copyrighted work in copies or phonorecords;
>
> (2) to prepare derivative works based upon the copyrighted work;
>
> (3) to distribute copies or phonorecords of the copyrighted work to the public by sale or other transfer of ownership, or by rental, lease, or lending;
>
> (4) in the case of literary, musical, dramatic, and choreographic works, pantomimes, and motion pictures and other audiovisual works, to perform the copyrighted work publicly; and
>
> (5) in the case of literary, musical, dramatic, and choreographic works, pantomimes, and pictorial, graphic, or sculptural works, including the individual images of a motion picture or other audiovisual work, to display the copyrighted work publicly.

6. REMEDIES

The Copyright Act of 1976 provides numerous remedies for copyright infringement. Sections 502–503 provide for an injunction against further infringement as well as destruction of all existing infringing materials. Under § 504, the copyright owner may elect to receive either the damages actually suffered plus any additional profits of the infringer or statutory damages of not less than $250 or more than $10,000. The court may also at its discretion award costs and attorney's fees.

In the case of willful infringement for commercial advantage or private financial gain, criminal sanctions are also available. Section 506 provides for fines of up to $50,000 and imprisonment for up to 2 years, depending on the type of work infringed and the prior record of the defendant.

7. DEFENSES

Independent Creation. Copyright protection extends only to copying the work in question. If someone independently creates a similar work, there is no copyright infringement. Thus, in any copyright suit the plaintiff must show that the defendant had access to the plaintiff's work. However, as former Beatle George Harrison learned, plaintiff does not have to prove that defendant intentionally or even consciously copied it. Bright Tunes Music Corp. v. Harrisongs Music, Ltd., 420 F.Supp. 177 (S.D.N.Y.1976).

Fair Use. As noted, the grant of rights to the owner of the copyright is conditioned on a series of limitations expressed in §§ 107–118. These include permitting libraries to make one photocopy of an article and permitting persons to make phonograph records of music without permission upon payment of certain royalties. Section 111 deals with the cable television problem. Probably the most important of these limitations is found in § 107, dealing with the problem of fair use. Until the 1976 statute, the problem of fair use had been left to develop as a judicially created exception to the rights of the copyright owner. There was great controversy over whether to recognize the defense explicitly and, if so, how to do it. The result is § 107:

> Notwithstanding the provisions of section 106, the fair use of a copyrighted work, including such use by reproduction in copies or phonorecords or by any other means specified by that section, for purposes such as criticism, comment, news reporting, teaching (including multiple copies for classroom use), scholarship, or research, is not an infringement of copyright. In determining whether the use made of a work in any particular case is a fair use the factors to be considered shall include—
>
> > (1) the purpose and character of the use, including whether such use is of a commercial nature or is for nonprofit educational purposes;
> >
> > (2) the nature of the copyrighted work;
> >
> > (3) the amount and substantiality of the portion used in relation to the copyrighted work as a whole; and
> >
> > (4) the effect of the use upon the potential market for or value of the copyrighted work.

Most observers have concluded that the statute does not change the previous approach to fair use. A sampling of recent fair use cases follows.

a. Plaintiff specialized in preparing copyrighted "in-depth analytical reports on approximately 275 industrial, financial, utility and railroad corporations." The reports, up to 40 pages long and involving months of an analyst's time, were used by 900 clients of plaintiff, including banks, insurance companies and mutual funds. Defendant, a weekly financial newspaper, featured a column called "Wall Street Roundup" that consisted almost exclusively of abstracts of institutional research reports. Defendant's advertising promised readers "a fast-reading, pinpointed account of heavyweight reports from the top institutional research firms."

Plaintiff sued for infringement and sought a preliminary injunction. The trial judge granted it and was upheld on appeal. Defendant argued that it was simply covering the financial news. The court disagreed. Although a news event cannot be copyrighted, the expression used by the author may be protected. Here, defendant was found to have copied the manner of expression used by plaintiff's analysts. The court noted that, unlike traditional news coverage, defendant provided no independent analysis or research; it carried no industry comments on the reports and included no criticism or praise of the reports. "Rather, the Transcript appropriated almost verbatim the most creative and original aspects of the reports, the financial analyses and predictions, which represent a substantial investment of time, money and labor." Wainwright Securities, Inc., v. Wall Street Transcript Corp., 558 F.2d 91 (2d Cir.1977), certiorari denied 434 U.S. 1014 (1978).

b.　Defendant wrote a book about Julius and Ethel Rosenberg: their trial, conviction, and execution for conspiring to transmit national defense information to the Soviet Union. The book quoted verbatim from 28 copyrighted letters written by the Rosenbergs while in prison—a total of 1,957 words. The plaintiffs, sons of the Rosenbergs, claimed the copyright in the letters, which had been published as the book "Death House Letters." The trial judge dismissed the claim but was reversed on appeal.

The court noted that although the letters represented less than one percent of the defendant's book, they were featured prominently in promotional literature for the book. Several questions of fact had to be resolved before the fair use question could be answered: the purpose for which the letters were used in the defendant's book, the need for verbatim copying of the letters; and the effect of their use on the future market for Death House Letters. The fact that Death House Letters had been out of print for 20 years did not necessarily mean that the letters had no future market. The possibilities of republication, and sale of motion picture rights, might have been affected by their use in defendant's book. Meeropol v. Nizer, 560 F.2d 1061 (2d Cir.1977), certiorari denied 434 U.S. 1013 (1978).

c.　When an undisclosed source gave Victor Navasky, editor of *The Nation*, an unauthorized copy of Former President Ford's memoirs, Navasky prepared an article comprised of quotations from and paraphrases of the manuscript. The article was published in *The Nation* prior to the book publication of President Ford's memoirs by Harper & Row. As a direct result of *The Nation* article, an agreement between Harper & Row and *Time* magazine selling *Time* certain prepublication rights was cancelled. *The Nation's* fair use defense was rejected by the trial court. On appeal the Second Circuit Court of Appeals reversed 2–1. Relying on the fact that much of what was discussed in the article was historical fact, the majority concluded that only a small portion of the article constituted copyrightable material.

> Where information concerning important matters of state is accompanied by a minimal borrowing of expression, the economic impact of which is dubious at best, the copyright holder's monopoly must not be permitted to prevail over a journalist's communication. To decide otherwise would be to ignore those values of free expression which have traditionally been accommodated by the statute's "fair use" provisions. [ ] We conclude, accordingly, that there was a "fair use" of copyrighted material in this case.

Judge Meskill's dissent argued that the majority was mistaken in characterizing much of the material taken as uncopyrightable.

> The majority is correct in suggesting that the fair use doctrine is used to reconcile competing claims of freedom of the press and ownership of intellectual labor. But the result reached by [the trial court] does not "threaten press freedom or obstruct the citizens' access to vital facts and historical observations about the nation's life." The publication of the book itself and the other authorized uses of the copyrighted material would only chill chiseling for personal profit.

Harper & Row v. Nation Enterprises, 723 F.2d 195 (2d Cir.1983). The Supreme Court has granted certiorari.

d. In 1977, after an arrest in the famous "Son of Sam" murder case, five strips of "Doonesbury" were devoted to commentary on the way a columnist for the *New York Daily News* behaved during the search for the killer. The *News*, which held the New York City rights to the strip, decided not to use the five strips. The *New York Post* reported the action of the *News* and, since "censorship is news," the *Post* reprinted the five deleted strips to show its readers what the *News* had refused to carry. No suit resulted. Might the copyright owner have successfully sued the *Post*?

e. When a network televised a parade during which music copyrighted by plaintiff was being played, the court held that the fair use doctrine protected the network. Italian Book Corp. v. American Broadcasting Companies, Inc., 458 F.Supp. 65 (S.D.N.Y.1978).

The traditional view has been that if the defendant has extensively copied plaintiff's expression and cannot rely on the defense of fair use, the plaintiff would succeed in the infringement action. But some situations may exist in which, although the defendant's use of the copyrighted material cannot be justified as "fair use," the public's need to have the information is so great that *perhaps* the First Amendment would serve as a defense to an infringement action. Although such a situation would be rare because one can always use the facts and simply alter the form of expression, there may be situations in which the form of presentation cannot be paraphrased with the same effect as the original presentation.

The best examples of such a case may be photographs, such as the Zapruder photographs of the John Kennedy assassination or the photographs of the MyLai massacre in Vietnam. The best evidence for the public to have in debating the assassination or the massacre may be all of the actual photographs rather than another's attempted verbal description of what the photographs purport to show—even though the copier, by using all the photographs, exceeds the bounds of fair use. This problem may be unique to the visual representations. The subject is well discussed, using these examples, in Nimmer, Does Copyright Abridge the First Amendment Guarantees of Free Speech and Press?, 17 U.C.L.A.L.Rev. 1180 (1970).

Another important question—one requiring a balancing of property rights and First Amendment rights—is to what extent a news organization can make unauthorized use of the research and labor of a competitor by either directly copying the work of its competitor or by "appropriating" the facts contained in a competitor's news release. Although the substance of news cannot be protected by copyright, the doctrine of unfair competition has been used to protect the gatherer of news from the direct, unauthorized reproduction of its material for commercial use. In International News Service v. Associated Press, 248 U.S. 215 (1918), I.N.S. was enjoined from copying news from A.P. bulletin boards and early editions of A.P. member newspapers until "the commercial value" of the news to the complainant and all of its members had passed. The Court found unfair competition in the taking of material acquired through the expenditure of skill, labor, and money by A.P. for the purpose of diverting "a material portion of the profit" to I.N.S. Although the Court condemned the "habitual failure" of I.N.S. to give credit to A.P. as the source of its news, the misrepresentation was not considered essential to a finding of unfair competition: "It is something more than the advantage of celebrity of which complainant is being deprived."

This type of protection has been extended to other areas. Radio stations may not broadcast news items taken verbatim from a local newspaper, and a second publisher may not photograph an existing edition of a book in order to save the cost of setting type, whether or not the first edition was copyrighted. Where words and ideas are involved, the courts have been quite protective of the initiator, perhaps because of the fragile and ephemeral nature of the finished product.

The doctrine does not inhibit the traditional practice of getting "tips" or "leads" from any source and then going out to research and write the story. The courts in the A.P. case barred only the taking of news "either bodily or in substance, from bulletins issued by [AP] or any of its members, or from editions of their newspapers, 'until its commercial value as news to the complainant and all its members has passed away.' " The Supreme Court drew a distinction "between the utilization of tips and the bodily appropriation of news matter, either in its original form or after rewriting and without independent investigation and verification . . . ." See Sullivan, News Piracy: An Interpretation of the Misappropriation Doctrine, 54 Journ.Q. 682 (1977).

B. PROBLEMS OF NEW TECHNOLOGIES

Perhaps the biggest problem Congress faced in drafting the Copyright Act of 1976 was providing for new technologies. As a result the courts are now having to answer difficult questions concerning the application of copyright law to these new technologies. The following is a perfect example.

SONY CORP. v. UNIVERSAL CITY STUDIOS

Supreme Court of the United States, 1984.
464 U.S. 417, 104 S.Ct. 774, 78 L.Ed.2d 574.

JUSTICE STEVENS delivered the opinion of the Court.

Petitioners manufacture and sell home video tape recorders. Respondents own the copyrights on some of the television programs that are broadcast on the public airwaves. Some members of the general public use video tape recorders sold by petitioners to record some of these broadcasts, as well as a large number of other broadcasts. The question presented is whether the sale of petitioners' copying equipment to the general public violates any of the rights conferred upon respondents by the Copyright Act.

Respondents commenced this copyright infringement action against petitioners in the United States District Court for the Central District of California in 1976. Respondents alleged that some individuals had used Betamax video tape recorders (VTR's) to record some of respondents' copyrighted works which had been exhibited on commercially sponsored television and contended that these individuals had thereby infringed respondents' copyrights. Respondents further maintained that petitioners were liable for the copyright infringement allegedly committed by Betamax consumers because of petitioners' marketing of the Betamax VTR's. Respondents sought no relief against any Betamax consumer. Instead, they sought money damages and an equitable accounting of profits from petitioners, as well as an injunction against the manufacture and marketing of Betamax VTR's.

. . .

An explanation of our rejection of respondents' unprecedented attempt to impose copyright liability upon the distributors of copying equipment requires a quite detailed recitation of the findings of the District Court. In summary, those findings reveal that the average member of the public uses a VTR principally to record a program he cannot view as it is being televised and then to watch it once at a later time. This practice, known as "time-shifting," enlarges the television viewing audience. For that reason, a significant amount of television programming may be used in this manner without objection from the owners of the copyrights on the programs. For the same reason, even the two respondents in this case, who do assert objections to time-shifting in this litigation, were unable to prove that the practice has impaired the commercial value of their copyrights or has created any likelihood of future harm. Given these findings, there is no basis in the Copyright Act upon which respondents can hold petitioners liable for distributing VTR's to the general public. The Court of Appeals' holding that respondents are entitled to enjoin the distribution of VTR's, to collect royalties on the sale of such equipment, or to obtain other relief, if affirmed, would enlarge the scope of respondents' statutory monopolies to encompass control over an article of commerce that is not the subject of copyright protection. Such an expansion of the copyright privilege is beyond the limits of the grants authorized by Congress.

.   .   .

II

Article I, Sec. 8 of the Constitution provides that:

"The Congress shall have Power .   . to Promote the Progress of Science and useful Arts, by securing for limited Times to Authors and Inventors the exclusive Right to their respective Writings and Discoveries."

The monopoly privileges that Congress may authorize are neither unlimited nor primarily designed to provide a special private benefit. Rather, the limited grant is a means by which an important public purpose may be achieved. It is intended to motivate the creative activity of authors and inventors by the provision of a special reward, and to allow the public access to the products of their genius after the limited period of exclusive control has expired.

"The copyright law, like the patent statute, makes reward to the owner a secondary consideration. In Fox Film Corp. v. Doyal, 286 U.S. 123, 127, Chief Justice Hughes spoke as follows respecting the copyright monopoly granted by Congress. 'The sole interest of the United States and the primary object in conferring the monopoly lie in the general benefits derived by the public from the labors of authors.' It is said that reward to the author or artist serves to induce release to the public of the products of his creative genius." [ ]

As the text of the Constitution makes plain, it is Congress that has been assigned the task of defining the scope of the limited monopoly that should be granted to authors or to inventors in order to give the public appropriate access to their work product. Because this task involves a difficult balance between the interests of authors and inventors in the control and exploitation of their writings and discoveries on the one hand, and society's competing interest in the free flow of ideas, information, and commerce on the other hand, our patent and copyright statutes have been amended repeatedly.

From its beginning, the law of copyright has developed in response to significant changes in technology. Indeed, it was the invention of a new form of copying equipment—the printing press—that gave rise to the original need for copyright protection. Repeatedly, as new developments have occurred in this country, it has been the Congress that has fashioned the new rules that new technology made necessary. Thus, long before the enactment of the Copyright Act of 1909, 35 Stat. 1075, it was settled that the protection given to copyrights is wholly statutory. [ ] The remedies for infringement "are only those prescribed by Congress." [ ]

The judiciary's reluctance to expand the protections afforded by the copyright without explicit legislative guidance is a recurring theme. [ ] Sound policy, as well as history, supports our consistent deference to Congress when major technological innovations alter the market for copyrighted materials. Congress has the constitutional authority and the institutional ability to accommodate fully the varied permutations of competing interests that are inevitably implicated by such new technology.

In a case like this, in which Congress has not plainly marked our course, we must be circumspect in construing the scope of rights created by a legislative enactment which never contemplated such a calculus of interests. In doing so, we are guided by Justice Stewart's exposition of the correct approach to ambiguities in the law of copyright:

> "The limited scope of the copyright holder's statutory monopoly, like the limited copyright duration required by the Constitution, reflects a balance of competing claims upon the public interest: Creative work is to be encouraged and rewarded, but private motivation must ultimately serve the cause of promoting broad public availability of literature, music, and the other arts. The immediate effect of our copyright law is to secure a fair return for an 'author's' creative labor. But the ultimate aim is, by this incentive, to stimulate artistic creativity for the general public good. 'The sole interest of the United States and the primary object in conferring the monopoly,' this Court has said, 'lie in the general benefits derived by the public from the labors of authors.' [ ] When technological change has rendered its literal terms ambiguous, the Copyright Act must be construed in light of this basic purpose." [ ]

. . .

The two respondents in this case do not seek relief against the Betamax users who have allegedly infringed their copyrights. Moreover, this is not a class action on behalf of all copyright owners who license their works for television broadcast, and respondents have no right to invoke whatever rights other copyright holders may have to bring infringement actions based on Betamax copying of their works. As was made clear by their own evidence, the copying of the respondents' programs represents a small portion of the total use of VTR's. It is, however, the taping of respondents own copyrighted programs that provides them with standing to charge Sony with contributory infringement. To prevail, they have the burden of proving that users of the Betamax have infringed their copyrights and that Sony should be held responsible for that infringement.

III

The Copyright Act does not expressly render anyone liable for infringement committed by another. In contrast, the Patent Act expressly brands anyone who "actively induces infringement of a patent" as an infringer, 35 U.S.C. § 271(b), and further imposes liability on certain individuals labeled "contributory" infringers, id., § 271(c). The absence of such express language in the copyright statute does not preclude the imposition of liability for copyright infringements on certain parties who have not themselves engaged in the infringing activity. For vicarious liability is imposed in virtually all areas of the law, and the concept of contributory infringement is merely a species of the broader problem of identifying the circumstances in which it is just to hold one individual accountable for the actions of another.

.   .   .

If vicarious liability is to be imposed on petitioners in this case, it must rest on the fact that they have sold equipment with constructive knowledge of the fact that their customers may use that equipment to make unauthorized copies of copyrighted material. There is no precedent in the law of copyright for the imposition of vicarious liability on such a theory. The closest analogy is provided by the patent law cases to which it is appropriate to refer because of the historic kinship between patent law and copyright law.

In the Patent Code both the concept of infringement and the concept of contributory infringement are expressly defined by statute. The prohibition against contributory infringement is confined to the knowing sale of a component especially made for use in connection with a particular patent. There is no suggestion in the statute that one patentee may object to the sale of a product that might be used in connection with other patents. Moreover, the Act expressly provides that the sale of a "staple article or commodity of commerce suitable for substantial noninfringing use" is not contributory infringement.

When a charge of contributory infringement is predicated entirely on the sale of an article of commerce that is used by the purchaser to infringe a patent, the public interest in access to that article of commerce is necessarily implicated. A finding of contributory infringement does not, of course, remove the article from the market altogether; it does, however, give the patentee effective control over the sale of that item. Indeed, a finding of contributory infringement is normally the functional equivalent of holding that the disputed article is within the monopoly granted to the patentee.

For that reason, in contributory infringement cases arising under the patent laws the Court has always recognized the critical importance of not allowing the patentee to extend his monopoly beyond the limits of his specific grant. These cases deny the patentee any right to control the distribution of unpatented articles unless they are "unsuited for any commercial noninfringing use." [ ]   Unless a commodity "has no use except through practice of the patented method," ibid., the patentee has no right to claim that its distribution constitutes contributory infringement. "To form the basis for contributory infringement the item must almost be uniquely suited as a component of the patented invention." [ ] "[A] sale of an article which though adapted to an infringing use is also adapted to other and lawful uses, is not enough to make the seller a contributory infringer. Such a rule would block the wheels of commerce." [ ]

We recognize there are substantial differences between the patent and copyright laws. But in both areas the contributory infringement doctrine is grounded on the recognition that adequate protection of a monopoly may require the courts to look beyond actual duplication of a device or publication to the products or activities that make such duplication possible. The staple article of commerce doctrine must strike a balance between a copyright holder's legitimate demand for effective—not merely symbolic—protection of the statutory monopoly, and the rights of others freely to engage in substantially unrelated areas of commerce. Accordingly, the sale of copying equipment, like the sale of other articles of commerce, does not constitute contributory infringement if the product is widely used for legitimate, unobjectionable purposes. Indeed, it need merely be capable of substantial noninfringing uses.

IV

The question is thus whether the Betamax is capable of commercially significant noninfringing uses. In order to resolve that question, we need not explore *all* the different potential uses of the machine and determine whether or not they would constitute infringement. Rather, we need only consider whether on the basis of the facts as found by the district court a significant number of them would be non-infringing. Moreover, in order to resolve this case we need not give precise content to the question of how much use is commercially significant. For one potential use of the Betamax plainly satisfies this standard, however it is understood: private, noncommercial time-shifting in the home. It does so both (A) because respondents have no right to prevent other copyright holders from authorizing it for their programs, and (B) because the District Court's factual findings reveal that even the unauthorized home time-shifting of respondents' programs is legitimate fair use.

. . .

The District Court's conclusions are buttressed by the fact that to the extent time-shifting expands public access to freely broadcast television programs, it yields societal benefits. Earlier this year, in Community Television of Southern California v. Gottfried, 459 U.S. 498, [at] n. 12 (1983), we acknowledged the public interest in making television broadcasting more available. Concededly, that interest is not unlimited. But it supports an interpretation of the concept of "fair use" that requires the copyright holder to demonstrate some likelihood of harm before he may condemn a private act of time-shifting as a violation of federal law.

When these factors are all weighed in the "equitable rule of reason" balance, we must conclude that this record amply supports the District Court's conclusion that home time-shifting is fair use. In light of the findings of the District Court regarding the state of the empirical data, it is clear that the Court of Appeals erred in holding that the statute as presently written bars such conduct.

In summary, the record and findings of the District Court lead us to two conclusions. First, Sony demonstrated a significant likelihood that substantial numbers of copyright holders who license their works for broadcast on free television would not object to having their broadcasts time-shifted by private viewers. And second, respondents failed to demonstrate that time-shifting would cause any likelihood of nonminimal harm to the potential market for, or the value of, their copyrighted works. The Betamax is, therefore, capable of substantial noninfringing uses. Sony's sale of such equipment to the general public does not constitute contributory infringement of respondent's copyrights.

V

"The direction of Art. I is that *Congress* shall have the power to promote the progress of science and the useful arts. When, as here, the Constitution is permissive, the sign of how far Congress has chosen to go can come only from Congress." Deepsouth Packing Co. v. Laitram Corp., 406 U.S. 518, 530 (1972).

One may search the Copyright Act in vain for any sign that the elected representatives of the millions of people who watch television every day have made it unlawful to copy a program for later viewing at home, or have enacted a flat prohibition against the sale of machines that make such copying possible.

It may well be that Congress will take a fresh look at this new technology, just as it so often has examined other innovations in the past. But it is not our job to apply laws that have not yet been written. Applying the copyright statute, as it now reads, to the facts as they have been developed in this case, the judgment of the Court of Appeals must be reversed.

[Justice Blackmun dissented in an opinion joined by Justices Marshall, Powell and Rehnquist. He believed that Universal had shown substantial harm to "potential markets for" Universal's copyrighted works and thus, taping of broadcast shows could not be considered a fair use. He argued that the majority had incorrectly focused on existing rather than potential markets.

He would have remanded the case for further proceedings on the issue of contributory infringement. In his view the unanswered question to be addressed was the proportion of VTR recording that constitutes infringement.]

Chapter VI

PROTECTING STATE SECRETS

In this Chapter we consider situations in which the government claims that disclosure of information will compromise or has already compromised an important state interest that requires secrecy. Although these matters are often gathered under the heading of "national security," that term is too narrow because secrecy may be claimed in areas far removed from national security or international relations. For example, the concern may be that identification of an undercover narcotics agent or of an informer will seriously impede or prematurely terminate an investigation into potential criminal offenses. In a different context, a government agency may assert that disclosure of projected freeway routings or land being considered for condemnation will jeopardize the implementation. It seems more appropriate, then, to gather these cases under the broader rubric of "state secrets." Of course, not all state secret claims that impinge on speech are equally powerful. Claims of serious danger to national security may receive greater consideration than the claim that an investigation of a misdemeanor has been thwarted by the identification of one government agent.

Disclosure of state secrets may occur apart from a property interest. Public disclosure by the press of a document from the foreign affairs ministry of another country might have implications for this country's national security or might seriously interfere with the conduct of foreign relations. Although the case would not involve government property, it would deal with an allegedly substantial harm to the national interest. Is such a concern beyond the reach of government sanction?

A. NATIONAL SECURITY AND INJUNCTIONS

NEW YORK TIMES CO. v. UNITED STATES

Supreme Court of the United States, 1971.
403 U.S. 713, 91 S.Ct. 2140, 29 L.Ed.2d 822.

PER CURIAM.

We granted certiorari in these cases in which the United States seeks to enjoin the New York Times and the Washington Post from publishing the contents of a classified study entitled "History of U.S. Decision-Making Process on Viet Nam Policy." [ ]

"Any system of prior restraints of expression comes to this Court bearing a heavy presumption against its constitutional validity." Bantam Books, Inc. v. Sullivan, 372 U.S. 58, 70 (1963); see also Near v. Minnesota, 283 U.S. 697 (1931). The Government "thus carries a heavy burden of showing justification for the imposition of

195

such a restraint." Organization for a Better Austin v. Keefe, 402 U.S. 415, 419 (1971). The District Court for the Southern District of New York in the *New York Times* case and the District Court for the District of Columbia and the Court of Appeals for the District of Columbia Circuit in the *Washington Post* case held that the Government had not met that burden. We agree.

The judgment of the Court of Appeals for the District of Columbia Circuit is therefore affirmed. The order of the Court of Appeals for the Second Circuit is reversed and the case is remanded with directions to enter a judgment affirming the judgment of the District Court for the Southern District of New York. The stays entered June 25, 1971, by the Court are vacated. The judgments shall issue forthwith.

So ordered.

MR. JUSTICE BLACK, with whom MR. JUSTICE DOUGLAS joins, concurring.

I adhere to the view that the Government's case against the Washington Post should have been dismissed and that the injunction against the New York Times should have been vacated without oral argument when the cases were first presented to this Court. I believe that every moment's continuance of the injunctions against these newspapers amounts to a flagrant, indefensible, and continuing violation of the First Amendment. Furthermore, after oral argument, I agree completely that we must affirm the judgment of the Court of Appeals for the District of Columbia Circuit and reverse the judgment of the Court of Appeals for the Second Circuit for the reasons stated by my Brothers Douglas and Brennan. In my view it is unfortunate that some of my Brethren are apparently willing to hold that the publication of news may sometimes be enjoined. Such a holding would make a shambles of the First Amendment.

. . .

In other words, we are asked to hold that despite the First Amendment's emphatic command, the Executive Branch, the Congress, and the Judiciary can make laws enjoining publication of current news and abridging freedom of the press in the name of "national security." The Government does not even attempt to rely on any act of Congress. Instead it makes the bold and dangerously far-reaching contention that the courts should take it upon themselves to "make" a law abridging freedom of the press in the name of equity, presidential power and national security, even when the representatives of the people in Congress have adhered to the command of the First Amendment and refused to make such a law. . . . To find that the President has "inherent power" to halt the publication of news by resort to the courts would wipe out the First Amendment and destroy the fundamental liberty and security of the very people the Government hopes to make "secure." No one can read the history of the adoption of the First Amendment without being convinced beyond any doubt that it was injunctions like those sought here that Madison and his collaborators intended to outlaw in this Nation for all time.

The word "security" is a broad, vague generality whose contours should not be invoked to abrogate the fundamental law embodied in the First Amendment.   The guarding of military and diplomatic secrets at the expense of informed representative government provides no real security for our Republic.   The Framers of the First Amendment, fully aware of both the need to defend a new nation and the abuses of the English and Colonial governments, sought to give this new society strength and security by providing that freedom of speech, press, religion, and assembly should not be abridged. . . .

Mr. Justice Douglas, with whom Mr. Justice Black joins, concurring.

While I join the opinion of the Court I believe it necessary to express my views more fully.

It should be noted at the outset that the First Amendment provides that "Congress shall make no law . . . abridging the freedom of speech, or of the press."   That leaves, in my view, no room for governmental restraint on the press.

There is, moreover, no statute barring the publication by the press of the material which the Times and the Post seek to use.   Title 18 U.S.C. § 793(e) provides that "[w]hoever having unauthorized possession of, access to, or control over any document, writing . . . or information relating to the national defense which information the possessor has reason to believe could be used to the injury of the United States or to the advantage of any foreign nation, willfully communicates . . . the same to any person not entitled to receive it . . . [s]hall be fined not more than $10,000 or imprisoned not more than ten years, or both."

The Government suggests that the word "communicates" is broad enough to encompass publication.

There are eight sections in the chapter on espionage and censorship, §§ 792–799.   In three of those eight "publish" is specifically mentioned: § 794(b) applies to "Whoever, in time of war, with intent that the same shall be communicated to the enemy, collects, records, *publishes*, or communicates . . . [the disposition of armed forces]."

Section 797 applies to whoever "reproduces, *publishes*, sells, or gives away" photographs of defense installations.

Section 798 relating to cryptography applies to whoever: "communicates, furnishes, transmits, or otherwise makes available . . . or *publishes*" the described material.   (Emphasis added.)

Thus it is apparent that Congress was capable of and did distinguish between publishing and communication in the various sections of the Espionage Act.

. . .

So any power that the Government possesses must come from its "inherent power."

The power to wage war is "the power to wage war successfully." See Hirabayashi v. United States, 320 U.S. 81, 93 (1943). But the war power stems from a declaration of war. The Constitution by Art. I, § 8, gives Congress, not the President, power "[t]o declare War." Nowhere are presidential wars authorized. We need not decide therefore what leveling effect the war power of Congress might have.

These disclosures [3] may have a serious impact. But that is no basis for sanctioning a previous restraint on the press. . . .

  . . .

The Government says that it has inherent powers to go into court and obtain an injunction to protect the national interest, which in this case is alleged to be national security. Near v. Minnesota, [ ], repudiated that expansive doctrine in no uncertain terms.

The dominant purpose of the First Amendment was to prohibit the widespread practice of governmental suppression of embarrassing information. It is common knowledge that the First Amendment was adopted against the widespread use of the common law of seditious libel to punish the dissemination of material that is embarrassing to the powers-that-be. [ ] The present cases will, I think, go down in history as the most dramatic illustration of that principle. A debate of large proportions goes on in the Nation over our posture in Vietnam. That debate antedated the disclosure of the contents of the present documents. The latter are highly relevant to the debate in progress.

Secrecy in government is fundamentally anti-democratic, perpetuating bureaucratic errors. Open debate and discussion of public issues are vital to our national health. On public questions there should be "uninhibited, robust, and wide-open" debate. [ ]

  . . .

MR. JUSTICE BRENNAN, concurring.

  . . .

The error that has pervaded these cases from the outset was the granting of any injunctive relief whatsoever, interim or otherwise. The entire thrust of the Government's claim throughout these cases has been that publication of the material sought to be enjoined "could," or "might," or "may" prejudice the national interest in various ways. But the First Amendment tolerates absolutely no prior judicial restraints of the press predicated upon surmise or

---

3. There are numerous sets of this material in existence and they apparently are not under any controlled custody. Moreover, the President has sent a set to the Congress. We start then with a case where there already is rather wide distribution of the material that is destined for publicity, not secrecy. I have gone over the material listed in the *in camera* brief of the United States. It is all history, not future events. None of it is more recent than 1968.

conjecture that untoward consequences may result.* Our cases, it is true, have indicated that there is a single, extremely narrow class of cases in which the First Amendment's ban on prior judicial restraint may be overridden. Our cases have thus far indicated that such cases may arise only when the Nation "is at war," Schenck v. United States, [ ], during which times "[n]o one would question but that a government might prevent actual obstruction to its recruiting service or the publication of the sailing dates of transports or the number and location of troops." Near v. Minnesota, [ ]. Even if the present world situation were assumed to be tantamount to a time of war, or if the power of presently available armaments would justify even in peacetime the suppression of information that would set in motion a nuclear holocaust, in neither of these actions has the Government presented or even alleged that publication of items from or based upon the material at issue would cause the happening of an event of that nature. . . .

MR. JUSTICE STEWART, with whom MR. JUSTICE WHITE joins, concurring.

. . .

In the absence of the governmental checks and balances present in other areas of our national life, the only effective restraint upon executive policy and power in the areas of national defense and international affairs may lie in an enlightened citizenry—in an informed and critical public opinion which alone can here protect the values of democratic government. For this reason it is perhaps here that a press that is alert, aware, and free most vitally serves the basic purpose of the First Amendment. For without an informed and free press there cannot be an enlightened people.

Yet it is elementary that the successful conduct of international diplomacy and the maintenance of an effective national defense require both confidentiality and secrecy. . . .

I think there can be but one answer to this dilemma, if dilemma it be. The responsibility must be where the power is. If the Constitution gives the Executive a large degree of unshared power in the conduct of foreign affairs and the maintenance of our national defense, then under the Constitution the Executive must have the largely unshared duty to determine and preserve the degree of internal security necessary to exercise that power successfully. . . .

* Freedman v. Maryland, 380 U.S. 51 (1965), and similar cases regarding temporary restraints of allegedly obscene materials are not in point. For those cases rest upon the proposition that "obscenity is not protected by the freedoms of speech and press." Roth v. United States, 354 U.S. 476, 481 (1957). Here there is no question but that the material sought to be suppressed is within the protection of the First Amendment; the only question is whether, notwithstanding that fact, its publication may be enjoined for a time because of the presence of an overwhelming national interest. . . .

This is not to say that Congress and the courts have no role to play. Undoubtedly Congress has the power to enact specific and appropriate criminal laws to protect government property and preserve government secrets. Congress has passed such laws, and several of them are of very colorable relevance to the apparent circumstances of these cases. And if a criminal prosecution is instituted, it will be the responsibility of the courts to decide the applicability of the criminal law under which the charge is brought. Moreover, if Congress should pass a specific law authorizing civil proceedings in this field, the courts would likewise have the duty to decide the constitutionality of such a law as well as its applicability to the facts proved.

But in the cases before us we are asked neither to construe specific regulations nor to apply specific laws. We are asked, instead, to perform a function that the Constitution gave to the Executive, not the Judiciary. We are asked, quite simply, to prevent the publication by two newspapers of material that the Executive Branch insists should not, in the national interest, be published. I am convinced that the Executive is correct with respect to some of the documents involved. But I cannot say that disclosure of any of them will surely result in direct, immediate, and irreparable damage to our Nation or its people. That being so, there can under the First Amendment be but one judicial resolution of the issues before us. I join the judgments of the Court.

MR. JUSTICE WHITE, with whom MR. JUSTICE STEWART joins, concurring.

I concur in today's judgments, but only because of the concededly extraordinary protection against prior restraints enjoyed by the press under our constitutional system. I do not say that in no circumstances would the First Amendment permit an injunction against publishing information about government plans or operations.[1] Nor, after examining the materials the Government charac-

---

1. The Congress has authorized a strain of prior restraints against private parties in certain instances. The National Labor Relations Board routinely issues cease-and-desist orders against employers who it finds have threatened or coerced employees in the exercise of protected rights. See 29 U.S.C. § 160(c). Similarly, the Federal Trade Commission is empowered to impose cease-and-desist orders against unfair methods of competition. 15 U.S.C. § 45(b). Such orders can, and quite often do, restrict what may be spoken or written under certain circumstances. See, e.g., NLRB v. Gissel Packing Co., 395 U.S. 575, 616–620 (1969). Article I, § 8, of the Constitution authorizes Congress to secure the "exclusive right" of authors to their writings, and no one denies that a newspaper can properly be enjoined from publishing the copyrighted works of another. See Westermann Co. v. Dispatch Printing Co., 249 U.S. 100 (1919). Newspapers do themselves rely from time to time on the copyright as a means of protecting their accounts of important events. However, those enjoined under the statutes relating to the National Labor Relations Board and the Federal Trade Commission are private parties, not the press; and when the press is enjoined under the copyright laws the complainant is a private copyright holder enforcing a private right. These situations are quite distinct from the Government's request for an injunction against publishing information about the affairs of government, a request admittedly not based on any statute.

terizes as the most sensitive and destructive, can I deny that revelation of these documents will do substantial damage to public interests. Indeed, I am confident that their disclosure will have that result. But I nevertheless agree that the United States has not satisfied the very heavy burden that it must meet to warrant an injunction against publication in these cases, at least in the absence of express and appropriately limited congressional authorization for prior restraints in circumstances such as these.

. . .

At least in the absence of legislation by Congress, based on its own investigations and findings, I am quite unable to agree that the inherent powers of the Executive and the courts reach so far as to authorize remedies having such sweeping potential for inhibiting publications by the press. Much of the difficulty inheres in the "grave and irreparable danger" standard suggested by the United States. If the United States were to have judgment under such a standard in these cases, our decision would be of little guidance to other courts in other cases, for the material at issue here would not be available from the Court's opinion or from public records, nor would it be published by the press. . . .

It is not easy to reject the proposition urged by the United States and to deny relief on its good-faith claims in these cases that publication will work serious damage to the country. But that discomfiture is considerably dispelled by the infrequency of prior-restraint cases. Normally, publication will occur and the damage be done before the Government has either opportunity or grounds for suppression. So here, publication has already begun and a substantial part of the threatened damage has already occurred. The fact of a massive breakdown in security is known, access to the documents by many unauthorized people is undeniable, and the efficacy of equitable relief against these or other newspapers to avert anticipated damage is doubtful at best.

. . .

The Criminal Code contains numerous provisions potentially relevant to these cases. Section 797 [5] makes it a crime to publish certain photographs of drawings of military installations. Section 798,[6] also

---

5. Title 18 U.S.C. § 797 provides:

"On and after thirty days from the date upon which the President defines any vital military or naval installation or equipment as being within the category contemplated under section 795 of this title, whoever reproduces, publishes, sells, or gives away any photograph, sketch, picture, drawing, map, or graphical representation of the vital military or naval installations or equipment so defined, without first obtaining permission of the commanding officer of the military or naval post, camp, or station concerned, or higher authority, unless such photograph, sketch, picture, drawing, map, or graphical representation has clearly indicated thereon that it has been censored by the proper military or naval authority, shall be fined not more than $1,000 or imprisoned not more than one year or both."

6. In relevant part 18 U.S.C. § 798 provides:

"(a) Whoever knowingly and willfully communicates, furnishes, transmits,

in precise language, proscribes knowing and willful publication of any classified information concerning the cryptographic systems or communication intelligence activities of the United States as well as any information obtained from communication intelligence operations.[7] If any of the material here at issue is of this nature, the newspapers are presumably now in full notice of the position of the United States and must face the consequences if they publish. I would have no difficulty in sustaining convictions under these sections on facts that would not justify the intervention of equity and the imposition of a prior restraint.

The same would be true under those sections of the Criminal Code casting a wider net to protect the national defense. Section 793(e) makes it a criminal act for any unauthorized possessor of a document "relating to the national defense" either (1) willfully to communicate or cause to be communicated that document to any person not entitled to receive it or (2) willfully to retain the document and fail to deliver it to an officer of the United States entitled to receive it. The subsection was added in 1950 because pre-existing law provided no penalty for the unauthorized possessor unless demand for the documents was made. "The dangers surrounding the unauthorized possession of such items are self-evident, and it is deemed advisable to require their surrender in such a case, regardless of demand, especially since their unauthorized possession may be unknown to the authorities who would otherwise make the demand." S.Rep. No. 2369, pt. 1, 81st Cong., 2d Sess., 9 (1950). . . .[10]

or otherwise makes available to an unauthorized person, or publishes, or uses in any manner prejudicial to the safety or interest of the United States or for the benefit of any foreign government to the detriment of the United States any classified information—

"(1) concerning the nature, preparation, or use of any code, cipher, or cryptographic system of the United States or any foreign government; or

"(2) concerning the design, construction, use, maintenance, or repair of any device, apparatus, or appliance used or prepared or planned for use by the United States or any foreign government for cryptographic or communication intelligence purposes; or

"(3) concerning the communication intelligence activities of the United States or any foreign government; or

"(4) obtained by the process of communication intelligence from the communications of any foreign government, knowing the same to have been obtained by such processes.

"Shall be fined not more than $10,000 or imprisoned not more than ten years, or both."

7. The purport of 18 U.S.C. § 798 is clear. . . .

Section 798 obviously was intended to cover publications by non-employees of the Government and to ease the Government's burden in obtaining convictions.

10. Also relevant is 18 U.S.C. § 794. Subsection (b) thereof forbids in time of war the collection or publication, with intent that it shall be communicated to the enemy, of any information with respect to the movements of military forces, "or with respect to the plans or conduct . . . of any naval or military operations . . . or any other information relating to the public defense, which might be useful to the enemy. . . ."

It is thus clear that Congress has addressed itself to the problems of protecting the security of the country and the national defense from unauthorized disclosure of potentially damaging information. [ ] It has not, however, authorized the injunctive remedy against threatened publication. It has apparently been satisfied to rely on criminal sanctions and their deterrent effect on the responsible as well as the irresponsible press. I am not, of course, saying that either of these newspapers has yet committed a crime or that either would commit a crime if it published all the material now in its possession. That matter must await resolution in the context of a criminal proceeding if one is instituted by the United States. In that event, the issue of guilt or innocence would be determined by procedures and standards quite different from those that have purported to govern these injunctive proceedings.

MR. JUSTICE MARSHALL, concurring.

. . .

In these cases there is no problem concerning the President's power to classify information as "secret" or "top secret." Congress has specifically recognized Presidential authority, which has been formally exercised in Exec.Order 10501 (1953), to classify documents and information. See, e.g., 18 U.S.C. § 798; 50 U.S.C. § 783. Nor is there any issue here regarding the President's power as Chief Executive and Commander in Chief to protect national security by disciplining employees who disclose information and by taking precautions to prevent leaks.

. . .

It would, however, be utterly inconsistent with the concept of separation of powers for this Court to use its power of contempt to prevent behavior that Congress has specifically declined to prohibit. There would be a similar damage to the basic concept of these co-equal branches of Government if when the Executive Branch has adequate authority granted by Congress to protect "national security" it can choose instead to invoke the contempt power of a court to enjoin the threatened conduct. The Constitution provides that Congress shall make laws, the President execute laws, and courts interpret laws. Youngstown Sheet & Tube Co. v. Sawyer, 343 U.S. 579 (1952). It did not provide for government by injunction in which the courts and the Executive Branch can "make law" without regard to the action of Congress. It may be more convenient for the Executive Branch if it need only convince a judge to prohibit conduct rather than ask the Congress to pass a law, and it may be more convenient to enforce a contempt order than to seek a criminal conviction in a jury trial. Moreover, it may be considered politically wise to get a court to share the responsibility for arresting those who the Executive Branch has probable cause to believe are violating the law. But convenience and political considerations of the moment do not justify a basic departure from the principles of our system of government.

. . .

MR. CHIEF JUSTICE BURGER, dissenting.

So clear are the constitutional limitations on prior restraint against expression, that from the time of Near v. Minnesota, [ ], until recently in Organization for a Better Austin v. Keefe, 402 U.S. 415 (1971), we have had little occasion to be concerned with cases involving prior restraints against news reporting on matters of public interest. There is, therefore, little variation among the members of the Court in terms of resistance to prior restraints against publication. Adherence to this basic constitutional principle however, does not make these cases simple. In these cases, the imperative of a free and unfettered press comes into collision with another imperative, the effective functioning of a complex modern government and specifically the effective exercise of certain constitutional powers of the Executive. Only those who view the First Amendment as an absolute in all circumstances—a view I respect, but reject—can find such cases as these to be simple or easy.

These cases are not simple for another and more immediate reason. We do not know the facts of the cases. No District Judge knew all the facts. No Court of Appeals judge knew all the facts. No member of this Court knows all the facts.

Why are we in this posture, in which only those judges to whom the First Amendment is absolute and permits of no restraint in any circumstances or for any reason, are really in a position to act?

I suggest we are in this posture because these cases have been conducted in unseemly haste. . . .

. . .

It is not disputed that the Times has had unauthorized possession of the documents for three to four months, during which it has had its expert analysts studying them, presumably digesting them and preparing the material for publication. During all of this time, the Times, presumably in its capacity as trustee of the public's "right to know," has held up publication for purposes it considered proper and thus public knowledge was delayed. No doubt this was for a good reason; the analysis of 7,000 pages of complex material drawn from a vastly greater volume of material would inevitably take time and the writing of good news stories takes time. But why should the United States Government, from whom this information was illegally acquired by someone, along with all the counsel, trial judges, and appellate judges be placed under needless pressure? After these months of deferral, the alleged "right to know" has somehow and suddenly become a right that must be vindicated instanter.

. . .

The consequence of all this melancholy series of events is that we literally do not know what we are acting on. As I see it, we have been forced to deal with litigation concerning rights of great magnitude without an adequate record, and surely without time for adequate treatment either in the prior proceedings or in this Court. It is interesting to note that counsel on both sides, in oral argument before this Court, were frequently unable to respond to questions on factual points. Not surprisingly they pointed out that they had been working literally "around the clock" and simply were unable to review the documents that give rise to these cases and were not familiar with them. This Court is in no better posture. I agree generally with Mr. Justice Harlan and Mr. Justice Blackmun but I am not prepared to reach the merits.[3]

I would affirm the Court of Appeals for the Second Circuit and allow the District Court to complete the trial aborted by our grant of certiorari, meanwhile preserving the status quo in the *Post* case. I would direct that the District Court on remand give priority to the *Times* case to the exclusion of all other business of that court but I would not set arbitrary deadlines.

I should add that I am in general agreement with much of what Mr. Justice White has expressed with respect to penal sanctions concerning communication or retention of documents or information relating to the national defense.

We all crave speedier judicial processes but when judges are pressured as in these cases the result is a parody of the judicial function.

MR. JUSTICE HARLAN, with whom THE CHIEF JUSTICE and MR. JUSTICE BLACKMUN join, dissenting.

These cases forcefully call to mind the wise admonition of Mr. Justice Holmes, dissenting in Northern Securities Co. v. United States, 193 U.S. 197, 400–401 (1904):

> "Great cases like hard cases make bad law. For great cases are called great, not by reason of their real importance in shaping the law of the future, but because of some accident of immediate overwhelming interest which appeals to the feelings and distorts the judgment. These immediate interests exercise a kind of hydraulic pressure which makes what previously was clear seem doubtful, and before which even well settled principles of law will bend."

With all respect, I consider that the Court has been almost irresponsibly feverish in dealing with these cases.

---

3. With respect to the question of inherent power of the Executive to classify papers, records, and documents as secret, or otherwise unavailable for public exposure, and to secure aid of the courts for enforcement, there may be an analogy with respect to this Court. No statute gives this Court express power to establish and enforce the utmost security measures for the secrecy of our deliberations and records. Yet I have little doubt as to the inherent power of the Court to protect the confidentiality of its internal operations by whatever judicial measures may be required.

Both the Court of Appeals for the Second Circuit and the Court of Appeals for the District of Columbia Circuit rendered judgment on June 23. The New York Times' petition for certiorari, its motion for accelerated consideration thereof, and its application for interim relief were filed in this Court on June 24 at about 11 a.m. The application of the United States for interim relief in the *Post* case was also filed here on June 24 at about 7:15 p.m. This Court's order setting a hearing before us on June 26 at 11 a.m., a course which I joined only to avoid the possibility of even more peremptory action by the Court, was issued less than 24 hours before. The record in the *Post* case was filed with the Clerk shortly before 1 p.m. on June 25; the record in the *Times* case did not arrive until 7 or 8 o'clock that same night. The briefs of the parties were received less than two hours before argument on June 26.

This frenzied train of events took place in the name of the presumption against prior restraints created by the First Amendment. Due regard for the extraordinarily important and difficult questions involved in these litigations should have led the Court to shun such a precipitate timetable. In order to decide the merits of these cases properly, some or all of the following questions should have been faced:

1. Whether the Attorney General is authorized to bring these suits in the name of the United States. . . .

2. Whether the First Amendment permits the federal courts to enjoin publication of stories which would present a serious threat to national security. See Near v. Minnesota, [ ], (dictum).

3. Whether the threat to publish highly secret documents is of itself a sufficient implication of national security to justify an injunction on the theory that regardless of the contents of the documents harm enough results simply from the demonstration of such a breach of secrecy.

4. Whether the unauthorized disclosure of any of these particular documents would seriously impair the national security.

5. What weight should be given to the opinion of high officers in the Executive Branch of the Government with respect to questions 3 and 4.

6. Whether the newspapers are entitled to retain and use the documents notwithstanding the seemingly uncontested facts that the documents, or the originals of which they are duplicates, were purloined from the Government's possession and that the newspapers received them with knowledge that they had been feloniously acquired. Cf. Liberty Lobby, Inc. v. Pearson, 129 U.S.App.D.C. 74, 390 F.2d 489 (1967, amended 1968).

7.   Whether the threatened harm to the national security or the Government's possessory interest in the documents justifies the issuance of an injunction against publication in light of—

    a.   The strong First Amendment policy against prior restraints on publication;

    b.   The doctrine against enjoining conduct in violation of criminal statutes; and

    c.   The extent to which the materials at issue have apparently already been otherwise disseminated.

These are difficult questions of fact, of law, and of judgment; the potential consequences of erroneous decision are enormous. The time which has been available to us, to the lower courts, and to the parties has been wholly inadequate for giving these cases the kind of consideration they deserve. It is a reflection on the stability of the judicial process that these great issues—as important as any that have arisen during my time on the Court—should have been decided under the pressures engendered by the torrent of publicity that has attended these litigations from their inception.

Forced as I am to reach the merits of these cases, I dissent from the opinion and judgments of the Court. Within the severe limitations imposed by the time constraints under which I have been required to operate, I can only state my reasons in telescoped form, even though in different circumstances I would have felt constrained to deal with the cases in the fuller sweep indicated above.

.   .   .

.   .   . It is plain to me that the scope of the judicial function in passing upon the activities of the Executive Branch of the Government in the field of foreign affairs is very narrowly restricted. This view is, I think, dictated by the concept of separation of powers upon which our constitutional system rests.

.   .   .

The power to evaluate the "pernicious influence" of premature disclosure is not, however, lodged in the Executive alone. I agree that, in performance of its duty to protect the values of the First Amendment against political pressures, the judiciary must review the initial Executive determination to the point of satisfying itself that the subject matter of the dispute does lie within the proper compass of the President's foreign relations power. Constitutional considerations forbid "a complete abandonment of judicial control." Cf. United States v. Reynolds, 345 U.S. 1, 8 (1953). Moreover, the judiciary may properly insist that the determination that disclosure of the subject matter would irreparably impair the national security be made by the head of the Executive Department concerned—here the Secretary of State or the Secretary of Defense—after actual personal consideration by that officer. This safeguard is required in the

analogous area of executive claims of privilege for secrets of state.
[   ]

But in my judgment the judiciary may not properly go beyond these two inquiries and redetermine for itself the probable impact of disclosure on the national security. . . .

Even if there is some room for the judiciary to override the executive determination, it is plain that the scope of review must be exceedingly narrow. I can see no indication in the opinions of either the District Court or the Court of Appeals in the *Post* litigation that the conclusions of the Executive were given even the deference owing to an administrative agency, much less that owing to a co-equal branch of the Government operating within the field of its constitutional prerogative.

. . .

MR. JUSTICE BLACKMUN, dissenting.

I join MR. JUSTICE HARLAN in his dissent. I also am in substantial accord with much that MR. JUSTICE WHITE says, by way of admonition, in the latter part of his opinion.

. . .

With such respect as may be due to the contrary view, this, in my opinion, is not the way to try a lawsuit of this magnitude and asserted importance. . . .

The First Amendment, after all, is only one part of an entire Constitution. Article II of the great document vests in the Executive Branch primary power over the conduct of foreign affairs and places in that branch the responsibility for the Nation's safety. Each provision of the Constitution is important, and I cannot subscribe to a doctrine of unlimited absolutism for the First Amendment at the cost of downgrading other provisions. First Amendment absolutism has never commanded a majority of this Court. See for example, Near v. Minnesota, [   ], and Schenck v. United States, [   ]. What is needed here is a weighing, upon properly developed standards, of the broad right of the press to print and of the very narrow right of the Government to prevent. Such standards are not yet developed. The parties here are in disagreement as to what those standards should be. But even the newspapers concede that there are situations where restraint is in order and is constitutional. . . .

. . .

I strongly urge, and sincerely hope that these two newspapers will be fully aware of their ultimate responsibilities to the United States of America. Judge Wilkey, dissenting in the District of Columbia case, after a review of only the affidavits before his court (the basic papers had not then been made available by either party), concluded that there were a number of examples of documents that, if in the possession of the Post, and if published, "could clearly result in great harm to the nation," and he defined "harm" to mean "the

death of soldiers, the destruction of alliances, the greatly increased
difficulty of negotiation with our enemies, the inability of our diplomats to negotiate. . . ." I, for one, have now been able to give at
least some cursory study not only to the affidavits, but to the
material itself. I regret to say that from this examination I fear that
Judge Wilkey's statements have possible foundation. I therefore
share his concern. I hope that damage has not already been done.
If, however, damage has been done, and if, with the Court's action
today, these newspapers proceed to publish the critical documents
and there results therefrom "the death of soldiers, the destruction of
alliances, the greatly increased difficulty of negotiation with our
enemies, the inability of our diplomats to negotiate," to which list I
might add the factors of prolongation of the war and of further delay
in the freeing of United States prisoners, then the Nation's people
will know where the responsibility for these sad consequences rests.

Notes and Questions

1. How many votes might have shifted had Congress enacted a
statute explicitly authorizing the government to seek an injunction to
bar release of information once the Attorney General determined that
release would pose a "grave and immediate danger" to national
security?

2. How many votes might have shifted if a criminal statute explicitly covering the behavior of the newspapers in this case rendered
them subject to criminal prosecution? Would prosecution under such
a statute have raised other constitutional questions?

3. Louis Henkin, in The Right to Know and the Duty to Withhold:
The Case of the Pentagon Papers, 120 U.Pa.L.Rev. 271 (1971), criticized the emphasis on the distinction between enjoining speech and
punishing it after the fact because "while a criminal penalty more
readily permits 'civil disobedience,' or reliance on the jury to acquit,
stiff penalties will deter—and deny the right to know—almost as
effectively as any injunction." In this case what are the differences
between enjoining and punishing afterward?

4. Henkin had another criticism of the decision (278–80):

> More important, the upshot of the Court's apparent constitu-
> tional doctrine is unsatisfying. For, as regards governmental
> documents and information, the Constitution is apparently inter-
> preted as ordaining that a branch of government can properly
> conceal even from other branches, surely from the public; but
> the Press is free to try to uncover, and if it succeeds it is free to
> publish. That kind of trial by battle and cleverness between the
> three estates and the fourth hardly seems the way best to
> further the various aims of a democratic society. It does not
> ensure that what should be concealed will not be uncovered.
> And, on the other hand, the rare, haphazard, fortuitous, journal-
> istic uncovering will hardly achieve effective public knowledge of

all that should be known, for almost all that is concealed (needfully or not) will continue to be effectively withheld. (That some bits of it are sometimes selectively revealed by official "leaks" to chosen journalists only underscores the haphazard quality of what is disclosed.)

Nor does the implication that the courts will be available to adjust the competing interests promise an effective accommodation. The difficulty is not with judicial balancing in principle: that, we have accepted (*pace* Mr. Justice Black), is what the Constitution orders even as regards the "preferred freedoms" of the first amendment. But, one may ask, can courts meaningfully weigh the Government's "need" to conceal, the Press's "need" to publish, the people's "need" to know? If, on the one hand, the need for military secrecy in time of war seems obvious and paramount; if, on the other hand, as in the *Pentagon Papers* Case, many could not see why the Government should conceal documents several years old relating to an issue that had become of great national moment; who can meaningfully weigh the less obvious, less dramatic consequences of disclosure of any one of millions of documents that are the stuff of governing and of international relations? . . .

But public knowledge will not flourish even if the Court continues to insist that the Constitution requires judicial review of the Government's determination that national interest in concealment outweighs the freedom of the Press to publish. Inevitably the courts will have to legislate gross categories ("diplomatic correspondence," "internal memoranda") and even then virtually rubber stamp (and legitimate) governmental concealment. In the result, there will be few instances of Press uncovering and divulging, few cases in which the Executive will seek to bar or punish publication, few cases in which the Court will in fact reverse the Executive.

. . .

There is no happy solution, only the eternal cry and quest for better government. But surely Congress and the President could do more than they have done. The *Pentagon Papers* Case has dramatized issues, admonished bureaucrats, and created an atmosphere receptive to a major effort to increase public and scholarly knowledge even while reinforcing secrecy where it is necessary. There is need for measures to rebuild confidence in government, including confidence in its policies of disclosure and concealment. At least there ought to be provision for automatic declassification of many categories of documents, putting the burden on the bureaucracy to determine and maintain the need for reclassifying. Until Congress and Presidents turn a hard face to unnecessary classification, bureaucrats will not learn the habit of disclosure. The unhappy game of trial by cleverness between Executive and Press with an infrequent journalistic success will do little to support the people's right to know when Government abuses its responsibility to withhold.

5. Compare Justice Stewart's opinion in *Landmark,* p. 218, infra.

6. Is the Chief Justice correct in suggesting an analogy between the Pentagon Papers case and the Supreme Court's power to protect the confidentiality of its internal operations?

7. Note that the pivotal opinions of Justices Stewart, White, and Marshall stress the absence of Congressional authorization for the action. Compare the reactions of several of the Justices when President Truman seized the struck steel mills without Congressional authorization. Youngstown Sheet & Tube Co. v. Sawyer, 343 U.S. 579 (1952). When the analysis emphasizes separation of powers does it matter that one case involved First Amendment interests and the other involved property interests of the owners of steel mills?

8. Many who had hoped for a definitive ruling on the legitimacy of "prior restraint" were disappointed with the strategy of Alexander Bickel, who argued the case for the *Times.* A lawyer who represented the *Washington Post* explained the litigation strategy in Godofsky, Protection of the Press From Prior Restraint and Harassment Under Libel Laws, 29 U.Miami L.Rev. 462, 471–72 (1975):

> I am aware of the fact that members of academia and others have criticized those who briefed and argued this case in the Supreme Court because none of us urged adoption of a rule which would prohibit prior restraints, even in circumstances such as those suggested by Chief Justice Hughes in Near v. Minnesota. I don't think I should attempt to explain the position of the *New York Times,* but I would like to tell you something of what went into our own thinking.

> In the first place we did not need an absolute ban on prior restraints to win the case. The district court had found, after an evidentiary hearing, that the only danger involved in publication was the embarrassment which the United States would suffer in attempting to explain to foreign governments why the United States government could not censor its press. We did not think that any court in this country would be prepared to support a prior restraint on this basis.

> Second, the court of appeals had also found, by a lopsided majority, that the government had failed to meet the *Near* test.
> . . . .

> Third, we knew from the Supreme Court memorandum setting the case for argument that four of the nine justices (Black, Douglas, Brennan and Marshall), would almost certainly hold that there was no basis for continuing the restraint which had been in effect during the pendency of the litigation, and we did not wish to take a position which might conceivably alienate the

critical fifth vote we needed to win. After all, unless you accept the position of Justices Black and Douglas, it's pretty hard to argue that papers can publish the sailing dates of troopships and the number and location of troop positions.

Finally, we knew that Justices Black and Douglas had long been advocates of the absolute position with respect to the first amendment. We also knew that these two eminent Justices had never convinced any of their brethren of the correctness of their views. We believed that Justices Black and Douglas would almost certainly continue to urge that view on their brethren in this case. We were of the view that if Justices Black and Douglas were unable, over a period of several decades, to convince their brethren that the first amendment was absolute, we certainly would not be able to devise a series of arguments which would do so between 3:30 P.M. Friday and 5 A.M. Saturday morning.

Professor Bickel discussed the significance of the case he argued successfully in A. Bickel, The Morality of Consent 79–88 (1976).

9. Although the government never sought to invoke criminal sanctions against the media in the Pentagon Papers episode, it did file charges against Daniel Ellsberg and Anthony Russo. Ellsberg, a consultant to the Rand Corporation, had been authorized to possess the papers, provided he kept them on the premises of Rand and in his safe when not in use. He was not to reproduce them, but he removed them from Rand and had them reproduced with Russo's help. The government relied primarily on 18 U.S.C. § 641, charging that Ellsberg did "embezzle, steal and knowingly convert to his own use and the use of another" the documents known as the Pentagon Papers, and on 18 U.S.C.A. § 793(d) and (e). Subsection (e) is discussed in Justice White's opinion. Subsection (d) involves communication and transmission of "any document, writing . . . or note relating to the national defense . . . which . . . the possessor has reason to believe could be used to the injury of the United States or to the advantage of any foreign nation. . . ." The charges against Ellsberg and Russo were dismissed because of government misconduct. The case is discussed in Nimmer, National Security Secrets v. Free Speech: The Issues Left Undecided in the Ellsberg Case, 26 Stan.L.Rev. 311 (1974).

10. *The Progressive's* H-Bomb Case. In March 1979, a federal district judge in Wisconsin issued a preliminary injunction, apparently the first of its kind, restraining a magazine from printing an article on national security grounds. The article by Howard Morland, entitled "The H Bomb Secret: How We Got It, Why We're Telling It," was to have appeared in *The Progressive*, a monthly magazine of political and social commentary with a circulation of 40,000.

The government relied on statutory authorization in the Atomic Energy Act, 42 U.S.C.A. § 2011 et seq., to seek the injunction. Section 2274 provides in part:

> Whoever, lawfully or unlawfully, having possession of, access to, control over, or being entrusted with any document, writing, sketch, photograph, plan, model, instrument, appliance, note, or information involving or incorporating Restricted Data—
>
> . . .
>
> (b) communicates, transmits, or discloses the same to any individual or person, or attempts or conspires to do any of the foregoing, with reason to believe such data will be utilized to injure the United States or to secure an advantage to any foreign nation, shall, upon conviction, be punished by a fine of not more than $10,000 or imprisonment for not more than ten years, or both.

"Restricted Data" is defined in § 2014(y) to include "all data concerning (1) design, manufacture or utilization of atomic weapons; (2) the production of special nuclear material; or (3) the use of special nuclear fuels in the production of energy . . .." In § 2014(aa), "special nuclear material" includes "plutonium, uranium enriched in the isotope 233 or in the isotope 235," and other materials that may be designated.

The specific authority for an injunction is found in § 2280 of the Act:

> Whenever in the judgment of the Commission any person has engaged or is about to engage in any acts or practices which constitute or will constitute a violation of any provision of this chapter, or any regulation or order issued thereunder, the Attorney General on behalf of the United States may make application to the appropriate court for an order enjoining such acts or practices, or for an order enforcing compliance with such provision, and upon a showing by the Commission that such person has engaged or is about to engage in any such acts or practices, a permanent or temporary injunction, restraining order, or other order may be granted.

The judge ruled that the government had met its burden under § 2274 of the statute, which he held was not vague or overbroad. The word "communicates," which had disturbed some justices in *New York Times*, was easily resolved here: "The Court is convinced that the terms used in the statute—'communicates, transmits or discloses'—include publishing in a magazine." The judge found that the government had "met the test enunciated by two Justices in the New York Times case, namely, grave, direct, immediate and irreparable harm to the United States."

The Pentagon Papers case was distinguishable because the information at issue there was historical data. The only cogent national security reason for restraining its publication was embarrassment to the United States. The information in *The Progressive* article concerned "the most destructive weapon in the history of mankind, information of sufficient destructive potential to nullify the right to free speech and to endanger the right to life itself."

> The Secretary of State states that publication would increase thermonuclear proliferation and that this would "irreparably impair the national security of the United States." The Secretary of Defense says that dissemination of the Morland article will mean a substantial increase in the risk of thermonuclear proliferation and lead to use or threats that could "adversely affect the national security of the United States."

The Judge recognized that a "mistake in ruling against *The Progressive* will seriously infringe cherished First Amendment rights." But "a mistake in ruling against the United States could pave the way for thermonuclear annihilation for us all. In that event, our right to life is extinguished and the right to publish becomes moot." He found the dictum of Near v. Minnesota applicable because "war by foot soldiers has been replaced in large part by war by machines and bombs." The "publication of the technical information on the hydrogen bomb contained in the article is analogous to publication of troop movements or locations in time of war and falls within the extremely narrow exception of the rule against prior restraint." The judge was also influenced by his belief that the purpose of the Morland article, to stimulate debate on nuclear nonproliferation, could be achieved without revealing the method of making such arms.

The reporter and the magazine argued that the information had been obtained from public sources, such as articles in encyclopedias. The judge responded that an affidavit from Dr. Hans Bethe asserted that "the design and operational concepts described in the manuscript are not expressed or revealed in the public literature nor do I believe they are known to scientists not associated with the government weapons program."

After study, the judge found "concepts within the article that [he did] not find in the public realm—concepts that are vital to the operation of the bomb." Although it has been asserted that the "secret" is nothing more than a few insights drawn from other scientific areas, the judge noted that sometimes what is obvious in one context may not be so obvious in another context. He cited a report that in the 1930's French scientists trying to develop a nuclear chain reaction were stymied for a year by their failure to grasp an "elementary" idea.

Although the judge recognized that it might only be a matter of time before other countries acquired their own hydrogen bombs, and that a "large, sophisticated industrial capacity" was required together with imaginative scientists, the article "could accelerate the membership of a candidate nation in the thermonuclear club." Moreover, "there are times in the course of human history when time itself may be very important." He mentioned the importance of Hitler's failure "to get his V–1 and V–2 bombs operational quickly enough to materially affect the outcome of World War II."

In prior restraint cases such as *Nebraska Press,* in Chapter IX, the Court considers among other issues, whether the restraint is likely to be effective. That matter is particularly important here because the information in question apparently involves common sense ideas applied in unexpected ways. Writing after the decision, Morland stated that "the secret" could be said in a single sentence— and that he first heard that sentence from a student in the rear of the audience at a talk he was giving at the University of Alabama. He also says that he submitted to the court four encyclopedia articles on the subjects "Comet" and "Sun" with pertinent passages underlined. He says that government attorneys asserted that the underlinings constituted a security violation and clean copies had to be found before the articles could be released to the press. Newsweek, Apr. 9, 1979 at 14. Could Morland be restrained from telling this episode? In "national security" cases, is likely effectiveness of the restraint a relevant consideration?

The Progressive appealed the granting of the preliminary injunction. After refusing a government request to bar the public from the argument, the court of appeals heard oral argument on September 13, 1979. The magazine asserted that the government had to prove that the publication would "surely result in direct, immediate and irreparable damage to our nation or its people," but had proven only that "in some unspecified time, some nations might acquire the capability to build a hydrogen bomb."

Just after the argument, the *Madison Press Connection* published a letter containing information that *The Progressive* had been enjoined from publishing. *The Chicago Tribune* then announced that it planned to publish the same letter. Once the information had been made public, any justification for enjoining its publication collapsed. The government then announced that it was withdrawing its complaint and the case was dismissed. Although the government reserved its right to bring criminal charges, no such case has been brought.

11. In May, 1980, Public Broadcasting Service broadcast a "documentary drama" portraying a love affair between a Saudi princess and a commoner, and their subsequent execution. The program also dwelt on some aspects of Saudi Arabian life that the Saudi government asserted were totally misrepresented. The program was patterned on a true story.

If the Saudi government had made a credible threat to cut off all oil shipments to the United States immediately upon the presentation of the program, and if the best evidence had been that such a cutoff would cripple the American economy, would the government have been able to obtain an injunction against the showing of the program?

Is it crucial that no "secret" is involved?

12.   After a spate of publications that named several United States covert foreign intelligence agents, presumably in an effort to undermine the U.S. intelligence activity, Congress took steps to criminalize such disclosures with the Intelligence Identities Protection Act of 1982.   Press groups, however, protested fiercely that too wide a ban would affect legitimate news accounts, based on information on the public record, of intelligence agency abuses.   A critical question is whether a reporter who writes a story about the CIA violates that statute if that story contains information that identifies a covert agent.   No litigation has occurred.

Government Authors

In national security cases the government has been more successful when seeking to enjoin disclosures by its employees.   United States v. Marchetti, 466 F.2d 1309 (4th Cir.1972), involved an injunction obtained by the government against publication of Marchetti's book about the Central Intelligence Agency, his former employer.   At the time he joined, he promised not to divulge any classified information unless specifically authorized in writing by the director.   When he resigned from the CIA he signed a secrecy oath.   Although recognizing that prior restraints were rarely justifiable, the court upheld this one because of the government's right to secrecy in foreign affairs.   A confidential relationship inhered in the employment and "the law would probably imply a secrecy agreement had there been no formal expressed agreement."   The government need not resort to ordinary criminal sanctions because of the great risk of harm from disclosure.   The court recognized that by joining the CIA, Marchetti did not relinquish his rights to free speech.   He might write about CIA operations and criticize the agency as any citizen might, but he could not disclose classified information obtained during his employment unless the material was already in the public domain.   The court concluded that judicial review of agency objections to the text was available, but that the court could determine only whether the material was classified and if so, whether it had previously been made public.   The Supreme Court denied certiorari, 409 U.S. 1063 (1972), Justices Douglas, Brennan, and Stewart dissenting.

On remand, the judge permitted publication of all but 26 of the 168 items still in question.   The director of the CIA and the Secretary of State appealed and the judgment was reversed.   Alfred A. Knopf, Inc. v. Colby, 509 F.2d 1362 (4th Cir.), certiorari denied 421 U.S. 992 (1975), Justice Douglas dissenting.   Apparently the trial judge could find little to explain why particular documents or parts of documents had been classified, and often the classification officer could not be identified or was unavailable. The court of appeals observed that in its earlier decision in *Marchetti* it had assumed that all information in a classified document should be held to be classified and not subject to disclosure. On this appeal the court decided that the trial judge had imposed an excessive burden on the government because he refused to recognize that there "is a presumption of regularity in the performance by a public official of his public duty. . . . That presumption leaves no room for speculation that information which the district court can recognize as proper for top secret classification was not classified at all by the official who placed the 'Top Secret' legend on the document."

The Snepp Case. A book by a former CIA agent was published before the CIA learned of it. The government sued the agent for breach of his employment contract, which barred publication of information learned while working at the CIA, without prepublication approval. The government did not contend that any classified information had been revealed. The judge held that the contract was enforceable and had been breached. He enjoined violation of the contract as to future works and established a constructive trust that required Snepp to pay the CIA all royalties the book produced. United States v. Snepp, 456 F.Supp. 176 (E.D.Va.1978).

The court of appeals agreed that a valid contract had been breached but disagreed, 2–1, on the damages question. The majority concluded that the government was entitled to try the case as a normal breach of contract case with the possibility of persuading the jury to award punitive damages, but that the constructive trust theory was not available. 595 F.2d 926 (4th Cir.1979).

Snepp sought certiorari to determine whether his agreement with the CIA was enforceable and, if so, whether punitive damages were recoverable in the government's case. The government filed a conditional cross-petition seeking certiorari to review the constructive trust question if the court granted Snepp's petition.

The Supreme Court granted both petitions and, without oral argument, reinstated the district court's judgment permitting the constructive trust theory. The Court largely rejected Snepp's claim that the CIA contract amounted to prior restraint in a lengthy footnote:

> When Snepp accepted employment with the CIA, he voluntarily signed the agreement that expressly obligated him to submit any proposed publication for prior review. He does not claim that he executed this agreement under duress. Indeed, he voluntarily reaffirmed his obligation when he left the Agency. We agree with the Court of Appeals that Snepp's agreement is an "entirely appropriate" exercise of the CIA Director's statutory mandate to "protect intelligence sources and methods from unauthorized disclosure." [ ] Moreover, this Court's cases

make clear that—even in the absence of an express agreement—the CIA could have acted to protect substantial governmental interests by imposing reasonable restrictions on employee activities that in other contexts might be protected by the First Amendment. [ ] The Government has a compelling interest in protecting both the secrecy of information important to our national security and the appearance of confidentiality so essential to the effective operation of our foreign intelligence service. [ ] The agreement that Snepp signed is a reasonable means for protecting this vital interest.

The Court's *per curiam* opinion noted that "Snepp's employment with the CIA involved an extremely high degree of trust." He published the book "on the basis of his background and exposure" to CIA activities and "deliberately and surreptitiously violated his obligation to submit all material for prepublication review." The violation of trust "does not depend upon whether his book actually contained classified information." The claim is that he should have given the CIA a chance to see whether anything he wrote "would compromise classified information or sources." 444 U.S. 507 (1980).

Justice Stevens, joined by Justices Brennan and Marshall, dissented. They stressed that "the Government has conceded that the book contains no classified, nonpublic material. Thus, by definition, the interest in confidentiality that Snepp's contract was designed to protect has not been compromised." They argued that the remedy of constructive trust was not authorized "by any applicable law and [that] it is most inappropriate for the Court to dispose of this novel issue summarily on the Government's conditional cross-petition for certiorari." Each point was discussed at length.

See Comments, 81 Colum.L.Rev. 662 (1981) and 59 N.C.L.Rev. 417 (1981).

B. OTHER SECRETS AND CRIMINAL LAW

LANDMARK COMMUNICATIONS, INC. v. VIRGINIA

Supreme Court of the United States, 1978.
435 U.S. 829, 98 S.Ct. 1535, 56 L.Ed.2d 1.

[The Virginia constitution directed the legislature to create a commission to investigate charges against judges—and decreed that proceedings before the commission "shall be confidential." A statute creating the commission declared that the proceedings were confidential "and shall not be divulged by any person to anyone except the Commission, except that the record of any proceeding filed with the Supreme Court shall lose its confidential character." A proceeding is filed with the Supreme Court only when the commission finds grounds for filing a formal complaint.

Landmark's newspaper, the Virginia Pilot, accurately reported that a named judge was under investigation by the Commission.

Landmark was found guilty of a misdemeanor for divulging forbidden information and fined $500 plus costs of prosecution. The Supreme Court of Virginia affirmed.

On appeal, the Supreme Court of the United States noted that virtually every state had such a commission, and that all provided for confidentiality. The accepted reasons for confidentiality were (1) it is thought to encourage the filing of complaints and willing participation of witnesses; (2) judges are protected from injury by publication of unexamined complaints until the meritorious can be separated from the unjustified; and (3) confidence in the judiciary is maintained by avoiding premature announcement of groundless claims. In addition, when removal is justified judges are more likely to resign voluntarily or retire if publicity can be avoided.

But even accepting the value of confidentiality, the Court considered this "only the beginning of the inquiry." Landmark was not attacking the confidentiality requirement. It was objecting to making it a crime to divulge or publish the information—a step taken by only Virginia and Hawaii.]

MR. CHIEF JUSTICE BURGER delivered the opinion of the Court.

. . . .

III.

The narrow and limited question presented, then, is whether the First Amendment permits the criminal punishment of third persons who are strangers to the inquiry, including the news media, for divulging or publishing truthful information regarding confidential proceedings of the Judicial Inquiry and Review Commission. We are not here concerned with the possible applicability of the statute to one who secures the information by illegal means and thereafter divulges it. We do not have before us any constitutional challenge to a State's power to keep the Commission's proceedings confidential or to punish participants for breach of this mandate.[10] Cf. Nebraska Press Assn. v. Stuart, 427 U.S. 539, 564 (1976); id., at 601 n. 27 (Brennan, J., concurring); Wood v. Georgia, 370 U.S. 375, 393–394 (1962). Nor does Landmark argue for any constitutionally compelled right of access for the press to those proceedings. Cf. Saxbe v. Washington Post Co., 417 U.S. 843 (1974); Pell v. Procunier, 417 U.S. 817 (1974). Finally, as the Supreme Court of Virginia held, and appellant does not dispute, the challenged statute does not constitute a prior restraint or attempt by the State to censor the news media.

Landmark urges as the dispositive answer to the question presented that truthful reporting about public officials in connection with their public duties is always insulated from the imposition of

10. At least two categories of "participants" come to mind: Commission members and staff employees, and witnesses or putative witnesses not officers or employees of the Commonwealth. No issue as to either of these categories is presented by this case.

criminal sanctions by the First Amendment. It points to the solicitude accorded even untruthful speech when public officials are its
subjects, see, e.g., New York Times Co. v. Sullivan, [ ], and the
extension of First Amendment protection to the dissemination of
truthful commercial information, see, e.g., Virginia State Board of
Pharmacy v. Virginia Citizens Consumer Council, 425 U.S. 748 (1976);
Linmark Associates, Inc. v. Willingboro, 431 U.S. 85 (1977), to support its contention. We find it unnecessary to adopt this categorical
approach to resolve the issue before us. We conclude that the
publication Virginia seeks to punish under its statute lies near the
core of the First Amendment, and the Commonwealth's interests
advanced by the imposition of criminal sanctions are insufficient to
justify the actual and potential encroachments on freedom of speech
and of the press which follow therefrom. [ ]

A.

In Mills v. Alabama, 384 U.S. 214, 218 (1966), this Court observed: "Whatever differences may exist about interpretations of the
First Amendment, there is practically universal agreement that a
major purpose of that Amendment was to protect the free discussion
of governmental affairs." . . .

The operations of the courts and the judicial conduct of judges
are matters of utmost public concern. . . .

The operation of the Virginia Commission, no less than the
operation of the judicial system itself, is a matter of public interest,
necessarily engaging the attention of the news media. The article
published by Landmark provided accurate factual information about
a legislatively authorized inquiry pending before the Judicial Review
and Inquiry Commission, and in so doing clearly served those interests in public scrutiny and discussion of governmental affairs which
the First Amendment was adopted to protect. See New York Times
Co. v. Sullivan, [ ].

B.

. . .

The Commonwealth . . . focuses on what it perceives to be the
pernicious effects of public discussion of Commission proceedings to
support its argument. It contends that the public interest is not
served by discussion of unfounded allegations of misconduct which
defames honest judges and serves only to demean the administration
of justice. The functioning of the Commission itself is also claimed
to be impeded by premature disclosure of the complainant, witnesses,
and the judge under investigation. Criminal sanctions minimize these
harmful consequences, according to the Commonwealth, by ensuring
that the guarantee of confidentiality is more than an empty promise.

It can be assumed for purposes of decision that confidentiality of Commission proceedings serves legitimate state interests. The question, however, is whether these interests are sufficient to justify the encroachment on First Amendment guarantees which the imposition of criminal sanctions entails with respect to nonparticipants such as Landmark. The Commonwealth has offered little more than assertion and conjecture to support its claim that without criminal sanctions the objectives of the statutory scheme would be seriously undermined. While not dispositive, we note that more than 40 States having similar commissions have not found it necessary to enforce confidentiality by use of criminal sanctions against nonparticipants.

Moreover, neither the Commonwealth's interest in protecting the reputation of its judges, nor its interest in maintaining the institutional integrity of its courts is sufficient to justify the subsequent punishment of speech at issue here, even on the assumption that criminal sanctions do in fact enhance the guarantee of confidentiality. Admittedly, the Commonwealth has an interest in protecting the good repute of its judges, like that of all other public officials. Our prior cases have firmly established, however, that injury to official reputation is an insufficient reason "for repressing speech that would otherwise be free." New York Times Co. v. Sullivan, [   ]. See also Garrison v. Louisiana, [   ]. The remaining interest sought to be protected, the institutional reputation of the courts, is entitled to no greater weight in the constitutional scales. . . . Mr. Justice Frankfurter, in his dissent in *Bridges*, [314 U.S. 252 (1941)] agreed that speech cannot be punished when the purpose is simply "to protect the court as a mystical entity or the judges as individuals or as anointed priests set apart from the community and spared the criticism to which in a democracy other public servants are exposed." [   ]

The Commonwealth has provided no sufficient reason for disregarding these well-established principles. We find them controlling and, on this record, dispositive.

IV.

The Supreme Court of Virginia relied on the clear-and-present-danger test in rejecting Landmark's claim. We question the relevance of that standard here; moreover we cannot accept the mechanical application of the test which led that court to its conclusion. Mr. Justice Holmes' test was never intended "to express a technical legal doctrine or to convey a formula for adjudicating cases." Pennekamp v. Florida, 328 U.S. 331, 353 (1946) (Frankfurter, J., concurring). Properly applied, the test requires a court to make its own inquiry into the imminence and magnitude of the danger said to flow from the particular utterance and then to balance the character of the evil, as well as its likelihood, against the need for free and unfettered expression. The possibility that other measures will serve the State's interests should also be weighed.

Landmark argued in the Supreme Court of Virginia that "before a state may punish expression, it must prove by 'actual facts' the existence of a clear and present danger to the orderly administration of justice." [ ] The court acknowledged that the record before it was devoid of such "actual facts," but went on to hold that such proof was not required when the legislature itself had made the requisite finding "that a clear and present danger to the orderly administration of justice would be created by divulgence of the confidential proceedings of the Commission." [ ] This legislative declaration coupled with the stipulated fact that Landmark published the disputed article was regarded by the court as sufficient to justify imposition of criminal sanctions.

Deference to a legislative finding cannot limit judicial inquiry when First Amendment rights are at stake. . . . A legislature appropriately inquires into and may declare the reasons impelling legislative action but the judicial function commands analysis of whether the specific conduct charged falls within the reach of the statute and if so whether the legislation is consonant with the Constitution. Were it otherwise, the scope of freedom of speech and of the press would be subject to legislative definition and the function of the First Amendment as a check on legislative power would be nullified.

It was thus incumbent upon the Supreme Court of Virginia to go behind the legislative determination and examine for itself "the particular utteranc[e] here in question and the circumstances of [its] publication to determine to what extent the substantive evil of unfair administration of justice was a likely consequence, and whether the degree of likelihood was sufficient to justify [subsequent] punishment." Bridges v. California, 314 U.S., at 271. Our precedents leave little doubt as to the proper outcome of such an inquiry.

In a series of cases raising the question of whether the contempt power could be used to punish out-of-court comments concerning pending cases or grand jury investigations, this Court has consistently rejected the argument that such commentary constituted a clear and present danger to the administration of justice. . . .

The efforts of the Supreme Court of Virginia to distinguish those cases from this case are unpersuasive. The threat to the administration of justice posed by the speech and publications in *Bridges*, *Pennekamp*, *Craig*, and *Wood* was, if anything, more direct and substantial than the threat posed by Landmark's article. If the clear-and-present-danger test could not be satisfied in the more extreme circumstances of those cases, it would seem to follow that the test cannot be met here. It is true that some risk of injury to the judge under inquiry, to the system of justice, or to the operation of the Judicial Review and Inquiry Commission may be posed by premature disclosure, but the test requires that the danger be "clear and present" and in our view the risk here falls far short of that requirement. Moreover, much of the risk can be eliminated through careful internal procedures to protect the confidentiality of Commission proceedings. Cf. Nebraska Press Assn. v. Stuart, 427 U.S., at 564; id., at 601 n. 27 (Brennan, J., concurring in judgment). In any event, we must conclude as we did in Wood v. Georgia, that "[t]he type of 'danger' evidenced by the record is precisely one of the types of activity envisioned by the Founders in presenting the First Amendment for ratification." 370 U.S., at 388.

Accordingly, the judgment of the Supreme Court of Virginia is reversed, and the case remanded for further proceedings not inconsistent with this opinion.

MR. JUSTICE BRENNAN and MR. JUSTICE POWELL took no part in the consideration or decision of this case.

MR. JUSTICE STEWART, concurring in the judgment.

Virginia has enacted a law making it a criminal offense for "any person" to divulge confidential information about proceedings before its Judicial Inquiry and Review Commission. I cannot agree with the Court that this Virginia law violates the Constitution.

There could hardly be a higher governmental interest than a State's interest in the quality of its judiciary. Virginia's derivative interest in maintaining the confidentiality of the proceedings of its Judicial Inquiry and Review Commission seems equally clear. Only such confidentiality, the State has determined, will protect upright judges from unjustified harm and at the same time insure the full and fearless airing in Commission proceedings of every complaint of judicial misconduct. I find nothing in the Constitution to prevent Virginia from punishing those who violate this confidentiality. [ ]

But in this case Virginia has extended its law to punish a newspaper, and that it cannot constitutionally do. If the constitutional protection of a free press means anything, it means that government cannot take it upon itself to decide what a newspaper may and may not publish. Though government may deny access to information and punish its theft, government may not prohibit or punish the publication of that information once it falls into the hands of the press, unless the need for secrecy is manifestly overwhelming.*

It is on this ground that I concur in the judgment of the Court.

Notes and Questions

1. What was the "categorical" approach that the majority rejected? Why did it reject it?

2. Under the majority's approach, who can be punished for revealing the judge's name?

---

* National defense is the most obvious justification for government restrictions on publication. Even then, distinctions must be drawn between prior restraints and subsequent penalties. See, e.g., [*Times* and *Near*].

3. Why does Chief Justice Burger "question" the relevance of the clear and present danger standard to this case? Assuming its applicability, what was Virginia's error in applying it?

4. As we shall see later, the Supreme Court has not yet addressed the question of gathering information by illegal or tortious means. Early in this opinion, the Chief Justice notes that the information was not gathered by "illegal means." This theme recurs in the *Daily Mail* case, infra, and is raised by Justice Stevens in his separate opinion in Nebraska Press Ass'n v. Stuart, in Chapter IX. Why might the legality of the gathering process affect the outcome of *Landmark?*

SMITH v. DAILY MAIL PUBLISHING CO.

Supreme Court of the United States, 1979.
443 U.S. 97, 99 S.Ct. 2667, 61 L.Ed.2d 399, 5 Med.L.Rptr. 1305.

[A West Virginia statute made it a crime for a "newspaper" to publish the names of juveniles in connection with juvenile proceedings without a written order of the court. The respondent newspapers learned over a police radio about a killing at a junior high school. Reporters went to the scene and obtained the name of the suspect by asking witnesses, the police and a prosecuting attorney. The name was revealed thereafter in the newspapers and over several broadcast stations.

After being indicted, the newspapers obtained an order from the state supreme court barring any prosecution on the ground that the statute was unconstitutional.]

MR. CHIEF JUSTICE BURGER delivered the opinion of the Court.

We granted certiorari to consider whether a West Virginia statute violates the First and Fourteenth Amendments of the United States Constitution by making it a crime for a newspaper to publish, without the written approval of the juvenile court, the name of any youth charged as a juvenile offender.

. . .

(2)

Respondents urge this Court to hold that because § 49–7–3 requires court approval prior to publication of the juvenile's name it operates as a "prior restraint" on speech.[1] [ ] Respondents concede that this statute is not in the classic mold of prior restraint, there being no prior injunction against publication. Nonetheless, they

---

1. Respondents do not argue that the statute is a prior restraint because it imposes a criminal sanction for certain types of publication. At page 11 of their brief they state: "The statute in question is, to be sure, not a prior restraint be- cause it subjects newspapers to criminal punishments for what they print" after the event.

. . .

contend that the prior-approval requirement acts in "operation and effect" like a licensing scheme and thus is another form of prior restraint. See Near v. Minnesota [   ]. As such, respondents argue, the statute bears "a 'heavy presumption' against its constitutional validity." [   ] They claim that the State's interest in the anonymity of a juvenile offender is not sufficient to overcome that presumption.

Petitioners do not dispute that the statute amounts to a prior restraint on speech. Rather, they take the view that even if it is a prior restraint the statute is constitutional because of the significance of the State's interest in protecting the identity of juveniles.

(3)

The resolution of this case does not turn on whether the statutory grant of authority to the juvenile judge to permit publication of the juvenile's name is, in and of itself, a prior restraint. First Amendment protection reaches beyond prior restraints, [*Landmark* and *Cox Broadcasting*], and respondents acknowledge that the statutory provision for court approval of disclosure actually may have a less oppressive effect on freedom of the press than a total ban on the publication of the child's name.

Whether we view the statute as a prior restraint or as a penal sanction for publishing lawfully obtained, truthful information is not dispositive because even the latter action requires the highest form of state interest to sustain its validity. Prior restraints have been accorded the most exacting scrutiny in previous cases. [   ]. However, even when a state attempts to punish publication after the event it must nevertheless demonstrate that its punitive action was necessary to further the state interests asserted. [*Landmark*]. Since we conclude that this statute cannot satisfy the constitutional standards defined in *Landmark Communications, Inc.*, we need not decide whether, as argued by respondents, it operated as a prior restraint.

Our recent decisions demonstrate that state action to punish the publication of truthful information seldom can satisfy constitutional standards. In *Landmark Communications* we declared unconstitutional a Virginia statute making it a crime to publish information regarding confidential proceedings before a state judicial review commission that heard complaints about alleged disabilities and misconduct of state-court judges. In declaring that statute unconstitutional, we concluded:

> "[T]he publication Virginia seeks to punish under its statute lies near the core of the First Amendment, and the Commonwealth's interests advanced by the imposition of criminal sanctions are insufficient to justify the actual and potential encroachments on freedom of speech and of the press which follow therefrom." 435 U.S., at 838.

In Cox Broadcasting Corp. v. Cohn, supra, we held that damages could not be recovered against a newspaper for publishing the name of a rape victim. The suit had been based on a state statute that made it a crime to publish the name of the victim; the purpose of the statute was to protect the privacy right of the individual and the family. The name of the victim had become known to the public through official court records dealing with the trial of the rapist. In declaring the statute unconstitutional, the Court, speaking through Mr. Justice White, reasoned:

> "By placing the information in the public domain on official court records, the State must be presumed to have concluded that the public interest was thereby being served. . . . States may not impose sanctions on the publication of truthful information contained in official court records open to public inspection." 420 U.S., at 495.

One case that involved a classic prior restraint is particularly relevant to our inquiry. In Oklahoma Publishing Co. v. District Court, 430 U.S. 308 (1977), we struck down a state-court injunction prohibiting the news media from publishing the name or photograph of an 11-year-old boy who was being tried before a juvenile court. The juvenile judge had permitted reporters and other members of the public to attend a hearing in the case, notwithstanding a state statute closing such trials to the public. The court then attempted to halt publication of the information obtained from that hearing. We held that once the truthful information was "publicly revealed" or "in the public domain" the court could not constitutionally restrain its dissemination.

None of these opinions directly controls this case; however, all suggest strongly that if a newspaper lawfully obtains truthful information about a matter of public significance then state officials may not constitutionally punish publication of the information, absent a need to further a state interest of the highest order. These cases involved situations where the government itself provided or made possible press access to the information. That factor is not controlling. Here respondents relied upon routine newspaper reporting techniques to ascertain the identity of the alleged assailant. A free press cannot be made to rely solely upon the sufferance of government to supply it with information. See Houchins v. KQED, Inc., 438 U.S. 1, 11 (1978) (plurality opinion); Branzburg v. Hayes, 408 U.S. 665, 681 (1972). If the information is lawfully obtained, as it was here, the state may not punish its publication except when necessary to further an interest more substantial than is present here.

(4)

The sole interest advanced by the State to justify its criminal statute is to protect the anonymity of the juvenile offender. It is asserted that confidentiality will further his rehabilitation because publication of the name may encourage further antisocial conduct and also may cause the juvenile to lose future employment or suffer other consequences for this single offense. In Davis v. Alaska, 415 U.S. 308 (1974), similar arguments were advanced by the State to justify not permitting a criminal defendant to impeach a prosecution witness on the basis of his juvenile record. We said there that "[w]e do not and need not challenge the State's interest as a matter of its own policy in the administration of criminal justice to seek to preserve the anonymity of a juvenile offender." Id., at 319. However, we concluded that the State's policy must be subordinated to the defendant's Sixth Amendment right of confrontation. Ibid. The important rights created by the First Amendment must be considered along with the rights of defendants guaranteed by the Sixth Amendment. See Nebraska Press Assn. v. Stuart, 427 U.S., at 561. Therefore, the reasoning of *Davis* that the constitutional right must prevail over the state's interest in protecting juveniles applies with equal force here.

The magnitude of the State's interest in this statute is not sufficient to justify application of a criminal penalty to respondents. Moreover, the statute's approach does not satisfy constitutional requirements. The statute does not restrict the electronic media or any form of publication, except "newspapers," from printing the names of youths charged in a juvenile proceeding. In this very case, three radio stations announced the alleged assailant's name before the Daily Mail decided to publish it. Thus, even assuming the statute served a state interest of the highest order, it does not accomplish its stated purpose.

In addition, there is no evidence to demonstrate that the imposition of criminal penalties is necessary to protect the confidentiality of juvenile proceedings. . . . [A]ll 50 states have statutes that provide in some way for confidentiality, but only five, including West Virginia, impose criminal penalties on nonparties for publication of the identity of the juvenile. Although every state has asserted a similar interest, all but a handful have found other ways of accomplishing the objective. See Landmark Communications, Inc. v. Virginia, 435 U.S., at 843.[3]

(5)

Our holding in this case is narrow. There is no issue before us of unlawful press access to confidential judicial proceedings, see Cox Broadcasting Corp. v. Cohn, 420 U.S., at 496 n. 26; there is no issue here of privacy or prejudicial pretrial publicity. At issue is simply the power of a state to punish the truthful publication of an alleged

3. The approach advocated by the National Council of Juvenile Court Judges is based on cooperation between juvenile court personnel and newspaper editors. It is suggested that if the courts make clear their purpose and methods then the press will exercise discretion and generally decline to publish the juvenile's name without some prior consultation with the juvenile court judge.

juvenile delinquent's name lawfully obtained by a newspaper.[4] The asserted state interest cannot justify the statute's imposition of criminal sanctions on this type of publication. Accordingly, the judgment of the West Virginia Supreme Court of Appeals is

Affirmed.

MR. JUSTICE POWELL took no part in the consideration or decision of this case.

[Justice Rehnquist, who concurred in the judgment, filed the only separate opinion. He believed that protecting juveniles in this type of case was an interest of the "highest order" and "far outweighs any minimal interference with freedom of the press . . . ." He also noted that the Court's decision "renders nugatory" state expungement laws, because a potential employer may now obtain information on juvenile offenses by visiting the morgue of the local newspaper. Also, in future cases the "press will still be able to obtain the child's name in the same manner as it was acquired in this case. [ ] Thus, the Court's reference to effective alternatives [other than criminal punishment] for accomplishing the State's goal is a mere chimera."

He did concur, however, because the state's statute did not accomplish its stated purpose. Since broadcasters could, and did, identify the juvenile, it was "difficult to take very seriously West Virginia's asserted need to preserve the anonymity of its youthful offenders when it permits other, equally, if not more, effective means of mass communication to distribute this information without fear of punishment."]

Notes and Questions

1. What are the arguments for and against treating this criminal statute as some form of prior restraint?

2. How does this case differ from *Landmark?* From *Cox Broadcasting?* From *Oklahoma Publishing?*

3. What is the significance of the statute's failure to bar broadcasts of this information?

4. Compare Justice Rehnquist's view of the importance of this statute with Justice Stewart's opinion in *Landmark* about the importance of that statute.

5. Chief Justice Burger ends by stressing the "narrow" nature of the holding. What makes the decision narrow? Could this case have been decided differently if the state's claim had been coupled with an invasion of privacy claim by the juvenile offender?

4. In light of our disposition of the First and Fourteenth Amendment issue, we need not reach respondents' claim that the statute violates equal protection by being applicable only to newspapers but not other forms of journalistic expression.

6. Again, note the same stress on legal acquisition of the material that we saw in *Landmark*. Why might legality of acquisition matter here?

7. In Kansas v. Stauffer Communications, Inc., 225 Kan. 540, 592 P.2d 891 (1979), defendant newspaper was prosecuted for violating a statute that barred reporting the issuance of search or arrest warrants before they had been executed. During a murder investigation, a reporter learned that officers were looking for a stolen car and that car's two occupants. Warrants were issued for their arrest and the county attorney wanted them executed before the occupants could be alerted. The reporter learned the names of the two men. To check her information she went to the clerk of the local district court. The criminal appearance docket book was in the back of the room—which was entered by a swinging gate. "It was the general practice for reporters from the news media to go through the gate, proceed to the table where the criminal appearance docket was kept and look through its pages. It is a public document or record which is kept by the clerk of the district court."

Although warned by county officials not to publish the names, the newspaper did publish them. One occupant was never located. The other was located several weeks later in another state.

The state supreme court held that the statute could not constitutionally be applied in a case in which the information published was obtained from a public record. It relied primarily on *Cox Broadcasting* and *Oklahoma Publishing*. Cases in which the information was obtained from sources other than a public record were not discussed.

Two justices concurred. They noted that since this case all records of warrants were unavailable until after execution. This would delay accurate reporting to the public. They noted that clerks previously gave information to reporters, who treated it as confidential until an arrest was made. The reporter prepared background material so that a story could appear promptly after the arrest. "Courthouse reporters were regarded as special people, and were treated as such." But now all must be treated alike. The "determination of one reporter and one newspaper to publish one perhaps obscure item, will have a direct effect upon all Kansas courthouse reporters, and will in some instances result in a slowing of the news-gathering process. It marks the passing of an era."

8. Many states do have expungement statutes of one type or another. Some apply only to juveniles, while others apply to adults who were arrested but not convicted, or to adults who were convicted of certain offenses. The theory behind the statutes is that, at least in the case of adult offenders, once rehabilitated, they deserve a chance to be free of their past. Records may be sealed, segregated, or withheld from the public eye in other ways. In a sense the state seeks to declare what had been previously public—the conviction or arrest—now a state secret.

Chapter VII

OBSCENITY

Recall that in 1942 in the famous quotation from *Chaplinsky*, p. 35, supra, Justice Murphy stated that "lewd and obscene" words were among those "certain well-defined and narrowly limited classes of speech, the prevention and punishment of which have never been thought to raise any Constitutional problem." That may explain why, even though laws against obscenity had been in effect in this country since Colonial times, it was not until 1957 that the Supreme Court confronted the question of the impact of the First Amendment on the law of obscenity. In Roth v. United States, 354 U.S. 476 (1957), the Court held that even though it was "expression," obscenity was outside the protection of the First and Fourteenth Amendments. Yet, "sex and obscenity are not synonymous." Sex, "a great and mysterious motive force in human life, has indisputably been a subject of absorbing interest to mankind through the ages; it is one of the vital problems of human interest and public concern." Basically, the majority decided that obscenity could be determined by asking "whether to the average person, applying contemporary community standards, the dominant theme of the material taken as a whole appeals to prurient interest."

Shortly, thereafter, the majority consensus began to collapse as justices began groping for the line between the protected and the unprotected. For example, Justice Stewart, concurring in Jacobellis v. Ohio, 378 U.S. 184, 197 (1964), asserted that "hardcore pornography" was the only type of material that could be prohibited. He continued, "I shall not today attempt further to define the kinds of material I understand to be embraced within that shorthand description; and perhaps I could never succeed in intelligibly doing so. But I know it when I see it, and the motion picture involved in this case is not that."

In Memoirs v. Massachusetts, 383 U.S. 413 (1966), no majority opinion emerged as some justices began to diverge from the *Roth* approach. These developments will be discussed in the Miller case.

That same year, Justice Stewart tried to define the term in a dissenting opinion in Ginzburg v. United States, 383 U.S. 463, 499 (1966). He adopted a position put forward by the government that "Such materials include photographs, both still and motion picture, with no pretense of artistic value, graphically depicting acts of sexual intercourse, including various acts of sodomy and sadism, and sometimes involving several participants in scenes of orgy-like character." He also extended the class to drawings in comic-book format, and to some verbal descriptions of "such activities in a bizarre manner with no attempt whatsoever to afford portrayals of character or situation and with no pretense to literary value."

By 1967, the Court had been reduced to reversing convictions for obscenity without hearing oral argument or rendering written opinions whenever five members of the Court, using their own tests, concluded that the material in the case was not obscene. See Redrup v. New York, 386 U.S. 767 (1967).

In Kois v. Wisconsin, 408 U.S. 229 (1972), one count of defendant publisher's conviction was based on the fact that his underground newspaper ran two "relatively small pictures showing a nude man and nude woman embracing in a sitting position." The photographs accompanied an article about the arrest of one of the newspaper's photographers on a charge of possessing obscene material. The article said that the two photographs were "similar" to those taken from the photographer.

The Supreme Court summarily reversed the conviction. Relying on *Roth*, the Court concluded that it could not "fairly be said, either considering the article as it appears or the record before the state court, that the article was a mere vehicle for the publication of the pictures. A quotation from Voltaire in the flyleaf of a book will not constitutionally redeem an otherwise obscene publication," but these photographs were "rationally related to an article that itself was clearly" protected. There was no need to decide whether the dissemination of the photographs by themselves could be prohibited.

In 1973, the Supreme Court once again attempted to set up a clear definition of pornography. At the same time, the Court reexamined the rationale for excluding pornography from any First Amendment protection. It is important to remember that the standard set out in the following two cases is the current standard for obscenity.

MILLER v. CALIFORNIA

Supreme Court of the United States, 1973.
413 U.S. 15, 93 S.Ct. 2607, 37 L.Ed.2d 419.

MR. CHIEF JUSTICE BURGER delivered the opinion of the Court.

This is one of a group of "obscenity-pornography" cases being reviewed by the Court in a re-examination of standards enunciated in earlier cases involving what Mr. Justice Harlan called "the intractable obscenity problem." Interstate Circuit, Inc. v. Dallas, 390 U.S. 676, 704 (1968) (concurring and dissenting).

Appellant conducted a mass mailing campaign to advertise the sale of illustrated books, euphemistically called "adult" material. After a jury trial, he was convicted of violating California Penal Code § 311.2(a), a misdemeanor, by knowingly distributing obscene matter,[1] and the Appellate Department, Superior Court of California, County of Orange, summarily affirmed the judgment without opinion. Appellant's conviction was specifically based on his conduct in causing five unsolicited advertising brochures to be sent through the mail in an envelope addressed to a restaurant in Newport Beach, California. The envelope was opened by the manager of the restaurant and his mother. They had not requested the brochures; they complained to the police.

The brochures advertise four books entitled "Intercourse," "Man-Woman," "Sex Orgies Illustrated," and "An Illustrated History of Pornography," and a film entitled "Marital Intercourse." While the brochures contain some descriptive printed material, primarily they consist of pictures and drawings very explicitly depicting men and women in groups of two or more engaging in a variety of sexual activities, with genitals often prominently displayed.

I

This case involves the application of a State's criminal obscenity statute to a situation in which sexually explicit materials have been thrust by aggressive sales action upon unwilling recipients who had in no way indicated any desire to receive such materials. This Court has recognized that the States have a legitimate interest in prohibiting dissemination or exhibition of obscene material[2] when the mode

---

1. At the time of the commission of the alleged offense, which was prior to June 25, 1969, § 311.2(a) and § 311 of the California Penal Code read in relevant part:

"§ 311.2 Sending or bringing into state for sale or distribution; printing, exhibiting, distributing or possessing within state

"(a) Every person who knowingly: sends or causes to be sent, or brings or causes to be brought, into this state for sale or distribution, or in this state prepares, publishes, prints, exhibits, distributes, or offers to distribute, or has in his possession with intent to distribute or to exhibit or offer to distribute, any obscene matter is guilty of a misdemeanor. . . ."

"§ 311. Definitions

"As used in this chapter:

"(a) 'Obscene' means that to the average person, applying contemporary standards, the predominant appeal of the matter, taken as a whole, is to prurient interest, i.e., a shameful or morbid interest in nudity, sex, or excretion, which goes substantially beyond customary limits of candor in description or representation of such matters

and is matter which is utterly without redeeming social importance.

. . .

"(e) 'Knowingly' means having knowledge that the matter is obscene."

2. This Court has defined "obscene material" as "material which deals with sex in a manner appealing to prurient interest," *Roth v. United States, supra,* at 487, but the *Roth* definition does not reflect the precise meaning of "obscene" as traditionally used in the English language. Derived from the Latin *obscaenus, ob,* to, plus *caenum,* filth, "obscene" is defined in the Webster's Third New International Dictionary (Unabridged 1969) as "1a: disgusting to the senses . . . b: grossly repugnant to the generally accepted notions of what is appropriate . . . 2: offensive or revolting as countering or violating some ideal or principle." The Oxford English Dictionary (1933 ed.) gives a similar definition, "[o]ffensive to the senses, or to taste or refinement; disgusting, repulsive, filthy, foul, abominable, loathsome."

The material we are discussing in this case is more accurately defined as "pornography" or "pornographic material." "Pornography" derives from the Greek

of dissemination carries with it a significant danger of offending the sensibilities of unwilling recipients or of exposure to juveniles. [ ] It is in this context that we are called on to define the standards which must be used to identify obscene material that a State may regulate without infringing on the First Amendment as applicable to the States through the Fourteenth Amendment.

The dissent of Mr. Justice Brennan reviews the background of the obscenity problem, but since the Court now undertakes to formulate standards more concrete than those in the past, it is useful for us to focus on two of the landmark cases in the somewhat tortured history of the Court's obscenity decisions. In Roth v. United States, 354 U.S. 476 (1957), the Court sustained a conviction under a federal statute punishing the mailing of "obscene, lewd, lascivious or filthy . . ." materials. The key to that holding was the Court's rejection of the claim that obscene materials were protected by the First Amendment. Five Justices joined in the opinion stating:

> "All ideas having even the slightest redeeming social importance—unorthodox ideas, controversial ideas, even ideas hateful to the prevailing climate of opinion—have the full protection of the [First Amendment] guaranties, unless excludable because they encroach upon the limited area of more important interests. But implicit in the history of the First Amendment is the rejection of obscenity as utterly without redeeming social importance. . . . "We hold that obscenity is not within the area of constitutionally protected speech or press." 354 U.S., at 484–485 (footnotes omitted).

Nine years later, in Memoirs v. Massachusetts, 383 U.S. 413 (1966), the Court veered sharply away from the *Roth* concept and, with only three Justices in the plurality opinion, articulated a new test of obscenity. The plurality held that under the *Roth* definition

> "as elaborated in subsequent cases, three elements must coalesce: it must be established that (a) the dominant theme of the material taken as a whole appeals to a prurient interest in sex; (b) the material is patently offensive because it affronts contemporary community standards relating to the description or representation of sexual matters; and (c) the material is utterly without redeeming social value." Id., at 418.

. . .

(*porné*, harlot, and *graphos*, writing). The word now means "1: a description of prostitutes or prostitution 2: a depiction (as in writing or painting) of licentiousness or lewdness: a portrayal of erotic behavior designed to cause sexual excitement." Webster's Third New International Dictionary, supra. Pornographic material which is obscene forms a subgroup of all "obscene" expression, but not the whole, at least as the word "obscene" is now used in our language. We note, therefore, that the words "obscene material" as used in this case, have a specific judicial meaning which derives from the *Roth* case, i.e., obscene material "which deals with sex." *Roth*, supra, at 487. See also ALI Model Penal Code § 251.4(*l*) "Obscene Defined." (Official Draft 1962.)

While *Roth* presumed "obscenity" to be "utterly without redeeming social importance," *Memoirs* required that to prove obscenity it must be affirmatively established that the material is "*utterly* without redeeming social value." Thus, even as they repeated the words of *Roth*, the *Memoirs* plurality produced a drastically altered test that called on the prosecution to prove a negative, i.e., that the material was "*utterly* without redeeming social value"—a burden virtually impossible to discharge under our criminal standards of proof. Such considerations caused Mr. Justice Harlan to wonder if the "*utterly* without redeeming social value" test had any meaning at all. [ ]

Apart from the initial formulation in the Roth case, no majority of the Court has at any given time been able to agree on a standard to determine what constitutes obscene, pornographic material subject to regulation under the States' police power. [ ] We have seen "a variety of views among the members of the Court unmatched in any other course of constitutional adjudication." Interstate Circuit, Inc. v. Dallas, 390 U.S., at 704–705 (Harlan, J., concurring and dissenting) (footnote omitted).[3] This is not remarkable, for in the area of freedom of speech and press the courts must always remain sensitive to any infringement on genuinely serious literary, artistic, political, or scientific expression. This is an area in which there are few eternal verities.

The case we now review was tried on the theory that the California Penal Code § 311 approximately incorporates the three-stage *Memoirs* test, supra. But now the *Memoirs* test has been abandoned as unworkable by its author,[4] and no Member of the Court today supports the *Memoirs* formulation.

II

. . .

The basic guidelines for the trier of fact must be: (a) whether "the average person, applying contemporary community standards" would find that the work, taken as a whole, appeals to the prurient interest, [ ]; (b) whether the work depicts or describes, in a patently offensive way, sexual conduct specifically defined by the applicable state law; and (c) whether the work, taken as a whole, lacks serious literary, artistic, political, or scientific value. We do not adopt as a

---

3. In the absence of a majority view, this Court was compelled to embark on the practice of summarily reversing convictions for the dissemination of materials that at least five members of the Court, applying their separate tests, found to be protected by the First Amendment. Redrup v. New York, 386 U.S. 767 (1967). Thirty-one cases have been decided in this manner. Beyond the necessity of circumstances, however, no justification has ever been offered in support of the *Redrup* "policy." [ ] The *Redrup* procedure has cast us in the role of an unreviewable board of censorship for the 50 States, subjectively judging each piece of material brought before us.

4. See the dissenting opinion of Mr. Justice Brennan in Paris Adult Theatre I v. Slaton, [ ].

constitutional standard the *"utterly* without redeeming social value" test of Memoirs v. Massachusetts, 383 U.S., at 419; that concept has never commanded the adherence of more than three Justices at one time. . . .

We emphasize that it is not our function to propose regulatory schemes for the States. That must await their concrete legislative efforts. It is possible, however, to give a few plain examples of what a state statute could define for regulation under part (b) of the standard announced in this opinion, supra:

(a) Patently offensive representations or descriptions of ultimate sexual acts, normal or perverted, actual or simulated.

(b) Patently offensive representations or descriptions of masturbation, excretory functions, and lewd exhibition of the genitals.

Sex and nudity may not be exploited without limit by films or pictures exhibited or sold in places of public accommodation any more than live sex and nudity can be exhibited or sold without limit in such public places. At a minimum, prurient, patently offensive depiction or description of sexual conduct must have serious literary, artistic, political, or scientific value to merit First Amendment protection. [ ] For example, medical books for the education of physicians and related personnel necessarily use graphic illustrations and descriptions of human anatomy. In resolving the inevitably sensitive questions of fact and law, we must continue to rely on the jury system, accompanied by the safeguards that judges, rules of evidence, presumption of innocence, and other protective features provide, as we do with rape, murder, and a host of other offenses against society and its individual members.

Mr. Justice Brennan, [ ] [abandoning his former position], now maintains that no formulation of this Court, the Congress, or the States can adequately distinguish obscene material unprotected by the First Amendment from protected expression, [ ]. Paradoxically, Mr. Justice Brennan indicates that suppression of unprotected obscene material is permissible to avoid exposure to unconsenting adults, as in this case, and to juveniles, although he gives no indication of how the division between protected and nonprotected materials may be drawn with greater precision for these purposes than for regulation of commercial exposure to consenting adults only. Nor does he indicate where in the Constitution he finds the authority to distinguish between a willing "adult" one month past the state law age of majority and a willing "juvenile" one month younger.

Under the holdings announced today, no one will be subject to prosecution for the sale or exposure of obscene materials unless these materials depict or describe patently offensive "hard core" sexual conduct specifically defined by the regulating state law, as written or construed. We are satisfied that these specific prerequi-

sites will provide fair notice to a dealer in such materials that his public and commercial activities may bring prosecution. . . .
  . . .

III

Under a national Constitution, fundamental First Amendment limitations on the powers of the States do not vary from community to community, but this does not mean that there are, or should or can be, fixed, uniform national standards of precisely what appeals to the "prurient interest" or is "patently offensive." These are essentially questions of fact, and our nation is simply too big and too diverse for this Court to reasonably expect that such standards could be articulated for all 50 States in a single formulation, even assuming the prerequisite consensus exists. When triers of fact are asked to decide whether "the average person, applying contemporary community standards" would consider certain materials "prurient," it would be unrealistic to require that the answer be based on some abstract formulation. The adversary system, with lay jurors as the usual ultimate factfinders in criminal prosecutions, has historically permitted triers of fact to draw on the standards of their community, guided always by limiting instructions on the law. To require a State to structure obscenity proceedings around evidence of a *national* "community standard" would be an exercise in futility.
  . . .

It is neither realistic nor constitutionally sound to read the First Amendment as requiring that the people of Maine or Mississippi accept public depiction of conduct found tolerable in Las Vegas, or New York City. [ ] People in different States vary in their tastes and attitudes, and this diversity is not to be strangled by the absolutism of imposed uniformity. As the Court made clear in Mishkin v. New York, 383 U.S., at 508–509, the primary concern with requiring a jury to apply the standard of "the average person, applying contemporary community standards" is to be certain that, so far as material is not aimed at a deviant group, it will be judged by its impact on an average person, rather than a particularly susceptible or sensitive person—or indeed a totally insensitive one. [ ] We hold that the requirement that the jury evaluate the materials with reference to "contemporary standards of the State of California" serves this protective purpose and is constitutionally adequate.

IV

The dissenting Justices sound the alarm of repression. But, in our view, to equate the free and robust exchange of ideas and political debate with commercial exploitation of obscene material demeans the grand conception of the First Amendment and its high purposes in the historic struggle for freedom. It is a "misuse of the great guarantees of free speech and free press. . . ." Breard v.

Alexandria, 341 U.S., at 645.　The First Amendment protects works which, taken as a whole, have serious literary, artistic, political, or scientific value, regardless of whether the government or a majority of the people approve of the ideas these works represent.　"The protection given speech and press was fashioned to assure unfettered interchange of *ideas* for the bringing about of political and social changes desired by the people," Roth v. United States, supra, at 484 (emphasis added).　[　] But the public portrayal of hard core sexual conduct for its own sake, and for the ensuing commercial gain, is a different matter.

There is no evidence, empirical or historical, that the stern 19th century American censorship of public distribution and display of material relating to sex, [　] in any way limited or affected expression of serious literary, artistic, political, or scientific ideas.　.　.　.

Mr. Justice Brennan finds "it is hard to see how state-ordered regimentation of our minds can ever be forestalled."　Paris Adult Theatre I v. Slaton (Brennan, J., dissenting).　These doleful anticipations assume that courts cannot distinguish commerce in ideas, protected by the First Amendment, from commercial exploitation of obscene material.　Moreover, state regulation of hard core pornography so as to make it unavailable to nonadults, a regulation which Mr. Justice Brennan finds constitutionally permissible, has all the elements of "censorship" for adults; indeed even more rigid enforcement techniques may be called for with such dichotomy of regulation.
.　.　.

In sum, we (a) reaffirm the *Roth* holding that obscene material is not protected by the First Amendment; (b) hold that such material can be regulated by the States, subject to the specific safeguards enunciated above, without a showing that the material is *"utterly without redeeming social value"*; and (c) hold that obscenity is to be determined by applying "contemporary community standards," [　] not "national standards."　The judgment of the Appellate Department of the Superior Court, Orange County, California, is vacated and the case remanded to that court for further proceedings not inconsistent with the First Amendment standards established by this opinion.　[　]

Mr. Justice Douglas, dissenting.
.　.　.

Today the Court retreats from the earlier formulations of the constitutional test and undertakes to make new definitions.　This effort, like the earlier ones, is earnest and well intentioned.　The difficulty is that we do not deal with constitutional terms, since "obscenity" is not mentioned in the Constitution or Bill of Rights. And the First Amendment makes no such exception from "the press" which it undertakes to protect nor, as I have said on other occasions, is an exception necessarily implied, for there was no recognized exception to the free press at the time the Bill of Rights was adopted which treated "obscene" publications differently from other types of papers, magazines, and books. So there are no constitutional guidelines for deciding what is and what is not "obscene." The Court is at large because we deal with tastes and standards of literature. What shocks me may be sustenance for my neighbor. What causes one person to boil up in rage over one pamphlet or movie may reflect only his neurosis, not shared by others. We deal here with a regime of censorship which, if adopted, should be done by constitutional amendment after full debate by the people.

.   .   .

My contention is that until a civil proceeding has placed a tract beyond the pale, no criminal prosecution should be sustained. For no more vivid illustration of vague and uncertain laws could be designed than those we have fashioned.   .   .   .

While the right to know is the corollary of the right to speak or publish, no one can be forced by government to listen to disclosure that he finds offensive. That was the basis of my dissent in Public Utilities Comm'n v. Pollak, 343 U.S. 451, 467 (1952), where I protested against making a streetcar audience a "captive" audience. There is no "captive audience" problem in these obscenity cases. No one is being compelled to look or to listen. Those who enter news stands or bookstalls may be offended by what they see. But they are not compelled by the State to frequent those places; and it is only state or governmental action against which the First Amendment, applicable to the States by virtue of the Fourteenth, raises a ban.

.   .   .

MR. JUSTICE BRENNAN, with whom MR. JUSTICE STEWART and MR. JUSTICE MARSHALL join, dissenting.

In my dissent in Paris Adult Theatre I v. Slaton, decided this date, I noted that I had no occasion to consider the extent of state power to regulate the distribution of sexually oriented material to juveniles or the offensive exposure of such material to unconsenting adults. In the case before us, appellant was convicted of distributing obscene matter in violation of California Penal Code § 311.2, on the basis of evidence that he had caused to be mailed unsolicited brochures advertising various books and a movie. I need not now decide whether a statute might be drawn to impose, within the requirements of the First Amendment, criminal penalties for the precise conduct at issue here. For it is clear that under my dissent in *Paris Adult Theatre I*, the statute under which the prosecution was brought is unconstitutionally overbroad, and therefore invalid on its face. "[T]he transcendent value to all society of constitutionally protected expression is deemed to justify allowing 'attacks on overly broad statutes with no requirement that the person making the attack demonstrate that his own conduct could not be regulated by a statute drawn with the requisite narrow specificity.' "   .   .   .

PARIS ADULT THEATRE I v. SLATON

Supreme Court of the United States, 1973.
413 U.S. 49, 93 S.Ct. 2628, 37 L.Ed.2d 446.

[Respondents, a district attorney and a local court solicitor, filed civil complaints seeking injunctions against petitioners, two Atlanta movie theatres, on the ground they were exhibiting obscene motion pictures. Signs outside the theatres identified them as showing "mature feature films" and stated that entrants must be "21 and able to prove it. If viewing the nude body offends you, Please Do Not Enter." Nothing outside indicated the full nature of what was being shown. "In particular, nothing indicated that the films depicted as they did—scenes of simulated fellatio, cunnilingus, and group sex intercourse. There was no evidence that minors had ever entered the theatres." The trial court denied the injunction on the ground that the exclusion of minors and the general notice of content made the showing constitutionally permissible. The Georgia Supreme Court unanimously reversed on the grounds that the movies were "hard core pornography" and their exhibition was not protected by the First Amendment.]

MR. CHIEF JUSTICE BURGER delivered the opinion of the Court.
. . .

II

We categorically disapprove the theory, apparently adopted by the trial judge, that obscene, pornographic films acquire constitutional immunity from state regulation simply because they are exhibited for consenting adults only. This holding was properly rejected by the Georgia Supreme Court. Although we have often pointedly recognized the high importance of the state interest in regulating the exposure of obscene materials to juveniles and unconsenting adults, [ ] this Court has never declared these to be the only legitimate state interests permitting regulation of obscene material. The States have a long-recognized legitimate interest in regulating the use of obscene material in local commerce and in all places of public accommodation, as long as these regulations do not run afoul of specific constitutional prohibitions. . . .

In particular, we hold that there are legitimate state interests at stake in stemming the tide of commercialized obscenity, even assuming it is feasible to enforce effective safeguards against exposure to juveniles and to passersby.[7] Rights and interests "other than those

---

7. It is conceivable that an "adult" theater can—if it really insists—prevent the exposure of its obscene wares to juveniles. An "adult" bookstore, dealing in obscene books, magazines, and pictures, cannot realistically make this claim. The Hill-Link Minority Report of the Commission on Obscenity and Pornography emphasizes evidence (the Abelson National Survey of Youth and Adults) that, although most pornography may be bought by elders, "the heavy

of the advocates are involved." Breard v. Alexandria, 341 U.S. 622, 642 (1951). These include the interest of the public in the quality of life and the total community environment, the tone of commerce in the great city centers, and, possibly, the public safety itself. The Hill-Link Minority Report of the Commission on Obscenity and Pornography indicates that there is at least an arguable correlation between obscene material and crime. Quite apart from sex crimes, however, there remains one problem of large proportions aptly described by Professor Bickel:

> "It concerns the tone of the society, the mode, or to use terms that have perhaps greater currency, the style and quality of life, now and in the future. A man may be entitled to read an obscene book in his room, or expose himself indecently there. . . . We should protect his privacy. But if he demands a right to obtain the books and pictures he wants in the market, and to foregather in public places—discreet, if you will, but accessible to all—with others who share his tastes, *then to grant him his right is to affect the world about the rest of us, and to impinge on other privacies.* Even supposing that each of us can, if he wishes, effectively avert the eye and stop the ear (which, in truth, we cannot), what is commonly read and seen and heard and done intrudes upon us all, want it or not." 22 The Public Interest 25–26 (Winter 1971). (Emphasis added.)
> . . .

But, it is argued, there are no scientific data which conclusively demonstrate that exposure to obscene material adversely affects men and women or their society. It is urged on behalf of the petitioners that, absent such a demonstration, any kind of state regulation is "impermissible." We reject this argument. It is not for us to resolve empirical uncertainties underlying state legislation, save in the exceptional case where that legislation plainly impinges upon rights protected by the Constitution itself. . . . Although there is no conclusive proof of a connection between antisocial behavior and obscene material, the legislature of Georgia could quite reasonably determine that such a connection does or might exist. . . .

From the beginning of civilized societies, legislators and judges have acted on various unprovable assumptions. Such assumptions underlie much lawful state regulation of commercial and business affairs. [ ] The same is true of the federal securities and antitrust laws and a host of federal regulations. [ ] On the basis of these assumptions both Congress and state legislatures have, for example,

users and most highly exposed people to pornography are adolescent females (among women) and adolescent and young adult males (among men)." The Report of the Commission on Obscenity and Pornography 401 (1970). The legitimate interest in preventing exposure of juveniles to obscene material cannot be fully served by simply barring juveniles from the immediate physical premises of "adult" bookstores, when there is a flourishing "outside business" in these materials.

drastically restricted associational rights by adopting antitrust laws, and have strictly regulated public expression by issuers of and dealers in securities, profit sharing "coupons," and "trading stamps," commanding what they must and must not publish and announce. [ ] Understandably those who entertain an absolutist view of the First Amendment find it uncomfortable to explain why rights of association, speech, and press should be severely restrained in the marketplace of goods and money, but not in the marketplace of pornography.

Likewise, when legislatures and administrators act to protect the physical environment from pollution and to preserve our resources of forests, streams, and parks, they must act on such imponderables as the impact of a new highway near or through an existing park or wilderness area. . . . The fact that a congressional directive reflects unprovable assumptions about what is good for the people, including imponderable aesthetic assumptions, is not a sufficient reason to find that statute unconstitutional.

If we accept the unprovable assumption that a complete education requires certain books, see Board of Education v. Allen, 392 U.S. 236, 245 (1968) [ ], and the well nigh universal belief that good books, plays, and art lift the spirit, improve the mind, enrich the human personality, and develop character, can we then say that a state legislature may not act on the corollary assumption that commerce in obscene books, or public exhibitions focused on obscene conduct, have a tendency to exert a corrupting and debasing impact leading to antisocial behavior? . . . The sum of experience, including that of the past two decades, affords an ample basis for legislatures to conclude that a sensitive, key relationship of human existence, central to family life, community welfare, and the development of human personality, can be debased and distorted by crass commercial exploitation of sex. Nothing in the Constitution prohibits a State from reaching such a conclusion and acting on it legislatively simply because there is no conclusive evidence or empirical data.

It is argued that individual "free will" must govern, even in activities beyond the protection of the First Amendment and other constitutional guarantees of privacy, and that government cannot legitimately impede an individual's desire to see or acquire obscene plays, movies, and books. We do indeed base our society on certain assumptions that people have the capacity for free choice. Most exercises of individual free choice—those in politics, religion, and expression of ideas—are explicitly protected by the Constitution. Totally unlimited play for free will, however, is not allowed in our or any other society. We have just noted, for example, that neither the First Amendment nor "free will" precludes States from having "blue sky" laws to regulate what sellers of securities may write or publish about their wares. [ ] Such laws are to protect the weak, the uninformed, the unsuspecting, and the gullible from the exercise of

their own volition. Nor do modern societies leave disposal of garbage and sewage up to the individual "free will," but impose regulation to protect both public health and the appearance of public places.
States are told by some that they must await a "laissez faire" market
solution to the obscenity-pornography problem, paradoxically "by
people who have never otherwise had a kind word to say for laissez
faire," particularly in solving urban, commercial, and environmental
pollution problems. [ ]

The States, of course, may follow such a "laissez faire" policy
and drop all controls on commercialized obscenity, if that is what they
prefer, just as they can ignore consumer protection in the marketplace, but nothing in the Constitution *compels* the States to do so
with regard to matters falling within state jurisdiction. . . .

It is asserted, however, that standards for evaluating state
commercial regulations are inapposite in the present context, as state
regulation of access by consenting adults to obscene material violates
the constitutionally protected right to privacy enjoyed by petitioners'
customers. Even assuming that petitioners have vicarious standing
to assert potential customers' rights, it is unavailing to compare a
theater open to the public for a fee, with the private home of Stanley
v. Georgia, 394 U.S., at 568, and the marital bedroom of Griswold v.
Connecticut, [381 U.S.] at 485–486. This Court, has, on numerous
occasions, refused to hold that commercial ventures such as a motion-
picture house are "private" for the purpose of civil rights litigation
and civil rights statutes. [ ] The Civil Rights Act of 1964 specifically defines motion-picture houses and theaters as places of "public
accommodation" covered by the Act as operations affecting commerce. [ ]

Our prior decisions recognizing a right to privacy guaranteed by
the Fourteenth Amendment included "only personal rights that can
be deemed 'fundamental' or 'implicit in the concept of ordered liberty.' [ ]." [ ] This privacy right encompasses and protects the
personal intimacies of the home, the family, marriage, motherhood,
procreation, and child rearing. [ ] Nothing, however, in this Court's
decisions intimates that there is any "fundamental" privacy right
"implicit in the concept of ordered liberty" to watch obscene movies
in places of public accommodation.

If obscene material unprotected by the First Amendment in itself
carried with it a "penumbra" of constitutionally protected privacy,
this Court would not have found it necessary to decide *Stanley* on the
narrow basis of the "privacy of the home," which was hardly more
than a reaffirmation that "a man's home is his castle" Cf. Stanley v.
Georgia, supra, at 564.[13] Moreover, we have declined to equate the

---

13. The protection afforded by Stanley v. Georgia, 394 U.S. 557 (1969), is
restricted to a place, the home. In contrast, the constitutionally protected privacy of family, marriage, motherhood, procreation, and child rearing is not just
concerned with a particular place, but
with a protected intimate relationship.
Such protected privacy extends to the
doctor's office, the hospital, the hotel

privacy of the home relied on in *Stanley* with a "zone" of "privacy" that follows a distributor or a consumer of obscene materials wherever he goes. [ ] The idea of a "privacy" right and a place of public accommodation are, in this context, mutually exclusive. Conduct or depictions of conduct that the state police power can prohibit on a public street do not become automatically protected by the Constitution merely because the conduct is moved to a bar or a "live" theater stage, any more than a "live" performance of a man and woman locked in a sexual embrace at high noon in Times Square is protected by the Constitution because they simultaneously engage in a valid political dialogue.

. . .

Finally, petitioners argue that conduct which directly involves "consenting adults" only has for that sole reason, a special claim to constitutional protection. Our Constitution establishes a broad range of conditions on the exercise of power by the States, but for us to say that our Constitution incorporates the proposition that conduct involving consenting adults only is always beyond state regulation, is a step we are unable to take.[15] Commercial exploitation of depictions, descriptions, or exhibitions of obscene conduct on commercial premises open to the adult public falls within a State's broad power to regulate commerce and protect the public environment. The issue in this context goes beyond whether someone, or even the majority, considers the conduct depicted as "wrong" or "sinful." The States have the power to make a morally neutral judgment that public exhibition of obscene material, or commerce in such material, has a tendency to injure the community as a whole, to endanger the public safety, or to jeopardize, in Mr. Chief Justice Warren's words, the States' "right . . . to maintain a decent society." Jacobellis v. Ohio, 378 U.S., at 199 (dissenting opinion).

To summarize, we have today reaffirmed the basic holding of Roth v. United States, supra, that obscene material has no protection under the First Amendment. See Miller v. California. . . . In this case we hold that the States have a legitimate interest in regulating commerce in obscene material and in regulating exhibition of obscene material in places of public accommodation, including so-called "adult" theaters from which minors are excluded. In light of these holdings, nothing precludes the State of Georgia from the regulation

---

room, or as otherwise required to safeguard the right to intimacy involved. [ ] Obviously, there is no necessary or legitimate expectation of privacy which would extend to marital intercourse on a street corner or a theater stage.

15. The state statute books are replete with constitutionally unchallenged laws against prostitution, suicide, voluntary self-mutilation, brutalizing "bare fist" prize fights, and duels, although these crimes may only directly involve "consenting adults." . . .

As Professor Irving Kristol has observed: "Bearbaiting and cockfighting are prohibited only in part out of compassion for the suffering animals; the main reason they were abolished was because it was felt that they debased and brutalized the citizenry who flocked to witness such spectacles." On the Democratic Idea in America 33 (1972).

of the allegedly obscene material exhibited in Paris Adult Theatre I or II, provided that the applicable Georgia law, as written or authoritatively interpreted by the Georgia courts, meets the First Amendment standards set forth in Miller v. California, [ ]. The judgment is vacated and the case remanded to the Georgia Supreme Court for further proceedings not inconsistent with this opinion and Miller v. California, supra. [ ].

Vacated and remanded.

MR. JUSTICE DOUGLAS, dissenting.

My Brother Brennan is to be commended for seeking a new path through the thicket which the Court entered when it undertook to sustain the constitutionality of obscenity laws and to place limits on their application. I have expressed on numerous occasions my disagreement with the basic decision that held that "obscenity" was not protected by the First Amendment. I disagreed also with the definitions that evolved. Art and literature reflect tastes; and tastes, like musical appreciation, are hardly reducible to precise definitions. That is one reason I have always felt that "obscenity" was not an exception to the First Amendment. . . .

. . .

MR. JUSTICE BRENNAN, with whom MR. JUSTICE STEWART and MR. JUSTICE MARSHALL join, dissenting.

This case requires the Court to confront once again the vexing problem of reconciling state efforts to suppress sexually oriented expression with the protections of the First Amendment, as applied to the States through the Fourteenth Amendment. No other aspect of the First Amendment has, in recent years, demanded so substantial a commitment of our time, generated such disharmony of views, and remained so resistant to the formulation of stable and manageable standards. I am convinced that the approach initiated 16 years ago in Roth v. United States, 354 U.S. 476 (1957), and culminating in the Court's decision today, cannot bring stability to this area of the law without jeopardizing fundamental First Amendment values, and I have concluded that the time has come to make a significant departure from that approach.

. . .

. . . The essence of our problem in the obscenity area is that we have been unable to provide "sensitive tools" to separate obscenity from other sexually oriented but constitutionally protected speech, so that efforts to suppress the former do not spill over into the suppression of the latter. . . .

. . .

Of course, the vagueness problem would be largely of our own creation if it stemmed primarily from our failure to reach a consensus on any one standard. But after 16 years of experimentation and debate I am reluctantly forced to the conclusion that none of the available formulas, including the one announced today, can reduce the vagueness to a tolerable level while at the same time striking an acceptable balance between the protections of the First and Fourteenth Amendments, on the one hand, and on the other the asserted state interest in regulating the dissemination of certain sexually oriented materials. Any effort to draw a constitutionally acceptable boundary on state power must resort to such indefinite concepts as "prurient interest," "patent offensiveness," "serious literary value," and the like. The meaning of these concepts necessarily varies with the experience, outlook, and even idiosyncrasies of the person defining them. Although we have assumed that obscenity does exist and that we "know it when [we] see it," Jacobellis v. Ohio, supra, at 197 (Stewart, J., concurring), we are manifestly unable to describe it in advance except by reference to concepts so elusive that they fail to distinguish clearly between protected and unprotected speech.

. . . These considerations suggest that no one definition, no matter how precisely or narrowly drawn, can possibly suffice for all situations, or carve out fully suppressible expression from all media without also creating a substantial risk of encroachment upon the guarantees of the Due Process Clause and the First Amendment.[9]

The vagueness of the standards in the obscenity area produces a number of separate problems, and any improvement must rest on an understanding that the problems are to some extent distinct. First, a vague statute fails to provide adequate notice to persons who are engaged in the type of conduct that the statute could be thought to proscribe. . . .

In addition to problems that arise when any criminal statute fails to afford fair notice of what it forbids, a vague statute in the areas of speech and press creates a second level of difficulty. We have indicated that "stricter standards of permissible statutory vagueness may be applied to a statute having a potentially inhibiting effect on speech; a man may the less be required to act at his peril here, because the free dissemination of ideas may be the loser." Smith v. California, 361 U.S. 147, 151 (1959). . . .

. . .

The problems of fair notice and chilling protected speech are very grave standing alone. But it does not detract from their importance to recognize that a vague statute in this area creates a third, although admittedly more subtle, set of problems. These problems concern the institutional stress that inevitably results

9. Although I did not join the opinion of the Court in Stanley v. Georgia, 394 U.S. 557 (1969), I am now inclined to agree that "the Constitution protects the right to receive information and ideas," and that "[t]his right to receive information and ideas, regardless of their social worth . . . is fundamental to our free society." . . . Whether or not a class of "obscene" and thus entirely unprotected speech does exist, I am forced to conclude that the class is incapable of definition with sufficient clarity to withstand attack on vagueness grounds. Accordingly, it is on principles of the void-for-vagueness doctrine that this opinion exclusively relies.

where the line separating protected from unprotected speech is excessively vague. In *Roth* we conceded that "there may be marginal cases in which it is difficult to determine the side of the line on which a particular fact situation falls. . . ." 354 U.S., at 491–492. Our subsequent experience demonstrates that almost every case is "marginal." And since the "margin" marks the point of separation between protected and unprotected speech, we are left with a system in which almost every obscenity case presents a constitutional question of exceptional difficulty. . . .

. . .

. . . In addition, the uncertainty of the standards creates a continuing source of tension between state and federal courts, since the need for an independent determination by this Court seems to render superfluous even the most conscientious analysis by state tribunals. And our inability to justify our decisions with a persuasive rationale—or indeed, any rationale at all—necessarily creates the impression that we are merely second-guessing state court judges.

The severe problems arising from the lack of fair notice, from the chill on protected expression, and from the stress imposed on the state and federal judicial machinery persuade me that a significant change in direction is urgently required. I turn, therefore, to the alternatives that are now open.

IV

1. The approach requiring the smallest deviation from our present course would be to draw a new line between protected and unprotected speech, still permitting the States to suppress all material on the unprotected side of the line. In my view, clarity cannot be obtained pursuant to this approach except by drawing a line that resolves all doubt in favor of state power and against the guarantees of the First Amendment. We could hold, for example, that any depiction or description of human sexual organs, irrespective of the manner or purpose of the portrayal, is outside the protection of the First Amendment and therefore open to suppression by the States. That formula would, no doubt, offer much fairer notice of the reach of any state statute drawn at the boundary of the State's constitutional power. And it would also, in all likelihood, give rise to a substantial probability of regularity in most judicial determinations under the standard. But such a standard would be appallingly overbroad, permitting the suppression of a vast range of literary, scientific, and artistic masterpieces. Neither the First Amendment nor any free community could possibly tolerate such a standard. Yet short of that extreme it is hard to see how any choice of words could reduce the vagueness problem to tolerable proportions, so long as we remain committed to the view that some class of materials is subject to outright suppression by the State.

2. The alternative adopted by the Court today recognizes that a prohibition against any depiction or description of human sexual organs could not be reconciled with the guarantees of the First Amendment. But the Court does retain the view that certain sexually oriented material can be considered obscene and therefore unprotected by the First and Fourteenth Amendment. To describe that unprotected class of expression, the Court adopts a restatement of the *Roth-Memoirs* definition of obscenity. . . .

. . .

Although the Court's restatement substantially tracks the three-part test announced in Memoirs v. Massachusetts, supra, it does purport to modify the "social value" component of the test. Instead of requiring, as did *Roth* and *Memoirs*, that state suppression be limited to materials utterly lacking in social value, the Court today permits suppression if the government can prove that the materials lack "*serious* literary, artistic, political or scientific value." But the definition of "obscenity" as expression utterly lacking in social importance is the key to the conceptual basis of *Roth* and our subsequent opinions. In *Roth* we held that certain expression is obscene, and thus outside the protection of the First Amendment, precisely *because* it lacks even the slightest redeeming social value. [ ] The Court's approach necessarily assumes that some works will be deemed obscene—even though they clearly have *some* social value—because the State was able to prove that the value, measured by some unspecified standard, was not sufficiently "serious" to warrant constitutional protection. That result is not merely inconsistent with our holding in *Roth;* it is nothing less than a rejection of the fundamental First Amendment premises and rationale of the *Roth* opinion and an invitation to widespread suppression of sexually oriented speech. Before today, the protections of the First Amendment have never been thought limited to expressions of *serious* literary or political value. [ ]

. . .

4. Finally, I have considered the view, urged so forcefully since 1957 by our Brothers Black and Douglas, that the First Amendment bars the suppression of any sexually oriented expression. That position would effect a sharp reduction, although perhaps not a total elimination, of the uncertainty that surrounds our current approach. Nevertheless, I am convinced that it would achieve that desirable goal only by stripping the States of power to an extent that cannot be justified by the commands of the Constitution, at least so long as there is available an alternative approach that strikes a better balance between the guarantee of free expression and the States' legitimate interests.

V

Our experience since *Roth* requires us not only to abandon the effort to pick out obscene materials on a case-by-case basis, but also to reconsider a fundamental postulate of *Roth:* that there exists a definable class of sexually oriented expression that may be totally suppressed by the Federal and State Governments. Assuming that such a class of expression does in fact exist, I am forced to conclude that the concept of "obscenity" cannot be defined with sufficient specificity and clarity to provide fair notice to persons who create and distribute sexually oriented materials, to prevent substantial erosion of protected speech as a byproduct of the attempt to suppress unprotected speech, and to avoid very costly institutional harms. Given these inevitable side effects of state efforts to suppress what is assumed to be *unprotected* speech, we must scrutinize with care the state interest that is asserted to justify the suppression. For in the absence of some very substantial interest in suppressing such speech, we can hardly condone the ill effects that seem to flow inevitably from the effort.

Obscenity laws have a long history in this country. . . .

This history caused us to conclude in *Roth* "that the unconditional phrasing of the First Amendment [that "Congress shall make no law . . . abridging the freedom of speech, or of the press . . ."] was not intended to protect every utterance." . . .

Because we assumed—incorrectly, as experience has proved— that obscenity could be separated from other sexually oriented expression without significant costs either to the First Amendment or to the judicial machinery charged with the task of safeguarding First Amendment freedoms, we had no occasion in *Roth* to probe the asserted state interest in curtailing unprotected, sexually oriented speech. Yet, as we have increasingly come to appreciate the vagueness of the concept of obscenity, we have begun to recognize and articulate the state interests at stake. . . .

The opinions in *Redrup* and Stanley v. Georgia reflected our emerging view that the state interest in protecting children and in protecting unconsenting adults may stand on a different footing from the other asserted state interests. . . . Similarly, if children are "not possessed of that full capacity for individual choice which is the presupposition of the First Amendment guarantees," Ginsberg v. New York, 390 U.S., at 649–650 (Stewart, J., concurring), then the State may have a substantial interest in precluding the flow of obscene materials even to consenting juveniles. [ ]

But, whatever the strength of the state interests in protecting juveniles and unconsenting adults from exposure to sexually oriented materials, those interests cannot be asserted in defense of the holding of the Georgia Supreme Court in this case. . . .

At the outset it should be noted that virtually all of the interests that might be asserted in defense of suppression, laying aside the special interests associated with distribution to juveniles and unconsenting adults, were also posited in Stanley v. Georgia, supra, where we held that the State could not make the "mere private possession of obscene material a crime." Id., at 568. That decision presages the conclusions I reach here today.

In *Stanley* we pointed out that "[t]here appears to be little empirical basis for" the assertion that "exposure to obscene materials may lead to deviant sexual behavior or crimes of sexual violence." Id., at 566 and n. 9.[26] In any event, we added that "if the State is only concerned about printed or filmed materials inducing antisocial conduct, we believe that in the context of private consumption of ideas and information we should adhere to the view that '[a]mong free men, the deterrents ordinarily to be applied to prevent crime are education and punishment for violations of the law. . . . ' Whitney v. California, 274 U.S. 357, 378 (1927) (Brandeis, J., concurring)." Id., at 566–567.

Moreover, in *Stanley* we rejected as "wholly inconsistent with the philosophy of the First Amendment," id., at 566, the notion that there is a legitimate state concern in the "control [of] the moral content of a person's thoughts," id., at 565, and we held that a State "cannot constitutionally premise legislation on the desirability of controlling a person's private thoughts." Id., at 566. That is not to say, of course, that a State must remain utterly indifferent to—and take no action bearing on—the morality of the community. . . .

. . .

If, as the Court today assumes, "a state legislature may . . . act on the . . . assumption that commerce in obscene books, or public exhibitions focused on obscene conduct, have a tendency to exert a corrupting and debasing impact leading to antisocial behavior," then it is hard to see how state-ordered regimentation of our minds can ever be forestalled. For if a State may, in an effort to maintain or create a particular moral tone, prescribe what its citizens cannot read or cannot see, then it would seem to follow that in pursuit of that same objective a State could decree that its citizens must read certain books or must view certain films. . . .

---

26. Indeed, since *Stanley* was decided, the President's Commission on Obscenity and Pornography has concluded:

"In sum, empirical research designed to clarify the question has found no evidence to date that exposure to explicit sexual materials plays a significant role in the causation of delinquent or criminal behavior among youth or adults. The Commission cannot conclude that exposure to erotic materials is a factor in the causation of sex crime or sex delinquency." Report of the Commission on Obscenity and Pornography 27 (1970) (footnote omitted).

To the contrary, the Commission found that "[o]n the positive side, explicit sexual materials are sought as a source of entertainment and information by substantial numbers of American adults. At times, these materials also appear to serve to increase and facilitate constructive communication about sexual matters within marriage." Id., at 53.

Recognizing these principles, we have held that so-called themat-ic obscenity—obscenity which might persuade the viewer or reader to engage in "obscene" conduct—is not outside the protection of the First Amendment:

> "It is contended that the State's action was justified because the motion picture attractively portrays a relationship which is contrary to the moral standards, the religious precepts, and the legal code of its citizenry. This argument misconceives what it is that the Constitution protects. Its guarantee is not confined to the expression of ideas that are conventional or shared by a majority. It protects advocacy of the opinion that adultery may sometimes be proper, no less than advocacy of socialism or the single tax. And in the realm of ideas it protects expression which is eloquent no less than that which is unconvincing." Kingsley International Pictures Corp. v. Regents, 360 U.S. 684, 688–689 (1959).

Even a legitimate, sharply focused state concern for the morality of the community cannot, in other words, justify an assault on the protections of the First Amendment. [   ] Where the state interest in regulation of morality is vague and ill defined, interference with the guarantees of the First Amendment is even more difficult to justify.

In short, while I cannot say that the interests of the State—apart from the question of juveniles and unconsenting adults—are trivial or nonexistent, I am compelled to conclude that these interests cannot justify the substantial damage to constitutional rights and to this Nation's judicial machinery that inevitably results from state efforts to bar the distribution even of unprotected material to consenting adults. [   ] I would hold, therefore, that at least in the absence of distribution to juveniles or obtrusive exposure to unconsenting adults, the First and Fourteenth Amendments prohibit the State and Federal Governments from attempting wholly to suppress sexually oriented materials on the basis of their allegedly "obscene" contents. Nothing in this approach precludes those governments from taking action to serve what may be strong and legitimate interests through regulation of the manner of distribution of sexually oriented material.

.   .   . Difficult questions must still be faced, notably in the areas of distribution to juveniles and offensive exposure to unconsenting adults. Whatever the extent of state power to regulate in those areas,[29] it should be clear that the view I espouse today would introduce a large measure of clarity to this troubled area, would reduce the institutional pressure on this Court and the rest of the State and Federal Judiciary, and would guarantee fuller freedom of

---

29. The Court erroneously states, Miller v. California, ante, [   ], that the author of this opinion "indicates that suppression of unprotected obscene material is permissible to avoid exposure to unconsenting adults . . . and to juveniles. . . ." I defer expression of my views as to the scope of state power in these areas until cases squarely presenting these questions are before the Court. See n. 9, supra; Miller v. California, supra (dissenting opinion).

expression while leaving room for the protection of legitimate governmental interests. . . .

Notes and Questions

1. What changes are wrought by *Miller*? How are they justified?

2. What different question is raised in *Paris*? What motivates the majority's answer to that question?

3. What underlies Justice Douglas's argument that no prosecution for obscenity should be possible until after a particular tract has been declared "beyond the pale" in a civil proceeding?

4. Is the use of injunctions necessarily more restrictive of speech than prosecuting for an offense after publication? The Court, 5–4, has upheld a state procedure under which an ex parte injunction could be obtained against allegedly obscene material with trial to follow within a day after issue was joined, and decision within two days after the end of the trial. Kingsley Books, Inc. v. Brown, 354 U.S. 436 (1957). The trial judge in that case found the books obscene and ordered their destruction. The majority stressed that it "would be bold to assert that the *in terrorem* effect" of criminal statutes "less restrains booksellers in the period before the law strikes" than does this civil procedure. The majority also stressed that the statute did not operate on matter until after it had been published. The dissenters were concerned that the original injunction operated before there had been a finding that the material was unprotected speech.

5. In Jenkins v. Georgia, 418 U.S. 153 (1974), Jenkins had been convicted for showing the film "Carnal Knowledge." The state courts had relied on the jury's finding, but the Court reversed on the ground that the standards set in *Miller* did not justify the jury's verdict. Although "ultimate sexual acts" took place "the camera does not focus on the bodies of the actors at such times. There is no exhibition whatever of the actors' genitals, lewd or otherwise, during these scenes. There are occasional scenes of nudity, but nudity alone is not enough to make material legally obscene" under *Miller*. Was the Supreme Court back in the business of reviewing individual books and movies?

6. In *Miller*, California had chosen to use a statewide community standard and the Court had observed that a national standard was "hypothetical and unascertainable." In *Jenkins*, the majority had said that a state was not required to define the phrase "contemporary community standards" in more precise geographical terms. In Hamling v. United States, 418 U.S. 87 (1974), the Court interpreted a federal statute barring the mailing of obscene materials to make the relevant community the one from which the jury was drawn.

7. Perhaps because motion picture censorship was permissible, states attempted to regulate more than obscenity when reviewing films. Some attempts were struck down because the grounds other

than obscenity were found too vague. In Joseph Burstyn, Inc. v. Wilson, 343 U.S. 495 (1952), New York had banned a film on the grounds that it was "sacrilegious," which the state defined as treating religion with "contempt, mockery, scorn, and ridicule." The Court thought this gave the censor too much leeway, although it noted that the First Amendment did not allow freedom to exhibit "every motion picture of every kind at all times and all places."

8. The result is that although motion pictures may still be subject to administrative screening before public presentation, Times Film Corp. v. Chicago, 365 U.S. 43 (1961), they may be rejected only for those reasons that permit penalizing distributors of books and magazines after the fact: obscenity and pornography. The characteristics of different media of course, may still lead to different results. In addition, when preliminary obligations are imposed, speedy review of adverse decisions must be assured.

9. In Erznoznik v. Jacksonville, 422 U.S. 205 (1975), the Court struck down an ordinance forbidding the showing of nudity on drive-in theatre screens visible from public streets. After an unsuccessful captive audience justification, the city also asserted that the ordinance was justified as a protection of children. This also failed because the restriction was "broader than permissible. The ordinance is not directed against sexually explicit nudity, nor is it otherwise limited. Rather, it sweepingly forbids display of films containing any uncovered buttocks or breasts, irrespective of contexts or pervasiveness. Thus, it would bar a film containing a picture of a baby's buttocks, the nude body of a war victim, or scenes from a culture in which nudity is indigenous . . . Clearly all nudity cannot be deemed obscene even as to minors." In appropriately drafted statutes, it is possible to protect minors from obscenity even though such a statute could not apply to the general public. See Ginsberg v. New York, 390 U.S. 629 (1968) for a discussion of the states' power to regulate minors' access to obscene material.

10. An obscenity statute need not precisely describe the kinds of sexual conduct covered. In Ward v. Illinois, 431 U.S. 767 (1977), the petitioner alleged that an Illinois obscenity statute was void for vagueness because it did not explicitly include sado-masochistic material in its ban. The Court disagreed, 5–4.

Justice White, for the majority, held that the Illinois law was sufficiently explicit in referring to the "kinds" of barred materials and that, even if it were not, the defendant had ample guidance from the state courts prior to the sale for which he was convicted. In response to an argument that sado-masochistic materials cannot be proscribed because they were not mentioned in *Miller*, Justice White asserted that the specifics in *Miller* were offered only as "examples" and "were not intended to be exhaustive."

Justice Stevens, for the dissenters, viewed the failure to require specificity in the definition of offensive material as a major and unwarranted change that would hasten the "ultimate downfall" of the *Miller* standard. "Today, the Court silently abandons one of the cornerstones of the *Miller* test." He found nothing in the statute that "specifically defines" what is prohibited. Nor had the state's supreme court "remedied this deficiency by supplying a limiting construction." To say that the statute need contain only generic references to the "kinds" of materials that are barred, "is to hold that a person can be prosecuted although the materials he sells are not specifically described in the list. Only five years ago, the Court promised that 'no one' could be so prosecuted."

11. In Pinkus v. United States, 436 U.S. 293 (1978), the Court was reviewing a conviction under the federal statute against mailing obscene materials, 18 U.S.C. § 1461. The trial judge charged the jury that in considering community standards under the pre-*Miller* law, the jury should consider "the community as a whole, young and old, educated and uneducated, the religious and the irreligious, men, women, and children, from all walks of life." The Court held the inclusion of "children" to be reversible error. The concern was that the "average person" standard would be substantially diluted by including children. The jury should be restricted to adults where there is no evidence that children were the intended recipients of the material or the defendant had no reason to know that children were likely to receive the material.

The trial judge also charged that the material was to be judged "by the standard of the hypothetical average person in the community, but in determining this average standard you must include the sensitive and the insensitive, in other words, you must include everyone in the community." The defendant objected to focusing on sensitive persons, but the majority saw no problem so long as the jury was told to include both sensitive and insensitive persons.

The trial judge also charged that in determining the prurient interest aspect the jury should consider the "average person of the community as a whole" and also the "members of a deviant sexual group." Defendant claimed that "to support an instruction on appeal to the prurient interest of deviants, the prosecution must come forward with evidence to guide the jury in its deliberations, since jurors cannot be presumed to know the reaction of such groups to stimuli as they would that of the average person." The majority disagreed: "Concededly, in the past we have 'reserve[d] judgment . . . on the extreme case . . . where contested materials are directed at such a bizarre deviant group that the experience of the trier of fact would be plainly inadequate to judge whether the material appeals to the [particular] prurient interest.' Paris Adult Theatre I v. Slaton, 413 U.S. 49, 56 n. 6 (1973). But here we are not presented with that 'extreme' case because the government did in fact present expert testimony on rebuttal which, when combined with the exhibits themselves, sufficiently guided the jury. This instruction, therefore, was acceptable."

Finally, the majority upheld a part of the charge in which the judge told the jury that if it found this "to be a close case" it might consider whether the defendant was involved in pandering: "the business of purveying textual or graphic matter openly advertised to appeal to the erotic interest of their customers." This permitted the jurors to consider the "touting descriptions along with the materials themselves to determine whether they were intended to appeal to the recipient's prurient interest in sex. . . ." Here the majority followed Ginzburg v. United States, 383 U.S. 465 (1966), in which the use of evidence of pandering was first approved.

Justice Stevens, though indicating that he would prefer to reconsider the entire obscenity area, concurred to make a majority. Justices Brennan, Stewart, and Marshall concurred in reversal for the reasons they asserted in *Miller* and *Paris*. Justice Powell dissented on the ground that the charge about children was error but the error was "harmless beyond a reasonable doubt."

12. When evaluating allegedly obscene material, the jury may look for guidance beyond the material itself to the circumstances of its sale and distribution. Citing *Hamling* and *Ginzburg*, Justice Rehnquist, for the majority, in Splawn v. California, 431 U.S. 595 (1977), concluded that as "a matter of First Amendment law, evidence of pandering to prurient interests in the creation, promotion or dissemination of material is relevant in determining whether the material is obscene."

Justice Stevens, in a dissent joined by Justices Brennan, Stewart and Marshall, declared that the majority decision allowed non-obscene material to be classified as obscene solely because of truthful advertising that emphasized its sexually provocative nature. In a footnote, he asserted that *Virginia Pharmacy*, p. 285, infra, granted constitutional protection to truthful advertisements.

13. In a federal prosecution for the mailing of obscene materials, a state statute is not conclusive evidence of community standards, although it may be relevant to the jury's determination. In Smith v. United States, 431 U.S. 291 (1977), the Court, 5–4, held that mailing obscene materials from one part of Iowa to another violated federal law, even though Iowa did not then bar the distribution of such materials to adults.

For the majority, Justice Blackmun asserted the question to be "whether the jury is entitled to rely on its own knowledge of community standards, or whether a state legislature (or a smaller legislative body) may declare what the community standards shall be, and, if such a declaration has been made, whether it is binding in a federal prosecution under § 1461." He concluded that a permissive state could not force the federal government to allow its mails to be used for obscene materials. He also suggested that the Iowa statute might not show community standards at all, but indicate only "that the resources of its prosecutors' offices should be devoted to matters deemed to have greater priority than the enforcement of obscenity statutes." The statute could not be conclusive in this federal prosecution on issues of contemporary community standards for appeal to the prurient interest and patent offensiveness.

Justice Brennan, joined by Justices Stewart and Marshall, dissented on the ground that the statute was "clearly overbroad and unconstitutional on its face."

Justice Stevens, who joined the Court after *Miller*, used his dissent in *Smith* to point out "the need for a principled re-examination of the premises" on which *Miller* rests, and his belief that "criminal prosecutions are an unacceptable method of abating a public nuisance which is entitled to at least a modicum of First Amendment protection."

He seriously questioned the ability of jurors to determine community standards of offensiveness with "even-handed" consistency. He saw no reason why a standard for a metropolitan area was any less "hypothetical and unascertainable," than the national standard the Court had previously rejected. He feared subtle but powerful peer pressure in the jury room since "it is much more popular to be against sin than to be tolerant of it," and suggested that "a juror might well find certain materials appealing and yet be unwilling to say so."

Finally, Justice Stevens argued that the material in this case, which was requested by postal inspectors, should not provide the basis for a criminal prosecution since it was delivered in sealed envelopes and could hardly be expected to offend those who requested it.

14. One of the difficulties facing a jury in this area is determining the community standards of patent offensiveness. Not surprisingly, urban communities are reported to have less restrictive standards, perhaps because of greater exposure to a greater variety of sexually provocative material.

One study revealed significant polarization in all communities, making it very difficult to determine a community-wide standard. Depictions of homosexuality, oral sex and sado-masochism were more offensive than nudity or intercourse, and were more offensive when depicted visually rather than textually. For the majority of communities, depictions of intercourse were more offensive than depictions of nudity, irrespective of format. Glassman, Community Standards of Patent Offensiveness: Public Opinion Data and Obscenity Law 42 Public Opinion Q. 161 (1978).

15. Women's groups have long been concerned about a possible link between pornography and violence towards women. In the early 1980's this concern led to pressure in various cities to pass ordinances

defining pornography in terms of material that presented women as sexual objects or in positions of sexual subordination. In American Booksellers Association v. Hudnut, 598 F.Supp. 1316 (D.Ind.1984) the major trade association for publishers of general books, textbooks and educational materials challenged an Indianapolis statute that prohibited "all discriminatory practices of sexual subordination or inequality through pornography." Pornography was defined as "the graphic sexually explicit subordination of women." The court held the ordinance unconstitutional on several grounds including vagueness and overbreadth. Rejecting the city's attempt to characterize the ordinance as a discrimination ordinance, the court found that it restricted speech and thus, was subject to the *Miller* standard.

16. The Supreme Court is still trying to solve the definitional problem. The Washington Supreme Court declared the Washington obscenity statute unconstitutionally overbroad because it defined "prurient interest" in terms of "lust". The Court heard arguments in Brockett v. Spokane Arcades in February 1985.

Children. As Justice Brennan noted in his dissent in *Paris*, juveniles present special problems in the area of obscenity. Many have argued that *Miller* is not an adequate solution in this area. The following case is important not only for its holding on this question, but also for its discussion of the doctrine of overbreadth.

NEW YORK v. FERBER

Supreme Court of the United States, 1982.
458 U.S. 747, 102 S.Ct. 3348, 73 L.Ed.2d 1113.

[Ferber, the owner of a Manhattan bookstore was arrested for selling two sexually explicit films to an undercover policeman. He was acquitted on charges of promoting an obscene sexual performance under § 263.10 of the New York Penal Law, but convicted under § 263.15 of promoting a sexual performance by a child. The conviction was overturned by the N.Y. Court of Appeals which held that § 263.15 violated the First Amendment.]

JUSTICE WHITE delivered the opinion of the Court.

At issue in this case is the constitutionality of a New York criminal statute which prohibits a person from knowingly promoting sexual performances by children under the age of 16 by distributing material which depicts such performances.

. . .

II

The Court of Appeals proceeded on the assumption that the standard of obscenity incorporated in § 263.10, which follows the guidelines enunciated in Miller v. California [ ], constitutes the appropriate line dividing protected from unprotected expression by which to measure a regulation directed at child pornography. . . .

The Court of Appeals' assumption was not unreasonable in light of our decisions. This case, however, constitutes our first examination of a statute directed at and limited to depictions of sexual activity involving children. We believe our inquiry should begin with the question of whether a State has somewhat more freedom in proscribing works which portray sexual acts or lewd exhibitions of genitalia by children.

B

The *Miller* standard, like its predecessors, was an accommodation between the state's interests in protecting the "sensibilities of unwilling recipients" from exposure to pornographic material and the dangers of censorship inherent in unabashedly content-based laws. Like obscenity statutes, laws directed at the dissemination of child pornography run the risk of suppressing protected expression by allowing the hand of the censor to become unduly heavy. For the following reasons, however, we are persuaded that the States are entitled to greater leeway in the regulation of pornographic depictions of children.

First. It is evident beyond the need for elaboration that a state's interest in "safeguarding the physical and psychological well being of a minor" is "compelling." [ ] "A democratic society rests, for its continuance, upon the healthy well-rounded growth of young people into full maturity as citizens. Prince v. Massachusetts, 321 U.S. 158, 168 (1944). Accordingly, we have sustained legislation aimed at protecting the physical and emotional well-being of youth even when the laws have operated in the sensitive area of constitutionally protected rights. In Prince v. Massachusetts, supra, the Court held that a statute prohibiting use of a child to distribute literature on the street was valid notwithstanding the statute's effect on a First Amendment activity. In Ginsberg v. New York [ ] we sustained a New York law protecting children from exposure to non-obscene literature. Most recently, we held that the government's interest in the "well-being of its youth" justified special treatment of indecent broadcasting received by adults as well as children. FCC v. Pacifica Foundation, 438 U.S. 726 (1978).

The prevention of sexual exploitation and abuse of children constitutes a government objective of surpassing importance. . . . The legislative judgment, as well as the judgment found in the relevant literature, is that the use of children as subjects of pornographic materials is harmful to the physiological, emotional, and mental health of the child. That judgment, we think, easily passes muster under the First Amendment.

Second. The distribution of photographs and films depicting sexual activity by juveniles is intrinsically related to the sexual abuse of children in at least two ways. First, the materials produced are a permanent record of the children's participation and the harm to the child is exacerbated by their circulation. Second, the distribution network for child pornography must be closed if the production of material which requires the sexual exploitation of children is to be effectively controlled.

Respondent does not contend that the State is unjustified in pursuing those who distribute child pornography. Rather, he argues that it is enough for the State to prohibit the distribution of materials that are legally obscene under the *Miller* test. While some States may find that this approach properly accommodates its interests, it does not follow that the First Amendment prohibits a State from going further. The *Miller* standard, like all general definitions of what may be banned as obscene, does not reflect the State's particular and more compelling interest in prosecuting those who promote the sexual exploitation of children. Thus, the question under the *Miller* test of whether a work, taken as a whole, appeals to the prurient interest of the average person bears no connection to the issue of whether a child has been physically or psychologically harmed in the production of the work. Similarly, a sexually explicit depiction need not be "patently offensive" in order to have required the sexual exploitation of a child for its production. In addition, a work which, taken as a whole, contains serious literary, artistic, political, or scientific value may nevertheless embody the hardest core of child pornography. "It is irrelevant to the child [who has been abused] whether or not the material . . . has a literary, artistic, political, or social value." [ ] We therefore cannot conclude that the *Miller* standard is a satisfactory solution to the child pornography problem.

Third. The advertising and selling of child pornography provides an economic motive for and is thus an integral part of the production of such materials, an activity illegal throughout the nation. "It rarely has been suggested that the constitutional freedom for speech and press extends its immunity to speech or writing used as an integral part of conduct in violation of a valid criminal statute." [ ] . . .

Fourth. The value of permitting live performances and photographic reproductions of children engaged in lewd sexual conduct is exceedingly modest, if not *de minimus.* We consider it unlikely that visual depictions of children performing sexual acts or lewdly exhibiting their genitals would often constitute an important and necessary part of a literary performance or scientific or educational work. . . .

Fifth. Recognizing and classifying child pornography as a category of material outside the protection of the First Amendment is not incompatible with our earlier decisions. "The question whether speech is, or is not protected by the First Amendment often depends on the content of the speech." [ ] . . . Thus, it is not rare that a content-based classification of speech has been accepted because it may be appropriately generalized that within the confines of the given classification, the evil to be restricted so overwhelmingly outweighs the expressive interests, if any, at stake, that no process of case-by-case adjudication is required. When a definable class of material, such as that covered by § 263.15, bears so heavily and pervasively on the welfare of children engaged in its production, we think the balance of competing interests is clearly struck and that it is permissible to consider these materials as without the protection of the First Amendment.

C

There are, of course, limits on the category of child pornography which, like obscenity, is unprotected by the First Amendment. As with all legislation in this sensitive area, the conduct to be prohibited must be adequately defined by the applicable state law, as written or authoritatively construed. Here the nature of the harm to be combatted requires that the state offense be limited to works that *visually* depict sexual conduct by children below a specified age. The category of "sexual conduct" proscribed must also be suitably limited and described.

The test for child pornography is separate from the obscenity standard enunciated in *Miller*, but may be compared to it for purpose of clarity. The *Miller* formulation is adjusted to the following respects: A trier of fact need not find that the material appeals to the prurient interest of the average person; it is not required that sexual conduct portrayed be done so in a patently offensive manner; and the material at issue need not be considered as a whole. We note that the distribution of descriptions or other depictions of sexual conduct, not otherwise obscene, which do not involve live performance or photographic or other visual reproduction of live performances, retains First Amendment protection. . . .

. . . .

III

It remains to address the claim that the New York statute is unconstitutionally overbroad because it would forbid the distribution of material with serious literary, scientific or educational value or material which does not threaten the harms sought to be combatted by the State. Respondent prevailed on that ground below, and it is to that issue we now turn.

The New York Court of Appeals recognized that overbreadth scrutiny has been limited with respect to conduct-related regulation [ ], but it did not apply [that] test because the challenged statute, in its view, was directed at "pure speech." The Court went on to find that § 263.15 was fatally overbroad: "[T]he statute would prohibit the showing of any play or movie in which a child portrays a defined sexual act, real or simulated, in a nonobscene manner. It would also prohibit the sale, showing, or distributing of medical or educational materials containing photographs of such acts. Indeed, by its terms, the statute would prohibit those who oppose such portrayals from providing illustrations of what they oppose."

A

The traditional rule is that a person to whom a statute may constitutionally be applied may not challenge that statute on the ground that it may conceivably be applied unconstitutionally to others in situations not before the Court. [ ] . . .

What has come to be known as the First Amendment over-breadth doctrine is one of the few exceptions to this principle and must be justified by "weighty countervailing policies." [ ] The doctrine is predicated on the sensitive nature of protected expression: "persons whose expression is constitutionally protected may well refrain from exercising their rights for fear of criminal sanctions by a statute susceptible of application to protected expression." [ ] It is for this reason that we have allowed persons to attack overly broad statutes even though the conduct of the person making the attack is clearly unprotected and could be proscribed by a law drawn with the requisite specificity. [ ]

The scope of the First Amendment overbreadth doctrine, like most exceptions to established principles, must be carefully tied to the circumstances in which facial invalidation of a statute is truly warranted. Because of the wide-reaching effects of striking a statute down on its face at the request of one whose own conduct may be punished despite the First Amendment, we have recognized that the overbreadth doctrine is "strong medicine" and have employed it with hesitation, and then "only as a last resort." Broadrick v. Oklahoma, 413 U.S. 601 (1973). We have, in consequence, insisted that the overbreadth involved be "substantial" before the statute involved will be invalidated on its face.

. . .

Broadrick was a regulation involving restrictions on political campaign activity, an area not considered "pure speech," and thus it was unnecessary to consider the proper overbreadth test when a law arguably reaches traditional forms of expression such as books and films. As we intimated in *Broadrick*, the requirement of substantial overbreadth extended "at the very least," to cases involving conduct plus speech. This case, which poses the question squarely, convinces us that the rationale of *Broadrick* is sound and should be applied in the present context involving the harmful employment of children to make sexually explicit materials for distribution.

. . . The requirement of substantial overbreadth is directly derived from the purpose and nature of the doctrine. While a sweeping statute, or one incapable of limitation, has the potential to repeatedly chill the exercise of expressive activity by many individuals, the extent of deterrence of protected speech can be expected to decrease with the declining reach of the regulation. This observation appears equally applicable to the publication of books and films as it is to activities, such as picketing or participation in election campaigns, which have previously been categorized as involving conduct plus speech. . . .

. . .

IV

Because § 263.15 is not substantially overbroad, it is unnecessary to consider its application to material that does not depict sexual conduct of a type that New York may restrict consistent with the First Amendment. As applied to Paul Ferber and to others who distribute similar material, the statute does not violate the First Amendment as applied to the States through the Fourteenth. The decision of the New York Court of Appeals is reversed and the case is remanded to that Court for further proceedings not inconsistent with this opinion.

So ordered.

JUSTICE BLACKMUN concurs in the result.

[Justice O'Connor concurred separately to emphasize the narrowness of the Court's decision. In her view the case held only that even if the N.Y. statute made some constitutionally protected speech illegal, it was not sufficiently overbroad to justify facial invalidation. She then indicated that the compelling state interest in protecting minors might be sufficient to justify banning the works in question even if they had serious literary, artistic, political or scientific value.]

[Justice Brennan, joined by Justice Marshall concurred in the judgment, but argued that application of the statute to materials with serious literary, artistic, political or scientific value would violate the First Amendment.]

[Justice Stevens concurred in the judgment on the ground that the category of speech covered by the statute was of lower quality than other speech. Since such "marginal" speech falls near the bottom of the First Amendment hierarchy, according to Justice Stevens, the extraordinary protection of the overbreadth doctrine was not justified.]

Offensive Words. The relationship between obscenity and offensive speech is developed in Cohen v. California, 403 U.S. 15 (1971), involving the words on the jacket, in which the Court rejected a captive audience rationale, p. 57, supra.

Justice Harlan concluded that the controlling point was whether "the States, acting as guardians of public morality, may properly remove this offensive word from the public vocabulary." He began consideration of that question by reemphasizing the values of free expression "in a society as diverse and populous as ours," citing Justice Brandeis's concurrence in *Whitney*, p. 48 supra. He then turned to the specific facts of the case:

> Against this perception of the constitutional policies involved, we discern certain more particularized considerations that peculiarly call for reversal of this conviction. First, the principle contended for by the State seems inherently boundless. How is one to distinguish this from any other offensive word? Surely the State has no right to cleanse public debate to the point where it is grammatically palatable to the most squeamish among us. Yet no readily ascertainable general principle exists for stopping short of that result were we to affirm the judgment below. For, while the particular four-letter word being litigated here is perhaps more distasteful than most others of its genre, it is nevertheless often true that one man's vulgarity is another's lyric. Indeed, we think it is largely because governmental officials cannot make principled distinctions in this area that the Constitution leaves matters of taste and style so largely to the individual.

> Additionally, we cannot overlook the fact, because it is well illustrated by the episode involved here, that much linguistic expression serves a dual communicative function: it conveys not only ideas capable of relatively precise, detached explication, but otherwise inexpressible emotions as well. In fact, words are often chosen as much for their emotive as their cognitive force. We cannot sanction the view that the Constitution, while solicitous of the cognitive content of individual speech, has little or no regard for that emotive function which, practically speaking, may often be the more important element of the overall message sought to be communicated. . . .

Justice Blackmun's dissent, joined by Justice Black among others, argued mainly that "Cohen's absurd and immature antic . . . was mainly conduct and little speech. [ ] Further, the case appears to me to be well within the sphere of Chaplinsky v. New Hampshire. . . . As a consequence, this Court's agonizing over First Amendment values seems misplaced and unnecessary."

Some have pressed the importance of the Cohen case as one involving political speech—and the recognition that limits on political expression are particularly dangerous, as well as the difficulty government will have in deciding what words to bar. In addition, the use of offensive speech often reveals important information to the rest of society—sometimes the ugliness of the speaker's cause; sometimes the deep extent of the speaker's frustration, and sometimes the ugliness of the situation being challenged. On this analysis, efforts to prevent group libels and to purify political speech (except perhaps for captive audiences) would be impermissible. Compare Farber, Civilizing Public Discourse: An Essay on Professor Bickel, Justice Harlan, and the Enduring Significance of Cohen v. California, 1980 Duke L.J. 283 (rejecting limits on such speech) with Arkes, Civility and the Restriction of Speech: Rediscovering the Defamation of Groups, 1974 Sup.Ct.Rev. 281 (supporting statutes proscribing certain types of attacks on racial and religious groups).

The special problem of the use of four-letter words in broadcasting is explored in Chapter XVI.

Chapter VIII

ADVERTISING REGULATION

A. WHY IS REGULATION NEEDED?

Over $90 billion is spent annually on advertising in the United States, with about $70 billion going to buy time and space in the mass media (the rest primarily being used for direct mail and specialty advertising). Additional billions are spent preparing the advertisements. When this much money is spent to promote products and services, sometimes to millions of people at a time, there is a strong motivation to advertise as effectively as possible. Advertisers may be tempted to mislead or to lie in an attempt to win customers. Businesses of all sizes have fallen prey to this, attempting to induce the greatest possible number of people to buy what the business is selling. Some advertisements are blatantly deceptive, others simply ambiguous, some literally true but still misleading. All of these present problems to consumers who must decide what products and services to purchase, and from whom.

Since advertising has become a major force in American commerce, questions have emerged about how honest advertising can and should be. Advertising is one component of an overall marketing scheme designed to move products from manufacturers, through distributors, to retailers where, for a variety of reasons, including the impact of advertising, consumers purchase them. During the industrial revolution, two conditions emerged that made this marketing pattern practical. First, products identified by a brand label could be moved by new transportation systems from maker to seller throughout the country. Second, the mass media were developing as a means to inform consumers what products were available and, according to most advertisers, that one brand was "better" than the others.

Among the first to exploit this new vehicle for promoting products were patent medicine sellers. Most patent medicines contained a high percentage of alcohol (a 94-proof compound was not unusual) and were touted as able to cure almost every known ailment. From the Civil War to the early Twentieth Century, patent medicine ads ran in magazines and newspapers and were put on posters and in brochures. Some ads contained an early form of a now-popular advertising technique, the testimonial. Actors, Congressmen, and even clergymen were said to be satisfied users, though there is no way of knowing whether these people actually used or approved of the nostrums.

An example of irresponsible early advertising is one printed in a magazine in the 1880's for Dr. Scott's Electric Corset. The corset was said to "cure" problems of being too fat or too lean or "any bodily ailment." It could also "ward off and cure disease" by bringing "the magnetic power" of the corset "into constant contact with all vital organs." To reassure readers, the "doctor" claimed that "professional men affirmed that there is hardly a disease that electricity and magnetism will not benefit and cure." One of the "professional men" named was a former Surgeon General of the United States.

The success of patent medicines, spurred by outlandish advertising, prompted manufacturers of other products to begin advertising. In many cases, ads for cereal, clothing, and cough drops were just as deceiving as those for patent medicines.

Today, the excesses may not be as blatant as they were 100 years ago, but some advertisers still attempt to deceive the public. Considerable debate exists over how to minimize unfair and misleading advertising and who should exercise these controls. For example, can advertising be controlled at all in the face of First Amendment protections of free expression? May advertising to certain groups (such as young children) or for certain products (such as non-prescription drugs) be regulated or even forbidden? Should certain groups (such as doctors and lawyers) not be able to advertise?

These questions and others have drawn the attention of numerous people, from consumer groups to the Federal Trade Commission (FTC), the government agency most directly involved with advertising regulation. Other federal and state agencies have addressed the problem of deceptive advertising. The advertising industry has a self-regulation process, and the media and advertising agencies have codes identifying unacceptable practices.

B. THE FEDERAL TRADE COMMISSION

1. THE FTC's JURISDICTION

It was a 1906 series of article in *Colliers* on patent medicines, "The Great American Fraud," written by muckraker Samuel Hopkins Adams, along with similar pieces in other publications, that in part led to the passage of the Pure Food and Drug Act in 1906 and the Federal Trade Commission Act (FTCA) in 1914.

The FTC was established by the FTCA. The Commission was initially charged with prohibiting "unfair methods of competition in commerce." As originally conceived, this phrase had nothing to do with advertising, but was to allow the FTC to enforce antitrust laws that courts had viewed with some hostility. Soon the FTC attempted to regulate deceptive advertising as a form of "unfair competition." The Supreme Court upheld the FTC, but only as a means of eliminating unfair competition by one business against another. Protection of consumers, as such, was beyond FTC power. Federal Trade Commission v. Raladam Co., 283 U.S. 643 (1931).

Three years later the Court reversed itself and upheld the FTC's regulation of the marketing of candy to children in a way that involved "gambling" to receive a larger quantity of the product. Federal Trade Commission v. R.F. Keppel & Bro., Inc., 291 U.S. 304 (1934). In part, the Court justified the concern with customers because they were children, but this was a first step toward giving the FTC power to regulate advertising because of its effect on consumers.

Congress concurred in this extension of power by passing what are known as the Wheeler-Lea Amendments to the FTCA in 1938. One change allowed the Commission to prohibit "unfair methods of competition in commerce, and unfair or deceptive acts or practices in commerce." The omission of "competition" in the latter phrase allowed the Commission to "center its attention on the direct *protection of the consumer.*" Pep Boys—Manny, Moe & Jack v. Federal Trade Commission, 122 F.2d 158 (3d Cir.1941). False advertising of food, drugs, or cosmetics also became a violation of the law. The amendments allowed the FTC to take action against deceptive advertising that affected consumers.

The Supreme Court gave effect to this Congressional intent, noting that business practices can be unfair even if they violate no antitrust laws or other statutes and affect no competitors. Federal Trade Commission v. Sperry & Hutchinson Co., 405 U.S. 233 (1972). That is, some activities might be "unfair" even though not specifically proscribed by law. The Commission can regulate "unfairness," generating a new body of law, where practices are immoral, unethical, oppressive or unscrupulous.

Another set of amendments to the FTCA was added in 1975 by the Magnuson-Moss Act, 15 U.S.C.A. § 2301. This enlarged the Commission's powers to their present reach: "Unfair methods of competition in or *affecting* commerce and unfair or deceptive acts or practices in or *affecting* commerce are hereby declared unlawful." These changes allow the FTC to deal with unfair or deceptive practices that may be local, not directly interstate, in character, but which have an adverse impact on interstate commerce. In particular, the Commission can reach deceptive practices in large cities affecting the economically disadvantaged and poorly educated.

Overseeing advertising is just one FTC task. The agency is composed of five commissioners, including the chairman, appointed by the President for seven-year terms and confirmed by the Senate. It has a staff of over 1,650 and an annual budget of about $70 million (compare with $90 billion spent on advertising annually). Its other responsibilities include laws concerning antitrust violations, warranties, granting of credit, and label laws.

What is the "advertising" over which the FTC has jurisdiction? Courts view advertising as any public and deliberate effort to draw attention to a product or service, or even to a person or organization. This may include trading stamps, premiums, lotteries, and labels, as well as the more common newspaper and magazine ads, television commercials, and billboards.

The statute does not define "unfair" or "deceptive." Instead, the FTC has established criteria for use in determining whether an ad violates the standards, and courts usually defer to the agency's expertise in this area, overturning the Commission only when its decision is deemed arbitrary or capricious. Federal Trade Commission v. Mary Carter Paint Co., 382 U.S. 46 (1965).

Any action the FTC takes must be in the public interest. Since advertising certainly affects the public, most actions the FTC takes regarding misleading ads will meet this standard. Also, the ad must misrepresent a fact that is misleading in a material respect. 15 U.S.C. § 52. That is, something that would be a material factor in a consumer's decision to buy the product or service satisfies this standard. To look at it another way, is the misleading statement a material part of the ad? For example, a representative of Standard Oil Co. claimed to be standing in front of the firm's research laboratory when discussing Chevron F–310 gasoline. In fact, he was near a county court house. An FTC hearing examiner said this was not a material misleading fact, even though the ad was false in this respect.

The Commission need not prove that an advertisement actually deceived consumers, but simply that it had a tendency to do so. For example, in Charles of the Ritz v. Federal Trade Commission, 143 F.2d 676 (2d Cir.1944), a manufacturer said its skin cream could make facial skin more attractive by removing lines and rejuvenating the user's face. Although the FTC produced no witnesses who said they thought the cream could actually do all that, the court said such proof was not necessary—a "capacity to deceive" was sufficient.

Who needs to be misled? At one time the FTC and the courts said it was a "reasonable" person. Then the courts held that if even a particularly gullible person were misled, that was sufficient. GELB v. Federal Trade Commission, 144 F.2d 580 (2d Cir.1944). Today, it has been suggested that the Commission's standard is "the perception of commercially significant ordinary purchasers of the advertised goods or services at whom the advertising is directed or who can ordinarily be expected to read or view it." G. Rosden & P. Rosden, The Law of Advertising 18–46 (1984).

It is equally accurate to say that a literally true statement in an advertisement may be deceptive and that an absolutely untrue statement may not be deceptive.

For instance, references to Santa Claus or to a tooth fairy are not to be believed as real, but rather as fantasies, and are acceptable advertising techniques. Aside from fantasies, however, explicit untruths are deceptive in advertising unless they are immaterial or the FTC finds they do not affect the public interest. Falsely advertising something as an antique or as imported or saying a razor blade will shave effectively for six months, are all explicit untruths materially affecting a consumer's reaction to the ad and are adverse to the public interest.

Questions of truth and untruth are more difficult when they are implicit or subtle. Determining whether such an ad is misleading must be based on the entire advertisement, not just a portion of it. One apparently misleading statement may be clarified by another, but the latter must be as conspicuous as the first and similarly positioned.

Sometimes even an ad that is literally true may be misleading because of the way it is presented. A seller of photograph albums and family portraits was ordered to stop representing that the company sold only to selected customers and gave away the albums free. The impression given was that each family was carefully selected for the offer. In fact, the company simply chose people on a random basis or by referrals from other customers.

Also, the cost of the photographs included the "price" of the album; the portraits actually "should" have cost less by themselves. The court said that although the representations may have been true literally, the overall impression given—free gifts and special selection of customers—was misleading. Kalwajtys v. Federal Trade Commission, 237 F.2d 654 (7th Cir.1956).

Ambiguity in ads usually will be construed against the advertiser. The use of an explanatory phrase may protect the advertiser. For example, the Potato Chip Institute said a product made of dehydrated potatoes, instead of raw potatoes, should not be called "potato chips." The court held that the phrase, "fashioned from dried potato granules," on the product's label and in its advertising prevented incorrect inferences by the public. Potato Chip Institute v. General Mills, 461 F.2d 1088 (8th Cir.1972).

Finally, the advertiser need not intend to deceive, though intent may make the violation more severe. Chrysler Corp. v. Federal Trade Commission, 561 F.2d 357 (D.C.Cir.1977).

2. DECEPTIVE ADVERTISING TECHNIQUES

The FTC and the courts have found many advertising techniques to be misleading or deceptive. Major examples follow.

a. *Deception by Pictures*

Although early concern over misleading ads stressed the words used, the FTC also has found ads deceptive because of their illustrations. It is deceptive to show an automobile with a number of options—bumper guards, striping, special wheel covers—but quote the price for a stripped-down version. An ad showing a model wearing expensive, tailor-made clothes may be deceptive if the store sells modestly priced, factory-produced goods. Children's toys must be able to do what the pictures show them doing. It is considered deceptive to have special effects or film editing enhance the toys' capabilities.

One widespread violation of FTC standards involved actors dressed in white coats to give the appearance of being scientists or doctors, adding an aura of authority to the product.

Although anything that would be deceptive if said in words would be equally impermissible if pictured, television has aggravated the problem because of the medium's impact and its ubiquity. For instance, the FTC considered deceptive a commercial showing a can of liquid household cleaner on a radiator, on a kitchen stove and near a candle. The commercial did not say the product was not flammable, but the picture gave that impression. In fact, it was highly flammable. Adell Chemical Co., Inc., 54 F.T.C. 1801 (1958).

Television demonstrations are another source of misleading ads. The Commission prohibited a Prestone antifreeze commercial which showed two metal strips, one coated with Prestone, the other with another antifreeze, dipped into acid. The Prestone strip remained in one piece; the other disintegrated. The FTC said the ad was unfair, in part, because the acid was not found in automobiles and the metal strips were not made of the metal found in automobile cooling systems. Union Carbide Corp., 79 F.T.C. 124 (1971).

b. Deception Regarding Price

An effective way to lure customers to a store or to persuade them to allow salespeople into their homes is to offer something "free." Few businesses would stay solvent if they gave away merchandise or services. In fact, most "free" offers involve the purchasing of something first, such as a two-for-one sale.

Generally, the Commission holds that deception occurs when the cost of the "free" goods is added to other merchandise the consumer buys without the customer's knowledge. In two-for-one offers, the merchandiser must have sold one unit of a product at the same price charged for two units when the offer was made. Federal Trade Commission v. Mary Carter Paint Co., 382 U.S. 46 (1965).

Since customers have begun to question whether unusually low prices mean unusually low quality merchandise or services, businesses have started explaining how such a price can be charged. For example, they may say goods are repossessed or have been bought from a merchant who needed cash or are offered at factory prices. In these cases, the FTC has said the representation must be accurate or it constitutes deceptive advertising. Similarly, reduced or special prices must actually be below former prices, and those earlier prices cannot have been set high in order to later lower them for a "sale." Also, a "regular retail price" has to be that for which the item usually is sold in the retailer's trade area.

"Bait and switch" advertising is another technique based on price. The "bait" is an item advertised at a particularly attractive price, designed to persuade customers to come to the store. Once there, customers are told the advertised item is "out of stock" or otherwise unavailable, that it had limitations anyway, and that the customer should consider a different, more expensive, and available, model. The FTC considers it deceptive to advertise merchandise without a clear intention of selling it. For instance, a sewing machine company advertised for $39 a model claimed to be worth $120. The salesperson disparaged the machine to customers, showing no interest in selling it, and instead praised a more expensive model. The FTC said the company had no intention of selling the advertised model, using it only to lure customers and switch them to the more expensive machine. This practice is forbidden by the FTC, although it must be distinguished from convincing a customer to buy a more expensive item than advertised, where the retailer has a sufficient stock of the advertised model and will sell it to customers who choose it.

c. *Mockups*

Among new problems presented by television is the use of mockups. A mockup is more than just a demonstration. It is the use of an object to simulate something that is real, the technique being used because of television's technical limitations. For instance, orange juice may look drab, almost like milk, unless a coloring agent is added to it. Mockups are sometimes abused by advertisers, using deceptive techniques to sell a product. The FTC has had trouble specifying what is permitted and what is not.

The Supreme Court confronted the mockup problem in FTC v. Colgate-Palmolive Co., 380 U.S. 374 (1969), when Colgate wanted to show that its Rapid Shave could shave sandpaper. Three one-minute commercials showed the "sandpaper test," in which the announcer said that to prove the product's "super-moisturizing power, we put it right from the can onto this tough, dry sandpaper. It was apply . . . soak . . . and off in a stroke." In fact, the sandpaper depicted in the commercial had to be soaked for 80 minutes before it could be shaved clean. The substance actually used in the commercial was plexiglass to which sand had been applied. The evidence showed that Rapid Shave could shave sandpaper, though in a longer period than the commercial showed, and that if sandpaper had been used, "the inadequacies of television transmission would have made it appear to viewers to be nothing more than plain, colored paper."

The FTC found the commercials deceptive. The Supreme Court agreed. It found three representations being made in the commercials: that Rapid Shave could shave sandpaper; that an experiment had verified that claim; and that the viewer was seeing that experiment actually performed. Although Colgate argued that any deception did not relate to the product itself, the Court accepted the Commission's view that a misrepresentation of *"any* fact so long as it materially induces a purchaser's decision to buy is a deception prohibited by" the FTCA. The Court observed:

> Respondents claim that it will be impractical to inform the viewing public that it is not seeing an actual test, experiment or demonstration, but we think it inconceivable that the ingenious advertising world will be unable, if it so desires, to conform to the Commission's insistence that the public be not misinformed. If, however, it becomes impossible or impractical to show simulated demonstrations on television in a truthful manner, this indicates that television is not a medium that lends itself to this type of commercial, not that the commercial must survive at all costs. Similarly unpersuasive is respondents' objection that the Commission's decision discriminates against sellers whose product claims cannot be "verified" on television without the use of simulations. All methods of advertising do not equally favor every seller. If the inherent limitations of a method do not permit its use in the way a seller desires, the seller cannot by material misrepresentation compensate for those limitations.

The FTC also found mockups deceptive when marbles were put in the bottom of a soup bowl to push the solids in the soup closer to the surface. The advertiser claimed it was necessary because television would not show the soup to be as thick as it actually was. In the Matter of Campbell Soup Co., 77 F.T.C. 664 (1970). Television does have technical restraints that cause such problems. Is it deceptive to have people wear blue clothes, which appear white on black-and-white television, rather than white clothes, which appear somewhat dirty? In the Rapid Shave commercial, how could an effective, but not deceptive demonstration be staged?

The Court in the Rapid Shave case held that demonstrations proving a product claim must not be deceptive. Using wine to represent coffee because of its deeper color is acceptable if the coffee cup is a background object in a commercial for dinner plates, but not if the commercial is for the brand of coffee. In one case, an ad for glass showed the sponsor's product to be clear and undistorted when a television camera looked through a car window. A competitor's glass created distortion. In fact, different camera angles and petroleum jelly smeared on the competitor's glass created the effect for the camera. The court held the deception impermissible, even if the two products actually performed as shown. If deception was necessary to demonstrate the difference on television, perhaps because of television's inherent technical limitations, then the difference could not be shown. Libby-Owens-Ford Glass Co. v. Federal Trade Commission, 352 F.2d 415 (6th Cir.1965).

In 1969, the FTC announced that advertisers would have to tell viewers that a mockup was being used to simulate reality. Notice how this is done for simulated pictures when television sets are being advertised.

d. Endorsements

Sometimes it will appear that an advertiser is not extolling the product, but that someone else is—an entertainer or sports figure, or an expert or specialist in a certain field. These testimonials or endorsements are permitted as an advertising technique if not abused. The use of a testimonial that was never given would be deceptive because untrue. Also, it is a tort to appropriate a person's name or likeness for commercial purposes (see p. 170, supra). Usually, celebrities are paid for endorsing a product. This need not be revealed, since the FTC assumes the public expects such payment. But what if a detergent manufacturer says its product is recommended by a washing machine company? If, in fact, the soap company is paying for the recommendation, that has to be stated. Otherwise, consumers may think the washing machine manufacturer freely chose the detergent from among a number of competing brands.

FTC guidelines say that the average consumer must be able to expect the performance claimed in an endorsement. If an "actual consumer" claims a certain brand of television set was in the shop only once in two years, and that was for a $10 repair, this must be a fair representation of the set's quality. Also, that "actual consumer" must really be a member of the general public, or the ad must disclose an actor is playing the part.

Someone who endorses a product by saying he or she uses it must actually use it, and continue to use it, as long as the ad is running. This normally applies to celebrities whose name the advertiser wants to connect to the product. When the endorsement is by those who claim special knowledge or expertise to judge a product, the endorsers' qualifications must be pertinent to the item. For instance, the FTC has ruled that a famous racing car driver may not endorse a toy racing car set because the skill required to drive a race car had nothing to do with judging a toy. The decision might have been different if the driver said he and his children played with the toy and enjoyed it. Mattel, Inc., 79 F.T.C. 667 (1971).

If special expertise is required to evaluate a product, such a judgment must not come from a lay person. For instance, the FTC barred entertainer "Pat" Boone from endorsing an acne product when his knowledge of the product's effectiveness came exclusively from the advertiser's claims, not from "reliable sources independent of the advertiser."

e. Tests

The testimonial can be an effective advertising technique. Tests or surveys showing a product in its best light are equally effective.

First, tests must actually be conducted before an advertiser can imply that test results prove something about the product. At one time, *Good Housekeeping Magazine* would award its "Seal of Approval" to products not tested or inadequately tested. The FTC would not allow this. In the Matter of Hearst Magazine, 32 F.T.C. 1440 (1941). Second, tests must actually have been conducted against a competing product if the ad so claims. Third, test results must not be presented deceptively. An advertiser cannot say a pain product was shown effective for headaches when tests were conducted on patients with toothaches. Fourth, the test must be scientifically accurate. Bristol-Myers randomly selected 10,000 of the 66,000 dentists in America to ask about toothpaste preferences. Only 1,983 replied, and the company based advertisements on only a few hundred responses about the dentists' personal toothpaste and a few hundred more about the toothpaste each dentist recommended to patients. The FTC found this number to be too small to constitute a scientifically proper survey of dentists. In the Matter of Bristol-Myers Co., 185 F.2d 58 (4th Cir.1950).

f. Non-Disclosure

While the FTC and the courts look carefully at what advertisements say, they also look at what an ad does *not* say: "To tell less than the truth is a well-known method of deception." P. Lorillard Co. v. Federal Trade Commission, 186 F.2d 52 (4th Cir.1950).

For example, the *Reader's Digest* sponsored a study of the tars, nicotine, and resins in leading cigarettes. The published results noted that the differences in these elements among the various brands made little difference in the physical harm done to smokers. The study did show Old Gold ranked lowest in these substances, though the difference was not significant. Old Gold ran an extensive advertising campaign claiming that an "impartial test by *Reader's Digest*" showed the cigarette to be in the "best among" those tested.

The FTC said the small portion of the test referred to in the ads was misleading. The result of the test was to show that little difference existed among the various brands, not to show Old Gold was minutely "better." The Seventh Circuit upheld the Commission's decision, rejecting a defense of literal truth. The omission of the important findings of the study regarding the physical hazards of smoking was deceptive. Id.

In another case, the FTC ordered a company to reveal that the "majority of people who are tired and run-down . . . are not so because of iron deficiency anemia," a condition the producer claimed

Geritol would aid. Not disclosing this made the ads deceptive. J.B. Williams Co. v. Federal Trade Commission, 381 F.2d 884 (6th Cir. 1967). Similarly, a picture of a gold-colored ring without further explanation must be made of gold. If it is gold plated or gold-colored plastic, the ad must say so. Although this may not be an explicit half-truth, consumers would readily draw an incorrect inference.

g. Puffery

Although most advertising is misleading if it is untrue in one form or another, some overstatement is permitted. Thus, "puffing," or "sales talk," sometimes is considered an acceptable form of extolling a product's virtues. A toothpaste can "whiten and brighten," though, in fact, it could not have such an effect on the inherent qualities of teeth. A product can be a "good bargain" or "exceptional" or "wonderful." But puffing must be used very carefully.

Generally, an expression of opinion about a product or service which does not create a misleading impression in consumers' minds can be construed as puffing. It is a normal exaggeration. But when a false impression is created, the ad has gone beyond puffery to misrepresentation and is not permitted. The FTC is becoming increasingly less receptive to puffery. The Commission is wary of exaggerations because it believes that consumers do not see the exaggerated claim as "sales talk," but are instead deceived by it.

Also, the FTC discourages puffing in comparative advertising. The Commission may consider a statement that a certain felt-tip pen is "worth five of any other brand" to be too great an exaggeration. Customers may believe that one of this brand will last as long as five of the other brand. See Moretrench Corp. v. Federal Trade Commission, 127 F.2d 792 (2d Cir.1942).

h. Product Description

The line between puffery and misrepresentation is clearly overstepped when a rusty, dirty used car is described as "shiny and clean." But what if something is called "top quality"? This will not be permitted if a demonstrably better product exists. A television set without automatic fine tuning cannot be called "the best the industry has to offer." The FTC says only a product made from elephant tusks may be called "ivory," and "Vermont maple syrup" must come from Vermont. Such product descriptions must be truthful, not exaggerated.

In addition to the origin and quality of merchandise, its mode of manufacture must be advertised accurately. Products claimed to be handmade cannot be manufactured completely by machines in factories.

Half-truths are a problem here, as ITT Continental Baking Co. has learned. In 1971, the FTC said it was deceptive to advertise that

Profile Bread contained fewer calories per slice than other brands without revealing that the statement was true only because Profile was sliced thinner. In re ITT Continental Baking Co., 79 F.T.C. 248 (1971). Two years later, the FTC ruled Wonder Bread did not contain more vitamins and minerals than other commercially produced bread. Commercials saying Wonder created healthy bodies "twelve ways" were deceptive if viewers were not told this. ITT Continental Baking Co., 83 F.T.C. 1105 (1973).

i. Comparative Advertising

Not until the 1970's did advertisers go beyond the vague "Brand X" advertisement and begin comparing their own product with a specific competing brand. Initially, these ads were governed by internal policies within the advertising industry and the media. Two television networks, ABC and NBC, have comparative advertising guidelines, as does the American Association of Advertising Agencies. The development of these codes shows an increasing acceptance of comparative advertising, a technique once discouraged.

The FTC became concerned about comparative advertising in which test results are presented inaccurately, or in which nutritional or health claims, or claims of uniqueness, are made. The Commission looks to the ad's effect on the public, and is particularly wary if children are the intended audience. Also, the FTC prefers substantiation of claims by independent testing laboratories, indicating that objective, provable claims are safest to make in comparative ads.

Another danger of this type of advertising is not stopping at comparisons, but denigrating a competitor's product or business practices. Such comments can lead to actions for disparagement or trade libel. These actions require plaintiffs to prove false disparagement, identification, publication and special damages. In addition, some states require proof of intent to injure, while others only demand proof of negligent disparagement.

It does not appear that the constitutional protection applied to other defamation cases is available in trade libel. In late 1984 the Supreme Court heard additional argument in a case that may provide more explicit guidelines concerning the extent of constitutional protection in trade libel cases. Greenmoss Builders, Inc. v. Dun & Bradstreet, Inc., 143 Vt. 66, 461 A.2d 414, certiorari granted ___ U.S. ___ (1983). Other aspects of this case were discussed at p. 117, supra.

Disparaging competitors or their products can also lead to unfair competition actions under section 43(a) of the Lanham Trademark Act, as the makers of Anacin discovered. A few years ago, Anacin, an aspirin-based compound, became the best-selling pain reliever, surpassing Bayer Aspirin. In 1976, Tylenol, a non-aspirin compound, passed Anacin in sales. Shortly thereafter, Anacin initiated two advertising campaigns. The first was a thirty-second television commercial beginning, "Your body knows the difference between these pain relievers . . . and Adult Strength Anacin." It claimed superiority to several non-aspirin tablets, including Tylenol and Extra-Strength Tylenol. The second advertisement, designed for magazines, read "Anacin can reduce inflammation that comes with most pain," "Tylenol cannot."

Based on consumer reaction surveys, a federal district court ruled that the advertisements represented that Anacin was "a superior analgesic generally" and that it was superior because it reduced inflammation. The court held the claims to be false and ordered Anacin not to make them in future advertising. The Court of Appeals for the Second Circuit found the language of the ads to be ambiguous. But even if the claims were literally true, said the court, the overall impression of the ads was false. The appellate court said the lower court's use of consumer response data showed the ads had "a tendency to mislead, confuse or deceive." Because consumers could incorrectly infer that Anacin was better than Tylenol for reducing pain or inflammation, the advertised claims were deceptive. American Home Products Corp. v. Johnson & Johnson, 577 F.2d 160 (2d Cir.1978).

3. FTC REMEDIES

The FTC may use a wide range of methods to stop or punish false or deceptive advertisements. The public reaction generated when the FTC simply announces it is reviewing an ad campaign may cause the company to change or stop it. But the Commission has more formal ways of approaching the problem.

a. Suggestions, Orders, and Penalties

On the broadest level, the FTC can issue an industry guide that suggests how businesses should act with regard to a potential problem. This guide serves as a "roadmap" through Commission regulations. Further, a particular business may request an advisory opinion about something it proposes to do. The FTC response is directed toward one firm rather than a whole industry. Industry guides and advisory opinions are informal methods, not carrying the force of law. If an advertiser violates either, the FTC can proceed only as it would against any other ad it believes to be misleading.

A trade regulation rule (TRR), however, is a formal interpretation of FTC regulations. The Commission specifically describes practices it has determined violate the FTCA. For instance, it ruled that not posting octane ratings on gasoline pumps was an unfair method of competition and a deceptive practice. National Petroleum Refiners Association v. Federal Trade Commission, 482 F.2d 672 (D.C.Cir. 1973). When a firm violates a valid TRR, it has violated the FTCA. The Commission then simply can prove, for example, that the firm put out the advertisement. It does not have to prove the advertisement was deceptive—the TRR already said that such an ad violated the FTCA.

It is possible for a company to sign a voluntary letter of compliance. The advertiser does not admit the ad was deceptive, but agrees to stop the campaign and not to run similar ads in the future. This is advantageous for a firm if the campaign was about to end anyway, because it reduces the adverse publicity and legal fees involved in a formal FTC action.

A consent order is similar to voluntary compliance. This is an agreement between a firm and the Commission in which, for example, an advertiser agrees not to make certain claims or to advertise in a certain way again. However, unlike voluntary compliance, a consent order contains a "cease and desist" order, which tells the company to stop its illegal practices or face penalties. Thus, a consent order is as binding as if the dispute had gone to a full Commission hearing or to court, but the advertiser need not admit the ad was deceptive, and is saved legal costs.

Although the FTC usually uses the less formal approaches of voluntary compliance or consent orders, it also uses more formal approaches. It can issue a complaint against a company and have a hearing before an administrative law judge, whose decision is final unless it is appealed to the full Commission or the Commission itself decides to review the case. If the decision is against the firm, the Commission will issue a cease and desist order.

Once a cease and desist order has been issued by the Commission after a hearing, no company may engage in that proscribed practice, whether the order was actually issued against it or not. That is, the FTC considers the order to be like a TRR, binding against a whole industry.

Violations of cease and desist orders can be punished by fines up to $10,000 per offense per day. The FTC can also ask a court to issue an injunction, ordering a company to stop a certain practice while the question of its deceptiveness is being decided. Finally, the Commission can bring a court action against a company to obtain relief for a consumer injured by deceptive practices.

The procedures involved in stopping or punishing an allegedly deceptive advertising campaign can be very complex and lengthy. In an unusually complex case, the FTC filed a complaint against the J.B. Williams Co. in 1962 charging that its television commercials for Geritol were misleading. The Commission's cease and desist order was issued in 1964 and upheld by the Court of Appeals for the Sixth Circuit in 1967. J.B. Williams Co., Inc. v. Federal Trade Commission, 381 F.2d 884 (6th Cir.1967). Two years later the FTC found the company had not yet complied with the order and gave the case to the Justice Department. A United States District Court in New York fined the company $456,000 and its advertising agency $356,000 in 1973 for not complying with the FTC's order. The company appealed and the Court of Appeals for the Second Circuit held J.B. Williams Co. was entitled to a jury trial to determine whether the advertisements were deceptive. United States v. J.B. Williams Co., Inc., 498 F.2d 414 (2d Cir.1974). The case was finally settled in 1976 when the FTC reported the company had agreed to pay $302,000 in penalties and interest. In the fourteen years since the original complaint was filed, the company reportedly spent $60 million on advertising Geritol.

b. Affirmative Disclosure

In the Geritol case, the Commission ordered J.B. Williams Co. to reveal in its commercials that iron-poor blood was rarely the cause of tiredness, which the product purported to cure. This order was upheld in court, allowing the FTC the power to require an advertiser to disclose certain facts about a product or service necessary to correct deceptive advertisements. J.B. Williams Co., Inc. v. Federal Trade Commission, 381 F.2d 884 (6th Cir.1967).

Initially, affirmative disclosure orders required stating what a product would *not* do, to qualify broad claims made by advertisers. More recently, disclosure orders have required giving consumers information they would not otherwise have, including legal rights and remedies. For instance, an order might require a firm to tell customers they do not have to return or pay for unordered merchandise.

c. Corrective Advertising

Another, and more controversial, form of affirmative disclosure is corrective advertising, which is meant to correct misconceptions about a product that linger from misleading advertising. This differs from affirmative disclosure in that corrective advertising is meant to remedy past deception rather than prompt future ads to be truthful. Included as part of a cease and desist order, corrective advertising requires a firm to spend a specific amount of its advertising budget informing consumers that false information was disseminated in the past. The order may also specify the language to be used in correcting the misconceptions.

Corrective advertising was first suggested, though not used, in the Campbell Soup case when marbles were placed in the bottom of a bowl to make the solid ingredients in vegetable soup float to the top. Campbell Soup Co., 77 F.T.C. 664 (1970). The Commission first successfully used corrective advertising in ordering ITT Continental Baking Co. to spend one quarter of its advertising budget over a one-year period to inform consumers that Profile Bread had only seven fewer calories per slice than ordinary bread, a difference which would not cause significant weight loss. In re ITT Continental Baking Co., 79 F.T.C. 248 (1971).

Similarly, Ocean Spray Cranberries agreed to use one quarter of its media expenditures for one year to tell consumers that the term "food energy" used in past advertising meant calories, not vitamins and minerals.   Ocean Spray Cranberries, Inc., 70 F.T.C. 975 (1972).

Since Listerine mouthwash was introduced in 1879, it had been represented as being beneficial in fighting colds, cold symptoms and sore throats.   These claims were made in direct advertising to the consumers since 1921.   In 1975, the FTC ordered Listerine's manufacturer to stop making these claims and to state in future advertising that "Contrary to prior advertising, Listerine will not help prevent colds or sore throats or lessen their severity."   The language was to appear in every Listerine ad in type size at least as large as that of the principal text of the ad, yet be separated from that text so that it could be readily noticed.   In television commercials the disclosure had to be simultaneously presented in both audio and video portions—and during the audio portions on radio and television ads no other sounds, including music, were to occur.

In Warner-Lambert Co. v. Federal Trade Commission, 562 F.2d 749 (D.C.Cir.1977), cert. denied 435 U.S. 950 (1978), the Court upheld the FTC's power to order corrective advertising.   Section 5 of the FTCA authorized the FTC to shape remedies appropriate to the situation.   The court then rejected the claim that after *Virginia Pharmacy,* p. 285, infra, the First Amendment barred such an order. The court relied on the Supreme Court's assertion that the First Amendment presented "no obstacle" to government regulation of false or misleading advertising.   Government could assure "that the stream of commercial information flow[s] cleanly as well as freely."

The court of appeals asserted that corrective advertising was not "really such an innovation.   The label may be newly coined, but the concept is well established.   It is simply that under certain circumstances an advertiser may be required to make affirmative disclosure of unfavorable facts."   Here, the court relied on cases requiring advertisers to inform the public that a baldness cure would not work in the vast majority of cases because they involve hereditary baldness;   that a device to stop bedwetting would not work in cases involving organic defects or disease;   and that Geritol would help only the small minority whose tiredness resulted from iron deficiency anemia.

Other support was found in cases in which past advertisements might make current ads misleading unless further explained.   In one example, a baking powder maker had advertised extensively that its product was superior to others because it was made with cream of tartar, not phosphate.   Because of increased costs, the producer replaced the cream of tartar with phosphate.   The new advertising did not mention cream of tartar, and stressed the product's low cost. The new labels very closely resembled the old ones.   The FTC and the courts agreed that new ads can be deceptive in not advising consumers that their past reasons for buying the product were no longer valid. Royal Baking Powder Co. v. F.T.C., 281 F. 744 (2d Cir. 1922).

Both groups of precedents were thought to provide support for corrective advertising.

Finally, though, the court was troubled by the wording of the FTC's order. Given the presentation requirements as to type size and absence of competing sound, as well as the obligation to continue the ads until the advertiser had spent an amount equal to one year's average ad outlay during the 1962–72 period, the court concluded that the new ads would attract much attention.

> Given these safeguards, we believe the preamble "Contrary to prior advertising" is not necessary. It can serve only two purposes: either to attract attention or to humiliate the advertiser. The Commission claims only the first purpose for it, and this we think is obviated by the other terms of the order. The second purpose, if it were intended, might be called for in an egregious case of deliberate deception, but this is not one. . . . On these facts, the confessional preamble is not warranted.

Not all Commission orders to include corrective material in ads are upheld by the courts. The Seventh Circuit allowed the FTC to stop the National Commission on Egg Nutrition, a group of egg producers, from misrepresenting scientific findings concerning the relationship between cholesterol, eggs, and heart disease. But the court refused to force the egg group to include in future advertising that "many medical experts believe increased consumption of dietary cholesterol, including that in eggs, may increase the risk of heart disease." There was no long history of deception, such as in *Warner-Lambert*, requiring that false claims be erased from the public's mind. Corrective advertising in this case was too harsh a measure. National Commission on Egg Nutrition v. Federal Trade Commission, 570 F.2d 157 (7th Cir.1977), certiorari denied 439 U.S. 821 (1978).

d. Substantiating Advertising Claims

In 1971, the FTC began requiring certain businesses to substantiate advertising claims through tests or other documentation. This is not done only when the Commission believes an ad is misleading. The purpose, more generally, is to have advertisers prove what they claim about their products. Initially, entire industries from air-conditioning manufacturers to antiperspirant makers, were asked to supply substantiation. Now, the Commission requires proof of claims from those whose advertisements seem most open to doubt.

The program was given impetus when Pfizer, Inc., claimed its Un-Burn product anesthetized nerve endings to stop sunburn pain. The FTC said it was an unfair trade practice to make a claim without having a reasonable basis for believing it. The proof must be available before the claim is made, not after. In the Matter of Pfizer,

Inc., 81 F.T.C. 23 (1972). Testing and other forms of substantiation must precede dissemination of the ad and must be the foundation of the claims made.

One impact of the advertising substantiation approach is to replace the FTC's burden of proof to show an ad is deceptive, by forcing the company to prove it is true. If the case goes to a hearing or to court, the Commission again carries the burden, but most disputes are resolved before that time. Thus, to a point, the advertiser answers the question of an advertisement's truthfulness by supplying or not supplying substantiating evidence for the claim.

In the early 1980's the Commission has made less use of advertising substantiation and has even given consideration to abandoning it altogether. This is consistent with the more limited view of its role that the Commission currently seems to be taking.

C. OTHER REMEDIES FOR DECEPTIVE ADVERTISING

1. OTHER FEDERAL AGENCIES

While the FTC is the primary federal governmental agency charged with regulating false, deceptive and misleading advertising, there are over thirty statutes that give various other agencies some control in this area. For instance, the Federal Communications Commission can deal with advertising on radio and television, the Food and Drug Administration with food, drug, and cosmetic advertising, the Securities and Exchange Commission with the advertising of stocks, bonds, and securities for sale, and the Postal Service with mailed advertisements. Then there are statutes forbidding the use of copies of paper currency, Regan v. Time, Inc., 468 U.S. —— (1984), or the United States flag in an ad. All this, remember, predates the Supreme Court's increasing protection of commercial speech.

2. STATE AND LOCAL LAWS

The FTC was created by Congress to deal with interstate commerce. When its powers were expanded to include advertising, this generally meant advertising that crossed state lines or involved products that did so. Today, some local advertising also can come within its jurisdiction. But not all advertising can be dealt with by the Commission. State and local laws attempt to fill any gap.

In 1911, a New York lawyer wrote a model law making untrue, deceptive or misleading advertising a misdemeanor. The law was called the Printer's Ink Statute after the magazine that championed its passage. Eventually, all states except Arkansas, Delaware, and New Mexico passed some form of the statute. But enforcement is spotty; few state law enforcement officials take the time or trouble to prosecute under the statutes.

Beginning in the 1960's, states added other laws to protect consumers against deceptive advertising. Again, enforcement depends on the jurisdiction. Because different sets of laws enforced in different ways have proven not to be effective, the Uniform Deceptive Trade Practices Act was developed in 1964. This was intended to put the same law in force in states across the country, but only one-third of the states have adopted it, and the vigor of enforcement depends on local officials.

3. SELF REGULATION

Though most of this section on advertising regulation concerns how various governmental agencies oversee advertising, only a fraction of the ads that appear require scrutiny. Most advertisers are quite honest and want to abide by the law. That is, they regulate themselves, as do advertising agencies and the media carrying the ads. This is done both individually and through industry groups. Because what constitutes deceptive or misleading advertising is not always clear, self-regulatory groups aid advertisers, advertising agencies, and the media by supplying guidelines interpreting policies of governmental agencies, such as the FTC, state and federal laws, and court rulings. They also attempt to regulate deceptive advertising before the government intervenes.

The National Advertising Review Board (NARB) is a major self-regulatory group created in 1971 by the Better Business Bureau, the Association of National Advertisers, the American Association of Advertising Agencies (AAAA) and the American Advertising Foundation. Initially, complaints about ads are reviewed by the National Advertising Division (NAD) of the Better Business Bureau. The NAD uses persuasion to seek changes in misleading ads. If that fails, the NAD takes the case to the NARB. Whenever the NARB finds an advertisement untruthful or inaccurate, it reports that to the media, which are unlikely to accept the ad, and to the FTC.

Several local advertising review boards have also been established.

Advertising agencies review advertisements before submitting them to the media. In order to belong to their major trade organizations, agencies must subscribe to the AAAA's "Standards of Practice," which outlaw unfair, false, and deceptive practices.

4. CONSUMER ACTION

Even if it were legally possible for consumers to sue advertisers for misleading advertisements, and generally it is not, it would be impractical. An individual consumer's damages are usually small—a cleanser that does not make a sink sparkling white does not cause much harm—and lawyers' fees might be larger than the damages collected. For various legal reasons, it also is not practical for groups of consumers to sue in class actions. The FTC can sue on behalf of a consumer under some circumstances, but the effectiveness of this new power is untested.

Consumers can sue if a product fails to live up to its warranty, which may be indicated in an advertisement, but this is a different type of action than would be brought for false or deceptive advertising.

Some special interest groups have attempted to influence advertisers through consumer pressure. Usually, though, the target of such pressure is not an advertisement, but rather a show being sponsored by the advertiser. Thus, various groups have organized boycotts of products manufactured by firms who sponsor television shows the groups consider unacceptable because of, for example, excessive violence or sexual innuendos.

D.　FIRST AMENDMENT PROTECTION OF ADVERTISING

1.　DEVELOPMENT OF THE PROTECTION

It may seem surprising to discuss advertising *regulation*. Is it not protected by the First Amendment like other expression? Recall that some categories of speech, such as obscenity, are not protected, and that this used to be true of advertising.

Not until 1942 did the Supreme Court consider whether advertising came within the First Amendment. That case arose when a man bought a used Navy submarine and docked it in New York City. He passed out handbills urging the people to tour the ship for a fee. Police told him that a city ordinance barred distribution of commercial handbills on the streets; only handbills containing "information or public protest" were permitted. He then printed a protest against the city's refusal to rent him a particular pier on one side of the sheet and an advertisement for his submarine tours on the other side. When police stopped him again, he obtained an injunction against the city's interfering with his distribution of the handbill. The Supreme Court ruled that commercial speech had no First Amendment protection. Although local officials could not prohibit a city's streets from being used for exercising freedom of expression, the Constitution "imposes no such restraint on government as respects purely commercial advertising." The protest on one side of the handbill was merely a ruse to evade the ordinance. Valentine v. Chrestensen, 316 U.S. 52 (1942).

This attitude toward commercial speech may partially explain Breard v. City of Alexandria, 341 U.S. 622 (1951), in which the Court upheld an ordinance banning door-to-door solicitation for purposes of sales—as applied to solicitors of magazine subscriptions. This case followed shortly after Martin v. City of Struthers, 319 U.S. 141 (1943), in which the Court had invalidated the application of an ordinance against uninvited solicitors—as applied to members of a religious group.

For 22 years, then, courts followed the *Chrestensen* approach. But in 1964, the Court gave protection to editorial advertisements, those that promote ideas and causes rather than products or services. In New York Times Co. v. Sullivan, p. 78, supra, the Court said the publication "was not a 'commercial' advertisement in the sense in which the word was used in *Chrestensen.* It communicated information, expressed opinion, recited grievances, protested claimed abuses, and sought financial support on behalf of a movement whose existence and objectives are matters of the highest public interest and concern."

Pittsburgh Press Co. v. Pittsburgh Commission on Human Relations, 413 U.S. 376 (1973) was a step back toward *Chrestensen.* An ordinance barred employers from discriminating in employment and also barred others from aiding in such discrimination. The *Pittsburgh Press* carried Help Wanted advertisements in columns captioned "Jobs—Male Interest," "Jobs—Female Interest," and "Male—Female," according to the wishes of the advertiser. The Commission ordered the *Press* to stop using such captions except where the ordinance provided that "the employer or advertiser is free to make hiring or employment referral decisions on the basis of sex." The Supreme Court upheld the order, 5–4:

> In the crucial respects, the advertisements in the present record resemble the *Chrestensen* rather than the *Sullivan* advertisement. None expresses a position on whether, as a matter of social policy, certain positions ought to be filled by members of one or the other sex, nor does any of them criticize the Ordinance or the Commission's enforcement practices. Each is no more than a proposal of possible employment. The advertisements are thus classic examples of commercial speech.

The newspaper argued that the case involved an editorial judgment concerning the placement of such advertisements. Although the newspaper always acceded to the advertisers' requests, Justice Powell, for the majority, acknowledged that some editorial judgment was involved. He concluded, however, that in this case the newspaper was entitled to no greater protection than the advertiser itself:

> Discrimination in employment is not only commercial activity, it is *illegal* commercial activity under the Ordinance. We have no doubt that a newspaper constitutionally could be forbidden to publish a want ad proposing a sale of narcotics or soliciting prostitutes. Nor would the result be different if the nature of the transaction were indicated by placement under columns captioned "Narcotics for Sale" and "Prostitutes Wanted" rather than stated within the four corners of the advertisement.

> The illegality in this case may be less overt, but we see no difference in principle here. . . .

The Court emphasized that nothing in the holding allowed government to forbid the newspaper to "publish and distribute advertisements commenting on the Ordinance, the enforcement practices of the Commission, or the propriety of sex preferences in employment."

Bigelow v. Virginia, 421 U.S. 809 (1975), involved the publication in a Virginia newspaper of a New York group's advertisement stating that abortions were legal in New York with no residency requirement and offering to provide information and to arrange abortions in accredited hospitals at low cost. An address and telephone numbers were listed. Bigelow, the manager of the newspaper, was prosecuted under a statute making it a misdemeanor for "any person, by publication . . . or by the sale or circulation of any publication . . . [to] encourage or prompt the procuring of" an abortion. The state courts upheld the conviction and relied on the state's interest that women come to decisions about abortions "without the commercial advertising pressure usually incidental to the sale of a box of soap powder."

The Supreme Court reversed, 7–2. In his opinion for the Court, Justice Blackmun placed the advertisement closer to that in the New York Times case than to those of the other cases because it conveyed "information of potential interest and value to a diverse audience." The opinion also stressed that the activities advertised were legal in New York and that, although Virginia might be concerned about the health and welfare of its citizens, it could not keep from them information about legal activities in other states.

VIRGINIA STATE BOARD OF PHARMACY v. VIRGINIA CITIZENS CONSUMER COUNCIL, INC.

Supreme Court of the United States, 1976.
425 U.S. 748, 96 S.Ct. 1817, 48 L.Ed.2d 346.

[A Virginia statute declared any pharmacist who "advertises . . . any . . . price . . . for any drugs which may be dispensed only by prescription" guilty of "unprofessional conduct" punishable by penalties ranging from fines to revocation of license. The parties stipulated that "about 95% of all prescriptions are now filled with dosage forms prepared by the pharmaceutical manufacturer." They also stipulated that prices for the same drug in the same city varied greatly. The statute was challenged by consumer groups and an individual on the ground that the First Amendment entitled them to receive information that pharmacists wished to communicate to them. A three-judge district court agreed and invalidated the statute.]

MR. JUSTICE BLACKMUN delivered the opinion of the Court.
. . .

We begin with several propositions that already are settled or beyond serious dispute. It is clear, for example, that speech does not lose its First Amendment protection because money is spent to project it, as in a paid advertisement of one form or another. Buckley v. Valeo, 424 U.S. 1 (1976); Pittsburgh Press Co. v. Pittsburgh Comm'n on Human Relations, 413 U.S., at 384; New York Times Co. v. Sullivan, 376 U.S., at 266. Speech likewise is protected even though it is carried in a form that is "sold" for profit, [   ] and even though it may involve a solicitation to purchase or otherwise pay or contribute money.

If there is a kind of commercial speech that lacks all First Amendment protection, therefore, it must be distinguished by its content. Yet the speech whose content deprives it of protection cannot simply be speech on a commercial subject. No one would contend that our pharmacist may be prevented from being heard on the subject of whether, in general, pharmaceutical prices should be regulated, or their advertisement forbidden. Nor can it be dispositive that a commercial advertisement is uneditorial, and merely reports a fact. Purely factual matter of public interest may claim protection. Bigelow v. Virginia, [   ].

Our question is whether speech which does "no more than propose a commercial transaction," Pittsburgh Press Co. v. Pittsburgh Comm'n on Human Relations, [   ] is so removed from any "exposition of ideas," Chaplinsky v. New Hampshire, [   ] and from " 'truth, science, morality, and arts in general, in its diffusion of liberal sentiments on the administration of Government,' " Roth v. United States, [   ] that it lacks all protection. Our answer is that it is not.

Focusing first on the individual parties to the transaction that is proposed in the commercial advertisement, we may assume that the advertiser's interest is a purely economic one. That hardly disqualifies him for protection under the First Amendment. . . .

As to the particular consumer's interest in the free flow of commercial information, that interest may be as keen, if not keener by far, than his interest in the day's most urgent political debate. Appellees' case in this respect is a convincing one. Those whom the suppression of prescription drug price information hits the hardest are the poor, the sick, and particularly the aged. A disproportionate amount of their income tends to be spent on prescription drugs; yet they are the least able to learn, by shopping from pharmacist to pharmacist, where their scarce dollars are best spent. When drug prices vary as strikingly as they do, information as to who is charging what becomes more than a convenience. It could mean the alleviation of physical pain or the enjoyment of basic necessities.

Generalizing, society also may have a strong interest in the free flow of commercial information. Even an individual advertisement, though entirely "commercial," may be of general public interest. . . . Obviously, not all commercial messages contain the same or even a very great public interest element. There are few to which such an element, however, could not be added. Our pharmacist, for example, could cast himself as a commentator on store-to-store disparities in drug prices, giving his own and those of a competitor as proof. We see little point in requiring him to do so, and little difference if he does not.

. . .

In concluding that commercial speech, like other varieties, is protected, we of course do not hold that it can never be regulated in any way. Some forms of commercial speech regulation are surely permissible. We mention a few only to make clear that they are not before us and therefore are not foreclosed by this case.

There is no claim, for example, that the prohibition on prescription drug price advertising is a mere time, place, and manner restriction. We have often approved restrictions of that kind provided that they are justified without reference to the content of the regulated speech, that they serve a significant governmental interest, and that in so doing they leave open ample alternative channels for communication of the information. [   ] Whatever may be the proper bounds of time, place, and manner restrictions on commercial speech, they are plainly exceeded by this Virginia statute, which singles out speech of a particular content and seeks to prevent its dissemination completely.

Nor is there any claim that prescription drug price advertisements are forbidden because they are false or misleading in any way. Untruthful speech, commercial or otherwise, has never been protected for its own sake. [   ] Obviously, much commercial speech is not provably false, or even wholly false, but only deceptive or misleading. We foresee no obstacle to a State's dealing effectively with this problem.[24] The First Amendment, as we construe it today, does not

24. In concluding that commercial speech enjoys First Amendment protection, we have not held that it is wholly undifferentiable from other forms. There are commonsense differences between speech that does "no more than propose a commercial transaction," Pittsburgh Press Co. v. Pittsburgh Comm'n on Human Relations, 413 U.S., at 385, and other varieties. Even if the differences do not justify the conclusion that commercial speech is valueless, and thus subject to complete suppression by the State, they nonetheless suggest that a different degree of protection is necessary to insure that the flow of truthful and legitimate commercial information is unimpaired. The truth of commercial speech, for example, may be more easily verifiable by its disseminator than, let us say, news reporting or political commentary, in that ordinarily the advertiser seeks to disseminate information about a specific product or service that he himself provides and presumably knows more about than anyone else. Also, commercial speech may be more durable than other kinds. Since advertising is the *sine qua non* of commercial profits there is little likelihood of its being chilled by proper regulation and foregone entirely.

Attributes such as these, the greater objectivity and hardiness of commercial speech, may make it less necessary to tolerate inaccurate statements for fear of silencing the speaker. [   ] They may also make it appropriate to require that a commercial message appear in such a form, or include such additional information, warnings, and disclaimers, as are necessary to prevent its being deceptive. [   ] They may also make inapplicable the prohibition against prior restraints. [   ]

prohibit the State from insuring that the stream of commercial information flows cleanly as well as freely. [   ]

Also, there is no claim that the transactions proposed in the forbidden advertisements are themselves illegal in any way. . . .

What is at issue is whether a State may completely suppress the dissemination of concededly truthful information about entirely lawful activity, fearful of that information's effect upon its disseminators and its recipients. Reserving other questions [25] we conclude that the answer to this one is in the negative.

The judgment of the District Court is affirmed.

It is so ordered.

MR. JUSTICE STEVENS took no part in the consideration or decision of this case.

[Chief Justice Burger concurred separately to emphasize that "the Court wisely leaves" the question of medical and legal services "to another day." Because 95 percent of prescriptions are already in dosage units, he thought the pharmacist "no more renders a true professional service than does a clerk who sells lawbooks." He suggested that advertising of price by professionals might be inherently misleading since "what the professional must do will vary greatly in individual cases."

Justice Stewart concurred separately to explain why the decision did not destroy the "constitutional legitimacy of every state and federal law regulating false or deceptive advertising." He emphasized that such laws generally are aimed at commercial advertisers who know the product they are advertising and can more easily verify the accuracy of representations made, than can "the press, which must often attempt to assemble the true facts from sketchy and sometimes conflicting sources under the pressure of publication deadlines. . . ." There was little likelihood of chilling accurate advertising by proscribing false advertising. "Indeed, the elimination of false and deceptive claims serves to promote the one facet of commercial price and product advertising that warrants First Amendment protection—its contribution to the flow of accurate and reliable information relevant to public and private decisionmaking."

Justice Rehnquist dissented. He disagreed on the standing issue because those interested could get the information by other means. On the merits, the Constitution did not require "the Virginia Legislature to hew to the teachings of Adam Smith." Recognizing the difficulty of drawing the line between protected speech and commer-

---

25. We stress that we have considered in this case the regulation of commercial advertising by pharmacists. Although we express no opinion as to other professions, the distinctions, historical and functional, between professions, may require consideration of quite different factors. Physicians and lawyers, for example, do not dispense standardized products; they render professional *services* of almost infinite variety and nature with the consequent enhanced possibility for confusion and deception if they were to undertake certain kinds of advertising.

cial speech in previous cases, he nevertheless thought the majority had been unwise in drawing a new line between truthful commercial speech and false and misleading commercial speech. He understood the Court's view that the First Amendment was "primarily an instrument to enlighten public decisionmaking in a democracy" to refer to "political, social, and other public issues, rather than the decision of a particular individual as to whether to purchase one or another kind of shampoo. It is undoubtedly arguable that many people in the country regard the choice of shampoo as just as important as who may be elected to local, state, or national political office, but that does not automatically bring information about competing shampoos within the protection of the First Amendment." He was also concerned that pharmacists might use this opportunity to promote the use of drugs by such advertisements as "Don't spend another sleepless night. Ask your doctor to prescribe Seconal without delay."]

Notes and Questions

1. Justice Blackmun responded to the dissent's standing question in a footnote observing that there was "no general principle that freedom of speech may be abridged when the speaker's listeners could come by his message by some other means, such as seeking him out and asking him what it is." To Justice Rehnquist's claim that if plaintiffs needed the information so badly they might have called the pharmacy or set up canvassing groups, Justice Blackmun responded that if "the great need for the information . . . distinguishes our prior cases at all, it makes the appellees' First Amendment claim a stronger rather than a weaker one."

2. Does the majority opinion imply some constraints other than those relating to truthful as opposed to false and misleading advertisements? In what ways might the right to engage in commercial speech be less broad than the right to engage in other types of speech?

3. If the government could bar an activity such as the sale of cigarettes, would it follow that it could bar advertising of that activity? Assuming that the government could prohibit the manufacture and sale of cigarettes, may it instead permit their continued sale but bar manufacturers from advertising (and the press from carrying the advertisements)?

4. After *Virginia Pharmacy* what considerations should determine the constitutionality of a statute or regulation restricting some form of advertising? How much guidance is provided by the following case?

CENTRAL HUDSON GAS & ELECTRIC CORP. v. PUBLIC
SERVICE COMMISSION OF NEW YORK

Supreme Court of the United States, 1980.
447 U.S. 557, 100 S.Ct. 2343, 65 L.Ed.2d 341.

MR. JUSTICE POWELL delivered the opinion of the Court.

This case presents the question whether a regulation of the
Public Service Commission of the State of New York violates the
First and Fourteenth Amendments because it completely bans adver-
tising by an electric utility.

. . .

II

The Commission's order restricts only commercial speech, that is,
expression related solely to the economic interests of the speaker and
its audience. [ ] The First Amendment, as applied to the States
through the Fourteenth Amendment, protects commercial speech
from unwarranted governmental regulation. [ ] Commercial expression not only serves the economic interest of the speaker, but
also assists consumers and furthers the societal interest in the fullest
possible dissemination of information. In applying the First Amendment to this area, we have rejected the "highly paternalistic" view
that government has complete power to suppress or regulate commercial speech. "[P]eople will perceive their own best interests if
only they are well enough informed, and . . . the best means to
that end is to open the channels of communication, rather than to
close them. . . ." Id., at 770; see Linmark Associates, Inc. v.
Willingboro, 431 U.S. 85, 92 (1977). Even when advertising communicates only an incomplete version of the relevant facts, the First
Amendment presumes that some accurate information is better than
no information at all. Bates v. State Bar of Arizona, supra, at 374.

Nevertheless, our decisions have recognized "the 'commonsense'
distinction between speech proposing a commercial transaction, which
occurs in an area traditionally subject to government regulation, and
other varieties of speech." [ ] The Constitution therefore accords
a lesser protection to commercial speech than to other constitutionally guaranteed expression. [ ] The protection available for particular commercial expression turns on the nature both of the expression
and of the governmental interests served by its regulation.

The First Amendment's concern for commercial speech is based
on the informational function of advertising. [ ] Consequently,
there can be no constitutional objection to the suppression of commercial messages that do not accurately inform the public about lawful
activity. The government may ban forms of communication more
likely to deceive the public than to inform it, [ ] or commercial
speech related to illegal activity, [ ].

If the communication is neither misleading nor related to unlawful activity, the government's power is more circumscribed. The State must assert a substantial interest to be achieved by restrictions on commercial speech. Moreover, the regulatory technique must be in proportion to that interest. The limitation on expression must be designed carefully to achieve the State's goal. Compliance with this requirement may be measured by two criteria. First, the restriction must directly advance the state interest involved; the regulation may not be sustained if it provides only ineffective or remote support for the government's purpose. Second, if the governmental interest could be served as well by a more limited restriction on commercial speech, the excessive restrictions cannot survive.

Under the first criterion, the Court has declined to uphold regulations that only indirectly advance the state interest involved. In both *Bates* and *Virginia Pharmacy Board*, the Court concluded that an advertising ban could not be imposed to protect the ethical or performance standards of a profession. The Court noted in *Virginia Pharmacy Board* that "[t]he advertising ban does not directly affect professional standards one way or the other." In *Bates*, the Court overturned an advertising prohibition that was designed to protect the "quality" of a lawyer's work. "Restraints on advertising . . . are an ineffective way of deterring shoddy work." 433 U.S., at 378.

The second criterion recognizes that the First Amendment mandates that speech restrictions be "narrowly drawn." [ ] The regulatory technique may extend only as far as the interest it serves. The State cannot regulate speech that poses no danger to the asserted state interest, [ ] nor can it completely suppress information when narrower restrictions on expression would serve its interest as well. For example, in *Bates* the Court explicitly did not "foreclose the possibility that some limited supplementation, by way of warning or disclaimer or the like, might be required" in promotional materials. [ ] And in Carey v. Population Services International, 431 U.S. 678, 701–702 (1977), we held that the State's "arguments . . . do not justify the total suppression of advertising concerning contraceptives." This holding left open the possibility that the State could implement more carefully drawn restrictions. [ ][9]

In commercial speech cases, then, a four-part analysis has developed. At the outset, we must determine whether the expression is protected by the First Amendment. For commercial speech to come within that provision, it at least must concern lawful activity and not be misleading. Next, we ask whether the asserted governmental

9. We review with special care regulations that entirely suppress commercial speech in order to pursue a nonspeech-related policy. In those circumstances, a ban on speech could screen from public view the underlying governmental policy. See *Virginia Pharmacy Board*, 425 U.S., at 780, n. 8 (Stewart, J., concurring). Indeed, in recent years this Court has not approved a blanket ban on commercial speech unless the expression itself was flawed in some way, either because it was deceptive or related to unlawful activity.

interest is substantial. If both inquiries yield positive answers, we must determine whether the regulation directly advances the governmental interest asserted, and whether it is not more extensive than is necessary to serve that interest.

III

We now apply this four-step analysis for commercial speech to the Commission's arguments in support of its ban on promotional advertising.

A

The Commission does not claim that the expression at issue either is inaccurate or relates to unlawful activity. Yet the New York Court of Appeals questioned whether Central Hudson's advertising is protected commercial speech. Because appellant holds a monopoly over the sale of electricity in its service area, the state court suggested that the Commission's order restricts no commercial speech of any worth. The court stated that advertising in a "noncompetitive market" could not improve the decisionmaking of consumers. 47 N.Y.2d, at 110, 390 N.E.2d, at 757. The court saw no constitutional problem with barring commercial speech that it viewed as conveying little useful information.

This reasoning falls short of establishing that appellant's advertising is not commercial speech protected by the First Amendment. Monopoly over the supply of a product provides no protection from competition with substitutes for that product. Electric utilities compete with suppliers of fuel oil and natural gas in several markets, such as those for home heating and industrial power. This Court noted the existence of interfuel competition 45 years ago. [ ] Each energy source continues to offer peculiar advantages and disadvantages that may influence consumer choice. For consumers in those competitive markets, advertising by utilities is just as valuable as advertising by unregulated firms.

Even in monopoly markets, the suppression of advertising reduces the information available for consumer decisions and thereby defeats the purpose of the First Amendment. The New York court's argument appears to assume that the providers of a monopoly service or product are willing to pay for wholly ineffective advertising. Most businesses—even regulated monopolies—are unlikely to underwrite promotional advertising that is of no interest or use to consumers. Indeed, a monopoly enterprise legitimately may wish to inform the public that it has developed new services or terms of doing business. A consumer may need information to aid his decision whether or not to use the monopoly service at all, or how much of the service he should purchase. In the absence of factors that would distort the decision to advertise, we may assume that the willingness of a business to promote its products reflects a belief that consumers are interested in the advertising. Since no such extraordinary conditions have been identified in this case, appellant's monopoly position does not alter the First Amendment's protection for its commercial speech.

B

The Commission offers two state interests as justifications for the ban on promotional advertising. The first concerns energy conservation. Any increase in demand for electricity—during peak or off-peak periods—means greater consumption of energy. The Commission argues, and the New York court agreed, that the State's interest in conserving energy is sufficient to support suppression of advertising designed to increase consumption of electricity. In view of our country's dependence on energy resources beyond our control, no one can doubt the importance of energy conservation. Plainly, therefore, the state interest asserted is substantial.

The Commission also argues that promotional advertising will aggravate inequities caused by the failure to base the utilities' rates on marginal cost. The utilities argued to the Commission that if they could promote the use of electricity in periods of low demand, they would improve their utilization of generating capacity. The Commission responded that promotion of off-peak consumption also would increase consumption during peak periods. If peak demand were to rise, the absence of marginal cost rates would mean that the rates charged for the additional power would not reflect the true costs of expanding production. Instead, the extra costs would be borne by all consumers through higher overall rates. Without promotional advertising, the Commission stated, this inequitable turn of events would be less likely to occur. The choice among rate structures involves difficult and important questions of economic supply and distributional fairness. The State's concern that rates be fair and efficient represents a clear and substantial governmental interest.

C

Next, we focus on the relationship between the State's interests and the advertising ban. Under this criterion, the Commission's laudable concern over the equity and efficiency of appellant's rates does not provide a constitutionally adequate reason for restricting protected speech. The link between the advertising prohibition and appellant's rate structure is, at most, tenuous. The impact of promotional advertising on the equity of appellant's rates is highly speculative. Advertising to increase off-peak usage would have to increase peak usage, while other factors that directly affect the fairness and efficiency of appellant's rates remained constant. Such conditional and remote eventualities simply cannot justify silencing appellant's promotional advertising.

In contrast, the State's interest in energy conservation is directly advanced by the Commission order at issue here. There is an immediate connection between advertising and demand for electricity. Central Hudson would not contest the advertising ban unless it believed that promotion would increase its sales. Thus, we find a direct link between the state interest in conservation and the Commission's order.

D

We come finally to the critical inquiry in this case: whether the Commission's complete suppression of speech ordinarily protected by the First Amendment is no more extensive than necessary to further the State's interest in energy conservation. The Commission's order reaches all promotional advertising, regardless of the impact of the touted service on overall energy use. But the energy conservation rationale, as important as it is, cannot justify suppressing information about electric devices or services that would cause no net increase in total energy use. In addition, no showing has been made that a more limited restriction on the content of promotional advertising would not serve adequately the State's interests.

Appellant insists that but for the ban, it would advertise products and services that use energy efficiently. These include the "heat pump," which both parties acknowledge to be a major improvement in electric heating, and the use of electric heat as a "backup" to solar and other heat sources. Although the Commission has questioned the efficiency of electric heating before this Court, neither the Commission's Policy Statement nor its order denying rehearing made findings on this issue. In the absence of authoritative findings to the contrary, we must credit as within the realm of possibility the claim that electric heat can be an efficient alternative in some circumstances.

The Commission's order prevents appellant from promoting electric services that would reduce energy use by diverting demand from less efficient sources, or that would consume roughly the same amount of energy as do alternative sources. In neither situation would the utility's advertising endanger conservation or mislead the public. To the extent that the Commission's order suppresses speech that in no way impairs the State's interest in energy conservation, the Commission's order violates the First and Fourteenth Amendments and must be invalidated. [   ]

The Commission also has not demonstrated that its interest in conservation cannot be protected adequately by more limited regulation of appellant's commercial expression. To further its policy of conservation, the Commission could attempt to restrict the format and content of Central Hudson's advertising. It might, for example, require that the advertisements include information about the relative efficiency and expense of the offered service, both under current conditions and for the foreseeable future. [   ] In the absence of a showing that more limited speech regulation would be ineffective, we cannot approve the complete suppression of Central Hudson's advertising.

IV

Our decision today in no way disparages the national interest in energy conservation. We accept without reservation the argument that conservation, as well as the development of alternative energy sources, is an imperative national goal. Administrative bodies empowered to regulate electric utilities have the authority—and indeed the duty—to take appropriate action to further this goal. When, however, such action involves the suppression of speech, the First and Fourteenth Amendments require that the restriction be no more extensive than is necessary to serve the state interest. In this case, the record before us fails to show that the total ban on promotional advertising meets this requirement.

Accordingly, the judgment of the New York Court of Appeals is

Reversed.

MR. JUSTICE BRENNAN, concurring in the judgment.

One of the major difficulties in this case is the proper characterization of the Commission's Policy Statement. I find it impossible to determine on the present record whether the Commission's ban on all "promotional" advertising, in contrast to "institutional and informational" advertising, is intended to encompass more than "commercial speech." I am inclined to think that Mr. Justice Stevens is correct that the Commission's order prohibits more than mere proposals to engage in certain kinds of commercial transactions, and therefore I agree with his conclusion that the ban surely violates the First and Fourteenth Amendments. But even on the assumption that the Court is correct that the Commission's order reaches only commercial speech, I agree with Mr. Justice Blackmun that "[n]o differences between commercial speech and other protected speech justify suppression of commercial speech in order to influence public conduct through manipulation of the availability of information."

Accordingly, with the qualifications implicit in the preceding paragraph, I join the opinions of Mr. Justice Blackmun and Mr. Justice Stevens concurring in the judgment.

MR. JUSTICE BLACKMUN, with whom MR. JUSTICE BRENNAN joins, concurring in the judgment.

I agree with the Court that the Public Service Commission's ban on promotional advertising of electricity by public utilities is inconsistent with the First and Fourteenth Amendments. I concur only in the Court's judgment, however, because I believe the test now evolved and applied by the Court is not consistent with our prior cases and does not provide adequate protection for truthful, nonmisleading, noncoercive commercial speech.

The Court asserts, that "a four-part analysis has developed" from our decisions concerning commercial speech. Under this four-part test a restraint on commercial "communication [that] is neither misleading nor related to unlawful activity" is subject to an intermediate level of scrutiny, and suppression is permitted whenever it "directly advances" a "substantial" governmental interest and is "not more extensive than is necessary to serve that interest." I agree with the Court that this level of intermediate scrutiny is appropriate for a restraint on commercial speech designed to protect consumers from misleading or coercive speech, or a regulation related to the time, place, or manner of commercial speech. I do not agree, however, that the Court's four-part test is the proper one to be applied when a State seeks to suppress information about a product in order to manipulate a private economic decision that the State cannot or has not regulated or outlawed directly.

. . .

I seriously doubt whether suppression of information concerning the availability and price of a legally offered product is ever a permissible way for the State to "dampen" demand for or use of the product. Even though "commercial" speech is involved, such a regulatory measure strikes at the heart of the First Amendment. This is because it is a covert attempt by the State to manipulate the choices of its citizens, not by persuasion or direct regulation, but by depriving the public of the information needed to make a free choice. As the Court recognizes, the State's policy choices are insulated from the visibility and scrutiny that direct regulation would entail and the conduct of citizens is molded by the information that government chooses to give them. [ ]

If the First Amendment guarantee means anything, it means that, absent clear and present danger, government has no power to restrict expression because of the effect its message is likely to have on the public. [ ] Our cases indicate that this guarantee applies even to commercial speech. In Virginia Pharmacy Board v. Virginia Consumer Council, 425 U.S. 748 (1976), we held that Virginia could not pursue its goal of encouraging the public to patronize the "professional pharmacist" (one who provided individual attention and a stable pharmacist-customer relationship) by "keeping the public in ignorance of the entirely lawful terms that competing pharmacists are offering." Id., at 770. We noted that our decision left the State free to pursue its goal of maintaining high standards among its pharmacists by "requir[ing] whatever professional standards it wishes of its pharmacists." Ibid.

We went on in *Virginia Pharmacy Board* to discuss the types of regulation of commercial speech that, due to the "commonsense differences" between this form of speech and other forms, are or may be constitutionally permissible. We indicated that government may impose reasonable "time, place, and manner" restrictions, and that it can deal with false, deceptive, and misleading commercial speech. We noted that the question of advertising of illegal transactions and the special problems of the electronic broadcast media were not presented.

Concluding with a restatement of the type of restraint that is not permitted, we said: "What is at issue is whether a State may completely suppress the dissemination of concededly truthful information about entirely lawful activity, fearful of that information's effect upon its disseminators and its recipients. . . . [W]e conclude that the answer to this [question] is in the negative." Id., at 773.

. . .

. . . . No differences between commercial speech and other protected speech justify suppression of commercial speech in order to influence public conduct through manipulation of the availability of information. The Court stated in Carey v. Population Services International:

"Appellants suggest no distinction between commercial and noncommercial speech that would render these discredited arguments meritorious when offered to justify prohibitions on commercial speech. On the contrary, such arguments are clearly directed not at any commercial aspect of the prohibited advertising but at the ideas conveyed and form of expression—*the core of First Amendment values.*" 431 U.S., at 701, n. 28 (emphasis added).

It appears that the Court would permit the State to ban all direct advertising of air conditioning, assuming that a more limited restriction on such advertising would not effectively deter the public from cooling its homes. In my view, our cases do not support this type of suppression. If a governmental unit believes that use or overuse of air conditioning is a serious problem, it must attack that problem directly, by prohibiting air conditioning or regulating thermostat levels. Just as the Commonwealth of Virginia may promote professionalism of pharmacists directly, so too New York may *not* promote energy conservation "by keeping the public in ignorance." *Virginia Pharmacy Board*, 425 U.S., at 770.

MR. JUSTICE STEVENS, with whom MR. JUSTICE BRENNAN joins, concurring in the judgment.

Because "commercial speech" is afforded less constitutional protection than other forms of speech, it is important that the commercial speech concept not be defined too broadly lest speech deserving of greater constitutional protection be inadvertently suppressed. The issue in this case is whether New York's prohibition on the promotion of the use of electricity through advertising is a ban on nothing but commercial speech.

In my judgment one of the two definitions the Court uses in addressing that issue is too broad and the other may be somewhat too narrow. The Court first describes commercial speech as "expression related solely to the economic interests of the speaker and its audience." Although it is not entirely clear whether this definition uses the subject matter of the speech or the motivation of the speaker as the limiting factor, it seems clear to me that it encompasses speech that is entitled to the maximum protection afforded by the First Amendment. Neither a labor leader's exhortation to strike, nor an economist's dissertation on the money supply, should receive any lesser protection because the subject matter concerns only the economic interests of the audience. Nor should the economic motivation of a speaker qualify his constitutional protection; even Shakespeare may have been motivated by the prospect of pecuniary reward. Thus, the Court's first definition of commercial speech is unquestionably too broad.

The Court's second definition refers to " 'speech proposing a commercial transaction.' " A salesman's solicitation, a broker's offer, and a manufacturer's publication of a price list or the terms of his standard warranty would unquestionably fit within this concept. Presumably, the definition is intended to encompass advertising that advises possible buyers of the availability of specific products at specific prices and describes the advantages of purchasing such items. Perhaps it also extends to other communications that do little more than make the name of a product or a service more familiar to the general public. Whatever the precise contours of the concept, and perhaps it is too early to enunciate an exact formulation, I am persuaded that it should not include the entire range of communication that is embraced within the term "promotional advertising."

This case involves a governmental regulation that completely bans promotional advertising by an electric utility. This ban encompasses a great deal more than mere proposals to engage in certain kinds of commercial transactions. It prohibits all advocacy of the immediate or future use of electricity. It curtails expression by an informed and interested group of persons of their point of view on questions relating to the production and consumption of electrical energy—questions frequently discussed and debated by our political leaders. For example, an electric company's advocacy of the use of electric heat for environmental reasons, as opposed to wood-burning stoves, would seem to fall squarely within New York's promotional advertising ban and also within the bounds of maximum First Amendment protection. The breadth of the ban thus exceeds the boundaries of the commercial speech concept, however that concept may be defined.

The justification for the regulation is nothing more than the expressed fear that the audience may find the utility's message persuasive. Without the aid of any coercion, deception, or misinformation, truthful communication may persuade some citizens to consume more electricity than they otherwise would. I assume that such a consequence would be undesirable and that government may therefore prohibit and punish the unnecessary or excessive use of electricity. But if the perceived harm associated with greater electrical usage is not sufficiently serious to justify direct regulation, surely it does not constitute the kind of clear and present danger that can justify the suppression of speech.

. . .

In sum, I concur in the result because I do not consider this to be a "commercial speech" case. Accordingly, I see no need to decide whether the Court's four-part analysis, adequately protects commercial speech—as properly defined—in the face of a blanket ban of the sort involved in this case.

[Justice Rehnquist dissented. He thought that a state-created monopoly, which was the subject of a comprehensive regulatory scheme, was not entitled to First Amendment protection. He further argued that the state law was an economic regulation and thus, that the speech involved occupied an extremely subordinate position in the First Amendment hierarchy. Finally, he believed that the Court, in applying the four-part test, had improperly substituted its own judgment for that of the State.]

Notes and Questions

1. As Justice Stevens noted in his concurrence, the Court used two definitions of commercial speech. He argued that neither was adequate. Assuming he was right, is a clear definition of commercial speech possible?

2. Prior to the decisions in *Virginia Pharmacy* and *Central Hudson* a statute banning cigarette advertising from the electronic media was upheld. See Capital Broadcasting v. Mitchell, p. 574, infra. Would the Court still reach the same result? Faced with a similar question in Capital Cities Cable v. Crisp, 467 U.S. __ (1984) (Oklahoma statute banned electronic media advertising for alcoholic beverages), the Court invalidated the statute on other grounds and did not address the commercial speech issue.

3. The Court is still struggling with the commercial speech question. In Metromedia, Inc. v. San Diego, 453 U.S. 490 (1981), the Court struck down a city ordinance forbidding with certain limited exceptions, all outdoor or billboard advertising. The Justices were unable to agree on much more than the result. There were five different opinions and in his dissent Justice Rehnquist referred to them as "a virtual Tower of Babel."

4. In contrast, the Court upheld a prohibition against posting signs on public property in City Council v. Taxpayers for Vincent, __ U.S. __ (1984). Applying the *Central Hudson* four-part test, the Court concluded that the City had a substantial interest in restricting

"visual clutter and blight", that the ordinance directly advanced that interest, and that "by banning these signs, the City did no more than eliminate the exact source of evil it sought to remedy."

5. Recently, the Securities and Exchange Commission has issued decisions raising important First Amendment questions. In Securities and Exchange Commission v. Lowe, 556 F.Supp. 1359 (E.D.N.Y. 1983), the SEC requested an injunction prohibiting Lowe and his corporations from publishing investment advisory materials. The Commission argued that publication of the materials constituted working as an investment advisor without the registration required by the Investment Advisors Act. The court refused to issue the injunction sought on the grounds it would constitute an unconstitutional prior restraint.

The Second Circuit reversed on appeal. Holding Lowe's publications to be commercial speech, the Court found no First Amendment protection from the application of the Investment Advisors Act. Because Lowe had a "history of deceptive, criminal conduct as an investment advisor, his publications [could] fairly be characterized as potentially deceptive commercial speech." The history referred to consisted of prior convictions for bad checks and misappropriating funds. Securities and Exchange Commission v. Lowe, 725 F.2d 892 (2d Cir.1984). The case was appealed to the Supreme Court.

In a totally different context the SEC is involved in another case with First Amendment implications. Former *Wall Street Journal* reporter, R. Foster Winans, is under indictment for conspiracy, securities fraud and wire and mail fraud. The government has alleged that Winans, one of the authors of the *Journal's* "Heard on the Street" column, tried to take advantage of his position by passing to others information about forthcoming columns that would favorably affect the prices of the stocks mentioned.

2. PROFESSIONAL ADVERTISING

For a number of years, groups regulating law and medicine have not allowed their practitioners to advertise. This has been enforced through professional organizations, such as the American Bar Association and the American Medical Association, state licensing boards and sometimes by state statutes. These barriers to professional advertising have begun to fall as the Supreme Court changes its view of the First Amendment protection commercial speech enjoys. Beginning in the late 1970's, the Court began to balance the rights of professionals to convey their message to the public through advertising against the suggested needs of professional organizations to inhibit the "commercialization" of these areas.

The Legal Profession: The Supreme Court dealt with legal advertising in a case involving advertising by two lawyers who operated a "legal clinic" in which they tried to provide basic legal services to clients of moderate income. To sustain their business, they needed a large number of clients, which they felt could be attracted only through advertising. They placed "truthful advertisements concerning the availability and terms of routine legal services" in daily newspapers. The state supreme court censured the attorneys for violating the state bar's code of ethics. The Supreme Court reversed. Bates v. State Bar of Arizona, 433 U.S. 350 (1977).

First, the Court rejected the state's three justifications for banning the ads: that "legal clinic" was a confusing term; that the price advertised for uncontested divorces was not in fact "very reasonable"; and that the ads did not inform the public that some legal actions, such as name changes, could be handled without an attorney. Balancing in each case, the Court thought that the free speech interest prevailed.

The Court then noted that some ads for professional services might be found misleading in the future though the same words would not be misleading if standardized products were being offered. The Court was particularly concerned about advertising the "quality" of legal services that are "not susceptible to measurement or verification." Similarly, in-person solicitation might create coercive pressures that media advertising would not.

The Court relied heavily on footnote 24 of *Virginia Pharmacy*, p. 287, supra, in recognizing that commercial speech might well be less susceptible to chilling than non-commercial speech:

> [A]ny concern that strict requirements for truthfulness will undesirably inhibit spontaneity seems inapplicable because commercial speech generally is calculated. Indeed, the public and private benefits from commercial speech derive from confidence in its accuracy and reliability. Thus, the leeway for untruthful or misleading expression that has been allowed in other contexts has little force in the commercial arena.

The Supreme Court, then, allows attorneys to advertise "basic facts," such as name, telephone number, address and office hours, information concerning an attorney's educational background, and basic prices for initial consultations and "routine" legal services. In addition, a state may not restrict the distribution of professional announcement cards to a specified audience, prohibit attorneys from listing the courts in which they are admitted to practice, nor prescribe the specific wording lawyers may use to describe their areas of practice. In Re RMJ, 455 U.S. 191 (1982).

Restrictions may still be imposed on false or deceptive ads and on the way business is solicited. Indeed, the Court did rule that in-person solicitation could still be barred because of ethical considerations that differentiate solicitation from advertising. Moreover, unlike advertising, solicitation does not promote informed decision-making by the public. Ohralik v. Ohio State Bar Association, 436 U.S. 447 (1978).

The Medical Profession: State statutes that bar advertising by medical professionals present the additional element of the relationship between the First Amendment right to disseminate honest advertising and the state's right to protect the public's health and safety. Some contend that the latter interest is enhanced by legal and ethical bans on medical advertising.

Blanket prohibitions on ads for medical products are no longer possible after *Virginia Pharmacy.* In contrast, state bans on ads for medical services have not yet been considered by the Supreme Court.

In an optometry case, however, the Supreme Court offered some clues as to the limits of the *Bates* approach. A Texas statute banned optometrists from operating under any trade name (a fictitious company name) other than the names of the optometrists who participated in the activity. The asserted purpose was to provide information to the public about who was actually performing the work at each facility. The statute was challenged by optometrists operating under the name "Texas State Optical" on the ground that it interfered with their right of free speech. The Court disagreed and upheld the statute. Friedman v. Rogers, 440 U.S. 1 (1979).

The Court held that trade names can mislead the public because the people actually doing the work may change while the trade name does not. "The possibilities for deception are numerous." The use of trade names was different from the commercial speech involved in *Virginia Pharmacy* and *Bates.* Those "statements were self-contained and self-explanatory. Here, we are concerned with a form of commercial speech that has no intrinsic meaning." The meaning is acquired over the years from associations formed in the public mind:

> A trade name conveys no information about the price and nature of the services offered by an optometrist until it acquires meaning over a period of time by associations formed in the minds of the public between the name and some standard of price or quality. Because these ill-defined associations of trade names with price and quality information can be manipulated by the users of trade names, there is a significant possibility that trade names will be used to mislead the public.

Finally, in contrast to the earlier cases, the state restriction "has only the most incidental effect on the content of the commercial speech of Texas optometrists." The information associated with trade names, such as the kind and price of the available services, "may be communicated freely and explicitly to the public. An optometrist may advertise the type of service he offers, the prices he charges, and whether he practices as a partner, associate, or employee with other optometrists." This offers more accurate information than before the statute when "optometrists were allowed to convey the information through unstated and ambiguous associations with a trade name." The state's insistence on certain information to prevent optometrists from being deceptive was justifiable and, on balance, prevailed over the free speech claim.

The FTC issued orders prohibiting the AMA and the ADA from blanket restrictions on advertising by their members, although the Commission will allow reasonable ethical guidelines covering deceptive advertising and solicitation of especially vulnerable patients. The AMA appealed and the order was upheld with minor modifications by the Second Circuit Court of Appeals. American Medical Association v. Federal Trade Commission, 638 F.2d 443 (1980). The Supreme Court subsequently affirmed without opinion. 455 U.S. 676 (1982).

3.   CORPORATE SPEECH

Corporations are created by law. In some ways they take on lives of their own. They can sue and be sued, must pay taxes, can go bankrupt—all as individuals can. But do they have the same constitutional rights as individuals? On the one hand, the Supreme Court has said they do not have the Fifth Amendment right against self-incrimination, but that they are "persons" entitled to the protections of the Fourteenth Amendment. What about the First Amendment right of freedom of expression? The Court took a step toward answering this question in First National Bank of Boston v. Bellotti, 435 U.S. 765 (1978).

Several corporations wanted to spend money to publicize their opposition to a referendum proposal to authorize the Massachusetts legislature to enact a graduated income tax. A state statute barred business corporations from spending money to influence votes on referenda unless the question was one "materially affecting" the corporation's business or assets. This action was brought against the state Attorney General to declare the statute unconstitutional. The state court upheld the statute on the ground that a corporation's First Amendment rights are limited to issues that "materially affect" its business, property or assets. The Supreme Court, 5–4, reversed.

For the majority, Justice Powell asserted that corporations had rights of free speech equivalent to those of individual citizens. Here the speech involved the essence of self-government and was thus protected under the First Amendment. In response to the state's argument that "communication by corporate members of the institutional press is entitled to greater constitutional protection than the same communication" by other types of corporations, Justice Powell noted that banks and other corporations might be better informed on economic issues than media corporations.

The state also argued that even though the speech was entitled to First Amendment protection, it was more important for government to sustain the active role of individual citizens in the electoral process. The argument was that "corporations are wealthy and powerful and their views may drown out other points of view." But the record presented no such showing. Since Massachusetts allows corporations to lobby in the legislature and they are protected in petitioning government officials, a ban on communicating with the electorate directly could be defended only on the ground that the state lacks confidence in the ability of the electorate to evaluate the relative merits of conflicting arguments. Such a paternalistic argument contradicted First Amendment values.

Justice White, joined by Justices Brennan and Marshall, dissented. He stressed that many states limit corporate political activity— and that this was an arena in which the "expertise of legislators is at its peak and that of judges is at its very lowest." Corporations hardly need freedom of speech for self-fulfillment since, in the words of Professor Emerson, such speech is not "an integral part of the development of ideas, of mental exploration and of the affirmation of self." Justice White concluded that the public's right to receive communications financed by corporate expenditures is not necessarily of the same dimension as that to hear other forms of expression. The lack of individual self-expression is critical: "Ideas which are not a product of individual choice are entitled to less First Amendment protection." When this raised questions about media corporations, Justice White responded in a footnote:

> [N]ewspapers and other forms of literature obviously do not lose their First Amendment protection simply because they are produced or distributed by corporations. It is, of course, impermissible to restrict any communication, corporate or otherwise, because of displeasure with its content. I need not decide whether newspapers have a First Amendment right to operate in a corporate form.

Justice White stressed that "the special status of corporations has placed them in a position to control vast amounts of economic power which may, if not regulated, dominate not only the economy but also the very heart of our democracy, the electoral process." The state "need not permit its own creation to consume it." Massachusetts could reasonably have concluded that "not to impose limits upon the political activities of corporations would have placed it in a position of departing from neutrality and indirectly assisting the propagation of corporate views because of the advantages its laws give to the corporate acquisition of funds to finance such activities."

In a separate dissent, Justice Rehnquist contended that a state that charters corporations might reasonably conclude that "those properties, so beneficial in the economic sphere, pose special dangers in the political sphere." He drew a sharp distinction between the corporation's right of speech and its right to spend money for certain objects. Thus, he argued that although "a newspaper corporation must necessarily have the liberty to endorse a political candidate in its editorial columns, it need have no greater right than any other corporation to contribute money to that candidate's campaign."

Even though he concluded that the state might regulate the expenditure of corporate funds in an election campaign, he did not believe that the free flow of information would be diminished. "All natural persons, who owe their existence to a higher sovereign than the Commonwealth, remain as free as before to engage in political activity."

E. OTHER CONSIDERATIONS

1. RESPONSIBILITIES AND LIABILITIES OF ADVERTISING AGENCIES AND THE MEDIA

Advertising for products distributed nationally, and for some local businesses, is handled by advertising agencies. These firms, in consultation with the companies that have hired them, plan advertising campaigns, design the ads and contract for time and space in the media in which the ads are to run. Originally it was assumed the agency was a conduit for the manufacturer of the product or supplier of the service being advertised and that the agency was not liable for any deception in the ad.

Recently, the FTC has successfully entered orders against both the advertiser and the advertising agency. Agencies are liable if they know or have reason to know the advertising was false. In one case, the agency argued that it should not be a party to the case because the commercials for Sucrets lozenges were approved by the manufacturer's legal and medical departments. In finding both the agency and the manufacturer responsible for the deceptive advertisements, the court said the agency, better than anyone, should have known whether the commercials were misleading, since this "is an area in which the agency had expertise." The manufacturer's liability could not relieve the agency of responsibility for commercials that the agency had created. Merck & Co., Inc. v. Federal Trade Commission, 392 F.2d 921 (6th Cir.1968).

The FTC, then, can and usually does issue a cease and desist order against an advertising agency if it knew or should have known the advertisement was misleading. Violation of the order can be punished by a fine.

The media that carry advertisements are in a different position. For two reasons, media outlets are rarely cited in FTC complaints or in legal actions taken by consumers or governmental agencies. First, media are not seen as creators of advertisements. Second, there are First Amendment concerns when media are ordered not to disseminate something, even advertisements. In spite of this, television networks, large newspapers and magazines, and other media outlets generally have elaborate procedures to review advertisements for accuracy, taste, and deception. This is probably done both to protect relations with the public and to ensure that government agencies adhere to their current attitudes on this question.

However, even when advertising agencies or media outlets are found liable for deceptive advertising, advertisers usually reimburse them for any loss they suffer. This is stipulated in contracts between the advertiser and the agency or outlet.

2. LOTTERIES

Broadcasting of "any advertisement of or information concerning any lottery . . . ." is prohibited by 18 U.S.C.A. § 1304. In addition, postal regulations forbid mailing information that publicizes lotteries. 39 U.S.C.A. § 3005. Since most magazines and newspapers mail at least some of their copies, they must heed this law. A newsworthy story about a lottery, such as an interview with the winner, is not barred. The line between publicity and newsworthiness may be difficult to draw. New York State Broadcasters Association v. United States, 414 F.2d 990 (2d Cir.1969), certiorari denied 396 U.S. 1061 (1970).

A lottery is a game of chance involving three elements: 1) a prize, something of value offered as an inducement to enter the lottery, 2) chance as the method of awarding the prize, as opposed to the entrant's skill (in solving a puzzle or writing a poem), and 3) consideration, purchasing something or otherwise offering something of value as a prerequisite to participating in the lottery. Federal Communications Commission v. American Broadcasting Co., 347 U.S. 284 (1954). For example, a cereal company offering a chance to win a television set (prize) by means of a random drawing (chance) among those sending in a box top (consideration—the box of cereal was purchased) is conducting a lottery, and the media are forbidden to publicize it in any way, including disseminating advertisements for it. (This is why companies allow an index card hand-lettered with the company's name to substitute for the box top. This eliminates the consideration, making the contest no longer a lottery.)

When states began running their own lotteries, new questions arose concerning the ban on lottery information. After an early case that somewhat limited the scope of § 1304, New York State Broadcasters Association v. United States, 414 F.2d 990 (2d Cir.1969), the issue came to a head in New Jersey. During three consecutive news broadcasts each Thursday, the day of the drawing in the state lottery, a licensee wanted to announce: "The winning state lottery number drawn today is . . . ." The Commission, in a declaratory ruling concluded that such a statement would violate § 1304, even though it was presented as a news item. A main argument was that this was "news" only to those who held tickets. Experience had shown that the lottery's telephone lines were greatly overloaded on Thursdays as people called to learn the winning number. On a typical Thursday, there were 2,750,000 ticket-holders. On appeal, the court, sitting en banc, unanimously reversed the Commission's ban on such broadcasts. New Jersey State Lottery Commission v. United States, 491 F.2d 219 (3d Cir.1974). The court concluded that the Commission had misconstrued § 1304 by interpreting it to ban "news." Although the information here was of transitory value, the court noted that on Thursdays more people in New Jersey care about this information than care about any given stock market quotation. Thus, the size of the interested group could not be the test of news. Broadcasters should be free to decide what is news and what news will serve the public unless their decision is beyond the realm of reason. The court was also influenced by the no-censorship language of § 326, which reinforced its view that § 1304 should be limited to advertising and information meant to make a particular lottery more attractive to participants.

The government's petition for certiorari was granted to resolve the apparent conflict between the decisions of the Second and Third Circuits. After argument, but before decision, Congress passed a statute providing that § 1304 shall not apply to "an advertisement, list of prizes, or information concerning a lottery conducted by a State acting under the authority of State law . . . broadcast by a radio or television station licensed to a location in that State or an adjacent State which conducts such a lottery." 18 U.S.C. § 1307(a) (2). On the government's motion, the Court, over a dissent by Justice Douglas, vacated the judgment of the Third Circuit and remanded for its consideration of whether the case had become moot. United States v. New Jersey State Lottery Commission, 420 U.S. 371 (1975).

On remand, the court noted that states adjacent to New Jersey (and to intervenor New Hampshire) did not have state lotteries, so that broadcasters in those states were not permitted by § 1307 to broadcast information about the New Jersey (or New Hampshire) lottery. The concern about limited dissemination of "news" still existed and the case was not moot. The court reaffirmed its earlier decision rejecting the Commission's interpretation of § 1304. The result is reported in New Jersey State Lottery Commission v. United States, 519 F.2d 1398 (3d Cir.1975). The opinion is reported in 34 R.R.2d 825 (1975).

Could a statute constitutionally ban the type of statement the licensee wanted to make?

There are similar exceptions for state-run lotteries. When a state-run lottery exists in the state in which a newspaper is published, 39 U.S.C.A. § 3005(d), or in an adjacent state, 18 U.S.C.A. § 1307(a), Congress has allowed newspapers of general circulation containing information about the lottery to be mailed.

3. CHILDREN'S ADVERTISING

The law treats children differently from adults in many ways (e.g., see variable obscenity standards, in Chapter VII). There is considerable debate whether the same set of advertising rules should apply to both groups. Although the Supreme Court has said children must be treated with care as consumers since they are "unable to protect themselves," FTC v. R.F. Keppel & Bro., Inc., 291 U.S. 304 (1934), controversy exists over what, if any, protection to impose on advertising.

Nearly $600 million a year is spent on television advertising to children between the ages of two and twelve, who are exposed to about 20,000 commercials a year. Studies have shown that although younger children are unable to differentiate between program content and commercials, older children are skeptical about advertising claims. Studies of these and other psychological effects of television advertising are still inconclusive.

Some critics are concerned about health problems caused by commercials inducing children to eat sugared cereals, candy, and other products containing large amounts of processed sugar. Others wonder whether advertising helps children learn how to be careful consumers or teaches them greed and materialism. Since younger children do not usually buy the products themselves, still other critics worry about potential conflicts between children and parents.

Beginning in the late 1960's, a number of consumer groups advocated eliminating or severely regulating advertising directed toward children, particularly on children's television programs. The most active organization has been the Boston-based Action for Children's Television (ACT), which has petitioned both the FTC and FCC to curtail television advertising to children.

The economic impact of a ban or curtailment of advertising on children's programs is in dispute. Some argue that such an order would effectively take many children's programs off the air. The counter argument asserts that the economic burden on networks and local stations would be minimal. The impact of such a move on the sales of companies currently advertising to children is a different question.

In 1970, ACT asked the FCC to prohibit advertising on children's television shows. Preferring self-regulation, the Commission declined to do so in 1974, and was affirmed in Action for Children's Television v. Federal Communications Comm'n, 564 F.2d 458 (D.C.Cir. 1977).

The FTC has taken action on a case-by-case basis when it found children's advertising deceptive, ruling, for instance, that advertisers must consider the "knowledge, sophistication, maturity and experience of" young people. In the Matter of Mattel, Inc., 79 F.T.C. 667 (1971). The Commission has shown concern about commercials that make the taking of vitamins seem like eating candy, Hudson Pharmaceutical Corp., 89 F.T.C. 82 (1977), and ads showing a small child helping to make rice on a stove. Uncle Ben's, Inc., 89 F.T.C. 131 (1977).

All proposals to limit advertising to children must also consider the impact of Supreme Court decisions extending First Amendment protection to commercial speech. The extent to which honest advertising can be regulated, even when directed to children, remains an open question.

Chapter IX

PRESS COVERAGE OF THE ADMINISTRATION OF JUSTICE

Press coverage of the administration of justice poses special problems for the press and for the courts. It is easy to generalize about the openness of the judicial system and about Americans' distaste for secret courts, and it is easy to generalize about our proud tradition of protecting the fairness of civil and criminal trials. The generalizations too often ignore the reality: the First Amendment right to freedom of the press and the Sixth Amendment right to a fair trial sometimes appear to give rise to conflict.

Part of what we explore in this Chapter relates to government-sought constraints on the press—issues we confronted in Chapters III through VIII. Additional material in this Chapter relates to the legal rights and responsibilities of the press as it seeks to gather news prior to publication—issues we shall confront again in other contexts in Chapters X and XI. The special treatment in this Chapter is appropriate because the problems are unique to the judicial branch of government and may involve the question of contempt of court, rather than criminal or tort liability.

That there is conflict between the press and the courts is hardly surprising. Professionals in the law and professionals in journalism are both trained to seek the truth, but they do so in quite different ways. Judges and lawyers are accustomed to seeking the truth in a courtroom where hearsay and illegally-obtained evidence have no place; speed in arriving at the truth takes second place to faith that the process will lead eventually to the truth. For journalists, on the other hand, speed is of major importance, and even hearsay and illegally-obtained evidence may be deemed newsworthy.

As journalists tell the story of a crime or arrest prior to trial, they inevitably influence opinions in the area, and it can be difficult—perhaps even impossible—to find jurors who can ignore press reports and come to a fair verdict based on evidence presented in court. On the other hand, if judges try to shape or stop the news coverage of the administration of justice, they may be interfering with the First Amendment rights of the journalists.

As long as people have talked about the problems created by pre-trial and trial news coverage, they have suggested remedies. In this Chapter we will examine those remedies, and we will see that they have limited effectiveness and a variety of disadvantages. Some of the so-called remedies have to do with keeping prejudicial information from reaching the public. They include (1) cautioning police, prosecutors and others involved with the case about the impropriety of making comments to the press, (2) shielding witnesses from the press, (3) cautioning journalists about the dangers of prejudicial news accounts, and (4) encouraging the adoption of voluntary bench-bar-press guidelines. Other so-called remedies have to do with finding unbiased jurors despite the fact that news accounts may already have revealed prejudicial information. Among those are: (5) granting a change of venue, (6) granting a change of venire, (7) relying on the effectiveness of the *voir dire*, the examination of potential jurors, or (8) granting a continuance or delay. Additional remedies have to do with keeping jurors unbiased after their selection: (9) cautioning jurors who are allowed to leave the courtroom at the end of the day that they should not read or listen to press reports or other comment about the case, or a more effective and more costly alternative, (10) sequestering the jury. Theoretically, other more dramatic remedies might be used, but some of these are constitutionally suspect: (11) closing the courtroom to the press and public during pre-trial hearings, (12) closing the courtroom during trials, (13) imposing conditions on those allowed to enter the courtroom, and (14) ordering the press not to publish certain information. Traditionally, a way of protecting the defendant's rights has been to (15) maintain the decorum of the courtroom, and frequently judges have sought to do that by (16) keeping cameras out of the courtroom. Serving to protect the defendant's right is the court's authority to punish those who interfere with the administration by citing them for contempt of court.

A. BACKGROUND

The judicial branch has been the object of considerable litigation as to which of its functions are to be open to public scrutiny. A specific constitutional provision, held to be solely for the benefit of the accused and not addressed to the press, is basic to our discussion. The Sixth Amendment to the United States Constitution provides: "In all criminal prosecutions, the accused shall enjoy the right to a speedy and public trial, by an impartial jury of the State and district wherein the crime shall have been committed. . . ." No directive in the constitution affects the conduct of legislative or executive proceedings even to this extent.

The Sixth Amendment also provides for the accused to "be informed of the nature and cause of the accusation; to be confronted with the witnesses against him; to have compulsory process for obtaining Witnesses in his favor. . . ." As we see in Chapter X, the latter poses problems for journalists who wish not to testify about secret sources, notes, documents, etc. See, for example, *Farber*, p. 399, infra.

The emphasis throughout this section will be on criminal proceedings. The interest of the press in the judicial process, at least at the trial level, has been devoted almost exclusively to dramatic criminal cases involving either sensational crimes or prominent persons. The press has fought hard against exclusion from these cases. Some defendants in criminal cases have therefore sought to bar the press, and necessarily also the public, from various pretrial and trial phases of their cases lest publicity prejudice the judge or, far more likely, the jury that will ultimately hear the case. Thus, the role of the jury in criminal cases and the strong press (and presumably public) interest in particular criminal cases combine to create a potential conflict in criminal cases between defendants and the press. This conflict has been called "fair trial-free press" by the bar and "free press-fair trial" by the press. Many commentators suggest that the problem is monolithic: a broad confrontation between two important segments of society. This book regards the conflict as having several separable aspects and analyzes each one as it arises.

The major, but not the only argument of the press is framed in terms of the public's "right to know" about the functioning of the judiciary. In addition, the press argues that its presence may sometimes directly help the defendant. As well as serving a "watchdog" function just by being present, deterring potential judicial or prosecutorial excesses, a reporter sometimes learns enough about a case to be moved to investigate the charges and eventually find evidence that exonerates the defendant.

Closing civil proceedings has not been a problem, except when famous people are involved. The cases are either too uninteresting for press coverage, too complicated, or too lengthy to sustain a reader's interest. Even in the few civil cases that do interest the press, the likelihood of prejudice is small. Except for personal injury cases, which are usually uneventful for the observer, most civil cases do not involve juries, and other forms of prejudice are unlikely. The testimony of witnesses rarely involves emotional experiences similar to those in dramatic criminal cases. Thus, if the press wanted to attend civil trials there would be little objection.

Prejudicial publicity may arise in two contexts. One involves efforts to influence judicial behavior by writing articles or editorials about pending cases. This problem is discussed later in this Chapter. The second context centers on the institution of the jury. In the early days jurors were likely to know of the events in question, but for several centuries, the courts have insisted that jurors be impartial. This has not meant that they must be totally ignorant of the events in their community, but, rather, that they be willing and able to reach a verdict solely on the basis of the evidence presented at the trial. Of course jurors' biases might come from many sources other than publicity, such as the defendant's race, religion, occupation, accent, way of walking or dressing, or political affiliation. It is sometimes difficult to determine whether a juror will be impartial. The conventional approach has been to ask jurors questions during the preliminary screening, known as *voir dire*, that would enable the judge and the lawyers to detect bias. Jurors who convincingly deny bias and assert an ability to be "impartial" will be seated unless extrinsic evidence indicates that the juror either was dishonest or would probably not be psychologically able to disregard some ground for bias. If jurors turned out to be unable or unwilling to serve impartially after being selected, the defendant could seek a new trial.

In order to understand some of the problems raised in this area, it is necessary to know that certain types of evidence must be excluded from criminal trials. The rule of exclusion means that the information is not to be considered in determining the guilt or innocence of the defendant.

Three exclusions are most likely to cause possible problems of prejudicial publicity. One is the rule that an accused's prior record of convictions is not generally admissible in evidence unless the defendant chooses to testify. The fear is that if jurors learn that a defendant has a prior record they may be tempted to convict even though the prosecution may have failed to establish guilt beyond a reasonable doubt in this particular situation.

The second is that confessions made by the defendant before the trial are not admissible in evidence at the trial unless they have been voluntarily made and the accused has been properly advised of his rights (the so-called "Miranda warning"). Even if other evidence shows the confession accurate, to accept a coerced confession would encourage law enforcement agencies to abuse their authority.

The third major variety of inadmissible evidence involves items seized in an unlawful search. In these cases, the evidence is almost always trustworthy—and often devastating. Nonetheless, it is excluded if the search was illegal. Again, the point is to discourage the state from engaging in offensive behavior.

In all three situations, since the evidence is inadmissible in the courtroom, the courts hope to keep jurors from gaining access to such information by other means.

The legal community long has questioned whether a defendant can receive a fair trial in the face of pervasive publicity about the crime. Early in our history, in ruling on the trial of Aaron Burr, Chief Justice John Marshall set an early standard for juror impartiality. Marshall said a juror was impartial if free from the dominant influence of what was heard or read outside the courtroom. If jurors were able to base a decision on the testimony offered, the trial was not tainted by prejudice. United States v. Burr, 25 Fed.Cas. 49 No. 14692g (1807).

In recent decades, the question of prejudicial publicity has arisen concerning Lee Harvey Oswald, accused assassin of President John F. Kennedy; Jack Ruby, Oswald's killer; Sirhan Sirhan, convicted of slaying Robert Kennedy; Caryl Chessman, convicted rapist; Richard Speck, convicted of killing eight student nurses in Chicago; Charles Manson; David Berkowitz, the self-styled "Son of Sam"; James Earl

Ray, convicted of killing Martin Luther King; and Patty Hearst, among others. Although each controversy subsides, the issue reappears when another sensational crime is committed.

In considering pretrial publicity that might introduce bias into trials, an empirical question must be asked about the effect upon jurors of having read or heard certain information about the defendant or a forthcoming trial. The obvious importance of this recurring conflict between the rights of fair trial and free press makes it desirable to look beyond our intuition as to the role of the media in the community before a criminal trial. Many empirical studies have explored the impact on the later decisions of jurors of information disseminated before trial. At the very least, the techniques and the results do not dictate the conclusion that no prejudice results from the publication. Thus, the courts may well continue to upset convictions reflecting extensive prejudice—and we may expect lawyers and judges to seek ways to conduct proceedings that will minimize the likelihood that prejudicial publicity will reach the jurors. This may mean either silencing the media or withholding information. Since silencing the media has been thought more difficult to sustain, the latter course is being explored.

The Supreme Court's first confrontation with the problem in constitutional dimension was in the following case.

IRVIN v. DOWD

Supreme Court of the United States, 1961.
366 U.S. 717, 81 S.Ct. 1639, 6 L.Ed.2d 751.

[Irvin was convicted of murder in the state courts of Indiana and sentenced to death. Before the trial one change of venue had been granted—to Gibson County. Motions for another change and for continuances, delays in the start of the trial, were denied. The state courts affirmed his conviction. Irvin then sought to upset his conviction in the federal courts by claiming that the state had denied him his constitutional right to an impartial jury because the jury that convicted him had been biased. The court of appeals had rejected his application for habeas corpus, the technical term for a prisoner's claim that he is being restrained illegally.]

MR. JUSTICE CLARK delivered the opinion of the Court.

. . .

. . . In essence, the right to jury trial guarantees to the criminally accused a fair trial by a panel of impartial, "indifferent" jurors. The failure to accord an accused a fair hearing violates even the minimal standards of due process. . . .

It is not required, however, that the jurors be totally ignorant of the facts and issues involved. In these days of swift, widespread and diverse methods of communication, an important case can be expected to arouse the interest of the public in the vicinity, and scarcely any of those best qualified to serve as jurors will not have formed some impression or opinion as to the merits of the case. This is particularly true in criminal cases. To hold that the mere existence of any preconceived notion as to the guilt or innocence of an accused, without more, is sufficient to rebut the presumption of a prospective juror's impartiality would be to establish an impossible standard. It is sufficient if the juror can lay aside his impression or opinion and render a verdict based on the evidence presented in court. [ ]

. . .

. . . But as Chief Justice Hughes observed in United States v. Wood, 299 U.S. 123, 145–146 (1936): "Impartiality is not a technical conception. It is a state of mind. For the ascertainment of this mental attitude of appropriate indifference, the Constitution lays down no particular tests and procedure is not chained to any ancient and artificial formula."

Here the build-up of prejudice is clear and convincing. An examination of the then current community pattern of thought as indicated by the popular news media is singularly revealing. For example, petitioner's first motion for a change of venue from Gibson County alleged that the awaited trial of petitioner had become the *cause célèbre* of this small community—so much so that curbstone opinions, not only as to petitioner's guilt but even as to what punishment he should receive, were solicited and recorded on the public streets by a roving reporter, and later were broadcast over the local stations. A reading of the 46 exhibits which petitioner attached to his motion indicates that a barrage of newspaper headlines, articles, cartoons and pictures was unleashed against him during the six or seven months preceding his trial. The motion further alleged that the newspapers in which the stories appeared were delivered regularly to approximately 95% of the dwellings in Gibson County and that, in addition, the Evansville radio and TV stations, which likewise blanketed that county, also carried extensive newscasts covering the same incidents. These stories revealed the details of his background, including a reference to crimes committed when a juvenile, his convictions for arson almost 20 years previously, for burglary and by a court-martial on AWOL charges during the war. He was accused of being a parole violator. The headlines announced his police line-up identification, that he faced a lie detector test, had been placed at the scene of the crime and that the six murders were solved but petitioner refused to confess. Finally, they announced his confession to the six murders and the fact of his indictment for four of them in Indiana. They reported petitioner's offer to plead guilty if promised a 99-year sentence, but also the determination, on the other hand, of the prosecutor to secure the death penalty, and that petitioner had confessed to 24 burglaries (the *modus operandi* of these robberies was compared to that of the murders and the similarity noted). One story dramatically relayed the promise of a sheriff to devote his life to securing petitioner's execution by the State of Kentucky, where petitioner is alleged to have committed one of the six murders, if Indiana failed to do so. Another characterized petitioner as remorseless and without conscience but also as having been found sane by a court-appointed panel of doctors. In many of the stories petitioner was described as the "confessed slayer of six," a parole violator and fraudulent-check artist. Petitioner's court-appointed counsel was quoted as having received "much criticism over being Irvin's counsel" and it was pointed out, by way of excusing the attorney, that he would be subject to disbarment should he refuse to represent Irvin. On the day before the trial the newspapers carried the story that Irvin had orally admitted the murder of Kerr (the victim in this case) as well as "the robbery-murder of Mrs. Mary Holland; the murder of Mrs. Wilhelmina Sailer in Posey County, and the slaughter of three members of the Duncan family in Henderson County, Ky."

It cannot be gainsaid that the force of this continued adverse publicity caused a sustained excitement and fostered a strong prejudice among the people of Gibson County. In fact, on the second day devoted to the selection of the jury, the newspapers reported that "strong feelings, often bitter and angry, rumbled to the surface," and that "the extent to which the multiple murders—three in one family—have aroused feelings throughout the area was emphasized Friday when 27 of the 35 prospective jurors questioned were excused for holding biased pretrial opinions. . . ." A few days later the feeling was described as "a pattern of deep and bitter prejudice against the former pipe-fitter." Spectator comments, as printed by the newspapers, were "my mind is made up"; "I think he is guilty"; and "he should be hanged."

Finally, and with remarkable understatement, the headlines reported that "impartial jurors are hard to find." The panel consisted of 430 persons. The court itself excused 268 of those on challenges for cause as having fixed opinions as to the guilt of petitioner; 103 were excused because of conscientious objection to the imposition of the death penalty; 20, the maximum allowed, were peremptorily challenged by petitioner and 10 by the State; 12 persons and two alternates were selected as jurors and the rest were excused on personal grounds, e.g., deafness, doctor's orders, etc. An examination of the 2,783-page *voir dire* record shows that 370 prospective jurors or almost 90% of those examined on the point (10 members of the panel were never asked whether or not they had any opinion) entertained some opinion as to guilt—ranging in intensity from mere suspicion to absolute certainty. A number admitted that, if they were in the accused's place in the dock and he in theirs on the jury with their opinions, they would not want him on a jury.

Here the "pattern of deep and bitter prejudice" shown to be present throughout the community, [ ], was clearly reflected in the sum total of the *voir dire* examination of a majority of the jurors finally placed in the jury box. Eight out of the 12 thought petitioner was guilty. With such an opinion permeating their minds, it would be difficult to say that each could exclude this preconception of guilt from his deliberations. The influence that lurks in an opinion once formed is so persistent that it unconsciously fights detachment from the mental processes of the average man. See Delaney v. United States, 199 F.2d 107 (1st Cir.1952). Where one's life is at stake—and accounting for the frailties of human nature—we can only say that in the light of the circumstances here the finding of impartiality does not meet constitutional standards. Two-thirds of the jurors had an opinion that petitioner was guilty and were familiar with the material facts and circumstances involved, including the fact that other murders were attributed to him, some going so far as to say that it would take evidence to overcome their belief. One said that he "could not . . . give the defendant the benefit of the doubt that he is innocent." Another stated that he had a "somewhat" certain fixed opinion as to petitioner's guilt. No doubt each juror was sincere when he said that he would be fair and impartial to petitioner, but the psychological impact requiring such a declaration before one's fellows is often its father. Where so many, so many times, admitted prejudice, such a statement of impartiality can be given little weight. As one of the jurors put it, "You can't forget what you hear and see." With his life at stake, it is not requiring too much that petitioner be tried in an atmosphere undisturbed by so huge a wave of public passion and by a jury other than one in which two-thirds of the members admit, before hearing any testimony, to possessing a belief in his guilt. [   ]

. . . Therefore, on remand, the District Court should enter such orders as are appropriate and consistent with this opinion, [   ], which allow the State a reasonable time in which to retry petitioner. [   ]

Vacated and remanded.

MR. JUSTICE FRANKFURTER, concurring.

Of course I agree with the Court's opinion. But this is, unfortunately, not an isolated case that happened in Evansville, Indiana, nor an atypical miscarriage of justice due to anticipatory trial by newspapers instead of trial in court before a jury.

More than one student of society has expressed the view that not the least significant test of the quality of a civilization is its treatment of those charged with crime, particularly with offenses which arouse the passions of a community. One of the rightful boasts of Western civilization is that the State has the burden of establishing guilt solely on the basis of evidence produced in court and under circumstances assuring an accused all the safeguards of a fair procedure. These rudimentary conditions for determining guilt are inevitably wanting if the jury which is to sit in judgment on a fellow human being comes to its task with its mind ineradicably poisoned against him. How can fallible men and women reach a disinterested verdict based exclusively on what they heard in court when, before they entered the jury box, their minds were saturated by press and radio for months preceding by matter designed to establish the guilt of the accused. A conviction so secured obviously constitutes a denial of due process of law in its most rudimentary conception.

. . .

Notes and Questions

1. What warrants the Court's rejection of the jurors' statements that they could be fair to Irvin? What about the oath that jurors take and the admonition of the judge that they must decide the case solely on the evidence before them?

2. The preliminary screening of prospective jurors, whose names have been drawn from the lists of voters, is generally conducted by lawyers for the opposing parties, supervised by a trial judge who may participate in the questioning. Each side has a certain number of peremptory challenges that may be exercised to have prospective jurors barred without giving a reason. Other challenges may be permitted "for cause" by the court. It is at this stage that the trial judge may act to ensure the impartiality of the jury. The change of venue mentioned refers to a removal of the trial from one area to another within the same general jurisdiction. A related device is the change of venire, in which the trial remains at its initial site but panels of jurors, who are also known as veniremen, are brought in from other areas more removed from the event.

Given the publicity described in the Court's opinion, would it have made a difference if the jury had been sequestered—isolated from all media and other persons outside the courtroom—throughout the trial? Would a delay in the trial help? What about further changes of venue within Indiana? What about a change of venire? Could a well-conducted, albeit lengthy, *voir dire* produce an unbiased jury? What about waiving a jury?

3. Another troubling case occurred when Wilbert Rideau was arrested in Louisiana for bank robbery, kidnapping, and murder. The sheriff invited a film crew from the local television station to film the sheriff's "interview" with Rideau. During the 20-minute interrogation, Rideau confessed to the crimes. The station showed the interview three times. After a requested change of venue was denied, Rideau was convicted and sentenced to death. The Supreme Court overturned the conviction, noting that after drawing a jury from people who could have been exposed to the confession, any "court proceedings . . . could be but a hollow formality." The Court implied that nothing could have overcome the effects of the television film and that specific proof of juror prejudice was not necessary under such circumstances. Rideau v. Louisiana, 373 U.S. 723 (1963).

4. In Murphy v. Florida, 421 U.S. 794 (1975), the jurors in defendant's robbery trial had learned through news stories about some or

all of the defendant's earlier convictions for murder, securities theft, and for the 1964 theft of the Star of India sapphire from a New York museum. The majority stated that qualified jurors need not be totally ignorant of the facts surrounding the case. The Court found in the *voir dire* no showing of hostility to the defendant. Four of the six jurors had volunteered that defendant's past was irrelevant. Moreover, the defendant's attorney during *voir dire* informed several of the jurors of crimes they had not known about, leading the Court to observe "We will not readily discount the assurances of a juror insofar as his exposure to a defendant's past crimes comes from the defendant or counsel." The indicia of impartiality "might be disregarded in a case where the general atmosphere in the community or courtroom is sufficiently inflammatory, but the circumstances surrounding petitioner's trial are not at all of that variety." Only 20 of the 78 persons examined were excused because of an opinion of guilt. "This may indeed be 20 more than would occur in the trial of a totally obscure person, but it by no means suggests a community with sentiment so poisoned against petitioner as to impeach the indifference of jurors who displayed no hostile animus of their own." Only Justice Brennan dissented.

5. Soon after *Irvin,* the Court considered a case involving problems in the conduct of the trial itself.

SHEPPARD v. MAXWELL

Supreme Court of the United States, 1966.
384 U.S. 333, 86 S.Ct. 1507, 16 L.Ed.2d 600.

[In 1954, Sheppard was charged with murdering his wife. The case attracted great public attention and extensive media coverage beginning shortly after the murder, before any arrest had been made. The publicity continued through the pretrial and trial period. Sheppard was convicted of second-degree murder. After serving several years in prison he sought habeas corpus in the federal courts, claiming that the state had denied him his constitutional rights during the prosecution. The district court agreed and granted the writ, but the court of appeals reversed. The Supreme Court in turn reversed, and ordered Sheppard released unless the state gave him a new trial. The Court's lengthy opinion traced the facts in great detail and placed responsibility on the trial judge for failing to give Sheppard a fair trial:

> The fact is that bedlam reigned at the courthouse during the trial and newsmen took over practically the entire courtroom, hounding most of the participants in the trial, especially Sheppard. . . . Having assigned almost all of the available seats in the courtroom to the news media the judge lost his ability to supervise the environment. The movement of the reporters in and out

of the courtroom caused frequent confusion and disruption of the trial.

Beyond this concern with the judge's lack of control over the courtroom the Court was troubled by publicity during the trial.]

MR. JUSTICE CLARK delivered the opinion of the Court.

. . .

Much of the material printed or broadcast during the trial was never heard from the witness stand, such as the charges that Sheppard had purposely impeded the murder investigation and must be guilty since he had hired a prominent criminal lawyer; that Sheppard was a perjurer; that he had sexual relations with numerous women; that his slain wife had characterized him as a "Jekyll-Hyde"; that he was "a bare-faced liar" because of his testimony as to police treatment; and, finally, that a woman convict claimed Sheppard to be the father of her illegitimate child. As the trial progressed, the newspapers summarized and interpreted the evidence, devoting particular attention to the material that incriminated Sheppard, and often drew unwarranted inferences from testimony. At one point, a front-page picture of Mrs. Sheppard's blood-stained pillow was published after being "doctored" to show more clearly an alleged imprint of a surgical instrument.

Nor is there doubt that this deluge of publicity reached at least some of the jury. On the only occasion that the jury was queried, two jurors admitted in open court to hearing the highly inflammatory charge that a prison inmate claimed Sheppard as the father of her illegitimate child. Despite the extent and nature of the publicity to which the jury was exposed during trial, the judge refused defense counsel's other requests that the jurors be asked whether they had read or heard specific prejudicial comment about the case, including the incidents we have previously summarized. In these circumstances, we can assume that some of this material reached members of the jury. [ ]

VII.

The court's fundamental error is compounded by the holding that it lacked power to control the publicity about the trial. From the very inception of the proceedings the judge announced that neither he nor anyone else could restrict prejudicial news accounts. And he reiterated this view on numerous occasions. Since he viewed the news media as his target, the judge never considered other means that are often utilized to reduce the appearance of prejudicial material and to protect the jury from outside influence. We conclude that these procedures would have been sufficient to guarantee Sheppard a fair trial and so do not consider what sanctions might be available against a recalcitrant press nor the charges of bias now made against the state trial judge.

The carnival atmosphere at trial could easily have been avoided since the courtroom and courthouse premises are subject to the control of the court. . . .

[The Court asserted that the trial judge should have "made some effort to control the release of leads, information, and gossip to the press by police officers, witnesses, and counsel for both sides."]

The fact that many of the prejudicial news items can be traced to the prosecution, as well as the defense, aggravates the judge's failure to take any action. [ ] Effective control of these sources—concededly within the court's power—might well have prevented the divulgence of inaccurate information, rumors, and accusations that made up much of the inflammatory publicity, at least after Sheppard's indictment.

More specifically, the trial court might well have proscribed extrajudicial statements by any lawyer, party, witness, or court official which divulged prejudicial matters, such as the refusal of Sheppard to submit to interrogation or take any lie detector tests; any statement made by Sheppard to officials; the identity of prospective witnesses or their probable testimony; any belief in guilt or innocence; or like statements concerning the merits of the case. . . . Being advised of the great public interest in the case, the mass coverage of the press, and the potential prejudicial impact of publicity, the court could also have requested the appropriate city and county officials to promulgate a regulation with respect to dissemination of information about the case by their employees. . . . Had the judge, the other officers of the court, and the police placed the interest of justice first, the news media would have soon learned to be content with the task of reporting the case as it unfolded in the courtroom—not pieced together from extrajudicial statements.

From the cases coming here we note that unfair and prejudicial news comment on pending trials has become increasingly prevalent. Due process requires that the accused receive a trial by an impartial jury free from outside influences. Given the pervasiveness of modern communications and the difficulty of effacing prejudicial publicity from the minds of the jurors, the trial courts must take strong measures to ensure that the balance is never weighed against the accused. And appellate tribunals have the duty to make an independent evaluation of the circumstances. Of course, there is nothing that proscribes the press from reporting the events that transpire in the courtroom. But where there is a reasonable likelihood that prejudicial news prior to trial will prevent a fair trial, the judge should continue the case until the threat abates, or transfer it to another county not so permeated with publicity. In addition, sequestration of the jury was something the judge should have raised *sua sponte* with counsel. If publicity during the proceedings threatens the fairness of the trial, a new trial should be ordered. But we must remember that reversals are but palliatives; the cure lies in those

remedial measures that will prevent the prejudice at its inception.
The courts must take such steps by rule and regulation that will
protect their processes from prejudicial outside interferences.
Neither prosecutors, counsel for defense, the accused, witnesses,
court staff nor enforcement officers coming under the jurisdiction of
the court should be permitted to frustrate its function. Collaboration
between counsel and the press as to information affecting the fairness of a criminal trial is not only subject to regulation, but is highly
censurable and worthy of disciplinary measures.

Since the state trial judge did not fulfill his duty to protect
Sheppard from the inherently prejudicial publicity which saturated
the community and to control disruptive influences in the courtroom,
we must reverse the denial of the habeas petition. The case is
remanded to the District Court with instructions to issue the writ and
order that Sheppard be released from custody unless the State puts
him to its charges again within a reasonable time.

It is so ordered.

MR. JUSTICE BLACK dissents [without opinion].

Notes and Questions

1. On Sheppard's retrial he was acquitted and released—after having spent ten years in prison.

2. Note that because the Court thinks that action by the trial judge
would have met the problem, it has no need to discuss "what
sanctions might be available against a recalcitrant press."

3. Note also that the Court recognizes that nothing "proscribes the
press from reporting the events that transpire in the courtroom."
This is the lesson from Craig v. Harney, discussed later in this
Chapter.

B. SO–CALLED REMEDIES FOR THE FAIR TRIAL–FREE PRESS PROBLEM

1. THE STANDARD REMEDIES

Although the judge's failure to maintain proper decorum during
the trial was viewed as his major error in *Sheppard*, the Court
devoted extensive consideration to the behavior of the media, and
suggested techniques by which the judge might have better insulated
the trial. Some of those suggestions were among those listed as so-
called remedies earlier in this Chapter which can now be examined
more thoroughly.

a. *Cautioning, Police, Prosecutors, etc.*

Cutting off information at its source is an obvious way of trying
to curtail its dissemination by the news media, and police and prose-

cutors sometimes are the sources of news stories about confessions and probable guilt, but gags on police and attorneys may be challenged by those gagged on the ground that they interfere with the First Amendment rights of the police and attorneys to express themselves. Furthermore, to the extent that the process of news-gathering may be protected by the First Amendment (see discussion of *Richmond Newspapers* later in this Chapter), such restrictive orders may be seen as interference with that right.

b. Shielding Witnesses

Shielding witnesses from the press similarly may interfere with the witnesses' own First Amendment rights and may interfere with a press right to gather news. On the other hand, of course, witnesses are under no obligation to answer questions from journalists.

c. Cautioning Journalists

If the court cautions journalists prior to publication of prejudicial information, the warning can seem to imply the threat of punishment by the contempt powers and may smack of an unconstitutional form of prior restraint on the press (see Chapter II). If the warning is made after some prejudicial information has already been published, the warning is likely to be ineffective because the damage has already been done.

d. Encouraging the Use of Guidelines

When the Supreme Court in *Sheppard* suggested techniques for insulating trials, it also cited the Report of the President's Commission on the Assassination of President John F. Kennedy, in which the Commission, chaired by Chief Justice Earl Warren, expressed grave concern about whether Lee Harvey Oswald could possibly have gotten a fair trial after all the publicity that followed the assassination. The discussion in *Sheppard* plus the observation that "reversals are still but palliatives" led the bar to begin investigating new courses of action in greater detail. The first such effort was made by the American Bar Association, which created a committee that became known as the Reardon Committee after its chairman, Justice Paul Reardon of Massachusetts.

The Reardon Report. The American Bar Association (ABA) is a private organization that has no lawmaking powers. After it undertakes research projects, however, it often tries to persuade the state courts or legislatures to adopt the ABA's solution as law in each state. In the case of the Reardon Report, the ABA met with mixed success. We shall briefly summarize some of its provisions—and then turn to consider recent litigation concerning the perceived problem of prejudicial publicity.

On the question of controlling the flow of information from court officials and those under control of the court, the Reardon Report recommended that the canons of ethics in the various states provide that after arrest and until trial in criminal cases lawyers release no extrajudicial statements relating to (1) prior criminal record of the accused; (2) existence or contents of any confession; (3) performance of any examinations or tests or the defendant's refusal to undergo them; (4) identity, testimony, or credibility of prospective witnesses; (5) possibility of a guilty plea to the charge or a lesser offense; or (6) any opinion as to the accused's guilt or innocence. The lawyer was permitted to make a factual statement of the accused's name, age, residence, occupation, and family status. Also, if the accused has not been apprehended a lawyer for the prosecution may release information necessary to aid in apprehension or to warn the public of danger. Upon arrest the facts of arrest, including whether there was resistance and what physical evidence was seized, may be released. (§ 1.1).

Another section recommended that law enforcement agencies place similar constraints on their officers. (§ 2.1). Court employees were to be ordered not to disclose information "not part of the public records of the court that may tend to interfere with the right of the people or of the defendant to a fair trial." (§ 2.3).

In 1978, the ABA adopted significant changes in the Reardon standards of a decade earlier for criminal cases. The second edition is part of a revised set of Standards Relating to the Administration of Criminal Justice. Attorneys are not to release information if it "would pose a clear and present danger to the fairness of the trial." (Standard 8–1.1). Subject to that basic provision, a lawyer who reveals information on the basic six items from the earlier version may be disciplined. The comments indicate that the previously used "reasonable likelihood" standard was altered to provide "greater weight to the attorney's right under the first amendment to make public, extrajudicial statements about criminal investigations or litigation." The new standards, which apply to both jury and bench trials, draw no distinctions among various stages of the litigation (as was done in the earlier version).

Regulations should be promulgated barring law enforcement agencies from identifying a wanted suspect unless the identification would aid the investigation, assist in apprehension, or warn the public of danger. (§ 8–2.1(a)). Regulations should ban the "deliberate posing of a person in custody" for photographing by media and interviews requested by news media unless the person has consented after being informed of his right to consult with counsel and to refuse to grant an interview. (§ 8–2.1(b)).

Regulations should bar law enforcement agencies from making statements that pose a clear and present danger to the fairness of the trial. "In no event, however, shall a law enforcement officer make an extrajudicial statement concerning" the existence or contents of any statement or refusal to make a statement and "the possibility of a plea of guilty to the offense charged or a lesser offense or other disposition." These two of the basic six areas of concern would be barred absolutely to law enforcement officers, though attorneys would be covered only under the clear and present danger test. The other four areas would be under the clear and present danger test for both law enforcement officers and attorneys. (§ 8–2.1(c)).

The comments suggest that judicial authority to use regulations to control law enforcement agencies is "dubious." "Outside the context of a case or controversy . . . or its counterpart at the state level, separation of powers principles cast serious doubt on the constitutionality of administrative regulations imposed upon law enforcement agencies by the courts." This question "is more serious than the commentary to the first edition indicated."

Court personnel are to be restricted from disclosing any information not part of the public records in the case that "may be prejudicial to the right of the people or the defendant to a fair trial." (§ 8–2.2).

There has been relatively little litigation challenging a court's power to order its employees, such as clerks and marshals, or witnesses not to reveal prejudicial information about a pending case. Courts have not generally tried to issue orders to the police (in the executive branch). Rather, efforts have been made to get the executive branch to issue its own orders.

It seems clear that the court may order the prosecutor not to divulge certain potentially prejudicial information. It is not clear that a similar order could be imposed on an unwilling defendant. The defendant may argue that he is entitled to waive protections promulgated for his benefit, and he may feel compelled to speak to counter what he perceives to be prejudicial pretrial information.

Finally, attorneys, although officers subject to orders of the court, have contested orders that they not reveal information. Some have been upheld. Some have been upset on the ground that they swept beyond the needs of the case; some on the ground that they were unduly vague.

State guidelines. Because some journalists resented what they saw as an ABA attempt to tell them how to report news, the Reardon Report had more influence on those in the legal community than on the journalists. In the late 1960's and early 1970's, however, voluntary bench-bar-press-law enforcement groups were begun in many states to increase the dialogue about the problems. Some of those groups adopted guidelines that addressed many of the same problems addressed in the Reardon guidelines but reflected the input of journalists by affirming the right of the journalists to make the ultimate decisions about what they publish and by including references to the openness of the judicial system and the right of the public and press to observe it.

The effectiveness of the guidelines as a way of protecting defendants' rights, of course, is directly related to the fact that the guidelines are voluntary. Even in states in which they are followed with some regularity on criminal cases of routine interest, they tend to lose their effectiveness when sensational crimes are committed. There is also some danger that courts may use the guidelines in ways the journalists never envisioned; see Nebraska Press Association v. Stuart and Federated Publications v. Swedberg later in this Chapter.

e. Granting Change of Venue

Where news accounts in an area may have created a situation in which it is unlikely that the accused can obtain a fair trial, a judge can transfer a trial to another area less touched by the publicity. A constitutional problem may arise in such instances, because the Sixth Amendment provides for one's trial "by an impartial jury of the State and district wherein the crime shall have been committed." Furthermore, such changes of venue are costly and bothersome to both the prosecution and the defense. If news accounts have already been state-wide or national, the change is unlikely to do much to mitigate the damage. Even if the new site of the trial has been untouched by earlier news accounts, the scheduling of the trial there becomes a news event in that area, and the problem may begin anew, though with less attention because the victim(s) are not local people.

f. Granting Change of Venire

Rather than moving the trial, it is theoretically possible to import a panel of jurors—or veniremen—from another area where they are less likely to have formed opinions about the case. In practice, this is extremely rare, and it raises questions as to whether the jurors from the remote area are really the accused's peers.

g. Relying on the Voir Dire

During the *voir dire*, the process under which prospective jurors are screened, attempts are made to exclude from the jury those people whose previously formed opinions will preclude their reaching a fair verdict based on the evidence presented during the trial. The *voir dire* may be successful in keeping truly biased people off a jury, but it is less successful when potential jurors have heard a specific piece of information. Also, the criticism is sometimes made that it can tend to eliminate from the jury those potential jurors who follow the news in their community most closely and who form intelligent opinions based on what they read or hear. The remaining potential jurors may be atypical of the population.

h.   Cautioning Jurors

The Court in *Sheppard* was critical of the trial judge for failing to give the jurors sufficient instruction about not reading media accounts of the trial or listening to comment outside the courtroom. Despite the fact that most judges today can be expected to give careful instructions, and most have faith in jurors to follow those instructions, there are undoubtedly instances in which jurors fail to heed those instructions and do see prejudicial news accounts outside the courtroom.

i.   Sequestering the Jury

Sequestering the jury—keeping them in a hotel during the trial— greatly reduces the risk of improper exposure to media accounts of the trial. Because the public reads about sequestration of jurors in some highly publicized cases, it seems to perceive sequestration as a more common practice than it is. Its high cost precludes its use in all but a few cases, and defense attorneys are sometimes reluctant even to suggest it because of unsureness about the effect on the jury. As some say, a juror who is unhappy about being confined for the duration of a trial cannot take out his frustrations on the judge or prosecutor and just may take them out on the accused.

2.   RESTRAINTS ON PUBLICATION

Because the First Amendment has traditionally been seen as a protection for the freedom to publish, restraints on the publication of information are undoubtedly the least desirable and most constitutionally suspect of the theoretically-available remedies for the fair trial-free press problem. Two cases that illustrate the problem are United States v. Dickinson and Nebraska Press Association v. Stuart, below.

The press calls them gag orders, lawyers and judges call them restrictive orders or protective orders. By whatever name, such an order directs the press (and often others) not to disseminate information a judge thinks may prejudice jurors in a forthcoming or present trial. Violating an order can lead to a contempt citation.

a.   Obeying Court Orders

These orders forcefully came to the attention of journalists in a federal courtroom in Louisiana. A hearing was being held to determine whether the state might properly prosecute a suspect for the attempted murder of the mayor of Baton Rouge. The federal judge ordered the press not to publish any testimony taken at the hearing for fear it might prejudice any forthcoming state trial. Two reporters violated the order, were cited for criminal contempt, and were fined $300 each. On appeal, the court of appeals held the order unconstitutional, but ruled that it had to be obeyed until overturned on appeal. United States v. Dickinson, 465 F.2d 496 (5th Cir.1972).

The court relied on Walker v. City of Birmingham, 388 U.S. 307 (1967), in which marchers violated a state court injunction against holding the march. The marchers did not pursue appellate routes available for contesting the injunction. The Supreme Court upheld as constitutional the Alabama requirement that court orders be obeyed until overturned on appeal—so long as there are ways to obtain rapid reversals and "stays" of lower court orders.

The court in *Dickinson* applied these rules to federal judicial orders. "Absent a showing of 'transparent invalidity' or patent frivolity surrounding the order, *it must be obeyed* until reversed by orderly review or disrobed of authority by delay or frustration in the appellate process" whether or not the original order was valid. The *Dickinson* court explained its reasoning as follows:

> The criminal contempt exception requiring compliance with court orders, while invalid non-judicial directives may be disregarded, is not the product of self-protection or arrogance of Judges. Rather it is born of an experience-proved recognition that this rule is essential for the system to work. Judges, after all, are charged with the final responsibility to adjudicate legal disputes. It is the judiciary which is vested with the duty and the power to interpret and apply statutory and constitutional law. Determinations take the form of orders. The problem is unique to the judiciary because of its particular role. Disobedience to a legislative pronouncement in no way interferes with the legislature's ability to discharge its responsibilities (passing laws). The dispute is simply pursued in the judiciary and the legislature is ordinarily free to continue its function unencumbered by any burdens resulting from the disregard of its directives. Similarly, law enforcement is not prevented by failure to convict those who disregard the unconstitutional commands of a policeman.

> On the other hand, the deliberate refusal to obey an order of the court without testing its validity through established processes requires further action by the judiciary, and therefore directly affects the judiciary's ability to discharge its duties and responsibilities. Therefore, "while it is sparingly to be used, yet the power of courts to punish for contempts is a necessary and integral part of the independence of the judiciary, and is absolutely essential to the performance of the duties imposed on them by law. Without it they are mere boards of arbitration whose judgments and decrees would be only advisory."

Finally, the court saw no impediment to applying the requirement to newsmen. The situation did present "thorny problems" because "timeliness of publication is the hallmark of 'news' and the difference between 'news' and 'history' is merely a matter of hours. . . . But in the absence of strong indications that the appellate process was being deliberately stalled . . . violation with impunity does not occur simply because immediate decision is not forthcoming, even though the communication enjoined is 'news.' " The court noted that "newsmen are citizens, too. [ ] They too may sometimes have to wait. They are not yet wrapped in an immunity or given the absolute right to decide with impunity whether a Judge's order is to be obeyed or whether an appellate court is acting promptly enough."

On remand the trial judge refused to alter the sentences. He said that they had been based on wilful disobedience rather than on any harm that occurred. 349 F.Supp. 227 (M.D.La.1972). The court of appeals affirmed, 476 F.2d 373 (5th Cir.1973), and the Supreme Court denied certiorari with Justice Douglas noting that he would have granted the writ. 414 U.S. 979 (1973).

The Supreme Court so far has said only that it was not unconstitutional for a state to follow such an approach so long as certain conditions, such as speedy appeals, were met. Several states reject this approach and allow parties who disobey injunctions to argue later that the injunctions were invalid. The California Supreme Court, for example, observed that it followed a rule "considerably more consistent with the exercise of First Amendment freedoms" than that adopted in other states. In re Berry, 68 Cal.2d 137, 65 Cal. Rptr. 273, 436 P.2d 273 (1968).

States need not follow *Dickinson*, though they may. Remember, however, that even *Dickinson* provided protection if the violator could show "transparent invalidity or patent frivolity surrounding the order." This means that as the substantive protections of the press grow, the number of instances of transparently invalid restrictions may grow. Keep this in mind as we proceed through this section.

In jurisdictions that follow *Dickinson*, another critical question is how rapidly a trial court's injunction can be "stayed" or "vacated" by an appellate court or judge. A "stay" involves delaying the effect of the lower court's order until later appellate review. "Vacate" is more drastic and occurs when the lower court's error is clear on cursory inspection. In each state, procedures are available that would permit efforts to stay or vacate a lower court's order within minutes or, at most, hours—though an immediate ruling is not guaranteed.

In State v. Coe, 101 Wn.2d 364, 679 P.2d 353 (1984), a trial judge's order holding a broadcaster in contempt for playing tapes which had been played in open court was reversed on appeal. The judge had ordered that the tapes not be played on the air because the defendant might be suicidal. The appellate court majority held that the state permitted those cited for contempt to violate the order and then challenge it if the order was "patently invalid or 'void' as outside the court's power."

b. *Validity of Restrictive Orders*

After *Sheppard*, the Supreme Court did not get involved in publicity problems for several years. Then, in the early 1970's, some courts began ordering the press not to report information it had obtained or might obtain. Some of these cases reached the state appellate courts but no clear pattern emerged. A few reached individual justices of the Supreme Court when newspapers asked them to "stay" a restrictive order issued by a state court pending review by the full Supreme Court. These did not result in the Court's addressing the issue until a major case developed in 1976.

NEBRASKA PRESS ASSOCIATION v. STUART

Supreme Court of the United States, 1976.
427 U.S. 539, 96 S.Ct. 2791, 49 L.Ed.2d 683.

MR. CHIEF JUSTICE BURGER delivered the opinion of the Court.

The respondent State District Judge entered an order restraining the petitioners from publishing or broadcasting accounts of confessions or admissions made by the accused or facts "strongly implicative" of the accused in a widely reported murder of six persons. We granted certiorari to decide whether the entry of such an order on the showing made before the state court violated the constitutional guarantee of freedom of the press.

I

On the evening of October 18, 1975, local police found the six members of the Henry Kellie family murdered in their home in Sutherland, Neb., a town of about 850 people. Police released the description of a suspect, Erwin Charles Simants, to the reporters who had hastened to the scene of the crime. Simants was arrested and arraigned in Lincoln County Court the following morning, ending a tense night for this small rural community.

The crime immediately attracted widespread news coverage, by local, regional, and national newspapers, radio and television stations. Three days after the crime, the County Attorney and Simants' attorney joined in asking the County Court to enter a restrictive order relating to "matters that may or may not be publicly reported or disclosed to the public," because of the "mass coverage by news media" and the "reasonable likelihood of prejudicial news which would make difficult, if not impossible, the impaneling of an impartial jury and tend to prevent a fair trial." The County Court heard oral argument but took no evidence; no attorney for members of the press appeared at this stage. The County Court granted the prosecutor's motion for a restrictive order and entered it the next day,

October 22. The order prohibited everyone in attendance from "releas[ing] or authoriz[ing] for public dissemination in any form or manner whatsoever any testimony given or evidence adduced"; the order also required members of the press to observe the Nebraska Bar-Press Guidelines.[1]

Simants' preliminary hearing was held the same day, open to the public but subject to the order. The County Court bound over the defendant for trial to the State District Court. The charges, as amended to reflect the autopsy findings, were that Simants had committed the murders in the course of a sexual assault.

Petitioners—several press and broadcast associations, publishers, and individual reporters—moved on October 23 for leave to intervene in the District Court, asking that the restrictive order imposed by the County Court be vacated. The District Court conducted a hearing, at which the County Judge testified and newspaper articles about the Simants case were admitted in evidence. The District Judge granted petitioners' motion to intervene and, on October 27, entered his own restrictive order. The judge found "because of the nature of the crimes charged in the complaint that there is a clear and present danger that pretrial publicity could impinge upon the defendant's right to a fair trial." The order applied only until the jury was impaneled and specifically prohibited petitioners from reporting five subjects: (1) the existence or contents of a confession Simants had made to law enforcement officers, which had been introduced in open court at arraignment; (2) the fact or nature of statements Simants had made to other persons; (3) the contents of a note he had written the night of the crime; (4) certain aspects of the medical testimony at the preliminary hearing; and (5) the identity of the victims of the alleged sexual assault and the nature of the assault. It also prohibited reporting the exact nature of the restrictive order itself. Like the County Court's order, this order incorporated the Nebraska Bar-Press Guidelines. Finally, the order set out a plan for attendance, seating and courthouse traffic control during the trial.

Four days later, on October 31, petitioners asked the District Court to stay its order. At the same time, they applied to the Nebraska Supreme Court for a writ of mandamus, a stay, and an expedited appeal from the order. The State of Nebraska and the defendant Simants intervened in these actions. The Nebraska Su-

---

1. The Nebraska Guidelines are voluntary standards adopted by members of the state bar and news media to deal with the reporting of crimes and criminal trials. They outline the matters of fact that may appropriately be reported, and also list what items are not generally appropriate for reporting, including: confessions, opinions on guilt or innocence, statements that would influence the outcome of a trial, the results of tests or examinations, comments on the credibility of witnesses, and evidence presented in the jury's absence. The publication of an accused's criminal record should, under the Guidelines, be "considered very carefully." The Guidelines also set out standards for taking and publishing photographs, and set up a joint bar-press committee to foster cooperation in resolving particular problems that emerge.

preme Court heard oral argument on November 25, and issued its *per curiam* opinion December 2. State ex rel. Nebraska Press Assn. v. Stuart, 194 Neb. 783, 236 N.W.2d 794 (1975).

The Nebraska Supreme Court balanced the "heavy presumption against . . . constitutional validity" that an order restraining publications bears, New York Times v. United States, 403 U.S. 713, 714 (1971), against the importance of the defendant's right to trial by an impartial jury. Both society and the individual defendant, the court held, had a vital interest in assuring that Simants be tried by an impartial jury. Because of the publicity surrounding the crime, the court determined that this right was in jeopardy. The court noted that Nebraska statutes required the District Court to try Simants within six months of his arrest, and that a change of venue could move the trial only to adjoining counties, which had been subject to essentially the same publicity as Lincoln County. The Nebraska Supreme Court held, "Unless the absolutist position of the relators was constitutionally correct, it would appear that the District Court acted properly." 194 Neb., at 797.

The Nebraska Supreme Court rejected that "absolutist position," but modified the District Court's order to accommodate the defendant's right to a fair trial and the petitioners' interest in reporting pretrial events. The order as modified prohibited reporting of only three matters: (a) the existence and nature of any confessions or admissions made by the defendant to law enforcement officers, (b) any confessions or admissions made to any third parties, except members of the press, and (c) other facts "strongly implicative" of the accused. The Nebraska Supreme Court did not rely on the Nebraska Bar-Press Guidelines. After construing Nebraska law to permit closure in certain circumstances, the court remanded the case to the District Judge for reconsideration of the issue whether pretrial hearings should be closed to the press and public.

We granted certiorari to address the important issues raised by the District Court order as modified by the Nebraska Supreme Court, but we denied the motion to expedite review or to stay entirely the order of the State District Court pending Simants' trial. 423 U.S. 1027 (1975). We are informed by the parties that since we granted certiorari, Simants has been convicted of murder and sentenced to death. His appeal is pending in the Nebraska Supreme Court.

II

[The Court concluded that the controversy was not moot because the dispute was "capable of repetition."]

III

The problems presented by this case are almost as old as the Republic. Neither in the Constitution nor in contemporaneous writ-

ings do we find that the conflict between these two important rights was anticipated, yet it is inconceivable that the authors of the Constitution were unaware of the potential conflicts between the right to an unbiased jury and the guarantee of freedom of the press.
. . .

The trial of Aaron Burr in 1807 presented Chief Justice Marshall, presiding as a trial judge, with acute problems in selecting an unbiased jury. Few people in the area of Virginia from which jurors were drawn had not formed some opinions concerning Mr. Burr or the case, from newspaper accounts and heightened discussion both private and public. The Chief Justice conducted a searching *voir dire* of the two panels eventually called, and rendered a substantial opinion on the purposes of *voir dire* and the standards to be applied. [ ]. Burr was acquitted, so there was no occasion for appellate review to examine the problem of prejudicial pretrial publicity. Chief Justice Marshall's careful *voir dire* inquiry into the matter of possible bias makes clear that the problem is not a new one.

The speed of communication and the pervasiveness of the modern news media have exacerbated these problems, however, as numerous appeals demonstrate. The trial of Bruno Hauptmann in a small New Jersey community, for the abduction and murder of the Charles Lindberghs' infant child, probably was the most widely covered trial up to that time, and the nature of the coverage produced widespread public reaction. Criticism was directed at the "carnival" atmosphere that pervaded the community and the courtroom itself. Responsible leaders of press and the legal profession—including other judges—pointed out that much of this sorry performance could have been controlled by a vigilant trial judge and by other public officers subject to the control of the court. [ ].

The excesses of press and radio and lack of responsibility of those in authority in the Hauptmann case and others of that era led to efforts to develop voluntary guidelines for courts, lawyers, press and broadcasters. . . .

In practice, of course, even the most ideal guidelines are subjected to powerful strains when a case such as Simants' arises, with reporters from many parts of the country on the scene. Reporters from distant places are unlikely to consider themselves bound by local standards. They report to editors outside the area covered by the guidelines, and their editors are likely to be guided only by their own standards. To contemplate how a state court can control acts of a newspaper or broadcaster outside its jurisdiction, even though the newspapers and broadcasts reach the very community from which jurors are to be selected, suggests something of the practical difficulties of managing such guidelines.

The problems presented in this case have a substantial history outside the reported decisions of courts, in the efforts of many responsible people to accommodate the competing interests. We cannot resolve all of them, for it is not the function of this Court to write a code. We look instead to this particular case and the legal context in which it arises.

IV

[The Court reviewed its cases touching this problem in which it upset convictions, including Irvin v. Dowd, Estes v. Texas, p. 371, infra, and Sheppard v. Maxwell, and quoted the passage from *Sheppard* requiring the trial judge to take "strong measures" to protect the defendants. It then cited another group of cases, including Murphy v. Florida, in which publicity did not lead to reversals of convictions.]

Taken together, these cases demonstrate that pretrial publicity—even pervasive, adverse publicity—does not inevitably lead to an unfair trial. The capacity of the jury eventually impaneled to decide the case fairly is influenced by the tone and extent of the publicity, which is in part and often in large part, shaped by what attorneys, police, and other officials do to precipitate news coverage. The trial judge has a major responsibility. What the judge says about a case, in or out of the courtroom, is likely to appear in newspapers and broadcasts. More important, the measures a judge takes or fails to take to mitigate the effects of pretrial publicity—the measures described in *Sheppard*—may well determine whether the defendant receives a trial consistent with the requirements of due process. That this responsibility has not always been properly discharged is apparent from the decisions just reviewed.

The costs of failure to afford a fair trial are high. . . .

The state trial judge in the case before us acted responsibly, out of a legitimate concern, in an effort to protect the defendant's right to a fair trial.[4] What we must decide is not simply whether the Nebraska courts erred in seeing the possibility of real danger to the defendant's rights, but whether in the circumstances of this case the means employed were foreclosed by another provision of the Constitution.

V

[The Court here reviewed its cases considering the imposition of a prior restraint against publishing certain material, primarily Near v. Minnesota and New York Times Co. v. United States, discussed at pp. 39 and 195, supra.]

The thread running through all these cases is that prior restraints on speech and publication are the most serious and the least tolerable infringement on First Amendment rights. A criminal penal-

---

4. The record also reveals that counsel for both sides acted responsibly in this case, and there is no suggestion that either sought to use pretrial news coverage for partisan advantage. . . .

ty or a judgment in a defamation case is subject to the whole panoply of protections afforded by deferring the impact of the judgment until all avenues of appellate review have been exhausted. Only after judgment has become final, correct or otherwise, does the law's sanction become fully operative.

A prior restraint, by contrast and by definition, has an immediate and irreversible sanction. If it can be said that a threat of criminal or civil sanctions after publication "chills" speech, prior restraint "freezes" it at least for the time.

The damage can be particularly great when the prior restraint falls upon the communication of news and commentary on current events. Truthful reports of public judicial proceedings have been afforded special protection against subsequent punishment. See Cox Broadcasting Corp. v. Cohn, 420 U.S. 469, 492–493 (1975); see also, Craig v. Harney, 331 U.S. 367, 374 (1947). For the same reasons the protection against prior restraint should have particular force as applied to reporting of criminal proceedings, whether the crime in question is a single isolated act or a pattern of criminal conduct. . . . The extraordinary protections afforded by the First Amendment carry with them something in the nature of a fiduciary duty to exercise the protected rights responsibly—a duty widely acknowledged but not always observed by editors and publishers. It is not asking too much to suggest that those who exercise First Amendment rights in newspapers or broadcasting enterprises direct some effort to protect the rights of an accused to a fair trial by unbiased jurors.

Of course, the order at issue . . . does not prohibit but only postpones publication. Some news can be delayed and most commentary can even more readily be delayed without serious injury, and there often is a self-imposed delay when responsible editors call for verification of information. But such delays are normally slight and they are self-imposed. Delays imposed by governmental authority are a different matter. . . . As a practical matter, moreover, the element of time is not unimportant if press coverage is to fulfill its traditional function of bringing news to the public promptly.

The authors of the Bill of Rights did not undertake to assign priorities as between First Amendment and Sixth Amendment rights, ranking one as superior to the other. In this case, the petitioners would have us declare the right of an accused subordinate to their right to publish in all circumstances. But if the authors of these guarantees, fully aware of the potential conflicts between them, were unwilling or unable to resolve the issue by assigning to one priority over the other, it is not for us to rewrite the Constitution by undertaking what they declined. It is unnecessary, after nearly two centuries, to establish a priority applicable in all circumstances. Yet it is nonetheless clear that the barriers to prior restraint remain high unless we are to abandon what the Court has said for nearly a

quarter of our national existence and implied throughout all of it.
. . .
. . .

VI

We turn now to the record in this case to determine whether, as Learned Hand put it, "the gravity of the 'evil,' discounted by its improbability, justifies such invasion of free speech as is necessary to avoid the danger." Dennis v. United States, 183 F.2d 201, 212 (1950), aff'd, 341 U.S. 494 (1951); see also L. Hand, The Bill of Rights 58–61 (1958). To do so, we must examine the evidence before the trial judge when the order was entered to determine (a) the nature and extent of pretrial news coverage; (b) whether other measures would be likely to mitigate the effects of unrestrained pretrial publicity; (c) how effectively a restraining order would operate to prevent the threatened danger. The precise terms of the restraining order are also important. We must then consider whether the record supports the entry of a prior restraint on publication, one of the most extraordinary remedies known to our jurisprudence.

A

In assessing the probable extent of publicity, the trial judge had before him newspapers demonstrating that the crime had already drawn intensive news coverage, and the testimony of the County Judge, who had entered the initial restraining order based on the local and national attention the case had attracted. The District Judge was required to assess the probable publicity that would be given these shocking crimes prior to the time a jury was selected and sequestered. He then had to examine the probable nature of the publicity and determine how it would affect prospective jurors.

Our review of the pretrial record persuades us that the trial judge was justified in concluding that there would be intense and pervasive pretrial publicity concerning this case. He could also reasonably conclude, based on common human experience, that publicity might impair the defendant's right to a fair trial. He did not purport to say more, for he found only "a clear and present danger that pretrial publicity *could* impinge upon the defendant's right to a fair trial." (Emphasis added.) His conclusion as to the impact of such publicity on prospective jurors was of necessity speculative, dealing as he was with factors unknown and unknowable.

B

We find little in the record that goes to another aspect of our task, determining whether measures short of an order restraining all publication would have insured the defendant a fair trial. Although the entry of the order might be read as a judicial determination that other measures would not suffice, the trial court made no express findings to that effect; the Nebraska Supreme Court referred to the issue only by implication. [   ]

Most of the alternatives to prior restraint of publication in these circumstances were discussed with obvious approval in Sheppard v. Maxwell, 384 U.S., at 357–362: (a) change of trial venue to a place less exposed to the intense publicity that seemed imminent in Lincoln County; [7] (b) postponement of the trial to allow public attention to subside; (c) use of searching questioning of prospective jurors, as Chief Justice Marshall did in the *Burr* case, to screen out those with fixed opinions as to guilt or innocence; (d) the use of emphatic and clear instructions on the sworn duty of each juror to decide the issues only on evidence presented in open court. Sequestration of jurors is, of course, always available. Although that measure insulates jurors only after they are sworn, it also enhances the likelihood of dissipating the impact of pretrial publicity and emphasizes the elements of the jurors' oaths.

This Court has outlined other measures short of prior restraints on publication tending to blunt the impact of pretrial publicity. See Sheppard v. Maxwell, 384 U.S. at 361–362. Professional studies have filled out these suggestions, recommending that trial courts in appropriate cases limit what the contending lawyers, the police, and witnesses may say to anyone. See American Bar Association, Standards for Criminal Justice, Fair Trial and Free Press 2–15 (Approved Draft, 1968).[8]

We have noted earlier that pretrial publicity, even if pervasive and concentrated, cannot be regarded as leading automatically and in every kind of criminal case to an unfair trial. . . .

We have therefore examined this record to determine the probable efficacy of the measures short of prior restraint on the press and speech. There is no finding that alternative measures would not have protected Simants' rights, and the Nebraska Supreme Court did

----

7. The respondent and intervenors argue here that a change of venue would not have helped, since Nebraska law permits a change only to adjacent counties, which had been as exposed to pretrial publicity in this case as Lincoln County. We have held that state laws restricting venue must on occasion yield to the constitutional requirement that the State afford a fair trial. Groppi v. Wisconsin, 400 U.S. 505 (1971). We note also that the combined population of Lincoln County and the adjacent counties is over 80,000, providing a substantial pool of prospective jurors.

8. Closing of pretrial proceedings with the consent of the defendant when required is also recommended in guidelines that have emerged from various studies. At oral argument petitioners' counsel asserted that judicially imposed restraints on lawyers and others would be subject to challenge as interfering with press rights to news sources. [   ] We are not now confronted with such issues.

We note that in making its proposals, the American Bar Association recommended strongly against resort to direct restraints on the press to prohibit publication. ABA Standards, at 68–73. Other groups have reached similar conclusions. [   ]

no more than imply that such measures might not be adequate. Moreover, the record is lacking in evidence to support such a finding.

C

We must also assess the probable efficacy of prior restraint on publication as a workable method of protecting Simants' right to a fair trial, and we cannot ignore the reality of the problems of managing and enforcing pretrial restraining orders. The territorial jurisdiction of the issuing court is limited by concepts of sovereignty [ ]. The need for *in personam* jurisdiction also presents an obstacle to a restraining order that applies to publication at-large as distinguished from restraining publication within a given jurisdiction. [ ]

The Nebraska Supreme Court narrowed the scope of the restrictive order, and its opinion reflects awareness of the tensions between the need to protect the accused as fully as possible and the need to restrict publication as little as possible. The dilemma posed underscores how difficult it is for trial judges to predict what information will in fact undermine the impartiality of jurors, and the difficulty of drafting an order that will effectively keep prejudicial information from prospective jurors. When a restrictive order is sought, a court can anticipate only part of what will develop that may injure the accused. But information not so obviously prejudicial may emerge, and what may properly be published in these "gray zone" circumstances may not violate the restrictive order and yet be prejudicial.

Finally, we note that the events disclosed by the record took place in a community of 850 people. It is reasonable to assume that, without any news accounts being printed or broadcast, rumors would travel swiftly by word of mouth. One can only speculate on the accuracy of such reports, given the generative propensities of rumors; they could well be more damaging than reasonably accurate news accounts. But plainly a whole community cannot be restrained from discussing a subject intimately affecting life within it.

Given these practical problems, it is far from clear that prior restraint on publication would have protected Simants' rights.

D

Finally, another feature of this case leads us to conclude that the restrictive order entered here is not supportable. At the outset the County Court entered a very broad restrictive order, the terms of which are not before us; it then held a preliminary hearing open to the public and the press. There was testimony concerning at least two incriminating statements made by Simants to private persons; the statement—evidently a confession—that he gave to law enforcement officials was also introduced. The State District Court's later order was entered after this public hearing and, as modified by the

Nebraska Supreme Court, enjoined reporting of (1) "[c]onfessions or admissions against interest made by the accused to law enforcement officials"; (2) "[c]onfessions or admissions against interest, oral or written, if any, made by the accused to third parties, excepting any statements, if any, made by the accused to representatives of the news media"; and (3) all "[o]ther information strongly implicative of the accused as the perpetrator of the slayings."

To the extent that this order prohibited the reporting of evidence adduced at the open preliminary hearing, it plainly violated settled principles: "there is nothing that proscribes the press from reporting events that transpire in the courtroom." Sheppard v. Maxwell, [ ]. See also Cox Broadcasting Corp. v. Cohn, [ ]; Craig v. Harney, [ ]. The County Court could not know that closure of the preliminary hearing was an alternative open to it until the Nebraska Supreme Court so construed state law; but once a public hearing had been held, what transpired there could not be subject to prior restraint.

The third prohibition of the order was defective in another respect as well. As part of a final order, entered after plenary review, this prohibition regarding "implicative" information is too vague and too broad to survive the scrutiny we have given to restraints on First Amendment rights. [ ] The third phase of the order entered falls outside permissible limits.

E

The record demonstrates, as the Nebraska courts held, that there was indeed a risk that pretrial news accounts, true or false, would have some adverse impact on the attitudes of those who might be called as jurors. But on the record now before us it is not clear that further publicity, unchecked, would so distort the views of potential jurors that 12 could not be found who would, under proper instructions, fulfill their sworn duty to render a just verdict exclusively on the evidence presented in open court. We cannot say on this record that alternatives to a prior restraint on petitioners would not have sufficiently mitigated the adverse effects of pretrial publicity so as to make prior restraint unnecessary. Nor can we conclude that the restraining order actually entered would serve its intended purpose. Reasonable minds can have few doubts about the gravity of the evil pretrial publicity can work, but the probability that it would do so here was not demonstrated with the degree of certainty our cases on prior restraint require.

Of necessity our holding is confined to the record before us. But our conclusion is not simply a result of assessing the adequacy of the showing made in this case; it results in part from the problems inherent in meeting the heavy burden of demonstrating, in advance of trial, that without prior restraint a fair trial will be denied. The practical problems of managing and enforcing restrictive orders will always be present. In this sense, the record now before us is illustrative rather than exceptional. It is significant that when this Court has reversed a state conviction because of prejudicial publicity, it has carefully noted that some course of action short of prior restraint would have made a critical difference. [ ] However difficult it may be, we need not rule out the possibility of showing the kind of threat to fair trial rights that would possess the requisite degree of certainty to justify restraint. This Court has frequently denied that First Amendment rights are absolute and has consistently rejected the proposition that a prior restraint can never be employed. [ ]

Our analysis ends as it began, with a confrontation between prior restraint imposed to protect one vital constitutional guarantee and the explicit command of another that the freedom to speak and publish shall not be abridged. We reaffirm that the guarantees of freedom of expression are not an absolute prohibition under all circumstances, but the barriers to prior restraint remain high and the presumption against its use continues intact. We hold that, with respect to the order entered in this case prohibiting reporting or commentary on judicial proceedings held in public, the barriers have not been overcome; to the extent that this order restrained publication of such material, it is clearly invalid. To the extent that it prohibited publication based on information gained from other sources, we conclude that the heavy burden imposed as a condition to securing a prior restraint was not met and the judgment of the Nebraska Supreme Court is therefore

Reversed.

MR. JUSTICE BRENNAN, with whom MR. JUSTICE STEWART and MR. JUSTICE MARSHALL concur, concurring in the judgment.

. . . The right to a fair trial by a jury of one's peers is unquestionably one of the most precious and sacred safeguards enshrined in the Bill of Rights. I would hold, however, that resort to prior restraints on the freedom of the press is a constitutionally impermissible method for enforcing that right; judges have at their disposal a broad spectrum of devices for ensuring that fundamental fairness is accorded the accused without necessitating so drastic an incursion on the equally fundamental and salutary constitutional mandate that discussion of public affairs in a free society cannot depend on the preliminary grade of judicial censors.

[After a most extensive review of the facts, Justice Brennan turned to a consideration of the values protected by the Sixth and First Amendments.]

II

A

. . . So basic to our jurisprudence is the right to a fair trial that it has been called "the most fundamental of all freedoms."

Estes v. Texas, 381 U.S. 532, 540 (1965). It is a right essential to the preservation and enjoyment of all other rights, providing a necessary means of safeguarding personal liberties against Government oppression. [   ]

The First Amendment to the United States Constitution, however, secures rights equally fundamental in our jurisprudence, and its ringing proclamation that "Congress shall make no law . . . abridging the freedom of speech or of the press . . ." has been both applied through the Fourteenth Amendment to invalidate restraints on freedom of the press imposed by the States, [   ]; and interpreted to interdict such restraints imposed by the courts [   ]. Indeed, it has been correctly perceived that a "responsible press has always been regarded as the handmaiden of effective judicial administration, especially in the criminal field. . . . The press does not simply publish information about trials but guards against the miscarriage of justice by subjecting the police, prosecutors, and judicial processes to extensive public scrutiny and criticism." Sheppard v. Maxwell, 384 U.S. 333, 350 (1966). See also, e.g., Cox Broadcasting Corp. v. Cohn, 420 U.S. 469, 491–496 (1975). Commentary and reporting on the criminal justice system is at the core of First Amendment values, for the operation and integrity of that system is of crucial import to citizens concerned with the administration of Government. Secrecy of judicial action can only breed ignorance and distrust of courts and suspicion concerning the competence and impartiality of judges; free and robust reporting, criticism, and debate can contribute to public understanding of the rule of law and to comprehension of the functioning of the entire criminal justice system, as well as improve the quality of that system by subjecting it to the cleansing effects of exposure and public accountability. [   ]

. . . Settled case law concerning the impropriety and constitutional invalidity of prior restraints on the press compels the conclusion that there can be no prohibition on the publication by the press of any information pertaining to pending judicial proceedings or the operation of the criminal justice system, no matter how shabby the means by which the information is obtained.[15] This does not imply, however, any subordination of Sixth Amendment rights, for an accused's right to a fair trial may be adequately assured through methods that do not infringe First Amendment values.

B

. . . A commentator has cogently summarized many of the reasons for this deep-seated American hostility to prior restraints:

---

15. Of course, even if the press cannot be enjoined from reporting certain information, that does not necessarily immunize it from civil liability for libel or invasion of privacy or from criminal liability for transgressions of general criminal laws during the course of obtaining that information.

"A system of prior restraints is in many ways more inhibiting than a system of subsequent punishment: It is likely to bring under government scrutiny a far wider range of expression; it shuts off communication before it takes place; suppression by a stroke of the pen is more likely to be applied than that suppression through criminal process; the procedures do not require attention to the safeguards of the criminal process; the system allows less opportunity for public appraisal and criticism; the dynamics of the system drive toward excesses, as the history of all censorship shows." T. Emerson, The System of Freedom of Expression 506 (1970).

Respondents correctly contend that "the [First Amendment] protection even as to prior restraint is not absolutely unlimited." Near v. Minnesota, supra, at 716. However, the exceptions to the rule have been confined to "exceptional cases." . . .

[Justice Brennan discussed these situations at length, particularly *Near* and *New York Times*.]

I would decline [an invitation to create a new category for the use of prior restraints]. In addition to the almost insuperable presumption against the constitutionality of prior restraints even under a recognized exception, and however laudable the State's motivation for imposing restraints in this case, there are compelling reasons for not carving out a new exception to the rule against prior censorship of publication.

1

Much of the information that the Nebraska courts enjoined petitioners from publishing was already in the public domain, having been revealed in open court proceedings or through public documents. . . .

2

The order of the Nebraska Supreme Court also applied, of course, to "confessions" and other information "strongly implicative" of the accused which was obtained from sources other than official records or open court proceedings. But for the reasons that follow—reasons equally applicable to information obtained by the press from official records of public court proceedings—I believe that the same rule against prior restraints governs *any* information pertaining to the criminal justice system, even if derived from nonpublic sources and regardless of the means employed by the press in its acquisition. . . .

A judge importuned to issue a prior restraint in the pretrial context will be unable to predict the manner in which the potentially prejudicial information would be published, the frequency with which it would be repeated or the emphasis it would be given, the context in which or purpose for which it would be reported, the scope of the audience that would be exposed to the information,[22] or the impact, evaluated in terms of current standards for assessing juror impartiality, the information would have on that audience. These considerations would render speculative the prospective impact on a fair trial of reporting even an alleged confession or other information "strongly implicative" of the accused. Moreover, we can take judicial notice of the fact that given the prevalence of plea bargaining, few criminal cases proceed to trial, and the judge would thus have to predict what the likelihood was that a jury would even have to be impaneled.[24] Indeed, even in cases that do proceed to trial, the material sought to be suppressed before trial will often be admissible and may be admitted in any event. And, more basically, there are adequate devices for screening from jury duty those individuals who have in fact been exposed to prejudicial pretrial publicity.

Initially, it is important to note that once the jury is impaneled, the techniques of sequestration of jurors and control over the courtroom and conduct of trial should prevent prejudicial publicity from infecting the fairness of judicial proceedings. Similarly, judges may stem much of the flow of prejudicial publicity at its source, before it is obtained by representatives of the press.[27] But even if the press nevertheless obtains potentially prejudicial information and decides to publish that information, the Sixth Amendment rights of the accused may still be adequately protected. In particular, the trial judge should employ the *voir dire* to probe fully into the effect of publicity. The judge should broadly explore such matters as the extent to which prospective jurors had read particular news accounts or whether they had heard about incriminating data such as an alleged confession or statements by purportedly reliable sources concerning the defendant's guilt. . . . Moreover, *voir dire* may indicate the need to grant a brief continuance[28] or to grant a change of venue,[29] tech-

---

22. It is suggested that prior restraints are really only necessary in "small towns," since media saturation would be more likely and incriminating materials that are published would therefore probably come to the attention of all inhabitants. Of course, the smaller the community, the more likely such information would become available through rumors and gossip, whether or not the press is enjoined from publication. . . .

24. Of course, judges accepting guilty pleas must guard against the danger that pretrial publicity has effectively coerced the defendant into pleading guilty.

27. A significant component of prejudicial pretrial publicity may be traced to public commentary on pending cases by court personnel, law enforcement officials, and the attorneys involved in the

case. . . . As officers of the court, court personnel and attorneys have a fiduciary responsibility not to engage in public debate that will redound to the detriment of the accused or that will obstruct the fair administration of justice. It is very doubtful that the court would not have the power to control release of information by these individuals in appropriate cases, [ ], and to impose suitable limitations whose transgression could result in disciplinary proceedings. [ ] Similarly, in most cases courts would have ample power to control such actions by law enforcement personnel.

28. Excessive delay, of course, would be impermissible in light of the Sixth Amendment right to a speedy trial. [ ] However, even short continuances can be effective in attenuating the impact of publicity, especially as other news

niques that can effectively mitigate any publicity at a particular time or in a particular locale. Finally, if the trial court fails or refuses to utilize these devices effectively, there are the "palliatives" of reversals on appeal and directions for a new trial. . . .

For these reasons alone I would reject the contention that speculative deprivation of an accused's Sixth Amendment right to an impartial jury is comparable to the damage to the Nation or its people that *Near* and *New York Times* would have found sufficient to justify a prior restraint on reporting. Damage to that Sixth Amendment right could never be considered so direct, immediate and irreparable, and based on such proof rather than speculation, that prior restraints on the press could be justified on this basis.

C

There are additional, practical reasons for not starting down the path urged by respondents.[32] . . .

. . .

There is, beyond peradventure, a clear and substantial damage to freedom of the press whenever even a temporary restraint is imposed on reporting of material concerning the operations of the criminal justice system, an institution of such pervasive influence in our constitutional scheme. And the necessary impact of reporting even confessions can never be so direct, immediate and irreparable that I would give credence to any notion that prior restraints may be imposed on that rationale. It may be that such incriminating material would be of such slight news value or so inflammatory in particular cases that responsible organs of the media, in an exercise of self-restraint, would choose not to publicize that material, and not make the judicial task of safeguarding precious rights of criminal defendants more difficult. Voluntary codes such as the Nebraska Bar-Press Guidelines are a commendable acknowledgement by the media that constitutional prerogatives bring enormous responsibilities, and I would encourage continuation of such voluntary cooperative efforts

crowds past events off the front pages. And somewhat substantial delays designed to ensure fair proceedings need not transgress the speedy trial guarantee. See Groppi v. Wisconsin, 400 U.S. 505, 510 (1971); [ ].

29. In Rideau v. Louisiana, 373 U.S. 723 (1963), we held that it was a denial of due process to deny a request for a change of venue that was necessary to preserve the accused's Sixth Amendment rights. And state statutes may not restrict changes of venue if to do so would deny an accused a fair trial. Groppi v. Wisconsin, 400 U.S. 505 (1971).

32. I include these additional considerations, many of which apply generally to any system of prior restraints, only because of the fundamentality of the Sixth Amendment right invoked as the justification for imposition of the restraints in this case; the fact that there are such overwhelming reasons for precluding *any* prior restraints even to facilitate preservation of such a fundamental right reinforces the longstanding constitutional doctrine that there is effectively an absolute prohibition against prior restraints against publication of *any* material otherwise covered within the meaning of the free press guarantee of the First Amendment. [ ]

between the bar and the media. However, the press may be arrogant, tyrannical, abusive, and sensationalist, just as it may be incisive, probing, and informative. But at least in the context of prior restraints on publication, the decision of what, when, and how to publish is for editors, not judges. [ ] Every restrictive order imposed on the press in this case was accordingly an unconstitutional prior restraint on the freedom of the press, and I would therefore reverse the judgment of the Nebraska Supreme Court and remand for further proceedings not inconsistent with this opinion.

MR. JUSTICE WHITE, concurring.

Technically there is no need to go farther than the Court does to dispose of this case, and I join the Court's opinion. I should add, however, that for the reasons which the Court itself canvasses there is grave doubt in my mind whether orders with respect to the press such as were entered in this case would ever be justifiable. It may be the better part of discretion, however, not to announce such a rule in the first case in which the issue has been squarely presented here. Perhaps we should go no farther than absolutely necessary until the federal courts, and ourselves, have been exposed to a broader spectrum of cases presenting similar issues. If the recurring result, however, in case after case is to be similar to our judgment today, we should at some point announce a more general rule and avoid the interminable litigation that our failure to do so would necessarily entail.

MR. JUSTICE POWELL, concurring.

Although I join the opinion of the Court, in view of the importance of the case I write to emphasize the unique burden that rests upon the party, whether it be the state or a defendant, who undertakes to show the necessity for prior restraint on pretrial publicity.

In my judgment a prior restraint properly may issue only when it is shown to be necessary to prevent the dissemination of prejudicial publicity that otherwise poses a high likelihood of preventing, directly and irreparably, the impaneling of a jury meeting the Sixth Amendment requirement of impartiality. This requires a showing that (i) there is a clear threat to the fairness of trial, (ii) such a threat is posed by the actual publicity to be restrained, and (iii) no less restrictive alternatives are available. Notwithstanding such a showing, a restraint may not issue unless it also is shown that previous publicity or publicity from unrestrained sources will not render the restraint inefficacious. The threat to the fairness of the trial is to be evaluated in the context of Sixth Amendment law on impartiality, and any restraint must comply with the standards of specificity always required in the First Amendment context.

I believe these factors are sufficiently addressed in the Court's opinion to demonstrate beyond question that the prior restraint here was impermissible.

MR. JUSTICE STEVENS, concurring in the judgment.

For the reasons eloquently stated by Mr. Justice Brennan, I agree that the judiciary is capable of protecting the defendant's right to a fair trial without enjoining the press from publishing information in the public domain, and that it may not do so. Whether the same absolute protection would apply no matter how shabby or illegal the means by which the information is obtained, no matter how serious an intrusion on privacy might be involved, no matter how demonstrably false the information might be, no matter how prejudicial it might be to the interests of innocent persons, and no matter how perverse the motivation for publishing it, is a question I would not answer without further argument. [ ] I do, however, subscribe to most of what Mr. Justice Brennan says and, if ever required to face the issue squarely, may well accept his ultimate conclusion.

Notes and Questions

1. What is the essential difference between Chief Justice Burger's approach and Justice Brennan's approach? What is the effect of the other concurring opinions?

2. Is it still permissible to issue restrictive orders preventing lawyers and other court officials from making certain types of statements?

3. As the opinions note, the press, bench and bar in Nebraska had collaborated on a set of voluntary guidelines. Such agreements exist in about half of the states, but this case is apparently the first in which a judge attempted to make the guidelines mandatory. In passing on the application for a stay, Justice Blackmun rejected this attempt out of hand, largely on the ground that the guidelines, since they were intended to be voluntary, used terms such as "consider carefully" that did not lend themselves to incorporation into a judicial order. Some members of the press had warned that guidelines might be misused in this way, and noted that guidelines had failed to deter judges from issuing restrictive orders.

4. Note that Justice Stevens suggests a possible connection between the way information is obtained and the freedom to publish that information. Recall *Landmark*, p. 218, supra.

5. When all the votes are counted in this case does the Chief Justice have more adherents than Justice Brennan?

6. As the result of the Nebraska Press case, the revised Reardon recommendations provide that no restrictions are to be imposed on the power of the news media to communicate "any information in their possession relating to criminal trial." (§ 8–3.2). Motions for change of venue and continuance are to be granted whenever "because of the dissemination of potentially prejudicial material, there is a substantial likelihood that, in the absence of such relief, a fair trial by an impartial jury cannot be had." No showing of actual prejudice is required. (§ 8–3.3).

7. If restrictive orders are not available against the press in dramatic murder trials, it is even clearer that they are not proper in cases involving much less potential public attention and prejudice.

In Goldblum v. National Broadcasting Co., 584 F.2d 904 (9th Cir. 1978), plaintiff, former executive officer of Equity Funding Corp., was serving a sentence for fraudulent activity in connection with the corporation's insolvency. NBC produced a "docudrama" based on the case, using the names of plaintiff and the corporation. Plaintiff, alleging that the program was inaccurate, sought an injunction against the showing of the program on the ground that it might inflame public opinion against him, jeopardize his release on parole, and adversely affect jury selection in any future criminal or civil cases arising out of the episode.

The district judge ordered NBC to produce the movie for review the day its presentation was scheduled. When NBC refused, the judge ordered counsel for the network imprisoned until the film was produced. A few hours later, a panel of the court of appeals granted an application for relief and freed the attorney. In a subsequent opinion, the court said that it found "no authority which is even a remote justification" for issuing a prior restraint on the theory that parole officials might become inflamed or that jury selection in some "wholly speculative criminal prosecution" might be adversely affected. The order to produce and the imprisonment were invalid.

8. Restrictive orders are rarely sought in civil litigation. The most important involved an attempt to stop a series of advertisements an insurance company was placing in national magazines. Their thrust was that when jurors in accident cases award large verdicts, they are really hurting themselves: "Every payer of liability insurance premiums is a loser." Several plaintiffs, whose accident cases were pending, sought to enjoin the insurer from placing, and the magazines from carrying, the advertisements. At an earlier stage, the case against the magazines was dismissed. Then the case against the insurer was dismissed on the ground that it was an unjustified prior restraint. Any claim that this was commercial speech and thus less protected than other types of speech fell because of *Virginia Pharmacy*, p. 285, supra. Moreover, the ads were couched in general language that was not aimed at a particular trial and resembled protected commentary on desirable social attitudes. Quinn v. Aetna Life & Casualty Co., 616 F.2d 38 (2d Cir.1980).

9. Soon after *Nebraska Press*, the Court had occasion to pass on a related problem. In a juvenile proceeding, an Oklahoma state judge ordered the press not to publish the name of an 11-year-old boy who was accused of firing a shot that killed a railroad switchman. His identity had been disclosed earlier during an open hearing. After the Oklahoma Supreme Court upheld the order, the press applied to the Supreme Court to stay the trial judge's order pending the filing and disposition of a petition for certiorari. In an unsigned order, the

Supreme Court granted the stay on the ground that the name had already been made public. Citing *Nebraska Press* and Cox Broadcasting Corp. v. Cohn, p. 158, supra, the Court's short opinion noted that the press did not challenge the judge's order silencing counsel or public employees, or an Oklahoma statute requiring that juvenile proceedings be held in private unless specified otherwise by the judge. Oklahoma Publishing Co. v. District Court, 429 U.S. 967 (1976).

When the petition for certiorari was filed, the Court granted it and summarily reversed. The First Amendment "will not permit a state court to prohibit the publication of widely disseminated information obtained at court proceedings which were in fact open to the public." The Oklahoma court had rejected *Nebraska Press* and *Cox Broadcasting* because here there was no showing that the judge had "distinctly and expressly ordered the hearing to be public." The Supreme Court concluded that the two cases controlled nonetheless: "Whether or not the trial judge expressly made such an order, members of the press were in fact present at the hearing with the full knowledge of the presiding judge, the prosecutor, and the defense counsel. No objection was made to the presence of the press in the courtroom . . .." Oklahoma Publishing Co. v. District Court, 430 U.S. 308 (1977).

c. Gag Orders on Litigants

A special problem arises when the media are themselves parties to litigation and want to report on the case. In Seattle Times v. Rinehart, 467 U.S. ___ (1984), the Supreme Court held that a protective order by a trial court in the state of Washington did not violate the First Amendment even though it prohibited the *Seattle Times* newspaper from publishing certain information related to a libel case against them. The information in question had been obtained by the newspaper as part of the discovery process prior to the libel trial, and the Court reasoned that there was a sufficient showing of good cause for the order and that the rights of a litigant do not necessarily include the right to disseminate information obtained through the "legislative grace" of the discovery process. Although most journalists and attorneys representing media clients consider it a disturbing trend, lower courts in other cases have also affirmed orders gagging litigants or trial participants.

3. DENIALS OF ACCESS TO THE COURTROOM AND CONDITIONAL ACCESS

As judges faced the reality that other means of solving the fair trial-free press problems were either undesirable or ineffective, some turned to excluding the press and public from the courtroom during pretrial hearings or during trials themselves, or granted access to the courtroom only on the acceptance of conditions.

a. Pretrial Proceedings

Journalists, of course, are also members of the public. But more, they see themselves as the eyes and ears of the public, surrogates for those who cannot attend a hearing or trial. They brought the first major challenge to closed pretrial proceedings.

Gannett Co. v. DePasquale, 443 U.S. 368 (1979), presented the question whether members of the public are constitutionally entitled to attend a pretrial hearing. The issue arose out of a murder prosecution in upstate New York.

Wayne Clapp, a resident of a suburb of Rochester, New York, disappeared in 1976 after last being seen alive when he went fishing with two men. The boat they had used was found full of bullet holes, and police searched for both Clapp and his missing companions. Clapp's truck was found in Michigan, and the two missing young men and a female companion were apprehended there. Newspapers in New York State reported the arrest and police theories of the crime.

The two men moved to suppress statements they had made to the Michigan police, on the ground that they had been given involuntarily. They also moved to suppress the gun that had been obtained as the fruit of the allegedly involuntary confession. The motions came before Judge DePasquale, and defense counsel asked the judge to close the hearing because "the unabated buildup of adverse publicity had jeopardized the ability of the defendants to receive a fair trial." The prosecutor did not object. Nor did the Gannett reporter in the courtroom. The judge removed press and public from the courtroom.

On the next day, the reporter complained to the judge, but the hearing had already concluded and the judge refused to release a transcript. Three days later, counsel for Gannett appeared and asked that the ruling be vacated and that a transcript of the hearing be provided. The judge held a formal hearing on these requests and denied both, concluding that an open hearing would create "a reasonable probability of prejudice to these defendants."

The New York Court of Appeals upheld the judge's action. It noted that in the interim the two defendants had pleaded guilty to lesser crimes and that the transcripts had then been released.

The Supreme Court affirmed, 5–4, in an opinion by Justice Stewart. He began by stating the dangers to a fair trial from reports about a suppression hearing. He concluded that the Sixth Amendment's provision that "the accused shall enjoy the right to a speedy and public trial by an impartial jury" extended no rights whatever to the public. "The Constitution nowhere mentions any right of access to a criminal trial on the part of the public; its guarantee, like the others enumerated [in the Sixth Amendment], is personal to the accused."

He recognized that the "strong societal interest in public trials" is based on several important considerations. The recognition of that interest "is a far cry, however, from the creation of a constitutional right on the part of the public. In an adversary system of criminal justice, the public interest in the administration of justice is protected by the participants in the litigation." If the defendant, the prosecutor, and the judge agree, the public interest is fully protected.

"Even if" the public were deemed to have any Sixth Amendment right to attend "trials," it would not extend to "pretrial" proceedings because they "were never characterized by the same degree of openness as were actual trials." Note that although the case involved only pretrial proceedings, part of Justice Stewart's analysis, since it is based on a reading of the Sixth Amendment, extends to trials as well.

Then Justice Stewart turned to Gannett's alternate argument based on the First Amendment:

The petitioner in this case urges us to narrow our rulings in *Pell, Saxbe,* and *Houchins* at least to the extent of recognizing a First and Fourteenth Amendment right to attend criminal trials. We need not decide in the abstract, however, whether there is any such constitutional right. For even assuming, *arguendo,* that the First and Fourteenth Amendments may guarantee such access in some situations, a question we do not decide, this putative right was given all appropriate deference by the state [trial judge].

Several factors lead to the conclusion that the actions of the trial judge here were consistent with any right of access the petitioner may have had under the First and Fourteenth Amendments. First, none of the spectators present in the courtroom, including the reporter employed by the petitioner, objected when the defendants made the closure motion. Despite this failure to make a contemporaneous objection, counsel for the petitioner was given an opportunity to be heard at a proceeding where he was allowed to voice the petitioner's objections to closure of the pretrial hearing. At this proceeding, which took place after the filing of briefs, the trial court balanced the "constitutional rights of the press and the public" against the "defendants' right to a fair trial." The trial judge concluded after making this appraisal that the press and the public could be excluded from the suppression hearing and could be denied immediate access to a transcript, because an open proceeding would pose a "reasonable probability of prejudice to these defendants." Thus, the trial court found that the representatives of the press did have a right of access of constitutional dimension, but held, under the circumstances of this case, that this right was outweighed by the defendants' right to a fair trial. In short, the closure decision was based "on an assessment of the competing societal interests involved . . . rather than on any determination that First Amendment freedoms were not implicated." *Saxbe,* supra, at 860 (Powell, J., dissenting).

Furthermore, any denial of access in this case was not absolute but only temporary. Once the danger of prejudice had dissipated, a transcript of the suppression hearing was made available. The press and the public then had a full opportunity to scrutinize the suppression hearing. Unlike the case of an absolute ban on access, therefore, the press here had the opportunity to inform the public of the details of the pretrial hearing accurately and completely. Under these circumstances, any First and Fourteenth Amendment right of the petitioner to attend a criminal trial was not violated.

Of the four Justices who joined Justice Stewart's opinion, all but Justice Stevens also wrote separately.

Chief Justice Burger joined Justice Stewart but also stressed that the case involved only "pretrial hearings" and thus was not covered by the Sixth Amendment's "trial" language in any event.

Justice Powell, who also joined the majority, wrote separately on the First Amendment point. Although Justice Stewart had "assumed" for purposes of argument a First Amendment right of access, Justice Powell "would hold explicitly that Gannett's reporter had an interest protected by the First and Fourteenth Amendments in being present at the pretrial suppression hearing." But this claim was not absolute. "It is limited both by the constitutional right of defendants to a fair trial . . . and by the needs of government to obtain just convictions and to preserve the confidentiality of sensitive information and the identity of informants."

To give the lower courts guidelines, Justice Powell would have ordered judges to "consider whether there are means reasonably available by which the fairness of the trial might be preserved without interfering substantially with the public's interest in prompt access to information concerning the administration of justice." Any exclusion must extend no farther than appears necessary. In addition, members of the public and press must have an opportunity to present their claims to access before the judge decides what to do. At this hearing, the criminal defendant must show that public access is "likely" to prejudice the fairness of his trial. Members of the press and public who object to closure must satisfy the court that "alternative procedures are available that would eliminate the dangers shown by the defendant and the State."

Applying these principles to this case, Justice Powell concluded that the judge properly held a hearing when requested to do so. "In the court's view, the nature of the evidence to be considered at the hearing would substantially jeopardize the fairness of the defendants' subsequent trial." The substantive standard used by the judge "was essentially correct." Thus, under Justice Powell's First Amendment approach, the closure was justified.

The fifth signer on the majority opinion, Justice Rehnquist, also wrote separately. He noted that "since the public does not have *any* Sixth Amendment right of access to such proceedings, it necessarily follows that if the parties agree on a closed proceeding, the trial court is not required by the Sixth Amendment to advance any reason whatsoever for declining to open a pretrial hearing or trial to the public."

As to the First Amendment, he noted that in *Pell, Saxbe,* and *Houchins* and other cases, the Court "repeatedly has held that there is no First Amendment right of access in the public or the press to judicial or other governmental proceedings."

The four dissenters, Justices Brennan, White, Marshall, and Blackmun, all joined in a lengthy dissent by Justice Blackmun. The basic points were (1) that the Sixth Amendment should be read to define trials as including suppression hearings because of the critical importance of such hearings; and (2) that the Sixth Amendment guarantee of a public trial extended to the public as well as to the accused. As noted earlier, all five members of the majority rejected the idea that the Sixth Amendment applied to this suppression hearing.

Justice Blackmun recognized that his Sixth Amendment right was not absolute. But any exceptions must be "narrowly drawn. It comports with the Sixth Amendment to require an accused who seeks closure to establish that it is strictly and inescapably necessary in order to protect the fair trial guarantee." He would have trial judges find facts showing a "substantial probability that irreparable damage" to defendant's fair-trial right will result from having an open proceeding. This would depend on such things as the size of the jury pool, the impact of the coverage, and the amount of information already known by the public. In addition, the usual judicial procedures, including changes in venue, *voir dire*, and peremptory challenges, should be explored.

After the decision in *Gannett,* many thought the matter was left to each state. In those states that are influenced by the revised Reardon Report, the presumption is that pretrial proceedings and their records "shall be open to the public, including representatives of the news media." If material is adduced "that is likely to threaten the fairness of a trial," the judge shall seek voluntary cooperation of the news media "in delaying dissemination of potentially prejudicial information . . . until the impaneling of the jury or until an earlier time consistent with the fair administration of justice." The proceeding may be closed and the record sealed only if the dissemination would create a "clear and present danger to the fairness of the trial, and the prejudicial effect of such information on trial fairness cannot be avoided by any reasonable alternative means." In such cases a complete record shall be kept and made available after the trial or earlier if consistent with trial fairness. (§ 8–3.2).

Note that the *Gannett* majority included three justices (the Chief Justice, Stewart and Rehnquist), who, in *Pell* and *Houchins*, pp. 427–431, infra., had rejected a First Amendment right of access to government activities or facilities, and two justices (Powell and Stevens) who had dissented in those earlier cases. This internal dispute may explain why Justice Stewart in *Gannett* "assumed" but did not decide, that the First Amendment claims applied—and treated the claim so casually. The *Gannett* dissenters relied solely on the Sixth Amendment, in part, because they, too, had previously disagreed about the role of the First Amendment. For whatever reason, the *Gannett* decision caused considerable confusion. Some were concerned by the general failure to address the First Amendment claim. Others were confused by Justice Stewart's 12 references to "trials" when the case involved "pretrial" proceedings.

The confusion in *Gannett* was not only over what the case meant for the future. It extended to the question of who had really won. Although a majority of five had decided the specific case against the press claim, the dissenters plus Justice Powell all found some constitutional right to access. Indeed, four dissenters found the case so strong they would have ruled for the newspaper. Justice Powell's pivotal opinion concluded that the "likelihood" of subsequent prejudice justified the actions of the trial judge in the case.

Adding these votes together led some commentators to argue that in the future the press and public had to be admitted to pretrial suppression hearings unless the judge could find the "likelihood" of prejudice that Justice Powell found in *Gannett*. Thus, some argued that the press and public had lost the *Gannett* battle but had won the access war. Others were reading *Gannett* as leaving the issue to the states.

In addition, *Gannett* apparently encouraged judges to close both pretrial proceedings and trials with little or no explanation, and several Supreme Court justices, delivering speeches shortly after *Gannett*, seemed to disagree about the meaning of their decision.

b. Trials

Soon after *Gannett*, the Court agreed to hear a case that involved related issues. Richmond Newspapers, Inc. v. Virginia, 448 U.S. 555 (1980). Stevenson had been indicted for murder. The conviction for second degree murder was overturned on appeal because improper evidence had been admitted. The second and third trials resulted in mistrials. At the start of the fourth trial, defense counsel moved to exclude the press and public from the courtroom because he did not want witnesses to compare stories or information to leak out and be learned by the jurors (who were not sequestered). The prosecutor offered no objection and the judge closed the courtroom. Although reporters were present they did not object at the time. Later that afternoon, however, their attorney argued that the trial should be opened. The defendant's attorney repeated the arguments he had made earlier, including the fact that this was the defendant's fourth trial and he wanted to avoid any more mistrials. The judge observed that, apparently because the jury box faced the audience, "having people in the Courtroom is distracting to the jury. . . . When we get into our new Court Building, people can sit in the audience so the jury can't see them. The rule of the Court may be different under those circumstances."

The judge concluded that "if I feel that the rights of the defendant are infringed in any way, . . . I'm inclined to go along with the defendant's motion" when it "doesn't completely override all rights of everyone else." He refused to open the courtroom. After the state's evidence was in, the trial judge dismissed the case, found the defendant not guilty and released him. Apparently, a tape of the proceedings was made available as soon as the trial terminated.

The newspaper appealed the reporters' exclusion to the state's supreme court, which concluded that the trial judge had committed no reversible error, and affirmed. By a vote of 7–1, the Supreme Court reversed the judgment of the Virginia Supreme Court. Justice Rehnquist dissented and Justice Powell did not participate. It is not easy to explain the reasoning that lay behind the decision because the seven justices in the majority wrote six opinions and there was no majority opinion.

Chief Justice Burger wrote the plurality opinion, joined by Justices White and Stevens. He stressed that *Gannett* had involved "pretrial" proceedings while this case involved a trial. He then traced at length the history of public criminal trials that ran back at least to the 13th century in England. (Note that no such history could be shown for pretrial proceedings because they are a recent development in criminal law.)

The reasons for this long tradition included the greater likelihood that witnesses would tell the truth and the therapeutic value of having open criminal trials that provide "an outlet for community concern, hostility, and emotion." No "community catharsis can occur if justice is" done in the dark. Public acceptance was a third reason for open trials. "People in an open society do not demand infallibility from their institutions, but it is difficult for them to accept what they are prohibited from observing. When a criminal trial is conducted in the open, there is at least an opportunity both for understanding the system in general and its workings in a particular case. . . ."

The tradition of openness was also explained by the fact that "in earlier times, both in England and America, attendance at court was a common mode of 'passing the time.' [ ] With the press, cinema, and electronic media now supplying the representations or reality of the real life drama once available only in the courtroom, attendance at court is no longer a widespread pastime." Instead of acquiring information about courts by firsthand observation or word of mouth, people now acquire such information from the media. "In a sense this validates the media claim of functioning as surrogates for the public. While media representatives enjoy the same right of access as the public, they often are provided special seating and priority of entry so that they may report what people in attendance have seen and heard."

His review of history and modern justifications led the Chief Justice to conclude that "a presumption of openness inheres in the very nature of a criminal trial under our system of justice."

The state countered that no provision of the United States Constitution guarantees the public the right to attend criminal trials. The Chief Justice's response began with the First Amendment, whose express provisions "share a common core purpose of assuring freedom of communication on matters relating to the functioning of government." He quoted from the Bellotti case, p. 303 supra, that the "First Amendment goes beyond protection of the press and the self-expression of individuals to prohibit government from limiting the stock of information from which members of the public may draw." He also drew on cases that had discussed a "right to listen" or a right to "receive information and ideas." It was not crucial whether the right be called a "right of access" or a "right to gather information." The "explicit, guaranteed rights to speak and to publish concerning what takes place at a trial would lose much meaning if access to observe the trial could, as it was here, be foreclosed arbitrarily."

The Chief Justice also saw an affinity between the right to attend criminal trials and freedom of assembly:

> Subject to the traditional time, place and manner restrictions, [ ], streets, sidewalks, and parks are places traditionally open, where First Amendment rights may be exercised [ ]; a trial courtroom also is a public place where the people generally—and representatives of the media—have a right to be present, and where their presence historically has been thought to enhance the integrity and quality of what takes place.

After finding support in the First Amendment, the Chief Justice asserted that the framers had worried that expressing some protections might lead to the argument that nothing else was to be protected. He concluded that efforts "culminating in the Ninth Amendment, served to allay the fears of those who were concerned that expressing certain guarantees could be read as excluding others." The Ninth Amendment provides that "The enumeration in the Constitution, of certain rights, shall not be construed to deny or disparage others retained by the people."

In a third response to the lack of an express constitutional guarantee of the public's right to attend criminal trials, the Chief

Justice noted that the Court had recognized several other rights despite a similar lack of express provisions:

> Notwithstanding the appropriate caution against reading into the Constitution rights not explicitly defined, the Court has acknowledged that certain unarticulated rights are implicit in enumerated guarantees. For example, the rights of association and of privacy, the right to be presumed innocent and the right to be judged by a standard of proof beyond a reasonable doubt in a criminal trial, as well as the right to travel, appear nowhere in the Constitution or Bill of Rights. Yet these important but unarticulated rights have nonetheless been found to share constitutional protection in common with explicit guarantees. The concerns expressed by Madison and others have thus been resolved; fundamental rights, even though not expressly guaranteed, have been recognized by the Court as indispensable to the enjoyment of rights explicitly defined.

This brought the Chief Justice to the last step in the analysis— applying the principles to the record in the case:

> Despite the fact that this was the fourth trial of the accused, the trial judge made no findings to support closure; no inquiry was made as to whether alternative solutions would have met the need to ensure fairness; there was no recognition of any right under the Constitution for the public or press to attend the trial. In contrast to the pretrial proceeding dealt with in *Gannett*, supra, there exist in the context of the trial itself various tested alternatives to satisfy the constitutional demands of fairness. See, e.g., Nebraska Press Association v. Stuart, [ ]; Sheppard v. Maxwell, [ ]. There was no suggestion that any problems with witnesses could not have been dealt with by their exclusion from the courtroom or their sequestration during the trial. See Sheppard v. Maxwell, [ ]. Nor is there anything to indicate that sequestration of the jurors would not have guarded against their being subjected to any improper information. All of the alternatives admittedly present difficulties for trial courts, but none of the factors relied on here was beyond the realm of the manageable. Absent an overriding interest articulated in findings, the trial of a criminal case must be open to the public. Accordingly, the judgment under review is reversed.

In a footnote to that passage, the Chief Justice stated that although he had "no occasion here to define the circumstances in which all or part of a criminal trial may be closed to the public, . . . our holding today does not mean that [the rights granted] are absolute." Reasonable regulations may be necessary in the interest of the "fair administration of justice" and it is "far more important that trials be conducted in a quiet and orderly setting than it is to preserve that atmosphere on city streets." He recognized that limited capacity of courtrooms may mean that all who wish to attend are not able to do so. "In such situations, reasonable restrictions on general access are traditionally imposed, including preferential seating for media representatives."

Although joining the plurality opinion, Justice White wrote separately to emphasize that if the dissenters' Sixth Amendment argument in *Gannett* had prevailed, this case would not have been necessary.

Justice Stevens, though joining the plurality opinion, also wrote separately. This was a "watershed case" because no prior case had "squarely held that the acquisition of newsworthy matter is entitled to any constitutional protection whatsoever." Then:

> It is somewhat ironic that the Court should find more reason to recognize a right of access today than it did in *Houchins*. [See p. 431, infra.] For *Houchins* involved the plight of a segment of society least able to protect itself, an attack on a longstanding policy of concealment, and an absence of any legitimate justification for abridging public access to information about how government operates. In this case we are protecting the interests of the most powerful voices in the community, we are concerned with an almost unique exception to an established tradition of openness in the conduct of criminal trials, and it is likely that the closure order was motivated by the judge's desire to protect the individual defendant from the burden [of another trial.]

He concurred in the reversal because of "the total absence of any record justification for the closure order entered in this case." (In a footnote he adhered to his view that the Sixth Amendment applied only to the accused—"the party who has the greatest interest in the right to a public trial.")

Justice Brennan, joined by Justice Marshall, concurred in an opinion that developed a "structural" view of the First Amendment. Although the First Amendment is usually "interposed to protect communication between speaker and listener," it "embodies more than a commitment to free expression and communicative interchange for their own sakes; it has a *structural* role to play in securing and fostering our republican system of government":

> Implicit in this structural role is not only "the principle that debate on public issues should be uninhibited, robust, and wide-open," New York Times Co. v. Sullivan, [   ], but the antecedent assumption that valuable public debate—as well as other civic behavior—must be informed. The structural model links the First Amendment to that process of communication necessary for a democracy to survive, and thus entails solicitude not only for communication itself, but for the indispensable conditions of meaningful communication.

However, because "the stretch of this protection is theoretically endless," [ ], it must be invoked with discrimination and temperance. For so far as the participating citizen's need for information is concerned, "[t]here are few restrictions on action which could not be clothed by ingenious argument in the garb of decreased data flow." Zemel v. Rusk, [ ]. An assertion of the prerogative to gather information must accordingly be assayed by considering the information sought and the opposing interests invaded.

This judicial task is as much a matter of sensitivity to practical necessities as it is of abstract reasoning. But at least two helpful principles may be sketched. First, the case for a right of access has special force when drawn from an enduring and vital tradition of public entry to particular proceedings or information. [ ] Such a tradition commands respect in part because the Constitution carries the gloss of history. More importantly, a tradition of accessibility implies the favorable judgment of experience. Second, the value of access must be measured in specifics. Analysis is not advanced by rhetorical statements that all information bears upon public issues; what is crucial in individual cases is whether access to a particular government process is important in terms of that very process.

To resolve the case before us, therefore, we must consult historical and current practice with respect to open trials, and weigh the importance of public access to the trial process itself.

Applying the model to this case, Justice Brennan first traced the history and tradition of public criminal trials. For Justice Brennan the major lesson was that earlier cases had recognized that "open trials are bulwarks of our free and democratic government: public access to court proceedings is one of the numerous 'checks and balances' of our system, because 'contemporaneous review in the forum of public opinion is an effective restraint on possible abuse of judicial power.'"

In addition, Justice Brennan mentioned the fear that closed trials may "breed suspicion of prejudice and arbitrariness, which in turn spawns disrespect for law." Also, in our system, "judges are not mere umpires, but, in their own sphere, lawmakers—a coordinate branch of government." This gave the trial structural importance as a "genuine governmental proceeding." Some of these factors established Justice Brennan's second point—the importance of public access to criminal trials.

Turning to the facts of the case, Justice Brennan said that whatever "countervailing interests might be sufficiently compelling to reverse" a presumption in favor of open trials "need not concern us now," for Virginia law authorized closures in the "unfettered discretion of the judge and parties." In a footnote, he suggested that "national security concerns about confidentiality may sometimes warrant closures during sensitive portions of trial proceedings, such as testimony about state secrets."

Justice Stewart, concurring, briefly noted that whatever the First Amendment may ultimately have to say about pretrial proceedings, the question avoided in *Gannett,* the First and Fourteenth Amendments "clearly give the press and the public a right of access to trials themselves, civil as well as criminal." He was persuaded by the history and the reasons discussed in the other opinions. "With us, a trial is by very definition a proceeding open to the press and to the public." He also recognized that limitations inappropriate for a city street might be appropriate in a courtroom. Where a courtroom cannot accommodate all who wish to attend, his view in *Houchins* requires that "representatives of the press must be assured access." A trial judge may "impose reasonable limitations upon the unrestricted occupation of a courtroom" by members of the press and public. Reversal was required here because "the trial judge appears to have given no recognition to the right of representatives of the press and members of the public to be present" at the trial.

Justice Blackmun, concurring, restated his preference that courts be opened under the Sixth Amendment as he had argued in his dissent in *Gannett.* He thought that reliance in this case on various clauses in the First Amendment, the Ninth Amendment, and a "cluster of penumbral guarantees recognized in past decisions" would prove "troublesome." Setting his losing reliance on the Sixth Amendment to one side, he concluded that "the First Amendment must provide some measure of protection for public access to the trial." But he did note that the fragmented approach here would spawn uncertainty over what must be shown before this new right may be limited in a particular case.

Justice Rehnquist, the lone dissenter, could find no public right to attend criminal trials in any provision of the Constitution. He argued that the Court's effort "over the past generation" to gather to itself "all of the ultimate decisionmaking power over how justice shall be administered, not merely in the federal system, but in each of the 50 states, is a task that no Court consisting of nine persons, however gifted, is equal to." Later: "it is basically unhealthy to have so much authority concentrated in a small group of lawyers who have been appointed to the Supreme Court and enjoy life tenure." There was no reason for the Court to "smother a healthy pluralism which would ordinarily exist in a national government embracing 50 states." Since Justice Rehnquist could find nothing in the Constitution to bar what the Virginia courts had done, he would have affirmed.

Notes and Questions

1. When may a trial be closed after *Richmond Newspapers?* Justice Blackmun, in his separate opinion, sought to show why the result was "troublesome":

> I need do no more than observe that uncertainty marks the nature—and strictness—of the standard of closure the Court adopts. The plurality opinion speaks of "an overriding interest articulated in findings," [　] Mr. Justice Stewart reserves, perhaps not inappropriately, "reasonable limitations," [　]; Mr. Justice Brennan presents his separate analytical framework; Mr. Justice Powell in *Gannett* was critical of those Justices who, relying on the Sixth Amendment, concluded that closure is authorized only when "strictly and inescapably necessary," [　] and Mr. Justice Rehnquist continues his flat rejection of, among others, the First Amendment avenue.

2. Although Justice Powell took no part in *Richmond Newspapers,* is it possible to predict how he would have voted based on his opinion in *Gannett?*

3. Does *Richmond Newspapers* suggest that a judge might prefer the press to the public in making certain decisions about admission to a trial? What about preferring the public to the press?

4. In a footnote, Chief Justice Burger observed that "whether the public has a right to attend trials of civil cases is a question not raised by this case, but we note that historically both civil and criminal trials have been presumptively open." When Justice Stewart treated civil and criminal trials in the same way in his concurring opinion, he observed in a footnote that both free speech and press are involved: "The right to speak implies a freedom to listen. [　] The right to publish implies a freedom to gather information."

The reasoning that brings a justice to his views about criminal trials is likely to control whether he will extend that analysis to civil trials in some later case. The issue of access to civil trials has arisen a few times, mostly involving contested divorce cases or cases involving celebrities. Prejudicial publicity is typically less of a concern in civil cases than in criminal cases. This is partially because juries are used in few civil cases other than personal injury cases, and there is generally low public interest. The Burnett, Sharon and Westmoreland libel cases all attracted considerable public interest, however, and demonstrate that there can be considerable news attention when public officials and public figures are litigants.

5. Those who thought that a right of access had been embedded in the result of *Gannett* because of Justice Powell's analysis, found support in *Richmond Newspapers* for requiring some more rigorous standard than "likelihood" of harm before judges could close pretrial proceedings. Others were not sure.

6. Some sections of the revised Reardon Report address questions about conduct of a trial in which possibly prejudicial publicity has occurred.

Standard 8–3.5 addresses the *voir dire* and the acceptability of jurors who have been exposed to potentially prejudicial material:

> Both the degree of exposure and the prospective juror's testimony as to state of mind are relevant to the determination of acceptability. A prospective juror testifying to an inability to overcome preconceptions shall be subject to challenge for cause no matter how slight the exposure. If the prospective juror remembers information that will be developed in the course of the trial, or that may be inadmissible but does not create a substantial risk of impairing judgment, that person's acceptability shall turn on the credibility of testimony as to impartiality. If the formation of an opinion is admitted, the prospective juror shall be subject to challenge for cause unless the examination shows unequivocally the capacity to be impartial. A prospective juror who has been exposed to and remembers reports of highly significant information, such as the existence or contents of a confession, or other incriminating matters that may be inadmissible in evidence, or substantial amounts of inflammatory material, shall be subject to challenge for cause without regard to the prospective juror's testimony as to state of mind.

Standard 8–3.5(c) recommends that the number of peremptory challenges be increased in cases in which there is a "substantial likelihood" that pretrial publicity has made the normal number of such challenges inadequate. The comments indicate the belief that the first version's faith in *voir dire* was "excessive."

7. Do the opinions in *Richmond Newspapers* suggest that any justice might change his mind in the prison access cases discussed at p. 427, infra? Do the arguments in favor of finding a First Amendment right of access to criminal trials extend to prisons?

8. Does Justice Brennan's structural analysis reflect the influence of Alexander Meiklejohn? Does it reflect other viewpoints that we explored in Chapter II?

9. In Globe Newspaper Co. v. Norfolk County Superior Court, 457 U.S. 596 (1982), the Supreme Court held for *The Boston Globe* in a challenge to a Massachusetts statute that provided for automatic closure of rape and other sexual assault trials during the testimony of minors who are victims. Wrote Justice Brennan for the six-member majority, "We agree with respondent that the first interest—safe-guarding the physical and psychological well-being of a minor—is a compelling one. But as compelling as that interest is, it does not justify a mandatory-closure rule, for it is clear that the circumstances of the particular case may affect the significance of the interest. A

trial court can determine on a case-by-case basis whether closure is necessary to protect the welfare of a minor victim. . . ."

In such closure decisions, the First Amendment requires that any such restriction on access to criminal trials be necessitated by compelling state interest and be narrowly tailored to serve that interest.

10. In Press-Enterprise Co. v. Superior Court, 464 U.S. 501 (1984), the Supreme Court dealt with the issue of the closing of the *voir dire* examination of potential jurors. Holding that such proceedings in criminal trials are presumptively open to the public, the Court said that closure would be justified only where there is an overriding interest, where the closure is narrowly tailored, and where alternatives to closure have been considered. The court found no support for the trial court's conclusion that an open proceeding would have threatened the prospective jurors' interests in privacy in this case. (The problem was compounded, from the press's point of view, by the fact that the trial court had refused to release the transcript of the *voir dire* as well.)

11. In Waller v. Georgia, 467 U.S. —— (1984), the Supreme Court addressed the problem of a closure of pretrial suppression hearings over the objection of the defendant. The case involved allegations of racketeering and gambling, and a pretrial hearing was held to consider suppression of wiretaps and evidence seized during searches at the defendants' homes. The hearing was closed when the prosecution moved for closure alleging that unnecessary "publication" of information obtained under the wiretaps would render the information inadmissible as evidence, and that the wiretap evidence would "involve" the privacy interests of some persons who were indicted but were not then on trial, and some who were not then indicted. Citing *Press-Enterprise*, supra, the court held the closure of the suppression hearing was unjustified, noting that the entire seven-day hearing had been closed even though the tapes were played for less than 2½ hours.

c. Conditional Access

With a variety of precedents holding that trial court judges should not gag journalists and should not keep them or other members out of courtrooms during trials, it was perhaps inevitable that a trial judge would find still another way of trying to solve the fair trial free press problems. A trial court judge in the State of Washington decided to use the voluntary bench-bar-media guidelines adopted in that state as a basis for granting access to his courtroom, allowing only reporters who agreed to abide by the guidelines into the room.

The Washington Supreme Court upheld the trial judge's order in Federated Publications v. Swedberg, 96 Wash.2d 13, 633 P.2d 74

(1981), certiorari denied 456 U.S. 984 (1982). Critics of bench-bar-press guidelines said that one of the envisioned dangers of such guidelines—their misuse by the courts—had become a reality. Early predictions of a trend toward such conditions on access to courtrooms proved premature, however. Adoption of amendments to state bench-bar-press guidelines, specifically precluding their use by courts for any purpose, lessened the likelihood that the guidelines, which media representatives had adopted in good faith, might be used against them in this way.

Conditional access also arises in juvenile proceedings. In many states, hearings in juvenile cases are confidential on the ground that they are primarily to rehabilitate and are clinical rather than punitive. The Supreme Court has said that a state may "continue, if it deems it appropriate, to provide and to improve provision for the confidentiality of records of police contracts and court action relating to juveniles." In re Gault, 387 U.S. 1, 25 (1967). Judges in many states will permit reporters to attend juvenile proceedings on the condition that they agree not to reveal the names of the juveniles involved.

d. The Defendant's Preference

For obvious reasons, the press always wants public, open trials. What about the defendant's choice? The defendant also may want an open trial, desiring publicity for reasons ranging from a belief that it may help establish innocence to a desire to humiliate the government's witnesses. Or the defendant may prefer a closed trial, perhaps not wanting to testify in front of the public and press.

(1) Defendant Wants a Public Trial

The Sixth Amendment to the United States Constitution provides that "the accused shall enjoy the right to a speedy and public trial, by an impartial jury of the State and district wherein the crime shall have been committed. . . ." A similar provision exists in several state constitutions, but recent constitutional decisions indicate that, in any event, this part of the Sixth Amendment applies to the states. The Supreme Court's first significant venture into this area was In re Oliver, 333 U.S. 257 (1948):

> The traditional Anglo-American distrust for secret trials has been variously ascribed to the notorious use of this practice by the Spanish Inquisition, to the excesses of the English Court of Star Chamber, and to the French monarchy's abuse of the *lettre de cachet*. All of these institutions obviously symbolize a menace to liberty. In the hands of despotic groups each of them had became an instrument for the suppression of political and religious heresies in ruthless disregard of the right of an accused to a fair trial. Whatever other benefits the guarantee to an accused that his trial be conducted in public may confer upon our society, the guarantee has always been recognized as a safe-

guard against any attempt to employ our courts as instruments of persecution. The knowledge that every criminal trial is subject to contemporaneous review in the forum of public opinion is an effective restraint on possible abuse of judicial power.

By the time of Duncan v. Louisiana, 391 U.S. 145 (1968), the Court was enumerating a public trial as one of the rights included within the Fourteenth Amendment.

This "right," like most, is not absolute. Various state interests have been held to be so compelling as to justify the exclusion of the public and the press regardless of the defendant's wishes. These state interests include the fact that a prosecution witness is young or frightened, or the crime is an embarrassing one; that a witness for the state is an undercover agent whose identity must remain secret; that the discussion will involve information that should be kept secret, such as the components of the skyjacker profile; that the litigation will entail disclosure of a carefully guarded trade secret; or that spectators are threatening witnesses or disrupting the proceedings. In each of these cases, the trial may be closed for as long as is necessary to meet the need that dictates closure. Cases discussing the various justifications are collected in United States ex rel. Lloyd v. Vincent, 520 F.2d 1272 (2d Cir.), certiorari denied 423 U.S. 937 (1975).

Courts once closed trials if the subject matter involved sexual misbehavior. Later they barred minors in such cases, but no longer automatically closed such trials. Mandatory exceptions to public trials, again defined in terms of sexually-oriented subject matter, ended with *Globe Newspapers*, supra.

Note that most of the state's reasons for closing trials are not related to the fear of prejudicial publicity.

(2) Defendant Wants a Closed Trial

The Supreme Court has stated that "The ability to waive a constitutional right does not ordinarily carry with it the right to insist upon the opposite of that right. For example, although a defendant can, under some circumstances, waive his constitutional right to a public trial, he has no absolute right to compel a private trial. . . ." Singer v. United States, 380 U.S. 24, 34–35 (1965). The normal reason for such a request, assuming that the jury is not sequestered, is to prevent the jury from learning about prejudicial information that may be discussed out of the jury's hearing but not admitted in evidence. This does not apply to information that the press may have learned earlier or from other sources, such as a prior criminal record or what happened at a hearing on motions to suppress, because that can be printed even if the trial is closed. The defendant may also seek closure for reasons having nothing to do with the fear of prejudicial publicity—such as to obtain essential testimony. Thus, in Kirstowsky v. Superior Court, 143 Cal.App.2d

745, 300 P.2d 163 (1956), the defendant in a murder trial wanted the public excluded because she would be testifying about "revolting" sexual practices the decedent forced her to perform. Her emotional state was such that if forced to testify in public she would be unable to do so effectively. The court held that the trial should have been closed, but only for her testimony. The concern involved an aspect of fair trial unrelated to prejudicial publicity.

Although we have been emphasizing prejudice to the defendant, it is possible that some cases may involve publicity prejudicial to the government. One obvious difference is that if prejudice enters the case as a result of media statements and leads to an acquittal, the rule against double jeopardy prevents holding a new trial.

4. DENIALS OF ACCESS TO COURT RECORDS

a. Transcript of Voir Dire—The Press Enterprise Case

Although there is a tradition of openness of court records, there are instances in which courts have withheld certain information during and sometimes after trials. Two reasons offered for withholding such information are the protection of candor in the *voir dire* proceedings and protection of the privacy of those actually seated as jurors. See the discussion of the Press-Enterprise case, p. 362, supra.

b. Jurors' Privacy

Not all limits on information about the judicial process relate to fears of the prejudicial effect of publicity. A judge may bar release of the names of jurors in notorious cases to protect their privacy and impartiality.

For example, a trial court judge in Iowa, concerned about retaliation against jurors, ordered reporters not to print the names, addresses, or phone numbers of jurors in a murder trial involving the widow of a slain motorcycle gang member. The judge also barred photographs of the jurors entering and leaving the courthouse. The press appealed the order and it was overturned in light of *Nebraska Press*. The Iowa Supreme Court found that no juror had expressed fear of retaliation, that other methods of preventing the suggested evil had not been tried, and that jurors' names and addresses could be published *after* the trial in any case, blunting the rationale for the order. Also, said the court, jury lists are public information in Iowa. Des Moines Register & Tribune Co. v. Osmundson, 248 N.W.2d 493 (Iowa 1976).

If a judge cannot prevent the press from reporting the names of jurors that have become public, the next step might be to try to prevent the names from becoming public in a state in which juror's names are not public property. This was approved in a criminal prosecution of major narcotics suspects in New York City. The trial judge gave each prospective juror a number and never released their names or addresses. The judge did conduct a *voir dire* based on his own questions and some submitted by counsel. He asked jurors, among other things, the county of their residence and if they were prejudiced against blacks (14 defendants were black). He asked about education and group memberships, but he refused to ask the jurors about their own ethnic or religious backgrounds.

After conviction, the defendants appealed asserting, as one ground, that they had been deprived of a meaningful opportunity to use their challenges in selecting a jury. The lack of name and address meant that the defendants could not question neighbors and learn on their own about the prospective jurors.

The defendants relied in part on a 1936 statement of Clarence Darrow's that a juror's "nationality, his business, religion, politics, social standing, family ties, friends, habits of life and thought; the books and newspapers he likes and reads . . . [his] method of speech, the kind of clothes he wears, the style of haircut" were important subjects for questioning.

The court affirmed the convictions. United States v. Barnes, 604 F.2d 121 (2d Cir.1979), certiorari denied 446 U.S. 907 (1980). The judge had grounds to fear threats of retaliation against the jury if it convicted. Since possible prejudice was explored, the court could see no added benefits from asking jurors about their own ethnic backgrounds. As to names and addresses, the defendants argued that "jurors must publicly disclose their identities and publicly take responsibility for the decisions they are about to make." The court disagreed. Jurors who fear retribution cannot be impartial. If an anonymous juror feels less pressure as the result of anonymity "this is as it should be—a factor contributing to his impartiality." As to religion, "our jury selection system was not designed to subject prospective jurors to a catechism of their tenets of faith."

Defendants are entitled to a fair and impartial jury and must have enough information to enable them to use their challenges sensibly. In this case the defendants had enough information to meet their needs. "Clarence Darrow's ideal has already yielded to what has been thought to be the greater necessity, *i.e.*, the need to streamline the *voir dire* process by resting the control of it in the district judge [ ], subject to the demand that the essentials of the case should be the subject of inquiry." (The court noted that a federal statute required that the names and addresses of prospective jurors in capital cases be disclosed three days before trial.)

An editorial in *The New York Times* observed that the dangers to jurors in certain types of cases "are real; but the decision is disturbing." It referred to situations in which the public loses because it cannot learn about jury behavior. The best-known example is the 1975 bribery trial of John Connally in the District of Columbia. The judge impounded the jurors' names. After acquittal, he refused to release them, in order to protect the jurors from harassment.   The *Times* noted that the judge's decision "left the public guessing why the jury had so quickly acquitted" Connally. N.Y. Times, May 10, 1979 at A22.

5.   USE OF THE CONTEMPT POWER

Courts have long been concerned about efforts by the parties and press to influence judges to decide pending cases in a certain way. The traditional approach was that such efforts either influenced the judge or appeared to influence the judge—and that either view seriously impaired the functioning of the judicial branch.   The technique for handling the problem was to hold the perpetrator in contempt of court and impose appropriate sanctions.   Before considering the power of courts to protect judges from such influence, we look at the nature of the contempt power—which is relevant not only here but at other points in this Chapter.

a.   Contempt of Court

Contempt of court involves a variety of actions that substantially obstruct the administration of justice.   These include disturbance of a judicial proceeding by shouting in the courtroom, wilful refusal to obey a court order to pay alimony, and refusal to answer a grand jury question after a judge has ordered the witness to do so.   If a court were to punish a member of the press for contempt, it would be more likely to be for disobeying an order of the court (not to bring equipment into the courtroom, for instance), for interfering with the administration of justice by publishing or broadcasting something prejudicial (the power is generally *not* used in such instances but might be), or for refusing to answer a question about a secret source, secret notes, etc. (see discussion in the chapter on confidentiality in newsgathering in Chapter X).

Limitations on the contempt power.   The power of federal courts to enforce contempt citations is based on a 1789 act by the first United States Congress establishing a federal judicial system. The statute allowed judges to punish "all contempts of authority." The statute stood until 1830 when federal Judge James H. Peck held an attorney in contempt for publishing an article criticizing him. Congress was so incensed by Peck's action that it impeached him and came within one vote of convicting him.   Congress also passed a law in 1831 limiting the use of contempt power by federal judges to matters happening in the presence of the court "or so near thereto as to obstruct the administration of justice."

b.   Comment on Pending Cases

The meaning of "so near thereto" was unclear.   Did it carry a geographical meaning—near to the courtroom—or a causal construction—closely related to the case before the court?   Did the "contemptuous act" have to happen close to the judge or could it be far away but something the judge thought affected the administration of justice? The Supreme Court first chose the latter interpretation, allowing judges to punish for contempts happening outside the courtroom. Toledo Newspaper Co. v. United States, 247 U.S. 402 (1918).

In 1941, however, the Court reversed itself and held that the phrase was to be given a geographical meaning—summary contempt could be used only for happenings within or close to the courtroom. Nye v. United States, 313 U.S. 33 (1941).

In 1941, the Court began using the First Amendment to restrict the contempt power. Labor leader Harry Bridges had been held in contempt for threatening to have his dockworkers go on strike if the courts enforced a judicial order unfavorable to the union. In a second case decided by the Court as part of the *Bridges* decision, the *Los Angeles Times* had been held in contempt for editorials a state court believed were aimed at influencing the outcome of certain decisions it was to make. The Supreme Court ruled that the contempt power could be used against published or spoken comments made outside the courtroom only when they presented a "clear and present danger" of obstructing justice. Bridges v. California, 314 U.S. 252 (1941).

The newspaper editorial had said that a judge would "make a serious mistake if he granted probation to" two Teamsters accused of assaulting non-union truck drivers. The majority said that given the newspaper's well-known hostility toward unions, "it is inconceivable that any judge in Los Angeles would expect anything but adverse criticism from it in the event probation were granted. Yet such criticism after final disposition of the proceedings would clearly have been privileged." The four dissenters stressed that the judge in question was facing reelection in a year and that the editorial "was hardly an exercise in futility."

The Court reiterated this stance in Pennekamp v. Florida, 328 U.S. 331 (1946). *Miami Herald* editorials accusing the Dade County judges of coddling criminals had been based on incorrect statements. In overturning the contempt citation against the paper's editor, the Supreme Court said that the editorials did not present "a clear and present danger to the fair administration of justice in Florida." The errors were inconsequential, said the Court, in the face of a commitment to free and open discussion of the judiciary.

A year later, in Craig v. Harney, 331 U.S. 367 (1947), the Court was confronted with another contempt citation against a paper that had criticized a judge during a trial. A lay judge was conducting a trial in which a landlord, claiming non-payment of rent, sought to regain possession of a building from a tenant who at the time was overseas in the armed forces. The judge directed the jury to find for the landlord. Twice the jury returned a verdict for the tenant and the judge refused to accept it. The third time the jury complied but stated that it was acting against its conscience. Two days later, the tenant's attorney moved for a new trial. During the jury's recalcitrance and the pendency of the motion for new trial, the newspaper published several articles and an editorial. The judge denied the motion for a new trial. He then adjudged petitioners in contempt of court for the publications and sentenced each to jail for three days. The Supreme Court reversed:

> The only substantial question raised pertains to the editorial. It called the judge's refusal to hear both sides "high handed," a "travesty on justice," and the reason that public opinion was "outraged." It said that his ruling properly "brought down the wrath of public opinion upon his head" since a serviceman "seems to be getting a raw deal." The fact that there was no appeal from his decision to a "judge who is familiar with proper procedure and able to interpret and weigh motions and arguments by opposing counsel and to make his decisions accordingly" was a "tragedy." It deplored the fact that the judge was a "layman" and not a "competent attorney." It concluded that the "first rule of justice" was to give both sides an opportunity to be heard and when that rule was "repudiated," there was "no way of knowing whether justice was done."
>
> This was strong language, intemperate language, and, we assume, an unfair criticism. But a judge may not hold in contempt one "who ventures to publish anything that tends to make him unpopular or to belittle him . . . ." [ ] The vehemence of the language used is not alone the measure of the power to punish for contempt. The fires which it kindles must constitute an imminent, not merely a likely, threat to the administration of justice. The danger must not be remote or even probable; it must immediately imperil.
>
> . . . [T]he law of contempt is not made for the protection of judges who may be sensitive to the winds of public opinion. Judges are supposed to be men of fortitude, able to thrive in a hardy climate. . . .
>
> . . . Judges who stand for reelection run on their records. That may be a rugged environment. Criticism is expected. Discussion of their conduct is appropriate, if not necessary. The fact that the discussion at this particular point of time was not in good taste falls far short of meeting the clear and present danger test.

The dissenters objected that the majority "appears to sponsor the myth that judges are not as other men are, and that therefore newspaper attacks . . . do not penetrate the judicial armor." Further:

> From our sheltered position, fortified by life tenure and other defenses to judicial independence, it is easy to say that this local judge ought to have shown more fortitude in the face of

criticism. But he had no such protection. He was an elective judge, who held [office] for a short term. I do not take it that an ambition of a judge to remain a judge is either unusual or dishonorable. Moreover, he was not a lawyer, and I regard this as a matter of some consequence. A lawyer may gain courage to render a decision that temporarily is unpopular because he has confidence that his profession over the years will approve it, despite its unpopular reception, as has been the case with many great decisions. But this judge had no anchor in professional opinion. Of course, the blasts of these little papers in this small community do not jolt us, but I am not so confident that we would be indifferent if a news monopoly in our entire jurisdiction should perpetrate this kind of an attack on us.

Notes and Questions

1. At one point, the majority stated that "A trial is a public event. What transpires in the court room is public property. . . . Those who see and hear what transpired can report it with impunity. There is no special perquisite of the judiciary which enables it, as distinguished from other institutions of democratic government, to suppress, edit, or censor events which transpire in proceedings before it." This was uttered in connection with a part of the case in which the court sought to impose contempt citations because of news reports of what had happened in the courtroom.

2. Is there much difference between saying that if the judge does not rule in a particular way the paper will oppose him in the next election, and saying after the decision that the paper disagrees with it so strongly that it will oppose him in the next election? Does it matter if the paper's position was entirely predictable although not previously articulated?

3. No case involving a contempt citation against media for influencing a judicial decision has reached the Supreme Court since *Craig.*

4. In many states judges are elected competitively—and for short terms. A few states have the "Missouri plan" whereby an incumbent judge seeks electoral approval of his record, but runs unopposed. Does the citizens' need to be informed about government justify the behavior of the papers in these cases?

6. RESTRICTIONS ON CAMERAS AND OTHER EQUIPMENT

When Bruno Hauptmann was brought to trial for kidnapping and slaying the son of Charles and Anne Morrow Lindbergh in 1932, journalists and photographers packed the courtroom. Hauptmann, found guilty and sentenced to death, may not have gotten a fair trial because of the adverse publicity. In response, the American Bar Association adopted Canon 35 in 1937. Together with amendments in 1952 and 1963, this ethical stricture bans radio and television broadcasting and still cameras from courtrooms. Although ABA canons have no effect of their own, the Judicial Conference of the United States, an organization of the country's federal judges, subsequently adopted similar provisions, as did most state courts. In 1979, an ABA committee proposed that Canon 3A(7), the successor to Canon 35, be amended to allow televising of trials at the judge's discretion. The ABA rejected the recommendation.

In the first Supreme Court case, Estes v. Texas, 381 U.S. 532 (1965), defendant had been indicted in the Texas state courts for "swindling"—inducing farmers to buy nonexistent fertilizer tanks and then to deliver to him mortgages on the property. The nature of the charges and the large sums of money involved, attracted nation-wide interest. Texas was one of the two states that then permitted televised trials. Over defendant's objection, the trial judge permitted televising of a two-day hearing before trial.

The Supreme Court reversed, 5–4, and upset the conviction. In his majority opinion Justice Clark concluded that the use of television at the trial involved "such a probability that prejudice will result that it is deemed inherently lacking in due process" even without any showing of specific prejudices. He was concerned about the impact on jurors, judges, parties, witnesses, and lawyers.

Justice Harlan, who provided the crucial fifth vote for reversal, joined the majority opinion only to the extent that it applied to televised coverage of "courtroom proceedings of a criminal trial of widespread public interest," "a criminal trial of great notoriety," and "a heavily publicized and highly sensational affair." In such cases he was worried about the impact on jurors.

In Chandler v. Florida, 449 U.S. 560 (1981), the Court unanimously rejected the view that televising a criminal trial over the objections of the defendant automatically rendered the trial unfair. (In Florida, only the consent of the trial judge is required to allow a trial to be televised.) The defendants had argued that the impact of television on the participants introduced potentially prejudicial but unidentifiable aspects into the trial. The majority, in an opinion by Chief Justice Burger, first concluded that *Estes* did not stand for the proposition that broadcasting was barred "in all cases and under all circumstances." Because of Justice Harlan's narrow views in that case, the ruling in *Estes* should apply only to cases of widespread interest. (On this point, two Justices insisted that *Chandler* over-ruled *Estes* and should say so.)

Then, Chief Justice Burger continued that the risk of prejudice from press coverage of a trial was not limited to broadcasting. "The risk of juror prejudice in some cases does not justify an absolute ban on news coverage of trials by the printed media; so also the risk of such prejudice does not warrant an absolute constitutional ban on all broadcast coverage." A case attracts attention because of its intrinsic interest to the public. The "appropriate safeguard" against prejudice in such cases "is the defendant's right to demonstrate that the media's coverage of his case—be it printed or broadcast—compromised the ability of the particular jury that heard the case to adjudicate fairly." The Court also observed that the changes in technology since *Estes* supported the state's argument it now be permitted to allow television in the courtroom.

Since the defendants in *Chandler*—two former city policemen accused of burglarizing a restaurant—showed no adverse impact from the television, the convictions were upheld.

Notice that this case involved criminal defendants attacking their convictions. The case did not involve a First Amendment claim by broadcasters claiming a right to bring their equipment into the courtroom in a state that barred such entry. The Court did not discuss the impact of *Richmond Newspapers* or other First Amendment cases. As of the time *Chandler* was decided, over half the states were permitting television in the courtroom either on an experimental basis or on a permanent basis after a successful experiment had ended. In many of these states, the consent of a criminal defendant was required before entry could be allowed. Many states that barred entry or required consent of a party before entry have continued their practices after *Chandler*. Cameras are not permitted in federal courts, and special attempts for permission—including in the 1984 Westmoreland libel trial—have thus far failed.

Courtroom Sketching. Television news directors have resorted to sketching of the courtroom scene to provide a visual dimension to their reports of judicial proceedings. That practice came under attack during the pretrial proceedings involving the trial of the "Gainesville Eight," who were charged with conspiring to disrupt the 1972 Republican National Convention. The trial judge decreed that no sketches be drawn in the courtroom. On appeal, the court refused to accept "a sweeping prohibition of in-court sketching where there has been no showing whatsoever that sketching is in any way obtrusive or disruptive." United States v. Columbia Broadcasting System, Inc., 497 F.2d 102 (5th Cir.1974).

The Nixon Tapes in the Courts. As we will see later, the saga of the Nixon tapes reached its first significant stage when the Supreme Court ordered the then President to honor a subpoena from the Watergate special prosecutor to deliver tapes of a large group of conversations for use in the so-called Watergate trial. United States v. Nixon, 418 U.S. 683 (1974). In 1974 Congress passed the Presidential Recordings and Materials Preservation Act, directing the Administrator of General Services to take custody of the former President's tapes and documents. The Administrator was directed to submit to Congress regulations governing access to Presidential materials of historical value. That act was upheld in Nixon v. Administrator of General Services, 433 U.S. 425 (1977). That was chapter two.

The third episode took shape during the Watergate trial. The tape reels obtained from the President were played in the judge's chambers before trial. Some conversations were declared irrelevant or privileged and were not reproduced. The other conversations were rerecorded on new tapes designated Copy A for the district court and Copy B for the special prosecutor. Some but not all of the conversations on Copy A were admitted into evidence. Some but not all of these were played to the jury. Some were played in full; others only in part. "Deletions were effected not by modifying the exhibit itself, but by skipping deleted portions on the tape or by interrupting the sound transmission to the jurors' headphones." Written transcripts of the conversations being played to the jurors were provided to the jurors and others in the court—all of whom heard the tapes over headphones.

During the trial, broadcasters approached Judge Sirica to obtain copies of the 22 hours of tapes played to the jury. After extensive proceedings, he denied the request for immediate access to the tapes on the ground that the convicted defendants had appeals pending and release of the tapes might prejudice their rights.

The court of appeals reversed, relying on the importance of the common law privilege of inspecting and copying judicial records. The fear of prejudice to the defendants did not outweigh the public's right to access.

The Supreme Court reversed the court of appeals. Nixon v. Warner Communications, Inc., 435 U.S. 589 (1978). Justice Powell, writing for the majority, began by discussing the asserted common law right to inspect judicial records. Although he found some case support, the right was not absolute. "Every court has supervisory power over its own records and files and access has been denied where court files might have become a vehicle for improper purposes." Common law rights to inspect had given way in cases in which the record might be used to "gratify private spite or promote public scandal" as in divorce cases; where the record contained libelous statements; and where the record contained "business information that might harm a litigant's competitive standing." Although he thought the cases showed that the decision was "one best left to the sound discretion of the trial court," Justice Powell was willing to assume that some right to inspect the tapes existed.

The Court then reviewed Nixon's arguments against disclosure. First, he argued that he had a property interest in his voice that the broadcasters should not be allowed to exploit for commercial gain. Second, he asserted a right of privacy. (The court of appeals had rejected that argument on the grounds that the passage of the Presidential Recordings Act contemplated release of the tapes at some time and that presidential documents are not subject to ordinary privacy claims. The broadcasters added that the privacy claim was overridden by the fact that the tapes would provide added understanding with the nuances and inflections. Nixon disagreed on the ground that out of 22 hours of tapes, broadcasters and record makers would use fractions, necessarily taken out of context.) Third, Nixon argued that United States v. Nixon authorized use of the tapes only for the trial since they were obtained from a third party. Finally, he argued that it would be unseemly for the courts to "facilitate the commercialization" of the tapes for presentation "at cocktail parties" or in "comedy acts or dramatic productions." Justice Powell continued:

> At this point, we normally would be faced with the task of weighing the interests advanced by the parties in light of the public interest and the duty of the courts.[14] On respondents' side of the scales is the incremental gain in public understanding of an immensely important historical occurrence that arguably would flow from the release of aural copies of these tapes, a gain said to be not inconsequential despite the already widespread dissemination of printed transcripts. Also on respondents' side is the presumption—however gauged—in favor of public access to judicial records. On petitioner's side are the arguments identified above, which must be assessed in the context of court custody of the tapes. Underlying each of petitioner's arguments is the crucial fact that respondents require a court's cooperation in furthering their commercial plans. The court—as custodian of tapes obtained by subpoena over the opposition of a sitting President, solely to satisfy "fundamental demands of due process of law in the fair administration of criminal justice," United States v. Nixon, 418 U.S., at 713—has a responsibility to exercise an informed discretion as to release of the tapes, with a sensitive appreciation of the circumstances that led to their production. This responsibility does not permit copying upon demand. Otherwise, there would exist a danger that the court could become a partner in the use of the subpoenaed material "to gratify private spite or promote public scandal." [ ], with no corresponding assurance of public benefit.

Having set the stage, Justice Powell announced that the Court need not decide the case because of a "unique element that was neither advanced by the parties nor given appropriate consideration by the courts below." Although the parties argued that the Presidential Recordings Act did not cover these tapes, the Court found a Congressional intent to create an administrative procedure for processing all the Nixon documents, including these recordings. (Why might each party have argued against the Act's relevance?) "The presence of an alternative means of public access tips the scales in favor of denying release." Questions concerning the regulations prepared by the Administrator of General Services were reserved "for future consideration in appropriate proceedings."

14. Judge Sirica's principal reason for refusing to release the tapes—fairness to the defendants, who were appealing their convictions—is no longer a consideration. All appeals have been resolved.

The broadcasters argued that even the presence of the Act could not destroy their constitutional claims to inspect the documents. First, the broadcasters relied on Cox Broadcasting Corp. v. Cohn, 420 U.S. 469 (1975), p. 158, supra, which barred damage liability against a broadcaster that named a rape victim whose name was obtained from official court records. The broadcasters argued that this gave them a right to copy anything displayed in open court. Justice Powell disagreed: the case gave the press only the right to copy records "open to the public." Here, reporters heard the tapes and were given transcripts, and could comment on each. *Cox Broadcasting* did not require that copies of the tapes "to which the public has never had *physical* access" be made available for copying. "The First Amendment generally grants the press no right to information about a trial superior to that of the general public."

In their second constitutional argument, the broadcasters relied on the Sixth Amendment's guarantee of a public trial, asserting that public understanding of the trial is incomplete if the public cannot hear the tapes that the jury heard. Justice Powell thought this proved too much—because it would require recording testimony of live witnesses at trials. Also, the guarantee is to avoid the use of "courts as instruments of persecution" and confers no special benefit on the press. Finally, the right to public trial does not require that the trial be broadcast or recorded for the public. The requirement "is satisfied by the opportunity of members of the public and the press to attend the trial and to report what they have observed. [ ] That opportunity abundantly existed here."

Although the lower court decision favoring the broadcasters was reversed, the Court did not decide how the district court should dispose of the tapes. Justices White and Brennan dissented in part on the reading of the Recordings Act and would have ordered the tapes delivered immediately to the Administrator. Justices Marshall and Stevens, in separate opinions, would have affirmed the court of appeals.

During 1980, a federal investigation of corruption among Congressmen (Abscam) produced several cases in which Congressmen took bribes from FBI agents posing as wealthy Arabs. The meetings were videotaped secretly and provided strong evidence at the trials—at which several Congressmen were convicted. After one early trial, the networks sought, and obtained, permission to make copies of the tapes for showing on television. The argument against the showing was that this might prejudice trials still to come or retrials of those convicted if their appeals should succeed. The tapes were shown, apparently the first case in which court evidence was later telecast.

In this Chapter we have seen some of the ways the courts try to protect defendants' rights to a fair trial, insulated so much as possible from the effects of prejudicial news coverage and public opinion. In the next Chapter we will see that the courts are also concerned with protecting judicial access to information relevant to court proceedings, and they must weigh the judicial interest in obtaining information against journalists' claims of an immunity from testifying about confidential sources, documents, notes, and other aspects of the newsgathering process.

Chapter X

CONFIDENTIALITY IN NEWSGATHERING

Related to the fair trial-free press issues discussed in the last Chapter, in the sense that both relate to the administration of justice, are problems relating to judicial access to evidence in the hands of journalists. Constitutional guarantees of a fair trial are meant to allow the parties a complete, objective hearing on the issues. A complete hearing may require full access to all relevant evidence—including that possessed by journalists. What if a journalist refuses to divulge certain information that may be pertinent to a case? What about photographs in a newspaper's file that shed light on an incident being considered by a court? Should the paper supply the photographs so that all relevant information is before the judge and jury, or should freedom of the press also be considered? Answers to these questions, and others to be discussed in this section, will affect the completeness of the information a court has before it when it makes decisions affecting litigants' finances, freedom, even their lives.

Journalists traditionally have sought recognition of a special privilege not to have to reveal their confidential sources, even when the identity of the source is part of the evidence sought by a court, a grand jury, or a legislative committee, but confidential sources are just part of a larger problem. In addition to being asked to reveal sources, journalists have been asked for their notes, for documents and other evidence which they obtained in the course of newsgathering, for unpublished materials (negatives of photos not used, outtakes of television productions, etc.), and for testimony as to their thoughts during the newsgathering and editing processes. In addition, there have been attempts to gather evidence by police searches of newsrooms or by obtaining reporters' travel records or telephone records in an attempt to deduce their sources.

A. JOURNALIST'S PRIVILEGE

1. THE ROLE OF CONFIDENTIALITY

It has been generally accepted that persons thought to have relevant information may be subpoenaed to testify as witnesses at certain governmental proceedings. Nevertheless, some relationships have been held to give rise to "privileges" permitting a party to withhold information he has learned in a confidential relationship. The most venerable of these relationships have been those of physician and patient, lawyer and client, and priest and penitent. In each of these the recipient may be prevented by the source from testifying as to information learned in confidence in that professional capacity.

Under common law, an assertion by journalists of a similar privilege from testifying was generally rejected. Critics of a privilege for journalists sometimes point out that professionals in medicine and law typically must meet certain educational requirements, be certified to practice, and be subject to disciplinary action if they fail to adhere to professional standards. Journalists, on the other hand, have no minimum education requirement, require no certification or license to be journalists, and are not subject to the same kinds of peer review to which doctors and lawyers are subject. So long as freedom of press belongs to everyone, not just to a few licensed to be journalists, professional standards are difficult to police. Although one likes to believe that the vast majority of journalists are ethical and truthful, such incidents as that involving the Janet Cooke Pulitzer Prize-winning story on the juvenile heroin addict (who turned out not to be a real child) in the *Washington Post* attract public attention and are sometimes pointed to by critics of a privilege for journalists.

Despite the rejection of the privilege at common law, it has made headway as a statutory protection. Since the first reporter's privilege statute was enacted in Maryland in 1896, half the states have enacted so-called "shield" laws. As we shall see, these statutes may have limited utility in certain situations.

In states without privilege statutes, reporters tried, with little success, to claim such a privilege under common law. Then in 1958 columnist Marie Torre tried a different approach. She had reported that a CBS executive had made certain disparaging remarks about Judy Garland. Garland sued CBS for defamation and sought by deposition to get Torre to identify the particular executive. Torre attacked the effort as a threat to freedom of the press, refused to answer the question, and asserted that the First Amendment protected her refusal. The court, though seeing some constitutional implications, held that even if the First Amendment were to provide some protection, the reporter must testify when the information sought goes to the "heart" of the plaintiff's claim. Garland v. Torre, 259 F.2d 545 (2d Cir.), certiorari denied 358 U.S. 910 (1958). Torre ultimately served ten days in jail for criminal contempt.

After *Garland*, reporters continued to assert First Amendment claims, still with little success. In the late 1960's the situation became more serious as the federal government began to serve subpoenas on reporters more frequently. The media asserted that this made previously willing sources of information unwilling because of fear that the courts would not protect the reporter or the source and reporters would violate confidences when pressed by the government.

This raised an empirical question about the effect of subpoenas on the flow of information. Professor Vince Blasi explored this in a study that pursued three paths. First he conducted 47 interviews with reporters and editors of newspapers in seven large cities. Second, he sent a questionnaire to 67 reporters familiar with the subpoena problem. The questionnaire was designed to elicit "qualitative" rather than "quantitative" information. Finally, he sent 1470 questionnaires to reporters on large newspapers, editors of underground papers, news magazine and broadcasting journalists. Before he could publish the results, the Supreme Court announced that it would review three cases dealing with reporters' subpoenas. Branzburg v. Hayes, infra. In the following excerpts, Professor Blasi summarizes his general empirical conclusions.

THE NEWSMAN'S PRIVILEGE: AN EMPIRICAL STUDY

Vince Blasi

70 Michigan Law Review 229, 231–232, 284 (1971).

The three cases on the Court's docket all concern one variant of the press subpoena problem: a grand jury's effort to acquire from a reporter information about possible law violations committed by his news sources. While this is currently the most common posture in which the issue presents itself, one must take cognizance of many other manifestations of the controversy before deciding what general principles, let alone detailed standards, ought to govern press subpoena disputes. Congressional committees, such as the panel that was looking into the CBS documentary *The Selling of the Pentagon*, may wish to subpoena newsmen to scrutinize the accuracy and balance of certain reporting efforts. Criminal defendants have an explicit sixth amendment right to compel the attendance of witnesses in their favor; this right may at times conflict with the reporter's interest in honoring confidences with sources, such as police officers or prosecutors, who may have given the reporter information that would be helpful to the defense. On occasion, information in the hands of newsmen might enable the police to prevent future crimes or to apprehend fugitive felons. Some journalistic endeavors border on criminal activity, such as participation in acts of demonstrative vandalism or receiving stolen documents. . . . These and other situations raise considerations that are not present in the cases that are currently before the Court, and that may call for a quite different reconciliation of the conflicting interests.

. . .

The results of a wide-ranging empirical study of the sort that I have undertaken cannot be telescoped into a tidy conclusion. Nevertheless, it may be useful for me to identify those findings and impressions that I regard as the most important and the most interesting. They are as follows: (1) good reporters use confidential source relationships mainly for the assessment and verification opportunities that such relationships afford rather than for the purpose of gaining access to highly sensitive information of a newsworthy character; (2) the adverse impact of the subpoena threat has been primarily in "poisoning the atmosphere" so as to make insightful, interpretive reporting more difficult rather than in causing sources to "dry up" completely; (3) understandings of confidentiality in reporter-source relationships are frequently unstated and imprecise; (4) press subpoenas damage source relationships primarily by compromising the reporter's independent or compatriot status in the eyes of sources rather than by forcing the revelation of sensitive information; (5) only one segment of the journalism profession, characterized by certain reporting traits (emphasis on interpretation and verification) more than type of beat, has been adversely affected by the subpoena threat; (6) reporters feel very strongly that any resolution of their conflicting ethical obligations to sources and to society should be a matter for personal rather than judicial determination, and in consonance with this belief these reporters evince a high level of asserted willingness to testify voluntarily and also a very high level of asserted willingness to go to jail if necessary to honor what they perceive to be their obligation of confidentiality; (7) newsmen prefer a flexible ad hoc qualified privilege to an inflexible per se qualified privilege; (8) newsmen regard protection for the *identity* of anonymous sources as more important than protection for the *contents* of confidential information given by known sources; (9) newsmen object most of all to the frequency with which press subpoenas have been issued in what these reporters regard as unnecessary circumstances when they have no important information to contribute; and (10) newsmen fear that an outright rejection by the Supreme Court of any sort of newsman's privilege would "poison the atmosphere" considerably and thus they regard the symbolic aspect of the current constitutional litigation to be of the utmost importance.

---

2. THE SUPREME COURT CONSIDERS THE PRIVILEGE

The first Supreme Court case to consider whether the First Amendment supports privileges claimed by reporters involved grand jury testimony. A grand jury is a group of citizens who receive evidence of alleged crimes brought to them by the prosecutor. If the grand jury believes that this evidence, uncontroverted by the accused, would justify conviction, it will return an "indictment"—a formal accusation of crime. This will set the criminal prosecution in operation. The Fifth Amendment to the United States Constitution provides that no one be brought to trial for "a capital, or otherwise infamous crime" unless first indicted by a grand jury. States need not, and some do not, use grand juries. (Where the grand jury is not used, the prosecutor instead files an "information" against the accused to get the case started.) Grand juries are able to subpoena witnesses, and all testimony before grand juries is to be kept secret.

In part, this confidentiality requirement is to prevent a stigma from attaching to those whom the grand jury refuses to indict.

BRANZBURG v. HAYES

(Together with In re Pappas and United States v. Caldwell.)

Supreme Court of the United States, 1972.
408 U.S. 665, 92 S.Ct. 2646, 33 L.Ed.2d 626.

[This group of cases involved demands on three reporters by grand juries. In *Branzburg,* the reporter wrote a newspaper article about persons supposedly using a chemical process to change marijuana into hashish. He was called before a grand jury and directed to identify the two individuals. He refused and sought an order from the Kentucky Court of Appeals prohibiting the trial judge from insisting that he answer the questions. He based his claim on both the Kentucky privilege statute and the First Amendment. The Court of Appeals construed the statute to protect a reporter who refused to divulge the identity of an informant who supplied him with information but not to protect the silence of a reporter about his personal observations. Constitutional arguments were rejected.

In a second episode, Branzburg wrote a story after interviewing drug users and watching some of them smoking marijuana. He was again subpoenaed before a grand jury but before he was due to appear he again asked the Kentucky Court of Appeals to prevent the grand jury from forcing him to appear. Again the court denied his requested relief.

In *Pappas,* a Massachusetts television reporter recorded and photographed statements of local Black Panther Party officials during a period of racial turmoil. He was allowed to enter the Party's headquarters to cover an expected police raid in return for his promise to disclose nothing he observed within. He stayed three hours, no raid occurred, and he wrote no story. He was summoned before the county grand jury but refused to answer any questions about what had taken place while he was there. When he was recalled, he moved to quash the second summons. The motion was denied by the trial judge, who noted the absence of a statutory newsman's privilege in Massachusetts and denied the existence of a constitutional privilege. The Supreme Judicial Court of Massachusetts affirmed.

In the third case, Caldwell had been assigned by the New York Times to cover the Black Panther Party and other black militant groups. He was subpoenaed to appear before a federal grand jury and to bring with him notes and tape recordings of interviews given to him for publication by officers and spokesmen of the Black Panther Party concerning aims, purposes and activities of the group. The court held that in the absence of a compelling showing of need by the prosecution, Caldwell need not even appear before the grand jury, much less answer its questions.]

Opinion of the Court by MR. JUSTICE WHITE, announced by the CHIEF JUSTICE [BURGER].

. . .

II

. . . Although the newsmen in these cases do not claim an absolute privilege against official interrogation in all circumstances, they assert that the reporter should not be forced either to appear or to testify before a grand jury or at trial until and unless sufficient grounds are shown for believing that the reporter possesses information relevant to a crime the grand jury is investigating, that the information the reporter has is unavailable from other sources, and that the need for the information is sufficiently compelling to override the claimed invasion of First Amendment interests occasioned by the disclosure. Principally relied upon are prior cases emphasizing the importance of the First Amendment guarantees to individual development and to our system of representative government, decisions requiring that official action with adverse impact on First Amendment rights be justified by a public interest that is "compelling" or "paramount," and those precedents establishing the principle that justifiable governmental goals may not be achieved by unduly broad means having an unnecessary impact on protected rights of speech, press, or association. The heart of the claim is that the burden on news gathering resulting from compelling reporters to disclose confidential information outweighs any public interest in obtaining the information.

We do not question the significance of free speech, press, or assembly to the country's welfare. Nor is it suggested that news gathering does not qualify for First Amendment protection; without some protection for seeking out the news, freedom of the press could be eviscerated. But these cases involve no intrusions upon speech or assembly, no prior restraint or restriction on what the press may publish, and no express or implied command that the press publish what it prefers to withhold. No exaction or tax for the privilege of publishing, and no penalty, civil or criminal, related to the content of published material is at issue here. The use of confidential sources by the press is not forbidden or restricted; reporters remain free to seek news from any source by means within the law. No attempt is made to require the press to publish its sources of information or indiscriminately to disclose them on request.

The sole issue before us is the obligation of reporters to respond to grand jury subpoenas as other citizens do and to answer questions relevant to an investigation into the commission of crime. Citizens generally are not constitutionally immune from grand jury subpoenas; and neither the First Amendment nor any other constitutional provision protects the average citizen from disclosing to a grand jury information that he has received in confidence. . . .

It is clear that the First Amendment does not invalidate every incidental burdening of the press that may result from the enforcement of civil or criminal statutes of general applicability. Under prior cases, otherwise valid laws serving substantial public interests may be enforced against the press as against others, despite the possible burden that may be imposed. [The Court here referred to the taxation, labor, and antitrust cases discussed in Chapter XII.] . . .

It has generally been held that the First Amendment does not guarantee the press a constitutional right of special access to information not available to the public generally. Zemel v. Rusk, 381 U.S. 1, 16–17 (1965); [ ]. In Zemel v. Rusk, supra, for example, the Court sustained the Government's refusal to validate passports to Cuba even though that restriction "render[ed] less than wholly free the flow of information concerning that country." Id., at 16. The ban on travel was held constitutional, for "[t]he right to speak and publish does not carry with it the unrestrained right to gather information." Id., at 17.[22]

Despite the fact that news gathering may be hampered, the press is regularly excluded from grand jury proceedings, our own conferences, the meetings of other official bodies gathered in executive session, and the meetings of private organizations. Newsmen have no constitutional right of access to the scenes of crime or disaster when the general public is excluded, and they may be prohibited from attending or publishing information about trials if such restrictions are necessary to assure a defendant a fair trial before an impartial tribunal. . . .

It is thus not surprising that the great weight of authority is that newsmen are not exempt from the normal duty of appearing before a grand jury and answering questions relevant to a criminal investigation. At common law, courts consistently refused to recognize the existence of any privilege authorizing a newsman to refuse to reveal confidential information to a grand jury. . . .

The prevailing constitutional view of the newsman's privilege is very much rooted in the ancient role of the grand jury that has the dual function of determining if there is probable cause to believe that a crime has been committed and of protecting citizens against unfounded criminal prosecutions. Grand jury proceedings are constitutionally mandated for the institution of federal criminal prosecutions for capital or other serious crimes. . . . The Fifth Amendment

---

22. "There are few restrictions on action which could not be clothed by ingenious argument in the garb of decreased data flow. For example, the prohibition of unauthorized entry into the White House diminishes the citizen's opportunities to gather information he might find relevant to his opinion on the way the country is being run, but that does not make entry into the White House a First Amendment right." 381 U.S., at 16–17.

provides that "[n]o person shall be held to answer for a capital, or otherwise infamous crime, unless on a presentment or indictment of a Grand Jury." . . . Although state systems of criminal procedure differ greatly among themselves, the grand jury is similarly guaranteed by many state constitutions and plays an important role in fair and effective law enforcement in the overwhelming majority of the States. Because its task is to inquire into the existence of possible criminal conduct and to return only well-founded indictments, its investigative powers are necessarily broad. . . .

A number of States have provided newsmen a statutory privilege of varying breadth, but the majority have not done so, and none has been provided by federal statute. Until now the only testimonial privilege for unofficial witnesses that is rooted in the Federal Constitution is the Fifth Amendment privilege against compelled self-incrimination. We are asked to create another by interpreting the First Amendment to grant newsmen a testimonial privilege that other citizens do not enjoy. This we decline to do.[29] Fair and effective law enforcement aimed at providing security for the person and property of the individual is a fundamental function of government, and the grand jury plays an important, constitutionally mandated role in this process. On the records now before us, we perceive no basis for holding that the public interest in law enforcement and in ensuring effective grand jury proceedings is insufficient to override the consequential, but uncertain, burden on news gathering that is said to result from insisting that reporters, like other citizens, respond to relevant questions put to them in the course of a valid grand jury investigation or criminal trial.

. . .

. . . It would be frivolous to assert—and no one does in these cases—that the First Amendment, in the interest of securing news or otherwise, confers a license on either the reporter or his news sources to violate valid criminal laws. Although stealing documents or private wire tapping could provide newsworthy information, neither reporter nor source is immune from conviction for such conduct, whatever the impact on the flow of news. Neither is immune, on First Amendment grounds, from testifying against the other, before the grand jury or at a criminal trial. . . .

Thus, we cannot seriously entertain the notion that the First Amendment protects a newsman's agreement to conceal the criminal conduct of his source, or evidence thereof, on the theory that it is better to write about crime than to do something about it. . . .

There remain those situations where a source is not engaged in criminal conduct but has information suggesting illegal conduct by others. Newsmen frequently receive information from such sources pursuant to a tacit or express agreement to withhold the source's

---

29. The creation of new testimonial privileges has been met with disfavor by commentators since such privileges obstruct the search for truth. . . .

name and suppress any information that the source wishes not published. . . .

The argument that the flow of news will be diminished by compelling reporters to aid the grand jury in a criminal investigation is not irrational, nor are the records before us silent on the matter. But we remain unclear how often and to what extent informers are actually deterred from furnishing information when newsmen are forced to testify before a grand jury. The available data indicate that some newsmen rely a great deal on confidential sources and that some informants are particularly sensitive to the threat of exposure and may be silenced if it is held by this Court that, ordinarily, newsmen must testify pursuant to subpoenas, but the evidence fails to demonstrate that there would be a significant constriction of the flow of news to the public if this Court reaffirms the prior common-law and constitutional rule regarding the testimonial obligations of newsmen. Estimates of the inhibiting effect of such subpoenas on the willingness of informants to make disclosures to newsmen are widely divergent and to a great extent speculative.[32] It would be difficult to canvass the views of the informants themselves; surveys of reporters on this topic are chiefly opinions of predicted informant behavior and must be viewed in the light of the professional self-interest of the interviewees.[33] Reliance by the press on confidential informants does not mean that all such sources will in fact dry up because of the later possible appearance of the newsman before a grand jury. The reporter may never be called and if he objects to testifying, the prosecution may not insist. . . . Moreover, grand juries characteristically conduct secret proceedings, and law enforcement officers are themselves experienced in dealing with informers, and have their own methods for protecting them without interference with the effective administration of justice. . . .

. . .

32. Cf. e.g., the results of a study conducted by Guest & Stanzler, which appears as an appendix to their article, [64 Nw.U.L.Rev. 18]. A number of editors of daily newspapers of varying circulation were asked the question, "Excluding one- or two-sentence gossip items, on the average how many stories based on information received in confidence are published in your paper each year? Very rough estimate." Answers varied significantly, e.g., "Virtually innumerable," Tucson Daily Citizen (41,969 daily circ.), "Too many to remember," Los Angeles Herald-Examiner (718,221 daily circ.), "Occasionally," Denver Post (252,084 daily circ.), "Rarely," Cleveland Plain Dealer (370,499 daily circ.), "Very rare, some politics," Oregon Journal (146,403 daily circ.). This study did not purport to measure the extent of deterrence of informants caused by subpoenas to the press.

33. In his Press Subpoenas: An Empirical and Legal Analysis, Study Report of the Reporters' Committee on Freedom of the Press 6–12, Prof. Vince Blasi discusses these methodological problems. Prof. Blasi's survey found that slightly more than half of the 975 reporters questioned said that they relied on regular confidential sources for at least 10% of their stories. Id., at 21. Of this group of reporters, only 8% were able to say with some certainty that their professional functioning had been adversely affected by the threat of subpoena; another 11% were not certain whether or not they had been adversely affected. Id., at 53.

We are admonished that refusal to provide a First Amendment reporter's privilege will undermine the freedom of the press to collect and disseminate news. But this is not the lesson history teaches us. As noted previously, the common law recognized no such privilege, and the constitutional argument was not even asserted until 1958. From the beginning of our country the press has operated without constitutional protection for press informants and the press has flourished. The existing constitutional rules have not been a serious obstacle to either the development or retention of confidential news sources by the press.

It is said that currently press subpoenas have multiplied, that mutual distrust and tension between press and officialdom have increased, that reporting styles have changed, and that there is now more need for confidential sources, particularly where the press seeks news about minority cultural and political groups or dissident organizations suspicious of the law and public officials. These developments, even if true, are treacherous grounds for a far-reaching interpretation of the First Amendment fastening a nationwide rule on courts, grand juries, and prosecuting officials everywhere. . . .

. . .

The privilege claimed here is conditional, not absolute; given the suggested preliminary showings and compelling need, the reporter would be required to testify. Presumably, such a rule would reduce the instances in which reporters could be required to appear, but predicting in advance when and in what circumstances they could be compelled to do so would be difficult. Such a rule would also have implications for the issuance of compulsory process to reporters at civil and criminal trials and at legislative hearings. If newsmen's confidential sources are as sensitive as they are claimed to be, the prospect of being unmasked whenever a judge determines the situation justifies it is hardly a satisfactory solution to the problem. For them it would appear that only an absolute privilege would suffice.

We are unwilling to embark the judiciary on a long and difficult journey to such an uncertain destination. The administration of a constitutional newsman's privilege would present practical and conceptual difficulties of a high order. Sooner or later, it would be necessary to define those categories of newsmen who qualified for the privilege, a questionable procedure in light of the traditional doctrine that liberty of the press is the right of the lonely pamphleteer who uses carbon paper or a mimeograph just as much as of the large metropolitan publisher who utilizes the latest photocomposition methods. . . . The informative function asserted by representatives of the organized press in the present cases is also performed by lecturers, political pollsters, novelists, academic researchers, and dramatists. Almost any author may quite accurately assert that he is contributing to the flow of information to the public, that he relies on confidential sources of information, and that these sources will be silenced if he is forced to make disclosures before a grand jury.

. . .

Thus, in the end, by considering whether enforcement of a particular law served a "compelling" governmental interest, the courts would be inextricably involved in distinguishing between the value of enforcing different criminal laws. By requiring testimony from a reporter in investigations involving some crimes but not in others, they would be making a value judgment that a legislature had declined to make since in each case the criminal law involved would represent a considered legislative judgment, not constitutionally suspect, of what conduct is liable to criminal prosecution. The task of judges, like other officials outside the legislative branch, is not to make the law but to uphold it in accordance with their oaths.

At the federal level, Congress has freedom to determine whether a statutory newsman's privilege is necessary and desirable and to fashion standards and rules as narrow or broad as deemed necessary to deal with the evil discerned and, equally important, to refashion those rules as experience from time to time may dictate. There is also merit in leaving state legislatures free, within First Amendment limits, to fashion their own standards in light of the conditions and problems with respect to the relations between law enforcement officials and press in their own areas. It goes without saying, of course, that we are powerless to bar state courts from responding in their own way and construing their own constitutions so as to recognize a newsman's privilege, either qualified or absolute.

In addition, there is much force in the pragmatic view that the press has at its disposal powerful mechanisms of communication and is far from helpless to protect itself from harassment or substantial harm. . . .

Finally, as we have earlier indicated, news gathering is not without its First Amendment protections, and grand jury investigations if instituted or conducted other than in good faith, would pose wholly different issues for resolution under the First Amendment. Official harassment of the press undertaken not for purposes of law enforcement but to disrupt a reporter's relationship with his news sources would have no justification. Grand juries are subject to judicial control and subpoenas to motions to quash. We do not expect courts will forget that grand juries must operate within the limits of the First Amendment as well as the Fifth.

III

We turn, therefore, to the disposition of the cases before us. From what we have said, it necessarily follows that the decision in United States v. Caldwell, must be reversed. . . .

The decisions in Branzburg v. Hayes and Branzburg v. Meigs must be affirmed. . . . In both cases, if what petitioner wrote was true, he had direct information to provide the grand jury concerning the commission of serious crimes.

The only question presented at the present time in In re Pappas is whether petitioner Pappas must appear before the grand jury to testify pursuant to subpoena. . . . We affirm the decision of the Massachusetts Supreme Judicial Court and hold that petitioner must appear before the grand jury to answer the questions put to him, subject, of course, to the supervision of the presiding judge as to "the propriety, purposes, and scope of the grand jury inquiry and the pertinence of the probable testimony." [   ]

So ordered.

MR. JUSTICE POWELL, concurring.

I add this brief statement to emphasize what seems to me to be the limited nature of the Court's holding. The Court does not hold that newsmen, subpoenaed to testify before a grand jury, are without constitutional rights with respect to the gathering of news or in safeguarding their sources. Certainly, we do not hold, as suggested in Mr. Justice Stewart's dissenting opinion, that state and federal authorities are free to "annex" the news media as "an investigative arm of government." The solicitude repeatedly shown by this Court for First Amendment freedoms should be sufficient assurance against any such effort, even if one seriously believed that the media—properly free and untrammeled in the fullest sense of these terms—were not able to protect themselves.

As indicated in the concluding portion of the opinion, the Court states that no harassment of newsmen will be tolerated. If a newsman believes that the grand jury investigation is not being conducted in good faith he is not without remedy. Indeed, if the newsman is called upon to give information bearing only a remote and tenuous relationship to the subject of the investigation, or if he has some other reason to believe that his testimony implicates confidential source relationships without a legitimate need of law enforcement, he will have access to the court on a motion to quash and an appropriate protective order may be entered. The asserted claim to privilege should be judged on its facts by the striking of a proper balance between freedom of the press and the obligation of all citizens to give relevant testimony with respect to criminal conduct. The balance of these vital constitutional and societal interests on a case-by-case basis accords with the tried and traditional way of adjudicating such questions.*

---

* It is to be remembered that Caldwell asserts a constitutional privilege not even to appear before the grand jury unless a court decides that the Government has made a showing that meets the three preconditions specified in the dissenting opinion of Mr. Justice Stewart. To be sure, this would require a "balancing" of interests by the court, but under circumstances and constraints significantly different from the balancing that will be appropriate under the court's decision.

In short, the courts will be available to newsmen under circumstances where legitimate First Amendment interests require protection.

MR. JUSTICE DOUGLAS, dissenting in United States v. Caldwell [and the other two cases].

. . .

It is my view that there is no "compelling need" that can be shown which qualifies the reporter's immunity from appearing or testifying before a grand jury, unless the reporter himself is implicated in a crime. His immunity in my view is therefore quite complete, for absent his involvement in a crime, the First Amendment protects him against an appearance before a grand jury and if he is involved in a crime, the Fifth Amendment stands as a barrier. Since in my view there is no area of inquiry not protected by a privilege, the reporter need not appear for the futile purpose of invoking one to each question. . . .

The starting point for decision pretty well marks the range within which the end result lies. The New York Times, whose reporting functions are at issue here, takes the amazing position that First Amendment rights are to be balanced against other needs or conveniences of government. My belief is that all of the "balancing" was done by those who wrote the Bill of Rights. By casting the First Amendment in absolute terms, they repudiated the timid, watered-down, emasculated versions of the First Amendment which both the Government and the New York Times advance in the case.

. . .

The press has a preferred position in our constitutional scheme, not to enable it to make money, not to set newsmen apart as a favored class, but to bring fulfillment to the public's right to know. The right to know is crucial to the governing powers of the people, to paraphrase Alexander Meiklejohn. Knowledge is essential to informed decisions.

. . .

MR. JUSTICE STEWART, with whom MR. JUSTICE BRENNAN and MR. JUSTICE MARSHALL, join, dissenting.

The Court's crabbed view of the First Amendment reflects a disturbing insensitivity to the critical role of an independent press in our society. The question whether a reporter has a constitutional

The newsman witness, like all other witnesses, will have to appear; he will not be in a position to litigate at the threshold the State's very authority to subpoena him. Moreover, absent the constitutional preconditions that Caldwell and that dissenting opinion would impose as heavy burdens of proof to be carried by the State, the court—when called upon to protect a newsman from improper or prejudicial questioning—would be free to balance the competing interests on their merits in the particular case. The new constitutional rule endorsed by that dissenting opinion would, as a practical matter, defeat such a fair balancing and the essential societal interest in the detection and prosecution of crime would be heavily subordinated.

right to a confidential relationship with his source is of first impression here, but the principles that should guide our decision are as basic as any to be found in the Constitution.   While Mr. Justice Powell's enigmatic concurring opinion gives some hope of a more flexible view in the future, the Court in these cases holds that a newsman has no First Amendment right to protect his sources when called before a grand jury.   The Court thus invites state and federal authorities to undermine the historic independence of the press by attempting to annex the journalistic profession as an investigative arm of government.   Not only will this decision impair performance of the press' constitutionally protected functions, but it will, I am convinced, in the long run harm rather than help the administration of justice.

I respectfully dissent.

I

The reporter's constitutional right to a confidential relationship with his source stems from the broad societal interest in a full and free flow of information to the public.   .   .   .

Enlightened choice by an informed citizenry is the basic ideal upon which an open society is premised,[3] and a free press is thus indispensable to a free society.   Not only does the press enhance personal self-fulfillment by providing the people with the widest possible range of fact and opinion, but it also is an incontestable precondition of self-government.   .   .   . As private and public aggregations of power burgeon in size and the pressures for conformity necessarily mount, there is obviously a continuing need for an independent press to disseminate a robust variety of information and opinion through reportage, investigation, and criticism, if we are to preserve our constitutional tradition of maximizing freedom of choice by encouraging diversity of expression.

A

In keeping with this tradition, we have held that the right to publish is central to the First Amendment and basic to the existence of constitutional democracy.   [   ]

.   .   .

No less important to the news dissemination process is the gathering of information.   News must not be unnecessarily cut off at its source, for without freedom to acquire information the right to publish would be impermissibly compromised.   Accordingly, a right to gather news, of some dimensions, must exist.   .   .   .

---

3. See generally Z. Chafee, Free Speech in the United States (1941); A. Meiklejohn, Free Speech and Its Relation to Self-Government (1948); T. Emerson, Toward a General Theory of the First Amendment (1963).

B

The right to gather news implies, in turn, a right to a confidential relationship between a reporter and his source. This proposition follows as a matter of simple logic once three factual predicates are recognized: (1) newsmen require informants to gather news; (2) confidentiality—the promise or understanding that names or certain aspects of communications will be kept off the record—is essential to the creation and maintenance of a news-gathering relationship with informants; and (3) an unbridled subpoena power—the absence of a constitutional right protecting, in *any* way, a confidential relationship from compulsory process—will either deter sources from divulging information or deter reporters from gathering and publishing information.

It is obvious that informants are necessary to the news-gathering process as we know it today. If it is to perform its constitutional mission, the press must do far more than merely print public statements or publish prepared handouts. Familiarity with the people and circumstances involved in the myriad background activities that result in the final product called "news" is vital to complete and responsible journalism, unless the press is to be a captive mouthpiece of "newsmakers."

It is equally obvious that the promise of confidentiality may be a necessary prerequisite to a productive relationship between a newsman and his informants. An officeholder may fear his superior; a member of the bureaucracy, his associates; a dissident, the scorn of majority opinion. All may have information valuable to the public discourse, yet each may be willing to relate that information only in confidence to a reporter whom he trusts, either because of excessive caution or because of a reasonable fear of reprisals or censure for unorthodox views. The First Amendment concern must not be with the motives of any particular news source, but rather with the conditions in which informants of all shades of the spectrum may make information available through the press to the public. [ ]

In *Caldwell*, the District Court found that "confidential relationships . . . are commonly developed and maintained by professional journalists, and are indispensable to their work of gathering, analyzing and publishing the news." Commentators and individual reporters have repeatedly noted the importance of confidentiality. And surveys among reporters and editors indicate that the promise of nondisclosure is necessary for many types of news gathering.

Finally, and most important, when governmental officials possess an unchecked power to compel newsmen to disclose information received in confidence, sources will clearly be deterred from giving information, and reporters will clearly be deterred from publishing it, because uncertainty about exercise of the power will lead to "self-censorship." [ ] The uncertainty arises, of course, because the judiciary has traditionally imposed virtually no limitations on the grand jury's broad investigatory powers. [ ]

After today's decision, the potential informant can never be sure that his identity or off-the-record communications will not subsequently be revealed through the compelled testimony of a newsman. A public-spirited person inside government, who is not implicated in any crime, will now be fearful of revealing corruption or other governmental wrongdoing, because he will now know he can subsequently be identified by use of compulsory process. The potential source must, therefore, choose between risking exposure by giving information or avoiding the risk by remaining silent.

The reporter must speculate about whether contact with a controversial source or publication of controversial material will lead to a subpoena. In the event of a subpoena, under today's decision, the newsman will know that he must choose between being punished for contempt if he refuses to testify, or violating his profession's ethics [10] and impairing his resourcefulness as a reporter if he discloses confidential information.

. . .

The impairment of the flow of news cannot, of course, be proved with scientific precision, as the Court seems to demand. Obviously, not every news-gathering relationship requires confidentiality. And it is difficult to pinpoint precisely how many relationships do require a promise or understanding of nondisclosure. But we have never before demanded that First Amendment rights rest on elaborate empirical studies demonstrating beyond any conceivable doubt that deterrent effects exist; we have never before required proof of the exact number of people potentially affected by governmental action, who would actually be dissuaded from engaging in First Amendment activity.

. . .

To require any greater burden of proof is to shirk our duty to protect values securely embedded in the Constitution. We cannot await an unequivocal—and therefore unattainable—imprimatur from empirical studies.[19] We can and must accept the evidence developed in the record, and elsewhere, that overwhelmingly supports the

10. The American Newspaper Guild has adopted the following rule as part of the newsman's code of ethics: "[N]ewspapermen shall refuse to reveal confidences or disclose sources of confidential information in court or before other judicial or investigating bodies." G. Bird & F. Merwin, The Press and Society 592 (1971).

19. Empirical studies, after all, can only provide facts. It is the duty of courts to give legal significance to facts; and it is the special duty of this Court to understand the constitutional significance of facts. We must often proceed in a state of less than perfect knowledge, either because the facts are murky or the methodology used in obtaining the facts is open to question. It is then that we must look to the Constitution for the values that inform our presumptions. And the importance to our society of the full flow of information to the public has buttressed this Court's historic presumption in favor of First Amendment values.

premise that deterrence will occur with regularity in important types of news-gathering relationships.

Thus, we cannot escape the conclusion that when neither the reporter nor his source can rely on the shield of confidentiality against unrestrained use of the grand jury's subpoena power, valuable information will not be published and the public dialogue will inevitably be impoverished.

II

Posed against the First Amendment's protection of the newsman's confidential relationships in these cases is society's interest in the use of the grand jury to administer justice fairly and effectively. The grand jury serves two important functions: "to examine into the commission of crimes" and "to stand between the prosecutor and the accused, and to determine whether the charge was founded upon credible testimony or was dictated by malice or personal ill will." Hale v. Henkel, 201 U.S. 43, 59. And to perform these functions the grand jury must have available to it every man's relevant evidence. [ ]

Yet the longstanding rule making every person's evidence available to the grand jury is not absolute. The rule has been limited by the Fifth Amendment, the Fourth Amendment, and the evidentiary privileges of the common law. . . . And in United States v. Bryan, 339 U.S. 323, the Court observed that any exemption from the duty to testify before the grand jury "presupposes a very real interest to be protected." Id., at 332.

Such an interest must surely be the First Amendment protection of a confidential relationship that I have discussed above in Part I. As noted there, this protection does not exist for the purely private interests of the newsman or his informant, nor even, at bottom, for the First Amendment interests of either partner in the news-gathering relationship. Rather, it functions to insure nothing less than democratic decisionmaking through the free flow of information to the public, and it serves, thereby, to honor the "profound national commitment to the principle that debate on public issues should be uninhibited, robust, and wide-open." New York Times Co. v. Sullivan, 376 U.S., at 270.

In striking the proper balance between the public interest in the efficient administration of justice and the First Amendment guarantee of the fullest flow of information, we must begin with the basic proposition that because of their "delicate and vulnerable" nature, NAACP v. Button, 371 U.S., at 433, and their transcendent importance for the just functioning of our society, First Amendment rights require special safeguards.

A

This Court has erected such safeguards when government, by legislative investigation or other investigative means, has attempted to pierce the shield of privacy inherent in freedom of association. In no previous case have we considered the extent to which the First Amendment limits the grand jury subpoena power. . . .

. . .

Thus, when an investigation impinges on First Amendment rights, the government must not only show that the inquiry is of "compelling and overriding importance" but it must also "convincingly" demonstrate that the investigation is "substantially related" to the information sought.

Government officials must, therefore, demonstrate that the information sought is *clearly* relevant to a *precisely* defined subject of governmental inquiry. [ ] They must demonstrate that it is reasonable to think the witness in question has that information. [ ] And they must show that there is not any means of obtaining the information less destructive of First Amendment liberties. [ ]

These requirements, which we have recognized in decisions involving legislative and executive investigations, serve established policies reflected in numerous First Amendment decisions arising in other contexts. . . .

I believe the safeguards developed in our decisions involving governmental investigations must apply to the grand jury inquiries in these cases. Surely the function of the grand jury to aid in the enforcement of the law is no more important than the function of the legislature, and its committees, to make the law. . . .

Accordingly, when a reporter is asked to appear before a grand jury and reveal confidences, I would hold that the government must (1) show that there is probable cause to believe that the newsman has information that is clearly relevant to a specific probable violation of law; (2) demonstrate that the information sought cannot be obtained by alternative means less destructive of First Amendment rights; and (3) demonstrate a compelling and overriding interest in the information.

This is not to say that a grand jury could not issue a subpoena until such a showing were made, and it is not to say that a newsman would be in any way privileged to ignore any subpoena that was issued. Obviously, before the government's burden to make such a showing were triggered, the reporter would have to move to quash the subpoena, asserting the basis on which he considered the particular relationship a confidential one.

B

The crux of the Court's rejection of any newsman's privilege is its observation that only "where news sources themselves are implicated in crime or possess information *relevant* to the grand jury's task need they or the reporter be concerned about grand jury subpoenas." See ante, at 691 (emphasis supplied). But this is a most misleading construct. For it is obviously not true that the only persons about whom reporters will be forced to testify will be those "confidential informants involved in actual criminal conduct" and those having "information suggesting illegal conduct by others." See ante, at 691, 693. As noted above, given the grand jury's extraordinarily broad investigative powers and the weak standards of relevance and materiality that apply during such inquiries, reporters, if they have no testimonial privilege, will be called to give information about informants who have neither committed crimes nor have information about crime. It is to avoid deterrence of such sources and thus to prevent needless injury to First Amendment values that I think the government must be required to show probable cause that the newsman has information that is clearly relevant to a specific probable violation of criminal law.

. . .

Both the "probable cause" and "alternative means" requirements would thus serve the vital function of mediating between the public interest in the administration of justice and the constitutional protection of the full flow of information. . . . No doubt the courts would be required to make some delicate judgments in working out this accommodation. But that, after all, is the function of courts of law. Better such judgments, however difficult, than the simplistic and stultifying absolutism adopted by the Court in denying any force to the First Amendment in these cases.

The error in the Court's absolute rejection of First Amendment interests in these cases seems to me to be most profound. For in the name of advancing the administration of justice, the Court's decision, I think, will only impair the achievement of that goal. People entrusted with law enforcement responsibility, no less than private citizens, need general information relating to controversial social problems. Obviously, press reports have great value to government, even when the newsman cannot be compelled to testify before a grand jury. The sad paradox of the Court's position is that when a grand jury may exercise an unbridled subpoena power, and sources involved in sensitive matters become fearful of disclosing information, the newsman will not only cease to be a useful grand jury witness; he will cease to investigate and publish information about issues of public import. I cannot subscribe to such an anomalous result, for, in my view, the interests protected by the First Amendment are not antagonistic to the administration of justice. Rather, they can, in the long run, only be complementary, and for that reason must be given great "breathing space." NAACP v. Button, 371 U.S., at 433.

Notes and Questions

1. Since Justice Powell's was the vital fifth vote that made Justice White's opinion an opinion for the Court, it becomes important to understand his position. Is Justice White's opinion based on balancing? Is it the same kind of balancing that Justice Powell calls for in his concurring opinion? Recall the different types of balancing discussed at p. 43, supra.

2. Justice Powell suggests some grounds for protecting reporters from grand jury investigations. Does Justice White's opinion suggest the same protections?

3. In what ways do Justices Powell and Stewart disagree?

4. Justice Douglas notes with obvious dismay that the reporters did not seek "absolute" privilege. What would such a privilege have meant in this case? Why do you think such an argument was not made?

5. How important are the empirical questions? In addition to Blasi's work, see the study in D. Gordon, Newsman's Privilege and the Law (1974).

6. Justice White observes that the Court would get into "practical and conceptual difficulties of a high order" if it were to develop a constitutional privilege for newsmen. Among the problems he sees is that of having to decide who is entitled to such a privilege. Could the Supreme Court rule that the privilege belongs to reporters who work for mass media but not to "the lonely pamphleteer who uses carbon paper or a mimeograph?" What about academic researchers?

7. The Supreme Court is generally skeptical about claims of privilege. In United States v. Nixon, 418 U.S. 683 (1974), the special prosecutor served a subpoena on then President Nixon seeking certain tapes and documents that might be relevant to the Watergate cover-up trial. The President asked the courts to have the subpoena withdrawn—or quashed—on the grounds (1) that the separation of powers doctrine precluded judicial review of the President's decision that it would not be in the public interest to disclose the contents of confidential conversations between a President and his close advisers, and (2) that as a matter of constitutional law, executive privilege prevailed over the subpoena. Although granting that the need for "complete candor and objectivity from advisers calls for great deference from the courts," the Court decided that absent a claim of "need to protect military, diplomatic, or sensitive national security secrets," the Court must weigh the competing interests to determine which should prevail:

. . . We have elected to employ an adversary system of criminal justice in which the parties contest all issues before a court of law. The need to develop all relevant facts in the adversary system is both fundamental and comprehensive. The ends of criminal justice would be defeated if judgments were to be founded on a partial or speculative presentation of the facts. The very integrity of the judicial system and public confidence in the system depend on full disclosure of all the facts, within the framework of the rules of evidence. To ensure that justice is done, it is imperative to the function of courts that compulsory process be available for the production of evidence needed either by the prosecution or by the defense.

Only recently the Court restated the ancient proposition of law, albeit in the context of a grand jury inquiry rather than a trial,

> "that 'the public . . . has a right to every man's evidence,' except for those persons protected by a constitutional, common-law, or statutory privilege, [ ] . . .." Branzburg v. Hayes, 408 U.S. 665, 688 (1972).
>
> . . .

In this case we must weigh the importance of the general privilege of confidentiality of Presidential communications in performance of his responsibilities against the inroads of such a privilege on the fair administration of criminal justice. The interest in preserving confidentiality is weighty indeed and entitled to great respect. However, we cannot conclude that advisers will be moved to temper the candor of their remarks by the infrequent occasions of disclosure because of the possibility that such conversations will be called for in the context of a criminal prosecution.

On the other hand, the allowance of the privilege to withhold evidence that is demonstrably relevant in a criminal trial would cut deeply into the guarantee of due process of law and gravely impair the basic function of the courts. A President's acknowledged need for confidentiality in the communications of his office is general in nature, whereas the constitutional need for production of relevant evidence in a criminal proceeding is specific and central to the fair adjudication of a particular criminal case in the administration of justice. Without access to specific facts a criminal prosecution may be totally frustrated. The President's broad interest in confidentiality of communications will not be vitiated by disclosure of a limited number of conversations preliminarily shown to have some bearing on the pending criminal cases.

8. The problem of reporter's privilege arises most frequently in the context of material that has been published without attribution of source. In *Branzburg,* however, several of the cases involved incom-

plete reports and efforts to get more information, such as what happened inside the building in *Pappas*. This may involve "outtakes," a term usually used to refer to parts of film or videotape that have been cut and not shown on the air. It may indeed refer to film, but might also refer to notes taken by a reporter that never appear in the story, or, indeed, perceptions or observations that are not even written down. Are government efforts to obtain this unpublished or unrecorded information different from the more conventional effort to get a reporter to identify a source of published information? Does Justice White suggest a distinction between the two situations? Outtakes are essential when the goal is to try to judge the fairness of what was actually presented. This was the situation when a House committee sought outtakes from the CBS program, The Selling of the Pentagon, referred to by Blasi. On outtakes, see Schonfeld, The Film on the Cutting Room Floor, Columbia Journalism Rev. (Nov./ Dec. 1974) at 52.

9. The courts are even less sympathetic when unsolicited information has been thrust on the reporter. See Lewis v. United States, 517 F.2d 236 (9th Cir.1975), upholding the contempt conviction of a manager of a radio station for refusing to produce the original of a "communique" he received from an underground group that claimed responsibility for a bombing. Does this situation differ greatly from those presented in *Branzburg?*

10. As we have seen, journalists' claims to a common law privilege not to testify, such as that enjoyed under some circumstances by doctors, lawyers, and clergy, have usually been unsuccessful. An appeal to a First Amendment privilege was not accepted by the Supreme Court in the context of the *Branzburg* facts. In the face of such uncertainty, and perhaps responding to the suggestion in *Branzburg*, several states passed some form of a shield law. About half the states now have them. Shield laws vary in detail but generally are statutory attempts to exempt journalists from divulging certain information—usually confidential sources or the information itself. The exemption can only apply to *state* proceedings, such as state grand juries or state trials.

11. Professor Blasi observes that the *Branzburg* group all involved the same limited question: appearance before a grand jury investigating possible crimes. How different is a demand that a reporter testify at a trial from a demand he testify before a grand jury? Might it matter if the defendant is the one seeking the testimony? Consider the defendant's Sixth Amendment right to call witnesses in his own defense. We turn to these variations now.

The state laws can have loopholes. For instance, the definition of who is a journalist and therefore protected by the law can be either narrow or broad. Should a shield law include college journalists? Annette Buchanan, editor of the University of Oregon *Daily Emerald*, was subpoenaed to reveal the source of her story about the use of marijuana on the campus. She refused and was cited for contempt. The Oregon Supreme Court ruled that there is no constitutional privilege, but specifically refused to rule on who is and is not a journalist. State v. Buchanan, 250 Or. 244, 436 P.2d 729, certiorari denied 392 U.S. 905 (1968). A maker of documentary films was held to be a journalist who could assert a claim of privilege in Silkwood v. Kerr-McGee, 563 F.2d 433 (10th Cir.1977).

A state shield law that is strong from a journalist's point of view should make clear which journalists are protected (reporters, editors, free-lancers, television cameramen?), should include temporarily unemployed or ex-journalists, should cover all of the media (including wire services and, perhaps, the non-fiction books), and should offer protection for professionals who are free-lancers.

Among possible limits on state shield laws is the Sixth Amendment right of defendants in criminal cases to have compulsory process to obtain witnesses in their favor. Another is the limited value of state statutes, because the reporter may be called before a federal grand jury or asked to testify in a federal court or in another state without similar protection to what exists in his home state.

3. AFTER BRANZBURG: OTHER CONTEXTS

a. *Criminal Trials and Shield Laws*

The conflict between the Sixth Amendment rights of defendants in criminal trials and First Amendment claims to testimonial privilege is well illustrated in the Farber case.

The Farber Case. Myron Farber, a reporter for the *New York Times*, began investigating a series of mysterious deaths that had occurred several years earlier at a hospital in New Jersey. His investigations led to a series of articles and to murder indictments against a physician. During the six-month-long murder trial, the defendant's attorney had subpoenas served on the reporter and the newspaper demanding that they produce certain documents relating to interviews with witnesses at the trial. Motions to quash the subpoenas were denied, but the trial judge did order that the documents be delivered to him for *in camera* inspection. Farber and the *Times* refused. Efforts to stay the order pending appeals were denied by the state appellate courts and Justices White and Marshall.

Farber and the *Times* refused to comply and were held in civil and criminal contempt. The civil contempt involved a fine of $5,000 per day on the *Times* and a flat $1,000 on Farber, who was sentenced to jail until he complied. The criminal penalties were $100,000 on the newspaper, and $1,000 on Farber plus six months in jail. On review, the New Jersey Supreme Court affirmed, 5–2. Matter of Farber, 78 N.J. 259, 394 A.2d 330 (1978).

The court rejected the argument that the First Amendment protected Farber's refusal because of the need to keep newsgathering and dissemination from being substantially impaired. It concluded that *Branzburg* "squarely held that no such First Amendment right exists." "Thus we do no weighing or balancing of societal interests in reaching our determination that the First Amendment does not afford appellants the privilege they claim." Moreover, "the obligation to appear at a criminal trial on behalf of a defendant who is enforcing his Sixth Amendment rights is at least as compelling as the duty to appear before a grand jury."

The court then turned to the state "shield law" providing that persons employed by media are privileged to refuse to disclose "in any legal . . . proceeding . . . including, but not limited to, any court, grand jury, petit jury, . . . or elsewhere" the source of information acquired or "any news or information obtained in the course of pursuing his professional activities whether or not it is disseminated." The court found a legislative desire to protect sources and information obtained by reporters "to the greatest extent permitted" by the state and federal constitutions. Since Farber was clearly covered by the statute, the court turned to the constitutional question.

The criminal defendant argued that the right to have compulsory process for obtaining witnesses in his favor prevailed over the statute if there was a conflict. The court agreed, noting that in the Nixon tapes case, the Supreme Court ordered the President to deliver materials to the special prosecutor although the President claimed an executive privilege and the prosecutor had nothing like the Sixth Amendment to support his demand.

The court concluded that the state constitution afforded a criminal defendant the right to compel witnesses to attend and to compel the production of documents "for which he may have, or may believe he has, a legitimate need in preparing or undertaking his defense." Witnesses properly summoned must testify or produce material demanded by a properly phrased subpoena. The state constitutional provision "prevails over" the shield statute, "but in recognition of the strongly expressed legislative viewpoint favoring confidentiality, we prescribe the imposition" of some procedural safeguards.

The court directed that in similar cases in the future the reporter would be "entitled to a preliminary determination before being compelled to submit the subpoenaed materials to a trial judge." The court reiterated that this result was based on its obligation to give as much effect to the shield statute as possible consistent with the conflicting constitutional provisions. The hearing was not mandated by the First Amendment.

In such a hearing, the defendant would have to show "by a fair preponderance of the evidence, including all reasonable inferences, that there was a reasonable probability or likelihood that the information sought by the subpoena was material and relevant to his defense, that it could not be secured from any less intrusive source and that the defendant had a legitimate need to see and otherwise use it."

In Farber's case, the trial judge's failure to accord such a hearing was not error because "it is perfectly clear that on the record before him a conclusion of materiality, relevancy, unavailability of another source, as well as need was quite inescapable." The judge had been trying the case for 18 weeks. "His knowledge of the factual background and of the part Farber had played was intimate and pervasive. Perhaps most significant is the trial court's thorough awareness of appellant Farber's close association with the Prosecutor's office since a time preceding the indictment." The court then listed the claims asserted by the defendant in the criminal case and considered the role of each witness and why the defendant might want Farber's files. These included some who admitted having spoken to Farber at various times, and one who refused to speak with the defense. Since there was enough to have persuaded a trial judge to order *in camera* submission of the materials had a hearing been held before such an order, and since Farber knew of all these facts, the court concluded that the requirements for an *in camera* order had been met.

The civil and criminal contempt convictions were upheld. (The majority did not mention the fact that Farber had signed a contract to write a book about the case. That issue emerged in a federal court hearing and did not enter into the state court proceeding.)

The Supreme Court denied certiorari sub nom. New York Times Co. v. New Jersey, 439 U.S. 997 (1978). Justice Brennan took no part in the decision.

As a result of the case, Mr. Farber spent several days in county jail on the civil contempt before the state court case just summarized. He was then released pending the outcome of that case. After the adverse decision, he returned to jail. He was released after the jury received the murder case since he could no longer effectively comply with the court's order to turn over the documents. He spent a total of 40 days in jail. The *Times* paid civil and criminal fines totalling $285,000. After the criminal trial was over—the jury having acquitted the physician—several other pending citations for contempt of court against Farber were dismissed and the sentence for criminal contempt was suspended without probation.

After *Farber*, the New Jersey Legislature amended its shield law to provide more clearly that a showing of need must be made before the reporter can be required to reveal confidential information even to the trial judge in chambers, much less the litigants. The state's supreme court twice upheld and applied the statute shortly thereafter.

C.B.S., Inc. v. Superior Court, 85 Cal.App.3d 241, 149 Cal.Rptr. 421 (1978), involved an arrangement between CBS and the Santa Clara County sheriff's department under which CBS was permitted to photograph meetings between undercover agents and two men. The meetings led to the arrest of both men for selling controlled substances—and CBS showed the arrest sequence on its program "60 Minutes." Before the criminal trial, the attorney for one defendant sought the CBS "outtakes"—film shot but not shown on the broadcast. CBS refused. The trial judge ordered the outtakes turned over to the defense.

On appeal, the court concluded that under state law, "where a criminal defendant has demonstrated a *reasonable possibility* that evidence sought to be discovered might result in his exoneration, he is entitled to its discovery." The court ordered the judge to conduct a preliminary screening of the film and to consider whether delivery of voice clips alone would satisfy the defendant's needs.

On remand, the tapes were made available to the parties. As a result, the prosecutor dropped the charges against the defendant who had sought the film. That defendant's attorney is reported to have said that the film clips showed that although the defendant was present, "he didn't participate" in the transaction, contrary to the officers' version. S.F. Chronicle, Feb. 24, 1979 at 4.

b. Civil Cases

When we turn to civil cases, the justifications change for insisting on a reporter's testimony. Since the case is not criminal, society's interest may be less direct and no one's freedom or life is at stake. Instead, a private person or group is suing for injury to person, property, privacy or reputation. What happens to the *Branzburg* rationale in this situation?

Shortly after *Branzburg*, an action was brought on behalf of "all Negroes in the City of Chicago who purchased homes from approximately 60 named defendants between 1952 and 1969." The claim was that the real estate brokers had engaged in "blockbusting," a discriminatory practice that involved buying homes at low prices and reselling them at high prices. To help prove their case the plaintiffs asked a reporter, Balk, to identify the source of an article he wrote in 1962 about real estate practices in Chicago, entitled "Confessions of a Block-Buster." Although sympathetic to the plaintiffs' position, Balk refused to testify because he got the story in confidence. The trial judge's refusal to order Balk to testify was affirmed on appeal. Baker v. F & F Investment, 470 F.2d 778 (2d Cir.1972).

The court read *Branzburg* as offering reporters some First Amendment protection and relied heavily on Justice Powell's statement that "these vital constitutional and societal interests" should be decided on a case-by-case basis. The court observed the great weight that Justice White gave to the role of the grand jury and to the

"importance of combatting crime."   Since Justice Powell suggested
that for him (and also the four dissenters) situations existed in
criminal cases in which the First Amendment might override the
interest in disclosure of information about crime, "surely in civil
cases, courts must recognize that the public interest in non-disclosure
of journalists' confidential sources will often be weightier than the
private interest in compelled disclosure."   The court found no compelling interest in disclosure in the facts of the case because the identity
of the source "simply did not go to the heart of" plaintiffs' case.

A qualified privilege also was found in Democratic National
Committee v. McCord, 356 F.Supp. 1394 (D.D.C.1973).   The Committee for the Re-election of the President (President Nixon's reelection
committee) was defending several suits arising out of the Watergate
break-in.   To obtain evidence for use in the trials, the committee
caused subpoenas to be issued against a number of journalists.   On
motions to quash the subpoenas, a federal court held that since all
other means had not been used to obtain the material before requesting it from reporters, and since the Committee had not shown clearly
that the material was relevant to the trials, the subpoenas should not
be issued.   In so ruling, the court discussed "the right of the press to
gather and publish, and that of the public to receive, news from
. . . ofttimes confidential sources."   The court also noted that the
suits in question were civil, not criminal, and that the media were not
parties to the suits.

The court thus adapted to civil cases the thrust of Justice
Stewart's dissent in *Branzburg,* in which he contended that three
conditions be met before a journalist is forced to testify or submit
material: "the government must (1) show that there is probable
cause to believe that the newsman has information that is clearly
relevant to a specific probable violation of law; (2) demonstrate that
the information sought cannot be obtained by alternative means less
destructive of First Amendment rights; and (3) demonstrate a compelling and overriding interest in the information."   (See p. 394,
supra.)   A number of federal cases involving subpoenas to reporters
in civil suits have followed the *McCord* approach.

c.   The Reporter as Plaintiff

What if the reporter *is* a party in the case?   Syndicated columnist Jack Anderson sued several officials of the Nixon administration
for conspiring to harass him.   The defendants asserted that the
statute of limitations had run and denied the merits of the claims.
As part of their defense they asked plaintiff when and how he
learned about the alleged harassment and also sought information on
other aspects of his claims.   Several of these questions required
disclosure of confidential sources but plaintiff refused to reveal them.
The judge ordered Anderson to reveal the sources on the ground that
they were central to the defenses being raised:

Here the newsman is not being obliged to disclose his sources. Plaintiff's pledge of confidentiality would have remained unchallenged had he not invoked the aid of the Court seeking compensatory and punitive damages based on his claim of conspiracy. Plaintiff is attempting to use the First Amendment simultaneously as a sword and a shield. He believes he was wronged by a conspiracy that sought to retaliate against his sources and to undermine his reliability and professional standing before the public because what he said was unpopular with the conspirators. But when those he accuses seek to defend by attempting to discover who his sources were, so that they may find out what the sources knew, their version of what they told him and how they were hurt, plaintiff says this is off limits—a forbidden area of inquiry. He cannot have it both ways. Plaintiff is not a bystander in the process but a principal. He cannot ask for justice and deny it to those he accuses.

The judge rejected plaintiff's claim that the conflicting claims should be "balanced." This was "most unrealistic. Having chosen to become a litigant, the newsman is not exempt from those obligations imposed by the rule of law on all litigants. . . ." The choice was plaintiff's: reveal the sources or have the case dismissed. Anderson v. Nixon, 444 F.Supp. 1195 (D.D.C.1978). The case was subsequently dismissed.

d. Press as Defamation Defendant

One complex question that cuts across several areas we have discussed is whether media defendants in defamation cases are privileged to refuse to identify confidential sources who gave them the allegedly defamatory information. The philosophy of New York Times v. Sullivan counsels that debate should be open and robust—but that the press should be liable for defamations that are deliberately or recklessly false. What if the public figure plaintiff must know the source of the story to prove that the falsehood was deliberate or reckless? On the other hand, if the plaintiff can expose confidential sources simply by the expedient of suing for libel, such sources may disappear. Is *Branzburg* relevant on this aspect of reporters' privileges?

Several courts struggled with this matter in the early and mid-1970's. (Recall that in the Judy Garland case, the paper was not sued.) In 1979, Herbert v. Lando, p. 118 supra, shed some light on the question. Recall that the Supreme Court held that the First Amendment did not protect a journalist from having to testify about his thoughts, opinions and conclusions as he was researching and preparing a story, and about his intra-office communications with others working on the story. The Court stressed that a plaintiff operating under the *New York Times* standard had a difficult task and should be able to seek direct evidence of constitutional malice.

The Court's suggestion that relevant evidence should be available to the plaintiff would suggest that confidential sources not be protected. On the other hand, the Herbert case involved little or no potential for chilling information sources because it involved only the professional journalist's thoughts and communications. The compelled identification of confidential sources would raise a different question.

These cases present two different questions. The first is when may courts order journalists to reveal confidential sources. It is highly unlikely that any court will allow a person to sue a newspaper for libel and then immediately learn all the confidential sources that were involved in the creation of the story. Much more likely, whether under state law or the First Amendment, courts will require the plaintiff to show his need for the information. The role the source played in the story's development and the article will be crucial.

The second question is what sanction should be imposed on a defendant who refuses to obey an order to disclose the identity of its confidential sources. Since Herbert v. Lando, a few state and lower federal courts have begun to address both questions.

In Miller v. Transamerican Press, Inc., 621 F.2d 721, rehearing denied, 628 F.2d 932 (5th Cir.1980), the court read the *Times* sequence of cases, *Branzburg*, and *Herbert* to create a First Amendment privilege:

> *Herbert* held that the press had no First Amendment privilege against discovery of mental processes where the discovery was for the purpose of determining whether malice existed.
>
> The policies supporting a First Amendment privilege would appear to be stronger here, where a defamation plaintiff seeks to compel disclosure of the name of a confidential informant, than they were in either *Branzburg* or *Herbert.* In *Herbert,* the Supreme Court reasoned that requiring disclosure of journalists' thought processes would have no chilling effect on the editorial process; the only effect would be to deter recklessness. However, forced disclosure of journalists' sources might deter informants from giving their stories to newsmen, except anonymously. This might cause the press to face the unwelcome alternatives of not publishing because of the inherent unreliability of anonymous tips, or publishing anonymous tips and becoming vulnerable to charges of recklessness.
>
> Similarly, there is a more apparent interest in protecting the confidentiality of journalists' sources in libel cases than in grand jury proceedings. In *Branzburg,* the prosecutor had an interest in keeping the informant's identity secret in order to protect him from reprisal. The government and the press had a similar purpose, both were ferreting out wrongdoing and seeking to correct it. In a libel case, the plaintiff and the press are on

opposite sides. And a defamed plaintiff might relish an opportunity to retaliate against the informant.

. . .

A final First Amendment consideration, in a case involving a public figure, is that it will often be possible to establish malice or lack of malice without disclosure of the identity of the informant. A plaintiff may be able to find other evidence of malice, or a defendant may be able to come forward with sufficient evidence of prudence in printing which would carry the burden in support of a motion for summary judgment.

The privilege, however, was not absolute. The court drew on a passage in *Herbert:* "Evidentiary privileges in litigation are not favored, and even those rooted in the Constitution must give way in proper circumstances." In *Miller,* the facts indicated that (1) the identity was relevant; (2) the plaintiff had exhausted other efforts to obtain the information; and (3) on balance, after considering other fact situations, the plaintiff's need to learn the identity was compelling. The source was central to the defendant's story and plaintiff could not prove the required type of falsity without knowing the source's identity. In addition, plaintiff must present "substantial evidence" that the statement "is both factually untrue and defamatory."

After ordering the defendant to reveal the source, the court observed the judge "should protect the informant by restricting the information about the informant's identity to counsel and requiring that it be used strictly for the litigation." Is this likely to induce disclosure?

In Downing v. Monitor Publishing Co., 120 N.H. 383, 415 A.2d 683 (1980), the court refused to require the plaintiff to prove the statement false before the defendant had to disclose the source. Plaintiff need only "satisfy the trial court that he has evidence to establish that there is a genuine issue of fact regarding" falsity. Then the court anticipated the question of what should happen if the defendant refused to disclose the source:

> We come to the question of enforcement of the court's order. Of course, the trial court is free to exercise its contempt power to enforce its order. We are aware, however, that most media personnel have refused to obey court orders to disclose, electing to go to jail instead. Confining newsmen to jail in no way aids the plaintiff in proving his case. Although we do not say that the contempt power should not be exercised, we do say that something more is required to protect the rights of a libel plaintiff. Therefore, we hold that when a defendant in a libel action, brought by a plaintiff who is required to prove actual malice under *New York Times,* refuses to declare his sources of information upon a valid order of the court, there shall arise a presumption that the defendant had no source. This presumption may be removed by a disclosure of the sources a reasonable

time before trial. Because such a disclosure may, for the press, be similar to the disclosure of a "trade secret," there may be circumstances under which an appropriate order limiting outside access to the informant's name when disclosed would not be improper.

In one highly publicized case a trial judge, to punish the defendant for refusal to reveal the source, ordered all of the defendant's defenses to be struck—and awarded judgment for plaintiff. On appeal, the state's highest court reversed. First, it doubted the need for the identity of the source, which apparently only told the newspaper where the relevant information could be found. But even if the order to disclose was valid, the appropriate remedy for disobedience was to tailor the sanction to those aspects of the case in which plaintiff was hampered by the defendant's refusal to disclose the essential information. Sierra Life Insurance Co. v. Magic Valley Newspapers, 101 Idaho 795, 623 P.2d 103 (1980).

The results in these cases appear to permit the defendant who refuses to obey an order still to prevail on the truth-falsity issue, or to prove that the damages claimed were not caused by the defamation.

State shield laws may affect this question if they directly create a testimonial privilege for reporters that extends to cases where the reporter is a party. Otherwise, even the most elaborate shield statutes will not be used in libel cases. California's version states: "A . . . reporter . . . cannot be adjudged in contempt by a judicial . . . body . . . for refusing to disclose . . . the source of any information procured . . . ." A legislative report stated that although the purpose of the statute was to protect the reporter from being held in contempt, "it does not create a privilege. Thus, the section will not prevent the use of other sanctions for refusal of a newsman to make discovery when he is a party to a civil proceeding." The California statute was discussed in Miller v. Transamerican Press, supra. See also Rancho LaCosta v. Penthouse Int'l, Ltd., (Cal. Super.Ct.1980), ordering the defendant to disclose its sources. If it failed to do so, the jury would be told it had no source. The appellate courts refused to review the case—even though just before the case the California shield law had been adopted verbatim as part of the state Constitution.

e. *Identifying Violators of Judicial Orders*

Another issue of privilege arises when a judge or a grand jury wants to learn who told a reporter information that was supposed to be secret. The problem is illustrated by the case of William Farr, a newspaper reporter covering the lurid Manson trial in Los Angeles. To reduce potentially prejudicial publicity in that case, the trial judge ordered the attorneys and certain others not to speak about specific phases of the case. Farr reported certain facts that he could only have learned from a person covered by the judge's order. The judge demanded that Farr identify his source despite the California privilege statute: "A publisher, editor, reporter . . . cannot be adjudged in contempt by a court . . . for refusing to disclose the source of any information procured for publication and published in a newspaper . . . ." Farr stated that the information had come from forbidden sources including two of the six attorneys. Each attorney denied having been a source. The judge again asked Farr to identify the individuals. Farr refused and was held in contempt.

The statute was held inapplicable because the legislature had no power to prohibit the court from seeking to preserve the integrity of its own operations. The legislature's efforts to immunize persons from punishment for violation of court orders, violated the separation of powers. To immunize Farr "would severely impair the trial court's discharge of a constitutionally compelled duty to control its own officers. The trial court was enjoined by controlling precedent of the United States Supreme Court to take reasonable action to protect the defendants in the Manson case from the effects of prejudicial publicity." Farr v. Superior Court, 22 Cal.App.3d 60, 99 Cal.Rptr. 342 (1971). The Supreme Court of California denied a hearing and the Supreme Court of the United States denied certiorari 409 U.S. 1011 (1972).

In a later proceeding Farr argued that a contempt citation upon him was essentially a sentence of imprisonment for life because he clearly would not comply. The court noted that an order committing a person until he complies with a court order is "coercive and not penal in nature." The purpose of this sanction is not to punish but to obtain compliance with the order. Where an individual demonstrates conclusively that the coercion will fail, the contempt power becomes penal and comes within a five-day maximum sentence set by California statute. The case was remanded to determine whether coercion could be justified. In re Farr, 36 Cal.App.3d 577, 111 Cal.Rptr. 649 (1974).

Farr was followed by Rosato v. Superior Court, 51 Cal.App.3d 190, 124 Cal.Rptr. 427 (1975), in which four employees of the *Fresno Bee* were ordered to testify about how they obtained a copy of a grand jury report that had been ordered sealed. The reporters' privilege did not apply to questions directed at learning whether persons under the court's sealing order had violated it. Hearing was denied and a petition for certiorari was denied, 427 U.S. 912 (1976). Two reporters and two editors served 15 days in jail. The judge then held a hearing and concluded that they would not testify. They were found in criminal contempt, sentenced to five-day terms, given credit for time served, and released.

f. Disclosing Information to Other Bodies

Not only do courts ask journalists for information, so do legislatures and administrative agencies. In 1971, the House of Representatives Commerce Committee subpoenaed then-CBS president Frank

Stanton, ordering him to produce portions of film shot for, but not shown on, the documentary "The Selling of the Pentagon." When Stanton refused to give the "outtakes" to the Committee, it voted 25–13 to recommend that Congress issued a contempt citation. The House refused to do so.

Later, Daniel Schorr, a former CBS journalist, obtained a copy of a "secret" report of the House Intelligence Committee concerning the Central Intelligence Agency. He gave the report to the *Village Voice*, which published it in 1976. When asked by the House Ethics Committee to name the person from whom he received the report, Schorr declined. The Committee did not vote to ask for a contempt citation.

In Massachusetts, a television reporter prepared a story on alleged misconduct by a state judge. The state Commission on Judicial Conduct allowed the judge to prepare a defense by asking the reporter to identify those to whom he spoke. Upon his refusal, he was held in contempt. Justice Brennan of the Supreme Court of the United States, acting as Circuit Justice, stayed the imposition of the contempt citation. He pointed to the four dissents and Justice Powell's concurrence in *Branzburg* to suggest "at least a limited First Amendment right to resist intrusion into newsgatherers' confidences. . . ." He believed that at least four Justices would vote to hear the case on appeal. In re Roche, 448 U.S. 1312 (1980). The Massachusetts Supreme Judicial Court, however, citing *Branzburg*, subsequently affirmed the contempt order. In re Roche, 381 Mass. 624, 411 N.E.2d 466 (1980).

g. *The Future of Shield Laws*

There remains substantial disagreement about whether a statutory privilege would be desirable, and, if so, the extent and nature of the privilege. As noted earlier, scholars of the law of evidence tend to oppose all privileges as obstacles to the search for truth. The legal profession has accepted some privileges but has refused to endorse a privilege for reporters. At its February 1974 meeting, the House of Delegates of the American Bar Association voted 157–122 to reject the proposition that a reporter's privilege is essential "to protect the public interest . . . in the free dissemination of news and information to the American people on matters of public importance." Editor & Publisher, Feb. 9, 1974 at 11.

Privilege legislation has also been opposed by a few representatives of the press: in 1974 the *Washington Post* in an editorial argued that the "best shield is the First Amendment, without the supposed reinforcement of even the purest form of shield law." Editor & Publisher, Mar. 30, 1974 at 15. The justification for this position is the belief that Congress has no business legislating about the press, whether protectively or otherwise. If Congress is conceded power to help the press now it may later be assumed to have power to enact legislation hostile to the press. This concern was also raised during the debate over the Newspaper Preservation Act. Those holding this view would prefer to litigate each case in the courts solely in terms of the First Amendment.

This view is likely to produce more litigation than would a statute that provided protection—even if limited to certain types of cases. Some media representatives, particularly those from smaller newspapers and broadcasters, believe a limited statute would help avoid expensive litigation without creating new dangers.

After rejecting the case-by-case approach because of its legal cost and uncertainties, a media lawyer considered objections to legislation in Paul, Why a Shield Law? 29 U.Miami L.Rev. 459 (1975):

> There is, however, the Graham-Knight argument which frets about compromising a basic constitutional right by allowing the legislature to tinker. This problem could be solved by adding two sentences to any shield legislation: "No provision of this act shall be construed to create or imply any limitations upon or otherwise affect any rights secured by the Constitution of the United States. The rights provided by this Act shall be in addition to any rights provided by the Constitution." . . .

> The Graham-Knight theorists are also worried about putting reporters in a special class. This ignores what the first amendment is all about. Gatherers and disseminators of information are already in a special class under the first amendment, as are people who insist on religious freedom. The founding fathers put them there. Of course it would be a terrible mistake to draw shield legislation so narrowly that it would apply only to reporters. A broad, one sentence shield law might serve the purpose:

>> No person shall be required in any federal or state proceeding to disclose either the source of any published or unpublished information obtained for any medium offering communication to the public, or any unpublished information obtained or prepared in gathering or processing information for any public medium of communication.

A shield law should be short, simple, and absolute because it must be a badge which a reporter can carry and completely understand without having to hire a lawyer or go to court. Some individuals, however, have argued that other factors should be balanced against the first amendment to justify shield law exceptions when: (1) the only way to prove that the defendant is innocent is to have the reporter testify; (2) the reporter is the only source concerning a committed crime; or (3) national security is involved. I do not accept any of these exceptions. They would create loopholes which would destroy the privilege and bring us back to the case-by-case method. While this might result in some miscarriages of justice, so does the privilege against self-incrimination. The fact that a person is the only witness to a crime does not mean he is required to waive his privilege against self-incrimination.

Would you support an absolute statute? If not, in which of the situations we have been discussing should reporters be fully protected? Partially protected?

Congress has considered federal shield laws since *Branzburg.* None has been enacted because of the lack of consensus similar to that we have just considered among lawyers, scholars, and journalists.

B. USE OF SEARCH WARRANTS AGAINST THE PRESS

Basically, law enforcement officials may choose from among three methods for obtaining relevant evidence. The first is simply to ask the person who probably has it to turn it over. This technique was used in the AT&T case p. 112, infra. The lack of formality simplifies and expedites the process. The drawback is that if the possessor of the information decides not to cooperate he may legally destroy or transfer possession of the material after learning that the police want it.

The second procedure is the subpoena, discussed in *Branzburg* and *Farber.* Prosecutorial officials ask either the court or grand jury for authority to issue a subpoena for evidence sought in connection with an investigation, or act under delegated authority. The recipient may not legally destroy the material after being served with the subpoena. A recipient who thinks the subpoena asks something illegal, may challenge it. If the recipient claims not to have the material or information being sought, he makes a statement to that effect under oath. It may be difficult to prove whether the person illegally destroyed the material after receiving the subpoena.

The third method, the search warrant, plays the central role in the case involving *The Stanford Daily*, the campus newspaper at Stanford University. A magistrate must decide whether a police request for a search warrant establishes probable cause to believe that the material sought is at the named location. If the magistrate is persuaded, the police may execute the warrant by appearing at the specified location without prior notice and may search the premises until they find the identified material.

Police believed that *Stanford Daily* photographers had taken photographs that would aid in identifying persons who had assaulted policemen during a violent demonstration. The police obtained a search warrant and served it on the *Daily*. After the search, the *Daily* brought an action against the chief of police and other local officials, and the case, Zurcher v. Stanford Daily, 436 U.S. 547 (1978), eventually reached the Supreme Court. Justice White wrote for the majority that valid warrants may be issued to search *any* property, and that even though the Fourth Amendment may protect the materials sought to be seized, nothing in the First Amendment bars searches of newspaper offices.

After the decision, a few states enacted bans on the issuance of search warrants against media, and Congress passed the Privacy Protection Act of 1980, which makes it unlawful for an official of any government to search or seize "any work product material possessed by a person reasonably believed to have a purpose to disseminate to the public a newspaper, book, broadcast, or other similar form of public communication, in or affecting interstate or foreign commerce," except in special circumstances.

Notes and Questions

1. *Telephone Records.* The government may learn about reporters' sources and activities in ways that do not involve search warrants or subpoenas. Reporters Committee for Freedom of the Press v. American Telephone & Telegraph Co., 593 F.2d 1030 (D.C.Cir.1978), involved government requests for records of long distance calls charged to (but perhaps not made to or from) certain telephone numbers. Reporters charged that the First and Fourth Amendments required that subscribers be given notice before AT & T honored the government's request for toll-call records. The court, 2–1, concluded that balancing was not appropriate because "Government access to third-party evidence in the course of a good faith felony investigation in no sense 'abridges' plaintiffs' information-gathering activities." The possibility of bad-faith investigations (to harass reporters) did not warrant prior judicial intervention unless the reporter could establish "a clear and imminent threat of such future misconduct." The dissenter would have afforded reporters the opportunity to have prior judicial decisions made on such requests on a case-by-case basis. Certiorari was denied. 440 U.S. 949 (1979), Brennan, Marshall and Stewart, JJ., dissenting.

2. *Department of Justice Guidelines.* After *Branzburg,* the Attorney General of the United States, in 1973, adopted guidelines to regulate the issuance of subpoenas to members of the news media. The main point was that, except for cooperating reporters, no subpoena could be issued to any member of the news media "without the express authorization of the Attorney General." In requesting such authorization, subordinates were told to do so in criminal cases only if there is reasonable ground to believe that a crime has occurred and that the information sought is essential to a successful investigation, particularly with respect to guilt or innocence, and only after efforts to obtain the information from alternative nonmedia sources have failed. In civil cases, the litigation must be "of substantial importance." Even subpoena authorization requests for publicly disclosed information "should be treated with care to avoid claims of harassment." All requests should be directed at limited subject matter, should cover a limited period of time and "should avoid requiring production of a large volume of unpublished material."

After the Department of Justice, in 1979, obtained records of a reporter's toll calls from the local telephone company, the press urged government attention to the problem. The result was the promulgation, in November, 1980, of amendments to the subpoena guidelines to provide that discussions with the reporter should precede any subpoena to the telephone company where the appropriate Assistant Attorney General concludes that such disclosure would not jeopardize the investigation. Before any subpoena is issued, the "express authorization of the Attorney General" is required. Such authorization should not be requested from the Attorney General unless there is reason to believe a crime has been committed, the need is clear, and alternative investigation steps have been unsuccessfully explored. The reporter should be informed within 45 days (though that may be delayed another 45 days) and the information obtained shall be closely held to prevent unauthorized persons from learning what the records reveal. The amended guidelines, which may be altered by any successor Attorney General, are in 45 Federal Register 76436 (Nov. 19, 1980), are codified in 28 Code of Federal Regulations 50.10, and are reprinted in 6 Media L.Rptr. 2153 (1980).

C. IMPLICATIONS FOR JOURNALISTS

No journalist would want to go through his career in constant fear of a subpoena or a jail term; that sort of "chill" would seriously damage the newsgathering process and the free flow of information to the public. On the other hand, journalists handling sensitive material or dealing with confidences would be foolish not to make themselves aware of the shield law protection or lack thereof in the state(s) in which they work. Journalists sometimes will find that their sources, particularly those in official positions who are experienced at dealing with the press, are themselves familiar with the state shield laws.

Legalities aside, identifiable sources and attributable quotes strengthen good news stories. That is enough reason not to promise confidentiality to every source who asks for such a promise. Even in those instances in which a reporter believes that a pledge of confidentiality is the only way he can get information from a source, he should be certain he has authorization from his employer before making such a promise. As we have seen from the cases, reporters and their employer publications or stations are often "in it together" when a court seeks evidence in their hands. News organizations are well advised to be sure that editors, news directors, reporters, and others are all aware of the organization's policy on confidential sources and information before pledges are made or subpoenas are served.

Although journalists can reasonably expect their employers to be supportive when subpoena problems arise, legal problems can create stress. When a reporter's notes are subpoenaed, who owns the notes—the reporter or his employer?   Absent any formal understanding to the contrary, the employer may assert that he has "bought" them as part of the reporter's work product when the reporter endorsed his pay checks, even though the employer does not normally ask for the notes.   The journalist may be more likely to feel that he has "sold" only his finished stories and that the notes are still his personal property.   Should it make any difference whether the reporter has taken notes in a notebook from the employer's supply room or in a notebook he bought himself?

Obviously, where sensitive material is concerned, journalists should be careful about what materials they create and where they store them.   Generating photocopies of confidential materials or writing memos within the news organization which might reveal or tend to reveal confidential information are examples of creating additional pieces of paper which could be subject to subpoena and should therefore not be done unnecessarily.   Despite the protection against newsroom searches afforded by 1980 Congressional action, a journalist may prefer to keep his most confidential notes or documents away from his office—even away from his home, in a safe deposit box, for instance.   This is not to suggest that paranoia should be the order of the day, and most reporters will never face such problems, but caution is in order for those handling the most sensitive information.

Computers also raise questions.   If the confidential information is stored in the computer, can the journalist be compelled to create a print-out?   In the event of a newsroom search, could the journalist be compelled to give law enforcement agents the password?

Even where there is no subpoena or search, journalists will sometimes find themselves having to make difficult decisions about the release of unpublished (not necessarily confidential) information. Suppose, for example, a newspaper photographer arriving at the scene of a fatal auto accident shoots a 36-exposure roll of film.   Only one of the photos is published in the newspaper.   An insurance company, involved in subsequent litigation, asks the newspaper if it can buy prints of the other photographs, because they are believed to show some details of the accident better than the police photos. Should the newspaper turn over the unpublished photos?   Would doing so be a harmless extension of the newspaper's usual role of disseminating the truth about events?   Would the fact that the newspaper last week turned over unpublished photos of a children's Halloween party to the children play any part in the decision?   Would accident victims or other news subjects be less cooperative with press photographers if they thought the latter might give or sell the photographs for non-journalistic purposes, including use in litigation?

These questions and others relating to the confidentiality problems are difficult to answer.   While it may at first be easy for journalists to say they would go to jail rather than to reveal a source or break a confidence, that becomes more difficult when relatives, neighbors, and friends outside of journalism ask how journalists think they are "above the law" and not subject to the same obligations that other citizens have. And, while a few journalists have briefly become famous by going to jail and have written about the experience, the fact is that the experience is inconvenient and disruptive at the least and quite difficult at the worst.

Chapter XI

NEWSGATHERING FROM PUBLIC SOURCES

Journalists obtain news from government sources and government-controlled places the same way they obtain news of other kinds—by cultivating sources, making phone calls, asking questions, observing. Sometimes government and the people in it are reluctant sources, and the journalist can use legal help in obtaining access to the information. The recognition by the Supreme Court in Richmond Newspapers v. Virginia (see Chapter IX) of a First Amendment right of the public to attend trials is still an unusual recognition of a constitutional protection for newsgathering; more typically, the First Amendment has been recognized only as a right to publish news that one already possesses. Because a constitutional right of newsgathering was far from clearly established, journalists and others interested in observing the workings of government lobbied successfully in the 1960's and later for legislation at both the federal and state levels to provide access to government information.

In this Chapter we consider access to public records, access to public meetings, and access to public places. Refer to the related discussion in Chapter IX on access to courtrooms and to Chapter IV for discussion of access to private places.

A. ACCESS TO PUBLIC RECORDS

1. FREEDOM OF INFORMATION ACT

As long as legislatures were the preeminent lawmakers in the country, persons concerned with government actions could follow the process. With the New Deal, however, vast numbers of administrative agencies and organizations emerged. Congress empowered most to promulgate their own internal rules, to issue substantive regulations, to enforce laws, to adjudicate some controversies, and take other action of great importance to citizens. The sheer number of regulations and orders being promulgated made it difficult to keep track of the process. In addition, some of the agencies were not open about their operations.

In 1946, Congress passed the Administrative Procedure Act to require all administrative agencies to follow certain procedures in the adoption of regulations and in their adjudicative hearings. Congress also sought to make the internal rules and procedures of agencies more readily available to the public.

For a variety of reasons, this first effort at openness was not notably successful. In 1967, Congress responded to growing criticism by adopting the first version of the Freedom of Information Act. The FOIA was amended in 1974 to expand its scope.   5 U.S.C.A. § 552.

The FOIA applies to all federal government agencies except Congress, the courts, the government of the District of Columbia, and courts martial or the military during wartime.   The Act requires each agency to publish in the Federal Register a description of its organization and a list of its personnel through whom the public can obtain information.   Each agency must also explain the procedures by which it will furnish information.   Each agency must make available to the public staff manuals and internal instructions that affect members of the public, final opinions in adjudicated cases, and current indexes.

Agencies may set reasonable fees for finding and copying material requested by the public.   These fees are to be waived when the information will be of primary benefit to the general public.

Agencies must respond quickly to requests for information. Should an agency not comply with the FOIA, a member of the public may ask a federal district court to enforce the act.   The court may review in private the material the agency wishes to withhold, but it is the agency that bears the burden of showing that the material may be withheld under one of the exemptions to the Act discussed below. If the court decides the information should be released, it can order the government to pay all costs associated with the court action. Additionally, the agency employee who authorized the improper withholding of the information may be punished.

The FOIA contains nine exemptions—categories of material that need not be made available to the public.   Several of these exemptions were amended in 1974 to require more material to be given to the public.   The current exemptions are:

(b) This section does not apply to matters that are—

(1)(A) specifically authorized under criteria established by an Executive order to be kept secret in the interest of national defense or foreign policy and (B) are in fact properly classified pursuant to such Executive order;

(2) related solely to the internal personnel rules and practices of an agency;

(3) specifically exempted from disclosure by statute (other than [the Privacy Act]), provided that such statute (A) requires that the matters be withheld from the public in such a manner as to leave no discretion on the issue, or (B) establishes particular criteria for withholding or refers to particular types of matters to be withheld;

(4) trade secrets and commercial or financial information obtained from a person and privileged or confidential;

(5) inter-agency or intra-agency memorandums or letters which would not be available by law to a party other than an agency in litigation with the agency;

(6) personnel and medical files and similar files the disclosure of which would constitute a clearly unwarranted invasion of personal privacy;

(7) investigatory records compiled for law enforcement purposes, but only to the extent that the production of such records would (A) interfere with enforcement proceedings, (B) deprive a person of a right to a fair trial or an impartial adjudication, (C) constitute an unwarranted invasion of personal privacy, (D) disclose the identity of a confidential source and, in the case of a record compiled by a criminal law enforcement authority in the course of a criminal investigation, or by an agency conducting a lawful national security intelligence investigation, confidential information furnished only by the confidential source, (E) disclose investigative techniques and procedures, or (F) endanger the life or physical safety of law enforcement personnel;

(8) contained in or related to examination, operating, or condition reports prepared by, on behalf of, or for the use of an agency responsible for the regulation or supervision of financial institutions; or

(9) geological and geophysical information and data, including maps, concerning wells.

[Any reasonably segregable portion of a record must be provided to any person requesting such record after deletion of the portions that are exempt under this subsection.]

Notes and Questions

1. Notice that nothing in the Act gives any special rights to the press as opposed to the public generally. Is that surprising?

2. What appear to be the critical limitations of the Act?

3. Needless to say, each exemption has produced its share of litigation. Those causing the most difficulty appear to be the first, third, fifth, and seventh exemptions. In some cases amendments have already altered interpretations when Congress disagreed with a judicial interpretation. The procedures under the Act can get quite complicated. Several organizations have prepared handbooks that provide guidance through the process.

The Supreme Court has had occasion to pass on several cases interpreting the Act. These are often technical in nature and not particularly useful for our purposes. It does not seem rewarding to recount these battles except to report that the courts are having difficulty with the Act.

2. THE PRIVACY ACT

The movement toward openness in government has been tempered by growing concern about the dangers to individual privacy resulting from the growing number of records and federal agencies keeping records. In response to these concerns, Congress passed the Privacy Act of 1974. 5 U.S.C. § 552a. One major part of the Act permits subjects of records to see their files, obtain copies, and to correct inaccuracies. The individual is not required to give the agency any reason for wanting to see his file. Civil actions may be brought for improper refusals to provide the file and for improper refusals to make corrections.

The part of the Act of most interest to the press, however, is the part that restricts disclosure of the contents of records unless certain conditions are met:

(b) Conditions of disclosure.—No agency shall disclose any record which is contained in a system of records by any means of communication to any person, or to another agency, except pursuant to a written request by, or with the prior written consent of, the individual to whom the record pertains, unless disclosure of the record would be—

(1) to those officers and employees of the agency which maintains the record who have a need for the record in the performance of their duties;

(2) required under section 552 of this title [FOIA];

(3) for a routine use as defined . . .;

(4) to the Bureau of the Census for purposes of planning or carrying out a census or survey or related activity . . .;

(5) to a recipient who has provided the agency with advance adequate written assurance that the record will be used solely as a statistical research or reporting record, and the record is to be transferred in a form that is not individually identifiable;

(6) to the National Archives of the United States as a record which has sufficient historical or other value to warrant its continued preservation by the United States Government, or for evaluation by the Administrator of General Services or his designee to determine whether the record has such value;

(7) to another agency or to an instrumentality of any governmental jurisdiction within or under the control of the United States for a civil or criminal law enforcement activity if the activity is authorized by law, and if the head of the agency or instrumentality has made a written request to the agency which maintains the record specifying the particular

portion desired and the law enforcement activity for which the record is sought;

(8) to a person pursuant to a showing of compelling circumstances affecting the health or safety of an individual if upon such disclosure notification is transmitted to the last known address of such individual;

(9) to either House of Congress, or, to the extent of matter within its jurisdiction, any committee or subcommittee thereof, any joint committee of Congress or subcommittee of any such joint committee;

(10) to the Comptroller General, or any of his authorized representatives, in the course of the performance of the duties of the General Accounting Office; or

(11) pursuant to the order of a court of competent jurisdiction.

Attempts by the Reagan administration in the 1980's to reduce disclosure of information by the federal government under the Freedom of Information Act have also had an impact on use of the Privacy Act as a reason for non-disclosure.

3. STATE OPEN RECORDS STATUTES

Although they vary a great deal, state access to information statutes exist in every state, and they are frequently parallel to the federal statute by beginning with a premise that all government records should be publicly available and then listing a series of exceptions or exemptions. These statutes are generally still new enough that they are subject to frequent amendment, and journalists are well advised to obtain copies of the open records statute for their state to see just what is available.

4. USING THE STATUTES

Freedom of information legislation can sometimes be helpful to a journalist—or, for that matter, any other member of the public seeking information—but that is not to say that it is frequently relied upon by the average journalist covering government. Establishing a good relationship with friendly sources inside government is a much more common way of obtaining information than using the statutes. When, however, the information would otherwise be unavailable, the reporter needs to know how to use the statute.

Freedom of information requests often have to be put into writing. Requestors of information are advised to make their requests as simple as possible, specify the records wanted as specifically as possible, cite the statute under which the records are sought, ask to whom an appeal should be addressed should access to the records be denied, and either put a dollar limit on the amount he is willing to pay or ask to be advised of the cost before the request is filled.

Even with attempts to strengthen the federal statute in 1974 and the state statutes in other years, a number of problems remain. Among those most frequently cited are (1) charging excessive fees for the records, (2) taking delays in filling requests, (3) demanding unreasonable specificity in identifying the records sought, (4) contaminating otherwise releasable records by filing them with classified information, and (5) applying the exemptions too broadly.

Regrettable though it may be, it is a fact of life that the level of compliance with the state statutes is sometimes a factor of the level of government from which information is sought. Small town officials are still heard to deny access to information and to respond to mentions of their states' freedom of information laws by saying, "That's just some law passed in the state capital. What are they going to do to me about it?" With few penalties built into the state laws for non-compliance and little enforcement, the freedom of information legislation still has a long way to go before it becomes very helpful from the journalists' point of view.

B. ACCESS TO PUBLIC MEETINGS

Guidelines for access to meetings of Congress or its committees and access to information about Congressional proceedings are prescribed initially in the Constitution. (Art. I, § 5):

Each House may determine the Rules of its Proceedings. . . . Each House shall keep a Journal of its Proceedings, and from time to time publish the same, excepting such Parts as may in their Judgment require Secrecy; and the Yeas and Nays of the Members of either House on any question shall, at the Desire of one fifth of those Present, be entered on the Journal.

From the earliest days, sessions of the full House or Senate have usually been open to the public. Senate sessions were occasionally closed for discussion of treaties or nominations, and in the 30 years between 1945 and 1975, the Senate held 17 closed sessions, devoted usually to foreign relations or defense questions. Guide to the Congress of the United States 73 (2d ed. 1976).

Although most sessions of the full House and Senate have been open, most committee meetings were closed unless hearings were being held. Since 1970, there has been a sharp increase in open committee meetings, extending first to mark-up sessions (in which a pending bill may be approved, amended or rewritten), and later to conference committee meetings in which representatives of the two houses try to reconcile two different versions of proposed legislation. In 1975 the House and Senate voted to require open conferences unless a majority of conferees from either chamber vote in public to close a session. Can such negotiations be conducted effectively in open sessions? Should all meetings of all committees and subcommittees be open?

A different problem arises out of the conduct of Congressional investigations. The power to legislate implies the power to inquire into subjects that may require legislation and allows Congress to conduct investigations and hold hearings. Congress may compel the attendance of witnesses and the production of documents at these hearings under threat of citation for contempt. The arguments against open hearings do not involve national security or the inhibiting effect of publicity on legislative compromise. Rather they reflect a concern for the privacy of witnesses and those whose behavior is under scrutiny. The advent of television coverage of some Congressional hearings has made this concern more significant and has led to some restrictions on coverage.

1. The "Sunshine" Act

At the urging of Congressmen and Senators from Florida, which had had good experience with its "Sunshine" Law, Congress, in 1976, passed a federal "Government in the Sunshine Act." 5 U.S.C. § 552b. The statement of purpose accompanying the Act declares that "the public is entitled to the fullest practicable information regarding the decision-making processes of the Federal Government." The Act sought to "provide the public with such information while protecting the rights of individuals and the ability of the Government to carry out its responsibilities."

Essentially, the Act provides that all federal agencies headed by boards of two or more persons appointed by the President—approximately 50 agencies—must hold "every portion of every meeting" open to the public. Adequate advance notice must be given of each meeting. Even if a meeting is closed because it falls within one of the ten exemptions to be noted, the agency must make public a transcript or minutes of all parts of the meeting that do not contain exempt material. Meetings may be closed only after a publicly recorded vote of a majority of the full membership of the agency.

The exemptions apply where the agency "properly determines" that a portion of its meeting "is likely to" result in the disclosure of specified information. The exemptions include verbatim copies of several FOIA exemptions—(1) involving national defense or foreign policy; (2) involving internal rules and practices of the agency; (3) matters specifically exempted from disclosure by another statute; (4) trade secrets; (7) law enforcement investigatory records; and (8) involving financial institutions. In addition, another exemption tracks very closely the "clearly unwarranted invasion of personal privacy" language of the sixth exemption of the FOIA. Given the similar goals of the two statutes it is not surprising that they contain similar exemptions.

In addition, the Sunshine Act contains the following summarized exemptions not found in the FOIA:

(5) disclosures that "involve accusing any person of a crime, or formally censuring any person;"

(9) "premature disclosures" involving agencies that regulate currencies, securities, commodities, or financial institutions, where the disclosure would be likely to (i) lead to "significant financial speculation" in these items or (ii) "significantly endanger the financial stability of any financial institution" or where the disclosure would be likely to "significantly frustrate implementation of a proposed agency action."

(10) information concerning an agency's issuance of a subpoena or its participation in a civil action or proceeding.

2. STATE OPEN MEETINGS STATUTES

Clearly, less governmental business is conducted by the state legislature than by the multitude of agencies created by the legislature or by the executive branch under legislative authorization. In an effort to bring these agencies and their decision-making processes under public scrutiny many state legislatures have adopted "open meeting" or "sunshine" laws. These vary greatly and are summarized in "State Open Meeting Laws: An Overview" by Prof. John B. Adams (Freedom of Information Foundation Series No. 3, July, 1974).

Enforcement provisions of the state laws vary. Some statutes provide that actions improperly taken in closed meetings can be declared null and void. Journalists generally favor fines or other penalties for public officials who disregard the open meetings statutes.

C. ACCESS TO PUBLIC PLACES

In addition to keeping records and holding meetings, governments also control access to their owned or leased buildings and grounds. No general legislation covers these situations. Instead, each has been handled under regulations issued by the person in control or by specific departments of the government, such as the Bureau of Prisons.

For example, in 1974, President Ford excluded all reporters from mingling with guests at White House receptions. In 1975, he announced new rules under which a small pool of reporters, carrying only notebooks, might circulate at such events "with the understanding that the pool reporters will respect the privacy of personal communications between myself or Mrs. Ford and our guests." Editor & Publisher, Sept. 13, 1975 at 15.

In 1979 when President Carter took a steamer trip down the Mississippi River, he set rules for reporters who wished to accompany him: that the White House must approve all photographs, that no photos be bought from tourists, and that national organizations not distribute photos taken by local photographers along the way. As a result, several organizations refused to send their staffs on the trip. N.Y. Times, Aug. 15, 1979 at A18. These conditions are enforced, if challenged, by White House security personnel or by physical barriers.

Access and Terrorism. Recent terrorist activity has shown the tension between the efforts of the press to gather news and the desire of law enforcement officials to isolate the terrorists and to prevent them from learning in advance what action the police are planning to take. The problem is, of course, aggravated if the terrorists have taken hostages whose lives are now in danger. Some have suggested that reporters covering such events receive training in psychology so that they understand the impact their coverage may have on the situation itself. Some police officials have proposed guidelines for handling future episodes, such as requiring that broadcast journalists be kept farther from the scene than are print reporters so that officials could brief the print press without risking the possibility that important information would reach the terrorists prematurely.

Many reporters have objected to plans that keep reporters from the scene. They urge that the matter be left to the sense of responsibility of the reporters. One journalist has said that "suppressing news of terrorism would be a denial of democracy that could take more lives than it saves. It is unworkable and philosophically unthinkable." The Quill (Dec. 1977) at 23.

Much discussion followed the seizure by Hanafi Muslims of B'nai B'rith headquarters in Washington, D.C. in 1977. Among the hostages taken was a reporter. His views are expressed in Fenyvesi, Looking Into the Muzzle of Terrorists, The Quill (July-Aug. 1977) at 16. In discussing the tension between newsgathering and the safety of hostages, he cited three "egregious examples" of press behavior during the siege. One involved a group of persons who had eluded the terrorists and had hidden, undiscovered, on a lower floor. A reporter saw a basket of supplies being lifted to a floor not known to be inhabited. The reporter's story to that effect was heard by supporters of the terrorists who informed those in the building, who then sought—but failed—to capture the group.

The second example involved a reporter who asked the leader whether he had set a deadline for compliance with his demands—at a time when the police and "all the other experts had thought that the absence of a deadline was one encouraging sign." In the third example, a reporter suggested over the telephone to the leader that the police were trying "to trick" him and "pulling a fast one" while pretending to negotiate in good faith. The leader "flew into a rage" and selected ten older male hostages for execution if the police tried

to fool him.   Several other articles in the same issue of The Quill
discuss other aspects of covering terrorism.

Although the wisdom of police action in these episodes is much
debated, there has been little legal challenge to police decisions that
prevent reporters from entering the building in question or getting
too close to the building.   Almost all states have statutes that
authorize police to bar access and provide that failure to obey an
order to remain outside is punishable as failing to obey lawful police
orders.

Obeying Lawful Orders.   The same principles would appear to
apply when a reporter has lawfully entered an area—and is then
asked to leave because of danger or for some other reason.   The
issue is analyzed in State v. Lashinsky, 81 N.J. 1, 404 A.2d 1121
(1979).   In a fatal freeway accident, a car left the road, ran down an
embankment and overturned.   Lashinsky, a news photographer,
came upon the scene and, believing that the event was worthy of
news coverage, parked 150 feet away, put his press card in his
windshield, walked toward the wreckage and began taking several
photographs.   Fifteen or 20 minutes later a state trooper arrived.
By this time 40 or 50 people had gathered.   A member of a local first
aid squad that had reached the scene before the trooper reported that
there were casualties.   A seriously injured girl, who was going into
shock, was pinned inside the automobile against the corpse of her
mother who had been decapitated.

The trooper returned to his car and radioed for an ambulance and
more police.   On returning to the scene he noticed gas and oil were
leaking from the car and that the battery had cracked open.   In
addition, much personal property was strewn around the site.   Fear-
ing a fire and wanting to protect the property and preserve the area
for investigation, the trooper ordered everyone not involved in first
aid to leave the area.   Lashinsky and some others refused.   The
trooper asked Lashinsky individually to leave.   He retreated five feet
but refused to move further.   When he showed his press pass issued
by the state police, the trooper said "I don't care at this point" and
again asked him to leave.   There was evidence that the reporter then
engaged the trooper in a heated argument lasting three or more
minutes telling the trooper to "do his own job and let Lashinsky do
his."

Lashinsky was arrested and convicted of violating a statute
providing that "Any person who in any place, public or private . . .
obstructs, molests or interferes with any person lawfully therein
. . . is a disorderly person."   The conviction was affirmed, 4–3.
Although not directly addressing the situation of a policeman's orders, the statute was broad enough to cover the "interference"
involved in this case.   The photographer's failure to obey prevented
the first aid team from getting the trooper's assistance in their work
and kept the trooper from helping.   The court held that the statute

had been violated. In passing it noted that an officer could not make someone a criminal simply by issuing an order. In each case there must be "an assessment of defendant's actions in light of *all* the surrounding circumstances—the activity giving rise to a policeman's order, the reasonableness of that order itself and the defendant's reaction to it." The conditions were met in this case because of the fire danger, property strewn around, the need to preserve the area for investigation, and the crowd control problem faced by a single officer.

The reporter then argued that the statute did not apply to him because he was a member of the press. The majority said that an officer who is made aware that a member of the press is gathering news should "be mindful that such an individual has a legitimate and proper reason to be where he is and, if possible, this important interest should be accommodated." But here, the officer "virtually working alone, could not, in his professional judgment, have permitted defendant to remain, even as a member of the press, and still discharged his own paramount responsibilities for the safety and welfare of those who were his immediate concern." Under these circumstances the reporter was obligated to retreat. Although under state law a right to gather news is protected, "the liberty which the press seeks to assure our people can be meaningfully enjoyed only in a society where there is an adequate measure or order."

Finally, the majority held the statute was not unconstitutionally vague.

Justice Pashman agreed with the standard being used but dissented from its application to this case. He found no "interference" or "obstruction" by the reporter. "Defendant's actions . . . constitute the precise type of conduct in which any media photographer must engage if he is to adequately report a news event." The justice concluded that although the order was reasonable as to non-media bystanders his request to the defendant "although given in good faith, was clearly unreasonable." Since the original order to withdraw was unreasonable as to the defendant, he could not be punished for standing up for his rights against it.

A major disagreement between the majority and Justice Pashman involved the role of the bystanders. The trooper testified that when he asked people to clear the scene 15 or 20 bystanders stayed with defendant. Apparently, the trooper was concerned that if Lashinsky stayed some bystanders would stay and perhaps others would return. The dissenter argued that in such a case the trooper may properly arrest the bystanders. But it "would be absurd to rule that a media representative forfeits this special access right merely because others over whose actions he has no control refuse to abide by a reasonable police request."

Finally, since the trooper knew defendant was a member of the press, the trooper should have realized that defendant was "sufficiently mature to evaluate the safety risks posed by the overturned vehicle and to position himself so as to minimize those risks. This is not to say that newsmen must be allowed access to any site, no matter what the risk of harm might be. Where, however, as in the present case, the risk is not substantial, a media representative should be allowed to situate himself" near the vehicle, according to Justice Pashman.

The other two dissenters agreed with the majority that the defendant's conduct "hardly brings credit or distinction to the press." Nonetheless, his "arrogant behavior" did not violate the criminal statute under which he was charged because that requires a "physical interference." They argued that the state could punish Lashinsky's behavior but had not passed an appropriate statute prior to this case.

After this case arose, but before the decision, the legislature did pass a statute providing: "A person in a gathering commits a petty disorderly persons offense if he refuses to obey a reasonable official request or order to move: (1) To prevent obstruction of a highway or other public passage; or (2) To maintain public safety by dispersing those gathered in dangerous proximity to a fire or other hazard . . . ."

Of course, a state may, if it wishes, provide special access rights for reporters. Under California Penal Code, § 409(a), for example, whenever "a menace to the public health or safety is created by a calamity such as flood, storm, fire, earthquake, explosion, accident or other disaster, [a law enforcement officer] may close the area where the menace exists for the duration thereof by means of ropes, markers or guards to any and all persons not authorized by such officer to enter or remain within the closed area."

Subsection (b) provides for closing areas around any "emergency field command post" established as the result of a calamity "or any riot or other civil disturbance."

Subsection (d), however, provides that "nothing in this section shall prevent a duly authorized representative of any news service . . . from entering the areas closed pursuant to this section."

Access to Prisons. As we saw in some detail at p. 353, supra, a series of Supreme Court cases suggested a possible right to receive information separate from the interest of the speaker or supplier of that information. In 1974, the Supreme Court decided two companion cases involving efforts to obtain information from inmates confined in prisons. Pell v. Procunier, 417 U.S. 817 (1974), involved a ban on press interviews with named inmates in the California prison system. Saxbe v. Washington Post Co., 417 U.S. 843 (1974), involved a similar ban in the federal prison system. The Court concluded in *Pell* that the security and penological considerations of incarceration were sufficient to justify rejection of the inmates' claims that the interview ban violated their First Amendment rights.

Justice Stewart, writing for the Court in *Pell* and in *Saxbe*, then turned to the claims raised by the press. He noted that "this regulation is not part of an attempt by the State to conceal the conditions in its prisons or to frustrate the press' investigation and reporting of those conditions." Reporters could visit the institutions and "speak about any subject to any inmates whom they might encounter." Interviews with inmates selected at random were also permitted and both the press and the public could take tours through the prisons. "In short, members of the press enjoy access to California prisons that is not available to other members of the public." Indeed, the only apparent restriction was the one being challenged.

The majority placed great weight on Branzburg v. Hayes, 408 U.S. 665 (1972), involving the question of a reporter's privilege not to disclose confidential information to grand juries. We considered this case at length in Chapter X. *Branzburg* contained a passage that said:

> It has generally been held that the First Amendment does not guarantee the press a constitutional right of special access to information not available to the public generally . . . . Despite the fact that newsgathering may be hampered, the press is regularly excluded from grand jury proceedings, our own conferences, the meetings of other official bodies in executive session, and the meetings of private organizations. Newsmen have no constitutional right of access to the scenes of crime or disaster when the general public is excluded.

This passage led Justice Stewart to add: "Similarly, newsmen have no constitutional right of access to prisons or their inmates beyond that afforded the general public." He reached this conclusion even though another part of *Branzburg* had observed that "without some protection for seeking out the news, freedom of the press could be eviscerated." Justice Stewart continued:

> The First and Fourteenth Amendments bar government from interfering in any way with a free press. The Constitution does not, however, require government to accord the press special access to information not shared by members of the public generally. It is one thing to say that a journalist is free to seek out sources of information not available to members of the general public, that he is entitled to some constitutional protection of the confidentiality of such sources, cf. Branzburg v. Hayes, supra, and that government cannot restrain the publication of news emanating from such sources. Cf. N.Y. Times v. United States, supra. It is quite another thing to suggest that the Constitution imposes upon government the affirmative duty to make available to journalists sources of information not available to members of the public generally. That proposition finds

no support in the words of the Constitution or in any decision of this Court. Accordingly, since § 415.071 does not deny the press access to sources of information available to members of the general public, we hold that it does not abridge the protections that the First and Fourteenth Amendments guarantee.

Four Justices dissented on the press question. Justice Powell (writing in dissent in *Saxbe*) asserted:

> The specific issue here is whether the Bureau's prohibition of prisoner-press interviews gives rise to a claim of constitutional dimensions. The interview ban is categorical in nature. Its consequence is to preclude accurate and effective reporting on prison conditions and inmate grievances. These subjects are not privileged or confidential. The Government has no legitimate interest in preventing newsmen from obtaining the information that they may learn through personal interviews or from reporting their findings to the public. Quite to the contrary, federal prisons are public institutions. The administration of these institutions, the effectiveness of their rehabilitative programs, the conditions of confinement that they maintain, and the experiences of the individuals incarcerated therein are all matters of legitimate societal interest and concern. . . .
>
> . . .
>
> . . . An informed public depends on accurate and effective reporting by the news media. No individual can obtain for himself the information needed for the intelligent discharge of his political responsibilities. For most citizens the prospect of personal familiarity with newsworthy events is hopelessly unrealistic. In seeking out the news the press therefore acts as an agent of the public at large. It is the means by which the people receive that free flow of information and ideas essential to intelligent self-government. By enabling the public to assert meaningful control over the political process, the press performs a crucial function in effecting the societal purpose of the First Amendment. . . .
>
> This constitutionally established role of the news media is directly implicated here. For good reasons, unrestrained public access is not permitted. The people must therefore depend on the press for information concerning public institutions. The Bureau's absolute prohibition of prisoner-press interviews negates the ability of the press to discharge that function and thereby substantially impairs the right of the people to a free flow of information and ideas on the conduct of their Government. The underlying right is the right of the public generally. The press is the necessary representative of the public's interest in this context and the instrumentality which effects the public's right. I therefore conclude that the Bureau's ban against per-

sonal interviews must be put to the test of First Amendment review.

> There seems to be little question that "big wheels" do exist and that their capacity to influence their fellow inmates may have a negative impact on the correctional environment of penal institutions. . . .

Justice Powell concluded, however, that prison authorities could handle that situation by narrow rules barring interviews with inmates under disciplinary suspension and limiting the number of interviews with any given inmate within a specified time period.

The Bureau of Prisons also argued that a case-by-case assessment of each interview request would be administratively burdensome and correctionally unsound. Justice Powell responded that the Bureau could meet its obligations by promulgating rules setting up reasonable restrictions on the time, place and manner of conducting interviews much as it was already doing in the case of interviews with family, friends, attorneys and clergy. Finally, the Bureau objected that it was difficult to tell "who constitutes the press." Justice Powell responded that although the concept was vague and many might claim to be included, the Bureau could define the term in a rule like the one it was already using for another purpose: "A newspaper entitled to second class mailing privileges; a magazine or periodical of general distribution; a national or international news service; a radio or television network or station." If too many qualified persons wanted interviews, Justice Powell suggested that media representatives might form pools as they do for news events when press access is limited.

Justices Brennan and Marshall joined Justice Powell's dissent. They also joined a dissent by Justice Douglas that emphasized the absolute nature of the ban and the importance of the information.

As emerged in later cases, the majority opinions in *Pell* and *Saxbe* contained a serious ambiguity. If the First Amendment did not authorize a right of access in these cases, why did it matter that the prisons had generally operated quite openly? In other words, was the majority decision based on the fact that the prisons in these cases already were fairly generous in allowing outsiders to visit, or on the view that no right of access could be found in the Constitution? Subsequent cases reveal a second ambiguity—does the press lose these cases because it is asking for a special privilege that members of the general public do not have? If members of the public had sought entry to interview a specific named and willing prisoner, and the prison authorities had responded in the same fashion, would the Supreme Court majority have written its opinion any differently?

A few years later, the Supreme Court returned to the prison question in a slightly different context.

HOUCHINS v. KQED, INC.

Supreme Court of the United States, 1978.
438 U.S. 1, 98 S.Ct. 2588, 57 L.Ed.2d 553.

[A suicide occurred at the Alameda County Jail at Santa Rita, California. KQED, licensee of a television station in nearby San Francisco, reported the story and quoted a psychiatrist as saying that conditions at the Little Greystone building were responsible for the illnesses of his patient-prisoners at the jail. In an earlier proceeding, a federal judge had ruled that the conditions at Greystone constituted cruel and unusual punishment. Houchins, the county sheriff, refused to admit a camera crew KQED sent to get the story and to photograph the facilities, including Greystone. At the time, no public tours of the jail were permitted.

KQED and the NAACP filed suit under 42 U.S.C. § 1983 claiming violation of their First Amendment rights. The NAACP claimed that information about the jail was essential to permit public debate on jail conditions in Alameda County. The complaint requested preliminary and permanent injunctions to prevent the sheriff from "excluding KQED news personnel from the Greystone cells and Santa Rita facilities and generally preventing full and accurate news coverage of the conditions prevailing therein."

Shortly after suit was filed, the sheriff announced a program of monthly tours. The press received advance notice, and several reporters, including one from KQED, went on the first tour. Each tour was limited to 25 persons and did not include Little Greystone. Cameras and tape recorders were barred, though the sheriff did supply photographs of some parts of the jail. Tour members "were not permitted to interview inmates and inmates were generally removed from view."

KQED argued that the tours were unsatisfactory because advance scheduling prevented timely access and because photography and interviewing were barred. The sheriff defended his policy on grounds of "inmate privacy," the danger of creating "jail celebrities" who would "undermine jail security," and the concern that unscheduled tours would "disrupt jail operations."

The district judge issued a preliminary injunction barring the sheriff from denying access to "responsible representatives" of the news media "at reasonable times and hours" and "from preventing KQED news personnel and responsible representatives of the news media from utilizing photographic and sound equipment or from utilizing inmate interviews in providing full and accurate coverage of the Santa Rita facilities." He found that a more flexible policy was "both desirable and attainable" without danger to prison discipline. The court of appeals, in three separate opinions, rejected the sheriff's argument that *Pell* and *Saxbe* controlled, and affirmed the injunction.]

MR. CHIEF JUSTICE BURGER announced the judgment of the Court and delivered an opinion, in which MR. JUSTICE WHITE and MR. JUSTICE REHNQUIST joined.

The question presented is whether the news media have a constitutional right of access to a county jail, over and above that of other persons, to interview inmates and make sound recordings, films, and photographs for publication and broadcasting by newspapers, radio and television.

. . .

III

We can agree with many of the respondents' generalized assertions; conditions in jails and prisons are clearly matters "of great public importance." Pell v. Procunier, supra, at 830 n. 7. Penal facilities are public institutions which require large amounts of public funds, and their mission is crucial in our criminal justice system. Each person placed in prison becomes in effect, a ward of the state for whom society assumes broad responsibility. It is equally true that with greater information, the public can more intelligently form opinions about prison conditions. Beyond question, the role of the media is important; acting as the "eyes and ears" of the public, they can be a powerful and constructive force, contributing to remedial action in the conduct of public business. They have served that function since the beginning of the Republic, but like all other components of our society media representatives are subject to limits.

The media are not a substitute for or an adjunct of government, and like the courts, they are "ill-equipped" to deal with problems of prison administration. Cf. Procunier v. Martinez, [ ]. We must not confuse the role of the media with that of government; each has special, crucial functions each complementing—and, sometimes conflicting with—the other.

The public importance of conditions in penal facilities and the media's role of providing information afford no basis for reading into the Constitution a right of the public or the media to enter these institutions, with camera equipment, and take moving and still pictures of inmates for broadcast purposes. This Court has never intimated a First Amendment guarantee of a right of access to all sources of information within government control. Nor does the rationale of the decisions upon which respondents rely lead to the implication of such a right.

. . .

The right to *receive* ideas and information is not the issue in this case. [ ] The issue is a claimed special privilege of access which the Court rejected in *Pell* and *Saxbe*, a right which is not essential to guarantee the freedom to communicate or publish.

IV

. . .

Unarticulated but implicit in the assertion that media access to the jail is essential for informed public debate on jail conditions is the assumption that media personnel are the best qualified persons for the task of discovering malfeasance in public institutions. But that assumption finds no support in the decisions of this Court or the First Amendment. Editors and newsmen who inspect a jail may decide to publish or not to publish what information they acquire. [ ] Public bodies and public officers, on the other hand, may be coerced by public opinion to disclose what they might prefer to conceal. No comparable pressures are available to anyone to compel publication by the media of what they might prefer not to make known.

There is no discernible basis for a constitutional duty to disclose, or for standards governing disclosure of or access to information. Because the Constitution affords no guidelines, absent statutory standards, hundreds of judges would, under the Court of Appeals' approach, be at large to fashion ad hoc standards, in individual cases, according to their own ideas of what seems "desirable" or "expedient." We, therefore, reject the Court of Appeals' conclusory assertion that the public and the media have a First Amendment right to government information regarding the conditions of jails and their inmates and presumably all other public facilities such as hospitals and mental institutions.

"There is no constitutional right to have access to particular government information, or to require openness from the bureaucracy. [Citing Pell v. Procunier, supra.] The public's interest in knowing about its government is protected by the guarantee of a Free Press, but the protection is indirect. The Constitution itself is neither a Freedom of Information Act nor an Official Secrets Act.

"The Constitution, in other words, establishes the contest, not its resolution. Congress may provide a resolution, at least in some instances, through carefully drawn legislation. For the rest, we must rely, as so often in our system we must, on the tug and pull of the political forces in American society." Stewart, "Or of the Press," 26 Hastings L.J. 631, 636 (1975).

Petitioner cannot prevent respondents from learning about jail conditions in a variety of ways, albeit not as conveniently as they might prefer. Respondents have a First Amendment right to receive letters from inmates criticizing jail officials and reporting on conditions. See Procunier v. Martinez, [ ]. Respondents are free to interview those who render the legal assistance to which inmates are entitled. See id., at 419. They are also free to seek out former inmates, visitors to the prison, public officials, and institutional personnel, as they sought out the complaining psychiatrist here.

Moreover, California statutes currently provide for a prison Board of Corrections that has the authority to inspect jails and prisons and *must* provide a public report at regular intervals. . . .

Neither the First Amendment nor the Fourteenth Amendment mandates a right of access to government information or sources of information within the government's control. Under our holdings in *Pell* [and *Saxbe*], until the political branches decree otherwise, as they are free to do, the media have no special right of access to the Alameda County Jail different from or greater than that accorded the public generally.

The judgment of the Court of Appeals is reversed and the case is remanded for further proceedings.

Reversed.

MR. JUSTICE MARSHALL and MR. JUSTICE BLACKMUN took no part in the consideration or decision of this case.

MR. JUSTICE STEWART, concurring in the judgment.

I agree that the preliminary injunction issued against the petitioner was unwarranted, and therefore concur in the judgment. In my view, however, KQED was entitled to injunctive relief of more limited scope.

The First and Fourteenth Amendments do not guarantee the public a right of access to information generated or controlled by government, nor do they guarantee the press any basic right of access superior to that of the public generally. The Constitution does no more than assure the public and the press equal access once government has opened its doors. Accordingly, I agree substantially with what the opinion of The Chief Justice has to say on that score.

We part company, however, in applying these abstractions to the facts of this case. Whereas he appears to view "equal access" as meaning access that is identical in all respects, I believe that the concept of equal access must be accorded more flexibility in order to accommodate the practical distinctions between the press and the general public.

When on assignment, a journalist does not tour a jail simply for his own edification. He is there to gather information to be passed on to others, and his mission is protected by the Constitution for very specific reasons. "Enlightened choice by an informed citizenry is the basic ideal upon which an open society is premised . . . ." Branzburg v. Hayes, 408 U.S. 665, 726 (dissenting opinion). Our society depends heavily on the press for that enlightenment. . . .

That the First Amendment speaks separately of freedom of speech and freedom of the press is no constitutional accident, but an acknowledgment of the critical role played by the press in American society. The Constitution requires sensitivity to that role, and to the special needs of the press in performing it effectively. A person touring Santa Rita Jail can grasp its reality with his own eyes and ears. But if a television reporter is to convey the jail's sights and sounds to those who cannot personally visit the place, he must use cameras and sound equipment. In short, terms of access that are reasonably imposed on individual members of the public may, if they impede effective reporting without sufficient justification, be unreasonable as applied to journalists who are there to convey to the general public what the visitors see.

Under these principles, KQED was clearly entitled to some form of preliminary injunctive relief. At the time of the District Court's decision, members of the public were permitted to visit most parts of the Santa Rita Jail, and the First and Fourteenth Amendments required the Sheriff to give members of the press *effective* access to the same areas. The Sheriff evidently assumed that he could fulfill this obligation simply by allowing reporters to sign up for tours on the same terms as the public. I think he was mistaken in this assumption, as a matter of constitutional law.

The District Court found that the press required access to the jail on a more flexible and frequent basis than scheduled monthly tours if it was to keep the public informed. By leaving the "specific methods of implementing such a policy . . . [to] Sheriff Houchins," the Court concluded that the press could be allowed access to the jail "at reasonable times and hours" without causing undue disruption. The District Court also found that the media required cameras and recording equipment for effective presentation to the viewing public of the conditions at the jail seen by individual visitors, and that their use could be kept consistent with institutional needs. These elements of the Court's order were both sanctioned by the Constitution and amply supported by the record.

In two respects, however, the District Court's preliminary injunction was overbroad. It ordered the Sheriff to permit reporters into the Little Greystone facility and it required him to let them interview randomly encountered inmates. In both these respects, the injunction gave the press access to areas and sources of information from which persons on the public tours had been excluded, and thus enlarged the scope of what the Sheriff and Supervisors had opened to public view. The District Court erred in concluding that the First and Fourteenth Amendments compelled this broader access for the press.

Because the preliminary injunction exceeded the requirements of the Constitution in these respects, I agree that the judgment of the Court of Appeals affirming the District Court's order must be reversed. But I would not foreclose the possibility of further relief for KQED on remand. In my view, the availability and scope of future permanent injunctive relief must depend upon the extent of access then permitted the public, and the decree must be framed to accommodate equitably the constitutional role of the press and the institutional requirements of the jail.

MR. JUSTICE STEVENS, with whom MR. JUSTICE BRENNAN and MR. JUSTICE POWELL join, dissenting.

The Court holds that the scope of press access to the Santa Rita jail required by the preliminary injunction issued against petitioner is inconsistent with the holding in Pell v. Procunier, [   ], that "newsmen have no constitutional right of access to prisons or their inmates beyond that afforded the general public" and therefore the injunction was an abuse of the District Court's discretion. I respectfully disagree.

. . .

For two reasons, which shall be discussed separately, the decisions in *Pell* and *Saxbe* do not control the propriety of the District Court's preliminary injunction. First, the unconstitutionality of petitioner's policies which gave rise to this litigation does not rest on the premise that the press has a greater right of access to information regarding prison conditions than do other members of the public. Second, relief tailored to the needs of the press may properly be awarded to a representative of the press which is successful in proving that it has been harmed by a constitutional violation and need not await the grant of relief to members of the general public who may also have been injured by petitioner's unconstitutional access policy but have not yet sought to vindicate their rights.

. . .

It is well settled that a defendant's corrective action in anticipation of litigation or following commencement of suit does not deprive the court of power to decide whether the previous course of conduct was unlawful. . . .

In Pell v. Procunier, [   ], the Court stated that "newsmen have no constitutional right of access to prisons or their inmates beyond that afforded the general public." But the Court has never intimated that a nondiscriminatory policy of excluding entirely both the public and the press from access to information about prison conditions would avoid constitutional scrutiny. Indeed, *Pell* itself strongly suggests the contrary.

. . .

The decision in *Pell*, therefore, does not imply that a state policy of concealing prison conditions from the press, or a policy denying the press any opportunity to observe those conditions, could have been justified simply by pointing to like concealment from, and denial to, the general public. If that were not true, there would have been no need to emphasize the substantial press and public access reflected in the record of that case. What *Pell* does indicate is that the question whether respondents established a probability of prevailing on their constitutional claim is inseparable from the question whether petitioner's policies unduly restricted the opportunities of the general public to learn about the conditions of confinement in Santa Rita jail.

As in *Pell*, in assessing its adequacy, the total access of the public and the press must be considered.

Here, the broad restraints on access to information regarding operation of the jail that prevailed on the date this suit was instituted are plainly disclosed by the record. . . . Petitioner's no-access policy, modified only in the wake of respondents' resort to the courts, could survive constitutional scrutiny only if the Constitution affords no protection to the public's right to be informed about conditions within those public institutions where some of its members are confined because they have been charged with or found guilty of criminal offenses.

II

The preservation of a full and free flow of information to the general public has long been recognized as a core objective of the First Amendment to the Constitution. It is for this reason that the First Amendment protects not only the dissemination but also the receipt of information and ideas. . . .

In addition to safeguarding the right of one individual to receive what another elects to communicate, the First Amendment serves an essential societal function. Our system of self-government assumes the existence of an informed citizenry.[21] . . . It is not sufficient, therefore, that the channels of communication be free of governmental restraints. Without some protection for the acquisition of information about the operation of public institutions such as prisons by the public at large, the process of self-governance contemplated by the Framers would be stripped of its substance.[22]

For that reason information-gathering is entitled to some measure of constitutional protection. See, e.g., Branzburg v. Hayes, [ ]; Pell v. Procunier, [ ]. As this Court's decisions clearly indicate, however, this protection is not for the private benefit of those who might qualify as representatives of the "press" but to insure that the citizens are fully informed regarding matters of public interest and importance.

A recognition that the "underlying right is the right of the public generally" is also implicit in the doctrine that "newsmen have no constitutional right of access to prisons or their inmates beyond that afforded the general public." Pell v. Procunier, [ ]. In *Pell* it was

21. See A. Meiklejohn . . . .

22. Admittedly, the right to receive or acquire information is not specifically mentioned in the Constitution. But "the protection of the Bill of Rights goes beyond the specific guarantees to protect from . . . abridgment those equally fundamental personal rights necessary to make the express guarantees fully meaningful. . . . The dissemination of ideas can accomplish nothing if otherwise willing adherents are not free to receive and consider them. It would be a barren marketplace of ideas that had only sellers and no buyers." Lamont v. Postmaster General, 381 U.S., at 308 (Brennan, J., concurring). It would be an even more barren marketplace that had willing buyers and sellers and no meaningful information to exchange.

unnecessary to consider the extent of the public's right of access to information regarding the prison and its inmates in order to adjudicate the press claim to a particular form of access, since the record demonstrated that the flow of information to the public, both directly and through the press, was adequate to survive constitutional challenge; institutional considerations justified denying the single, additional mode of access sought by the press in that case.

Here, in contrast, the restrictions on access to the inner portions of the Santa Rita jail that existed on the date this litigation commenced concealed from the general public the conditions of confinement within the facility. The question is whether petitioner's policies, which cut off the flow of information at its source, abridged the public's right to be informed about those conditions.

The answer to that question does not depend upon the degree of public disclosure which should attend the operation of most governmental activity. Such matters involve questions of policy which generally must be resolved by the political branches of government.[25] Moreover, there are unquestionably occasions when governmental activity may properly be carried on in complete secrecy. For example, the public and the press are commonly excluded from "grand jury proceedings, our own conferences, [and] the meetings of other official bodies gathering in executive session . . . ." Branzburg v. Hayes . . . .

In this case, however, "[r]espondents do not assert a right to force disclosure of confidential information or to invade in any way the decisionmaking processes of governmental officials."[28] They simply seek an end to petitioner's policy of concealing prison conditions from the public. Those conditions are wholly without claim to confidentiality. While prison officials have an interest in the time and manner of public acquisition of information about the institutions they administer, there is no legitimate, penological justification for concealing from citizens the conditions in which their fellow citizens are being confined.

The reasons which militate in favor of providing special protection to the flow of information to the public about prisons relate to the unique function they perform in a democratic society. Not only are they public institutions, financed with public funds and administered by public servants; they are an integral component of the criminal justice system. . . .

. . .

In this case, the record demonstrates that both the public and the press had been consistently denied any access to the inner portions of the Santa Rita jail, that there had been excessive censorship of

25. In United States v. Nixon, 418 U.S. 683, 705 n. 15, we pointed out that the Founders themselves followed a policy of confidentiality . . . .

28. Saxbe v. Washington Post Co. [   ] (Powell, J. dissenting).

inmate correspondence, and that there was no valid justification for these broad restraints on the flow of information. An affirmative answer to the question whether respondent established a likelihood of prevailing on the merits did not depend, in final analysis, on any right of the press to special treatment beyond that accorded the public at large. Rather, the probable existence of a constitutional violation rested upon the special importance of allowing a democratic community access to knowledge about how its servants were treating some of its members who have been committed to their custody. An official prison policy of concealing such knowledge from the public by arbitrarily cutting off the flow of information at its source abridges the freedom of speech and of the press protected by the First and Fourteenth Amendments to the Constitution.

. . .

I would affirm the judgment of the Court of Appeals.

Notes and Questions

1. What part of the majority opinion in *Pell* does Chief Justice Burger utilize? What part does Justice Stewart utilize? What part does Justice Stevens utilize?

2. To what extent does Justice Stewart agree with Chief Justice Burger? With Justice Stevens?

3. Under Justice Stewart's view, why can't the KQED crew go into Little Greystone?

4. Would any of the three opinions treat the NAACP differently from KQED, if it had asked to send a small group into the jail to investigate conditions?

5. What opinions would have been affected if the sheriff had decided to discontinue the public tours before the Supreme Court decided the case? What if the sheriff discontinues the tours after the decision?

6. How many other types of government facilities come within Justice Stevens's analysis? Could the sheriff have asserted any legitimate need for secrecy in running the jail?

D. DISCRIMINATORY ACCESS TO INFORMATION

Our focus has been on the question whether any statute or constitutional provision requires unwilling government officials to reveal information or to permit the press or public to gather information from government files, meetings, or areas under government control. (Occasionally, a statute like the Privacy Act bars willing officials from supplying information.) The situation was one in which government officials wanted nobody to learn certain information.

A quite different question arises when government officials are willing to part with information that they are not required to divulge—but want to discriminate among the prospective gatherers. The government's interest in this situation is no longer that the material should remain confidential or that secrecy is needed, because the official is quite prepared to divulge the information. The claim of government secrecy has been replaced by the desire of a government official to play favorites in the disclosure process either for personal or political reasons.

Reporters have no right to force an unwilling private person to reveal information. If the private source does decide to speak, there is no reason why he cannot decide to sell the story to the highest bidder or to give it first to a reporter who is a close friend.

But government traditionally must not behave in a discriminatory fashion. Even though the government official may not be required by statute or constitution to reveal certain information, he does not have unlimited control over the method of dissemination.

The starting point in general is that unless an official can demonstrate some reason for treating two apparently similar persons differently, the one who is being treated less well is not receiving equal protection of the laws. Notice that this constitutional protection in the Fourteenth Amendment applies broadly to all government action. If a government welfare program were arbitrarily to pay more money to redheads than to other recipients, the others would be able to claim a denial of equal protection.

We have already seen situations in which this rule of law might operate. If, in the Lashinsky case, two press photographers had been taking photographs and the state trooper had ordered Lashinsky to leave the scene while allowing his competitor to stay, the case would have been very different. Unless Lashinsky's behavior justified that different treatment, the trooper's actions would have amounted to unacceptable discrimination against Lashinsky. The trooper's action could not be justified on his or the state's disapproval of the editorial policy of Lashinsky's newspaper or on official disapproval of the gory photos that Lashinsky might have been attempting to obtain.

But all distinctions may not be invidious. Where press cards must be limited for some reasons, some government agencies may prefer media organizations that regularly cover the situations in which the cards will be needed. For example, if media representatives need press cards to get through police lines at emergencies, the police might give several cards to media that cover fires, police emergencies, and disasters before granting any press cards to a newspaper that stressed political or fashion news and did not regularly cover emergencies. Drawing these lines may be quite difficult. This situation is explored in Los Angeles Free Press, Inc. v. City of Los Angeles, 9 Cal.App.3d 448, 88 Cal.Rptr. 605 (1970), certiorari denied 401 U.S. 982 (1971), Justices Black, Douglas, and Brennan dissenting.

Sometimes gender differences between reporters have been asserted to justify unequal treatment.   The question of admitting women sports reporters to locker rooms went to court when the New York Yankees refused to allow them in after games.   (This is not a case of private discrimination because Yankee Stadium was located on property owned by the city and thus involved governmental action.)   The judge ordered that the women be admitted when the men were admitted.   The players' privacy could be protected in less restrictive ways than by totally excluding women reporters.   "The other two interests asserted by defendants, maintaining the status of baseball as a family sport and conforming to traditional notions of decency and propriety, are clearly too insubstantial to merit serious consideration."   Ludtke v. Kuhn, 461 F.Supp. 86 (S.D.N.Y.1978).

The issue may arise in a variety of contexts.   For example, a public official may not like the way a particular newspaper has been treating him or a friend.   He may respond by holding a press conference and ordering guards not to admit anyone from that newspaper.   At the other extreme, an official may decide to reveal information in a private talk with one reporter in his office.   Other reporters seek entry to the meeting.   Is there a critical difference between holding a public meeting and excluding one person and holding a private meeting and excluding all others?

Sometimes the different treatment may be based on characteristics of the individual.   For example, in Sherrill v. Knight, 569 F.2d 124 (D.C.Cir.1977), Sherrill, Washington correspondent for *The Nation,* had credentials for the House and Senate press galleries but was denied a White House press pass because of Secret Service objections.   He was said to be a security risk because he had assaulted the press secretary to the governor of Florida and also faced assault charges in Texas.

The Secret Service had been ordered by the trial court to formulate "narrow and specific" standards for deciding who posed a sufficient danger to the President to be denied a press card.   Security officials were the appellants in the court of appeals.   That court began by discussing the claim and distinguishing several matters that were not involved in this case:

> These considerations can perhaps be best understood by first recognizing what this case does *not* involve.   It is not contended that standards relating to the security of the President are the sole basis upon which members of the general public may be refused entry to the White House, or that members of the public must be afforded notice and hearing concerning such refusal. The first amendment's protection of a citizen's right to obtain information concerning "the way the country is being run" does not extend to every conceivable avenue a citizen may wish to employ in pursuing this right.   Nor is the discretion of the President to grant interviews or briefings with selected journal-

ists challenged. It would certainly be unreasonable to suggest that because the President allows interviews with some bona fide journalists, he must give this opportunity to all. Finally, appellee's first amendment claim is not premised upon the assertion that the White House must open its doors to the press, conduct press conferences, or operate press facilities.

Rather, we are presented with a situation where the White House has voluntarily decided to establish press facilities for correspondents who need to report therefrom. These press facilities are perceived as being open to all bona fide Washington-based journalists, whereas most of the White House itself, and press facilities in particular, have not been made available to the general public. White House press facilities having been made publicly available as a source of information for newsmen, the protection afforded newsgathering under the first amendment guarantee of freedom of the press, see [Branzburg and Pell], requires that this access not be denied arbitrarily or for less than compelling reasons. [ ] Not only newsmen and the publications for which they write, but also the public at large have an interest protected by the first amendment in assuring that restrictions on newsgathering be no more arduous than necessary, and that individual newsmen not be arbitrarily excluded from sources of information.

The court recognized that the safety of the President was a compelling, indeed overwhelming, interest that would justify restrictions on a reporter's access to the White House. But simply telling the reporter that he was barred "for reasons of security" did not meet the procedural safeguards that were required in this case. The court ordered the Secret Service to "publish or otherwise make publicly known the actual standard employed in determining whether an otherwise eligible journalist will obtain a White House pass." This did not lend itself to the narrow specifications required by the trial judge. It is enough if the Service is guided by the standard of whether the applicant "presents a potential source of physical danger . . . so serious as to justify his exclusion." In addition, a reporter who is barred must get notice of the facts the Service is relying on and have a chance to rebut them.

Occasionally, the basis for the different treatment is to be found in the nature of the media involved. Some states have barred journalists with tape recorders from legislative chambers, though they have allowed reporters to use pencil and pad. These limits, which have rarely been challenged, have usually been upheld.

Television has presented special problems. In Chapter IX, we considered the question of television cameras in the courtroom. Television has also raised questions in connection with the coverage of executions. In Garrett v. Estelle, 556 F.2d 1274 (5th Cir.1977), certiorari denied 438 U.S. 914 (1978), the court upheld Texas' refusal to allow cameras or tape recorders into the execution chamber. The state was willing to allow press pool reporters into the chamber and to permit other reporters to view the events over simultaneous closed circuit television. The court held, following *Pell* and *Saxbe*, that "the first amendment does not accompany the press where the public may not go." There was no public right to entry or to film the event.

The reporter then argued that he was being denied equal protection of the law because "other members of the press are allowed free use of their usual reporting tools." The court disagreed because the regulation also denied "the print reporter use of his camera and the radio reporter use of his tape recorder. Garrett is free to make his report by means of anchor desk or stand-up delivery on the TV screen, or even by simulation."

The final argument was that Texas had already chosen to make executions public by televising them over a closed circuit. Texas responded that legislation closing executions had already been upheld, Holden v. Minnesota, 137 U.S. 483 (1890), and that the limited televising of the execution should not be equated with making the event public. The court agreed that the closed circuit television was for those allowed to be present and should not be used to justify opening the event to the public.

Televising Congress. In early 1979, the House of Representatives began television coverage of its proceedings. The House decided to maintain control over the cameras and allow broadcasters to use whatever footage they wanted. The entire proceedings are available to subscribers to a special cable network. An early dispute involved the practice of blacking out the picture during votes. At these times the screen shows only the ongoing tally. Speaker O'Neill explained that since members may change their votes at the end of the 15-minute voting period only by "going to the well" and informing the clerk, they may be reluctant to do that with the cameras focused on them. Attempts to introduce cameras in the Senate have thus far failed.

Chapter XII

OWNERSHIP OF THE MEDIA AND
RELATED PROBLEMS

Although the press is the only industry mentioned by name in the U.S. Constitution, and the First Amendment gives it a unique protection from a great deal of government intrusion, the media are still businesses and as such are subject to antitrust laws, certain tax laws, and some other laws affecting business. Although there is, of course, no Federal Print Commission regulating the print media, there is a Federal Communications Commission regulating the electronic media. In this Chapter we will look at some of these ownership/business concerns.

A. NEWSPAPER ECONOMICS AND ANTITRUST LAW

In the next Chapter we will address the issue presented in Miami Herald Publishing Co. v. Tornillo, 418 U.S. 241 (1974): can one successfully assert a legal right to use print media owned by another? The problem of limited access to the print media is more often a local, rather than regional or national, concern. The reason, simply, is that the United States has increasingly become a country of one newspaper cities—in all but the largest cities. Even in many cities with two newspapers, both are owned by the same company and often speak with the same editorial voice. Although persons who want access to media can sometimes find a measure of relief from local broadcasters, for reasons discussed later, many still think the problem is serious. It is worthwhile to consider how the economic structure of the newspaper industry has produced a situation that antitrust laws could not avoid.

The goals of American antitrust law were set in 1890, with the enactment of the Sherman Antitrust Act, 15 U.S.C.A. §§ 1 and 2. Section 1 states a desire to "protect trade and commerce against unlawful restraints and monopolies," and then declares illegal "every contract, combination in the form of trust or otherwise, or conspiracy, in restraint of trade, or commerce." Section 2 provides that "Every person who shall monopolize, or attempt to monopolize, or combine or conspire with any other person or persons, to monopolize any part of the trade or commerce . . . . shall be guilty of a misdemeanor."

During the early 1800's, more dailies appeared. The period up to the Civil War was one in which "the newspaper was still basically individualistic and political—the creature of an individual editor/publisher, devoted to his personal views and those of his friends." B. Owen, Economics and Freedom of Expression 45 (1975). Changes began around 1880 that continued well into this century. Economies of scale in printing and distribution favored newspapers with large circulations and competition in the cities intensified. By 1920 newspaper circulation was at a saturation point and there was no further opportunity to produce a specialized product for a specific untapped audience. As Owen put it (at 47):

> Editors could no longer afford to put the stamp of their personal biases on the entire range of editorial content; they had increasingly to include content of appeal to diverse groups. The editor as an institution receded into the background. The publisher's success formula was to take advantage of scale economies with respect to the physical size of the newspaper by including content that was specialized to serve subgroups of the population, and at the same time to generate demand for circulation by broadening (and perhaps lowering) the appeal of the basic news content of the newspaper. The newspapers in their search for mass audiences interacted directly with the political environment of the day: boosterism, muck-raking, progressivism, yellow journalism, even a war promoted by a newspaper publisher. Newspaper publishers scrambled for huge circulation because that was the key to profit and survival and the newspaper ceased to be the instrument of an individualistic editor or his political cronies.

These developments led to the inevitable demise of many city newspapers, first in the smaller cities where the more homogeneous population included few specialized audiences. Thus, Owen reported that while in 1923, 60 percent of newspaper publishers had direct competition, by 1973 the figure had dropped to 5.4 percent. But this small percentage produced 32 percent of the nation's circulation. (p. 49) Virtually all American cities have one newspaper or combined ownership of more than one, but these few surviving urban papers compete for circulation and advertising with suburban papers and for advertising with broadcasting as well. Economists suggest that the economies of scale were bound to reduce the number of newspapers regardless of efforts of the antitrust law to save competition. Professor Owen provided extensive discussion of the economics of newspapers in his book at pp. 33–85.

The quoted provisions of the Sherman Act have been applied against business enterprises engaged in manufacturing or marketing tangible products. Whether they can as readily be invoked against organizations involved in gathering and disseminating news was first considered in the early 1940's when the Associated Press was charged with violating both sections by creating a system of by-laws that prohibited local AP members from selling "spontaneous" news (as opposed to researched news) to non-members, and granted to its one member in each city the effective power to block all non-member local competitors from membership in AP. Among other findings, the lower court determined that because of these restrictions 1,179

English language dailies with a circulation of 42 million were obligated not to supply AP news or their own "spontaneous" news to any nonmembers of AP. The lower court (Learned Hand, J.) concluded that the AP By-Laws "unlawfully restricted admission to AP membership, and violated the Sherman Act insofar as the By-Laws' provisions clothed a member with powers to impose or dispense with conditions upon the admission of his business competitor." Over three dissents, the Supreme Court affirmed. Associated Press v. United States, 326 U.S. 1 (1945). In doing so, the majority had to respond to the wire service's First Amendment argument:

> That Amendment rests on the assumption that the widest possible dissemination of information from diverse and antagonistic sources is essential to the welfare of the public, that a free press is a condition of a free society. Surely a command that the government itself shall not impede the free flow of ideas does not afford non-governmental combinations a refuge if they impose restraints upon that constitutionally guaranteed freedom. Freedom to publish means freedom for all and not for some. Freedom to publish is guaranteed by the Constitution, but freedom to combine to keep others from publishing is not.

In a concurring opinion, Justice Frankfurter observed:

> To be sure, the Associated Press is a cooperative organization of members who are "engaged in a commercial business for profit." [ ] But in addition to being a commercial enterprise, it has a relation to the public interest unlike that of any other enterprise pursued for profit. A free press is indispensable to the workings of our democratic society. The business of the press, and therefore the business of the Associated Press, is the promotion of truth regarding public matters by furnishing the basis for an understanding of them. Truth and understanding are not wares like peanuts or potatoes. And so, the incidence of restraints upon the promotion of truth through denial of access to the basis for understanding calls into play considerations very different from comparable restraints in a cooperative enterprise having merely a commercial aspect. I find myself entirely in agreement with Judge Learned Hand that "neither exclusively, nor even primarily, are the interests of the newspaper industry conclusive; for that industry serves one of the most vital of all general interests: the dissemination of news from as many different sources, and with as many different facets and colors as is possible. That interest is closely akin to, if indeed it is not the same as, the interest protected by the First Amendment; it presupposes that right conclusions are more likely to be gathered out of a multitude of tongues, than through any kind of authoritative selection. To many this is, and always will be, folly; but we have staked upon it our all." 52 F.Supp. 362, 372.

The Supreme Court has decided a variety of newspaper antitrust cases since Associated Press v. United States.

One type is suggested by Lorain Journal v. United States, 342 U.S. 143 (1951), in which the Justice Department charged that the *Lorain* (Ohio) *Journal*'s conduct constituted an attempt to monopolize interstate commerce in violation of the Sherman Act. From 1933 to 1948, the *Journal* had a substantial monopoly of the mass dissemination of news and advertising in Lorain. In 1948, however, the FCC licensed the Elyria-Lorain Broadcasting Company to operate WEOL radio in Elyria, Ohio, eight miles south of Lorain. In an effort to preserve its monopoly, the *Lorain Journal* attempted to prevent WEOL from selling any advertising, by refusing to accept advertising from any Lorain County advertiser who advertised or whom the newspaper believed to be about to advertise over WEOL. The trial court found that "the purpose and intent of this procedure was to destroy the broadcasting company," and issued an injunction enjoining such behavior. The Supreme Court affirmed, noting that the *Journal*'s coverage of 99 percent of Lorain families made it a critical medium of advertising for Lorain businesses, and that the publisher's refusals to print advertising of those also using WEOL, if unchecked, would cut off WEOL's revenues and destroy it as a competitor.

In Times-Picayune Publishing Co. v. United States, 345 U.S. 594 (1953), the publisher of a morning and an afternoon paper in New Orleans set a unit rate that required an advertiser to place his ads in both papers or in neither but did not bar those who also chose to advertise in the one afternoon competitor. The Department of Justice claimed that unit rates were really "tying agreements" that violated the Sherman Act. The District Court agreed that the power of the unopposed morning paper was forcing advertisers to place ads in the related afternoon paper, hurting the other afternoon paper because some advertisers who wanted the morning space would not also be able to afford both afternoon papers. On appeal, the Supreme Court, 5–4, reversed and held that the government had failed to establish its case. The majority viewed the "market" as including all three dailies, which meant that the morning paper did not hold a dominant position in the market, and therefore that the fairly strong afternoon partner was not being forced on unwilling advertisers. The dissenters thought the morning and afternoon markets were separate and agreed with the government's and the District Court's view of the case.

Another type of problem is suggested by United States v. Times Mirror Co., 274 F.Supp. 606 (C.D.Cal.1967), affirmed without opinion 390 U.S. 712 (1968). The Justice Department sought to prevent the Times Mirror Company, publisher of the *Los Angeles Times*, the largest daily newspaper in southern California, from acquiring the Sun Company, publisher of the largest "independent" daily newspaper in southern California. The Justice Department charged that the effect of the acquisition would be to "substantially lessen competition" in violation of Section 7 of the Clayton Act, 15 U.S.C. § 18, a major addition to the antitrust arsenal. The District Court focused on the elements of the acquisition relevant to the effects on competition: whether the *Times* and the *Sun* were in the same product and geographical markets so as to be in competition for the consumer's dollar, the existing concentration in the southern California newspaper industry, and the degree of control exercised by Times Mirror over the *Sun*'s policies. The District Court concluded that the acquisition would substantially lessen competition in violation of the Clayton Act.

The Newspaper Preservation Act

The most significant recent antitrust confrontation between the Justice Department and the newspaper industry occurred in Citizen Publishing Co. v. United States, 394 U.S. 131 (1969). In 1940, the only two daily newspapers in Tucson, Arizona, the *Citizen*, an evening paper, and the *Star*, a daily and Sunday paper, negotiated a 25-year joint operating agreement. The agreement provided that each paper would retain its own editorial and news departments and its corporate identity, but that business operations would be integrated "to end any business or commercial competition between the two papers." The agreement was implemented in three ways. One was price fixing. Newspapers were sold and distributed by a single circulation department and advertising placed in either paper was sold through a single advertising department. Second, all profits realized were pooled and distributed to the *Star* and *Citizen* pursuant to an agreed ratio. Third, the *Star* and the *Citizen* agreed that neither paper nor any person affiliated with either would engage in any business in the metropolitan area of Tucson in conflict with the agreement. Prior to 1940 the two papers competed vigorously with each other. Though their circulations were about equal, the *Star* sold 50 percent more advertising than the *Citizen* and operated at an annual profit of about $26,000, while the *Citizen*'s annual losses averaged about $23,550. Following the agreement, all commercial rivalry between the papers ceased. Combined profits rose from $27,531 in 1940 to $1,727,217 in 1964.

The government charged violations of the Sherman and Clayton Acts. The District Court found that the agreement violated the antitrust laws and the Supreme Court affirmed. Its opinion focused on the applicability to the defendants of the "failing company doctrine." This judicially created doctrine held that the acquisition of one company by another did not violate the antitrust laws when "the resources of the one company were so depleted and the prospect of rehabilitation so remote that 'it faced the grave probability of a business failure,'" and there was "no other prospective purchaser." But the District Court had found that at the time the *Star* and

Citizen entered into the operating agreement, there was no serious probability that the *Citizen* was on the verge of going out of business or that, even had the *Citizen* been contemplating liquidation, the *Star* was the only available purchaser. The Supreme Court rejected the defense and affirmed the lower court's decree.

Congressional reaction was swift, largely because the decision raised doubt about the validity of similar agreements in 22 other cities. The result was the passage, in 1970, of the Newspaper Preservation Act, 15 U.S.C. § 1801 et seq. Congress declared its purpose to maintain "a newspaper press editorially and reportorially independent and competitive in all parts of the United States." Joint newspaper operating agreements were authorized to link virtually all mechanical and commercial aspects of the newspaper but there was to be no combination of editorial or reportorial staffs. A "failing newspaper" was defined as one that "regardless of its ownership or affiliation, is in probable danger of financial failure." The Act provided that joint agreements previously entered into are valid if when started, "not more than one of the newspaper publications involved . . . was likely to remain or become a financially sound publication." Future joint operating agreements required the approval of the Attorney General, who must first "determine that not more than one of the newspaper publications involved in the arrangement is a publication other than a failing newspaper" and that approval of the agreement would advance the policy of the Act. Predatory practices that would be unlawful if engaged in by a single entity may not be engaged in by the members of the joint operating agreement.

This Act is an exception to the general hostility between press and government. Here, the press actively sought Congressional intervention, whereas the press is usually protesting against government action and relying upon the First Amendment for protection. Apart from the obvious political pressures, why might Congress have passed such legislation? The Act has had its most important role in preserving the 22 joint operating agreements that were in existence at the time of *Citizen Publishing*. Only a handful of new agreements have been proposed and approved since the Act went into effect.

A few figures will show the effect of these agreements on advertisers and potential competitors. Studies have shown that advertising provides 75 to 80 percent of the income of most newspapers. Joint operators and monopolists are asserted to charge about the same advertising rates—rates significantly higher than duopolists. Owen, Newspaper and Television Station Joint Ownership, 18 Antitrust Bull. 787 (1973). The situation in San Francisco is illustrative. The basic display rate of the *Chronicle* rose from $1.20 a line to $2.32 per line ten months after the agreement. The *Chronicle*'s increase may well have been due to the fact that as part of the agreement a third paper ceased publication and the *Chronicle* obtained a monopoly in the morning. The afternoon paper's rate rose from $1.03 to $1.55 during the same period. More significantly, an advertiser could buy space in both papers for $2.50 per line after the agreement. This is the common result of such agreements and presents obvious problems to prospective competitors.

The first major challenge to the Act came in San Francisco. A small paper that had hoped to move into competition with the large papers filed an antitrust action claiming that their agreement made it virtually impossible for another paper to break in. Advertisers whose rates had been increased by the agreement joined the challenge. The defendants asserted that the Act validated their agreement. Plaintiffs moved to dismiss the defense on the ground that the Act was unconstitutional. Bay Guardian Co. v. Chronicle Publishing Co., 344 F.Supp. 1155 (N.D.Cal.1972). A First Amendment challenge to the Act was rejected:

> Plaintiffs contend that the Act is unconstitutional because it permits the defendant newspapers to combine so as to prevent the plaintiffs' newspaper from publishing. This effect of the Act, they contend, causes it to be in violation of the freedom of the press guarantee of the First Amendment.

> The simple answer to the plaintiffs' contention is that the Act does not authorize any conduct. It is a narrow exception to the antitrust laws for newspapers in danger of failing. Thus it is in many respects merely a codification of the judicially created "failing company" doctrine. See, 83 Harv.L.R. 673 (1970).

> . . .

> Here the Act was designed to preserve independent editorial voices. Regardless of the economic or social wisdom of such a course, it does not violate the freedom of the press. Rather it is merely a selective repeal of the antitrust laws. It merely looses the same shady market forces which existed before the passage of the Sherman, Clayton and other antitrust laws.

> Such a repeal, even when applicable only to the newspaper industry, does not violate the First Amendment.

The operation of the Newspaper Preservation Act is studied and criticized in Barnett, Monopoly Games—Where Failures Win Big, Columbia Journalism Review (May/June 1980) at 40.

The assistant general in charge of the antitrust division once commented upon the limited power of antitrust law to prevent the decline of newspaper competition:

> In some instances, this decline can be attributed to the higher average costs imposed on a smaller paper as a result of the existence of economies of scale and the disposition of many large advertisers to place a disproportionately large portion of their advertising dollars with the newspaper having the larger circula-

tion.   In addition, the decline may be in part a result of increased competition from the broadcasting media and from weekly or free-distribution newspapers, the latter being particularly a phenomenon of suburban areas.   There is, however, some reasons to hope that new, more efficient printing technology will ease the economies of scale problem and, in the long run, lead to a rebirth of competing daily newspapers.

Shenefield, Ownership Concentration in Newspapers, 65 A.B.A.J. 1332 (1979).   He noted that his division was trying to preserve the opportunity for such a development by closely scrutinizing mergers and joint operating agreements; by making sure that dominant daily newspapers do not use their power to erect barriers to entry by newcomers; and to reduce and limit joint ownership of newspaper and broadcast facilities in the same market.   This latter concern is explored shortly.

To suggest the potential for revival within the industry, Shenefield noted that the circulation of weekly newspapers increased from 21.3 million to 37.9 million between 1960 and 1977.   During that same period, the circulation of daily newspapers rose only from 58.9 million to 61.7 million.

Considerable controversy arose over the 1981 application by the Seattle Times Company and the *Seattle Post-Intelligencer* for approval of a joint operating agreement for the two metropolitan daily newspapers in Seattle.   The Committee for an Independent P-I, made up of the newspaper's employees and advertisers, and the publishers of smaller newspapers, challenged the joint operating agreement on the ground that the owners had not made a good faith effort to sell the *Post-Intelligencer*.   The U.S. Court of Appeals for the Ninth Circuit held in 1983 that the Attorney General's finding that one of the newspapers was "failing" was justified by the showing that the newspaper would probably fail, even without evidence of greater effort to sell the paper.   Committee for an Independent P-I v. Hearst Corp., 704 F.2d 467 (9th Cir.1983).

Until now, we have been concerned with the demise of newspaper competition in all but our largest cities.   Another growing concern is the emergence of group ownership or "chains."   Shenefield reports that 1,095 of the 1,753 daily newspapers in 1977 were owned by a group that controlled two or more newspapers in different cities. Each chain controlled an average of 6.5 newspapers, ranging from several with two to Gannett with almost 80 in 1977.   Of the 53 dailies that changed hands in 1978, 47 were purchased by groups.

The top 20 groups are estimated to control about 50 percent of newspaper circulation—with the top chain controlling 6.3 percent of the daily circulation.   Since this degree of concentration is quite small, the antitrust division has been unable to move against this type of group ownership unless, in a specific case, it can show some probable anticompetitive effect.   Nonetheless, Shenefield observed:

"Control of all daily newspapers by five chains, for example, would cause me as an American citizen far greater concern than would control of a similarly sized manufacturing industry by five business entities."

The next step in the process is discussed in Bagdikian, Newspaper Mergers—The Final Phase, Columbia Journalism Review (March/April 1977) at 17. Now that most independent dailies have become parts of chains, the larger chains have begun acquiring smaller chains.

The magazine industry is more diverse than the newspaper industry. Most of that industry does not face the problem of competing local outlets. So far as group ownership is concerned, the 50 largest companies account for 65 percent of the industry's total revenues—a figure that has not grown over the years. The subject is explored in Smith and Fowler, Jr., The Status of Magazine Group Ownership, 56 Journ.Q. 572 (1979).

B. NEWSPAPER TAXATION PROBLEMS

Special problems arise with taxation of the press—particularly in instances in which the tax appears discriminatory. The first significant case involving taxation of the press arose from the efforts of Governor Huey Long of Louisiana to silence criticism of his actions by the state's larger newspapers. The Louisiana legislature enacted a gross receipts tax that was to apply to those newspapers, magazines and other periodicals having a circulation of more than 20,000 copies per week. The result was a tax limited to major newspapers. The Supreme Court unanimously rejected it. Grosjean v. American Press Co., 297 U.S. 233 (1936). Justice Sutherland's opinion did not rely on the political background, nor did it focus on equal protection. Instead it reviewed the history of press regulation and concluded that the tax operated as a prior restraint on publishing because it led publishers to reduce press runs to avoid the tax, thus limiting the public's access to information. Since the First Amendment was meant at least to avoid most types of prior restraint the Court had little difficulty in rejecting the tax. The Supreme Court's opinion has been criticized in C. Miller, The Supreme Court and the Uses of History, 78 (1969):

> It is evident that the Court's chief historical supports in this case, that early Americans valued their press as a vehicle for criticism of British policies and that the colonists were furious at the stamp tax (which included fees on newspapers), have no historical relationship to each other. Although these two cherished uprights were used in constructing the story of American freedom, it was the Court, not history, that built a crossbeam between them.

The very next year the Supreme Court made clear that *Grosjean* was not to be read as a general barrier to taxation of the media. Arizona had levied a tax on the sales or gross income of "practically every person or concern engaged in selling merchandise or services in the state." A newspaper publisher, relying on *Grosjean,* challenged the tax, but the Supreme Court of Arizona rejected the challenge and distinguished *Grosjean* on the ground that newspapers there had been singled out for special treatment. As a concurring justice observed, in *Grosjean* "a situation existed in the state of Louisiana which was unparalleled in American history. A single individual had obtained a control over the entire executive, legislative, and judicial machinery of that state as absolute as that exercised by any modern European dictatorship." Giragi v. Moore, 49 Ariz. 74, 64 P.2d 819 (1937). The publisher appealed to the Supreme Court of the United States, claiming a conflict with *Grosjean.* The appeal was dismissed by the Supreme Court for "want of a substantial federal question." 301 U.S. 670 (1937).

The following year the Supreme Court held that taxes levied by states and municipalities on gross advertising receipts of media having interstate circulation did not unconstitutionally burden interstate commerce. Western Live Stock v. Bureau of Revenue, 303 U.S. 250 (1938). See also, Matter of New Yorker Magazine, Inc. v. Gerosa, 3 N.Y.2d 362, 165 N.Y.S.2d 469, 144 N.E.2d 367 (1957), appeal dismissed for want of a substantial federal question, 356 U.S. 339 (1958). Fairly apportioned taxes that do not unfairly burden interstate enterprises are permissible and media receive no special protection.

In Minneapolis Star and Tribune Co. v. Minnesota Commissioner of Revenue, 460 U.S. 575 (1983), the Supreme Court held that a Minnesota tax violated the First Amendment. The tax was imposed on publications' use of paper and ink exceeding $100,000 annually. After the enactment of the tax, 11 publishers, producing 14 of the 388 paid circulation newspapers in the state, incurred a tax liability in 1974. The Star and Tribune Co. was only one of the 11 publishers, but the company paid approximately two-thirds of the revenue raised by the tax. In holding the tax unconstitutional, the Supreme Court noted that the press had been singled out for special treatment, that no adequate justification had been offered for the special treatment of newspapers, and that the tax targeted a small group of newspapers.

C. FCC OWNERSHIP LIMITATIONS

Our discussion so far has dealt with print media rather than with users of the broadcast spectrum, to the extent that legal controls for the two differ. At the heart of this distinction is the requirement that all broadcast facilities be licensed by the Federal Communications Commission. Under the Communications Act of 1934 the Commission has sole power to allocate the broadcast spectrum, to establish general standards of operation, and to license persons to use designated parts of the spectrum. Although the details of broadcast regulation are covered in Chapters XIII–XVI, it is appropriate to examine now the Commission's efforts to maximize diversity of ownership of broadcast facilities.

1. LOCAL CONCENTRATION

Local concentration of control of mass media facilities has been a problem for the Commission at least since 1938, when it received an application for a standard broadcasting station in Flint, Michigan from applicants who already controlled another corporation that operated a standard broadcasting station in the same area. Although there were no rival applicants the Commission refused to grant the second facility without a compelling showing that the public interest would be served in such a situation.

This was the beginning of the so-called "duopoly" rule, which the Commission formalized in a general rule that it would not grant a license to any applicant who already held a similar facility or license so located that the service areas of the two would overlap.

In the 1960's the Commission returned to this subject and recognized that the dwindling number of American newspapers made the impact of individual broadcasting stations "significantly greater." This reinforced the need for diversity in the broadcast media and led the Commission to announce that it would probably never again grant a duopoly.

During this period, however, the Commission was granting to the same applicant one AM, one FM and one television station in the same locality because this was not a duplication of facilities in the same service area. In 1970 the Commission moved the next step and adopted the so-called "one-to-a-customer" rule. This meant that in the future the Commission would not grant a television license to the owner of an AM station in the community, or vice-versa. The Commission rejected an argument "that the good profit position of a multiple owner in the same market results in more in-depth informational programs being broadcast and, thus, in more meaningful diversity. We do not doubt that some multiple owners may have a greater capacity to so program, but the record does not demonstrate that they generally do so. The citations and honors for exceptional programming appear to be continually awarded to a very few licensees—perhaps a dozen or so multiple owners out of a total of hundreds of such owners." In the Matter of Amendment of §§ 73.35, 73.240 and 73.636 of the Commission Rules Relating to Multiple Ownership of Standard, FM and Television Broadcast Stations, 22 F.C.C.2d 306 (1970).

When an AM licensee sought to add an FM station, that presented a special problem because traditionally FM had been weak as a competitive force, and indeed the Commission during the 1950's had encouraged AM stations to acquire FM stations. But by 1970 FM stations were becoming more powerful competitors and were becoming increasingly profitable. For that reason, the Commission did not automatically approve the continuation of AM–FM combinations—but neither did it ban the formation of new ones. Instead, it announced that it would continue to review these situations one by one.

As for UHF stations, the Commission acknowledged that they were still weak competitively and that few would go on the air unless affiliated with an established radio station. Therefore the Commission refused to adopt a firm rule against radio-UHF combinations but again indicated that it would review those on a case-by-case basis. Finally, the Commission announced that its ban on VHF-radio combinations would apply only in the future and no divestitures would be required, due to the large number of existing combinations and a sense that ordering divestiture for such a large group might very well create instability.

When the Commission adopted its one-to-a-customer rules, it also proposed the adoption of another set of rules that would proscribe common ownership of newspapers and broadcast facilities serving the same area, and require divestiture of prohibited combinations. Although the Commission had flirted with such a regulation in the early 1940's, it abandoned the attempt. The basis for the Commission movement in 1970 was an awareness that 94 television stations were affiliated through common control with newspapers in the same city. In addition, of course, "some newspapers own television stations in other cities, which also serve the city in which the newspaper is located." The Commission thought this situation was very similar to the joint ownership of two television stations in the same community, something the Commission has never permitted. "The functions of newspapers and television stations as journalists are so similar that their joint ownership is, in this respect, essentially the same as the joint ownership of two television stations." After extensive consideration the Commission adopted rules in 1975 that prohibit granting a license for a television or radio station to any applicant who already controls, owns, or operates a daily newspaper serving part of the same area.

The rule was to apply retroactively to only a few small communities where the sole newspaper owned the sole television station. Common ownership of the only newspaper and the only radio station was to be dissolved unless the community had an independently owned television station. Multiple Ownership Rules, Second Report and Order, 50 F.C.C.2d 1046, 32 R.R.2d 954 reconsidered, 53 F.C.C.2d 589, 33 R.R.2d 1603 (1975). The Commission rejected widespread divestiture as too "harsh" without a clear showing of need. Some appealed the prospective ban itself, others the refusal to order more divestitures.

The Supreme Court unanimously upheld the Commission's three-part rules on whether a newspaper should be permitted to hold a broadcasting license in the same community in which the newspaper is located. Federal Communications Commission v. National Citizens Committee for Broadcasting, 436 U.S. 775 (1978). In an opinion by Justice Marshall, the Court first held that the Commission had acted within its statutory and constitutional authority in promulgating a rule that prospectively barred newspaper owners from holding broadcast licenses in the same community. The statutory authority came from § 303(r) of the 1934 Act, which permitted the Commission to promulgate rules and regulations to give effect to the provisions of the Act. "It was not inconsistent with the statutory scheme . . . for the Commission to conclude that the maximum benefit to the 'public interest' would follow from allocation of broadcast licenses so as to promote diversification of the mass media as a whole." Even though the record was not conclusive on the point, the Commission "acted rationally in finding that diversification of ownership would enhance the possibility of achieving greater diversity of viewpoints." It was also permissible for the Commission to make diversification the controlling factor in selecting new applicants.

The Commission's constitutional power to exclude a class of applicants from holding licenses was upheld on the scarcity rationale of *Red Lion v. FCC*, (discussed at length in Chapter XIII), which rejected the claim of an "unabridgeable First Amendment right to broadcast comparable to the right of every individual to speak, write, or publish:"

> The physical limitations of the broadcast spectrum are well known. Because of problems of interference between broadcast signals, a finite number of frequencies can be used productively; this number is far exceeded by the number of persons wishing to broadcast to the public. In light of this physical scarcity, Government allocation and regulation of broadcast frequencies are essential, as we have often recognized. [ ] No one here questions the need for such allocation and regulation, and, given that need, we see nothing in the First Amendment to prevent the Commission from allocating licenses so as to promote the "public interest" in diversification of the mass communications media.

Efforts to affect the coverage of public issues in broadcasting "may be permissible where similar efforts to regulate the print media would not be." The basic thrust of the opinion was that since the Commission was being forced to choose among applicants for limited facilities, it was free to "enhance the diversity of information heard by the public without ongoing government surveillance of the content of speech."

Second, the Court upheld the Commission's decision to order divestiture in 16 "egregious" cases of small communities in which the newspaper owned the only television station or, if there was no television station, the only radio station. The danger in these situations was sufficient to warrant divestiture. Third, the Supreme

Court found that the Commission had adequately explained that diversification was not its only concern:

> The Order identified several specific respects in which the public interest would or might be harmed if a sweeping divestiture requirement were imposed: the stability and continuity of meritorious service provided by the newspaper owners as a group would be lost; owners who had provided meritorious service would unfairly be denied the opportunity to continue in operation; "economic dislocations" might prevent new owners from obtaining sufficient working capital to maintain the quality of local programming; and local ownership of broadcast stations would probably decrease. [ ] We cannot say that the Commission acted irrationally in concluding that these public interest harms outweighed the potential gains that would follow from increasing diversification of ownership.

The result, then, was to permit continuation of all but 16 existing combinations, but to bar future newspaper-broadcast co-located combinations.

The Court noted that the Commission's study of "existing co-located newspaper-television combinations showed that in terms of percentage of time devoted to several categories of local programming, these stations had displayed 'an undramatic but nonetheless statistically significant superiority' over other television stations."

The Court observed that remaining combinations still could be challenged on an individual basis. Diversification "will be a relevant but somewhat secondary factor." A challenger might also show that a common owner has "engaged in specific economic or programming abuses" attributable to the existence of its combination.

One study, Gormley, Jr., How Cross-Ownership Affects News-Gathering, Colum.J.Rev. (May/June 1977) at 38, indicates that cross-ownership means less diversity of information. The study showed much more sharing of news between co-owned newspapers and television stations than between independent entities. It also showed that 52 percent of the newspaper-owned television stations never editorialized as opposed to 25 percent of the stations not owned by newspapers. Another study suggests that newspapers affiliated with television stations do not report television network news interviews very differently from newspapers that have no such affiliations. Burriss and Williams, Use of Network News Material by Cross-Owned Newspapers, 56 Journ.Q. 567 (1979).

Television-Cable cross-ownership. In 1970, the Commission prospectively barred cross-ownership of a local cable system by a local television licensee.

After years of debate over whether or not to require divestiture of the existing combinations, the Commission finally decided to grandfather all cases in which a television station owns a cable system in an overlapping area—so long as the station is not the only commercial broadcast station serving the cable community. Where it is the only commercial broadcaster, the Commission is considering divestiture. It is also considering repealing the ban on all such cross-ownership situations. Cable/TV Cross-Ownership. Third Report and Order, 56 R.R.2d 87 (1984).

2. NATIONAL CONCENTRATION

The Commission has also demonstrated a continuing concern that a few nationwide entities might dominate broadcasting.

Beginning in 1940 the Commission adopted rules limiting the number of stations that might be held by a single owner. In 1953 the Commission resolved that the rules should prohibit the ownership or control, directly or indirectly, by any party of more than seven AM stations, seven FM stations, and seven television stations of which not more than five could be VHF. The Commission explained its position as follows:

> The vitality of our system of broadcasting depends in large part on the introduction into this field of licensees who are prepared and qualified to serve the varied and divergent needs of the public for radio service. Simply stated, the fundamental purpose of this facet of the multiple ownership rules is to promote diversification of ownership in order to maximize diversification of program and service viewpoints as well as to prevent any undue concentration of economic power contrary to the public interest. In this connection, we wish to emphasize that by such rules diversification of program services is furthered without any governmental encroachment on what we recognize to be the prime responsibility of the broadcast licensee. (See Section 326 of the Communications Act.) . . .

The Commission chose an equal number of AM and FM stations because at that time 538 of the 600 FM stations were owned by AM licensees, the result of a conscious Commission policy to encourage AM stations to put FM stations on the air since most of those operating FM stations alone were finding it extremely unprofitable. The number seven was chosen "in order that present holdings of such stations be not unduly disrupted." Very few owners had holdings in excess of seven and the Commission planned to hold a divestiture hearing for each of them. Rules and Regulations Relating to Multiple Ownership, 18 F.C.C. 288 (1953).

This limitation rule was challenged immediately by a group owner who claimed that the Commission was illegally using the rule procedure to foreclose the right of an applicant to a hearing as to whether the license would be in the public interest, by making a categorical judgment linking the public interest with a given maximum concentration of holdings. The Supreme Court rejected the challenge in United States v. Storer Broadcasting Co., 351 U.S. 192 (1956). The Court viewed the Commission's action as "but a rule that announces the Commission's attitude on public protection against such concentration." The opinion did state, however, that the Commission's responsibility to behave in the public interest required it to grant a hearing to an applicant who had already reached the maximum number of stations but nonetheless asserted sufficient reasons why the rule should be waived in its particular case.

In early 1984, the Commission voted to expand the limits on multiple ownership from 7–7–7 to 12–12–12. The new rule made no distinction between VHF and UHF television. Faced with mounting criticism of the new rule and threatened Congressional action, the Commission revised the television portion of the order. Effective April 2, 1985 one entity may own 12 television stations provided the total reach of these stations is less than 25% of the television households in the country. For the purposes of this rule, a UHF will be counted as covering only 50% of the television households in its market. In an attempt to encourage minority ownership, the Commission also decided to allow those who purchase interests in minority-controlled broadcast outlets to own 14 stations in any service and to reach up to 30% of the television households in the country as long as at least two of the stations in each service are more than half-owned by minorities. ___ F.C.C.2d ___ (1985).

3. Conglomerates in Broadcasting

Occasionally the problem has been raised, not in terms of multiple ownership of competing media, but concern about other businesses in which a prospective licensee is engaged. The prime example is a merger that was proposed between ABC, which in its capacity as group owner, owned seventeen broadcasting stations, and International Telephone and Telegraph, a vast conglomerate with manufacturing facilities, telecommunication operations and other activities in sixty-six countries throughout the world.

Critics were concerned that ITT would use the broadcasting facilities to further the interests of the parent corporation in ways that might include distorting the news and making editorial decisions on grounds other than professional journalistic criteria. The Commission rejected these concerns on the ground that "it is too late in the day to argue that such outside business interests are disqualifying. . . . We cannot in this case adopt standards which when applied to other cases would require us to restructure the industry unless we are prepared to undertake that task. We could not, in good conscience, forbid ABC to merge with ITT without instituting proceedings to separate NBC from RCA, both of which are bigger than the respective principals in this case." The Commission granted the application for transferring of the seventeen licenses by a 4 to 3 vote. Memorandum Opinion and Order 7 F.C.C.2d 245, 9 R.R.2d 12 (1966).

While an appeal by the Justice Department on antitrust grounds was pending, the parties abandoned their proposed merger. Would there be any problem if, for example, General Motors sought to acquire a television station in Detroit? Are different questions raised if a book publisher or motion picture producer seeks a television license?

The Gannett-Combined Communications Merger. In 1979, the FCC approved the largest deal in broadcasting history. The parties were Gannett, which at the time published 77 daily and 32 weekly newspapers and owned WHEC–TV in Rochester, N.Y., and Combined Communications Corp. which at the time owned newspapers in Cincinnati and Oakland (Cal.) plus five VHF, two UHF, six AM, and six FM stations. In addition, Gannett owned Louis Harris and Associates, the polling firm, and Combined was a major supplier of outdoor advertising. The deal called for $370 million in Gannett stock to go to Combined. After spin-offs to meet the FCC's cross-ownership policies, Gannett had 79 daily newspapers, seven television stations and 12 radio stations.

The final result, because of the spin-offs, violated no concentration rule. Nonetheless, the Commission considered whether granting the applications to transfer ownership of the stations would be in the "public interest." The majority concluded that the deal was not likely to adversely affect competition or raise antitrust concerns.

The First Amendment issue, however, raised harder questions. The FCC noted that Gannett had represented that "local autonomy will be the touchstone for the operation of each newspaper and broadcast property" and that the newspapers would operate separately from the broadcast properties. For example, Gannett asserted that in 1976, of its 35 papers that made endorsements, 22 endorsed Gerald Ford and 13 endorsed Jimmy Carter. Decentralized operation was the goal, although everyone recognized that under § 310 of the 1934 Act, Gannett had to retain ultimate control of its stations.

Some were concerned about the possibility that the size of the combination would lead advertisers and stock market investors to exercise more control over management than would occur with less centralized control. They feared that a large communications entity might "harm diversity of information and opinion through its institutional pressures rather than by any intentional acts of its corporate leadership."

The FCC stressed countervailing considerations: "Media chains may have more freedom and might be inclined to take more risks in their reporting of news and opinion because their financial health allows a degree of independence from the political views of their major advertisers." The size of the organization might permit more coverage of national news in competition with the wire services, the television networks, and the largest newspapers and magazines.

Since all of these newspapers and stations face "substantial local mixed-media competition," even if a "Gannett" view entered a new market it was not eliminating other views available in that market. Affirmatively, the Commission noted that the deal had resulted in the break-up of cross-ownership interests in Phoenix and St. Louis, as well as sale of WHEC–TV to a buyer controlled by a minority group. This made WHEC–TV the first network-affiliated major market television station controlled by a minority group. The merger was approved, 5–1.

The dissenter was greatly concerned by the "trend" toward placing "organs of information and news and opinion in this country in fewer and fewer hands. This is an unhealthy thing for a democracy: absentee ownership, on a vast scale, of newspapers and broadcasting stations. . . . Where are the William Allen Whites of 1979? Too many of them have been bought out, one by one, by the chains. They've been made offers they could not refuse."

The Capital Cities Communications-American Broadcasting Companies Merger. In March, 1985, Capital Cities Communications (CCC) announced plans to acquire American Broadcasting Companies, Inc. (ABC) for $3.5 billion. This transaction, by far the largest in broadcast history, will result in the formation of a new company, Capital Cities Communications/ABC, Inc. (CCC/ABC).

For the new company to meet the various FCC ownership rules, it is likely that over $1 billion worth of properties will be sold. While CCC and ABC only own 12 AM stations, 12 FM stations and 12 TV stations between them, the total reach of the TV stations is 28.59%. One or more of the TV stations will have to be sold to bring that figure down to the 25% maximum allowed by the new multiple ownership rules.

Furthermore, both CCC and ABC own FM stations or AM–FM combinations in Los Angeles, New York, Dallas-Fort Worth and Detroit. When the companies merge the resulting duplications would violate the duopoly rule. Furthermore, many of the ABC radio stations are co-located with ABC TV stations. Remember that the Commission did not require divestiture of existing TV-radio combinations when it modified the duopoly rule to prohibit them. However, if the transaction is viewed as CCC buying ABC, then the "grandfathered" status of these combinations will no longer be allowed and they will have to be broken up.

Another duopoly question is presented by the signal overlap of CCC's TV properties in Philadelphia and New Haven with WABC–TV in New York. Technically, these would also be a violation, but there is some indication that the Commission will grant a waiver because the overlap is not viewed as serious.

Several CCC newspapers may also be subject to divestiture requirements. The *Oakland Press* and *The Daily Register* are both published in suburbs of cities where ABC broadcast outlets are located.

Finally, CCC/ABC may have to sell all the cable properties owned by CCC. Another FCC media concentration rule prohibits network ownership of cable.

Assuming that CCC/ABC divests itself of all properties failing to conform to the various FCC ownership restrictions, the Commission is expected to approve the merger. There does not seem to be much concern with the more general media concentration issues addressed in the Gannett case. If approved, the merger may herald a new wave of acquisitions and mergers, further concentrating the ownership of the nation's media in the hands of a few large corporations. The CCC/ABC merger and its implications are discussed at length in Broadcasting, Mar. 25, 1985 at 31.

Chapter XIII

ACCESS TO THE MEDIA

As we noted in our discussion of the philosophical justifications for the First Amendment, many people believe that the intended beneficiary of the First Amendment was the public not the press. Traditionally, protecting the press was seen as benefitting the public. However, some have come to question this latter idea. According to scholars like law professor Jerome Barron, the development of mass media has reduced the "marketplace of ideas" to nothing more than a romantic fantasy. Reasoning that increased concentration in media ownership had resulted in a marketplace failure, Barron contends that a government-created right of access to the media is not just allowed, but indeed required by the First Amendment. See page 27, supra. In 1973, Barron had the chance to argue this point before the Supreme Court on behalf of Pat Tornillo.

A. ACCESS TO PRINT MEDIA

MIAMI HERALD PUBLISHING CO. v. TORNILLO

Supreme Court of the United States, 1974.
418 U.S. 241, 94 S.Ct. 2831, 41 L.Ed.2d 730.

MR. CHIEF JUSTICE BURGER delivered the opinion of the Court.

The issue in this case is whether a state statute granting a political candidate a right to equal space to reply to criticism and attacks on his record by a newspaper, violates the guarantees of a free press.

I

In the fall of 1972, appellee, Executive Director of the Classroom Teachers Association, apparently a teachers' collective-bargaining agent, was a candidate for the Florida House of Representatives. On September 20, 1972, and again on September 29, 1972, appellant printed editorials critical of appellee's candidacy.* In response to these editorials appellee demanded that appellant print verbatim his replies, defending the role of the Classroom Teachers Association and the organization's accomplishments for the citizens of Dade County. Appellant declined to print the appellee's replies, and appellee brought suit in Circuit Court, Dade County, seeking declaratory and

---

* [The editorials are reprinted in the opinion. The proposed replies are printed in Lange, The Role of the Access Doctrine in the Regulation of the Mass Media: A Critical Review and Assessment, 52 N.C.L.Rev. 1, 60 n. 272 (1973)—ed.]

injunctive relief and actual and punitive damages in excess of $5,000. The action was premised on Florida Statute § 104.38 (1973), a "right of reply" statute which provides that if a candidate for nomination or election is assailed regarding his personal character or official record by any newspaper, the candidate has the right to demand that the newspaper print, free of cost to the candidate, any reply the candidate may make to the newspaper's charges. The reply must appear in as conspicuous a place and in the same kind of type as the charges which prompted the reply, provided it does not take up more space than the charges. Failure to comply with the statute constitutes a first-degree misdemeanor.[2]

Appellant sought a declaration that § 104.38 was unconstitutional. After an emergency hearing requested by appellee, the Circuit Court denied injunctive relief because, absent special circumstances, no injunction could properly issue against the commission of a crime, and held that § 104.38 was unconstitutional as an infringement on the freedom of the press under the First and Fourteenth Amendments to the Constitution. 38 Fla.Supp. 80 (1972). The Circuit Court concluded that dictating what a newspaper must print was no different from dictating what it must not print. The Circuit Judge viewed the statute's vagueness as serving "to restrict and stifle protected expression." Id., at 83. Appellee's cause was dismissed with prejudice.

On direct appeal, the Florida Supreme Court reversed, holding that § 104.38 did not violate constitutional guarantees. 287 So.2d 78 (1973). It held that free speech was enhanced and not abridged by the Florida right-of-reply statute, which in that court's view, furthered the "broad societal interest in the free flow of information to the public." Id., at 82. It also held that the statute is not impermissibly vague; the statute informs "those who are subject to it as to what conduct on their part will render them liable to its penalties." Id., at 85.[4] Civil remedies, including damages, were held to be available under this statute; the case was remanded to the trial court

2. "104.38 *Newspaper assailing candidate in an election; space for reply*—If any newspaper in its columns assails the personal character of any candidate for nomination or for election in any election, or charges said candidate with malfeasance or misfeasance in office, or otherwise attacks his official record, or gives to another free space for such purpose, such newspaper shall upon request of such candidate immediately publish free of cost any reply he may make thereto in as conspicuous a place and in the same kind of type as the matter that calls for such reply, provided such reply does not take up more space than the matter replied to. Any person or firm failing to comply with the provisions of this section shall be guilty of a misdemeanor of the first degree, punishable as provided in § 775.082 or § 775.083."

4. The Supreme Court placed the following limiting construction on the statute:

"[W]e hold that the mandate of the statute refers to 'any reply' which is wholly responsive to the charge made in the editorial or other article in a newspaper being replied to and further that such reply will be neither libelous nor slanderous of the publication nor anyone else, nor vulgar nor profane." Id., at 86.

for further proceedings not inconsistent with the Florida Supreme Court's opinion.

. . .

III

A

The challenged statute creates a right to reply to press criticism of a candidate for nomination or election. The statute was enacted in 1913 and this is only the second recorded case decided under its provisions.

Appellant contends the statute is void on its face because it purports to regulate the content of a newspaper in violation of the First Amendment. Alternatively it is urged that the statute is void for vagueness since no editor could know exactly what words would call the statute into operation. It is also contended that the statute fails to distinguish between critical comment which is and which is not defamatory.

B

The appellee and supporting advocates of an enforceable right of access to the press vigorously argue that government has an obligation to ensure that a wide variety of views reach the public.[8] The contentions of access proponents will be set out in some detail.[9] It is urged that at the time the First Amendment to the Constitution was enacted in 1791 as part of our Bill of Rights the press was broadly representative of the people it was serving. While many of the newspapers were intensely partisan and narrow in their views, the press collectively presented a broad range of opinions to readers. Entry into publishing was inexpensive; pamphlets and books provided meaningful alternatives to the organized press for the expression of unpopular ideas and often treated events and expressed views not covered by conventional newspapers. A true marketplace of ideas existed in which there was relatively easy access to the channels of communication.

Access advocates submit that although newspapers of the present are superficially similar to those of 1791 the press of today is in reality very different from that known in the early years of our national existence. In the past half century a communications revolution has seen the introduction of radio and television into our lives, the promise of a global community through the use of communications satellites, and the specter of a "wired" nation by means of

8. See generally Barron, Access to the Press—A New First Amendment Right, 80 Harv.L.Rev. 1641 (1967).

9. For a good overview of the position of access advocates see Lange, The Role of the Access Doctrine in the Regulation of the Mass Media: A Critical Review and Assessment, 52 N.C.L.Rev. 1, 8–9 (1973) (hereinafter Lange).

an expanding cable television network with two-way capabilities. The printed press, it is said, has not escaped the effects of this revolution. Newspapers have become big business and there are far fewer of them to serve a larger literate population. Chains of newspapers, national newspapers, national wire and news services, and one-newspaper towns,[13] are the dominant features of a press that has become noncompetitive and enormously powerful and influential in its capacity to manipulate popular opinion and change the course of events. Major metropolitan newspapers have collaborated to establish news services national in scope. Such national news organizations provide syndicated "interpretive reporting" as well as syndicated features and commentary, all of which can serve as part of the new school of "advocacy journalism."

The elimination of competing newspapers in most of our large cities, and the concentration of control of media that results from the only newspaper's being owned by the same interests which own a television station and a radio station, are important components of this trend toward concentration of control of outlets to inform the public.

The result of these vast changes has been to place in a few hands the power to inform the American people and shape public opinion.[15] Much of the editorial opinion and commentary that is printed is that of syndicated columnists distributed nationwide and, as a result, we are told, on national and world issues there tends to be a homogeneity of editorial opinion, commentary, and interpretive analysis. The abuses of bias and manipulative reportage are, likewise, said to be the result of the vast accumulations of unreviewable power in the modern media empires. In effect, it is claimed, the public has lost any ability to respond or to contribute in a meaningful way to the debate on issues. The monopoly of the means of communication allows for little or no critical analysis of the media except in professional journals of very limited readership. . . .

The obvious solution, which was available to dissidents at an earlier time when entry into publishing was relatively inexpensive, today would be to have additional newspapers. But the same economic factors which have caused the disappearance of vast numbers

13. "Nearly half of U.S. daily newspapers, representing some three-fifths of daily and Sunday circulation, are owned by newspaper groups and chains, including diversified business conglomerates. One-newspaper towns have become the rule with effective competition operating in only 4 percent of our large cities." Background Paper by Alfred Balk in Twentieth Century Fund Task Force Report for a National News Council, A Free and Responsive Press 18 (1973).

15. "Local monopoly in printed news raises serious questions of diversity of information and opinion. What a local newspaper does not print about local affairs does not see general print at all. And, having the power to take initiative in reporting and enunciation of opinions, it has extraordinary power to set the atmosphere and determine the terms of local consideration of public issues." B. Bagdikian, The Information Machines 127 (1971).

of metropolitan newspapers,[16] have made entry into the marketplace of ideas served by the print media almost impossible. It is urged that the claim of newspapers to be "surrogates for the public" carries with it a concomitant fiduciary obligation to account for that steward-ship. From this premise it is reasoned that the only effective way to insure fairness and accuracy and to provide for some accountability is for government to take affirmative action. The First Amendment interest of the public in being informed is said to be in peril because the "marketplace of ideas" is today a monopoly controlled by the owners of the market.

Proponents of enforced access to the press take comfort from language in several of this Court's decisions which suggests that the First Amendment acts as a sword as well as a shield, that it imposes obligations on the owners of the press in addition to protecting the press from government regulation. In Associated Press v. United States, [ ], the Court, in rejecting the argument that the press is immune from the antitrust laws by virtue of the First Amendment, stated:

> "The First Amendment, far from providing an argument against application of the Sherman Act, here provides powerful reasons to the contrary. That Amendment rests on the assumption that the widest possible dissemination of information from diverse and antagonistic sources is essential to the welfare of the public, that a free press is a condition of a free society. Surely a command that the government itself shall not impede the free flow of ideas does not afford non-governmental combinations a refuge if they impose restraints upon that constitutionally guar-anteed freedom. Freedom to publish means freedom for all and not for some. Freedom to publish is guaranteed by the Constitu-tion, but freedom to combine to keep others from publishing is not. Freedom of the press from governmental interference under the First Amendment does not sanction repression of that freedom by private interests." (Footnote omitted.)

In New York Times Co. v. Sullivan, [ ], the Court spoke of "a profound national commitment to the principle that debate on public issues should be uninhibited, robust and wide-open." It is argued that the "uninhibited, robust" debate is not "wide-open" but open only to a monopoly in control of the press. Appellee cites the plurality opinion in Rosenbloom v. Metromedia, Inc., 403 U.S. 29, 47, and n. 15 (1971), which he suggests seemed to invite experimentation by the States in right-to-access regulation of the press.[18]

---

16. The newspapers have persuaded Congress to grant them immunity from the antitrust laws in the case of "failing" newspapers for joint operations. 84 Stat. 466, 15 U.S.C. § 1801 et seq.

18. "If the States fear that private citizens will not be able to respond ade-quately to publicity involving them, the solution lies in the direction of ensuring their ability to respond, rather than in stifling public discussion of matters of public concern.[*]

"[*] Some states have adopted retraction statutes or right-of-reply statutes . . . .

Access advocates note that Mr. Justice Douglas a decade ago expressed his deep concern regarding the effects of newspaper monopolies:

> "Where one paper has a monopoly in an area, it seldom presents two sides of an issue. It too often hammers away on one ideological or political line using its monopoly position not to educate people, not to promote debate, but to inculcate in its readers one philosophy, one attitude—and to make money." "The newspapers that give a variety of views and news that is not slanted or contrived are few indeed. And the problem promises to get worse . . . .." The Great Rights 124–125, 127 (E. Cahn ed. 1963).

They also claim the qualified support of Professor Thomas I. Emerson, who has written that "[a] limited right of access to the press can be safely enforced," although he believes that "[g]overnment measures to encourage a multiplicity of outlets, rather than compelling a few outlets to represent everybody, seems a preferable course of action." T. Emerson, The System of Freedom of Expression 671 (1970).

IV

However much validity may be found in these arguments, at each point the implementation of a remedy such as an enforceable right of access necessarily calls for some mechanism, either governmental or consensual. If it is governmental coercion, this at once brings about a confrontation with the express provisions of the First Amendment and the judicial gloss on that Amendment developed over the years.[20]

The Court foresaw the problems relating to government-enforced access as early as its decision in Associated Press v. United States, supra. There it carefully contrasted the private "compulsion to print" called for by the Association's bylaws with the provisions of the District Court decree against appellants which "does not compel AP or its members to permit publication of anything which their 'reason' tells them should not be published." 326 U.S., at 20 n. 18. In Branzburg v. Hayes, [ ], we emphasized that the cases then before us "involve no intrusions upon speech or assembly, no prior

"One writer, in arguing that the First Amendment itself should be read to guarantee a right of access to the media not limited to a right to respond to defamatory falsehoods, has suggested several ways the law might encourage public discussion. Barron, Access to the Press—A New First Amendment Right, 80 Harv.L.Rev. 1641, 1666–1678 (1967). It is important to recognize that the private individual often desires press exposure either for himself, his ideas, or his causes. Constitutional adjudication must take into account the individual's interest in access to the press as well as the individual's interest in preserving his reputation, even though libel actions by their nature encourage a narrow view of the individual's interest since they focus only on situations where the individual has been harmed by undesired press attention. A constitutional rule that deters the press from covering the ideas or activities of the private individual thus conceives the individual's interest too narrowly."

20. Because we hold that § 104.38 violates the First Amendment's guarantee of a free press we have no occasion to consider appellant's further argument that the statute is unconstitutionally vague.

restraint or restriction on what the press may publish, and no express or implied command that the press publish what it prefers to withhold." In Columbia Broadcasting System, Inc. v. Democratic National Committee, 412 U.S. 94, 117 (1973), the plurality opinion as to Part III noted:

> "The power of a privately owned newspaper to advance its own political, social, and economic views is bounded by only two factors: first, the acceptance of a sufficient number of readers— and hence advertisers—to assure financial success; and, second, the journalistic integrity of its editors and publishers."

An attitude strongly adverse to any attempt to extend a right of access to newspapers was echoed by several Members of this Court in their separate opinions in that case. Id., at 145 (Stewart, J., concurring); id., at 182 n. 12 (Brennan, J., dissenting). Recently, while approving a bar against employment advertising specifying "male" or "female" preference, the Court's opinion in Pittsburgh Press Co. v. Human Relations Comm'n, 413 U.S. 376, 391 (1973), took pains to limit its holding within narrow bounds:

> "Nor, *a fortiori*, does our decision authorize any restriction whatever, whether of content or layout, on stories or commentary originated by Pittsburgh Press, its columnists, or its contributors. On the contrary, we reaffirm unequivocally the protection afforded to editorial judgment and to the free expression of views on these and other issues, however controversial."

Dissenting in *Pittsburgh Press*, Mr. Justice Stewart, joined by Mr. Justice Douglas, expressed the view that no "government agency— local, state, or federal—can tell a newspaper in advance what it can print and what it cannot." [ ]

We see that beginning with *Associated Press*, supra, the Court has expressed sensitivity as to whether a restriction or requirement constituted the compulsion exerted by government on a newspaper to print that which it would not otherwise print. The clear implication has been that any such a compulsion to publish that which " 'reason' tells them should not be published" is unconstitutional. A responsible press is an undoubtedly desirable goal, but press responsibility is not mandated by the Constitution and like many other virtues it cannot be legislated.

Appellee's argument that the Florida statute does not amount to a restriction of appellant's right to speak because "the statute in question here has not prevented the *Miami Herald* from saying anything it wished" begs the core question. Compelling editors or publishers to publish that which " 'reason' tells them should not be published" is what is at issue in this case. The Florida statute operates as a command in the same sense as a statute or regulation forbidding appellant to publish specified matter. Governmental restraint on publishing need not fall into familiar or traditional patterns to be subject to constitutional limitations on governmental powers.

Grosjean v. American Press Co., [ ]. The Florida statute exacts a penalty on the basis of the content of a newspaper. The first phase of the penalty resulting from the compelled printing of a reply is exacted in terms of the cost in printing and composing time and materials and in taking up space that could be devoted to other material the newspaper may have preferred to print. It is correct, as appellee contends, that a newspaper is not subject to the finite technological limitations of time that confront a broadcaster but it is not correct to say that, as an economic reality, a newspaper can proceed to infinite expansion of its column space to accommodate the replies that a government agency determines or a statute commands the readers should have available.[22]

Faced with the penalties that would accrue to any newspaper that published news or commentary arguably within the reach of the right-of-access statute, editors might well conclude that the safe course is to avoid controversy. Therefore, under the operation of the Florida statute, political and electoral coverage would be blunted or reduced. Government-enforced right of access inescapably "dampens the vigor and limits the variety of public debate," New York Times Co. v. Sullivan, [ ]. The Court, in Mills v. Alabama, 384 U.S. 214, 218 (1966), stated that

> "there is practically universal agreement that a major purpose of [the First] Amendment was to protect the free discussion of governmental affairs. This of course includes discussions of candidates . . .."

Even if a newspaper would face no additional costs to comply with a compulsory access law and would not be forced to forego publication of news or opinion by the inclusion of a reply, the Florida statute fails to clear the barriers of the First Amendment because of its intrusion into the function of editors. A newspaper is more than a passive receptacle or conduit for news, comment, and advertising. The choice of material to go into a newspaper, and the decisions made as to limitations on the size and content of the paper, and treatment of public issues and public officials—whether fair or unfair—constitute the exercise of editorial control and judgment. It has yet to be demonstrated how governmental regulation of this crucial process can be exercised consistent with First Amendment guarantees of a

---

22. "However since the amount of space a newspaper can devote to 'live news' is finite,* if a newspaper is forced to publish a particular item, it must as a practical matter, omit something else.

"[*]The number of column inches available for news is predetermined by a number of financial and physical factors, including circulation, the amount of advertising, and increasingly, the availability of newsprint. . . ." Note, 48 Tulane L.Rev. 433, 438 (1974) (one footnote omitted).

Another factor operating against the "solution" of adding more pages to accommodate the access matter is that "increasingly subscribers complain of bulky, unwieldly papers." Bagdikian, Fat Newspapers and Slim Coverage, Columbia Journalism Review 19 (Sept./Oct. 1973).

free press as they have evolved to this time. Accordingly, the judgment of the Supreme Court of Florida is reversed.

It is so ordered.

MR. JUSTICE BRENNAN, with whom MR. JUSTICE REHNQUIST joins, concurring.

I join the Court's opinion which, as I understand it, addresses only "right of reply" statutes and implies no view upon the constitutionality of "retraction" statutes affording plaintiffs able to prove defamatory falsehoods a statutory action to require publication of a retraction. See generally Note, Vindication of the Reputation of a Public Official, 80 Harv.L.Rev. 1730, 1739–1747 (1967).

MR. JUSTICE WHITE, concurring.

The Court today holds that the First Amendment bars a State from requiring a newspaper to print the reply of a candidate for public office whose personal character has been criticized by that newspaper's editorials. According to our accepted jurisprudence, the First Amendment erects a virtually insurmountable barrier between government and the print media so far as government tampering, in advance of publication, with news and editorial content is concerned. New York Times Co. v. United States, 403 U.S. 713 (1971). A newspaper or magazine is not a public utility subject to "reasonable" governmental regulation in matters affecting the exercise of journalistic judgment as to what shall be printed. Cf. Mills v. Alabama, 384 U.S. 214, 220 (1966). We have learned, and continue to learn, from what we view as the unhappy experiences of other nations where government has been allowed to meddle in the internal editorial affairs of newspapers. Regardless of how beneficent-sounding the purposes of controlling the press might be, we prefer "the power of reason as applied through public discussion" and remain intensely skeptical about those measures that would allow government to insinuate itself into the editorial rooms of this Nation's press. . . .

. . .

To justify this statute, Florida advances a concededly important interest of ensuring free and fair elections by means of an electorate informed about the issues. But prior compulsion by government in matters going to the very nerve center of a newspaper—the decision as to what copy will or will not be included in any given edition—collides with the First Amendment. Woven into the fabric of the First Amendment is the unexceptionable, but nonetheless timeless, sentiment that "liberty of the press is in peril as soon as the government tries to compel what is to go into a newspaper." 2 Z. Chafee, Government and Mass Communications 633 (1947).

The constitutionally obnoxious feature of § 104.38 is not that the Florida Legislature may also have placed a high premium on the protection of individual reputational interests; for government certainly has "a pervasive and strong interest in preventing and redressing attacks upon reputation." Rosenblatt v. Baer, 383 U.S. 75, 86 (1966). Quite the contrary, this law runs afoul of the elementary First Amendment proposition that government may not force a newspaper to print copy which, in its journalistic discretion, it chooses to leave on the newsroom floor. . . .

. . .

Reaffirming the rule that the press cannot be forced to print an answer to a personal attack made by it, however, throws into stark relief the consequences of the new balance forged by the Court in the companion case also announced today. Gertz v. Robert Welch, Inc., [ ], goes far toward eviscerating the effectiveness of the ordinary libel action, which has long been the only potent response available to the private citizen libeled by the press. Under *Gertz*, the burden of proving liability is immeasurably increased, proving damages is made exceedingly more difficult, and vindicating reputation by merely proving falsehood and winning a judgment to that effect are wholly foreclosed. Needlessly, in my view, the Court trivializes and denigrates the interest in reputation by removing virtually all the protection the law has always afforded.

Of course, these two decisions do not mean that because government may not dictate what the press is to print, neither can it afford a remedy for libel in any form. *Gertz* itself leaves a putative remedy for libel intact, albeit in severely emaciated form; and the press certainly remains liable for knowing or reckless falsehoods under New York Times Co. v. Sullivan, [ ], and its progeny, however improper an injunction against publication might be.

One need not think less of the First Amendment to sustain reasonable methods for allowing the average citizen to redeem a falsely tarnished reputation. . . . To me it is a near absurdity to so deprecate individual dignity, as the Court does in *Gertz*, and to leave the people at the complete mercy of the press, at least in this stage of our history when the press, as the majority in this case so well documents, is steadily becoming more powerful and much less likely to be deterred by threats of libel suits.

Notes and Questions

1. Although the statute was limited to attacks on candidates in election campaigns the majority treats the case as involving a general right of access to the press. Should it have mattered that the law was designed to assure the free flow of information to the public only in the political area and only at a specific point in the political process? The Florida Supreme Court had emphasized this aspect of the state's objective in upholding the statute (287 So.2d 78, 80–81, 86):

> The election of leaders of our government by a majority of the qualified electors is the fundamental precept upon which our system of government is based, and is an integral part of our nation's history. Recognizing that there is a right to publish

without prior governmental restraint, we also en
there is a correlative responsibility that the pu
informed.

The entire concept of freedom of expression
founding fathers rests upon the necessity for a fully unu...
electorate. James Madison wrote that, "A popular government
without popular information or the means of acquiring it is but a
prologue to a farce or tragedy; or, perhaps both. Knowledge
will forever govern ignorance; and a people who mean to be
their own governors, must arm themselves with the power which
knowledge gives" (to W.T. Barry, August 4, 1822).

The public *"need to know"* is most critical during an election campaign. By enactment of the first comprehensive corrupt
practices act relating to primary elections in 1909 our legislature
responded to the need for insuring free and fair elections. . . .
The statutory provision . . . was enacted not to punish, coerce
or censor the press but rather as a part of a centuries old
legislative task of *maintaining conditions conducive to free
and fair elections.* The Legislature in 1913 decided that owners
of the printing press had already achieved such political clout
that when they engaged in character assailings, the victim's
electoral chances were unduly and improperly diminished. To
assure fairness in campaigns, the assailed candidate had to be
provided an equivalent opportunity to respond; otherwise not
only the candidate would be hurt *but also* the people would be
deprived of both sides of the controversy.

What some segments of the press seem to lose sight of is
that the First Amendment guarantee is "not for the benefit of
the press so much as for the benefit of us all." [10] Speech
concerning public affairs is more than self expression. It is the
essence of self government.[11]

. . .

In conclusion, we do not find that the operation of the
statute would interfere with freedom of the press as guaranteed
by the Florida Constitution and the Constitution of the United
States. Indeed it strengthens the concept in that it presents both
views leaving the reader the freedom to reach his own conclusion. This decision will encourage rather than impede the wide
open and robust dissemination of ideas and counterthought
which the concept of free press both fosters and protects and
which is essential to intelligent self government.

Is the justification for an access statute strongest—or weakest—
when limited to election campaigns rather than being categorical?
For the legislative history of the statute, including the odd fact that it
was sponsored by an editor and that seven of the eight news-

10. Time, Inc. v. Hill, 385 U.S. 374,   11. Garrison v. Louisiana, 379 U.S.
389 (1967).   64, 74–75 (1964).

papermen in the legislature supported it, see Hoffer and Butterfield, The Right to Reply: A Florida First Amendment Aberration, 53 Journ.Q. 111 (1976).

2. In Mills v. Alabama, 384 U.S. 214 (1966), cited in *Tornillo,* the Court unanimously reversed the conviction of a newspaper editor for writing an editorial in violation of a statute prohibiting "electioneering" or solicitation of votes on election day:

> Suppression of the right of the press to praise or criticize governmental agents and to clamor and contend for or against change, which is all that this editorial did, muzzles one of the very agencies the Framers of our Constitution thoughtfully and deliberately selected to improve our society and keep it free. The Alabama Corrupt Practices Act by providing criminal penalties for publishing editorials such as the one here silences the press at a time when it can be most effective. It is difficult to conceive of a more obvious and flagrant abridgment of the constitutionally guaranteed freedom of the press.

The state claimed to be protecting the public from confusing "last minute charges" that could not be answered, but the Court noted that such charges could still be made on the day before the election. No "test of reasonableness can save" such a statute.

3. *Access in Electoral Campaigns.* Can a special case be made for requiring access to the media in election campaigns? On balance, is the right of reply likely to expand or contract the breadth of political debate?

4. How do the Florida court and the Supreme Court analyze the issue of "compulsion" to print in terms of the traditional First Amendment framework of prior restraints and subsequent punishment? Is an affirmative obligation to print something any more or less onerous than a negative ban on certain kinds of publication? From a philosophical standpoint, can *Tornillo* be seen as a conflict between "freedom from" and "freedom to?" Or a conflict between "press" and "speech?"

5. Might the statute in *Tornillo* have withstood attack if it had required a demonstration of "falsity"—or deliberate falsity—in the newspaper coverage before making access available?

6. Is there a basis for Justice Brennan's assertion that the Court's opinion does not bring into question a statute that would give defamation plaintiffs who prove falsity the right to a mandatory retraction? Consider the differences among statutes that required the paper to say "We were wrong" or "A court has ordered us to state that it has found that we were in error" or "A court has ordered us to retract our statement. . . ."

What about a statute that gave the publisher a choice between paying damages and issuing a retraction?

7. In a book devoted almost exclusively to the access question, it is claimed that the *Tornillo* ruling is "almost devoid of reasoned support, its use of precedent is disingenuous, and the constitutional principle announced is not consistent with other rules grounded in the First Amendment." B. Schmidt, Jr., Freedom of the Press vs. Public Access 13 (1976). Since unreasoned opinions are fragile, "the sweeping and conclusive fashion in which the Court rejected the constitutionality of access statutes may prove less durable than less categorical arguments against broad access requirements." Later, at p. 234, the author suggested that the Court may have written sweepingly to counter the broad claims of the Florida opinions and the academic supporters of access. Although the case does recognize "autonomy of the press" as a "guarantee of constitutional dimension," later cases may impose some limit on the broad proposition, as in other First Amendment areas.

One response to the *Tornillo* problem has been more discussion of unofficial "press councils" to pass upon complaints brought against media by members of the public. The subject was explored in Ritter and Leibowitz, Press Councils: The Answer to Our First Amendment Dilemma, 1974 Duke L.J. 845. Published reports by the National News Council, including those published in the 1970's in *Columbia Journalism Review*, demonstrate the results of the council's efforts. With the demise of the National News Council in the 1980's due to lack of interest and inadequate funding, hopes that press councils would solve access problems died too.

A public opinion survey undertaken by Public Agenda Foundation suggested that many respondents disagreed with the results in *Tornillo*. By overwhelming votes, the respondents rejected any kind of censorship or prohibition on what newspapers or television might report. But by even larger margins they wanted their media to be "fair." Thus, the following laws were supported: requiring newspapers to give major party candidates equal coverage (82% to 12%); requiring newspapers to give opponents of a controversial policy as much coverage as proponents (73% to 17%); requiring newspapers to cover activities of "major" third party candidates (63% in favor). Respondents expressed similar feelings about broadcasters' obligations. As we shall see, broadcasters are already under obligations similar to those that respondents would impose on newspapers.

On the other hand, "Most Americans have not worked through the complexities involved in government regulation of the media, and many of the respondents found questions about the problems of enforcing fairness to be frustrating and confusing." The Speaker and the Listener: A Public Perspective on Freedom of Expression 28–31 (1980).

One editorial response asserted that "The foundation's findings reveal what we consider a tremendous ignorance, or, more politely, misunderstanding, on the part of the public as to what freedom of the press is all about." S.F. Chronicle, Oct. 28, 1980 at 48.

The respondents also found newspapers "not usually fair" (54%) and "not usually accurate" (52%). The comparable figures for television were 46% and 37%.

8. *Paid Advertisements.* The statute in question in *Tornillo* applied to newspaper "columns" generally. Would a different question of access be raised if Tornillo wanted to purchase space for political advertising?

a. With the exception of one lower court case in 1919, courts have uniformly held that a private newspaper may reject advertising for any reason, or no reason, so long as its motive or effect is not anti-competitive, and most state action claims have been denied. When a litigant relied on the "access argument" to contend that a private paper that has established itself as a forum for advertising has an obligation to accept advertisements expressing opinions on matters of public concern, the court rejected it in a single paragraph: "We do not understand this to be the concept of freedom of the press recognized in the First Amendment." Chicago Joint Board, Amalgamated Clothing Workers of America v. Chicago Tribune Co., 435 F.2d 470 (7th Cir.1970), certiorari denied 402 U.S. 973 (1971).

b. A separate but related problem is presented when the government itself wishes to place official notices in local newspapers—often required by statute to do so. Though there are few cases it appears that the courts uniformly hold that newspapers may reject such advertising if they desire.

c. The rates that a newspaper may charge (if it does accept editorial advertising) are frequently regulated. A number of states as well as the federal government (Federal Election Campaign Act Amendments of 1974, § 205(a), 2 U.S.C. § 435) require that a periodical charge political advertisers no more than it charges others who make "comparable use" of the same space for other purposes. Constitutional attacks on these statutes have been rejected in both Massachusetts, Opinion of the Justices to the Senate, 363 Mass. 909, 298 N.E.2d 829, 835 (1973), and New Hampshire, Chronicle & Gazette Publishing Co., Inc. v. Attorney General, 94 N.H. 148, 48 A.2d 478 (1946), certiorari denied 329 U.S. 690 (1947), on the ground that the regulation dealt exclusively with commercial aspects of the operation of the periodical. Compare Gore Newspapers Co. v. Shevin, 397 F.Supp. 1253 (S.D.Fla.1975), invalidating Florida's statute requiring newspapers when they sold space to candidates to charge a rate that did not exceed "the lowest local rate available to advertisers otherwise qualifying for maximum frequency discounts, bulk discounts, and advertising packages. . . ." The court assumed that the "cheapest rate is not an unprofitable rate." Nonetheless, it declared the statute unconstitutional because it restrained the content of the publication. The judge relied on the *Tornillo* rationale that the access statute imposed a penalty on the press for printing certain types of material. Here, the restraint was aimed at revenue rather than content but the judge thought the same principle applicable.

B. ACCESS TO BROADCAST MEDIA

1. IS MANDATED ACCESS CONSTITUTIONAL?

Miami Herald v. Tornillo was not the first case to consider a forced right of access to the media. In 1969, the Court decided a similar case involving the broadcast media. The case, Red Lion Broadcasting v. FCC, involved a challenge to the personal attack part of the broader fairness doctrine. The case also refers to the "equal opportunities" rule (sometimes incorrectly called the "equal time" rule), which applies during election campaigns. Although we look at each of these doctrines in detail in Chapter XV, we must introduce each one now so that *Red Lion* can be fully understood.

As part of the first Communications Act, Congress passed what is now Section 315, which requires any broadcaster who sells or gives time for a candidate's use to treat all other candidates for the same office equally. This means that a broadcaster who sells a candidate for Congress 15 minutes of prime time, must be prepared to sell each opponent of that candidate the same amount of prime time at equivalent prices.

The fairness doctrine, on the other hand, was not imposed by Congress. Developed by the Commission on its own in the 1940's, the doctrine has two separate parts. One part requires the broadcaster to air issues that "are so critical or of such great public importance that it would be unreasonable for a licensee to ignore them completely." Much more attention has been paid to the second part of the doctrine—that if a broadcaster does cover a "controversial issue of public importance" it must take steps to assure that important contrasting views are also presented. These views may be presented by the licensee itself or by speakers chosen by the licensee.

The personal attack aspect of the fairness doctrine emerged in decisions in which the FCC ordered stations that had broadcast programs attacking a person's character during a discussion of a controversial issue of public importance to inform the person and offer him time to present his side. The Red Lion case arose from such a situation.

As the Red Lion case was being litigated, the FCC decided to promulgate a formal rule to make the personal attack doctrine more precise and more readily enforceable. The personal attack rule applied when "during the presentation of views on a controversial issue of public importance, an attack is made upon the honesty, character, integrity, or like personal qualities of an identified person or group." Notice and an opportunity to respond were required.

At the same time, the FCC decided to promulgate a formal political editorial rule providing that when a licensee editorially endorsed a candidate for political office, other candidates for the same office were to be advised of the endorsement and offered a reasonable opportunity to respond. The same opportunity was to be extended to any candidate who was attacked in an editorial.

As soon as these two formal rules were announced, the Radio Television News Directors Association (RTNDA) sued to declare the rules unconstitutional. The court of appeals agreed, and held that the rules violated the First Amendment. The Supreme Court heard both cases together and decided them in the same opinion.

RED LION BROADCASTING CO. v. FEDERAL COMMUNICATIONS COMMISSION

Supreme Court of the United States, 1969.
395 U.S. 367, 89 S.Ct. 1794, 23 L.Ed.2d 371.

MR. JUSTICE WHITE delivered the opinion of the Court.

The Federal Communications Commission has for many years imposed on radio and television broadcasters the requirement that discussion of public issues be presented on broadcast stations, and that each side of those issues must be given fair coverage. This is known as the fairness doctrine, which originated very early in the history of broadcasting and has maintained its present outlines for some time. It is an obligation whose content has been defined in a long series of FCC rulings in particular cases, and which is distinct from the statutory requirement of § 315 of the Communications Act that equal time be allotted all qualified candidates for public office. Two aspects of the fairness doctrine, relating to personal attacks in the context of controversial public issues and to political editorializing, were codified more precisely in the form of FCC regulations in 1967. The two cases before us now, which were decided separately below, challenge the constitutional and statutory bases of the doctrine and component rules. *Red Lion* involves the application of the fairness doctrine to a particular broadcast, and *RTNDA* arises as an action to review the FCC's 1967 promulgation of the personal attack and political editorializing regulations, which were laid down after the *Red Lion* litigation had begun.

I.

A.

The Red Lion Broadcasting Company is licensed to operate a Pennsylvania radio station, WGCB. On November 27, 1964, WGCB carried a 15-minute broadcast by the Reverend Billy James Hargis as part of a "Christian Crusade" series. A book by Fred J. Cook entitled "Goldwater—Extremist on the Right" was discussed by Hargis, who said that Cook had been fired by a newspaper for making false charges against city officials; that Cook had then worked for a Communist-affiliated publication; that he had defended Alger Hiss and attacked J. Edgar Hoover and the Central Intelligence Agency; and that he had now written a "book to smear and destroy Barry Goldwater." When Cook heard of the broadcast he concluded that he had been personally attacked and demanded free reply time, which the station refused. After an exchange of letters among Cook, Red Lion, and the FCC, the FCC declared that the Hargis broadcast constituted a personal attack on Cook; that Red Lion had failed to meet its obligation under the fairness doctrine as expressed in Times-Mirror Broadcasting Co., 24 P & F Radio Reg. 404 (1962), to send a tape, transcript, or summary of the broadcast to Cook and offer him reply time; and that the station must provide reply time whether or not Cook would pay for it. On review in the Court of Appeals for the District of Columbia Circuit, the FCC's position was upheld as constitutional and otherwise proper. [ ]

. . .

C.

Believing that the specific application of the fairness doctrine in *Red Lion*, and the promulgation of the regulations in *RTNDA*, are both authorized by Congress and enhance rather than abridge the freedoms of speech and press protected by the First Amendment, we hold them valid and constitutional, reversing the judgment below in *RTNDA* and affirming the judgment below in *Red Lion*.

II.

The history of the emergence of the fairness doctrine and of the related legislation shows that the Commission's action in the *Red Lion* case did not exceed its authority, and that in adopting the new regulations the Commission was implementing congressional policy rather than embarking on a frolic of its own.

A.

Before 1927, the allocation of frequencies was left entirely to the private sector, and the result was chaos. It quickly became apparent that broadcast frequencies constituted a scarce resource whose use could be regulated and rationalized only by the Government. Without government control, the medium would be of little use because of the cacaphony of competing voices, none of which could be clearly and predictably heard. Consequently, the Federal Radio Commission was established to allocate frequencies among competing applicants in a manner responsive to the public "convenience, interest, or necessity."

Very shortly thereafter the Commission expressed its view that the "public interest requires ample play for the free and fair competi-

tion of opposing views, and the commission believes that the principle applies . . . to all discussions of issues of importance to the public."
. . . After an extended period during which the licensee was obliged not only to cover and to cover fairly the views of others, but also to refrain from expressing his own personal views, Mayflower Broadcasting Corp., 8 F.C.C. 333 (1940), the latter limitation on the licensee was abandoned and the doctrine developed into its present form.

There is a twofold duty laid down by the FCC's decisions and described by the 1949 Report on Editorializing by Broadcast Licensees, 13 F.C.C. 1246 (1949). The broadcaster must give adequate coverage to public issues, [   ], and coverage must be fair in that it accurately reflects the opposing views. [   ] This must be done at the broadcaster's own expense if sponsorship is unavailable. [   ] Moreover, the duty must be met by programming obtained at the licensee's own initiative if available from no other source. . . .

When a personal attack has been made on a figure involved in a public issue, both the doctrine of cases such as *Red Lion* and *Times Mirror Broadcasting Co.*, 24 P & F Radio Reg. 404 (1962), and also the 1967 regulations at issue in *RTNDA* require that the individual attacked himself be offered an opportunity to respond. Likewise, where one candidate is endorsed in a political editorial, the other candidates must themselves be offered reply time to use personally or through a spokesman. These obligations differ from the general fairness requirement that issues be presented, and presented with coverage of competing views, in that the broadcaster does not have the option of presenting the attacked party's side himself or choosing a third party to represent that side. But insofar as there is an obligation of the broadcaster to see that both sides are presented, and insofar as that is an affirmative obligation, the personal attack doctrine and regulations do not differ from the preceding fairness doctrine. The simple fact that the attacked men or unendorsed candidates may respond themselves or through agents is not a critical distinction, and indeed, it is not unreasonable for the FCC to conclude that the objective of adequate presentation of all sides may best be served by allowing those most closely affected to make the response, rather than leaving the response in the hands of the station which has attacked their candidacies, endorsed their opponents, or carried a personal attack upon them.

B.

The statutory authority of the FCC to promulgate these regulations derives from the mandate to the "Commission from time to time, as public convenience, interest, or necessity requires" to promulgate "such rules and regulations and prescribe such restrictions and conditions . . . as may be necessary to carry out the provisions of this chapter. . . ." 47 U.S.C. § 303 and § 303(r). The Commission is specifically directed to consider the demands of the public interest in the course of granting licenses, 47 U.S.C. §§ 307(a), 309(a); renewing them, 47 U.S.C. § 307; and modifying them. Ibid. Moreover, the FCC has included among the conditions of the Red Lion license itself the requirement that operation of the station be carried out in the public interest, 47 U.S.C. § 309(h). This mandate to the FCC to assure that broadcasters operate in the public interest is a broad one, a power "not niggardly but expansive," National Broadcasting Co. v. United States, 319 U.S. 190, 219 (1943), whose validity we have long upheld. [   ] It is broad enough to encompass these regulations.

The fairness doctrine finds specific recognition in statutory form, is in part modeled on explicit statutory provisions relating to political candidates, and is approvingly reflected in legislative history.

In 1959 the Congress amended the statutory requirement of § 315 that equal time be accorded each political candidate to except certain appearances on news programs, but added that this constituted no exception *"from the obligation imposed upon them under this Act to operate in the public interest and to afford reasonable opportunity for the discussion of conflicting views on issues of public importance."* Act of September 14, 1959, § 1, 73 Stat. 557, amending 47 U.S.C. § 315(a) (emphasis added). This language makes it very plain that Congress, in 1959, announced that the phrase "public interest," which had been in the Act since 1927, imposed a duty on broadcasters to discuss both sides of controversial public issues. In other words, the amendment vindicated the FCC's general view that the fairness doctrine inhered in the public interest standard. Subsequent legislation declaring the intent of an earlier statute is entitled to great weight in statutory construction. And here this principle is given special force by the equally venerable principle that the construction of a statute by those charged with its execution should be followed unless there are compelling indications that it is wrong, especially when Congress has refused to alter the administrative construction. Here, the Congress has not just kept its silence by refusing to overturn the administrative construction, but has ratified it with positive legislation. Thirty years of consistent administrative construction left undisturbed by Congress until 1959, when that construction was expressly accepted, reinforce the natural conclusion that the public interest language of the Act authorized the Commission to require licensees to use their stations for discussion of public issues, and that the FCC is free to implement this requirement by reasonable rules and regulations which fall short of abridgment of the freedom of speech and press, and of the censorship proscribed by § 326 of the Act.

The objectives of § 315 themselves could readily be circumvented but for the complementary fairness doctrine ratified by § 315. The section applies only to campaign appearances by candidates, and not by family, friends, campaign managers, or other supporters. Without the fairness doctrine, then, a licensee could ban all campaign appearances by candidates themselves from the air and proceed to deliver over his station entirely to the supporters of one slate of candidates, to the exclusion of all others. In this way the broadcaster could have a far greater impact on the favored candidacy than he could by simply allowing a spot appearance by the candidate himself. It is the fairness doctrine as an aspect of the obligation to operate in the public interest, rather than § 315, which prohibits the broadcaster from taking such a step.

. . .

In light of the fact that the "public interest" in broadcasting clearly encompasses the presentation of vigorous debate of controversial issues of importance and concern to the public; the fact that the FCC has rested upon that language from its very inception a doctrine that these issues must be discussed, and fairly; and the fact that Congress has acknowledged that the analogous provisions of § 315 are not preclusive in this area, and knowingly preserved the FCC's complementary efforts, we think the fairness doctrine and its component personal attack and political editorializing regulations are a legitimate exercise of congressionally delegated authority. . . .

III.

The broadcasters challenge the fairness doctrine and its specific manifestations in the personal attack and political editorial rules on conventional First Amendment grounds, alleging that the rules abridge their freedom of speech and press. Their contention is that the First Amendment protects their desire to use their allotted frequencies continuously to broadcast whatever they choose, and to exclude whomever they choose from ever using that frequency. No man may be prevented from saying or publishing what he thinks, or from refusing in his speech or other utterances to give equal weight to the views of his opponents. This right, they say, applies equally to broadcasters.

A.

Although broadcasting is clearly a medium affected by a First Amendment interest, United States v. Paramount Pictures, Inc., 334 U.S. 131, 166 (1948), differences in the characteristics of new media justify differences in the First Amendment standards applied to them. [ ] For example, the ability of new technology to produce sounds more raucous than those of the human voice justifies restrictions on the sound level, and on the hours and places of use, of sound trucks so long as the restrictions are reasonable and applied without discrimination. [ ]

Just as the Government may limit the use of sound-amplifying equipment potentially so noisy that it drowns out civilized private speech, so may the Government limit the use of broadcast equipment. The right of free speech of a broadcaster, the user of a sound truck, or any other individual does not embrace a right to snuff out the free speech of others. Associated Press v. United States, 326 U.S. 1, 20 (1945).

When two people converse face to face, both should not speak at once if either is to be clearly understood. But the range of the human voice is so limited that there could be meaningful communications if half the people in the United States were talking and the other half listening. Just as clearly, half the people might publish and the other half read. But the reach of radio signals is incomparably greater than the range of the human voice and the problem of interference is a massive reality. The lack of know-how and equipment may keep many from the air but only a tiny fraction of those with resources and intelligence can hope to communicate by radio at the same time if intelligible communication is to be had, even if the entire radio spectrum is utilized in the present state of commercially acceptable technology.

It was this fact, and the chaos which ensued from permitting anyone to use any frequency at whatever power level he wished, which made necessary the enactment of the Radio Act of 1927 and the Communications Act of 1934, as the Court has noted at length before. National Broadcasting Co. v. United States, 319 U.S. 190, 210–214 (1943). It was this reality which at the very least necessitated first the division of the radio spectrum into portions reserved respectively for public broadcasting and for other important radio uses such as amateur operation, aircraft, police, defense, and navigation; and then the subdivision of each portion, and assignment of specific frequencies to individual users or groups of users. Beyond this, however, because the frequencies reserved for public broadcasting were limited in number, it was essential for the Government to tell some applicants that they could not broadcast at all because there was room for only a few.

Where there are substantially more individuals who want to broadcast than there are frequencies to allocate, it is idle to posit an unabridgeable First Amendment right to broadcast comparable to the right of every individual to speak, write, or publish. If 100 persons want broadcast licenses but there are only 10 frequencies to allocate, all of them may have the same "right" to a license; but if there is to be any effective communication by radio, only a few can be licensed and the rest must be barred from the airwaves. It would be strange if the First Amendment, aimed at protecting and furthering communications, prevented the Government from making radio communication possible by requiring licenses to broadcast and by limiting the number of licenses so as not to overcrowd the spectrum.

This has been the consistent view of the Court. Congress unquestionably has the power to grant and deny licenses and to eliminate existing stations. FRC v. Nelson Bros. Bond & Mortgage Co., 289 U.S. 266 (1933). No one has a First Amendment right to a license or to monopolize a radio frequency; to deny a station license because "the public interest" requires it "is not a denial of free speech." National Broadcasting Co. v. United States, 319 U.S. 190, 227 (1943).

By the same token, as far as the First Amendment is concerned those who are licensed stand no better than those to whom licenses are refused. A license permits broadcasting, but the licensee has no constitutional right to be the one who holds the license or to monopolize a radio frequency to the exclusion of his fellow citizens. There is nothing in the First Amendment which prevents the Government from requiring a licensee to share his frequency with others and to conduct himself as a proxy or fiduciary with obligations to present those views and voices which are representative of his community and which would otherwise, by necessity, be barred from the airwaves.

This is not to say that the First Amendment is irrelevant to public broadcasting. On the contrary, it has a major role to play as the Congress itself recognized in § 326, which forbids FCC interference with "the right of free speech by means of radio communication." Because of the scarcity of radio frequencies, the Government is permitted to put restraints on licensees in favor of others whose views should be expressed on this unique medium. But the people as a whole retain their interest in free speech by radio and their collective right to have the medium function consistently with the ends and purposes of the First Amendment. It is the right of the viewers and listeners, not the right of the broadcasters, which is paramount. See FCC v. Sanders Bros. Radio Station, 309 U.S. 470, 475 (1940); FCC v. Allentown Broadcasting Corp., 349 U.S. 358, 361–362 (1955); 2 Z. Chafee, Government and Mass Communications 546 (1947). It is the purpose of the First Amendment to preserve an uninhibited marketplace of ideas in which truth will ultimately prevail, rather than to countenance monopolization of that market, whether it be by the Government itself or a private licensee. Associated Press v. United States, 326 U.S. 1, 20 (1945); New York Times Co. v. Sullivan, 376 U.S. 254, 270 (1964); Abrams v. United States, 250 U.S. 616, 630 (1919) (Holmes, J., dissenting). "[S]peech concerning public affairs is more than self-expression; it is the essence of self-government." Garrison v. Louisiana, 379 U.S. 64, 74–75 (1964). See Brennan, The Supreme Court and the Meiklejohn Interpretation of the First Amendment, 79 Harv.L.Rev. 1 (1965). It is the right of the public to receive suitable access to social, political, esthetic, moral, and other ideas and experiences which is crucial here. That right may not constitutionally be abridged either by Congress or by the FCC.

B.

Rather than confer frequency monopolies on a relatively small number of licensees, in a Nation of 200,000,000, the Government could surely have decreed that each frequency should be shared among all or some of those who wish to use it, each being assigned a portion of the broadcast day or the broadcast week. The ruling and regulations at issue here do not go quite so far. They assert that under specified circumstances, a licensee must offer to make available a reasonable amount of broadcast time to those who have a view different from that which has already been expressed on his station. The expression of a political endorsement, or of a personal attack while dealing with a controversial public issue, simply triggers this time sharing. As we have said, the First Amendment confers no right on licensees to prevent others from broadcasting on "their" frequencies and no right to an unconditional monopoly of a scarce resource which the Government has denied others the right to use.

In terms of constitutional principle, and as enforced sharing of a scarce resource, the personal attack and political editorial rules are indistinguishable from the equal-time provision of § 315, a specific enactment of Congress requiring stations to set aside reply time under specified circumstances and to which the fairness doctrine and these constituent regulations are important complements. That provision, which has been part of the law since 1927, Radio Act of 1927, § 18, 44 Stat. 1170, has been held valid by this Court as an obligation of the licensee relieving him of any power in any way to prevent or censor the broadcast, and thus insulating him from liability for defamation. The constitutionality of the statute under the First Amendment was unquestioned. Farmers Educ. & Coop. Union v. WDAY, 360 U.S. 525 (1959).

Nor can we say that it is inconsistent with the First Amendment goal of producing an informed public capable of conducting its own affairs to require a broadcaster to permit answers to personal attacks occurring in the course of discussing controversial issues, or to require that the political opponents of those endorsed by the station be given a chance to communicate with the public.[18] Otherwise, station owners and a few networks would have unfettered power to make time available only to the highest bidders, to communicate only their own views on public issues, people and candidates, and to permit on the air only those with whom they agreed. There is no sanctuary

---

18. The expression of views opposing those which broadcasters permit to be aired in the first place need not be confined solely to the broadcasters themselves as proxies. "Nor is it enough that he should hear the arguments of adversaries from his own teachers, presented as they state them, and accompanied by what they offer as refutations. That is not the way to do justice to the arguments, or bring them into real contact with his own mind. He must be able to hear them from persons who actually believe them; who defend them in earnest, and do their very utmost for them." J. Mill, On Liberty 32 (R. McCallum ed. 1947).

in the First Amendment for unlimited private censorship operating in a medium not open to all. "Freedom of the press from governmental interference under the First Amendment does not sanction repression of that freedom by private interests." Associated Press v. United States, 326 U.S. 1, 20 (1945).

C.

It is strenuously argued, however, that if political editorials or personal attacks will trigger an obligation in broadcasters to afford the opportunity for expression to speakers who need not pay for time and whose views are unpalatable to the licensees, then broadcasters will be irresistibly forced to self-censorship and their coverage of controversial public issues will be eliminated or at least rendered wholly ineffective. Such a result would indeed be a serious matter, for should licensees actually eliminate their coverage of controversial issues, the purposes of the doctrine would be stifled.

At this point, however, as the Federal Communications Commission has indicated, that possibility is at best speculative. The communications industry, and in particular the networks, have taken pains to present controversial issues in the past, and even now they do not assert that they intend to abandon their efforts in this regard. It would be better if the FCC's encouragement were never necessary to induce the broadcasters to meet their responsibility. And if experience with the administration of these doctrines indicates that they have the net effect of reducing rather than enhancing the volume and quality of coverage, there will be time enough to reconsider the constitutional implications. The fairness doctrine in the past has had no such overall effect.

That this will occur now seems unlikely, however, since if present licensees should suddenly prove timorous, the Commission is not powerless to insist that they give adequate and fair attention to public issues. It does not violate the First Amendment to treat licensees given the privilege of using scarce radio frequencies as proxies for the entire community, obligated to give suitable time and attention to matters of great public concern. To condition the granting or renewal of licenses on a willingness to present representative community views on controversial issues is consistent with the ends and purposes of those constitutional provisions forbidding the abridgment of freedom of speech and freedom of the press. Congress need not stand idly by and permit those with licenses to ignore the problems which beset the people or to exclude from the airways anything but their own views of fundamental questions. The statute, long administrative practice, and cases are to this effect.

Licenses to broadcast do not confer ownership of designated frequencies, but only the temporary privilege of using them. 47 U.S.C. § 301. Unless renewed, they expire within three years. 47 U.S.C. § 307(d). The statute mandates the issuance of licenses if the "public convenience, interest, or necessity will be served thereby." 47 U.S.C. § 307(a). In applying this standard the Commission for 40 years has been choosing licensees based in part on their program proposals. In FRC v. Nelson Bros. Bond & Mortgage Co., 289 U.S. 266, 279 (1933), the Court noted that in "view of the limited number of available broadcasting frequencies the Congress has authorized allocation and licenses." In determining how best to allocate frequencies, the Federal Radio Commission considered the needs of competing communities and the programs offered by competing stations to meet those needs; moreover, if needs or programs shifted the Commission could alter its allocations to reflect those shifts. Id., at 285. . . .

D.

The litigants embellish their First Amendment arguments with the contention that the regulations are so vague that their duties are impossible to discern. Of this point it is enough to say that, judging the validity of the regulations on their face as they are presented here, we cannot conclude that the FCC has been left a free hand to vindicate its own idiosyncratic conception of the public interest or of the requirements of free speech. . . .

We need not and do not now ratify every past and future decision by the FCC with regard to programming. There is no question here of the Commission's refusal to permit the broadcaster to carry a particular program or to publish his own views; of a discriminatory refusal to require the licensee to broadcast certain views which have been denied access to the airwaves; of government censorship of a particular program contrary to § 326; or of the official government view dominating public broadcasting. Such questions would raise more serious First Amendment issues. But we do hold that the Congress and the Commission do not violate the First Amendment when they require a radio or television station to give reply time to answer personal attacks and political editorials.

E.

It is argued that even if at one time the lack of available frequencies for all who wished to use them justified the Government's choice of those who would best serve the public interest by acting as proxy for those who would present differing views, or by giving the latter access directly to broadcast facilities, this condition no longer prevails so that continuing control is not justified. To this there are several answers.

Scarcity is not entirely a thing of the past. Advances in technology, such as microwave transmission, have led to more efficient utilization of the frequency spectrum, but uses for that spectrum have also grown apace. Portions of the spectrum must be reserved for vital uses unconnected with human communication, such as radio-navigational aids used by aircraft and vessels. Conflicts have even emerged between such vital functions as defense preparedness and experimentation in methods of averting midair collisions through radio warning devices. "Land mobile services" such as police, ambulance, fire department, public utility, and other communications systems have been occupying an increasingly crowded portion of the frequency spectrum and there are, apart from licensed amateur radio operators' equipment, 5,000,000 transmitters operated on the "citizens' band" which is also increasingly congested. Among the various uses for radio frequency space, including marine, aviation, amateur, military, and common carrier users, there are easily enough claimants to permit use of the whole with an even smaller allocation to broadcast radio and television uses than now exists.

Comparative hearings between competing applicants for broadcast spectrum space are by no means a thing of the past. The radio spectrum has become so congested that at times it has been necessary to suspend new applications. The very high frequency television spectrum is, in the country's major markets, almost entirely occupied, although space reserved for ultra high frequency television transmission, which is a relatively recent development as a commercially viable alternative, has not yet been completely filled.[25]

The rapidity with which technological advances succeed one another to create more efficient use of spectrum space on the one hand, and to create new uses for that space by ever growing numbers of people on the other, makes it unwise to speculate on the future allocation of that space. It is enough to say that the resource is one

25. In a table prepared by the FCC on the basis of statistics current as of August 31, 1968, VHF and UHF channels allocated to and those available in the top 100 market areas for television are set forth:

Commercial

Market Areas	Channels Allocated		Channels On the Air, Authorized, or Applied for		Available Channels	
	VHF	UHF	VHF	UHF	VHF	UHF
Top 10	40	45	40	44	0	1
Top 50	157	163	157	136	0	27
Top 100	264	297	264	213	0	84

Noncommercial

Market Areas	Channels Reserved		Channels On the Air, Authorized, or Applied for		Available Channels	
	VHF	UHF	VHF	UHF	VHF	UHF
Top 10	7	17	7	16	0	1
Top 50	21	79	20	47	1	32
Top 100	35	138	34	69	1	69

1968 FCC Annual Report 132–135.

of considerable and growing importance whose scarcity impelled its regulation by an agency authorized by Congress. Nothing in this record, or in our own researches, convinces us that the resource is no longer one for which there are more immediate and potential uses than can be accommodated, and for which wise planning is essential. This does not mean, of course, that every possible wavelength must be occupied at every hour by some vital use in order to sustain the congressional judgment. The substantial capital investment required for many uses, in addition to the potentiality for confusion and interference inherent in any scheme for continuous kaleidoscopic reallocation of all available space may make this unfeasible. The allocation need not be made at such a breakneck pace that the objectives of the allocation are themselves imperiled.

Even where there are gaps in spectrum utilization, the fact remains that existing broadcasters have often attained their present position because of their initial government selection in competition with others before new technological advances opened new opportunities for further uses. Long experience in broadcasting, confirmed habits of listeners and viewers, network affiliation, and other advantages in program procurement give existing broadcasters a substantial advantage over new entrants, even where new entry is technologically possible. These advantages are the fruit of a preferred position conferred by the Government. Some present possibility for new entry by competing stations is not enough, in itself, to render unconstitutional the Government's effort to assure that a broadcaster's programming ranges widely enough to serve the public interest.

In view of the scarcity of broadcast frequencies, the Government's role in allocating those frequencies, and the legitimate claims of those unable without governmental assistance to gain access to those frequencies for expression of their views, we hold the regulations and ruling at issue here are both authorized by statute and constitutional.[28] The judgment of the Court of Appeals in *Red Lion* is affirmed and that in *RTNDA* reversed and the causes remanded for proceedings consistent with this opinion.

It is so ordered.

Not having heard oral argument in these cases, MR. JUSTICE DOUGLAS took no part in the Court's decision.

---

28. We need not deal with the argument that even if there is no longer a technological scarcity of frequencies limiting the number of broadcasters, there nevertheless is an economic scarcity in the sense that the Commission could or does limit entry to the broadcasting market on economic grounds and license no more stations than the market will support. Hence, it is said, the fairness doctrine or its equivalent is essential to satisfy the claims of those excluded and of the public generally. A related argument, which we also put aside, is that quite apart from scarcity of frequencies, technological or economic, Congress does not abridge freedom of speech or press by legislation directly or indirectly multiplying the voices and views presented to the public through time sharing, fairness doctrines, or other devices which limit or dissipate the power of those who sit astride the channels of communication with the general public. Cf. Citizen Pub. Co. v. United States, 394 U.S. 131 (1969).

Notes and Questions

1. The Court states that the differences among the technical aspects of media warrant different regulatory treatment. Compare Jackson, J., concurring, in Kovacs v. Cooper, 336 U.S. 77, 97 (1949): "The moving picture screen, the radio, the newspaper, the handbill, the sound truck and the street corner orator have differing natures, values, abuses and dangers. Each, in my view, is a law unto itself. . . ."

2. The Court states that only a tiny fraction of those who want to broadcast are able to do so "even if the entire radio spectrum is utilized. . . . " Who decided how much of the spectrum to allocate to radio? Could a niggardly or inefficient allocation of radio space justify government exercise of its regulatory power? The notion of "scarcity" plays a major role in the Court's analysis. What does the term appear to mean in the opinion?

Consider whether scarcity is present in the following contexts: (a) all three radio outlets allocated to a community are being used; (b) of the five radio outlets allocated three are being used; (c) all 40 radio outlets allocated to an urban area are being used; (d) seven of the 40 outlets are vacant.

3. Does Justice White's next-to-last paragraph suggest that the reality of scarcity in the past will be enough to justify continuing regulation even if it were determined that no scarcity exists today?

4. Accepting limits on the part of the spectrum allocated to radio, does it follow that government must be involved in assigning space to specific applicants? Even if government is involved in the individual assignments, might the channels be assigned by other devices, such as auctioning them off in perpetuity? Or for a period of years?

5. Justice White says that "It is the right of the viewers and listeners, not the right of the broadcasters, which is paramount. [ ] It is the purpose of the First Amendment to preserve an uninhibited marketplace of ideas in which truth will ultimately prevail, rather than to countenance monopolization of that market, whether it be by the Government itself or a private licensee." What philosophical strands are being brought together here?

When Justice White says that the "right" involved in the case belongs to "the public" and that this "right may not constitutionally be abridged either by Congress or by the FCC," is he suggesting that the absence of government control of broadcasters' programming would deny the public's constitutional right to "receive suitable access to social, political, esthetic, moral and other ideas and experiences?"

6. Is the Court's concern about licensees refusing to air controversial material if they must provide response time consistent with the Court's analysis in *Tornillo* ? Is it surprising that the Court did not cite *Red Lion* in its decision in *Tornillo*?

7.   There is reason to believe that Fred Cook's demand for reply time was part of a broader effort to use the fairness doctrine to soften attacks on the Kennedy administration by right-wing political commentators.   The plan was to monitor right-wing programs and then to demand reply time for personal attacks or to demand balance under the general fairness doctrine.   F. Friendly, The Good Guys, The Bad Guys and the First Amendment (1976).   If the result was that licensees cancelled several right-wing commentators would that affect your reaction to the *Red Lion* decision?   Did Cook misuse the doctrine?

8.   Aside from the spectrum scarcity arguments there are intrinsic differences between print and broadcast media.   There is a physical limit to the number of words that can be uttered intelligibly over a broadcasting facility during a 24-hour day.   Based on an estimate of about 200,000 words, using normal speaking patterns, one author suggests that a newspaper is the equivalent of between one and three 24-hour programs.   But the reader of a newspaper can at any time go directly to what interests him and skim or ignore the rest.   In broadcasting, the choice is made for the listener by the broadcaster; the speed, content, and sequence are fixed.   Baxter, Regulation and Diversity in Communications Media, 64 Am.Econ.Rev. 392 (1974).   Might such differences justify greater regulation of broadcasting?

9.   Other differences between the print and electronic media emphasize the greater impact of broadcasting in conveying certain types of information.   The vivid telecasts during the Vietnam War are thought to have been a strong factor in the shift of public attitude against that war, beyond the potential of any verbal journalism.   Another major difference is the role of sound in broadcasting, which makes it possible to use songs and jingles effectively in advertising.   During the discussion of the broadcast advertising of cigarettes, one court observed:

> Written messages are not communicated unless they are read, and reading requires an affirmative act.   Broadcast messages, in contrast, are "in the air."   In an age of omnipresent radio, there scarcely breathes a citizen who does not know some part of a leading cigarette jingle by heart.   Similarly, an ordinary habitual television watcher can *avoid* these commercials only by frequently leaving the room, changing the channel, or doing some other such affirmative act.   It is difficult to calculate the subliminal impact of this pervasive propaganda, which may be heard even if not listened to, but it may reasonably be thought greater than the impact of the written word.

Banzhaf v. Federal Communications Commission, 405 F.2d 1082, 1100–01 (D.C.Cir.1968), certiorari denied 396 U.S. 842 (1969).   Does this suggest an additional basis for regulating some aspects of broadcasting?

In considering this, recall the refusal of the Supreme Court to declare unconstitutional all motion picture censorship. In Times Film Corp. v. Chicago, 365 U.S. 43 (1961), the Court, 5–4, refused to hold "that the public exhibition of motion pictures must be allowed under any circumstances" and that the state may punish only after the fact. As the Pentagon Papers case, p. 195, supra, suggests, prior restraints may be permissible in some exceptional circumstances. Since the film producers were presumably not claiming greater protection than what was given print media, might the motion picture decision be simply an anticipation of that development? Or might the Court be concerned about the explicit and vivid depiction of sexual episodes— and fear the impact of the medium on viewers more than it fears the printed page in such circumstances? Might such a concern with motion pictures apply to television? Note that 47 U.S.C.A. § 326 bans the Commission from "censorship" of programming.

Does the *Banzhaf* view of broadcasting imply a "captive audience" comparable to the addresses of sound trucks in residential neighborhoods, or political advertisements in mass transit vehicles? Is turning off the program like averting your eyes from offensive wording on someone's jacket? Is it relevant to this aspect of the discussion that most television sets and radios are in private homes?

10. The Supreme Court returned to these questions once again in Columbia Broadcasting System, Inc. v. Democratic National Committee, 412 U.S. 94 (1973). The Court decided that broadcasters were not obligated to accept paid advertisements from "responsible" individuals and groups. The majority relied upon *Red Lion.*

Justice Stewart in a separate concurring opinion stated "I agreed with the Court in *Red Lion,* although with considerable doubt, because I thought that that much Government regulation of program content was within the outer limits of First Amendment tolerability."

In another concurring opinion, Justice Douglas stated of *Red Lion:* "I did not participate in that decision and, with all respect, would not support it. The Fairness Doctrine has no place in our First Amendment regime." He argued that the uniqueness of the spectrum was "due to engineering and technical problems. But the press in a realistic sense is likewise not available to all. Small or 'underground' papers appear and disappear; and the weekly is an established institution. But the daily papers now established are unique in the sense that it would be virtually impossible for a competitor to enter the field due to the financial exigencies of this era. The result is that in practical terms the newspapers and magazines, like TV and radio, are available only to a selected few."

2. Is Broadcasting "Government Action"?

The issues raised in *NBC* and *Red Lion* revolve around the broadcaster's claim that the First Amendment protects it from government regulation. Sometimes claims in the name of the First

Amendment are made by private citizens against the media. In *Tornillo*, the citizen's claim failed. But when such a claim is made against broadcast media a new element enters the picture. When government undertakes to provide a forum for discussion, or a street for parades, it must not discriminate among prospective users according to their views. Government must be neutral in such situations. If too many want to parade or use the forum, government might develop a lottery system or a queueing system; but it could not prefer those those views it liked. Some have argued that this analysis applies to broadcasters—that they are so closely related to, and regulated by, government that their actions are government action, and, thus, bound by the neutrality principle.

The Supreme Court avoided this question in Columbia Broadcasting System, Inc. v. Democratic National Comm., supra. DNC wanted to buy commercial time to urge financial support for the party. Another group (BEM) sought to buy time to oppose the war in Vietnam. The broadcasters refused to sell time to either group because the proposed commercials did not fit into the type of programming the broadcasters wanted to present. The DNC and BEM asked the FCC to order the broadcasters to take their commercials— at least as long as they were taking commercials from other sources. The FCC refused. The Supreme Court upheld the FCC's refusal.

The DNC–BEM claim that the broadcasters should be treated as government fragmented the Court badly. Three justices met it head on and rejected it. They were concerned that the "concept of journalistic independence could not co-exist with a reading of the challenged conduct of the licensee as government action" because a government medium could not exercise editorial judgment as to what content should be carried or excluded.

The three observed, however, that even if the First Amendment applied to this case, the groups were not entitled to access. Here, they relied on Meiklejohn's theme that the essential point was "not that everyone shall speak, but that everything worth saying shall be said." Congress and the Commission might reasonably conclude that "the allocation of journalistic priorities should be concentrated on the licensee rather than diffused among many. This policy gives the public some assurance that the broadcaster will be answerable if he fails to meet its legitimate needs. No such accountability attaches to the private individual. . . ."

Three other justices agreed that even if government action were involved in the case, there was no violation of the groups' rights under the First Amendment. They therefore refused to pass on the question of government involvement.

Justice Douglas, concurring, did not decide the question. He noted that if a licensee were to be considered a federal agency it would "within limits of its time be bound to disseminate all views." If a licensee was not considered a federal agency "I fail to see how constitutionally we can treat TV and radio differently than we treat newspapers." He agreed that "The Commission has a duty to encourage a multitude of voices but only in a limited way, viz., by preventing monopolistic practices and by promoting technological developments that will open up new channels. But censorship or editing or the screening by Government of what licensees may broadcast goes against the grain of the First Amendment."

In dissent Justice Brennan, with whom Justice Marshall concurred, disagreed:

> Thus, given the confluence of these various indicia of "governmental action"—including the public nature of the airwaves, the governmentally created preferred status of broadcasters, the extensive Government regulation of broadcast programming, and the specific governmental approval of the challenged policy—I can only conclude that the Government "has so far insinuated itself into a position" of participation in this policy that the absolute refusal of broadcast licensees to sell air time to groups or individuals wishing to speak out on controversial issues of public importance must be subjected to the restraints of the First Amendment.

The dissenters then concluded that the absolute refusal did violate the First Amendment. "The retention of such *absolute* control in the hands of a few Government licensees is inimical to the First Amendment, for vigorous, free debate can be attained only when members of the public have *some* opportunity to take the initiative and editorial control into their own hands." The emergence of broadcasting as "the public's prime source of information," has "made the soapbox orator and the leafleteer virtually obsolete."

The case, however, indicates only that the Constitution does not create a right of access to broadcasting. It does not address the question whether Congress might enact a statute requiring broadcasters as a condition of their licenses to give a certain period of time per day or week to members of the public. How might those who wish to speak be selected? Would such a statute be valid? Might the Commission issue a rule to the same effect? Even if such a statute or rule would be constitutional, would it be sound? What does this controversy say about the "agenda-setting" role of media?

In the DNC–BEM case much of the majority's approach was based on the power to enforce the broadcaster's responsibility to program in the public interest because of the two prongs of the fairness doctrine. It is ironic that the fairness doctrine, resisted by the broadcasters in *Red Lion*, also shields them from having to give unlimited access to their broadcasting facilities. As a broadcaster, which would you find a greater interference with your freedom—the fairness doctrine or a rule requiring you to give some persons or groups access to your facilities?

Chapter XIV

INTRODUCTION TO BROADCASTING

As *Red Lion* makes clear, legal controls for broadcasters differ significantly from those for print media. In this Chapter we consider how broadcasting operates and why this has led to legal regulation quite unlike that of the print sector. Major sections of the Communications Act of 1934 are reprinted in Appendix B. An organizational chart of the FCC is reprinted in Appendix D.

A. THE SPECTRUM AND ITS UTILIZATION

1. THE NATURE OF THE SPECTRUM

The electromagnetic spectrum is a unique natural resource. Utilization does not use it up or wear it out. It does not require continual maintenance to remain usable. It is subject to pollution (interference), but once the interference is removed the pollution totally disappears. The value of the spectrum lies primarily in its use for conveying a wide variety of information at varying speeds over varying distances: in other words, for communications.

All electromagnetic radiation is a form of radiant energy, similar in many respects to heat, light, or X-radiation. All of these types of radiation are considered by physicists to be waves resulting from the periodic oscillations of charged subatomic particles. All radiation has a measurable frequency, or rate of oscillation, which is measured in cycles per second, or hertz. One thousand cycles per second equals one kilocycle per second (1 kHz); 1,000 kilocycles per second equals one Megacycle per second (1 MHz); and 1,000 Megacycles per second equals one Gigacycle per second (1 GHz). The frequencies of electromagnetic radiation that comprise the radio spectrum span a wide range, from 10 kHz to 3,000,000,000,000 cycles per second (3,000 GHz), all of which are nearly incomprehensibly rapid. Present technology allows use of the spectrum only up to around 40 GHz.

The radio spectrum resource itself has three dimensions: space, time and frequency. Two spectrum users can transmit on the same frequency at the same time if they are sufficiently separate physically; the physical separation necessary will depend on the power at which each signal is transmitted. They then occupy different parts of the spectrum in the spatial sense. Similarly, the spectrum can be divided in terms of frequency, dependent on the construction of the transmitting and receiving equipment; or in a temporal sense, dependent largely on the hours of use.

The spectrum is subject to the phenomenon of interference. One radio signal interferes with another to the extent that both have the same dimensions. That is, two signals of the same frequency that occupy the same physical space at the same time will interfere with each other (co-channel interference). Signals on adjacent channels may also interfere with each other. Interference usually obscures or destroys any information that either signal is carrying. The degree to which two signals occupy the same physical space depends on the intensity of the radiated power at a given point, which in turn depends on the construction of the transmitting equipment and antenna.

The spectrum is divided into numbered bands, extending from Very Low Frequencies (VLF) to Very, Ultra, Super and Extremely High Frequencies (EHF) and beyond. The lower frequencies of the radio spectrum are used for "point-to-point" communications and for navigational aids. AM radio is located in the range between 300 and 3,000 kHz, known as the Medium Frequency band (MF). FM radio and VHF television (channels 2–13) are in the Very High Frequency band (VHF), from 30 to 300 MHz. The Ultra High Frequency band (UHF), from 300 to 3,000 MHz, is the location of UHF television (channels 14–69). Still higher frequencies are used for microwave relays and communication satellites.

The effective limitations on use of the radio spectrum are defined by (1) the propagation characteristics of the various frequencies and (2) the level of interference. Low frequency radio waves are best suited to long distance communications. In the lowest frequency bands the radio waves propagate primarily along the ground or water and follow the curvature of the earth. The attenuation of these "ground waves" generally increases with frequency; VLF waves may be propagated for thousands of miles, which explains their value for point-to-point communication. Ground waves in the HF band below VHF, can propagate no more than a few hundred miles and above that band they become unimportant. Sky wave propagation is important up to the start of the VHF band. These radio waves tend to depart from the earth's surface and are reflected by the ionosphere, an electrically charged region of the atmosphere 35 to 250 miles above the earth. The amount of reflection depends on the level of daily solar activity, the time of day, the season, and geographical location, as well as the length of the signal path and the angle at which the waves strike the ionosphere. The reflection of sky waves is much greater at night when they may be transmitted over great distances. Above 30 MHz, radio waves tend to pierce the ionosphere rather than to be reflected, and line of sight transmission becomes increasingly necessary. As the frequency increases above 30 MHz, surface objects absorb radiation at an increasing rate until a clear unobstructed line of sight becomes necessary at 1 GHz. In the very highest frequencies, the waves are subject to substantial absorption by water vapor and oxygen in the atmosphere and cannot be used for communication.

Interference constitutes the second major limitation on the use of the electromagnetic spectrum. As noted above, interference results when two signals attempt to occupy the same spectrum in all of its three dimensions. Even if two users wish to transmit on the same frequency, interference can be avoided by sufficient geographical separation between transmitters, limitations on the power radiated by each transmitter, limitations on antenna height, or separation of the signals in time. The first three techniques cause spatial differentiation; the last affects the temporal dimension.

Standard (AM) broadcasting propagates its waves by "amplitude modulation." The sound waves vary in power, producing variations in the height of the waves that are transmitted. The receiving unit decodes these height variations, reproducing the original sounds. AM transmissions occur in the MF band and thus have a long range primary service through ground waves, particularly near the lower end of the band. AM also can utilize sky waves to provide a secondary service at night.

FM broadcasting utilizes "frequency modulation" rather than "amplitude modulation." In this system the height of the wave is held constant but the frequency of the waves transmitted is varied. This type of broadcasting provides higher quality service with less interference than does AM, but it serves smaller areas, since the waves of the VHF band do not follow the surface of the earth and are not reflected by the ionosphere. This also means that FM service is unaffected by skywave interference at night.

Television utilizes separate signals for the visual and the sound components. The picture is transmitted by amplitude modulation and the sound by frequency modulation. Since the transmissions are either in the VHF or UHF bands, the range of the signal is short and television cannot utilize either long ground waves or sky waves.

2. ALLOCATION OF THE SPECTRUM

The method of dividing the spectrum resource among prospective users is enormously complex and highly controversial. The general term "allocation policy" comprehends three separate but not always distinct processes, each of which involves both technical and nontechnical considerations. The allocation process is the division of the spectrum into blocks of frequencies to be used by specified services or users. Thus, the television service is allocated certain frequencies in the VHF and UHF bands, microwave users are allocated frequencies in the UHF and SHF bands, and so on. The second process, allotment, involves the distribution of spectrum rights within allocated bands to users in various geographical areas. Assignment, the third process, denotes the choice among potential individual users of allocated and allotted channels or frequency bands. We usually refer to all three processes under the general label of "allocation policy."

Perhaps the most important objective consideration in formulating an allocation policy is the technical usability of the spectrum itself. Technical usability is dependent primarily on three factors: the propagation characteristics of each frequency range, interference problems and their resolution, and limitations imposed by the communications system itself, especially the transmitting and receiving equipment. In other words, it is dependent on the physics of radio waves, other users of the spectrum, and the technical state of the electronics industry. Frequency characteristics themselves seldom pose significant problems, for although there are optimal frequency ranges for various services, these tend to be broad ranges. Consequently, there is usually considerable flexibility in the initial choice of a frequency for a given service except for whatever priority is given to those already utilizing the space.

Several forms of interference may present problems since interference can be caused by an overcrowded frequency, insufficient geographical separation, or unduly strong power levels.

The third constraint on spectrum allocation involves the technology of the communications system used, especially the antenna system and the transmitting and receiving equipment. Any major change in receivers might create economic problems for the public and thus for the industry as a whole.

The problem of crowding in the broadcasting industry began early in the 1920's. The episode is recounted by Justice Frankfurter in his opinion for the Court in National Broadcasting Co. v. United States, 319 U.S. 190 (1943), a case to which we return later:

> Federal regulation of radio begins with the Wireless Ship Act of June 24, 1910, 36 Stat. 629, which forbade any steamer carrying or licensed to carry fifty or more persons to leave any American port unless equipped with efficient apparatus for radio communication, in charge of a skilled operator. The enforcement of this legislation was entrusted to the Secretary of Commerce and Labor, who was in charge of the administration of the marine navigation laws. But it was not until 1912 when the United States ratified the first international radio treaty, 37 Stat. 1565, that the need for general regulation of radio communication became urgent. In order to fulfill our obligations under the treaty, Congress enacted the Radio Act of August 13, 1912, 37 Stat. 302. This statute forbade the operation of radio apparatus without a license from the Secretary of Commerce and Labor; it also allocated certain frequencies for the use of the Government, and imposed restrictions upon the character of wave emissions, the transmission of distress signals and the like.

The enforcement of the Radio Act of 1912 presented no serious problems prior to the World War. Questions of interference arose only rarely because there were more than enough frequencies for all the stations then in existence. The war accelerated the development of the art, however, and in 1921 the first standard broadcast stations were established. They grew rapidly in number, and by 1923 there were several hundred such stations throughout the country. The Act of 1912 had not set aside any particular frequencies for the use of private broadcast stations; consequently, the Secretary of Commerce selected two frequencies, 750 and 833 kilocycles, and licensed all stations to operate upon one or the other of these channels. The number of stations increased so rapidly however, and the situation became so chaotic, that the Secretary, upon the recommendation of the National Radio Conferences which met in Washington in 1923 and 1924, established a policy of assigning specified frequencies to particular stations. The entire radio spectrum was divided into numerous bands, each allocated to a particular kind of service. The frequencies ranging from 550 to 1500 kilocycles (96 channels in all, since the channels were separated from each other by 10 kilocycles) were assigned to the standard broadcast stations. But the problems created by the enormously rapid development of radio were far from solved. The increase in the number of channels was not enough to take care of the constantly growing number of stations. Since there were more stations than available frequencies, the Secretary of Commerce attempted to find room for everybody by limiting the power and hours of operation of stations in order that several stations might use the same channel. The number of stations multiplied so rapidly, however, that by November, 1925, there were almost 600 stations in the country, and there were 175 applications for new stations. Every channel in the standard broadcast band was, by that time, already occupied by at least one station, and many by several. The new stations could be accommodated only by extending the standard broadcast band, at the expense of the other types of services, or by imposing still greater limitations upon time and power. The National Radio Conference which met in November, 1925, opposed both of these methods and called upon Congress to remedy the situation through legislation.

[During 1926, courts held that the Secretary of Commerce lacked the power to stem the tide, and his pleas for self-regulation went unheeded by the burgeoning new industry.]

From July, 1926, to February 23, 1927, when Congress enacted the Radio Act of 1927, 44 Stat. 1162, almost 200 new stations went on the air. These new stations used any frequencies they desired, regardless of the interference thereby caused to others. Existing stations changed to other frequencies and increased their power and hours of operation at will. The result

was confusion and chaos. With everybody on the air, nobody
could be heard. . . .

———

a. *The Federal Communications Commission*

Congress usually creates administrative agencies when the task
at hand requires continuing supervision, extensive technical considerations or the development of expert skills, or all of these. The
thought is that a group devoting full attention to such a problem may
do a better job than Congress might do in sporadic legislative forays
into an area. In 1927, Congress had no ability or time or desire to
unravel the mess that had developed on the airwaves. The basic
decision for Congress, in retrospect, was whether to decree a system
of private ownership for the airwaves and to allow the courts to
unravel the matters through lawsuits invoking property law, to opt
for outright public ownership, or to create an administrative body to
develop and enforce an allocation system that would bring order from
the chaos. Congress chose the last of these.

All agencies must function within the direction that the legislature gives them by statute. Here, Congress had no specific idea how
the FCC should proceed. Instead, Congress provided in § 303 that
"Except as otherwise provided in this Act, the Commission from time
to time, as public convenience, interest, or necessity requires shall
. . .." The list that followed included powers to: assign bands of
frequencies to the various classes of radio stations and assign individual frequencies; decide the times each station may operate; establish
areas to be served by any station; regulate the apparatus used with
respect to the sharpness of the transmissions; take steps to prevent
interference; suspend licenses upon a showing that the licensee
violated any statute or regulation or transmitted obscene communications; make rules and regulations that are necessary to carry out the
other provisions of the statute; and require licensees to keep records
the FCC may deem desirable.

Notice that all these powers are conditioned on a showing that
"public convenience, interest, or necessity requires" the regulation.
This is a vague standard and, as we shall see, the FCC has rarely
been barred from acting on the ground that Congress did not authorize the particular regulation.

An administrative agency such as the FCC, usually functions in a
variety of ways. Within its statutory authorization it may issue rules
or regulations that have the virtual effect of statutes. At other
times, it may have to choose between two applicants for a broadcasting license in what resembles a judicial proceeding. Still other times,
it performs executive branch functions, as when it seeks out broadcasters or ham operators who are violating their licenses by using
excessive power or using unauthorized frequencies.

This variety of regulatory patterns may not comport with traditional understandings about the separation of powers, but these multi-function agencies have been with us for so long that little concern remains about their structure. As we shall see, however, questions are continually raised about whether the agency followed the statutory requirements in performing its functions, whether it followed its own rules, and whether its processes comport with constitutional requirements.

In 1927, Congress created a five-member Federal Radio Commission to rationalize the radio spectrum and make allocations. In 1934, the agency was expanded to seven members, given jurisdiction over telephone and telegraph communication as well, and renamed the Federal Communications Commission. In 1982, Congress voted to return to a five-member commission. See 47 U.S.C. §§ 154, 155. Each member is appointed by the President for a seven-year term subject to Senate confirmation. No more than three members may be from the same political party. The terms are staggered so that no more than one expires in any year. If a member resigns in the middle of a term, the new appointment is for only the unexpired portion of that term. One consequence is that many of those appointed do not have the independence of beginning with a seven-year term. The Chairman, chosen by the President, is the chief executive officer and has major administrative responsibilities including the setting of the agenda. A chart showing the organization of the Commission is presented in Appendix D.

Of the agency's several offices and bureaus for its various functions, the most important for our purposes is the Mass Media Bureau, formed by the 1982 merger of the Broadcast Bureau and the Cable Bureau, which receives all applications for licenses, renewals and transfers. Under delegated authority from the Commission, the Bureau's staff is authorized to issue some licenses and renew others. In cases in which it has no such power, it may still recommend to the Commissioners which applications to grant and which to deny, thus assuming the position of an advocate within the agency. In addition, complaints of violations of the fairness doctrine or of the equal opportunities provision of § 315 are processed through the Mass Media Bureau.

When an adjudicatory hearing is required, usually in a licensing case, it is conducted by an Administrative Law Judge, formerly called a hearing examiner, who is an independent employee of the Commission. The Mass Media Bureau may also appear before the Administrative Law Judge to argue in favor of or against an applicant. The judge renders an initial decision that will become effective unless appealed. The appeal will be either to the Commission itself or to the Review Board. This Board, composed of senior employees of the Commission, sits in panels of three and reviews the initial decisions.

The Commission chooses whether or not to accept appeals from the Review Board.

Within the Commission the Mass Media Bureau takes positions and makes recommendations. Any applicant who is unhappy with the Commission's decision may then appeal to the courts—usually to the United States Court of Appeals for the District of Columbia. But once the Commission renders a decision the Bureau's role ceases. The General Counsel then takes over to represent the Commission in any litigation that results from the Commission's decision. The General Counsel may also advise the Commission as it prepares to promulgate rules. Sometimes one part of the agency may disagree with another. For example, during reconsideration of the Fairness Report, infra, the General Counsel's office proposed that complaints that a licensee had not sufficiently covered issues of public importance should be considered only at renewal time. The Bureau opposed the proposal and the Commissioners agreed with the Bureau.

The Radio Act of 1927 and the Communications Act of 1934 rejected the idea of a market system of spectrum allocation and of any property rights in the spectrum resource. The Federal Communications Commission has the sole power to allocate the radio spectrum, to establish general standards of operation, and to license persons to use designated parts of the spectrum.

Many services must be placed, but some critics of Commission policies charge undue reliance on the bloc allocation concept, which calls for allocating discrete frequency bands to classes of users essentially without regard to geographical location, and maintaining a relatively strict segregation among allocations. This can lead to such anomalous results as marine bands in Nebraska and forestry bands in New York City. These problems are exacerbated by the general administrative difficulty of changing an allocation once made: the start-up costs are so great and the capital investment is usually so heavy that there is a strong economic incentive not to move users from one frequency band to another. Thus, as new uses develop, they are allocated higher and higher frequencies, with little consideration of which frequencies are technically best suited for which services. For example, location of radio broadcasting in the AM band (535–1605 kHz) may be inefficient. Local broadcasting might be moved to the current FM band (88–108 MHz), which is much better suited technically to local radio, and long distance broadcasting might be moved to frequencies below 500 kHz to take advantage of the long distance ground wave propagation characteristics at those frequencies.

Another claim is that area coverage by broadcasting stations would require less spectrum if the Commission were to drop its socalled "local station goal." High powered stations in major urban centers could serve the entire country in only one-third the spectrum space presently used. Yet local stations are important; they are outlets for local news and forums for local citizens to express their views, they serve local advertisers, and they provide such local services as weather reports (which might be critical in areas subject to flash flooding or sudden tornadoes or storms).

---

b. *Radio Allocation*

AM broadcasting occupies slightly more than 1 MHz of spectrum in the Medium Frequency band between 535 kHz and 1605 kHz. This is divided into 107 assignable channels each with a bandwidth of 10 kHz. AM stations are divided into four major classes: Class I "clear channel" stations are high powered stations designed to provide primary (groundwave) service to a metropolitan area and its environs and secondary nighttime (skywave) service to an extended rural area. Class II stations also operate on clear channels with primary service areas limited by interference from Class I stations. A Class II station must usually avoid causing interference within the normally protected service areas of Class I or other Class II stations. Class III stations are medium powered and are designed to provide service primarily to larger cities and contiguous rural areas. Class IV stations are low powered and operate on local channels to provide service to a city or town and contiguous areas.

The 1927 Act creating the Federal Radio Commission had charged the Commission to provide "fair, efficient, and equitable radio service" to all areas of the country. The Commission then proceeded by establishing general engineering constraints such as maximum interference standards, and by allocating each of the 107 frequencies to a class of stations. Within these general constraints, the Commission adopted a first-come-first-served approach. An applicant who could find a promising community could apply for a license to serve that community if it could find a channel that would satisfy the various general constraints. An applicant must show that it will not interfere excessively with the signals of existing stations nor expose too many of its new listeners to interference beyond certain acceptable limits.

Clear Channels. As noted earlier, because of the skywave phenomenon, powerful AM stations can be received at great distances at night. In the 1940's, with an estimated 20 million persons uncovered by local radio service at night, the FCC created a group of 25 powerful stations operating at 50 kw. Each station shared its daytime channel frequency with other stations around the country. But at sundown all the others left the air so that the channel was clear except for the powerful station, which could reach distant and remote areas of the country.

With the development of FM radio and a surge in interest in AM radio, some argued that the clear channel stations should have their protections reduced to allow more diversity. In response, the clear channel stations argued that their power should be increased to 750 kw so that they could provide additional service. The FCC faced the issue in 1961 but reached no conclusion. In a compromise, it ordered that 13 of the 25 frequencies be shared with one or two other stations, but left the remainder fully protected, while it continued to consider the problem.

In 1980, the Commission acted decisively. The number of persons unserved by nighttime local radio was down to four million, and applicants were clamoring for space on the AM spectrum. The Commission decided to end the clear channel concept, but to protect those stations from interference for a radius of 750 miles. This would still permit them to reach larger areas than ordinary stations but it would permit an additional 125 stations to broadcast at night.

The new stations will be limited in power to 1 kw except in special cases. At the same time, the FCC explicitly refused to allow the clear channel stations to raise their power above 50 kw. (In the 1930's, an experiment permitted a Cincinnati station to broadcast at 500 kw. The station became the most popular in several Midwestern states. The experiment was terminated and a limit of 50 kw imposed for all stations.) By January, 1985, more than 300 applications were already on file or designated for hearing. Broadcasting, Jan. 7, 1985 at 39.

Expanding the Band. A second way to increase the number of AM stations is to expand the part of the spectrum available for such broadcasting. This occurred in 1979, when the World Administrative Radio Conference at its meeting (held once every 20 years) decided to increase the AM band in the Western Hemisphere so that it will run from 525 to 1705 kHz. Part would be used exclusively for AM radio, other parts would be shared, in a manner to be decided by a Western Hemispheric conference.

––––––––––

FM broadcasting, which began around 1940, is located in the VHF band. It occupies the frequencies between 88 and 108 MHz, which are excellent for aural broadcast service and allow an effective range of 30 to 75 miles. That spectrum space is divided into 100 assignable channels, each 200 kHz wide. The lowest 20 channels are reserved for noncommercial educational stations; the remaining 80 are given over to commercial use. Commercial FM channels were originally divided into three classes: A, B, and C. Class A channels are designed for use by low-power stations serving relatively small communities and the surrounding area. Class B channels are for medium-power stations intended to serve a sizable city or town or the principal city of an urbanized area. Class C channels are used by high-power stations serving a city and large surrounding areas. Noncommercial, educational FM stations operate with very low power on a fourth class of channel, Class D. Commercial FM assignments are based on a Table of Assignments, in which communities are assigned a specific number of FM stations of specified power and on specifc channels. Licenses are given only for stations within the communities listed in the Table of Assignments or within a 15 mile radius—unless an application to change the table is granted.

In the late 1970's the demand for FM licenses increased dramatically as FM outlets started to overcome the traditional dominance of AM stations. The superior quality of the FM signal and the availability of stereo were the keys to this change.

In an effort to meet the increased demand for FM stations the FCC adopted a drop-in rulemaking allowing new FM stations to be started without interfering with present broadcasters. FM Broadcast Stations (Additional Commercial Allocations), 53 R.R.2d 1550 (1983). 73 CFR 202 (1983). This rulemaking created three new intermediary classes of commercial licenses: B1, C1 and C2. In addition, Class A licenses will be permitted on channels previously set aside for Class B and Class C licenses. The FCC hired an outside contractor to supply the computer software that will determine the availability of these more closely spaced drop-ins. This new technology has made the FCC able to determine the coverage areas of these stations with greater accuracy. Broadcasting, Oct. 3, 1983 at 7.

In late 1984, the FCC approved a list of 689 locations, an initial step in the omnibus rulemaking process. Most of the new availabilities are Class A licenses in the southeast. The Commission will initiate the application process in mid-1985, but may stagger the applications for different channels over the next three years. Broadcasting Mar. 11, 1985 at 32.

Beneficiaries. Who are the likely beneficiaries of these attempts to increase the number of broadcast outlets? In radio, daytime AM broadcasters have argued forcefully that they deserve the opportunity to obtain fulltime outlets. Meanwhile, the Commission has long been concerned that minority groups are woefully underrepresented among the owners of broadcast licenses. Although minority ownership does not necessarily mean that a station's programming will take minority tastes into special account, the FCC believes that minority ownership itself is important—and that the other may follow. Other demonstrations of the FCC's concern about minorities in broadcasting are discussed elsewhere in this and later chapters.

In the FM drop-in rulemaking, supra, the Commission voted to give preference both to AM daytime broadcasters and to minority applicants. Broadcasting, March 18, 1985, at 27.

c. Television Allocation

The first licensing of television stations in this country occurred in 1941 and involved 18 channels. The first assignment plan was developed in 1945, based solely on the VHF channels. It involved the assignment of about 400 stations to 140 major market centers. Early comers quickly preempted the 100 choice assignments. In 1948, because of unexpected problems with tropospheric interference and concern that the 1945 assignment plan could cause problems, the Commission ordered a freeze on channel assignments. The freeze ended with the issuance of the Sixth Report and Order on Television Allocations, 17 Fed.Reg. 3905, 1 R.R. 91:601 (1952), creating the Table of Assignments.* The Commission rejected the idea of moving all television to the UHF band. Instead, the 12 VHF channels were retained and 70 new UHF channels were added, so that the Table provided for about 620 VHF and 1400 UHF stations. Television uses an enormous amount of spectrum compared to radio. One VHF channel uses six MHz—six times more than the entire AM band.

The Commission generated the Table of Assignments from its hierarchy of priorities: (1) to provide at least one television service to every part of the United States; (2) to provide each community with at least one television station; (3) to provide a choice of at least two television services to all parts of the U.S.; (4) to provide each community with at least two television stations; and (5) to assign remaining channels to communities on the basis of population, geographic location, and the number of television services already available to that community. Note the emphasis on "local" outlets. Is this a sound hierarchy?

In making these assignments the Commission decided to "intermix" VHF and UHF channels as a single service in the same markets. Many observers warned that the newer UHF channels could not survive but the Commission apparently believed that the demand for VHF would overflow into the UHF band and it also feared that failure to intermix would relegate UHF stations to markets overshadowed by VHF outlets in nearby metropolitan areas, or to remote rural areas. In any event, the Table of Assignments called for combined VHF and UHF channels in the following pattern: 6–10 for cities with population over 1,000,000; 4–6 for cities with 250,000 to 1,000,000; 2–4 for those with populations between 50,000 and 250,000; and 1–2 for communities under 50,000.

Because the Table tended to allot three VHF stations to most markets with only a few getting more than three, the three major

---

* The Commission's official reports are referred to by volume number, F.C.C. or F.C.C.2d, followed by page number. When the Commission proposes rules for possible adoption, formal notice of the pending action must be given to the public. This is done through the Federal Register (Fed.Reg. or F.R.) as above. The register is organized chronologically and covers all federal agencies and departments. Regulations adopted by the Commission as well as its rules of organization and internal operation are reported and grouped together in another official publication called the Code of Federal Regulations (C.F.R.). An unofficial service reports Commission rulemaking actions and case decisions. The full name of this service, Pike & Fischer's Radio Regulation, is abbreviated as R.R. or R.R.2d, and sometimes as P & F Radio Reg.

networks could now program almost entirely through VHF affiliates. This gave them strong audience and advertiser support. (In 1971, for example, 108 of the nation's 207 television markets, covering 58 percent of the nation's television households, could receive the three networks but no VHF independent stations. R. Noll, M. Peck, and J. McGowan, Economic Aspects of Television Regulation 168 (1973)). Without adequate set penetration, UHF stations found it difficult if not impossible to secure advertising revenues and network affiliation. By the end of 1956, there were 395 VHF stations and 96 UHF stations on the air. Almost 300 VHF stations had joined the 108 that already existed and 161 UHF stations had gone on the air; in that period, however, 65 UHFs were forced out of business, while only four VHFs left the air. By this time Dumont, a fourth network, had collapsed. By 1960 only 75 (15 percent) of the 575 commercial stations on the air were UHF, even though 70 percent of the total channel assignments were UHF.

The Commission recognized that intermixture was not working. In 1956, while considering broader solutions such as the transfer of all television to the UHF band, the Commission adopted deintermixture as an "interim" measure in several communities, making them all-UHF. In 1961, the Commission planned to deintermix eight more communities. This time, however, the opposition from established VHF stations was formidable. After a fierce battle, Congress entered the fray and enacted a compromise: the All Channel Receiver Act of 1962. The Act, which became § 303(s) of the Communications Act, authorized the Commission to order that all sets shipped in interstate commerce be capable of receiving both VHF and UHF signals. The VHF interests gave their support for the proposal in exchange for the Commission's indefinite suspension of deintermixture proposals. The Commission did require "all-channel" receivers and declared a moratorium on most pending deintermixture proposals. The Commission's regulation came too late for many of the UHF pioneers of the 1950's. In 1971, the Commission began steps to require detent ("click") dialing on all UHF receivers.

The continued underutilization of UHF spots led the FCC to begin to reallocate frequencies to competing uses of the airwaves. Channels 70–83 have been reassigned for land mobile use. In some cities Channels 14 to 20 are being used by land mobile operators and are being shared elsewhere. In 1980, 63 percent of the television assignments were UHF. The vacancy rates were as follows: 61 of the 578 commercial VHFs; 266 of the 648 commercial UHFs; 23 of the 136 noncommercial VHFs; and 374 of the 570 noncommercial UHFs. In the top 100 markets vacancies existed on 86 UHF channels but on no commercial VHF. In the top 200 markets, the comparable figures were 176 and six.

In addition to the intermixture problem, UHF stations are also more expensive to operate because it takes ten times as much power for a UHF transmitter to reach the same area as a VHF transmitter. Because of the inferior wave-propagation qualities of UHF signals compared to VHF signals, UHF stations are permitted to operate at a power of 5,000 kw compared to 100 or 316 kw for VHF stations. But the energy costs are so high that few UHF stations operate at maximum permitted power.

Since most network programs, the most popular, are on VHF stations, viewers in intermixed communities have little incentive to seek out UHF, even though by 1983, 96 percent of all homes with television could receive UHF. Until "click" dialing became common, some viewers trying to use UHF found it difficult to tune in the desired station.

In 1978, a Senate Committee observed that "the intent of the All Channel Receiver Act of 1962 has not been realized. UHF television broadcasting remains sorely disadvantaged within the national television system. The Committee directs that the Commission devise a plan for UHF to reach comparability with VHF in as short a time as practicable. . . ." In response the FCC began studies to reduce noise in UHF reception, to improve transmitting techniques, and into other matters.

During 1979, the future of UHF suddenly brightened.* Applicants sought stations that had gone begging since 1952; existing stations were sold at increasingly higher prices, and major broadcast owners became interested in UHF for the first time. The change in climate was apparently due to a variety of independent factors coming into play at the same time. Viewers were finding "click" dialing or newer digital dialing systems more attractive; cable television was improving the reception of the UHF stations. Another temporary boost came from the introduction of Subscription Television (STV), an over-the-air pay television system in which viewers who wish to buy the service are supplied decoders that unscramble the signal being transmitted. Although little original programming was being provided, the prospect of uncut motion pictures without commercials was sufficiently attractive to make the venture appear profitable.

However, the long-term viability of STV is now in doubt. Hurt by increasing cable penetration, piracy of signals, and increasing interest in Multi-channel Multipoint Distribution Service (see p. 654, infra), the STV subscriber base has dropped from 1.4 million in 1981 to about 400,000 in early 1985. There are only 12 STV stations still in operation. New Communication Technologies: What to Expect in 1985, Abel, John, 4th Annual ABA Legal Forum, Apr. 13, 1985.

* The press caught the change in mood. Compare UHF's Broadcasting Struggles: F.C.C. Help for Ailing Stations, N.Y. Times, Jan. 1, 1979 at 29 with Picture Turns Bright for UHF: Stations Draw High Prices in Heated Bidding, N.Y. Times, Dec. 20, 1979 at D1.

A few UHF stations have become profitable as the result of developments in cable television. Because of changes in FCC rules governing cable systems, it became possible for a single television station, in effect, to become a network by supplying its programs by satellite to cable systems throughout the country. The operation of these "superstations" is described more extensively in the discussion of cable television.

New Television Outlets. In March, 1982 the FCC approved the start of a new television service of perhaps as many as 4,000 low-power television (LPTV) stations throughout the country. These stations operate at a power sufficient to reach viewers within a radius of 10–15 miles. It is up to the applicant to find spots on the VHF and UHF bands in which such stations will not interfere with existing stations.

LPTV operators are permitted to join together by satellite to set up networks. Neither the duopoly or one-to-a-market rules discussed in Chapter XII apply to LPTV. There is no limit set on the number of LPTV licenses one entity can have. Programming restrictions are also minimal. The fairness doctrine and section 315 (see Chapter XV, infra) apply only to licensee-originated programming.

A lottery procedure for initial licensing of LPTV was approved by the Commission in March, 1983. Selection from Among Competing Applications Using Random Selection or Lotteries Instead of Comparative Hearings, 48 Fed.Reg. 27,182 (1983). This procedure was necessitated by the great number of applications for LPTV licenses. Applications for LPTV licenses were frozen in September, 1983 and the lottery is disposing of competing applications at a rate of 250–350 each month. Nevertheless, the backlog of applications was estimated at 23,000 in early 1985. Broadcasting, Jan. 7, 1985 at 46.

On the same day, the Commission, 4–3, approved four drop-ins on specific VHF channels in specific cities. These would be full-power stations that the Commission has decided would provide enough new service to viewers to outweigh any loss of service to some persons in areas near existing stations on the same channel. The drop-in is required to reduce its power in the direction of existing stations, but it would be far more powerful than a low-power station.

A general VHF drop-in plan by the FCC that could add up to 140 more drop-ins is still under consideration. Fear that the plan as originally proposed would not provide sufficient protection for existing television service caused Chairman Fowler to ask for a further notice of proposed rulemaking. Broadcasting, Oct. 1, 1984 at 83.

B. JUSTIFICATIONS FOR GOVERNMENT REGULATION

1. "Public Interest" and Government Regulation

We have just been considering the special nature of the spectrum and various actions that the FCC has taken to regulate the behavior of those who use part of the spectrum. We turn now to the legal question of what justifies the Commission in undertaking these forms of regulation, plus other types of regulation that we consider later. Although a few cases challenged this power early in the life of the FCC, the first major case to address the problem was National Broadcasting Co. v. United States, 319 U.S. 190 (1943).

After conducting a study of business practices and ownership patterns of radio networks in 1941, the Federal Communications Commission concluded that the major networks (NBC and CBS) exerted too much control over the broadcast industry through control over local station programming. To correct this situation, the Commission issued the Chain Broadcasting Regulations, which defined permissible relationships between networks and stations in terms of affiliation, network programming of affiliates' time, and network ownership of stations. These regulations were aimed at dissuading individual licensees from entering contracts that gave the networks the power to exert such control over licensees. NBC challenged the Commission's authority to adopt regulations controlling licensee behavior not related to technical and engineering matters.

The first claim was that Congress had not authorized the FCC to adopt these regulations. Section 303 of the Act provided that the Commission "as public interest, convenience, or necessity requires, shall . . . have authority to make special regulations applicable to radio stations engaged in chain broadcasting. . . ." NBC argued that the "public interest" language was to be read as limited to technical and engineering aspects of broadcasting—and that these were not the basis for the FCC's regulations in this case.

The Court noted that several sections of the Act authorized the FCC in furtherance of the "public interest, convenience, or necessity" to do such things as "study new uses for radio, . . . and generally encourage the larger and more effective use of radio in the public interest" and to provide a "fair, efficient and equitable distribution [of licenses] among the states." Building from these several grants of power, the Court rejected NBC's claim:

> The Act itself establishes that the Commission's powers are not limited to the engineering and technical aspects of regulation of radio communication. Yet we are asked to regard the Commission as a kind of traffic officer, policing the wave lengths to prevent stations from interfering with each other. But the Act does not restrict the Commission merely to supervision of the traffic. It puts upon the Commission the burden of determining

the composition of that traffic. The facilities of radio are not large enough to accommodate all who wish to use them. Methods must be devised for choosing from among the many who apply. And since Congress itself could not do this, it committed the task to the Commission.

. . .

. . . The Commission's licensing function cannot be discharged, therefore, merely by finding that there are no technological objections to the granting of a license. If the criterion of "public interest" were limited to such matters, how could the Commission choose between two applicants for the same facilities, each of whom is financially and technically qualified to operate a station? Since the very inception of federal regulation by radio, comparative considerations as to the services to be rendered have governed the application of the standard of "public interest, convenience, or necessity." [ ]

. . .

These provisions, individually and in the aggregate, preclude the notion that the Commission is empowered to deal only with technical and engineering impediments to the "larger and more effective use of radio in the public interest." We cannot find in the Act any such restriction of the Commission's authority. Suppose, for example, that a community can, because of physical limitations, be assigned only two stations. That community might be deprived of effective service in any one of several ways. More powerful stations in nearby cities might blanket out the signals of the local stations so that they could not be heard at all. The stations might interfere with each other so that neither could be clearly heard. One station might dominate the other with the power of its signal. But the community could be deprived of good radio service in ways less crude. One man, financially and technically qualified, might apply for and obtain the licenses of both stations and present a single service over the two stations, thus wasting a frequency otherwise available to the area. The language of the Act does not withdraw such a situation from the licensing and regulatory powers of the Commission, and there is no evidence that Congress did not mean its broad language to carry the authority it expresses.

The Court then considered NBC's claims that if Congress did authorize the FCC to do this, the statute was unconstitutional. The first argument was that the phrase "public interest" was too vague a standard for delegating functions to the FCC. The Court disagreed and relied on an earlier broadcasting case in which it had said that the phrase "is as concrete as the complicated factors for judgment in such a field of delegated authority permit." The phrase is not to be interpreted as giving the FCC "unlimited power."

Next, the Court rejected NBC's First Amendment claim:

We come, finally, to an appeal to the First Amendment. The Regulations, even if valid in all other respects, must fall because they abridge, say the appellants, their right of free speech. If that be so, it would follow that every person whose application for a license to operate a station is denied by the Commission is thereby denied his constitutional right of free speech. Freedom of utterance is abridged to many who wish to use the limited facilities of radio. Unlike other modes of expression, radio inherently is not available to all. That is its unique characteristic, and that is why, unlike other modes of expression, it is subject to governmental regulation. Because it cannot be used by all, some who wish to use it must be denied. But Congress did not authorize the Commission to choose among applicants upon the basis of their political, economic or social views, or upon any other capricious basis. If it did, or if the Commission by these Regulations proposed a choice among applicants upon some such basis, the issue before us would be wholly different. The question here is simply whether the Commission, by announcing that it will refuse licenses to persons who engage in specified network practices (a basis for choice, which we hold is comprehended within the statutory criterion of "public interest"), is thereby denying such persons the constitutional right of free speech. The right of free speech does not include, however, the right to use the facilities of radio without a license. The licensing system established by Congress in the Communications Act of 1934 was a proper exercise of its power over commerce. The standard it provided for the licensing of stations was the "public interest, convenience, or necessity." Denial of a station license on that ground, if valid under the Act, is not a denial of free speech.

Notes and Questions

1. The origin of the phrase, "public interest, convenience and necessity," § 309(a), or "public convenience, interest or necessity," § 307(a), is unclear from legislative documents. A former chairman of the Commission, Newton Minow, suggests the origin in Equal Time 8–9 (1964): Senator Clarence C. Dill, who had played a major part in the early legislation, told Minow that the drafters had reached an impasse in attempting to define a regulatory standard for this new, uncharted activity. A young lawyer who had been loaned to the Senate by the Interstate Commerce Commission proposed the words because they were used in other federal statutes.

Judge Henry Friendly, in The Federal Administrative Agencies 54–55 (1962), comments on the standard:

> The only guideline supplied by Congress in the Communications Act of 1934 was "public convenience, interest, or necessity." The standard of public convenience and necessity introduced into the federal statute book by Transportation Act, 1920,

conveyed a fair degree of meaning when the issue was whether new or duplicating railroad construction should be authorized or an existing line abandoned. It was to convey less when, as under the Motor Carrier Act of 1935, or the Civil Aeronautics Act of 1938, there would be the added issue of selecting the applicant to render a service found to be needed; but under those statutes there would usually be some demonstrable factors, such as, in air route cases, ability to render superior one-plane or one-carrier service because of junction of the new route with existing ones, lower costs due to other operations, or historical connection with the traffic, that ought to have enabled the agency to develop intelligible criteria for selection. The standard was almost drained of meaning under section 307 of the Communications Act, where the issue was almost never the need for broadcasting service but rather who should render it.

2. The Radio Commission's first obligation was to clear the airwaves to avoid destructive interference. It decided in 1928 that "as between two broadcasting stations with otherwise equal claims for privileges, the station which has the longest record of continuous service has the superior right." Great Lakes Broadcasting Co., 3 F.R.C.Ann.Rep. 32 (1929), modified on other grounds 37 F.2d 993 (D.C.Cir.), certiorari dismissed 281 U.S. 706 (1930). In that case, involving three competing stations, the Commission also stated, however, that if there was a "substantial disparity" in the services being offered by the stations, "the claim of priority must give way to the superior service." The Commission was soon evaluating service in terms of program content. In *Great Lakes*, the Commission contented itself with noting that stations using formats that appeal to only a "small portion" of the public were not serving the public interest because each member of the listening public is entitled to service from each station in the community.

3. In its early years the Radio Commission showed no hesitation in denying renewal of licenses because of the content of the speech uttered over the station. Section 29 of the 1927 Act, reenacted as § 326 of the 1934 Act, provided in relevant part:

>   Nothing in this Act shall be understood or construed to give the licensing authority the power of censorship over the radio communications or signals transmitted by any radio station, and no regulation or condition shall be promulgated or fixed by the licensing authority which shall interfere with the right of free speech by means of radio communication. . . .

In 1930 the Commission denied renewal of a license to KFKB on the ground that the station was being controlled and used by Dr. J.R. Brinkley to further his personal interest. Dr. Brinkley had three half-hour programs daily in which he answered anonymous inquiries on health and medicine and usually recommended several of his own tonics and prescriptions that were known to the public only by numerical designations.   Druggists paid a fee to Dr. Brinkley for each sale they made.

In affirming the denial of renewal, KFKB Broadcasting Association v. Federal Radio Commission, 47 F.2d 670 (D.C.Cir.1931), the court rejected the station's argument that the Commission had censored in violation of § 29:

> This contention is without merit.   There has been no attempt on the part of the commission to subject any part of appellant's broadcasting matter to scrutiny prior to its release.   In considering the question whether the public interest, convenience, or necessity will be served by a renewal of appellant's license, the commission has merely exercised its undoubted right to take note of appellant's past conduct, which is not censorship.

In Trinity Methodist Church, South v. Federal Radio Commission, 62 F.2d 850 (D.C.Cir.1932), certiorari denied 288 U.S. 599 (1933), the controlling figure was the minister of the church, Dr. Shuler, who regularly defamed government institutions and officials, and attacked labor groups and various religions.   The Commission's denial of renewal was affirmed.   The court concluded that the broadcasts "without facts to sustain or to justify them" might fairly be found not to be within the public interest:

> If it be considered that one in possession of a permit to broadcast in interstate commerce may, without let or hindrance from any source, use these facilities, reaching out, as they do, from one corner of the country to the other, to obstruct the administration of justice, offend the religious susceptibilities of thousands, inspire political distrust and civic discord, or offend youth and innocence by the free use of words suggestive of sexual immorality, and be answerable for slander only at the instance of the one offended, then this great science, instead of a boon, will become a scourge and the nation a theater for the display of individual passions and the collision of personal interests.   This is neither censorship nor previous restraint, nor is it a whittling away of the rights guaranteed by the First Amendment, or an impairment of their free exercise.   Appellant may continue to indulge his strictures upon the characters of men in public office.   He may just as freely as ever criticize religious practices of which he does not approve.   He may even indulge private malice or personal slander—subject, of course, to being required to answer for the abuse thereof—but he may not, as we think, demand, of right, the continued use of an instrumentality of commerce for such purposes, or any other, except in subordination to all reasonable rules and regulations Congress, acting through the Commission, may prescribe.

4.   The Supreme Court did not again consider the FCC's power until 26 years after *NBC*.   Many scholars view that case, *Red Lion*, as the most important broadcast regulation case ever decided.   We dis-

cussed *Red Lion* in Chapter XIII, supra, but it is worth revisiting. Examine again the Notes and Questions following *Red Lion.*

5. Consistent with the First Amendment is there any justification other than the scarcity rationale for regulating broadcasting differently than other media? See FCC v. Pacifica, reprinted in Chapter XVI.

6. The most recent extended discussion of the bases for regulating broadcasting occurred in FCC v. League of Women Voters of California, 468 U.S. ___ (1984). The three plaintiffs were the League, which wished to persuade public noncommercial educational broadcasters to take editorial positions; a listener who wished to hear such editorials; and a noncommercial broadcaster that wished to take editorial stands. The impediment was § 399 of the Public Broadcasting Act of 1967, as amended in 1981:

> No noncommercial educational broadcasting station which receives a grant from the Corporation for Public Broadcasting under subpart C of this part may engage in editorializing. No noncommercial educational broadcasting station may support or oppose any candidate for public office.

The case in fact centered on the first sentence of the section, which most of the justices thought severable from the second sentence. The core of the decision, centering on the nature of "public broadcasting," is reprinted in Chapter XV. Here we focus on the majority's background discussion of the bases for regulating broadcasting.

> The issue arose in the context of determining the "appropriate standard of review." The trial court, whose judgment of unconstitutionality was on direct review, had held that § 399 could survive constitutional scrutiny only if it served a "compelling" governmental interest. The FCC argued that a less demanding standard was appropriate. It based this argument in part on the "special characteristic" of spectrum scarcity and in part on the unique role of noncommercial broadcasting in this country.

> The response of the five-member majority follows.

FEDERAL COMMUNICATIONS COMMISSION v. LEAGUE OF WOMEN VOTERS OF CALIFORNIA

Supreme Court of the United States, 1984.
468 U.S. ___, 104 S.Ct. 3106, 82 L.Ed.2d 278.

[After setting forth the facts discussed in the introduction to this case, supra, and reviewing the history of noncommercial broadcasting, Justice Brennan addressed the appropriate standard of review in the following passage:]

JUSTICE BRENNAN delivered the opinion of the Court.

. . . .

At first glance, of course, it would appear that the District Court applied the correct standard. Section 399 plainly operates to restrict the expression of editorial opinion on matters of public importance, and, as we have repeatedly explained, communication of this kind is entitled to the most exacting degree of First Amendment protection. [ ] Were a similar ban on editorializing applied to newspapers and magazines, we would not hesitate to strike it down as violative of the First Amendment. E.g., Mills v. Alabama, 384 U.S. 214 (1966). But, as the Government correctly notes, because broadcast regulation involves unique considerations, our cases have not followed precisely the same approach that we have applied to other media and have never gone so far as to demand that such regulations serve "compelling" governmental interests. At the same time, we think the Government's argument loses sight of concerns that are important in this area and thus misapprehends the essential meaning of our prior decisions concerning the reach of Congress' authority to regulate broadcast communication.

The fundamental principles that guide our evaluation of broadcast regulation are by now well established. First, we have long recognized that Congress, acting pursuant to the Commerce Clause, has power to regulate the use of this scarce and valuable national resource. The distinctive feature of Congress' efforts in this area has been to ensure through the regulatory oversight of the FCC that only those who satisfy the "public interest, convenience and necessity" are granted a license to use radio and television broadcast frequencies. 47 U.S.C.A. § 309(a).[11]

Second, Congress may, in the exercise of this power, seek to assure that the public receives through this medium a balanced presentation of information on issues of public importance that otherwise might not be addressed if control of the medium were left entirely in the hands of those who own and operate broadcasting stations. Although such governmental regulation has never been allowed with respect to the print media, Miami Herald Publishing Co. v. Tornillo, 418 U.S. 241 (1974), we have recognized that "differences in the characteristics of new media justify differences in the First Amendment standards applied to them." Red Lion Broadcasting Co. v. FCC, 395 U.S. 367, 386 (1969). The fundamental distinguishing characteristic of the new medium of broadcasting that, in our view, has required some adjustment in First Amendment analysis is that

---

11. [ ].

The prevailing rationale for broadcast regulation based on spectrum scarcity has come under increasing criticism in recent years. Critics, including the incumbent Chairman of the FCC, charge that with the advent of cable and satellite television technology, communities now have access to such a wide variety of stations that the scarcity doctrine is obsolete. See, e.g., Fowler & Brenner, A Marketplace Approach to Broadcast Regulation, 60 Tex.L.Rev. 207, 221–226 (1982). We are not prepared, however, to reconsider our long-standing approach without some signal from Congress or the FCC that technological developments have advanced so far that some revision of the system of broadcast regulation may be required.

"[b]roadcasting frequencies are a scarce resource [that] must be portioned out among applicants." Columbia Broadcasting System, Inc. v. Democratic National Committee, 412 U.S. 94, 101 (1973). Thus, our cases have taught that, given spectrum scarcity, those who are granted a license to broadcast must serve in a sense as fiduciaries for the public by presenting "those views and voices which are representative of his community and which would otherwise, by necessity, be barred from the airwaves." *Red Lion*, supra, at 389. As we observed in that case, because "[i]t is the purpose of the First Amendment to preserve an uninhibited marketplace of ideas in which truth will ultimately prevail, . . . the right of the public to receive suitable access to social, political, esthetic, moral and other ideas and experiences [through the medium of broadcasting] is crucial here [and it] may not constitutionally be abridged either by the Congress or the FCC." Id., at 390.

Finally, although the government's interest in ensuring balanced coverage of public issues is plainly both important and substantial, we have, at the same time, made clear that broadcasters are engaged in a vital and independent form of communicative activity. As a result, the First Amendment must inform and give shape to the manner in which Congress exercises its regulatory power in this area. Unlike common carriers, broadcasters are "entitled under the First Amendment to exercise 'the widest journalistic freedom consistent with their public [duties].' " Columbia Broadcasting System, Inc. v. FCC, 453 U.S. 367, 395 (1981) (quoting Columbia Broadcasting System, Inc. v. Democratic National Committee, supra, at 110). See also FCC v. Midwest Video Corp., 440 U.S. 689, 703 (1979). Indeed, if the public's interest in receiving a balanced presentation of views is to be fully served, we must necessarily rely in large part upon the editorial initiative and judgment of the broadcasters who bear the public trust. See Columbia Broadcasting System, Inc. v. Democratic National Committee, supra, at 124–127.

Our prior cases illustrate these principles. In *Red Lion*, for example, we upheld the FCC's "fairness doctrine"—which requires broadcasters to provide adequate coverage of public issues and to ensure that this coverage fairly and accurately reflects the opposing views—because the doctrine advanced the substantial governmental interest in ensuring balanced presentations of views in this limited medium and yet posed no threat that a "broadcaster [would be denied permission] to carry a particular program or to publish his own views." Id., at 396.[12] Similarly, in Columbia Broadcasting System,

12. We note that the FCC, observing that "[i]f any substantial possibility exists that the [fairness doctrine] rules have impeded, rather than furthered, First Amendment objectives, repeal may be warranted on that ground alone," has tentatively concluded that the rules, by effectively chilling speech, do not serve the public interest, and has therefore proposed to repeal them. Notice of Proposed Rulemaking In re Repeal or Modification of the Personal Attack and Political Editorial Rules, 48 Fed.Reg. 28295, 28298, 28301 (June 21, 1983). Of course, the Commission may, in the exercise of its discretion, decide to modify or

Inc. v. FCC, supra, the Court upheld the right of access for federal candidates imposed by § 312(a)(7) of the Communications Act both because that provision "makes a significant contribution to freedom of expression by enhancing the ability of candidates to present, and the public to receive, information necessary for the effective operation of the democratic process," id., at 396, and because it defined a sufficiently *"limited* right of 'reasonable' access" so that "the discretion of broadcasters to present their views on any issue or to carry any particular type of programming" was not impaired. Id., at 396–397 (emphasis in original). Finally, in Columbia Broadcasting System, Inc. v. Democratic National Committee, supra, the Court affirmed the FCC's refusal to require broadcast licensees to accept all paid political advertisements. Although it was argued that such a requirement would serve the public's First Amendment interest in receiving additional views on public issues, the Court rejected this approach, finding that such a requirement would tend to transform broadcasters into common carriers and would intrude unnecessarily upon the editorial discretion of broadcasters. 412 U.S., at 123–125. The FCC's ruling, therefore, helped to advance the important purposes of the Communications Act, grounded in the First Amendment, of preserving the right of broadcasters to exercise "the widest journalistic freedom consistent with [their] public obligations," and of guarding against "the risk of an enlargement of Government control over the content of broadcast discussion of public issues." 412 U.S., at 110, 127.[13]

Thus, although the broadcasting industry plainly operates under restraints not imposed upon other media, the thrust of these restrictions has generally been to secure the public's First Amendment interest in receiving a balanced presentation of views on diverse matters of public concern. As a result of these restrictions, of

---

abandon these rules, and we express no view on the legality of either course. As we recognized in *Red Lion,* however, were it to be shown by the Commission that the fairness doctrine "has the effect of reducing rather than enhancing" speech, we would then be forced to reconsider the constitutional basis of our decision in that case. 395 U.S., at 393.

13. This Court's decision in FCC v. Pacifica Foundation, 438 U.S. 726 (1978), upholding an exercise of the Commission's authority to regulate broadcasts containing "indecent" language as applied to a particular afternoon broadcast of a George Carlin monologue, is consistent with the approach taken in our other broadcast cases. There, the Court focused on certain physical characteristics of broadcasting—specifically, that the medium's uniquely pervasive presence renders impossible any prior warning for those listeners who may be offended by indecent language, and, second, that the ease with which children may gain access to the medium, especially during daytime hours, creates a substantial risk that they may be exposed to such offensive expression without parental supervision. Id., at 748–749. The governmental interest in reduction of those risks through Commission regulation of the timing and character of such "indecent broadcasting" was thought sufficiently substantial to outweigh the broadcaster's First Amendment interest in controlling the presentation of its programming. Id., at 750. In this case, by contrast, we are faced not with indecent expression, but rather with expression that is at the core of First Amendment protections, and no claim is made by the Government that the expression of editorial opinion by noncommercial stations will create a substantial "nuisance" of the kind addressed in FCC v. Pacifica Foundation.

course, the absolute freedom to advocate one's own positions without also presenting opposing viewpoints—a freedom enjoyed, for example, by newspaper publishers and soapbox orators—is denied to broadcasters. But, as our cases attest, these restrictions have been upheld only when we were satisfied that the restriction is narrowly tailored to further a substantial governmental interest, such as ensuring adequate and balanced coverage of public issues. [ ] Making that judgment requires a critical examination of the interests of the public and broadcasters in light of the particular circumstances of each case. E.g., FCC v. Pacifica Foundation, supra.

[Justice Brennan then turned to a consideration of the specifics of this case. His discussion of this issue, and those of the dissenting justices are reprinted in Chapter XVI.]

C. INITIAL LICENSING

1. INTRODUCTION TO BASIC QUALIFICATIONS

In the 1934 Act, Congress empowered the Federal Communications Commission to grant licenses to applicants for radio stations for periods of up to three years "if public convenience, interest, or necessity will be served thereby." § 307(a). Section 307(b) requires the Commission to make "such distribution of licenses, frequencies, hours of operation, and of power among the several states and communities as to provide a fair, efficient, and equitable distribution of radio service to each of the same."

As we have seen, the Commission responded by allocating a portion of the spectrum for standard (AM) radio service and then subdividing that space further by requiring very powerful stations to use certain frequencies and weaker stations to utilize others and some stations to leave the air at sundown. The Commission used its rule-making powers to develop these allocations and then set engineering standards of separation and interference. The 1934 Act empowered the Commission to promulgate "such rules and regulations and prescribe such restrictions and conditions, not inconsistent with law, as may be necessary to carry out the provisions of this chapter. . . ." § 303(r).

In addition to requiring proof that a grant will serve the "public convenience, interest, or necessity," § 307(a), the Act also requires that each applicant demonstrate that it meets basic "citizenship, character, and financial, technical, and other qualifications," § 308(b). An applicant who fails to satisfy any one of the following "basic qualifications" is ineligible to receive a license.

a. *Legal Qualifications.* An applicant for a license must comply with the specific requirements of the Communications Act and the Commission's rules. For example, there are restrictions on permitting aliens to hold radio and broadcast licenses. § 310(b). Prior revocation of an applicant's license by a federal court for an antitrust violation precludes grant of a new application. § 313. An application will be denied if its grant would result in violation of the Commission's multiple ownership rules or chain broadcasting regulations.

b. *Technical Qualifications.* An applicant for a broadcast station must also comply with the Commission's standards for transmission. These standards include such issues as interference with existing or allocated stations and efficiency of operation, gains or losses of service to affected populations, structure, power and location of the antenna, coverage and quality of the signal in the areas to be served, and studio location and operating equipment utilized.

c. *Financial Qualifications.* Although the applicant must show that it has an adequate financial base to commence operations, it need not demonstrate that it can sustain operations indefinitely. The test applied by the Commission is that the applicant must have sufficient funds to operate a broadcast station for three months without advertising revenue. The Commission may also inquire into the applicant's estimates of the amounts that will be actually required to operate the station and the reliability of its proposed sources of funds, such as estimated advertising revenues.

d. *Character Qualifications.* Character issues that may be investigated by the Commission include past criminal convictions of the applicant, trafficking in broadcast licenses, anticompetitive business practices, lack of candor or misrepresentation to the Commission, failure to keep the Commission informed of changes in the applicant's status, and other situations that raise questions as to the integrity or reliability of the applicant in the broadcasting function.

e. The final category of basic qualifications, "other," has been interpreted to refer primarily to character issues but it may also overlap with public interest considerations. We return to the question of qualifications after a brief look at the FCC's procedures.

2. THE ADMINISTRATIVE PROCESS AT WORK

In this section we consider the process by which the Commission grants licenses to applicants. To seek a license for a broadcast frequency, an applicant first asks the Commission for a construction permit to build the facility. If the construction permit is granted, the license will then follow almost automatically if the facility is constructed on schedule. The process for such applications was discussed at p. 501, supra.

As noted earlier, anyone whose application for a construction permit or license is rejected may appeal to the courts.

An indication of how the United States Court of Appeals for the District of Columbia (which hears most of these appeals) views its role in reviewing broadcast licensing is found in Greater Boston

Television Corp. v. Federal Communications Commission, 444 F.2d 841, 850–53 (D.C.Cir.1970), certiorari denied 403 U.S. 923 (1971), (footnotes citing a wealth of authorities have been excluded):

> Assuming consistency with law and the legislative mandate, the agency has latitude not merely to find facts and make judgments, but also to select the policies deemed in the public interest. The function of the court is to assure that the agency has given reasoned consideration to all the material facts and issues. This calls for insistence that the agency articulate with reasonable clarity its reasons for decision, and identify the significance of the crucial facts, a course that tends to assure that the agency's policies effectuate general standards, applied without unreasonable discrimination. . . .
>
> Its supervisory function calls on the court to intervene not merely in case of procedural inadequacies or bypassing of the mandate in the legislative charter, but more broadly if the court becomes aware, especially from a combination of danger signals, that the agency has not really taken a "hard look" at the salient problems, and has not genuinely engaged in reasoned decision-making. If the agency has not shirked this fundamental task, however, the court exercises restraint and affirms the agency's action even though the court would on its own account have made different findings or adopted different standards. Nor will the court upset a decision because of errors that are not material, there being room for the doctrine of harmless error. . . .

This posture of self-restraint would apply to administrative agencies generally.

But the most complex cases before the Commission are those in which more than one applicant seeks a single vacant frequency or channel. These are called "mutually exclusive" applications because only one can be granted. These cases almost always raise serious fact questions that must be resolved in a hearing. These hearings can be very time-consuming because each of two or more parties not only attempts to present arguments why it should get the spot, but also may present evidence attacking each of the other applicants.

In these cases there may be specific questions, such as whether one of the applicants is an alien, or whether another is inadequately financed or proposes to use inadequate engineering equipment. But even if all the applicants meet every basic qualification, a hearing would still be needed to determine which qualified applicant should get the award.

We might note now that the same hearing process may be required at other stages in the licensing process. If a licensee applies for a renewal, if claims are made that the licensee has misbehaved in some way or should not get the license renewed, any fact questions that need to be resolved will be explored at a similar hearing conducted by an ALJ.

In the interests of simplicity, the foregoing description of the administrative process assumed that when the FCC decided to grant or renew a license to an applicant who had no competitors that was the end of the process. If the applicant had beaten out challengers they could carry the fight into the courts. But if the applicant had no challenger and the Commission decided in its favor, the Bureau— even if it had disagreed with that result—could not attack the decision of its agency. The Commission firmly rejected all efforts of listeners or citizen groups to take a formal part in the licensing process. Formally stated, the FCC denied outsiders "standing" to participate.

In 1966, however, the court of appeals ordered that citizen groups be allowed to participate in these proceedings. In Office of Communications of United Church of Christ v. Federal Communications Commission, 359 F.2d 994 (D.C.Cir.1966), the opinion by then Circuit Judge Burger said in part:

> The argument that a broadcaster is not a public utility is beside the point. True it is not a public utility in the same sense as strictly regulated common carriers or purveyors of power, but neither is it a purely private enterprise like a newspaper or an automobile agency. A broadcaster has much in common with a newspaper publisher, but he is not in the same category in terms of public obligations imposed by law. A broadcaster seeks and is granted the free and exclusive use of a limited and valuable part of the public domain; when he accepts that franchise it is burdened by enforceable public obligations. A newspaper can be operated at the whim or caprice of its owners; a broadcast station cannot. After nearly five decades of operation the broadcast industry does not seem to have grasped the simple fact that a broadcast license is a public trust subject to termination for breach of duty.

> . . .

> Public participation is especially important in a renewal proceeding, since the public will have been exposed for at least three years to the licensee's performance, as cannot be the case when the Commission considers an initial grant, unless the applicant has a prior record as a licensee. In a renewal proceeding, furthermore, public spokesmen, such as Appellants here, may be the only objectors. In a community served by only one outlet, the public interest focus is perhaps sharper and the need for airing complaints often greater than where, for example, several channels exist. Yet if there is only one outlet, there are no rivals at hand to assert the public interest, and reliance on opposing applicants to challenge the existing licensee for the channel would be fortuitous at best. Even when there are multiple competing stations in a locality, various factors may operate to inhibit the other broadcasters from opposing a renew-

al application. An imperfect rival may be thought a desirable rival, or there may be a "gentleman's agreement" of deference to a fellow broadcaster in the hope he will reciprocate on a propitious occasion.

He also noted that the fears of regulatory agencies that they will be flooded with applications are rarely borne out.

In the period since this case, the feared flood has not developed, though citizen groups are playing a much more active part in the regulatory processes of the Commission than ever before. The role of citizen groups is extensively discussed in D. Guimary, Citizens' Groups and Broadcasting (1975). Their most common legal action is the filing of a petition to deny a renewal application on the ground that the applicant has failed to meet the required level of public service.

Negotiation and Agreement. Another possibility is to negotiate. In order to avoid the expense of defending against petitions to deny renewals, broadcasters have begun entering into agreements with citizen groups that challenge their license applications or renewals. In return for withdrawal of the challenge, a broadcaster typically undertakes to make certain changes in its station's operation. The broadcaster may promise to change its employment policies, to support local production of broadcast programming, or to attempt to expand certain types of programming.

The Commission generally allows broadcasters to enter into the agreements if they maintain responsibility at all times for determining how best to serve the public interest. Does recognition of these private agreements serve the public interest? Does it allow a broadcaster to "buy off" citizen groups who may be in the best position to point out programming deficiencies or offensive overcommercialization?

Carroll Doctrine. Existing licensees have standing to object that the granting of a new license will cause technical interference with existing stations. But a competitor may also object that there is not enough potential advertising revenue in the community to support an added station. The FCC originally refused to consider this objection. The court of appeals, however, insisted, in what has become known as the *Carroll* doctrine, that the FCC inquire into these cases because "economic injury to an existing station, while not in and of itself a matter of moment, becomes important when on the facts it spells diminution or destruction of service." The public interest is the crucial concern, not an individual station's profitability.

The FCC, for its part, has reduced the number of these complaints by ruling that when such a complaint is made and the FCC agrees that the community cannot support both stations, the existing licensee's renewal application will be heard together with the new application. As we shall see shortly, this procedure might be risky for the existing licensee.

3. SUBSTANTIVE CONSIDERATIONS

So far in this section, we were introduced to a few basic qualifications that each applicant for a license must meet. Then we surveyed the procedure that the FCC follows to determine whether the basic qualifications are present—or which of several applicants should get the license. Now we return for a more extensive look at the substantive considerations in the process. We start with the single applicant for the single vacancy—an applicant who has met the basic qualifications, such as citizenship and financial security.

Still, as noted earlier, that applicant may not get the license. Since the FCC was created in large part to reduce crowding and eliminate chaos, what role may it play when only one applicant seeks an available spot? A first answer may be found in *NBC*, where the Court recognized that the FCC may act beyond its policeman's role and may consider the public interest. Sometimes the public interest might be better served by leaving a vacancy that a good applicant might later fill rather than taking the first comer.

But this, of course, requires that the FCC be able to identify a "good" applicant from a lesser one. From the very beginning the Commission has confronted the tension between using criteria that directly address programming considerations and the concern that too close a look at proposed programming may amount to government control.

The Commission believed that the "entire listening public within the service area of a station, or a group of stations in one community, is entitled to service from that station or stations." Specialized stations were entitled to little or no consideration. In the Commission's opinion "the tastes, needs, and desires of all substantial groups among the listening public should be met, in some fair proportion by a well-rounded program, in which entertainment, consisting of music of both classical and lighter grades, religion, education and instruction, important public events, discussions of public questions, weather, market reports and news, and matters of interest to all members of the family find a place." Recognizing that communities differed and that other variables were relevant, the Commission did not erect a "rigid schedule."

Over the years the Commission has taken different positions on what constitutes serving the public interest. The current position is that licensees are obligated to determine the needs and interests of their community and then present programs that meet those needs and interests. Until recently, the Commission also prescribed a specific methodology for determining the needs and interests of their community. The Primer on Ascertainment of Community Problems by Broadcast Applicants, 27 F.C.C.2d 650, 21 R.R.2d 1507 (1971). Amendment of the Primers on Ascertainment of Community Problems, 76 F.C.C.2d 401, 47 R.R.2d 189 (1980). These ascertainment requirements were eliminated for commercial broadcasting in two separate proceedings. In those proceedings the Commission emphasized that they were only eliminating formal ascertainment requirements, not the licensee's obligation to determine and serve the needs and interests of its community. Deregulation of Radio, 84 F.C.C.2d 968, 49 R.R.2d 1, reconsideration denied, 87 F.C.C.2d 797, 50 R.R.2d 93 (1981); Revision of Programming and Commercialization Policies, Ascertainment Requirements and Program Log Requirements for Commercial Television Stations, __ F.C.C.2d __, 56 R.R.2d 1005 (1984). Radio deregulation was upheld in Office of Communication of the United Church of Christ v. F.C.C., 707 F.2d 1413, 53 R.R.2d 1371 (D.C.Cir.1983). TV deregulation has been appealed.

Equal Employment Opportunity. In addition to the general public interest issues of employment discrimination by licensees, the Commission's rules generally require that each applicant for a broadcast license, for assignment or transfer of control of a license, and renewal applicants who have not previously done so "file with the Commission programs designed to provide equal employment opportunities for Blacks (not of Hispanic origin), Asians or Pacific Islanders, American Indians or Alaskan Natives, Hispanics, and women."

4. THE COMPARATIVE PROCEEDING

If two or more applicants file for use of the same or interfering facilities the Commission must proceed by way of comparative hearing among all qualified applicants to determine which will best serve the public interest. An applicant in a comparative proceeding must not only meet minimum qualifications but must also prevail when judged on the Commission's comparative criteria. These criteria, which involve considerations other than those applied in the noncomparative proceeding, evolved through adjudication rather than rule making.

POLICY STATEMENT ON COMPARATIVE BROADCAST HEARINGS

Federal Communications Commission, 1965.
1 F.C.C.2d 393, 5 R.R.2d 1901.

By the Commission: COMMISSIONERS HYDE and BARTLEY dissenting and issuing statements; COMMISSIONER LEE concurring and issuing a statement.

[The Commission noted that choosing one from among several qualified applicants for a facility was one of its primary responsibilities. The process involved an extended hearing in which the various applicants were compared on a variety of subjects. The "subject does not lend itself to precise categorization or to the clear making of precedent. The various factors cannot be assigned absolute values. . . ." Moreover, the membership of the Commission is continually changing and each member has his or her own idea of what factors are important. Thus, the statement is not binding and the Commission is not obligated to deal with all cases "as it has dealt in the past with some that seem comparable." Nonetheless, it is "important to have a high degree of consistency of decision and of clarity in our basic policies." The statement was to "serve the purpose of clarity and consistency of decision, and the further purpose of eliminating from the hearing process time-consuming elements not substantially related to the public interest." The Commission declared that this statement "does not attempt to deal with the somewhat different problems raised where an applicant is contesting with a licensee seeking renewal of license." The Commission then turned to the merits and identified "two primary objectives:" "best practicable service to the public" and "maximum diffusion of control of the media of mass communications."]

Several factors are significant in the two areas of comparison mentioned above, and it is important to make clear the manner in which each will be treated.

1. *Diversification of control of the media of mass communications.*—Diversification is a factor of primary significance since, as set forth above, it constitutes a primary objective in the licensing scheme.

2. *Full-time participation in station operation by owners.*— We consider this factor to be of substantial importance. It is inherently desirable that legal responsibility and day-to-day performance be closely associated. In addition, there is a likelihood of greater sensitivity to an area's changing needs, and of programming designed to serve these needs, to the extent that the station's proprietors actively participate in the day-to-day operation of the station. This factor is thus important in securing the best practicable service. It also frequently complements the objective of diversification, since concentrations of control are necessarily achieved at the expense of integrated ownership.

We are primarily interested in full-time participation. . . .

Attributes of participating owners, such as their experience and local residence, will also be considered in weighing integration of ownership and management. While, for the reasons given above, integration of ownership and management is important per se, its value is increased if the participating owners are local residents and if they have experience in the field. Participation in station affairs on the basis described above by a local resident indicates a likelihood of continuing knowledge of changing local interests and needs. . . .
. . .

3. *Proposed program service.*—. . . The importance of program service is obvious. The feasibility of making a comparative evaluation is not so obvious. Hearings take considerable time and precisely formulated program plans may have to be changed not only

in details but in substance, to take account of new conditions obtaining at the time a successful applicant commences operation. Thus, minor differences among applicants are apt to prove to be of no significance.

. . .

Decisional significance will be accorded only to material and substantial differences between applicants' proposed program plans. [ ] Minor differences in the proportions of time allocated to different types of programs will not be considered. Substantial differences will be considered to the extent that they go beyond ordinary differences in judgment and show a superior devotion to public service.

. . .

In light of the considerations set forth above, and our experience with the similarity of the program plans of competing applicants, taken with the desirability of keeping hearing records free of immaterial clutter, no comparative issue will ordinarily be designated on program plans and policies, or on staffing plans or other program planning elements, and evidence on these matters will not be taken under the standard issues. The Commission will designate an issue where examination of the applications and other information before it makes such action appropriate, and applicants who believe they can demonstrate significant differences upon which the reception of evidence will be useful may petition to amend the issues.

No independent factor of likelihood of effectuation of proposals will be utilized. The Commission expects every licensee to carry out its proposals, subject to factors beyond its control, and subject to reasonable judgment that the public's needs and interests require a departure from original plans. If there is a substantial indication that any party will not be able to carry out its proposals to a significant degree, the proposals themselves will be considered deficient.

4. *Past broadcast record.*—This factor includes past ownership interest and significant participation in a broadcast station by one with an ownership interest in the applicant. It is a factor of substantial importance upon the terms set forth below.

A past record within the bounds of average performance will be disregarded, since average future performance is expected. Thus, we are not interested in the fact of past ownership per se, and will not give a preference because one applicant has owned stations in the past and another has not.

We are interested in records which, because either unusually good or unusually poor, give some indication of unusual performance in the future. . . .

. . .

5. *Efficient use of frequency.*—In comparative cases where one of two or more competing applicants proposes an operation which, for

one or more engineering reasons, would be more efficient, this fact can and should be considered in determining which of the applicants should be preferred. . . .

6. *Character.*—The Communications Act makes character a relevant consideration in the issuance of a license. See section 308(b), 47 U.S.C. 308(b). Significant character deficiencies may warrant disqualification, and an issue will be designated where appropriate. Since substantial demerits may be appropriate in some cases where disqualification is not warranted, petitions to add an issue on conduct relating to character will be entertained. In the absence of a designated issue, character evidence will not be taken. Our intention here is not only to avoid unduly prolonging the hearing process, but also to avoid those situations where an applicant converts the hearing into a search for his opponents' minor blemishes, no matter how remote in the past or how insignificant.

7. *Other factors.*—As we stated at the outset, our interest in the consistency and clarity of decision and in expedition of the hearing process is not intended to preclude the full examination of any relevant and substantial factor. We will thus favorably consider petitions to add issues when, but only when, they demonstrate that significant evidence will be adduced.[13]

. . .

Notes and Questions

1. How well do these comparative criteria predict which applicant will best serve the public interest? Are each of these criteria equal or should more weight be given to certain ones? If so, which ones?

2. Although the Commission has emphasized localism, there has always been an undercurrent of doubt. In the early 1960's, when the Commission appeared to favor not only local programs but also live presentations, Judge Friendly observed, "I wonder also whether the Commission is really wise enough to determine that live telecasts, so much stressed in the decisions, e.g., of local cooking lessons, are always 'better' than a tape of Shakespeare's Histories." Friendly, The Federal Administrative Agencies: The Need for Better Definition of Standards, 75 Harv.L.Rev. 1055, 1071 (1962). This concern was restated in a different context by a former chairman of the Commission:

> [T]he automatic preference accorded local applicants disregards the possibility that, depending on the facts of a particular case, a competitor's proposed use of a professional employee-manager from outside the community might very well bring imagination,

---

13. Where a narrow question is raised, for example on one aspect of financial qualification, a narrowly drawn issue will be appropriate. In other cir-cumstances, a broader inquiry may be required. This is a matter for ad hoc determination.

an appreciation of the role of journalism, and sensitivity to social issues far exceeding that of a particular local owner-manager.

Hyde, FCC Policies and Procedures Relating to Hearings on Broadcast Applications, 1975 Duke L.J. 253, 277 (1975).

The Chairman of the House Communications Subcommittee once estimated that even now local television averages 80 percent nonlocal programming and "maybe that's the way the viewers want it." He was suggesting that Congress might reconsider the desirability of localism. See Broadcasting, Nov. 22, 1976 at 20.

3. *Minority Ownership.* New issues may reflect changes in licensing policy. In TV 9, Inc. v. Federal Communications Commission, 495 F.2d 929 (D.C.Cir.1973), rehearing and rehearing en banc denied (1974), certiorari denied 419 U.S. 986 (1974), Comint Corp., Mid-Florida Television Corporation, and six other applicants sought a construction permit for Channel 9 in Orlando, Florida. In making the award to Mid-Florida, the Commission rejected Comint's contention that it was entitled to special consideration because two of Comint's principals were local black residents and 25 percent of those to be served by Channel 9 were black. The Commission's position was that the Communications Act was "color blind" and did not permit considerations of color in the award of licenses. The court disagreed and ruled that the ownership interests and participation of the two black residents gave Comint an edge in providing "broader community representation and practicable service to the public by increasing diversity of content, especially of opinion and viewpoint."

D. RENEWAL OF LICENSES

1. INTRODUCTION

The initial license period was limited to three years by § 307(d), and the Commission considered renewal applications from about one-third of all licensees each year. In 1981, license terms were changed to five years for television and seven years for radio. At the outset, as it sought to unclutter the AM spectrum, the Commission frequently denied renewals, but after the initial flurry, denials were rare unless the broadcaster's behavior fell far below par. A study of denials and reasons for them is discussed at p. 531 infra. Due to the large volume of renewal applications now filed annually, the FCC staff cannot fully investigate the performance of each applicant. Instead, the Commission has relied increasingly on informal complaints from citizens or citizen groups, and on petitions to deny renewal that became possible after the United Church of Christ case, p. 522, supra. Section 307(d) authorizes renewals only on the same terms as initial grants—public interest, convenience, and necessity.

The FCC has been generally reluctant to deny renewals except in egregious cases. The reason is the size of the penalty that denial of renewal inflicts on the licensee in a world in which VHF stations may be worth $300 million and more, and even radio stations are often worth several million dollars or more.

Penalties and Short Renewals. Before 1960 the Commission had few weapons for dealing with misbehavior, since Congress assumed that denial of renewal would suffice in most cases, with revocation during the term to handle the most serious violations. But the Commission came to view denial of renewal as too harsh for all but the most serious violations of rules or other misbehavior. In the 1960 amendments to the Communications Act, Congress explicitly authorized shorter renewals by amending § 307(d), but this could not be utilized until the end of the license period. To fill this gap, Congress responded with §§ 503(b) et seq. to provide the Commission with "an effective tool in dealing with violations in situations where revocation or suspension does not appear to be appropriate." Under § 503(b), the Commission could impose a fine, called a forfeiture, against a licensee who had violated a specific rule. The maximum penalty is now "$2,000 for each violation. Each day of a continuing violation shall constitute a separate offense" but the total penalty shall not exceed $20,000 for licensees or cable operators.

The added array of sanctions reduced the likelihood that the denial of renewal would be used for what the Commission perceived to be lesser transgressions of the rules. The Commission has resorted extensively to the short-term renewal. The expectation is that if the licensee performs properly during that period it will then return to the regular renewal cycle. In addition to its probationary impact, a short renewal imposes burdens of legal expenses and administrative effort in preparing and defending the application.

Single instances of fraudulent behavior toward advertisers or conducting rigged contests were among the violations that traditionally led to forfeitures or short-term renewals. Among the most common types of fraud are billing advertisers for commercials that were never actually broadcast and the practice of "double-billing." This latter involves cooperative advertising in which a national manufacturer promises to share advertising expenses with its local retailers. The retailer gets a discount for volume, but the station sends it two bills—one for the actual discounted amount due and a second based on a higher non-discounted rate to be forwarded to the national manufacturer as the basis for the sharing.

After many years of warning against the practice and punishing violators with forfeitures and other minor penalties, the Commission, in the 1970's, began to deny license renewals to violators. The courts upheld the FCC. See White Mountain Broadcasting Co. v. Federal Communications Commission, 598 F.2d 274 (D.C.Cir.1979) (upholding denial of renewal where the practice had continued for 5½ years with full knowledge of the president and sole shareholder of licensee).

2. Substantive Grounds for Nonrenewal

a. Non-Speech Considerations

Just as the Commission may deny an uncontested application for a vacant channel, it may deny renewal when no other applicant seeks the spot and even when no complaint has been made. The Mass Media Bureau may argue against renewals when it believes that they would not serve the public interest.

Lying to the FCC may be the clearest basis for denying renewal. In its early years, the FCC did not treat dishonesty toward the Commission with heavy sanctions. This led to more examples of such behavior. Finally, the Commission denied the renewal of a station whose general manager for 12 years had concealed from the Commission the fact that a vice-president of a network secretly owned 24 percent of the station's stock. The station appealed on the grounds, among others, that the harsh treatment came without warning and that there was no indication that the FCC would not have renewed the station's application even if it had known the truth.

The Supreme Court upheld the denial of renewal. The fact that the FCC had previously dealt more mildly with similar cases did not prevent it from changing course without warning. Also, the "fact of concealment may be more significant than the facts concealed. The willingness to deceive a regulatory body may be disclosed by immaterial and useless deceptions as well as by material and persuasive ones." The fact that stockholders of a majority of the shares had no knowledge of the dishonesty did not bar the FCC from acting—"the fact that there are innocent stockholders can not immunize the corporation from the consequences of such deception." Stockholders often suffer from the misdeeds of their chosen officers. Federal Communications Commission v. WOKO, Inc., 329 U.S. 223 (1946).

Sometimes the Commission has held that the manager's deceit is the licensee's responsibility because of its failure to exercise adequate control and supervision consistent with its responsibilities as a licensee. Renewal was denied and the court affirmed in such a case. Continental Broadcasting, Inc. v. Federal Communications Commission, 439 F.2d 580 (D.C.Cir.), certiorari denied 403 U.S. 905 (1971).

Since the license is issued to the licensee, the licensee must meet the standards of the Communications Act and the FCC. Misbehavior of the officers may show either that the licensee knew of the misbehavior or a serious failure to control the station. In an appropriate situation, either may justify denial of renewal.

b. Speech Considerations

As you will recall, p. 513, supra, in its early days the Commission was not hesitant about denying license renewals when it disapproved of the speech being uttered. The potential implications of that practice were not tested because the situation eased after the famous Mayflower Broadcasting Corp., 8 F.C.C. 333 (1940), in which the Commission renewed a license but appeared to criticize the licensee for editorializing: "A truly free radio cannot be used to advocate the causes of the licensee. . . . In brief, the broadcaster cannot be an advocate." The case apparently deterred controversial discussion and therefore reduced the need for the Commission to judge speech directly. The situation changed after the Commission's Report on Editorializing by Broadcast Licensees, 13 F.C.C. 1246, 1 R.R. pt. 3, ¶ 91.21 (1949), which directed licensees to devote a reasonable portion of their broadcast time to the discussion of controversial issues of public importance and to encourage the presentation of various views on these questions. This has also affected renewal cases.

One study indicates that 64 radio and television licenses were revoked or not renewed between 1970 and 1978, compared with 78 during the years from 1934 to 1969. Weiss, Ostroff & Clift, Station License Revocations and Denials of Renewal, 1970–78, 24 J. Broadcasting 69 (1980). The authors analyzed the grounds for revocation or nonrenewal in the 64 cases. Since multiple grounds were common, 110 reasons were listed. The most common were misrepresentations to the FCC (18), failure to pursue the renewal procedure (16), fraudulent billing practices (11), departure from promised programming (11), and unauthorized transfer of control by the licensee (10).

Very few of the 64 involved speech grounds. Even those that did were commonly combined with other derelictions because the Commission has been reluctant to single out a speech basis for nonrenewal. For example, although the study shows that four licenses were lost for "news slanting," all four of these stations were also listed under "misrepresentations to the Commission," three were listed under character qualifications, and the fourth was also listed under failure to prosecute renewal. Similarly, although three cases listed "fairness" violation as grounds for nonrenewal, one of these was also one of the group of four listed above and had four separate reasons for nonrenewal. A second was also listed for misrepresentation. The third, the Brandywine case, is discussed shortly.

This situation is not surprising. First, a station that senses that it may be doing something wrong may seek to hide the matter without realizing that misrepresentation to the Commission may be much more serious that its substantive misbehavior. Recall the WOKO case. Second, misbehavior sometimes occurs because the licensee has not exerted sufficient control over management or employees. In such a case, the FCC combines the misbehavior with inadequate supervision as grounds for the denial of renewal. Third, the posture of the courts has not encouraged the FCC to deny renewals on pure speech grounds—as a few examples will make clear.

In one case, the FCC found that a disc jockey had been using vulgar and suggestive language. When the FCC began to investigate, the licensee denied all knowledge of the offending conduct. Because of the history of complaints, the Commission found that denial incredible, which raised a question about the licensee's character qualifications. After renewal was denied, the court affirmed but did so explicitly on the character ground, refusing to pass on whether the speech alone would have justified non-renewal. Robinson v. Federal Communications Commission, 334 F.2d 534 (D.C.Cir.), certiorari denied 379 U.S. 843 (1964).

In Walton Broadcasting, Inc., 78 F.C.C.2d 857, 47 R.R.2d 1233 (1980), the Commission denied renewal to a station that had tried to build upon the popularity of a new disc jockey by having him disappear and reporting that he had been kidnapped. Listeners jammed telephone lines to the police and the radio station. The licensee was an absentee owner who took no steps to rectify the matter until after the FCC began investigating. The renewal was denied because the licensee failed to exercise adequate control over the station's operations:

> The misconduct in this case, the hoax broadcast of news and the false announcement about the kidnapping or disappearance in a non-news context over a 4-day period, was designed to shock and alarm KIKX's listening public. The misconduct can be traced directly to the licensee's failure to require promotion formats be approved, its failure to transmit and to emphasize the substance of its policies to its station manager, its failure to insure that the manager understood its policies, its failure to check to see if he transmitted the information to on-the-air personnel, and its failure to understand and inculcate the most elementary principle of public trusteeship.

The licensee was also found responsible for six technical violations of the logging rules and 12 engineering violations. Since the control was inadequate and the resulting misconduct was quite serious, the penalty of nonrenewal was justified.

Another kind of deception was attempted by a minister whose initial efforts to acquire a station for his seminary were challenged by groups who believed that his past record showed that he would not honor the fairness doctrine or his other obligations. The prospective licensee responded by promising to provide balance. Within ten days of obtaining the license, the licensee began drastically altering its format and groups complained that the licensee was not living up to its obligations. The Commission denied renewal on two grounds:

alleged violations of the fairness doctrine, and deception practiced on the Commission in obtaining the license. On appeal, the court affirmed, 2–1. Two judges agreed on the deception ground while the dissenter found that ground "too narrow a ledge" for decision. He thought that the Commission had really denied renewal because of speech uttered on the station and he concluded that this was impermissible. Brandywine-Main Line Radio, Inc. v. Federal Communications Commission, 473 F.2d 16 (D.C.Cir.1972), certiorari denied 412 U.S. 922 (1973), Douglas, J. dissenting.

The most dramatic nonrenewal on speech grounds involved the station in Jackson, Mississippi that was the subject of the United Church of Christ case discussed at p. 522, supra. Strangely, the case did *not* involve a Commission decision not to renew. Groups claimed that the station had violated the fairness doctrine, had failed to air contrasting viewpoints on racial matters, had given blacks inadequate exposure, had generally been disrespectful to blacks, had discriminated against local Catholics, and had given inadequate time to public affairs. Blacks constituted 45 percent of the population of the station's primary service area. The FCC gave the licensee a short renewal and ordered it to honor its obligations.

After the FCC had been ordered to allow the citizen groups to participate and to reconsider the case, it decided that the station deserved renewal because the allegations had not been proven.

On a second appeal, the court reversed on the ground that the FCC's decision was not supported by substantial evidence. The FCC's errors included placing the burden of proof on the citizen groups rather than on the renewal applicant and failing to accept uncontradicted testimony about the station's practices, including cutting off national programs that showed blacks in a favorable light or that discussed racial issues. Sometimes the licensee falsely blamed technical difficulties for the interruptions in service. Office of Communication, United Church of Christ v. Federal Communications Commission, 425 F.2d 543 (D.C.Cir.1969).

Rather than remand again, the court itself vacated the license and ordered the FCC to invite applications for the now vacant channel—and to provide for interim operation of the facility. Finally, the station was taken over by a different licensee.

Surely the most widescale nonrenewal occurred when the Commission refused to renew licenses for eight educational stations in Alabama as well as an application for a construction permit for a ninth. Alabama Educational Television Commission, 50 F.C.C.2d 461, 32 R.R.2d 539 (1975). The Commission found that "blacks rarely appeared on AETC programs; that no black instructors were employed in connection with locally-produced in-school programs; and that unexplained decisions or inconsistently applied policies caused the preemption of almost all black-oriented network programming." The Commission concluded that the "licensee followed a racially discriminatory policy in its overall programming practices and, by reason of its pervasive neglect of a black minority consisting of approximately 30 percent of the population of Alabama, its programming did not adequately meet the needs of the public it was licensed to serve." Although a station need not meet minority needs by special programming, the licensee "cannot with impunity ignore the problems of significant minorities in its service areas." Two dissenters argued that the improvements in the last few years should justify more lenient treatment. The majority used that improvement, which came only after the challenges to renewal, to waive its usual rule that an applicant who is denied renewal is ineligible to reapply for that same station. The state agency here was permitted to reapply but it would be on an equal footing with any other applicant.

Generally, however, a licensee runs no risk of losing its license because of what it broadcasts so long as the content is not obscene or otherwise proscribed, as discussed in Chapter XVI. The clearest judicial exposition of this view occurred when a petition to deny renewal was filed against a radio station that had broadcast several programs that "made offensive comments concerning persons of the Jewish faith, equating Judaism with Socialism and Socialism with Communism." The Commission granted renewal without a hearing. The court of appeals affirmed. Anti-Defamation League of B'nai B'rith v. Federal Communications Commission, 403 F.2d 169 (D.C.Cir. 1968), certiorari denied 394 U.S. 930 (1969).

The court approvingly quoted from the Commission's opinion in the case:

> The Commission has long held that its function is not to judge the merit, wisdom or accuracy of any broadcast discussion or commentary but to insure that all viewpoints are given fair and equal opportunity for expression and that controverted allegations are balanced by the presentation of opposing viewpoints. Any other position would stifle discussion and destroy broadcasting as a medium of free speech. To require every licensee to defend his decision to present any controversial program that has been complained of in a license renewal hearing would cause most—if not all—licensees to refuse to broadcast any program that was potentially controversial or offensive to any substantial group. More often than not this would operate to deprive the public of the opportunity to hear unpopular or unorthodox views.

The court rejected the petitioner's main contention that "recurrent bigoted appeals to anti-Semitic prejudice" was a basis for denial of renewal. Here it quoted extensively from the opinion of a concurring Commissioner:

> It is not only impractical—and impossible in any ultimate sense—to separate an appeal to prejudice from an appeal to reason in this field, it is equally beyond the power or ability of authority to say what is religious or racial. There are centuries

of bloody strife to prove that man cannot agree on what is or is not "religion."

. . .

Nevertheless these subjects will and must be discussed. But they cannot be freely discussed if there is to be an official ban on the utterance of "falsehood" or an "appeal to prejudice" as officially defined. All that the government can properly do, consistently with the right of free speech, is to demand that the opportunity be kept open for the presentation of all viewpoints. Yet this would be impossible under the rule espoused by the ADL. . . . If what the ADL calls "appeals to racial or religious prejudice" is to be classed with hard-core obscenity, then it has no right to be heard on the air, and the only views which are entitled to be broadcast on matters of concern to the ADL are those which the ADL holds or finds acceptable. This is irreconcilable with either the Fairness Doctrine or the right of free speech.

Talk of "responsibility" of a broadcaster in this connection is simply a euphemism for self-censorship. It is an attempt to shift the onus of action against speech from the Commission to the broadcaster, but it seeks the same result—suppression of certain views and arguments. . . . Attempts to impose such schemes of self-censorship have been found as unconstitutional as more direct censorship efforts by government. [ ]

3. COMPARATIVE RENEWAL PROCEEDINGS

In the early years of regulation of each medium, except perhaps for AM, so many vacant frequencies existed that few applicants tried to oust incumbents. When such a challenge did occur, the Commission undertook the difficult comparison of the incumbent's actual performance and the challenger's proposed operation. In a major case involving renewal of the license of a Baltimore AM station, the Commission's analysis showed some reasons favoring the incumbent and others favoring the challenger. Hearst Radio, Inc. (WBAL), 15 F.C.C. 1149, 6 R.R. 994 (1951). Although the incumbent had not integrated ownership and management this did not matter because its actual performance was now available for review. Similarly, although the incumbent also controlled an FM station, a television station and a newspaper in Baltimore, it had not abused its power so this was not a serious problem. The Commission found little difference in programming despite the challenger's strong assertions to the contrary, and concluded:

We have found that both of the applicants are legally, technically, and financially qualified and must therefore choose between them as their applications are mutually exclusive. We have discussed at some length why the criteria which we may sometimes consider as determining factors when one of the applicants is not operating the facilities sought and where the applicants have not proved their abilities, are not controlling factors in the light of the record of operation of WBAL. The determining factor in our decision is the clear advantage of continuing the established and excellent service now furnished by WBAL and which we find to be in the public interest, when compared to the risks attendant on the execution of the proposed programming of Public Service Radio Corporation, excellent though the proposal may be.

This decision was thought to give renewal applicants such an advantage that prospective challengers sought entry by other means, such as buying an existing facility or seeking available, though less desirable, vacant frequencies. In its 1965 Policy Statement on Comparative Broadcast Hearings, p. 525, supra, the Commission noted that it was not attempting to deal with "the somewhat different problems raised where an applicant is contesting with a licensee seeking renewal of license." Yet, later that year, in a case in which two applicants were challenging the incumbent, the Commission stated that, on further consideration, it had "concluded that the policy statement should govern the introduction of evidence in this and similar proceedings where a renewal application is contested. . . . However, we wish to make it clear that the parties will be free to urge any arguments they may deem applicable concerning the relative weights to be afforded the evidence bearing on the various comparative factors." Seven (7) League Productions, Inc., 1 F.C.C.2d 1597 (1965).

Although the Commission might have developed a special set of standards governing renewal cases, it has found it quite difficult to do so. This was not a serious problem so long as few applicants challenged renewal applicants. But in the 1960's and early 1970's, those who wished to get into broadcasting were faced with virtually no vacancies on the spectrum (except UHF) and greatly increasing prices for existing stations. Despite the warning of *Hearst*, applicants began increasingly to challenge incumbents. Whether because the incumbents were superior—or at least equal—or because the denial of renewal imposed a serious financial penalty, the Commission continued to favor renewal applicants.

While everyone seemed to agree that giving some preference or "renewal expectancy" to the incumbent was reasonable, neither the Commission nor the courts could set up clear guidelines as to what level of performance entitled a licensee to renewal expectancy or how much weight to give renewal expectancy. In 1970 the FCC announced a policy statement stating that in any hearing between an incumbent and a challenger, the incumbent would obtain a controlling preference by demonstrating substantial past performance without serious deficiencies. If the incumbent's record met that non-comparative renewal standard, the Commission would not even consider the challenger's application.

The policy statement was challenged in the courts and overturned. Citizen's Communications Center v. Federal Communications Commission, 447 F.2d 1201 (D.C.Cir.1971). The Court ruled that the policy statement was inconsistent with the 1934 Act's requirement of a "full hearing" under § 309(e). This, together with a Supreme Court case, was understood to require that where "two or more applications for permits or licenses are mutually exclusive, the Commission must conduct one full comparative hearing of the applications." The hearing proposed in the policy statement was not "comparative" because it looked in the first instance only at the record of the incumbent.

While establishing that renewal expectancy should never reach the level of a controlling preference, the case did not state how much weight it could have in relation to the other comparative criteria. In subsequent decisions the FCC did little, if anything, to clarify the situation, but appeared nonetheless to be giving substantial weight to renewal expectancy. Finally, in a case where the incumbent was renewed despite a number of factors seemingly favoring the challenger, the court ordered the Commission to articulate and justify its comparative renewal policy.

CENTRAL FLORIDA ENTERPRISES, INC. v. FEDERAL COMMUNICATIONS COMMISSION

United States Court of Appeals, District of Columbia Circuit, 1982.
683 F.2d 503, certiorari denied 460 U.S. 1084, 103 S.Ct. 1774,
76 L.Ed.2d 346 (1983).

Before ROBINSON, CHIEF JUDGE, WILKEY, CIRCUIT JUDGE, and FLANNERY, DISTRICT JUDGE for the District of Columbia.

WILKEY, CIRCUIT JUDGE:

. . .

In its decision appealed in *Central Florida I* the FCC concluded that the reasons undercutting Cowles' bid for renewal did "not outweigh the substantial service Cowles rendered to the public during the last license period." Accordingly, the license was renewed. Our reversal was rooted in a twofold finding. First, the Commission had inadequately investigated and analyzed the four factors weighing against Cowles' renewal. Second, the process by which the FCC weighed these four factors against Cowles' past record was never "even vaguely described" and, indeed, "the Commission's handling of the facts of this case [made] embarrassingly clear that the FCC [had] practically erected a presumption of renewal that is inconsistent with the full hearing requirement" of the Communications Act. We remand[ed] with instructions to the FCC to cure these deficiencies.

On remand the Commission has followed our directives and corrected, point by point, the inadequate investigation and analysis of the four factors cutting against Cowles' requested renewal. The Commission concluded that, indeed, three of the four merited an advantage for Central Florida, and on only one (the mail fraud issue) did it conclude that nothing needed to be added on the scale to Central's plan or removed from Cowles'. We cannot fault the Commission's actions here.

We are left, then, with evaluating the way in which the FCC weighed Cowles' main studio move violation and Central's superior diversification and integration, on the one hand, against Cowles' substantial record of performance on the other. This is the most difficult and important issue in this case, for the new weighing process which the FCC has adopted will presumably be employed in its renewal proceedings elsewhere. We therefore feel that it is necessary to scrutinize carefully the FCC's new approach, and discuss what we understand and expect it to entail.

For some time now the FCC has had to wrestle with the problem of how it can factor in some degree of "renewal expectancy" for a broadcaster's meritorious past record, while at the same time undertaking the required comparative evaluation of the incumbent's probable future performance versus the challenger's. As we stated in *Central Florida I,* "the incumbent's past performance is some evidence, and perhaps the best evidence, of what its future performance would be." And it has been intimated—by the Supreme Court in FCC v. National Citizens Committee for Broadcasting (NCCB) and by this court in Citizens Communications Center v. FCC and *Central Florida I*—that some degree of renewal expectancy is permissible. But *Citizens and Central Florida I* also indicated that the FCC has in the past impermissibly raised renewal expectancy to an irrebuttable presumption in favor of the incumbent.

We believe that the formulation by the FCC in its latest decision, however, is a permissible way to incorporate some renewal expectancy while still undertaking the required comparative hearing. *The new policy, as we understand it, is simply this: renewal expectancy is to be a factor weighed with all the other factors, and the better the past record, the greater the renewal expectancy "weight."*

In our view [states the FCC], the strength of the expectancy depends on the merit of the past record. Where, as in this case, the incumbent rendered substantial but not superior service, the "expectancy" takes the form of a comparative preference weighed against [the] other factors . . . .. An incumbent performing in a superior manner would receive an even stronger preference. An incumbent rendering minimal service would receive no preference.

This is to be contrasted with Commission's *1965 Policy Statement on Comparative Broadcast Hearings*, where "[o]nly unusually good or unusually poor records have relevance."

If a stricter standard is desired by Congress, it must enact it. We cannot: the new standard is within the statute.

The reasons given by the Commission for factoring in some degree of renewal expectancy are rooted in a concern that failure to do so would hurt broadcast *consumers*.

> The justification for a renewal expectancy is three-fold. (1) There is no guarantee that a challenger's paper proposals will, in fact, match the incumbent's proven performance. Thus, not only might replacing an incumbent be entirely gratuitous, but *it might even deprive the community of an acceptable service and replace it with an inferior one*. (2) Licensees should be encouraged through the likelihood of renewal to make investments *to ensure quality service. Comparative renewal proceedings cannot function as a "competitive spur" to licensees if their dedication to the community is not rewarded.* (3) Comparing incumbents and challengers as if they were both new applicants could lead to a haphazard restructuring of the broadcast industry especially considering the large number of group owners. *We cannot readily conclude that such a restructuring could serve the public interest.*

We are relying, then, on the FCC's commitment that renewal expectancy will be factored in for the benefit of the public, not for incumbent broadcasters. . . . As we concluded in *Central Florida I,* "[t]he only legitimate fear which should move [incumbent] licensees is the fear of their own substandard performance, and that would be all to the public good."

There is a danger, of course, that the FCC's new approach could still degenerate into precisely the sort of irrebuttable presumption in favor of renewal that we have warned against. But this did not happen in the case before us today, and our reading of the Commission's decision gives us hope that if the FCC applies the standard in the same way in future cases, it will not happen in them either. The standard is new, however, and much will depend on how the Commission applies it and fleshes it out. Of particular importance will be the definition and level of service it assigns to "substantial"—and whether that definition is ever found to be "opaque to judicial review," "wholly unintelligible," or based purely on "administrative 'feel.'" [27]

---

27. Id. at 50 (quoting earlier proceeding, 60 F.C.C.2d 372, 422 (1976)). We think it would be helpful if at some point the Commission defined and explained the distinctions, if any, among: substantial, meritorious, average, above average, not above average, not far above average, above mediocre, more than minimal, solid, sound, favorable, not superior, not exceptional, and unexceptional—all terms used by the parties to describe what the FCC found Cowles' level of performance to have been. We are especially interested to know what the standard of comparison is in each case. "Average" compared to all applicants? "Mediocre"

In this case, however, the Commission was painstaking and explicit in its balancing. The Commission discussed in quite specific terms, for instance, the items it found impressive in Cowles' past record. It stressed and listed numerous programs demonstrating Cowles' "local community orientation" and "responsive[ness] to community needs," discussed the percentage of Cowles' programming devoted to news, public affairs, and local topics, and said it was "impressed by [Cowles'] reputation in the community. Seven community leaders and three public officials testified that [Cowles] had made outstanding contributions to the local community. Moreover, the record shows no complaints . . . ." The Commission concluded that "Cowles' record [was] more than minimal," was in fact " 'substantial,' i.e., 'sound, favorable and substantially above a level of mediocre service which might just minimally warrant renewal.' "

The Commission's inquiry in this case did not end with Cowles' record, but continued with a particularized analysis of what factors weighed against Cowles' record, and how much. The FCC investigated fully the mail fraud issue. It discussed the integration and diversification disadvantages of Cowles and conceded that Central had an edge on these issues—"slight" for integration, "clear" for diversification. But it reasoned that "structural factors such as [these]—of primary importance in a new license proceeding—should have lesser weight compared with the preference arising from substantial past service." [31] Finally, with respect to the illegal main studio move, the FCC found that "licensee misconduct" in general "may provide a more meaningful basis for preferring an untested challenger over a proven incumbent." The Commission found, however, that here the "comparative significance of the violation" was diminished by the underlying facts . . . . The FCC concluded that "the risk to the public interest posed by the violation seems small

compared to all incumbents? "Favorable" with respect to the FCC's expectations? We realize that the FCC's task is a subjective one, but the use of imprecise terms needlessly compounds our difficulty in evaluating what the Commission has done. We think we can discern enough to review intelligently the Commission's actions today, but if the air is not cleared or, worse, becomes foggier, the FCC's decisionmaking may again be adjudged "opaque to judicial review."

31. . . .

Here we have a caveat. We do not read the Commission's new policy as *ignoring* integration and diversification considerations in comparative renewal hearings. In its brief at page 6 the Commission states that "an incumbent's meritorious record should outweigh in the comparative renewal context a challenging applicant's advantages under the structural factors of integration and diversification." Ceteris paribus, this may be so—depending in part, of course, on how "meritorious" is defined. But where there are weights on the scales other than a meritorious record on the one hand, and integration and diversification on the other, the Commission must afford the latter two *some* weight, since while they alone may not outweigh a meritorious record they may tip the balance if weighed with something else. See *Citizens*, 447 F.2d at 1208–09 n. 23.

That, of course, is precisely the situation here, since the main studio move violation must also be balanced against the meritorious record. The Commission may not weigh the antirenewal factors separately against the incumbent's record, eliminating them as it goes along. It must weigh them all simultaneously. . . .

when compared to the actuality of depriving Daytona Beach of Cowles' tested and acceptable performance."

Having listed the relevant factors and assigned them weights, the Commission concluded that Cowles' license should be renewed. We note, however, that despite the finding that Cowles' performance was " 'substantial,' i.e., 'sound, favorable and substantially above a level of mediocre service,' " the combination of Cowles' main studio rule violation and Central's diversification and integration advantages made this a "close and difficult case." Again, we trust that this is more evidence that the Commission's weighing did not, and will not, amount to automatic renewal for incumbents.

We are somewhat reassured by a recent FCC decision granting, for the first time since at least 1961, on *comparative* grounds the application of the challenger for a radio station license and denying the renewal application of the incumbent licensee.[38] In that decision the Commission found that the *incumbent deserved no renewal expectancy* for his past program record and that his application was inferior to the challenger's on comparative grounds. Indeed, it was the *incumbent's* preferences on the diversification and integration factors which were overcome (there, by the challenger's superior programming proposals and longer broadcast week). The Commission found that the incumbent's "inadequate [past performance] reflects poorly on the *likelihood of future service in the public interest.*" Further, it found that the incumbent had no "legitimate renewal expectancy" because his past performance was neither "meritorious" nor "substantial."

We have, however, an important caveat. In the Commission's weighing of factors the scale mid-mark must be neither the factors themselves, nor the interests of the broadcasting industry, nor some other secondary and artificial construct, but rather the intent of Congress, which is to say the interests of the listening public. All other doctrine is merely a means to this end, and it should not become more. If in a given case, for instance, the factual situation is such that the denial of a license renewal would not undermine renewal expectancy *in a way harmful to the public interest*, then renewal expectancy should not be invoked.[40]

Finally, we must note that we are still troubled by the fact that the record remains that an incumbent *television* licensee has *never* been denied renewal in a comparative challenge. American television viewers will be reassured, although a trifle baffled, to learn that even

---

38. In re Applications of Simon Geller and Grandbanke Corp., FCC Docket Nos. 21104–05 (Released 15 June 1982). We intimate no view at this time, of course, on the soundness of the Commission's decision there; we cite it only as demonstrating that the Commission's new approach may prove to be more than a paper tiger.

40. Thus, the three justifications given by the Commission for renewal expectancy, [   ] should be remembered by the FCC in future renewal proceedings and, where these justifications are in a particular case attenuated, the Commission ought not to chant "renewal expectancy" and grant the license.

the worst television stations—those which are, presumably, the ones picked out as vulnerable to a challenge [42]—are so good that they never need replacing. We suspect that somewhere, sometime, somehow, some television licensee *should* fail in a comparative renewal challenge, but the FCC has never discovered such a licensee yet. As a court we cannot say that it must be Cowles here.

We hope that the standard now embraced by the FCC will result in the protection of the public, not just incumbent licensees. And in today's case we believe the FCC's application of the new standard was not inconsistent with the Commission's mandate. Accordingly the Commission's decision is

Affirmed.

———

Ironically, less than a year later, when the court was presented with the case where the Commission awarded a radio license to a new applicant rather than the incumbent, the court did not approve. Simon Geller had operated a one-man classical music FM station in Gloucester, Massachusetts since the early 1960's. In 1981, Grandebanke Corporation filed a competing application. The Commission held that because less than one percent of the station's programming was of a nonentertainment nature and the station broadcast no news, editorials, or locally produced programming, Geller was not entitled to the benefit of renewal expectancy. Simon Geller, 91 F.C.C.2d 1253, 52 R.R.2d 709 (1982).

On appeal the FCC's action was vacated and the case remanded. The court began by characterizing it as "yet another meandering effort by the [FCC] to develop a paradigm for its license renewal hearings."

> For years this court has urged the FCC to put some bite into its comparative hearings. [citing *Central Florida I*] Indeed, we have too long hungered for just one instance in which the FCC properly denied an incumbent's renewal expectancy. Unfortunately, in the process of seeking to respond to this court's signals with regard to renewal expectancy, the FCC ignored its own precedents as to the other factors that must be considered in conducting a comparative analysis.

The court of appeals agreed that Geller was entitled to no renewal expectancy because his programming did not even attempt to respond to ascertained community needs and problems. The FCC then properly turned to the comparative criteria. Here, however, the court concluded that the FCC had improperly diminished the value of Geller's obvious advantages of diversification and integration of

---

42. Counsel for the FCC conceded at oral argument, "I grant you, [competitors] wouldn't challenge the [incumbent] they thought was exceptional or far above average." The dissent from the Commission's decision declared it a "readily apparent fact that competing applicants file against only the ne'er-do-wells of the industry." 86 F.C.C.2d at 1055 n. 99.

ownership and management because it tied each to its view of Geller's programming. The FCC thus failed to accord to Geller the importance it had usually attached to diversification and integration in prior cases. The case was remanded for further consideration. Geller v. F.C.C., 737 F.2d 74 (D.C.Cir.1984).

E. TRANSFER OF LICENSES

In part because of the Commission's renewal policies, radio and television licenses have acquired substantial value. When a licensee decides to leave broadcasting altogether or to switch services or locations at the end of a license period, the licensee has no opportunity to reap profit. To reap profits, the licensee must seek renewal and, during the term, sell the facilities and goodwill and assign the license to a prospective buyer. In some ways this "transfer" procedure resembles the sale of any business, but the Commission's rules substantially affect the transaction.

Section 310(d) of the Communications Act requires the Commission to pass on all transfers and find that "the public interest, convenience, and necessity will be served thereby." But it also provides that in deciding whether the public interest would be served by the transfer the Commission "may not consider whether the public interest . . . might be served by the transfer . . . to a person other than the proposed transferee or assignee." Why might Congress have imposed this limitation?

When a transferee applies for its first full term, should it be judged as an original applicant who must compete in a comparative hearing without any advantage of incumbency or as a renewal applicant? What are the justifications for each view?

Despite the possible objections to transfer applications, most are granted, usually with little or no delay. This kind of turnover suggests a problem for the Commission. If licenses acquire substantial value a tendency may develop to build up stations and then sell them at a profit. This might be viewed as undermining the "public interest" philosophy of the licensing process. On the other hand, the public may benefit from someone building up a station, even though that person's motive is to sell it for a profit.

Chapter XV

LEGAL CONTROL OF BROADCAST PROGRAMMING: POLITICAL SPEECH

In this Chapter we consider direct regulation of content, but not necessarily prohibitions on speech. We begin, for example, with Congressional legislation to provide access and fairness in the electoral process. No speech is prohibited. Rather, broadcasters are told that they must allow certain candidates to use the station's facilities. In addition, if a candidate for an office is allowed to use the facilities his opponents must be allowed equal opportunities.

We then turn to doctrines developed by the Commission itself that require a broadcaster who has allowed certain types of comments to be made over his facilities to expose his listeners to contrasting viewpoints on that subject.

In each case consider whether the regulations, although not prohibitory, may nonetheless indirectly influence broadcasters to air or not to air certain types of content.

A. EQUAL OPPORTUNITIES AND ACCESS IN POLITICAL CAMPAIGNS

1. EQUAL OPPORTUNITIES—SECTION 315

In the Radio Act of 1927, § 18 provided:

> If any licensee shall permit any person who is a legally qualified candidate for any public office to use a broadcasting station, he shall afford equal opportunities to all other such candidates for that office in the use of such broadcasting station; . . . *Provided*, That such licensee shall have no power of censorship over the material broadcast under the provisions of this paragraph. No obligation is hereby imposed upon any licensee to allow the use of its station by any such candidate.

This became § 315 of the 1934 Act. Although the Commission has explicit rulemaking power to carry out the provisions of § 315(a), few rules have been promulgated. Most of the problems involve requests in the heat of an election campaign and for this reason few decisions have been reviewed by the courts until recently.

One major limitation on the applicability of § 315 was defined in 1951 when it was held that the section did not apply to uses of a broadcast facility on behalf of a candidate unless the candidate appeared personally during the program. This meant that friends and campaign committees could purchase time without triggering § 315. Felix v. Westinghouse Broadcasting Co., 186 F.2d 1 (3d Cir.

1951). This raised a separate set of problems discussed at p. 579, infra.

Another basic question was resolved in Farmers Educational & Cooperative Union v. WDAY, Inc., 360 U.S. 525 (1959), when the Court unanimously held that a licensee was barred from censoring the comments of a speaker exercising rights under § 315. The Court also held, 5–4, that the section preempted state defamation law and created an absolute privilege that protected the licensee from liability for statements made by such a candidate. Are these rulings sound? Because of the way the litigation arose, neither party challenged the constitutionality of § 315. Note, however, that although the station is protected from liability for defamation, the person who utters the statements is subject to liability under the general rules of defamation considered earlier.

During its early years the statute apparently caused few serious problems. The advent of television, however, changed matters dramatically. In 1956, the Commission issued two major rulings during the presidential campaign. In one it ruled that stations carrying President Eisenhower's appearance in a two-to-three minute appeal on behalf of the annual drive of the United Community Funds would be a "use" of the facility by a candidate that would trigger the equal opportunities provision. The section carried no exception for "public service" nor did it require the appearance to be "political." Columbia Broadcasting System (United Fund), 14 R.R. 524 (F.C.C.1956). One week before the election, President Eisenhower requested and received 15 minutes of free time from the three networks to discuss the sudden eruption of war in the Middle East. His Democratic opponent's request for equal time was rejected by the networks. One day before the election, the Commission, without opinion and with one dissent, upheld the networks' position. Columbia Broadcasting System (Suez Crisis), 14 R.R. 720 (F.C.C.1956).

This response to an incumbent speaking as President rather than as candidate was unusual for the Commission, which had interpreted "use" very broadly. It did so, again, in 1959 when a third-party candidate for mayor of Chicago, Lar Daly, asked equal time on the basis of two series of television clips of his opponents, incumbent Mayor Daley and the Republican challenger. One group of clips showed the two major candidates filing their papers (46 seconds); Mayor Daley accepting the nomination (22 seconds); and a one-minute clip asking the Republican why he was running. A second group of clips included "nonpolitical" activities such as a 29-second clip of Mayor Daley on a March of Dimes appeal and 21 seconds of his greeting President Frondizi of Argentina at a Chicago airport. The Commission, in a long opinion, ruled that both groups required equal time. Columbia Broadcasting System, Inc. (Lar Daly), 26 F.C.C. 715 (1959). It relied on the words "use" and "all" in the statute and thought the issue of who initiated the appearance (such as the March of Dimes asking the Mayor to appear) to be irrelevant. Although formal campaigning was the most obvious way of putting forward a candidacy, "of no less importance is the candidate's appearance as a public servant, as an incumbent office holder, or as a private citizen in a nonpolitical role." Such "appearances and uses of a nonpolitical nature may confer substantial benefits on a candidate who is favored."

Congressional response was swift—and negative. Hearings began within days after the decision and the result was an amended version of § 315:

> Sec. 315. (a) If any licensee shall permit any person who is a legally qualified candidate for any public office to use a broadcasting station, he shall afford equal opportunities to all other such candidates for that office in the use of such broadcasting station: *Provided,* That such licensee shall have no power of censorship over the material broadcast under the provisions of this section. No obligation is hereby imposed upon any licensee to allow the use of its station by any such candidate.* Appearance by a legally qualified candidate on any—
>
> (1) bona fide newscast,
>
> (2) bona fide news interview,
>
> (3) bona fide news documentary (if the appearance of the candidate is incidental to the presentation of the subject or subjects covered by the news documentary), or
>
> (4) on-the-spot coverage of bona fide news events (including but not limited to political conventions and activities incidental thereto),
>
> shall not be deemed to be use of a broadcasting station within the meaning of this subsection. Nothing in the foregoing sentence shall be construed as relieving broadcasters, in connection with the presentation of newscasts, news interviews, news documentaries, and on-the-spot coverage of news events, from the obligation imposed upon them under this chapter to operate in the public interest and to afford reasonable opportunity for the discussion of conflicting views on issues of public importance.

Recall the significance of this episode to the Court in *Red Lion,* p. 478, supra.

In 1960, Congress suspended the operation of § 315 so that the stations could give time to national candidates without creating a § 315 obligation. This permitted the Kennedy-Nixon debates to be held without need to provide free time for the many minority candidates. There was no incumbent and no major third party candidate— two factors that made the debates politically possible.

---

* In 1971 Congress amended this sentence by adding "under this subsection" after the word "imposed." The reason for this is explained when we consider § 312(a)(7) shortly.

Presidential election problems returned in 1964. First, the Commission ruled that coverage of an incumbent President's press conferences were not exempt under either § 315(a)(2) or (4). Nor were those of his main challenger. Columbia Broadcasting System (Presidential Press Conference), 3 R.R.2d 623 (F.C.C.1964). Then, two weeks before the election, the three networks granted President Johnson time to comment on two events that had just occurred: a sudden change of leadership was announced in Moscow, and China exploded a nuclear device. The Commission adhered to its 1956 ruling that this was not a "use." It also upheld a network claim that this program came within § 315(a)(4) as a bona fide news event. Republican National Committee (Dean Burch), 3 R.R.2d 647 (F.C.C.1964). An appeal of this ruling to the court of appeals led to an affirmance on a divided vote, 3–3, without opinion. A petition for certiorari was denied, Goldwater v. Federal Communications Commission 379 U.S. 893 (1964), with Justice Goldberg, joined by Justice Black, dissenting with opinion. They argued that the case presented substantial questions and that the Commission seemed not to be consistent in its own decisions.

In 1968, Senator Eugene McCarthy announced early that he was a candidate for the Democratic nomination for President against the incumbent, Lyndon Johnson. During a traditional year-end interview with television reporters, President Johnson criticized Senator McCarthy and made several political statements. McCarthy sought "equal time" but the Commission denied the request on the ground that the President had not announced that he was a candidate for re-election and thus did not come within the statute or the Commission's rules on who is a "legally qualified candidate" for office. Eugene McCarthy, 11 F.C.C.2d 511, 12 R.R.2d 106 (1968). On appeal, the Commission's position was affirmed. McCarthy v. Federal Communications Commission, 390 F.2d 471 (D.C.Cir.1968). Shortly thereafter, President Johnson abruptly announced that he would not seek reelection.

In 1972, the problems centered around the Democratic nomination. Just before the crucial California primary, CBS held a joint session of "Face the Nation", expanded from its regular half-hour to one hour, featuring Senators Humphrey and McGovern, the two leading candidates in the primary and for the nomination. The network claimed that this was a bona fide news interview and thus exempt under § 315(a)(2) from time requests by other Democratic candidates. Similar programs on other networks raised similar questions. The Commission found the changes did not deprive the programs of their bona fide character as interviews, and perceived and intended its opinion to accord "with the remedial purpose of the 1959 amendments to accord leeway to licensee journalistic decisions." Hon. Sam Yorty and Hon. Shirley Chisholm, 35 F.C.C.2d 572, 24 R.R.2d 447 (1972). On Chisholm's appeal, the FCC's ruling was vacated. Chisholm v. Federal Communications Commission, 24 R.R.2d 2061 (D.C.Cir.1972). The court thought the program more a debate than an interview. On remand, the Commission begrudgingly complied and ordered the networks to grant Chisholm one-half hour of prime time before the election. 35 F.C.C.2d 579, 24 R.R.2d 720 (1972).

Through the 1960's and 1970's various proposals were made in Congress to amend or repeal § 315. Nothing came of any of them. But in 1975, the Commission responded dramatically to two petitions. It overruled its 1962 decisions that coverage of a debate did not come within the exemption for on-the-spot coverage of bona fide news events. The Commission said that it had misinterpreted legislative history when it required the appearance of the candidate to be "incidental" to the coverage of a separate news event. The Commission now concluded that, in 1959, Congress intended to run the risks of political favoritism among broadcasters in an effort to allow broadcasters to "cover the political news to the fullest degree." Debates were exempt if controlled by someone other than the candidates or the broadcaster, as with the Economic Club and UPI convention, and if judged to be bona fide news events under § 315(a)(4).

In a companion ruling, the Commission overruled its 1964 decision on press conference coverage. It decided that full coverage of a press conference by any incumbent or candidate would come within the exemption for on-the-spot coverage of a bona fide news event if it "may be considered newsworthy and subject to on-the-spot coverage." But the Commission refused to bring a press conference within the exemption for bona fide news interviews because the licensee did not "control" the format and the event was not "regularly scheduled." Petitions of Aspen Institute and CBS, Inc., 55 F.C.C. 2d 697, 35 R.R.2d 49 (1975).

Appeals were taken against both parts of the Commission's 1975 rulings. The main contentions were that the Commission had not followed the Congressional mandate when it permitted the candidate to "become the event" under the (a)(4) exemption, and that the statute did not allow the Commission to uphold licensee decisions if only they are in "good faith"—that it is for the Commission to make these judgments. By a vote of 2–1, the court affirmed both rulings, Chisholm v. Federal Communications Commission, 538 F.2d 349 (D.C. Cir.1976). The opinions disagreed over the significance of the complex legislative history, with the majority concluding that the Commission's interpretation was "reasonable." Rehearing en banc was denied. A petition for certiorari was denied, 429 U.S. 890 (1976) White, J., dissenting.

Seizing on the Commission's rulings, the League of Women Voters set up "debates" between the two major Presidential candidates in 1976. They were held in auditoriums before invited audiences. The candidates were questioned by panelists selected by the League after consultation with the participants. Television was allowed to cover the events—but the League imposed restrictions against showing the audience or any audience reactions. Although the networks complained about the restrictions and about the way the panelists were selected, they did carry the programs live and in full.

Again in 1980, the League took steps to sponsor debates among the major candidates. It decided that John Anderson's showing in public opinion polls was sufficiently strong to warrant his inclusion in a three-way debate. When President Carter refused to participate in a debate with Anderson, the League went ahead anyway and staged an Anderson-Reagan debate. If networks decided to cover the event, as CBS and NBC did, the coverage would be exempt under (a)(4) because the networks and licensees were making the judgment it was a bona fide news event even without the President.

After Anderson's ratings fell to around 10 percent, the League invited Carter and Reagan to debate. Both accepted the invitation and held a single head-to-head debate a week before the election.

In 1980, just before the primaries began, President Carter, seeking renomination as Democratic candidate for President in a contest against Senator Edward M. Kennedy, held a press conference that was carried live in prime time by the three commercial networks and the Public Broadcasting Service. Senator Kennedy, claiming that President Carter had used more than five minutes on that occasion to attack him and to misstate several of his positions, sought relief from the FCC.

In Kennedy for President Committee v. Federal Communications Commission, 636 F.2d 432 (D.C.Cir.1980) (*Kennedy I*), the Senator asked for equal opportunities under § 315 to respond to the "calculated and damaging statements" and to "provide contrasting viewpoints." The FCC denied the request. On appeal, the court affirmed.

The press conference was exempt under § 315(a)(4) so long as the broadcasters reasonably believed that the conference was a "bona fide news event." The Commission said, in a passage approved by the court, that an incumbent President "may well have an advantage over his opponent in attracting media coverage" but "absent strong evidence that broadcasters were not exercising their bona fide news judgment, the Commission will not interfere with such judgments." The Senator was free to hold a press conference the next day to rebut the charges. Indeed, generally, Senator Kennedy was getting substantial media coverage.

The court traced the history of the exemptions to § 315 and adhered to its decision in *Chisholm* upholding the Commission's new approach to § 315. "The only inquiry now in order is whether there was anything so peculiar about the February 13 presidential press conference as to remove it from the ambit of *Aspen* and *Chisholm*." The court found no reason to doubt the broadcasters' good faith. It also concluded that the actual content of the event could not control the question of exemption. In addition to the difficult judgments about content, context and impact of particular statements that the Commission and the courts would have to make, the goal of the exemptions would be defeated if broadcasters could not know until after an event whether it was exempt.

Senator Kennedy then argued that the First Amendment required that he be granted time to respond, even if the statute did not. The court rejected the contention on the basis of CBS v. DNC, p. 492, supra:

> From its inception more than a half-century ago, federal regulation of broadcasting has largely entrusted protection of that public right to short-term station licensees functioning under Commission supervision, and with liberty as well as responsibility to determine who may get on the air and when. The history of this era portrays Congress' consistent refusal to mandate access to the air waves on a non-selective basis and, contrariwise, its decision "to permit private broadcasting to develop with the widest journalistic experience consistent with its public obligations." [CBS v. DNC] The Commission has honored that policy in a series of rulings establishing that a private right to utilize the broadcaster's facilities exists only when specially conferred. The net of these many years of legislative and administrative oversight of broadcasting is that "[o]nly when the interests of the public are found to outweigh the private journalistic interests of the broadcasters will government power be asserted within the framework of the Act."

The First Amendment permits Congress to enforce the public's primary interests by using broadcasters as public trustees, and CBS v. DNC shows that no one has a constitutional right to broadcast his own views on any matter.

In Petitions of Henry Geller et al., 54 R.R.2d 1246 (1983), the FCC reversed long-standing administrative decisions by permitting broadcasters themselves to sponsor debates between political candidates without having to provide uninvited candidates with equal broadcasting opportunities. Such debates may still fall within the § 315(a)(4) exemption. The Commission concluded that its previous interpretations neither represented the outer bounds of its legislated authority under the statute nor met the overriding Congressional mandate to encourage broadcast coverage of electoral issues. Third-party sponsorship was not the *sine qua non* of impartiality. For example, the risks of favoritism in the news interview format (§ 315(a)(3)) were thought to be no different than in the debate format and therefore disparate treatment was not justified. The League of Women Voters' argument that this approach creates too great a risk of favoritism was rejected. The risks inherent in broadcaster-sponsored debates were no greater than the *Chisholm* court had understood the 1959 amendments to be willing to accept.

The Commission also noted that in many cases a broadcaster may be "the ideal, and perhaps the only, entity interested in promoting a debate between candidates for a particular office, especially at the state or local level". Exempting broadcaster-sponsored debates would therefore increase the number of debates and ultimately benefit the public. Finally, a debate's exempt status "should not be contingent upon whether a broadcaster is the sponsoring or controlling entity—for such control generally would not affect the program's news value". The Commission also made clear that this new interpretation of § 315(a)(4) did not authorize licensees to favor or disfavor any candidate.

The League's expedited appeal was rejected without opinion. League of Women Voters v. FCC, 731 F.2d 995 (D.C.Cir.1984), Broadcasting, Mar. 12, 1984 at 69.

The "on the spot" language of § 315(a)(4) also has produced litigation. Groups afraid that an exempt program, such as a debate, might be recorded and played over several times to the detriment of excluded candidates, have argued that the statute permits only one showing—and that it must be live. The FCC rejected this and allowed the broadcaster to tape the live event and to present it once during the next 24 hours. When that ruling was challenged, the court affirmed the Commission. The agency had authority to develop a balance between rigidly equal opportunities and the new freedom provided by the 1959 exemptions. There was no showing that the FCC had misconstrued the law, and it had fully explained what it was doing. Office of Communication of the United Church of Christ v. Federal Communications Comm'n, 590 F.2d 1062 (D.C.Cir.1978).

The one-day rule was eliminated in *Henry Geller, supra*. The reasonableness of a delayed broadcast would now be left to the broadcaster's good faith determination that the delay of more than one day after the occurrence of the exempt debate would better serve the community. Such delay, however, must be motivated by concerns of informing the public, and not in order to favor or disfavor any candidate.

The other subdivisions, (a)(1) and (a)(3), have given rise to fewer problems. In 1976, supporters of Ronald Reagan complained when a Miami television station broadcast six-minute interviews with President Ford on five consecutive evening newscasts. The complaint asserted that the segments were from a single half-hour interview that had been broken up into five parts. The Commission held that even if the 30-minute interview would not have been exempt under § 315, inclusion of the segments within newscasts would not preclude "exempt status pursuant to § 315(a)(1) unless it has been shown that such a decision is clearly unreasonable or in bad faith." Even though this was broadcast during the last week of a primary campaign and might benefit President Ford, the complainants "have not shown that the licensee in deciding to air them, considered anything other than their newsworthiness." Citizens for Reagan, 58 F.C.C.2d 925, 36 R.R.2d 885 (1976). Does the statute's use of "bona fide" support the Commission's decision to leave the decision in the first instance with the licensee?

If a program is exempt, that status is not lost simply because its timing may help one candidate more than another. The day before the Iowa caucus vote in 1980, President Carter was the guest on NBC's "Meet the Press", a program normally exempt under (a)(2) as a bona fide news interview program. One of his opponents argued that the program lost its exemption because of the impact just before the critical first voting of the 1980 primary process.

The FCC rejected the complaint. So long as the format remains the same and is controlled by the broadcaster, and the choice of guest is based on newsworthiness, the FCC would not intervene. The spirit of the Aspen decision was to leave judgments of newsworthiness to the professionals. In this case, since there was no showing that the incumbent's appearance would not be newsworthy, the timing was not controlling.

The FCC has granted general exemptions under (a)(1) to such programs as "Today" and "Good Morning America." In each case, the FCC was influenced by the fact that the program was regularly scheduled and involved regular coverage of current news supplemented by interviews, commentary and discussions. The determinations of what to cover are made in the exercise of news judgment and not to further a particular candidate's advantage. On the other hand, the Commission denied such a general exemption to "Donahue" because both Donahue, the host, and the audience can, and often do, give their personal opinions about the subjects being discussed. Also, "Tonight" has been held to be a variety show and, thus, not entitled to exemption.

In 1984, the Commission unanimously overruled its earlier ruling denying an exemption to the Donahue show. Multimedia Entertainment, Inc., 56 R.R.2d 143 (1984). The Commission concluded that it "would appear immaterial" that some parts of the show have nothing to do with elections or politics. Also, the Commission now accepted the claim that Donahue would be able to control the audience to prevent anyone from using the show for partisan purposes. It noted that tickets are distributed months before any particular program. The Commission concluded that it would be unwise to bar exemptions to any program that did not rigidly adhere to a traditional news interview format.

The Commission appears to be holding firm to its earlier decisions broadly defining "use" in cases of "nonpolitical" appearances. Thus, in United Way of America, 35 R.R.2d 137 (F.C.C.1975), which was decided at about the same time as the Aspen-CBS petitions, the Commission, 4–3, adhered to its earlier rulings that an appearance by candidate Ford opening an annual charity fund drive came within

§ 315. The Commission has also adhered to its view that appearances by television personalities or film stars after they have announced their candidacy for office constitutes a "use" under § 315. In Adrian Weiss, 58 F.C.C.2d 342, 36 R.R.2d 292 (1976), the Broadcast Bureau ruled that the showing of old Ronald Reagan films on television would require the offering of equal opportunities to other Republican presidential aspirants. The Bureau relied heavily on the claim that non-political uses can be very effective. The Commission refused to review the Bureau's decision, with two Commissioners concurring separately and two dissenting. These four all thought that common sense dictated exempting movies made before Reagan actively entered politics but the two concurring Commissioners thought that any change should be made by Congress. In Pat Paulsen, 33 F.C.C.2d 297, affirmed 33 F.C.C.2d 835, 23 R.R.2d 861 (1972), affirmed 491 F.2d 887 (9th Cir.1974), the Commission rejected a comedian's argument that applying § 315 would deprive him of due process and equal protection by forcing him to give up his livelihood in order to run for public office. Their interpretation was held permissible "to achieve the important and legitimate objectives of encouraging political discussion and preventing unfair and unequal use of the broadcast media."

Content problems under § 315 are rare, but do arise. Among the candidates running in 1972 for the Democratic nomination for Senator from Georgia, one was broadcasting the following spot announcement:

> I am J.B. Stoner. I am the only candidate for U.S. Senator who is for the white people. I am the only candidate who is against integration. All of the other candidates are race mixers to one degree or another. I say we must repeal Gambrell's civil rights law. Gambrell's law takes jobs from us whites and gives those jobs to the niggers. The main reason why niggers want integration is because the niggers want our white women. I am for law and order with the knowledge that you cannot have law and order and niggers too. Vote white. This time vote your convictions by voting white racist J.B. Stoner into the run-off election for U.S. Senator. Thank you.

Several groups asked the Commission to rule that a licensee may, and has the responsibility to, withhold announcements under § 315 if they "pose an imminent and immediate threat to the safety and security of the public it serves." The groups alleged that the spot had created racial tension and that the Mayor of Atlanta had urged broadcasters not to air the advertisement. Letter to Lonnie King, 36 F.C.C.2d 635, 25 R.R.2d 54 (1972). The Commission refused to issue the requested order:

> The relief requested in your letter would amount to an advance approval by the Commission of licensee censorship of a candidate's remarks. By way of background, we note that

Constitutional guarantees do not permit the proscription of even the advocacy of force or of law violation "except where such advocacy is directed to inciting or producing imminent lawless action and is likely to incite or produce such action." Brandenburg v. Ohio, 395 U.S. 444, 447 (1969). And a prior restraint bears a heavy presumption against its constitutional validity. Carroll v. Princess Anne, 393 U.S. 175, 181 (1968). While there may be situations where speech is "so interlaced with burgeoning violence that it is not protected," Carroll v. Princess Anne, 393 U.S. at 180 and while a similar approach might warrant overriding the no-censorship command of Section 315, we need not resolve that difficult issue here, for we conclude on the basis of the information before us that there is no factual basis for the relief you request. Despite your report of threats of bombing and violence, there does not appear to be that clear and present danger of imminent violence which might warrant interfering with speech which does not contain any direct incitement to violence. A contrary conclusion here would permit anyone to prevent a candidate from exercising his rights under Section 315 by threatening a violent reaction. In view of the precise commands of Sections 315 and 326, we are constrained to deny your requests.

The FCC has also received occasional complaints about political announcements that contain indecent language. The problem of indecent and obscene political announcements will be discussed in Chapter XVI.

---

2. Reasonable Access—Section 312(a)(7)

In 1971, as part of legislation concerning election campaigning, Congress passed two statutes that affect broadcasting during political campaigns. One requires that candidates using broadcast facilities during the 45 days before a primary and the 60 days before a general election be charged rates not to exceed "the lowest unit charge of the station for the same class and amount of time for the same period. . . . ." At all other times, the rates charged candidates are not to exceed "the charges made for comparable use of such station by other users thereof." 47 U.S.C. § 315(b). The major difference between the two quoted passages is that during the 45 and 60 day periods, the candidate pays the rate that the highest-volume advertiser would pay for that time. At other times, the candidate pays the rates charged to those who advertise as little or as much as the candidate does.

At the same time, Congress adopted § 312(a)(7), providing that the Commission may revoke a license

(7) for willful or repeated failure to allow reasonable access to or to permit purchase of reasonable amounts of time for the use of a broadcasting station by a legally qualified candidate for Federal elective office on behalf of his candidacy.

The legislative history indicates that one purpose of the overall legislation was to "give candidates for public office greater access to the media so that they may better explain their stand on the issues and thereby more fully and completely inform the voters."

It was only in 1980, that cases involving the section began to reach the courts.

The first case raised the questions of when the campaign had begun and how requests should be treated. The Carter-Mondale Committee asked each major network to sell it 30 minutes of prime time in December, 1979 (just after the formal announcement that President Carter was seeking renomination), in order to show a documentary on President Carter's first term. CBS offered two five-minute segments, one of which would be in prime time. ABC indicated that it would make time available beginning in January, 1980. NBC said that it was "too early in the political season for nationwide broadcast time to be made available for paid political purposes." The Committee complained to the FCC, which found the stations in violation of § 312(a)(7), by a vote of 4–3.

The Supreme Court upheld the FCC decision. CBS, Inc. v. FCC, 453 U.S. 367 (1981). Chief Justice Burger, for the majority, agreed with the FCC that the section had "created an affirmative, promptly enforceable right of reasonable access to the use of broadcast stations for individual candidates seeking federal elective office" rather than simply codifying prior policies that the FCC had developed under the general public interest standard. The Court relied on the specific language of the statute itself, the legislative history, and what the Court found to be the FCC's consistent administrative interpretation of the language since the statute's enactment. Perhaps the "most telling evidence" of Congressional intent was the contemporaneous change in Section 315 from a statement that "No obligation is imposed upon any licensee to allow the use of its station by" a candidate to the statement that no such obligation "is imposed under this subsection [§ 315(a)]."

Next the Court rejected the contention that the FCC's interpretation under the statute, particularly its emphasis on case-by-case individualized analysis, intruded on editorial discretion and judgment to an extent not intended by Congress. The Court summarized the state of affairs under various FCC edicts as follows:

> Broadcasters are free to deny the sale of air time prior to the commencement of a campaign, but once a campaign has begun, they must give reasonable and good faith attention to access requests from "legally qualified" candidates for federal elective office. Such requests must be considered on an individu-

alized basis, and broadcasters are required to tailor their responses to accommodate, as much as reasonably possible, a candidate's stated purposes in seeking air time. In responding to access requests, however, broadcasters may also give weight to such factors as the amount of time previously sold to the candidate, the disruptive impact on regular programming, and the likelihood of requests for time by rival candidates under the equal opportunities provision of § 315(a). These considerations may not be invoked as pretexts for denying access; to justify a negative response, broadcasters must cite a realistic danger of substantial program disruption—perhaps caused by insufficient notice to allow adjustments in the schedule—or of an excessive number of equal time requests. Further, in order to facilitate review by the Commission, broadcasters must explain their reasons for refusing time or making a more limited counteroffer. If broadcasters take the appropriate factors into account and act reasonably and in good faith, their decisions will be entitled to deference even if the Commission's analysis would have differed in the first instance. But if broadcasters adopt "across-the-board policies" and do not attempt to respond to the individualized situation of a particular candidate, the Commission is not compelled to sustain their denial of access.

The Court upheld the process by which the FCC will decide whether an election campaign has, in fact, started. Such a decision "is not, and cannot be, purely one of editorial judgment." Moreover, by limiting access to the period after a campaign starts the FCC "has limited its impact on broadcasters and given substance to [the statute's] command of reasonable access."

Next the Court upheld the FCC's insistence that broadcasters respond to each request individually. The Court understood the FCC to be mandating "careful consideration of, not blind assent to, candidates' desires for air time." It quoted from FCC statements that although the broadcaster was not to "second guess" the "political wisdom" of a candidate's request, that request was "by no means conclusive of the question of how much time, if any, is appropriate. Other . . . factors, such as disruption or displacement of regular programming . . . must be considered in the balance." Although "the adoption of uniform policies might well prove more convenient for broadcasters, such an approach would allow personal campaign strategies and the exigencies of the political process to be ignored." Thus, a policy allowing program lengths of a single fixed duration might be "unreasonable" as to a candidate who wanted a different length.

The Court concluded that the Commission's actions were a "reasoned attempt to effectuate the statute's access requirement, giving broadcasters room to exercise their discretion but demanding that they act in good faith." These ground rules were sufficiently clear in late 1979 to permit the FCC to rule that the networks had violated the statute by failing to grant "reasonable access."

Finally, the Court rejected the network's assertion that § 312(a) (7) was unconstitutional.

> The First Amendment interests of candidates and voters, as well as broadcasters, are implicated by § 312(a)(7). We have recognized that "it is of particular importance that candidates have the . . . opportunity to make their views known so that the electorate may intelligently evaluate the candidates' personal qualities and their positions on vital public issues before choosing among them on election day." [Buckley v. Valeo]. [ ] Indeed, "speech concerning public affairs is . . . the essence of self-government." [Garrison v. Louisiana]. The First Amendment "has its fullest and most urgent application precisely to the conduct of campaigns for public office." [Monitor Patriot Co. v. Roy]. Section 312(a)(7) thus makes a significant contribution to freedom of expression by enhancing the ability of candidates to present, and the public to receive, information necessary for the effective operation of the democratic process.

> Petitioners are correct that the Court has never approved a *general* right of access to the media. [ ] Nor do we do so today. Section 312(a)(7) creates a *limited* right to "reasonable" access that pertains only to legally qualified federal candidates and may be invoked by them only for the purpose of advancing their candidacies once a campaign has commenced. The Commission has stated that, in enforcing the statute, it will "provide leeway to broadcasters and not merely attempt *de novo* to determine the reasonableness of their judgments . . ." If broadcasters have considered the relevant factors in good faith, the Commission will uphold their decisions. See 629 F.2d, at 25. Further, § 312(a)(7) does not impair the discretion of broadcasters to present their views on any issue or to carry any particular type of programming.

> Section 312(a)(7) represents an effort by Congress to assure that an important resource—the airwaves—will be used in the public interest. We hold that the statutory right of access, as defined by the Commission and applied in these cases, properly balances the First Amendment rights of federal candidates, the public, and broadcasters.

The relation between § 312(a)(7) and § 315 was central to Kennedy for President Committee v. Federal Communications Commission, 636 F.2d 417 (D.C.Cir.1980) (*Kennedy II*). On March 14, 1980, President Carter made a 30-minute speech in the afternoon and held a press conference from 9:00 to 9:30 p.m. that night. The three major commercial networks carried both programs live, except that ABC delayed the press conference for three hours. Senator Kennedy charged that these programs saturated the public with the President's views on the economy only four days before the Illinois primary. He asked for free time to reply under § 312(a)(7). The networks denied the request, the Commission refused to order that time be granted, and the court affirmed.

The court began by noting that Congress, in 1971, enacted § 312(a)(7) and § 315(b)(1), requiring lowest charges to candidates using broadcast facilities, because Congress was concerned about the rising cost of candidates' televised appearances:

> It was believed that the informational and educational aspects of political broadcasting could greatly be enhanced by ensuring that more time would be made available to candidates at lower rates. This expectably would encourage less dependence on thirty- to sixty-second "spots" necessarily little more than slogans—in favor of longer, more illuminating presentations; it would also enable more candidates to afford the television appearances so instrumental to present-day electioneering.

The court concluded that the "most straightforward reading" of § 312(a)(7) "is that broadcasters may fulfill their obligation thereunder either by allotting free time to a candidate *or* by selling the candidate time at the rates prescribed by Section 315(b). Considering the legislative history, the FCC's consistent administrative interpretations, and the apparent statutory scheme of the various provisions, the court concluded that § 312(a)(7), although seeking to assure federal candidates access to broadcasting, did not "confer the privilege of using the broadcaster's facilities without charge." The choice of giving or selling time is for the broadcaster:

> Should Section 312(a)(7) be construed as automatically entitling a candidate to responsive broadcast access whenever and for whatever reason his opponent has appeared on the air, Section 315(a)'s exemptions would soon become meaningless. Statutes are to be interpreted, if possible, to give operation to all of their parts, and to maintain them in harmonious working relationship.

Since Kennedy never claimed that he had not been given an opportunity to buy time, he could not invoke § 312(a)(7). Nor had he sought relief under § 315.

B. THE FAIRNESS DOCTRINE

1. IN GENERAL

Beginning in Chapter XIII with *Red Lion,* and at several points during the licensing discussion, we have had occasion to note the existence of, and to consider aspects of, the Commission-created fairness doctrine. We now consider the doctrine itself.

The Commission has been concerned with fairness and the exposure of varying views since its earliest days. Indeed, the Radio

Commission in 1928 indicated as much in a discussion of the implications of the limited spectrum. It observed that there was not room "for every school of thought, religious, political, social, and economic, each to have its separate broadcasting station, its mouthpiece in the ether." Such ideas "must find their way into the market of ideas by the existing public-service stations, and if they are of sufficient importance to the listening public the microphone will undoubtedly be available. If it is not, a well-founded complaint will receive the careful consideration of the commission in its future action with reference to the station complained of." Great Lakes Broadcasting Co., 3 F.R.C.Ann.Rep. 32 (1929), modified on other grounds 37 F.2d 993 (D.C.Cir.), certiorari dismissed 281 U.S. 706 (1930). The doctrine evolved through case law until it became the subject of a major report in 1949. In 1959, when § 315 was amended, p. 547, supra, many people interpreted the phrase, "nothing in the foregoing sentence shall be construed as relieving broadcasters . . . from the obligation under this chapter to operate in the public interest and to afford reasonable opportunity for the discussion of conflicting views on issues of public importance" as codifying the Fairness Doctrine in the Communication Act.

IN THE MATTER OF THE HANDLING OF PUBLIC ISSUES UNDER THE FAIRNESS DOCTRINE AND THE PUBLIC INTEREST STANDARDS OF THE COMMUNICATIONS ACT

(FAIRNESS REPORT)

Federal Communications Commission, 1974.
48 F.C.C.2d 1, 30 R.R.2d 1261.

By the Commission: COMMISSIONER HOOKS concurring in part and dissenting in part and issuing a separate statement; COMMISSIONER QUELLO concurring and issuing a separate statement.

[The Commission first restated its commitment to the goal of "uninhibited, robust, wide open" debate on public issues and the need to recognize that achievement of this goal must be compatible with the public interest in "the larger and more effective use of radio" § 303(g). This included the fact that "ours is a commercially-based broadcast system" and that the Commission's policies "should be consistent with the maintenance and growth of that system." The Commission then quoted a critical passage from its Report on Editorializing, 13 F.C.C. 1246, 1249 (1949), in which the fairness doctrine was formally announced:

It is axiomatic that one of the most vital questions of mass communication in a democracy is the development of an informed public opinion through the public dissemination of news and ideas concerning the vital public issues of the day. . . . The

Commission has consequently recognized the necessity for licensees to devote a reasonable percentage of their broadcast time to the presentation of news and programs devoted to the consideration and discussion of public issues of interest in the community served by the particular station. And we have recognized, with respect to such programs, the paramount right of the public in a free society to be informed and to have presented to it for acceptance or rejection the different attitudes and viewpoints concerning these vital and often controversial issues which are held by the various groups which make up the community. It is this right of the public to be informed, rather than any right on the part of the Government, any broadcast licensee or any individual member of the public to broadcast his own particular views on any matter, which is the foundation stone of the American system of broadcasting.

The 1974 Report stressed that two basic duties were involved: "(1) the broadcaster must devote a reasonable percentage of time to the coverage of public issues; and (2) his coverage of these issues must be fair in the sense that it provides an opportunity for the presentation of contrasting points of view." The Commission also noted that in 1970 it had described the two parts of the fairness doctrine "as the single most important requirement of operation in the public interest—the *sine qua non* for grant of a renewal of license." The Commission denied that imposition of these two duties could be inhibiting:

18. In evaluating the possible inhibitory effect of the fairness doctrine, it is appropriate to consider the specifics of the doctrine and the procedures employed by the Commission in implementing it. When a licensee presents one side of a controversial issue, he is not required to provide a forum for opposing views on that same program or series of programs. He is simply expected to make provision for the opposing views in his *overall programming.* Further, there is no requirement that any precisely equal balance of views be achieved, and all matters concerning the particular opposing views to be presented and the appropriate spokesmen and format for their presentation are left to the licensee's discretion subject only to a standard of reasonableness and good faith.

19. As a matter of general procedure, we do not monitor broadcasts for possible violations, but act on the basis of complaints received from interested citizens. These complaints are not forwarded to the licensee for his comments unless they present *prima facie* evidence of a violation. Allen C. Phelps, 21 FCC2d 12 (1969). Thus, broadcasters are not burdened with the task of answering idle or capricious complaints. By way of illustration, the Commission received some 2,400 fairness com-

plaints in fiscal 1973, only 94 of which were forwarded to licensees for their comments.

> 20. While there may be occasional exceptions, we find it difficult to believe that these policies add significantly to the overall administrative burdens involved in operating a broadcast station. . . . The Supreme Court has made it clear and it should be reemphasized here that "if present licensees should suddenly prove timorous, the Commission is not powerless to insist that they give adequate and fair attention to public issues." Red Lion Broadcasting Co. v. FCC, 395 U.S. at 393.

As to the first duty imposed, the Commission noted:

> We have, in the past, indicated that some issues are so critical or of such great public importance that it would be unreasonable for a licensee to ignore them completely. [ ] But such statements on our part are the rare exception, not the rule, and we have no intention of becoming involved in the selection of issues to be discussed, nor do we expect a broadcaster to cover each and every important issue which may arise in his community.

> 26. We wish to emphasize that the responsibility for the selection of program material is that of the individual licensee. That responsibility "can neither be delegated by the licensee to any network or other person or group, or be unduly fettered by contractual arrangements restricting the licensee in his free exercise of his independent judgments." Report on Editorializing, 13 FCC at 1248. We believe that stations, in carrying out this responsibility, should be alert to the opportunity to complement network offerings with local programming on these issues, or with syndicated programming.

The Commission then turned to the second, and more frequently litigated, aspect of the fairness doctrine.]

2. A Reasonable Opportunity for Opposing Viewpoints

. . .

28. It has frequently been suggested that individual stations should not be expected to present opposing points of view and that it should be sufficient for the licensee to demonstrate that the opposing viewpoint has been adequately presented on another station in the market or in the print media. See WSOC Broadcasting Co., 17 P & F Radio Reg. 548, 550 (1958). While we recognize that citizens receive information on public issues from a variety of sources, other considerations require the rejection of this suggestion. First, in amending section 315(a) of the Communications Act in 1959, Congress gave statutory approval to the fairness doctrine, including the requirement that broadcasters themselves provide an opportunity for opposing viewpoints. See BEM, 412 U.S. at 110, note 8. Second, it would be an administrative nightmare for this Commission to attempt to review the overall coverage of an issue in all of the broadcast stations

and publications in a given market. Third, and perhaps most importantly, we believe that the requirement that *each* station provide for contrasting views greatly increases the likelihood that individual members of the public will be exposed to varying points of view.
. . .

a. What is a "controversial issue of public importance"?

29. It has frequently been suggested that the Commission set forth comprehensive guidelines to aid interested parties in recognizing whether an issue is "controversial" and of "public importance." However, given the limitless number of potential controversial issues and the varying circumstances in which they might arise, we have not been able to develop detailed criteria which would be appropriate in all cases. For this very practical reason, and for the reason that our role must and should be limited to one of review, we will continue to rely heavily on the reasonable, good faith judgments of our licensees in this area.

30. Some general observations, however, are in order. First of all, it is obvious that an issue is not necessarily a matter of significant "public importance" merely because it has received broadcast or newspaper coverage. "Our daily papers and television broadcasts alike are filled with news items which good journalistic judgment would classify as newsworthy, but which the same editors would not characterize as containing important controversial public issues." Healey v. FCC, 460 F.2d 917, 922 (D.C.Cir.1972). Nevertheless, the degree of media coverage is one factor which clearly should be taken into account in determining an issue's importance. It is also appropriate to consider the degree of attention the issue has received from government officials and other community leaders. The principal test of public importance, however, is not the extent of media or governmental attention, but rather a subjective evaluation of the impact that the issue is likely to have on the community at large. If the issue involves a social or political choice, the licensee might well ask himself whether the outcome of that choice will have a significant impact on society or its institutions. It appears to us that these judgments can be made only on a case-by-case basis.

31. The question of whether an issue is "controversial" may be determined in a somewhat more objective manner. Here, it is highly relevant to measure the degree of attention paid to an issue by government officials, community leaders, and the media. The licensee should be able to tell, with a reasonable degree of objectivity, whether an issue is the subject of vigorous debate with substantial elements of the community in opposition to one another. It is possible, of course, that "programs initiated with no thought on the part of the licensee of their possible controversial nature will subsequently arouse controversy and opposition of a substantial nature which will merit presentation of opposing views." Report on Editori-

alizing, 13 FCC at 1251. In such circumstances, it would be appropriate to make provision for opposing views when the opposition becomes manifest.

b. *What specific issue has been raised?*

32. One of the most difficult problems involved in the administration of the fairness doctrine is the determination of the *specific* issue or issues raised by a particular program. This would seem to be a simple task, but in many cases it is not. . . .

. . .

c. *What is a "reasonable opportunity" for contrasting viewpoints?*

. . .

37. The first point to be made with regard to the obligation to present contrasting views is that it cannot be met "merely through the adoption of a general policy of not refusing to broadcast opposing views where a demand is made of the station for broadcast time." Report on Editorializing, 13 FCC at 1251. The licensee has a duty to play a conscious and positive role in encouraging the presentation of opposing viewpoints.[13] . . .

38. In making provision for the airing of contrasting viewpoints, the broadcaster should be alert to the possibility that a particular issue may involve more than two opposing viewpoints. Indeed, there may be several important viewpoints or shades of opinion which warrant broadcast coverage.

. . .

41. In providing for the coverage of opposing points of view, we believe that the licensee must make a reasonable allowance for presentations by genuine partisans who actually believe in what they are saying. The fairness doctrine does not permit the broadcaster "to preside over a 'paternalistic' regime," BEM, 412 U.S. at 130, and it would clearly not be acceptable for the licensee to adopt a "policy of excluding partisan voices and always itself presenting views in a bland, inoffensive manner. . . ." . . .

42. This does not mean, however, that the Commission intends to dictate the selection of a particular spokesman or a particular format, or indeed that partisan spokesmen must be presented in every instance. We do not believe that it is either appropriate or feasible for a governmental agency to make decisions as to what is

---

13. This duty includes the obligation defined in Cullman Broadcasting Co., 40 FCC 576, 577 (1963) . . . .

We do not believe that the passage of time since *Cullman* was decided has in any way diminished the importance and necessity of this principle. If the public's right to be informed of the contrasting views on controversial issues is to be truly honored, broadcasters must provide the forum for the expression of those viewpoints at their own expense if paid sponsorship is unavailable.

desirable in each situation. In cases involving personal attacks and political campaigns, the natural opposing spokesmen are relatively easy to identify. This is not the case, however, with the majority of public controversies. Ordinarily, there are a variety of spokesmen and formats which could reasonably be deemed to be appropriate. We believe that the public is best served by a system which allows individual broadcasters considerable discretion in selecting the manner of coverage, the appropriate spokesmen, and the techniques of production and presentation.

43. Frequently, the question of the reasonableness of the opportunity provided for contrasting viewpoints comes down to weighing the *time* allocated to each side. Aside from the field of political broadcasting, the licensee is not required to provide equal time for the various opposing points of view. Indeed, we have long felt that the basic goal of creating an informed citizenry would be frustrated if for every controversial item or presentation on a newscast or other broadcast the licensee had to offer equal time to the other side. . . . Similarly, we do not believe that it would be appropriate for this Commission to establish any other mathematical ratio, such as 3 to 1 or 4 to 1, to be applied in all cases. We believe that such an approach is much too mechanical in nature and that in many cases our pre-conceived ratios would prove to be far from reasonable. In the case of a 10-second personal attack, for example, fairness may dictate that more time be afforded to answer the attack than was given the attack itself.

. . .

E. Fairness and Accurate News Reporting

58. In our 1949 Report on Editorializing, we alluded to a licensee's obligation to present the news in an accurate manner:

> It must be recognized, however, that the licensee's opportunity to express his own views . . . does not justify or empower any licensee to exercise his authority over the selection of program material to distort or suppress the basic factual information upon which any truly fair and free discussion of public issues must necessarily depend. . . . A licensee would be abusing his position as public trustee of these important means of mass communication were he to withhold from expression over his facilities relevant news or facts concerning a controversy or to slant or distort the presentation of such news. No discussion of the issues involved in any controversy can be fair or in the public interest where such discussion must take place in a climate of false or misleading information concerning the basic facts of the controversy, 13 FCC at 1254–55.

It is a matter of critical importance to the public that the basic facts or elements of a controversy should not be deliberately suppressed or misstated by a licensee. But, we must recognize that such distortions are "so continually done in perfect good faith, by persons who are not considered . . . ignorant or incompetent, that it is rarely possible, on adequate grounds, conscientiously to stamp the misrepresentations as morally culpable. . . ." J.S. Mill, On Liberty 31 (People's ed. 1921). Accordingly, we do not believe that it would be either useful or appropriate for us to investigate charges of news misrepresentations in the absence of substantial extrinsic evidence or documents that on their face reflect deliberate distortion. See The Selling of the Pentagon, 30 FCC2d 150 (1971).

Notes and Questions

1. In 1976, the Commission denied reconsideration of the Report. 58 F.C.C.2d 691, 36 R.R.2d 1021 (1976). Commissioner Robinson dissented because he doubted the value of the efforts involved and was concerned about the intrusion into editorial decisions. He noted that in 1973 and 1974, of 4,280 formal fairness complaints only 19 resulted in findings adverse to the licensee. These included seven in the political editorial area, seven cases of personal attack, and five general fairness complaints. Of the 19 violations, only eight resulted in tangible penalty to the licensee—seven political editorializing cases and one personal attack case involved forfeitures under § 503. Since this sanction is available only for violations of formal rules, it is not available for violations of the uncodified general doctrine.

2. Commissioner Robinson asserted that so long as *Red Lion* was the law the Commission could not eliminate the fairness doctrine completely. He favored the suggestion made by the Committee for Open Media, under which a licensee might choose to meet its obligations under the fairness doctrine by allowing access to its facilities. The proposal was to allow 35 one-minute messages per week scheduled at different times, including prime time. Half the spots would be allocated on a first-come, first-served basis and the other half would use "a representative spokesperson" system. If an excessive number wanted to speak Commissioner Robinson suggested that speakers might be chosen by lot or by queueing so as to minimize licensee bias. Efforts would be made to prevent monopolization by one outside group. Commissioner Robinson thought few licensees would choose to relinquish their control in this way, but he thought it offered the Commission an opportunity to avoid judging content and he urged offering this alternative to licensees. For a study of the operation of Free Speech Messages in San Francisco, see Harris, Free Speech Messages: When the Public Gets Access, What Does It Say?, Access 34 at 20 (1976).

In a separate statement Chairman Wiley attacked the access proposal on grounds that it encouraged licensees to abdicate editorial control and emphasized a single programming technique: the access announcement. "In my opinion a more varied, interesting and informative coverage would be possible if professional journalists played a conscious and positive role in the process."

3. After the Commission's denial of reconsideration of the Fairness Report, the court of appeals generally affirmed that ruling. National Citizens Committee for Broadcasting v. Federal Communications Commission, 567 F.2d 1095 (D.C.Cir.1977). The court upheld the Commission's decision to discontinue applying the fairness doctrine to most commercial advertisements—a result already reached in the snowmobile case, infra. The court did remand two issues to the Commission for additional consideration. One was the COM proposal, discussed supra. The other was a proposal that the Commission order each licensee to "list annually the ten controversial issues of public importance, local and national, which it chose for the most coverage in the prior year, set out the offers for response made, and note representative programming that was presented on each issue."

The parties who were dissatisfied with the commercial advertisement part of the decision sought Supreme Court review but certiorari was denied. 436 U.S. 926 (1978).

On the remand, the Commission adhered to its earlier views. 74 F.C.C.2d 163, 46 R.R.2d 999 (1979). It rejected the COM proposal on the ground that "any system which has its emphasis on speakers rather than on ideas is at cross-purposes to that of the Fairness Doctrine. Since the goal of the Fairness Doctrine is to inform the public, any substitute means of compliance must do this." Studies of access usage in various cities provided no assurances that important and timely public issues would be discussed, that presentations on issues would be balanced, or that they would be informative and comprehensible. Even time assigned to spokespersons for issue-oriented groups might not be devoted to the discussion of important public issues.

Despite the acknowledged attractions of the access proposal, such as the opportunity for "true partisans" to express their views and the use of spot announcements "to reach larger and more diverse audiences than through program-length public affairs broadcasts", the defects were held to outweigh the potential gains.

Licensees who might choose to institute an access program must still comply with the fairness doctrine. "How the licensee achieves this mandate depends, as we have always stated, upon the journalistic discretion of each participating station."

The Commission again rejected the Geller proposal that television licensees be required to list annually the 10 community and national controversial issues of public importance that they chose for the most coverage in the prior year. The licensees would have been required to keep a record of their offers to the public for response, the representative programming that was devoted to each issue, the partisan spokespersons presented, and the sources and times of the broadcasts. Routine news coverage would have been excluded.

The Commission concluded that the added record keeping would not "necessarily enhance coverage" of controversial issues. The existing rules already required television licensees "to keep in their public inspection file a listing of no more than ten significant problems of the area served by the station during the preceding twelve months and to indicate typical and illustrative programming broadcast in response to those problems and needs." At renewal time the listings for the three prior years are sent to the Commission as part of the renewal process. In the absence of any showing that television licensees are not now covering controversial issues, the added burden was unwarranted.

Moreover, Geller's proposal was inconsistent with the goal of reviewing fairness doctrine complaints as they arise rather than waiting until renewal when the issues might have become stale.

4. *The Affirmative Duty to Raise Issues.* The Commission refers to the fairness doctrine as having two parts. Virtually all the litigation and discussion have involved the second part: the requirement that a licensee who has presented one side of a controversial issue of public importance must present contrasting views.

In 1976, for the first time, the Commission applied the first part. A Congresswoman sent an 11-minute tape opposing strip mining to West Virginia radio stations to counter a presentation in favor of strip mining that had been distributed to many stations by the U.S. Chamber of Commerce. One station, WHAR, refused to play the tape because it had not presented the first program. Indeed, it had presented nothing on the issue except items on regular newscasts taken from the AP news service. Several persons and groups complained to the Commission contending that in this part of West Virginia at this time the question of strip mining was of primary importance. In its renewal application WHAR had cited "development of new industry" and "air and water pollution" as issues of great concern to its listeners. In addition, bills on the subject were pending in Congress at the time and local newspapers were extensively discussing the question. (Presentation of a five-minute tape by an outspoken foe of strip mining was not relevant because he did not discuss the economic or ecological aspects of strip mining or the pending legislation.)

The Commission asserted that although a violation of the first part "would be an exceptional situation and would not counter our intention to stay out of decisions concerning the selection of specific programming matter," this was such a case and demonstrated an "unreasonable exercise" of discretion. The Commission quoted the passage from *Red Lion* that "if the present licensees should suddenly prove timorous, the Commission is not powerless to insist that they give adequate and fair attention to public issues." The lack of any prior request to program on this subject was irrelevant because "it is the station's obligation to make an affirmative effort to program on issues of concern to its community." The role of the AP news items was minimal because it was not even clear which ones were aired.

"Where, as in the present case, an issue has significant and possibly unique impact on the licensee's service area, it will not be sufficient for the licensee as an indication of compliance with the fairness doctrine to show that it may have broadcast an unknown amount of news touching on a general topic related to the issue cited in a complaint." The station was ordered to tell the Commission within 20 days how it intended to meet its fairness obligations. Rep. Patsy Mink, 59 F.C.C.2d 987, 37 R.R.2d 744 (1976).

What is the difference between saying (1) a station has an obligation to present programs on the need for good dental hygiene, even though the subject may not be controversial, and (2) a station must present programs on a controversial issue in the community? Are both covered by the fairness doctrine?

What is the justification for requiring each station in a community to present a range of views on controversial issues of public importance? Why is it not enough if the spectrum as a whole provides contrasting viewpoints? Is there more—or less—reason to require a station to raise important subjects when other stations in the community are doing so? Thus, in the strip mining case, should it matter that other broadcasters are devoting extensive coverage to the subject? What has this obligation to do with "fairness"?

5. *The duty to present contrasting views.* At one point the Commission quotes a court to the effect that not everything that is thought newsworthy by journalists necessarily presents a controversial issue of public importance. What are some examples of divergence between the two?

The Commission has never declared the fairness doctrine "applicable to issues involving the interpretation of religious doctrine." When a group complained that the program "In Search of Noah's Ark" presented one side of the issue of whether the Ark exists, and gave mistaken impressions about the attitudes of historians, archaeologists and scholars, the Broadcast Bureau responded: "While such issues may be widely and vigorously disputed in the religious community, they generally do not rise to the level of a controversial issue of public importance. . . . Although the issue has received media coverage in that the film itself was broadcast, you have not shown that government and community leaders have taken positions on the issue. Nor have you demonstrated that the issue has any particular impact on the community at large." The network's determination that the fairness doctrine did not apply was not unreasonable. Religion and Ethics Institute, Inc., 42 R.R.2d 1657 (Bd.Bur.1978).

6. *Defining the "Issue."* In American Sec. Council Educational Foundation v. Federal Communications Commission, 607 F.2d 438 (D.C.Cir.1979), the ASCEF analyzed a full year's news programming of CBS. It transcribed all CBS news reports, broke them into sentences, and then determined whether each was relevant to four topics: "United States military and foreign affairs; Soviet Union

military and foreign affairs; China military and foreign affairs; and Vietnam affairs." Each relevant sentence was put into one of three categories: Viewpoint A was that the "threat to U.S. security is more serious than perceived by the government or that the United States ought to *increase* its national security efforts." Viewpoint B was that the government's perception is essentially correct and viewpoint C was that the threat is less serious than perceived and national security efforts should be decreased. The ASCEF analysis put 3.54 percent of the content into viewpoint A; 34.63 percent into viewpoint B, and 61.83 percent into viewpoint C. Based on these results and claimed similar disparities for later years, ASCEF filed a fairness complaint with the FCC asking that CBS be ordered to provide a reasonable opportunity for the expression of "A viewpoints."

The FCC dismissed the complaint without calling for any response from CBS on the ground that the complaint did not identify "the particular issue of a controversial nature" that was involved. The court, 6–3, affirmed:

> We affirm the Commission's decision that ASCEF failed to base its complaint on a particular well-defined issue because (1) the indirect relationships among the issues aggregated by ASCEF under the umbrella of "national security" do not provide a basis for determining whether the public received a reasonable balance of conflicting views, and (2) a contrary result would unduly burden broadcasters without a countervailing benefit to the public's right to be informed.

Since the fairness doctrine is issue-oriented, it is essential that the "issue" be clearly identified. Here "national security" was an umbrella that held within it too many issues that were only tangentially related, such as detente with China, America's commitment to NATO, SALT, and response to the Soviet Union's role in the Middle East.

The court suggested that a fairness complaint could be based on an issue that consists of separately identifiable subissues only if the main issue was well defined. If ASCEF had used single issues it could have analyzed actual views "instead of superimposing artificial A, B, and C viewpoints on the broadcasts studied." Then the FCC could have determined the question of balance and, if necessary, framed a specific remedy.

Acceptance of ASCEF's approach would also burden broadcasters. "CBS could have had to review all of its news programming relevant to national security over at least a year's time. . . . It would have been virtually impossible to know which broadcasts should be included as relevant to national security, or how views discussed . . . should be tallied to measure 'balance' under the fairness doctrine."

Further burdens would fall on editors: "An editor preparing an evening newscast would be required to decide whether any of the day's newsworthy events is tied, even tangentially, to events covered in the past, and whether a report on today's lead story, in some remote way, balances yesterday's, last week's or last year's." Certiorari was denied, 444 U.S. 1013 (1980).

7. A potentially significant case involved a complaint that a network documentary about the failure of some private pension plans had been unfairly one-sided. The network responded that the program was about "some problems in some pension plans." The Commission concluded that the network had presented a one-sided program on the operation of the overall private pension system and must provide balance. On appeal, the court, 2–1, reversed the Commission on the ground that the Commission was wrong in thinking that it was the proper body to decide the subject of the program. Instead, the court held that it was for the network to decide what the program was about and the Commission could reject the network's characterization only if it was found to be unreasonable. Since that was not the case here, the Commission's order could not stand.

The entire court voted to review the panel's decision en banc. But at that stage the Commission asked that the case be remanded to be dismissed. That occasioned another round of judicial opinions but finally the case was remanded to the Commission and all decisions were vacated. All the action is reported in National Broadcasting Co. v. Federal Communications Commission, 516 F.2d 1101 (D.C.Cir.1974–75). An effort by the complainant, Accuracy in Media (AIM), to get the Supreme Court to reinstate the case, failed when the Court denied AIM's petition for certiorari. 424 U.S. 910 (1976).

Although the Pensions case was mooted, cases discussed later in this Chapter have reiterated the court's finding that licensee discretion is central to Fairness Doctrine questions. The Commission is limited to judging the reasonableness of a licensee's determination.

8. A San Francisco licensee's determination that programs advocating defeat of gay rights legislation elsewhere did not present a controversial question of public importance, was rejected by the Commission as unreasonable. The Commission stated that although the discussion was of "primary importance to the homosexual community . . . , the issue has had and continues to have a significant impact on the public at large." Council on Religion and the Homosexual, 68 F.C.C.2d 1500, 43 R.R.2d 1580 (1978).

The licensee had presented eight hours of programs (half original and half rebroadcasts) featuring Anita Bryant and others arguing against the proposed Dade County, Florida, ordinance barring discrimination on grounds of sexual preference. These programs were presented over a period of four months, with one and a half hours in prime time. The licensee presented a one-hour tape supporting gay rights, nine times over a period of four days, never in prime time. The complainants argued that this did not afford a reasonable opportunity for the presentation of opposing viewpoints. The Commission disagreed. It noted that the gay rights position had received more total time than the other side. Also, the licensee had advertised only the pro-gay talks in local newspapers.

When complainants objected to equating a single one-hour tape with more varied presentations on the other side, and four months on one side with four days on the other, the Commission noted that its role was "not to substitute our judgment for that of the licensee but merely to review that judgment for reasonableness." The Commission could not, and would not, "make the subjective determination of the relative impact of the pro or anti-gay rights programming presented on the station." The licensee's judgment could not be deemed unreasonable.

9. What constitutes balance? In paragraph 43 of the Fairness Report, p. 565, supra, the Commission rejected any strict mathematical determination of balance. Instead, in each case the Commission decides whether in its judgment the licensee acted reasonably in concluding that the coverage was balanced. The factors considered include the total amount of time devoted to each side, the frequency with which each side was presented and the size of audience for each presentation. For an extensive discussion of this process see Public Media Center v. Federal Communications Commission, 587 F.2d 1322 (D.C.Cir.1978).

10. Occasionally, entertainment programming may raise problems under the Fairness Doctrine. One typical example would be a story in which a character considers whether to seek an abortion. See Diocesan Union of Holy Name Societies, 41 F.C.C.2d 297, 28 R.R.2d 545 (1973) (involving a pro-abortion theme). Must contrasting views be presented? If so, must it be by other entertainment programming or will an interview program suffice? What about implicit presentations, such as a series featuring a happily married couple of different faiths? Must the licensee provide for contrasting views against interfaith marriages? The cases are collected and discussed in Rosenfeld, The Jurisprudence of Fairness: Freedom Through Regulation in the Marketplace of Ideas, 44 Ford.L.Rev. 877, 901–04 (1976).

11. The owner of a station in the same county as WXUR, which was denied renewal in Brandywine-Maine Line, p. 533, supra, wrote that his station presented two guests on a call-in show on consecutive days. The first day Dr. McIntire, the principal figure behind WXUR, appeared. Every question called in was favorable to his position. The next day, the guest was an opponent, who believed strongly in the fairness doctrine and who had attacked the operation of WXUR. He did not receive a single supportive call. The owner's point was that "liberal intellectuals" are most comfortable with each other and shy away from the less educated. When the "average liberal-intellectual" listens to radio he seeks out classical music or an all-news or educational station. "If he should tune in to a talk station and listen to some of the 'drivel' broadcast, he would become furious and switch to a station with which he is more at home." The conclusion was that

if the liberal hopes to convert others to his viewpoint he must become a proselytizer, and call-in shows are an easy way to reach large numbers of voters. Tannen, Liberals and the Media, The Progressive, April, 1974 at 11. Is this report an accurate picture of "liberal" attitudes? If so, does that affect your view of the fairness doctrine?

12. *Commercials.* In the 1960's the Commission decided that advertisements for cigarettes required stations to present some programming on the dangers of smoking. This ruling was upheld in Banzhaf v. Federal Communications Commission, 405 F.2d 1082 (D.C. Cir.1968), certiorari denied 396 U.S. 842 (1969). Although the licensee could decide how to meet this requirement, most licensees presented material that had been prepared by the American Cancer Society and similar organizations. We trace the future of cigarette advertising in the next note.

The Commission attempted to treat the cigarette case as unique. Thus, when opponents of high-powered automobiles wanted the FCC to require licensees to present contrasting views on the value of such cars, the FCC refused. On appeal, the court of appeals could not distinguish the cigarette situation from the high-powered car situation and ordered the FCC to be consistent. Friends of the Earth v. Federal Communications Commission, 449 F.2d 1164 (D.C.Cir.1971).

In 1974, the Commission, in an omitted portion of its Fairness Report, rethought the question of applying the fairness doctrine to commercials. It finally decided to divide commercials into those that simply try to sell products and those that present a "meaningful statement which obviously addresses, and advocates a point of view on, a controversial issue of public importance." The latter, also called "editorial advertisements", gave rise to obligations under the fairness doctrine. If an advertisement is false or misleading, it might give rise to some action by the Federal Trade Commission or by competitors, but the fairness doctrine was not the appropriate way to handle commercials that did not address public issues.

This position was quickly challenged in the courts in a case involving a commercial for snowmobiles. Environmental groups complained that the commercials showed only one side of the controversial issue of the desirability of snowmobiles. The FCC rejected the complaint on the ground that, although the environmental effects of snowmobiles might involve a controversial issue of public importance, the commercials themselves were not devoted to an obvious or meaningful discussion of that issue.

The court of appeals affirmed. Public Interest Research Group v. Federal Communications Commission, 522 F.2d 1060 (1st Cir.1975), certiorari denied 424 U.S. 965 (1976). The appellants argued that the FCC had no authority to retreat from its earlier rulings that selling commercials might invoke the fairness doctrine. The court disagreed. "In the absence of statutory or constitutional barriers, an agency may abandon earlier precedents and frame new policies."

Congress had not frozen the fairness doctrine in any particular form. Nor was there any reason to require the FCC to apply the doctrine to all commercials or to none.

Finally, the appellants argued that the First Amendment itself required that the fairness doctrine be rigorously enforced so that the airwaves would be true public forums for the presentation of divergent views. The court rejected this argument. Although the *Red Lion* approach might be furthered by extending the fairness doctrine to all advertising, the court did "not view that question, in the short and long run, as so free from doubt that courts should impose an inflexible response as a matter of constitutional law. We believe that the first amendment permitted the Commission not only to experiment with full-scale application of the fairness doctrine to advertising but also to retreat from its experiment when it determined from experience that the extension was unworkable."

13.   *Cigarettes.*   After the *Banzhaf* decision, Congress moved into the picture. In 1969, it adopted 15 U.S.C. § 1335: "After January 1, 1971, it shall be unlawful to advertise cigarettes on any medium of electronic communication subject to the jurisdiction of the Federal Communications Commission."

The statute was challenged by broadcasters—but not by cigarette manufacturers. It was upheld by a three judge court in Capital Broadcasting Co. v. Mitchell, 333 F.Supp. 582 (D.D.C.1971), affirmed without opinion 415 U.S. 1000 (1972). The dissenting opinion in the lower court suggested that the cigarette manufacturers were not at all unhappy to be ordered to stop advertising on radio and television because it had become unprofitable.

Now that commercial speech is being given more protection, might a ban on such advertising be invalid? See p. 299, supra. Could Congress ban programs devoted to a discussion of the pros and cons of smoking?

The court rejected the argument that this amounted to censorship in violation of § 326 because licensees were still free to present pro-smoking messages—except to the extent that Congress had forbidden commercial messages. The Commission was leaving that decision to the licensees. Moreover, some aspects of anti-smoking messages might still be found to invoke the fairness doctrine—but health danger was not one of them. Also, it was permissible to consider at renewal time whether a licensee carried programs on the dangers of smoking—not because it was a controversial issue, but because one aspect of meeting the public interest is to warn about dangers to health and safety, even if they are obvious and noncontroversial. What might the Commission do at renewal time if it found that a licensee had presented several debates on cigarette smoking in which half the speakers argued that there was no health hazard in smoking? Is there a tension between saying that licensees are free to program pro-smoking material if they wish and that they will be judged at renewal time on how they have programmed on matters of health and safety?

13. Chairman Wiley had urged abandoning the fairness doctrine for radio in the large major markets. He saw little reason for the doctrine in such markets as Chicago, with 65 commercial radio stations and New York, with 43 stations. Contrasting viewpoints were likely to emerge in such a situation and scarcity was not a sound rationale for the fairness doctrine. A majority of the Commission in denying reconsideration of the Fairness Report, rejected his proposal, saying only "The Commission has decided not to proceed at this time with a proposal by the Chairman for an experimental suspension of the fairness doctrine in larger radio markets." 58 F.C.C.2d 691, 699, n. 11, 36 R.R.2d 1021, 1033, n. 11 (1976). See also Broadcasting, Mar. 1, 1976, p. 49.

14. Recently, the fairness doctrine has come under renewed attack. In May 1984, the FCC released a notice of inquiry on the fairness doctrine stating that "continuance of these obligations now or in the future may be at odds not only with the very same First Amendment goals underlying their foundation but with other First Amendment principles in other areas of speech and expression. . . . [Q]uestions exist over the need for continued government interference into the private journalistic discretion that the fairness doctrine occasions." The notice sought comments as to whether the doctrine was essential, desirable, or required by section 315. Docket 84–282. Broadcasting, May 14, 1984 at 70.

Could a Commission decision that the Fairness Doctrine reduces rather than enhances speech lead the Supreme Court to overrule *Red Lion*? This possibility was raised in n. 12 of *League of Women Voters*, p. 517, supra.

Senator Packwood (R.-Ore.) introduced legislation in Congress to, among other things, repeal the fairness doctrine and sections 315 and 312(a)(7). Freedom of Expression Act of 1983, S.1917, 2d Sess. (1983). A diluted version of his bill, proposing the repeal of the equal opportunities provision and the fairness doctrine for radio only, was rejected by the Senate Commerce Committee on a vote of 11–6. Broadcasting, June 18, 1984 at 32.

At that time, Committee member Nancy Kassebaum (R.-Kans.), who holds ownership interests in several radio stations objected to the proposal believing some content regulation is required. She highlighted the case of KTTL(FM), Dodge City, Kansas, whose license is being challenged following the broadcasting of ethnic and racial slurs and possible encouragement of violence. Broadcasting, June 18, 1984 at 32.

2. PERSONAL ATTACK RULES

As we saw in *Red Lion*, p. 478, supra, the personal attack part of the general Fairness Doctrine has been crystallized into a rule, 47 C.F.R. § 73.123:

(a) When, during the presentation of views on a controversial issue of public importance, an attack is made upon the honesty, character, integrity or like personal qualities of an identified person or group, the licensee shall, within a reasonable time and in no event later than 1 week after the attack, transmit to the person or group attacked (1) notification of the date, time and identification of the broadcast; (2) a script or tape (or an accurate summary if a script or tape is not available) of the attack; and (3) an offer of a reasonable opportunity to respond over the licensee's facilities.

(b) The provisions of paragraph (a) of this section shall not be applicable (1) to attacks on foreign groups or foreign public figures; (2) to personal attacks which are made by legally qualified candidates, their authorized spokesmen, or those associated with them in the campaign, on other such candidates, their authorized spokesmen, or persons associated with the candidates in the campaign; and (3) to bona fide newscasts, bona fide news interviews, and on-the-spot coverage of a bona fide news event (including commentary or analysis contained in the foregoing programs, but the provisions of paragraph (a) of this section shall be applicable to editorials of the licensee).

The first point to note is that the episode must occur "during the presentation of views on a controversial issue of public importance." This limitation means that personal attacks unrelated to such a discussion do not invoke the rule—and presumably are left exclusively to defamation suits. Why is this distinction drawn?

Sometimes it is difficult to determine what constitutes "during the presentation of views on a controversial issue of public importance." In Straus Communications, Inc. v. Federal Communications Commission, 530 F.2d 1001 (D.C.Cir.1976), a licensee's argument that time for reply was not justified because the attack did not take place during such a discussion was rejected by the Commission. On appeal, the court ruled that the Commission had used the wrong standard when stating that it "believed" that the comment was sufficiently related to an earlier discussion of a meat boycott to justify the conclusion that the personal attack occurred during a continuation of that discussion. The court concluded that the proper approach was for the Commission to judge "the objective reasonableness of the licensee's determination" that the meat boycott discussion had long since ended.

See also Polish American Congress v. Federal Communications Comm'n, 520 F.2d 1248 (7th Cir.1975), certiorari denied 424 U.S. 927

(1976), in which the complainants had claimed that a skit of Polish jokes on television violated the personal attack part of the fairness doctrine. The Commission rejected the complaint. On appeal, the court stated that the order must be upheld "if the Commission properly determined that ABC's conclusion that the broadcast did not involve a controversial issue of public importance was not unreasonable nor in bad faith." The court concluded that "the Commission was correct in ruling that ABC did not overstep its discretion in failing to find a controversial issue of public importance." This was true whether the issue was stated to be (1) whether "Polish Americans are inferior to other human beings in terms of intelligence, personal hygiene, etc." or (2) whether "promulgating" Polish jokes by broadcasting them is desirable. If the former, ABC could reasonably conclude that even if some people felt that way they had not generated enough support to raise a controversial issue of public importance. Even if they had, ABC could conclude that the skit presented did not constitute a "discussion" of this issue. If the issue was the latter, no controversy was shown.

Another issue raised in *Polish American Congress* (although it was not addressed due to the lack of a controversial issue of public importance) was the size of the group attacked. Remember from the discussion of group libel, p. 66, supra, that once the group gets too large there is no identification—the individual plaintiff would have difficulty showing that his own personal reputation was harmed. Should the same apply to the personal attack rule when the attack is on a large group rather than on an individual or on a small group? In Diocese of Rockville Centre, 50 F.C.C.2d 330, 32 R.R.2d 376 (1973), a licensee had broadcast a statement that perhaps an earlier writer was correct when he stated "The Roman Church is filled with men who were led into it merely by ambition, who though they might have been useful and respectful as laymen, are hypocritical and immoral." The Commission ruled that the group is not sufficiently "identified" unless the licensee "could reasonably be expected to know exactly who or what finite group" is best able to inform the public of the contrasting viewpoint. The reference to "men" who fill the "Roman Church" was found too vague.

The Commission has made clear that attacks during discussion of controversial issues of public importance are not misbehavior—and wide-open debate is encouraged—so long as the rules are followed.

The FCC has begun rulemaking to modify or eliminate the personal attack and political editorializing rules, questioning whether they have enhanced diversity of expression. The National Association of Broadcasters has contended the personal attack rule has been misused by people more intent upon vindicating their reputations than in providing the public with information about their positions, and that the political editorializing rule has discouraged broadcasters from making political endorsements. Chairman Fowler has characterized the personal attack rule as mainly a "quasi-defamation" action because it is not being used to enlighten public debate.

Representatives Timothy Wirth (D.-Colo.) and John Dingell (D.-Mich.) opposed repeal in a letter to Fowler in June 1983. They said the proposals represent "yet another disturbing step in the Commission's pattern of systematic retreat from the principles of public service and accountability that form the cornerstone of a broadcaster's responsibilities under the Communications Act". Broadcasting, June 27, 1983 at 86. This view was joined by Accuracy in Media, the Conservative Caucus, the American Business Media Council, and the Telecommunications Research and Action Center, creating an alliance of both the right and left. Broadcasting, Aug. 22, 1983 at 48.

---

3. FAIRNESS IN POLITICAL CAMPAIGNS

The fairness doctrine enters into political issues in two ways. The first involves the use of broadcasting by the party in power, particularly the President, between political campaigns. The courts have taken the view that when the President speaks on an issue of national concern, the party out of power has no automatic right to reply. The only exception occurred when the President delivered five uninterrupted speeches during a seven-month period about the war in Indochina. Since broadcast coverage of that dispute had otherwise been roughly in balance, the FCC decided that the networks were obligated to provide free time for a spokesman from the other side of the issue.

But that instance aside, the courts have considered the speeches of a President just one factor to weigh in deciding whether the required rough balance in the presentation of contrasting views has been achieved. As usual, the FCC will generally defer to the views of the licensees, and the courts will generally defer to the views of the FCC. The subject is explored extensively in Democratic National Committee v. Federal Communications Commission, 481 F.2d 543 (D.C.Cir.1973) (unsuccessful Democratic attempt to obtain free reply time to counter President's speeches on economic policy.) The official use of television and the response of the networks to official requests are discussed in N. Minow, J.B. Martin, and L.M. Mitchell, Presidential Television (1973).

The second role of the fairness doctrine in politics involves the campaign itself. Since § 315 was construed not to cover appearances by anyone other than candidates, and since the section also does not cover ballot propositions, many important political campaign broadcasts must be regulated under provisions much less precise than § 315. Not surprisingly, as television has become increasingly important in election campaigns, questions not covered by § 315 have arisen more frequently.

Uses by Supporters. Turning first to a close parallel situation, what are the controlling principles when Candidate A's friends or campaign committee purchase time to further his candidacy or to attack B, his opponent? In its Letter to Nicholas Zapple, 23 F.C.C.2d 707, 19 R.R.2d 421 (1970), the Commission stated that the 1959 amendment to § 315 had explicitly recognized the operation of the fairness doctrine when the candidate's own appearance was exempted from § 315. The doctrine was thought equally applicable here. Moreover, when a candidate is supported or his opponent attacked, although the licensee has the responsibility of identifying suitable speakers for opposing views, "barring unusual circumstances, it would not be reasonable for a licensee to refuse to sell time to spokesmen for or supporters of candidate B comparable to that previously bought on behalf of candidate A." But there was no obligation to provide B's supporters with free time. Although usually requiring that time be given away, if necessary, to get contrasting views before the public, the Commission thought this unsound in the political arena. To hold otherwise would require licensees, or other advertisers, to subsidize B's campaign. The rejection of subsidization meant that even if A's friends mounted a personal attack on B, B would not get free time. The Commission has adhered closely to the *Zapple* ruling, which is sometimes referred to as the "quasi equal opportunities" or "political party" corollary to the fairness doctrine.

In 1979, the Commission decided that Congress intended that "uses" under § 315 and *Zapple* were to be mutually exclusive of the fairness doctrine. The Commission concluded that licensees should not be responsible for "uses" since they have no control over them. As a result, the personal attack rule was rewritten to provide that it did not apply to personal attacks occurring during uses under § 315 or those occurring under *Zapple* situations.

More generally, the fairness doctrine was declared not to apply to issues raised during "uses." The Commission believed that issues raised during "uses" were likely to be of such public interest that other views would be aired in due course without the goad of the fairness doctrine. Personal Attacks and Applicability of the Fairness Doctrine to Section 315 "Uses," 78 F.C.C.2d 457, 45 R.R.2d 1635 (1979).

Recall that § 315 itself explicitly provides that the fairness doctrine applies to programs that are exempted from the equal opportunities provision of § 315.

A new problem emerged in 1980 involving groups organized by friends of Ronald Reagan but not controlled by the candidate. These groups are not bound by spending limits that may bind the candidates themselves. When these groups began to buy time on broadcast stations, the Carter campaign committee complained to the FCC that the stations selling time to these "independent expenditure groups" should be required to make equal, and free, opportunities available to the Carter campaign (and presumably to all other campaigns). These should be free, the Carter committee asserted, because it and the Reagan campaign were each limited to $29.4 million for campaigning because they agreed to accept federal funds. As a result, they could not match both the money Reagan was spending and that being spent by the independent groups.

The FCC rejected the claim on the ground that friends of Carter could start comparable groups to match the expenditures being made by the Reagan groups. To allow the Carter campaign free time would put the Commission in the position of benefitting one of the candidates at the expense of the other, whose friends had been required to pay for his time.

In *Kennedy II*, p. 558, supra, after rejecting the candidate's claims under § 312 and § 315, the court turned to the role of the fairness doctrine in political campaigns. The Broadcast Bureau and the Commission had found three fatal flaws in Kennedy's reliance on the fairness doctrine in this case—and the court agreed. First, he had failed to define the particular controversial issue involved with sufficient specificity. Second, there was no showing that the networks had failed to present contrasting viewpoints on the national economy in their overall programming. The fairness doctrine "does not operate with the dissective focus of" § 315(a). "Intelligent assessment of the nature and caliber of a broadcaster's overall programming obviously cannot be confined to one program, or even to one day's presentations, so a failure to show some fairness deficiency on the whole is necessarily fatal."

Even if imbalance were established, the third flaw was that Senator Kennedy had no "individual right to broadcast his views on the current economic crisis." Kennedy did not show that he was "uniquely and singularly qualified to represent those who dispute the President's economic leadership or strategies."

Finally, the fairness doctrine extends to political campaigns since the question of which candidate should be elected may be considered a "controversial issue of public importance." This means that even if no requests for time are made under § 315 or § 312, a broadcaster might be required to introduce the issue under the first part of the fairness doctrine. If some views are expressed about the forthcoming campaign during non-uses, the licensee would be obligated under the second part of the doctrine to provide coverage of contrasting views. In determining what views should get how much time, the licensee must make good faith judgments about the importance of the race and the significance of each candidate.

The Commission's dismissal of a fairness complaint alleging unbalanced coverage of economic matters was upheld in DNC v.

Federal Communications Commission, 717 F.2d 1471, 54 R.R.2d 941 (1983). Disparities approximating 3:1 and 4:1 in favor of the pro-Administration economic view occurred on the networks. Compliance with fairness doctrine obligations was to be measured by a standard of good faith and reasonableness, not by reference to "rough approximations of equality." Since the disparities were not "glaring," and the audiences were not shown to be very different in size, the Commission's dismissal of the complaint was reasonable. Although the court cited data showing that fairness complainants prevail in roughly 1 in 1,000 cases, the court rejected Commission statements that fairness complaints will inevitably be futile.

Putting § 315, § 312, *Zapple*, and the general fairness doctrine together, does a coherent package result? What changes would you advocate?

Political Editorials. In a section of the personal attack rules, 47 C.F.R. § 73.123(c), the Commission covered political editorials:

> (c) Where a licensee, in an editorial (i) endorses or (ii) opposes a legally qualified candidate or candidates, the licensee shall, within 24 hours after the editorial, transmit to respectively (i) the other qualified candidate or candidates for the same office or (ii) the candidate opposed in the editorial (1) notification of the date and the time of the editorial; (2) a script or tape of the editorial; and (3) an offer of a reasonable opportunity for a candidate or a spokesman of the candidate to respond over the licensee's facilities: *Provided, however,* That where such editorials are broadcast within 72 hours prior to the day of the election, the licensee shall comply with the provisions of this paragraph sufficiently far in advance of the broadcast to enable the candidate or candidates to have a reasonable opportunity to prepare a response and to present it in a timely fashion.

Be sure to note that a single editorial on behalf of one candidate creates an opportunity to respond for *each* opposing candidate. This is true regardless of the number of opposing candidates. Friends of Howard Miller, 72 F.C.C.2d 508, 45 R.R.2d 1142 (1979).

Ballot Propositions. In an omitted part of the Fairness Report, the Commission reached the conclusion that such matters as referenda, initiative and recall propositions, bond proposals and constitutional amendments were to be regulated under the general fairness doctrine. The area was thought closer to general political discussion not involving elections than it was to the election of individuals to office. Thus, the *Cullman* doctrine requiring the licensee to present contrasting views, by the use of free time if necessary, was applicable. One argument against the *Cullman* doctrine was that some groups might spend their available money on non-broadcast media, wait for the other side to buy broadcast time, and then insist on free time under *Cullman* to counter their adversary. The Commission was not persuaded. First, this concern can always be raised against

Cullman but the Commission thought it most important that the public have access to contrasting views. On the tactical level, the Commission noted that the fairness doctrine does not guarantee equality of exposure of views nor who will be chosen as speakers. Those who rely solely on *Cullman* "have no assurance of obtaining equality by such means." Fairness Report, 48 F.C.C.2d 1, 33, 30 R.R.2d 1261, 1302 (1974).

C. NONCOMMERCIAL BROADCASTING AND POLITICAL SPEECH

Virtually all of our attention so far has been devoted to commercial broadcasting. Most of the litigation and regulation has involved commercial broadcasters and, in terms of viewers, commercial broadcasting is the preeminent part of the picture. But it is not the only part. AM broadcasting developed too early for the Commission to be able to consider reserving spots for noncommercial educational stations. In allocating FM and television, however, the Commission was able to plan in advance and reserved certain spots for educational broadcasters. These are usually operated by academic institutions, by governmental groups or by groups organized by private citizens. A station run by a sectarian academic institution may be eligible for a reserved educational spot in the community in which the school is located. If an organization's central purpose is religious it is not eligible for a reserved channel.

1. PUBLIC BROADCASTING

The development of public broadcasting and several questions it raises, are considered in the following case.

ACCURACY IN MEDIA, INC. v. FEDERAL COMMUNICATIONS COMMISSION

United States Court of Appeals, District of Columbia Circuit, 1975.
521 F.2d 288, certiorari denied 425 U.S. 934, 96 S.Ct. 1664,
48 L.Ed.2d 175 (1976).

Before BAZELON, CHIEF JUDGE, LEVENTHAL, CIRCUIT JUDGE and WEIGEL, UNITED STATES DISTRICT JUDGE for the Northern District of California.

BAZELON, CHIEF JUDGE.

Accuracy in Media, Inc. (AIM) filed two complaints with the FCC against the Public Broadcasting Service (PBS) concerning two programs distributed by PBS to its member stations. AIM alleged that the programs, dealing with sex education and the American system of criminal justice, were not a balanced or objective presentation of each subject and requested the FCC to order PBS to rectify the situation. The legal basis for AIM's complaints was the Fairness Doctrine and 47 U.S.C. § 396(g)(1)(A) (1970). On its initial hearing of the matter, the FCC concluded that the PBS had not violated the Fairness Doctrine and invited comments from interested parties on its authority to enforce whatever standard of program regulation was contained in § 396(g)(1)(A). AIM does not seek review of the Commission's decision on the Fairness Doctrine issue.

Section 396(g)(1)(A) is part of the Public Broadcasting Act of 1967, an act which created the Corporation for Public Broadcasting (CPB) and authorized it to fund various programming activities of local, non-commercial broadcasting licensees. Section 396(g)(1)(A) qualifies that authorization in the following language:

> In order to achieve the objectives and to carry out the purposes of this subpart, as set out in subsection (a) of this section, the Corporation is authorized to—
>
> > (A) facilitate the full development of educational broadcasting in which programs of high quality, obtained from diverse sources, will be made available to noncommercial educational television or radio broadcast stations, with strict adherence to objectivity and balance in all programs or series of programs of a controversial nature. . . .

AIM contends that since the above-mentioned PBS programs were funded by the CPB, pursuant to this authorization, the programs must contain "strict adherence to objectivity and balance", a requirement AIM contends is more stringent than the standard of balance and fairness in overall programming contained in the Fairness Doctrine. AIM alleges that the two relevant programs did not meet this more stringent standard of objectivity and balance.

After consideration of the comments received on the matter, invited in its preliminary decision discussed above, the Commission concluded that it had no jurisdiction to enforce the mandate of § 396(g)(1)(A) against CPB. . . .

I. THE ORGANIZATION OF PUBLIC BROADCASTING IN THE UNITED STATES

Resolution of the issues raised by AIM's petition requires an understanding of the operation of the public broadcasting system. There are three tiers to this operation, each reflecting a different scheme of governmental regulation. The basic level is comprised of the local, noncommercial broadcasting stations that are licensed by the FCC and, with a few exceptions, subject to the same regulations as commercial licenses. Through the efforts of former Commissioner Frieda Hennock, the FCC has reserved exclusive space in its allocation of frequencies for such noncommercial broadcasters. Other than this specific reservation, noncommercial licenses are still subject to the same renewal process and potential challenges as their commercial counterparts.

Such was the state of the public broadcasting system until the passage of the Educational Television Facilities Act in 1962. The Act added the element of government funding to public broadcasting by establishing a capital grant program for noncommercial facilities. This second level of the system was reorganized and expanded by the Public Broadcasting Act of 1967 which created the Corporation for Public Broadcasting (CPB). The Corporation, the product of a study made by the Carnegie Commission on Educational Television, was established as a funding mechanism for virtually all activities of noncommercial broadcasting. In setting up this nonprofit, private corporation, the Act specifically prohibited CPB from engaging in any form of "communication by wire or radio."

The third level of the public broadcasting system was added in 1970 when CPB and a group of noncommercial licensees formed the Public Broadcasting Service (PBS) and National Public Radio. The Public Broadcasting Service operates as the distributive arm of the public television system. As a nonprofit membership corporation, it distributes national programming to approximately 150 educational licensees via common carrier facilities. This interconnection service is funded by the Corporation (CPB) under a contract with PBS; in addition, much of the programming carried by PBS is either wholly or partially funded by CPB. National Public Radio provides similar services for noncommercial radio. In 1974, CPB and the member licensees of PBS agreed upon a station program cooperative plan [14] to insure local control and origination of noncommercial programming funded by CPB. Though PBS is the national coordinator under this scheme, it is not a "network" in the commercial broadcasting sense, and does not engage in "communication by wire or radio," except to the extent that it contracts for interconnection services.

II. FCC JURISDICTION OVER THE CORPORATION FOR PUBLIC BROADCASTING

With the structure of the public broadcasting system in view, we turn to AIM's contention that the FCC should enforce the mandate of § 396(g)(1)(A) against the CPB. Since the Section is clearly directed to the Corporation and its programming activities, we have no doubt that the Corporation must respect the mandate of the Section. However, we conclude that nothing in the language and legislative history

---

14. The Station Program Cooperative (SPC) is a unique concept in program selection and financing for public television stations. Though the idea of public television as a "fourth network" had been proposed at various times, the 1974 plan reversed this trend toward centralization. Under the SPC, certain programming will be produced only if the individual local stations decide together to fund the production. The local licensees will be financed through the CPB and other sources; the funding of specific programs will be by a 4 to 5 ratio (station funds to national cooperative funds). The aim of this cooperative is to reinforce the existing licensee responsibility for programming discretion. Through this plan the local stations will eventually assume the responsibility for support of the cooperative and the Corporation will concentrate on new programming development. [ ]

of the Federal Communications Act or the Public Broadcasting Act of 1967 authorizes the FCC to enforce that mandate against the CPB.

Section 398 of the Communications Act expresses the clear intent of Congress that there shall be no direct jurisdiction of the FCC over the Corporation. That section states that nothing in the 1962 or 1967 Acts "shall be deemed (1) to amend any other provision of, or requirement under this Act; or (2) to authorize any department, agency, officer, or employee of the United States to exercise any direction, supervision or control over educational television or radio broadcasting, or over the Corporation or any of its grantees or contractors . . . ." Since the FCC is obviously an "agency . . . of the United States" and since any enforcement of § 396(g)(1)(A) would necessarily entail "supervision" of the Corporation, the plain words of subsection (2) preclude FCC jurisdiction. . . .

Congress desired to establish a program funding agency which would be free from governmental influence or control in its operations. Yet, the lawmakers feared that such complete autonomy might lead to biases and abuses of its own. The unique position of the Corporation is the synthesis of these competing influences. Reference to the legislative history of the 1967 Act shows a deep concern that governmental regulation or control over the Corporation might turn the CPB into a Government spokesman. Congress thus sought to insulate CPB by removing its "programming activity from governmental supervision." . . .

. . .

AIM maintains that this view of FCC jurisdiction to enforce § 396(g)(1)(A) renders the Section nugatory and hence ignores the Congressional sentiment that biases and abuses within the public broadcasting system should be controlled. We do not view our holding on the FCC's jurisdiction as having that effect. Rather, we take notice of the carefully balanced framework designed by Congress for the control of CPB activities.

The Corporation was established as nonprofit and non-political in nature and is prohibited from owning or operating "any television or radio broadcast station, system or network, community antenna system, or interconnection, or production facility." Numerous statutory safeguards were created to insure against partisan abuses.[28] Ultimately, Congress may show its disapproval of any activity of the Corporation through the appropriation process.[29] This supervision of

---

28. Other statutory checks on the Corporation include: restricting the Board membership to no more than eight out of fifteen members from the same political party, § 396(c)(1). The composition of the Board was an important issue during debate and the decision to make the Board bipartisan was a significant addition to the original Carnegie Commission proposal. The Act also requires that the CPB's accounts be audited annually by an independent accountant, § 396(l)(1)(A), and *may* be audited by the General Accounting Office, § 396(l)(2)(A).

29. Section 396(k) assures that most of the CPB's operating budget be derived through the Congressional appropriation process.

CPB through its funding is buttressed by an annual reporting requirement.[30] Through these statutory requirements and control over the "purse-strings," Congress reserved for itself the oversight responsibility for the Corporation.

A further element of this carefully balanced framework of regulation is the accountability of the local noncommercial licensees under established FCC practice, including the Fairness Doctrine in particular. This existing system of accountability was clearly recognized in the 1967 legislative debates as a crucial check on the power of the CPB. . . .

. . .

The framework of regulation of the Corporation for Public Broadcasting we have described—maximum freedom from interference with programming coupled with existing public accountability requirements—is sensitive to the delicate constitutional balance between the First Amendment rights of the broadcast journalist and the concerns of the viewing public struck in Columbia Broadcasting System, Inc. v. Democratic National Committee, 412 U.S. 94 (1973). There the Supreme Court warned that "only when the interests of the public are found to outweigh the private journalistic interests of the broadcasters" will governmental interference with broadcast journalism be allowed. The Court on the basis of this rule rejected a right of access to broadcast air time greater than that mandated by the Fairness Doctrine as constituting too great a "risk of an enlargement of Government control over the content of broadcast discussion of public issues."

It is certainly arguable that FCC application of the standard—whatever that standard may be—of § 396(g)(1)(A) could "risk [an] enlargement of Government control over the content of broadcast discussion of public issues" in the following two ways: whereas the existing Fairness Doctrine requires only that the presentation of a controversial issue of public importance be balanced in *overall* programming, § 396(g)(1)(A) might be argued to require balance of controversial issues within each individual program. Administration of such a standard would certainly require a more active role by the FCC in oversight of programming. Furthermore, whereas the FCC has at present carefully avoided anything but the most limited inquiry into the factual accuracy of programming, § 396(g)(1)(A) by use of the term "objective" could be read to expand that inquiry and thereby expand FCC oversight of programming. Both of these potential enlargements of government control of programming, whether directed against the CPB, PBS or individual noncommercial licensees, threaten to upset the constitutional balance struck in *CBS*. We will not presume that Congress meant to thrust upon us the substantial constitutional questions such a result would raise. We

30. 47 U.S.C. § 396(i) (1970).

thus construe § 396(g)(1)(A) and the scheme of regulation for public broadcasting as a whole to avoid such questions.

. . . We hold today only that the FCC has no function in this scheme of accountability established by § 396(g)(1)(A) and the 1967 Act in general other than that assigned to it by the Fairness Doctrine. Therefore, we deny the petition for review and affirm the Commission's decision rejecting jurisdiction over the Corporation for Public Broadcasting.

So Ordered.

Notes and Questions

1. What is the difference between the Fairness Doctrine and AIM's reading of § 396(g)(1)(A)? Why does the court think that one would call for more Commission intervention in programming than the other?

2. The court suggests that, although thought of by many as a "fourth network," PBS does not properly fit such a description. Why not?

3. Since many of these stations are run by state and local governments, which also provide some of the financing, an additional set of problems has emerged with regard to the power of the state to impose restrictions more stringent than those imposed by Congress. In State of Maine v. University of Maine, 266 A.2d 863 (Me.1970), the state-run educational television system was partially financed from state funds. A statute ordered that no facilities "supported in whole or in part by state funds shall be used directly or indirectly for the promotion, advertisement or advancement of any political candidate . . . or for the purpose of advocating or opposing any specific program, existing or proposed, of governmental action which shall include, but shall not be limited to, constitutional amendments, tax referendums or bond issues."

The court concluded that the limitations ran counter to federal demands that a licensee operating in the public interest may not flatly ban all such programming. The role of state funding gave the state no added power in this area. Although the state "has a valid surviving power to protect its citizens in matters involving their health and safety or to protect them from fraud and deception, it has no such valid interest in protecting them from the dissemination of ideas as to which they may be called upon to make an informed choice."

4. Despite the ruling in the AIM case, the Commission retains several controls over public noncommercial broadcasters. The primary power is to be found in the licensing process. Recall the denial of renewal to the eight Alabama stations, p. 534, supra. A fundamental dispute over the proper role of educational stations emerged when WNET in New York was challenged on its application for renewal: Commissioner Hooks dissented from the approval on the ground that

the station was programming for a very small elite minority and essentially neglecting the needs of larger groups in the community who would benefit from language, vocational, and remedial programs. Elite programming is defended on the ground that the noncommercial stations do not get enough money from public sources and must solicit funds from their communities. It is thought that a station that presents culturally high-level programs for the wealthier segments of the community will have better success at raising the funds necessary to keep the station going. Is this a problem? How might the situation be changed?

5. Section 399(b) requires public broadcasters to make and retain for 60 days (to allow inspection by government or public) audio tapes for all programs "in which any issue of public importance is discussed." It has been declared unconstitutional in an en banc decision, 5–4. Community-Service Broadcasting of Mid-America, Inc. v. Federal Communications Commission, 593 F.2d 1102 (D.C.Cir.1978). The majority relied on equal protection grounds—that no similar burden was imposed on commercial broadcasters. Several members of the majority also expressed varying degrees of certainty that such a provision imposed on all broadcasters would violate the First Amendment. The dissenters thought that the statutory requirement of "objectivity and balance" justified the special obligation of § 399(b).

6. Another troublesome question in the 1967 Act involves § 399: "No noncommercial educational broadcast station may engage in editorializing or may support or oppose any candidate for political office." What arguments might be made against such a provision? What arguments to sustain it?

In late 1982, a district judge declared unconstitutional the ban on editorializing by stations accepting CPB grants. The Supreme Court, 5–4, affirmed.

FEDERAL COMMUNICATIONS COMMISSION v. LEAGUE OF WOMEN VOTERS OF CALIFORNIA

Supreme Court of the United States, 1984.
468 U.S. —, 104 S.Ct. 3106, 82 L.Ed.2d 278.

JUSTICE BRENNAN delivered the opinion of the Court.

[The background of the case and an excerpt from an earlier part of Justice Brennan's opinion appear at page 515, supra.

III

We turn now to consider whether the restraint imposed by § 399 satisfies the requirements established by our prior cases for permissible broadcast regulation. Before assessing the government's proffered justifications for the statute, however, two central features of the ban against editorializing must be examined, since they help to illuminate the importance of the First Amendment interests at stake in this case.

A

First, the restriction imposed by § 399 is specifically directed at a form of speech—namely, the expression of editorial opinion—that lies at the heart of First Amendment protection. In construing the reach of the statute, the FCC has explained that "although the use of noncommercial educational broadcast facilities by licensees, their management or those speaking on their behalf for the propagation of the licensee's own views on public issues is not permitted, such prohibition should not be construed to inhibit any *other* presentations on controversial issues of public importance." In re Complaint of Accuracy in Media, Inc., 45 F.C.C.2d 297, 302 (1973) (emphasis added). The Commission's interpretation of § 399 simply highlights the fact that what the statute forecloses is the expression of editorial opinion on "controversial issues of public importance." As we recently reiterated in NAACP v. Claiborne Hardware Co., 458 U.S. 886 (1982), "expression on public issues 'has always rested on the highest rung of the hierarchy of First Amendment values.'" Id., at 913 (quoting Carey v. Brown, 447 U.S. 455, 467 (1980)). And we have emphasized that:

> "The freedom of speech and of the press guaranteed by the Constitution embraces at least the liberty to discuss publicly and truthfully all matters of public concern without previous restraint or fear of subsequent punishment. . . . Freedom of discussion, if it would fulfill its historic function in this nation, must embrace all issues about which information is needed or appropriate to enable the members of society to cope with the exigencies of their period." Thornhill v. Alabama, 310 U.S. 88, 101–102 (1940).

The editorial has traditionally played precisely this role by informing and arousing the public, and by criticizing and cajoling those who hold government office in order to help launch new solutions to the problems of the time. Preserving the free expression of editorial opinion, therefore, is part and parcel of "our profound national commitment . . . that debate on public issues should be uninhibited, robust, and wide-open." New York Times v. Sullivan, 376 U.S. 254, 270 (1964). As we recognized in Mills v. Alabama, supra, the special place of the editorial in our First Amendment jurisprudence simply reflects the fact that the press, of which the broadcasting industry is indisputably a part, United States v. Paramount Pictures, Inc., 334 U.S. 131, 166 (1948), carries out a historic, dual responsibility in our society of reporting information and of bringing critical judgment to bear on public affairs. Indeed, the pivotal importance of editorializing as a means of satisfying the public's interest in receiving a wide variety of ideas and views through the medium of broadcasting has long been recognized by the FCC; the Commission has for the past 35 years actively encouraged commercial broadcast licensees to include editorials on public affairs in their programming. Because § 399 appears to restrict precisely that form of speech which the Framers of the Bill of Rights were most anxious to protect— speech that is "indispensable to the discovery and spread of political truth"—we must be especially careful in weighing the interests that are asserted in support of this restriction and in assessing the precision with which the ban is crafted. Whitney v. California, 274 U.S. 357, 375 (1927) (Brandeis, J., concurring).

Second, the scope of § 399's ban is defined solely on the basis of the content of the suppressed speech. A wide variety of non-editorial speech "by licensees, their management or those speaking on their behalf," In re Complaint of Accuracy in Media, Inc., supra, 45 F.C.C.2d, at 302, is plainly not prohibited by § 399. Examples of such permissible forms of speech include daily announcements of the station's program schedule or over-the-air appeals for contributions from listeners. Consequently, in order to determine whether a particular statement by station management constitutes an "editorial" proscribed by § 399, enforcement authorities must necessarily examine the content of the message that is conveyed to determine whether the views expressed concern "controversial issues of public importance." Ibid.

As Justice Stevens observed in Consolidated Edison Co. v. Public Service Commission, 447 U.S. 530 (1980), however, "[a] regulation of speech that is motivated by nothing more than a desire to curtail expression of a particular point of view on controversial issues of general interest is the purest example of a 'law . . . abridging the freedom of speech, or of the press.' A regulation that denies one group of persons the right to address a selected audience on 'controversial issues of public policy' is plainly such a regulation." Id., at 546 (concurring opinion); accord id., at 537–540 (majority opinion). Section 399 is just such a regulation, for it singles out noncommercial broadcasters and denies them the right to address their chosen audience on matters of public importance. . . .

B

In seeking to defend the prohibition on editorializing imposed by § 399, the Government urges that the statute was aimed at preventing two principal threats to the overall success of the Public Broadcasting Act of 1967. According to this argument, the ban was necessary, first, to protect noncommercial educational broadcasting stations from being coerced, as a result of federal financing, into becoming vehicles for government propagandizing or the objects of governmental influence; and, second, to keep these stations from becoming convenient targets for capture by private interest groups wishing to express their own partisan viewpoints.[16]   By seeking to safeguard the public's right to a balanced presentation of public issues through the prevention of either governmental or private bias, these objectives are, of course, broadly consistent with the goals identified in our earlier broadcast regulation cases.   But, in sharp contrast to the restrictions upheld in *Red Lion* or in Columbia Broadcasting System, Inc. v. FCC, which left room for editorial discretion and simply required broadcast editors to grant others access to the microphone, § 399 directly prohibits the broadcaster from speaking out on public issues even in a balanced and fair manner.   The Government insists, however, that the hazards posed in the "special" circumstances of noncommercial educational broadcasting are so great that § 399 is an indispensable means of preserving the public's First Amendment interests.   We disagree.

(1)

When Congress first decided to provide financial support for the expansion and development of noncommercial educational stations, all concerned agreed that this step posed some risk that these traditionally independent stations might be pressured into becoming forums devoted solely to programming and views that were acceptable to the Federal government.   That Congress was alert to these dangers cannot be doubted.   It sought through the Public Broadcasting Act to fashion a system that would provide local stations with sufficient funds to foster their growth and development while preserving their tradition of autonomy and community-orientation. . . .

The intended role of § 399 in achieving these purposes, however, is not as clear.   The provision finds no antecedent in the Carnegie Report, which generally provided the model for most other aspects of the Act.   It was not part of the Administration's original legislative proposal.   And it was not included in the original version of the Act passed by the Senate.   The provision found its way into the Act only as a result of an amendment in the House.   Indeed, it appears that, as the House Committee Report frankly admits, § 399 was added not because Congress thought it was essential to preserving the autonomy and vitality of local stations, but rather "out of an abundance of caution."   H.R.Rep. No. 572, 90th Cong., 1st Sess. 20 (1967).   [   ][18]

---

16. The Government also contends that § 399 is intended to prevent the use of taxpayer monies to promote private views with which taxpayers may disagree.   This argument is readily answered by our decision in Buckley v. Valeo, 424 U.S. 1, 90–93 (1976) (per curiam).   As we explained in that case, virtually every congressional appropriation will to some extent involve a use of public money as to which some taxpayers may object.   Id., at 91–92.   Nevertheless, this does not mean that those taxpayers have a consti-

tutionally protected right to enjoin such expenditures.   Nor can this interest be invoked to justify a congressional decision to suppress speech. . . .

18. . . .

Of course, as the Government points out, Congress has consistently retained the basic proscription on editorializing in § 399, despite periodic reconsiderations and modifications of the Act in 1973, 1978, and 1981.   Brief for the United States 25–27; see also n. 7, supra.   A

More importantly, an examination of both the overall legislative scheme established by the 1967 Act and the character of public broadcasting demonstrates that the interest asserted by the Government is not substantially advanced by § 399. First, to the extent that federal financial support creates a risk that stations will lose their independence through the bewitching power of governmental largesse, the elaborate structure established by the Public Broadcasting Act already operates to insulate local stations from governmental interference. Congress not only mandated that the new Corporation for Public Broadcasting would have a private, bipartisan structure, see §§ 396(c)–(f), but also imposed a variety of important limitations on its powers. The Corporation was prohibited from owning or operating any station, § 396(g)(3), it was required to adhere strictly to a standard of "objectivity and balance" in disbursing federal funds to local stations, § 396(g)(1)(A), and it was prohibited from contributing to or otherwise supporting any candidate for office, § 396(f)(3).

The Act also established a second layer of protections which serve to protect the stations from governmental coercion and interference. Thus, in addition to requiring the Corporation to operate so as to "assure the maximum freedom [of local stations] from interference with or control of program content or other activities," § 396(g)(1)(D), the Act expressly forbids "any department, agency, officer, or employee of the United States [from] exercis[ing] any direction, supervision, or control over educational television or radio broadcasting, or over the Corporation or any of its grantees or contractors . . .," § 398(a). . . . The principal thrust of the amendments, therefore, has been to assure long-term appropriations for the Corporation and, more importantly, to insist that it pass specified portions of these funds directly through to local stations to give them greater autonomy in defining the uses to which those funds should be put. Thus, in sharp contrast to § 399, the unifying theme of these various statutory provisions is that they substantially reduce the risk of governmental interference with the editorial judgments of local stations without restricting those stations' ability to speak on matters of public concern.[19]

reviewing court may not easily set aside such a considered congressional judgment. At the same time, "[d]eference to a legislative finding cannot limit judicial inquiry when First Amendment rights are at stake. . . . Were it otherwise, the scope of freedom of speech and of the press would be subject to legislative definition and the function of the First Amendment as a check on legislative power would be nullified." Landmark Communications, Inc. v. Virginia, 435 U.S. 829, 843–844 (1978).

19. Furthermore, the risk that federal coercion or influence will be brought to bear against local stations as a result of federal financing is considerably attenuated by the fact that CPB grants account for only a portion of total public broadcasting income. CPB, Public Broadcasting Income: Fiscal Year 1982, at Table 2 (Final Report, Dec. 1983) (noting that federal funds account for 23.4% of total income for all public broadcasting stations). The vast majority of financial support comes instead from state and local governments, as well as a wide variety of private sources, including foundations, businesses, and individual contributions; indeed, as the CPB recently noted, "[t]he diversity of support in America for public broadcasting is remarkable," CPB,

Even if these statutory protections were thought insufficient to the task, however, suppressing the particular category of speech restricted by § 399 is simply not likely, given the character of the public broadcasting system, to reduce substantially the risk that the Federal Government will seek to influence or put pressure on local stations. An underlying supposition of the Government's argument in this regard is that individual noncommercial stations are likely to speak so forcefully on particular issues that Congress, the ultimate source of the stations' Federal funding, will be tempted to retaliate against these individual stations by restricting appropriations for all of public broadcasting. But, as the District Court recognized, the character of public broadcasting suggests that such a risk is speculative at best. There are literally hundreds of public radio and television stations in communities scattered throughout the United States and its territories, see CPB, 1983–84 Public Broadcasting Directory 20–50, 66–86 (Sept. 1983). Given that central fact, it seems reasonable to infer that the editorial voices of these stations will prove to be as distinctive, varied, and idiosyncratic as the various communities they represent. More importantly, the editorial focus of any particular station can fairly be expected to focus largely on issues affecting only its community.[20] Accordingly, absent some showing by the Government to the contrary, the risk that local editorializing will place all of public broadcasting in jeopardy is not sufficiently pressing to warrant § 399's broad suppression of speech.

Indeed, what is far more likely than local station editorials to pose the kinds of dangers hypothesized by the Government are the wide variety of programs addressing controversial issues produced, often with substantial CPB funding, for national distribution to local stations. . . .

Furthermore, the manifest imprecision of the ban imposed by § 399 reveals that its proscription is not sufficiently tailored to the harms it seeks to prevent to justify its substantial interference with broadcasters' speech. Section 399 includes within its grip a potentially infinite variety of speech, most of which would not be related in any way to governmental affairs, political candidacies or elections. Indeed, the breadth of editorial commentary is as wide as human imagination permits. But the Government never explains how, say, an editorial by local station management urging improvements in a town's parks or museums will so infuriate Congress or other Federal officials that the future of public broadcasting will be imperiled unless such editorials are suppressed. Nor is it explained how the

1982 Annual Report 2 (1982). Given this diversity of funding sources and the decentralized manner in which funds are secured, the threat that improper federal influence will be exerted over local stations is not so pressing as to require the total suppression of editorial speech by these stations.

20. This likelihood is enhanced with respect to public stations because they are required to establish community advisory boards which must reasonably reflect the "diverse needs and interests of the communities served by such station[s]." § 396(k)(9)(A). . . .

suppression of editorials alone serves to reduce the risk of governmental retaliation and interference when it is clear that station management is fully able to broadcast controversial views so long as such views are not labelled as its own.[ ]

The Government appears to recognize these flaws in § 399, because it focuses instead on the suggestion that the source of governmental influence may well be state and local governments, many of which have established public broadcasting commissions that own and operate local noncommercial educational stations.[22] The ban on editorializing is all the more necessary with respect to these stations, the argument runs, because the management of such stations will be especially likely to broadcast only editorials that are favorable to the state or local authorities that hold the purse strings. The Government's argument, however, proves too much. First, § 399's ban applies to the many private noncommercial community organizations that own and operate stations that are not controlled in any way by state or local government. Second, the legislative history of the Public Broadcasting Act clearly indicates that Congress was concerned with "assur[ing] complete freedom from any *Federal Government influence.*" [ ] Consistently with this concern, Congress refused to create any federally owned stations and it expressly forbid the CPB to own or operate any television or radio stations, § 396(g)(3). By contrast, although Congress was clearly aware in 1967 that many noncommercial educational stations were owned by state and local governments, it did not hesitate to extend Federal assistance to such stations, it imposed no special requirements to restrict state or local control over these stations, and, indeed, it ensured through the structure of the Act that these stations would be as insulated from Federal interference as the wholly private stations.

Finally, although the Government certainly has a substantial interest in ensuring that the audiences of noncommercial stations will not be led to think that the broadcaster's editorials reflect the official view of the government, this interest can be fully satisfied by less restrictive means that are readily available. To address this important concern, Congress could simply require public broadcasting stations to broadcast a disclaimer every time they editorialize which would state that the editorial represents only the view of the station's management and does not in any way represent the views of the Federal Government or any of the station's other sources of funding. Such a disclaimer—similar to those often used in commercial and noncommercial programming of a controversial nature—would effectively and directly communicate to the audience that the editorial

---

22. As the Government points out in its Brief, at least two-thirds of the public television broadcasting stations in operation are licensed to (a) state public broadcasting authorities or commissions, in which commission members are often ap- pointed by the governor with the advice and consent of the state legislature, (b) state universities or educational commissions, or (c) local school boards or municipal authorities. [ ]

reflected only the views of the station rather than those of the government. . . .

In sum, § 399's broad ban on all editorializing by every station that receives CPB funds far exceeds what is necessary to protect against the risk of governmental interference or to prevent the public from assuming that editorials by public broadcasting stations represent the official view of government. The regulation impermissibly sweeps within its prohibition a wide range of speech by wholly private stations on topics that do not take a directly partisan stand or that have nothing whatever to do with federal, state or local government.

(2)

Assuming that the Government's second asserted interest in preventing noncommercial stations from becoming a "privileged outlet for the political and ideological opinions of station owners and management," Brief at 34, is legitimate, the substantiality of this asserted interest is dubious. The patent over⌐ and underinclusiveness of § 399's ban "undermines the likelihood of a genuine [governmental] interest" in preventing private groups from propagating their own views via public broadcasting. First National Bank of Boston v. Bellotti, supra, 435 U.S., at 793. If it is true, as the government contends, that noncommercial stations remain free, despite § 399, to broadcast a wide variety of controversial views through their power to control program selection, to select which persons will be interviewed, and to determine how news reports will be presented, Brief at 41, then it seems doubtful that § 399 can fairly be said to advance any genuinely substantial governmental interest in keeping controversial or partisan opinions from being aired by noncommercial stations. . . .

In short, § 399 does not prevent the use of noncommercial stations for the presentation of partisan views on controversial matters; instead, it merely bars a station from specifically communicating such views on its own behalf or on behalf of its management. If the vigorous expression of controversial opinions is, as the Government assures us, affirmatively encouraged by the Act, and if local licensees are permitted under the Act to exercise editorial control over the selection of programs, controversial or otherwise, that are aired on their stations, then § 399 accomplishes only one thing—the suppression of editorial speech by station management. It does virtually nothing, however, to reduce the risk that public stations will serve solely as outlets for expression of narrow partisan views. What we said in Columbia Broadcasting System, Inc. v. Democratic National Committee, supra, applies, therefore, with equal force here: the "sacrifice [of] First Amendment protections for so speculative a gain is not warranted. . . ." 412 U.S., at 127.

Finally, the public's interest in preventing public broadcasting stations from becoming forums for lopsided presentations of narrow partisan positions is already secured by a variety of other regulatory means that intrude far less drastically upon the "journalistic freedom" of noncommercial broadcasters. [ ]

The requirements of the FCC's fairness doctrine, for instance, which apply to commercial and noncommercial stations alike, ensure that such editorializing would maintain a reasonably balanced and fair presentation of controversial issues. Thus, even if the management of a noncommercial educational station were inclined to seek to further only its own partisan views when editorializing, it simply could not do so. . . . Since the breadth of § 399 extends so far beyond what is necessary to accomplish the goals identified by the Government, it fails to satisfy the First Amendment standards that we have applied in this area.

We therefore hold that even if some of the hazards at which § 399 was aimed are sufficiently substantial, the restriction is not crafted with sufficient precision to remedy those dangers that may exist to justify the significant abridgement of speech worked by the provision's broad ban on editorializing. The statute is not narrowly tailored to address any of the government's suggested goals. Moreover, the public's "paramount right" to be fully and broadly informed on matters of public importance through the medium of noncommercial educational broadcasting is not well served by the restriction, for its effect is plainly to diminish rather than augment "the volume and quality of coverage" of controversial issues. *Red Lion,* supra, at 393. Nor do we see any reason to deny noncommercial broadcasters the right to address matters of public concern on the basis of merely speculative fears of adverse public or governmental reactions to such speech.

IV

Although the Government did not present the argument in any form to the District Court, it now seeks belatedly to justify § 399 on the basis of Congress' Spending Power. Relying upon our recent decision in Regan v. Taxation With Representation, 461 U.S. 540 (1983), the Government argues that by prohibiting noncommercial educational stations that receive CPB grants from editorializing, Congress has, in the proper exercise of its Spending Power, simply determined that it "will not subsidize public broadcasting station editorials." Brief of the United States 42. In *Taxation With Representation,* the Court found that Congress could, in the exercise of its Spending Power, reasonably refuse to subsidize the lobbying activities of tax-exempt charitable organizations by prohibiting such organizations from using tax-deductible contributions to support their lobbying efforts. . . .

Of course, if Congress were to adopt a revised version of § 399 that permitted noncommercial educational broadcasting stations to establish "affiliate" organizations which could then use the station's facilities to editorialize with non-federal funds, such a statutory mechanism would plainly be valid under the reasoning of *Taxation With Representation.* Under such a statute, public broadcasting stations would be free, in the same way that the charitable organization in *Taxation With Representation* was free, to make known its views on matters of public importance through its non-federally funded, editorializing affiliate without losing federal grants for its non-editorializing broadcast activities. [ ]. But in the absence of such authority, we must reject the Government's contention that our decision in *Taxation With Representation* is controlling here.

V

In conclusion, we emphasize that our disposition of this case rests upon a narrow proposition. We do not hold that the Congress or the FCC are without power to regulate the content, timing, or character of speech by noncommercial educational broadcasting stations. Rather, we hold only that the specific interests sought to be advanced by § 399's ban on editorializing are either not sufficiently substantial or are not served in a sufficiently limited manner to justify the substantial abridgment of important journalistic freedoms which the First Amendment jealously protects. Accordingly, the judgment of the District Court is affirmed.

JUSTICE REHNQUIST, with whom THE CHIEF JUSTICE and JUSTICE WHITE join, dissenting.

All but three paragraphs of the Court's lengthy opinion in this case are devoted to the development of a scenario in which the government appears as the "Big Bad Wolf," and appellee Pacifica as "Little Red Riding Hood." In the Court's scenario the Big Bad Wolf cruelly forbids Little Red Riding Hood from taking to her grandmother some of the food that she is carrying in her basket. Only three paragraphs are used to delineate a truer picture of the litigants, wherein it appears that some of the food in the basket was given to Little Red Riding Hood by the Big Bad Wolf himself, and that the Big Bad Wolf had told Little Red Riding Hood in advance that if she accepted his food she would have to abide by his conditions. Congress in enacting § 399 of the Public Broadcasting Act, 47 U.S.C. (Supp. V) § 399, has simply determined that public funds shall not be used to subsidize noncommercial, educational broadcasting stations which engage in "editorializing" or which support or oppose any political candidate. I do not believe that anything in the First Amendment to the United States Constitution prevents Congress from choosing to spend public monies in that manner. Perhaps a more appropriate analogy than that of Little Red Riding Hood and the Big Bad Wolf is that of Faust and Mephistopheles; Pacifica, well aware of § 399's condition on its receipt of public money, nonetheless accepted the public money and now seeks to avoid the conditions which Congress legitimately has attached to receipt of that funding.

   . . .

    The Court's three-paragraph discussion of why § 399, repeatedly reexamined and retained by Congress, violates the First Amendment is to me utterly unpersuasive. Congress has rationally determined that the bulk of the taxpayers whose monies provide the funds for grants by the CPB would prefer not to see the management of local educational stations promulgate its own private views on the air at taxpayer expense. Accordingly Congress simply has decided not to subsidize stations which engage in that activity.

   . . .

    This is not to say that the government may attach *any* condition to its largess; it is only to say that when the government is simply exercising its power to allocate its own public funds, we need only find that the condition imposed has a rational relationship to Congress' purpose in providing the subsidy and that it is not primarily "aimed at the suppression of dangerous ideas." Cammarano v. United States, 358 U.S. 498, 513 (1959), quoting Speiser v. Randall, 357 U.S. 513, 519 (1958). In this case Congress' prohibition is directly related to its purpose in providing subsidies for public broadcasting, and it is plainly rational for Congress to have determined that taxpayer monies should not be used to subsidize management's views or to pay for management's exercise of partisan politics. Indeed, it is entirely rational for Congress to have wished to avoid the appearance of government sponsorship of a particular view or a particular political candidate. Furthermore, Congress' prohibition is strictly neutral. In no sense can it be said that Congress has prohibited only editorial views of one particular ideological bent. Nor has it prevented public stations from airing programs, documentaries, interviews, etc. dealing with controversial subjects, so long as management itself does not expressly endorse a particular viewpoint. And Congress has not prevented station management from communicating its own views on those subjects through any medium other than subsidized public broadcasting.

    For the foregoing reasons I find this case entirely different from the so-called "unconstitutional condition" cases, wherein the Court has stated that the government "may not deny a benefit to a person on a basis that infringes his constitutionally protected interests— especially his interest in freedom of speech." Perry v. Sinderman, 408 U.S. 593, 597 (1972). In those cases the suppressed speech was not content-neutral in the same sense as here, and in those cases, there is at best only a strained argument that the legislative purpose of the condition imposed was to avoid *subsidizing* the prohibited speech. Speiser v. Randall, supra, is illustrative of the difference. In that case California's decision to deny its property tax exemption to veterans who would not declare that they would not work to overthrow the government was plainly directed at suppressing what California regarded as speech of a dangerous content. And the condition imposed was so unrelated to the benefit to be conferred that it is difficult to argue that California's property tax exemption actually subsidized the dangerous speech.

Here, in my view, Congress has rationally concluded that the bulk of taxpayers whose monies provide the funds for grants by the CPB would prefer not to see the management of public stations engage in editorializing or the endorsing or opposing of political candidates. Because Congress' decision to enact § 399 is a rational exercise of its spending powers and strictly neutral, I would hold that nothing in the First Amendment makes it unconstitutional. Accordingly, I would reverse the judgment of the District Court.

JUSTICE WHITE: Believing that the editorializing and candidate endorsement proscription stand or fall together and being confident that Congress may condition use of its funds on abstaining from political endorsements, I join JUSTICE REHNQUIST's dissenting opinion.

JUSTICE STEVENS, dissenting.

The court jester who mocks the King must choose his words with great care. An artist is likely to paint a flattering portrait of his patron. The child who wants a new toy does not preface his request with a comment on how fat his mother is. Newspaper publishers have been known to listen to their advertising managers. Elected officials may remember how their elections were financed. By enacting the statutory provision that the Court invalidates today, a sophisticated group of legislators expressed a concern about the potential impact of government funds on pervasive and powerful organs of mass communication. One need not have heard the raucous voice of Adolph Hitler over Radio Berlin to appreciate the importance of that concern.

As Justice White correctly notes, the statutory prohibitions against editorializing and candidate endorsements rest on the same foundation. In my opinion that foundation is far stronger than merely "a rational basis" and it is not weakened by the fact that it is buttressed by other provisions that are also designed to avoid the insidious evils of government propaganda favoring particular points of view. The quality of the interest in maintaining government neutrality in the free market of ideas—of avoiding subtle forms of censorship and propaganda—outweigh the impact on expression that results from this statute. Indeed, by simply terminating or reducing funding, Congress could curtail much more expression with no risk whatever of a constitutional transgression.

.   .   .

Although appellees originally challenged the validity of the entire statute, in their amended complaint they limited their attack to the prohibition against editorializing. In its analysis of the case, the

Court assumes that the ban on political endorsements is severable from the first section and that it may be constitutional.[3] In view of the fact that the major difference between the ban on political endorsements is based on the content of the speech, it is apparent that the entire rationale of the Court's opinion rests on the premise that it may be permissible to predicate a statutory restriction on candidate endorsements on the difference between the content of that kind of speech and the content of other expressions of editorial opinion.

The Court does not tell us whether speech that endorses political candidates is more or less worthy of protection than other forms of editorializing, but it does iterate and reiterate the point that "the expression of editorial opinion" is a special kind of communication that "is entitled to the most exacting degree of First Amendment protection." [ ].[4]

Neither the fact that the statute regulates only one kind of speech, nor the fact that editorial opinion has traditionally been an important kind of speech, is sufficient to identify the character or the significance of the statute's impact on speech. Three additional points are relevant. First, the statute does not prohibit Pacifica from expressing its opinion through any avenue except the radio stations for which it receives federal financial support. It eliminates the subsidized channel of communication as a forum for Pacifica itself, and thereby deprives Pacifica of an advantage it would otherwise have over other speakers, but it does not exclude Pacifica from the marketplace for ideas. Second, the statute does not curtail the expression of opinion by individual commentators who participate in Pacifica's programs. The only comment that is prohibited is a statement that Pacifica agrees or disagrees with the opinions that others may express on its programs. Third, and of greatest significance for me, the statutory restriction is completely neutral in its operation—it prohibits all editorials without any distinction being drawn concerning the subject matter or the point of view that might be expressed.[5]

---

3. The Court actually raises the wrong severability issue. The serious question in this regard is whether the entire public funding scheme is severable from the prohibition on editorializing and political endorsements. The legislative history of the statute indicates the strength of the congressional aversion to these practices. . . .

4. Thus, once again the Court embraces the obvious proposition that some speech is more worthy of protection than other speech—that the right to express editorial opinion may be worth fighting to preserve even though the right to hear less worthy speech may not—a proposition that several members of today's ma-

jority could only interpret "as an aberration" in Young v. American Mini Theaters, 427 U.S. 50, 87 (1976) (dissenting opinion) ("The fact that the 'offensive' speech here may not address 'important' topics—'ideas of social and political significance,' in the Court's terminology, does not mean that it is less worthy of constitutional protection." Ibid.).

5. Section 399's ban on editorializing is a content based restriction on speech, but not in the sense that the majority implies. The majority speaks of "editorial opinion" as if it were some sort of special species of opinion, limited to issues of public importance. The majority confuses the typical content of editorials

II

The statute does not violate the fundamental principle that the citizen's right to speak may not be conditioned upon the sovereign's agreement with what the speaker intends to say. On the contrary, the statute was enacted in order to protect that very principle—to avoid the risk that some speakers will be rewarded or penalized for saying things that appeal to—or are offensive to—the sovereign.[7] The interests the statute is designed to protect are interests that underlie the First Amendment itself.

In my judgment the interest in keeping the Federal Government out of the propaganda arena is of overriding importance. That interest is of special importance in the field of electronic communication, not only because that medium is so powerful and persuasive, but also because it is the one form of communication that is licensed by the Federal Government.[8] When the Government already has great potential power over the electronic media, it is surely legitimate to enact statutory safeguards to make sure that it does not cross the threshold that separates neutral regulation from the subsidy of partisan opinion.

The Court does not question the validity of the basic interests served by § 399. Instead, it suggests that the statute does not substantially serve those interests because the Public Broadcasting Act operates in many other respects to insulate local stations from

with the meaning of editorial itself. An editorial is, of course, a statement of the *management's* opinion on any topic imaginable. The Court asserts that what the statute "forecloses is the expression of editorial opinion on 'controversial issues of public importance.' " The statute is not so limited. The content which is prohibited is that the station is not permitted to state its opinion with respect to any matter. In short, it may not be an on-the-air advocate if it accepts government funds for its broadcasts. The prohibition on editorializing is not directed at any particular message a station might wish to convey, ...

Paradoxically, section 399 is later attacked by the majority as essentially being underinclusive because it does not prohibit "controversial" national programming that is often aired with substantial federal funding. . . . Next, § 399's ban on editorializing is attacked by the majority on overinclusive grounds—because it is content-neutral—since it prohibits a "potentially infinite variety of speech, most of which would not be related in any way to governmental affairs, political candidacies or elections." . . .

7. . . .

Moreover, the statute will also protect the listener's interest in not having his tax payments used to finance the advocacy of causes he opposes. The majority gives extremely short shrift to the Government's interest in minimizing the use of taxpayer monies to promote private views with which the taxpayers may disagree. The Court briefly observes that the taxpayers do not have a constitutionally protected right to enjoin such expenditures and then leaps to the conclusion that given the fact that the funding scheme itself is not unconstitutional, this interest cannot be used to support the statute at issue here. The conclusion manifestly does not follow from the premise, and this interest is plainly legitimate and significant.

8. We have consistently adhered to the following guiding principles applicable to First Amendment claims in the area of broadcasting, and they bear repeating at some length: [quoting from *Red Lion*].

governmental interference. In my view, that is an indication of nothing more than the strength of the governmental interest involved here—Congress enacted many safeguards because the evil to be avoided was so grave. Organs of official propaganda are antithetical to this nation's heritage and Congress understandably acted with great caution in this area. It is no answer to say that the other statutory provisions "substantially reduce the risk of government interference with the editorial judgments of the local stations without restricting the stations' ability to speak out on matters of public concern." [ ]. The other safeguards protect the stations from interference with judgments that they will necessarily make in selecting programming, but those judgments are relatively amorphous. No safeguard is foolproof; and the fact that funds are dispensed according to largely "objective" criteria certainly is no guarantee. Individuals must always make judgments in allocating funds, and pressure can be exerted in subtle ways as well as through outright fund-cutoffs.

Members of Congress, not members of the Judiciary, live in the world of politics. When they conclude that there is a real danger of political considerations influencing the dispensing of this money and that this provision is necessary to insulate grantees from political pressures in addition to the other safeguards, that judgment is entitled to our respect.

The magnitude of the present danger that the statute is designed to avoid is admittedly a matter about which reasonable judges may disagree.[10] Moreover, I would agree that the risk would be greater if other statutory safeguards were removed. It remains true, however, that Congress has the power to prevent the use of public funds to subsidize the expression of partisan points of view, or to suppress the propagation of dissenting opinions. No matter how great or how small the immediate risk may be, there surely is more than a theoretical possibility that future grantees might be influenced by the ever present tie of the political purse strings, even if those strings are never actually pulled. . . .

III

The Court describes the scope of § 399's ban as being "defined solely on the basis of the content of the suppressed speech," ante, at 18, and analogizes this case to the regulation of speech we condemned in Consolidated Edison Co. v. Public Serv. Comm'n, 447 U.S.

---

10. The majority argues that the Government's concededly substantial interest in ensuring that audiences of educational stations will not perceive the station to be a government propaganda organ can be fully satisfied by requiring such stations to broadcast a disclaimer each time they editorialize stating that the editorial "does not in any way represent the views of the Federal Government. . . ." [ ]. This solution would be laughable were it not so Orwellian: the answer to the fact that there is a real danger that the editorials are really government propaganda is for the government to require the station to tell the audience that it is not propaganda at all!

530 (1980). This description reveals how the Court manipulates labels without perceiving the critical differences behind the two cases.

In *Consolidated Edison* the class of speakers that was affected by New York's prohibition consisted of regulated public utilities that had been expressing their opinion on the issue of nuclear power by means of written statements inserted in their customers' monthly bills. Although the scope of the prohibition was phrased in general terms and applied to a selected group of speakers, it was obviously directed at spokesmen for a particular point of view. The justification for the restriction was phrased in terms of the potential offensiveness of the utilities' messages to their audiences. It was a classic case of a viewpoint-based prohibition.

In this case, however, although the regulation applies only to a defined class of noncommercial broadcast licensees, it is common ground that these licensees represent heterogenous points of view.[12] There is simply no sensible basis for considering this regulation a viewpoint restriction—or, to use the Court's favorite phrase, to condemn it as "content-based"—because it applies equally to station owners of all shades of opinion. Moreover, the justification for the prohibition is not based on the "offensiveness" of the messages in the sense that that term was used in *Consolidated Edison*. Here, it is true that taxpayers might find it offensive if their tax monies were being used to subsidize the expression of editorial opinion with which they disagree, but it is the fact of the subsidy—not just the expression of the opinion—that legitimates this justification. Furthermore, and of greater importance, the principal justification for this prohibition is the overriding interest in forestalling the creation of propaganda organs for the Government.

I respectfully dissent.

———

The crucial difference between commercial and non-commercial broadcasting involves the question of the licensee's ability to control content and to reject programming. The issue arose in Muir v. Alabama Educational Television Commission, 688 F.2d 1033 (5th Cir.1982), cert. denied 460 U.S. 1023 (1983).

In *League of Women Voters* the Court was faced with the problem of indirect control of PBS stations through the CPB funding mechanism. Consider, however, that more than 140 PBS stations are under some form of government ownership. What effect should that have on the ability of those licensees to control content and reject programming? The issue was posed dramatically in May 1980, when several PBS stations decided to cancel a previously scheduled show-

---

12. That does not necessarily mean, however, "that the editorial voices of these stations will prove to be as distinctive, varied, and idiosyncratic as the var- ious communities they represent," [ ] at 25, given the potential effects of government funding, [ ].

ing of "Death of a Princess," a dramatization of the circumstances surrounding the 1977 execution for adultery of a Saudi Arabian princess and her commoner lover. Strong objections to the program had been voiced by the Saudi Arabian government.

Two separate actions requesting injunctions requiring the airing of the program were filed by viewers against PBS licensees, the Alabama Educational Television Commission (AETC) and the University of Houston. The denial of an injunction against AETC was upheld on appeal while a separate panel reversed the granting of an injunction against the University of Houston. The two cases were then consolidated for rehearing en banc.

The 22 judges who participated in the rehearing produced a total of six separate opinions. The majority of 15 viewed the central issue to be "whether the First Amendment rights of viewers impose limits on the programming discretion of public television stations licensed to state instrumentalities." In an opinion, written by Judge Hill, they determined that no such limits were imposed despite plaintiffs' argument that public television stations are public forums.

> A facility is a public forum only if it is designed to provide a general public right of access to its use, or if such public access has historically existed and is not incompatible with the facility's primary activity.

> • . . .

> . . . The pattern of usual activity for public television stations is the statutorily mandated practice of the broadcast licensee exercising sole programming authority. The general invitation extended to the public is not to schedule programs, but to watch or decline to watch what is offered. It is thus clear that the public television stations involved in the cases before us are not public forums.

Plaintiffs also tried to argue that cancelling a previously scheduled show constituted "censorship" in violation of the First Amendment. Again, the Court was not persuaded.

> We conclude that the defendants' editorial decisions to cancel "Death of a Princess" cannot be properly characterized as "censorship." Had the states of Alabama and Texas sought to prohibit the exhibition of the film by another party then indeed a question of censorship would have arisen. Such is not the case before us. The states have not sought to forbid or curtail the right of any person to show or view the film. . . . The state officials in charge of AETC and KUHT–TV have simply exercised their statutorily mandated discretion and decided not to show a particular program at a particular time. There is a clear distinction between a state's exercise of editorial discretion over its own expression, and a state's prohibition or suppression of the speech of another.

Other judges viewed the case as presenting a much narrower issue. In his concurrence, Judge Garwood stated:

> First, plaintiffs are not attacking governmental "public" broadcasting as such. Nor do they seek to require its operation to be on a pure "open forum" basis—like an empty stage available to all comers—where each citizen can cause the broadcast of his or her program of choice, with the inevitable selectivity determined by completely content neutral factors such as lot, or first come first served or the like. Rather, plaintiffs seek to become a part of governmental "public" broadcasting essentially as it is, except they want it to broadcast this particular program of their choice. However, there is simply no way for them— together with all others who might wish to assert similar rights for their favorite "dramatization"—to become a part of *such* "conventional" (as distinguished from pure "open forum") governmental broadcasting *except* on the basis of governmental selection of the individual programs.

The three dissenting opinions, for the seven dissenters, all focused on the state's ability to censor ideas. As Judge Johnson stated:

> The clearly defined issue in these appeals is whether the executive officers of a state operated public television station may cancel a previously scheduled program because it presents a point of view disagreeable to the religious and political regime of a foreign country. The majority opinion permitting cancellation on these grounds flies completely in the face of the First Amendment and our tradition of vigilance against governmental censorship of political and religious expression.

The dissenting judges argued that the majority's reliance on the editorial discretion conferred by the Communications Act on broadcast licensees elevated the Act above the Constitution. While disagreeing among themselves as to the exact standards for judging the programming decisions of state licensees, they all agreed that the editorial discretion of state broadcasters should be limited by the First Amendment.

---

2. RELIGIOUS BROADCASTING

As noted earlier, religious institutions may be eligible for reserved educational channels. The test used by the Commission to decide whether an institution is eligible for a reserved spot is "whether the primary thrust is educational, albeit with a religious aspect to the educational activity. Recognizing that some overlap in purposes is, or can be, involved, we look to the application as a whole to determine which is the essential purpose and which is incidental."

Bible Moravian Church, Inc., 28 F.C.C.2d 1, 21 R.R.2d 492 (1971) (rejecting an application for a reserved educational spot).

Some have argued that religious programming provides too narrow a base to justify the allocation of a license. An effort to persuade the Commission of this failed in 1975. Multiple and Religious Ownership of Educational Stations, 54 F.C.C.2d 941, 34 R.R.2d 1217 (1975). Two persons requested a "freeze" on all grants of reserved educational FM and television channels to religious institutions pending a study of their value. The Commission thought this would violate its obligation of "neutrality" toward sectarian applicants. The Commission concluded that no new policies were needed and decided to continue ad hoc enforcement of its existing policies, such as the Fairness Doctrine and "the principle that a broadcast station may not be used solely to promote the personal or partisan objectives of the broadcaster."

In its early days of reallocating frequencies when there were no spots reserved for educational broadcasting, the Radio Commission had occasion to consider the value of a station emphasizing religious programming. It decided that such programming was usually aimed at too narrow a base of listeners and this "discriminated against" the rest of the listeners. "In rare cases it is possible to combine a general public-service station and a high-class religious station in a division of time which will approximate a well-rounded program. In other cases religious stations must accept part time on inferior channels or daylight assignments . . . ." Great Lakes Broadcasting Co., 3 F.R.C.Ann.Rep. 32 (1929), modified on other grounds 37 F.2d 993 (D.C.Cir.), certiorari dismissed 281 U.S. 706 (1930). As the spectrum has expanded, religious broadcasting has gained a more secure footing.

Religious institutions that do not meet the educational qualifications are able to apply for other spots as noncommercial licensees. In such instances, the rules applicable to other broadcasters are applicable to religious broadcasters as well. The Commission has made one major exception in allowing a religious broadcaster to consider an applicant's religion for employment, but only for "those persons hired to espouse a particular religious philosophy over the air."

Chapter XVI

LEGAL CONTROL OF BROADCAST PROGRAMMING: NONPOLITICAL SPEECH

In Chapter XV we examined legal controls on broadcast programming that were primarily concerned with political speech. We now turn to other content regulation of broadcasting. Here, the restrictions often take the form of direct bans on speech. As we examine these cases ask yourself whether these restrictions are more, or less, justifiable than those covered in the previous Chapter.

A. DRUGS

YALE BROADCASTING CO. v. FEDERAL COMMUNICATIONS COMMISSION

United States Court of Appeals, District of Columbia Circuit, 1973.
478 F.2d 594, certiorari denied 414 U.S. 914, 94 S.Ct. 211, 38 L.Ed.2d 152 (1973).

Before DANAHER, SENIOR CIRCUIT JUDGE, and ROBINSON and WILKEY, CIRCUIT JUDGES.

WILKEY, CIRCUIT JUDGE:

The source of this controversy is a Notice issued by the Federal Communications Commission regarding "drug oriented" music allegedly played by some radio stations. This Notice and a subsequent Order, the stated purposes of which were to remind broadcasters of a pre-existing duty, required licensees to have knowledge of the content of their programming and on the basis of this knowledge to evaluate the desirability of broadcasting music dealing with drug use. Appellant, a radio station licensee, argues first that the Notice and the Order are an unconstitutional infringement of its First Amendment right to free speech. . . .

   .   .   .

Despite all its attempts to assuage broadcasters' fears, the Commission realized that if an Order can be misunderstood, it will be misunderstood—at least by some licensees. To remove any excuse for misunderstanding, the Commission specified examples of how a broadcaster could obtain the requisite knowledge. A licensee could fulfill its obligation through (1) pre-screening by a responsible station employee, (2) monitoring selections while they were being played, or (3) considering and responding to complaints made by members of the public. The Order made clear that these procedures were merely suggestions, and were not to be regarded as either absolute requirements or the exclusive means for fulfilling a station's public interest obligation.

Having made clear our understanding of what the Commission has done, we now take up appellant's arguments seriatim.

III. AN UNCONSTITUTIONAL BURDEN ON FREEDOM OF SPEECH

Appellant's first argument is that the Commission's action imposes an unconstitutional burden on a broadcaster's freedom of speech. This contention rests primarily on the Supreme Court's opinion in Smith v. California,[12] in which a bookseller was convicted of possession and selling obscene literature. The Supreme Court reversed the conviction. Although the State had a legitimate purpose in seeking to ban the distribution of obscene materials, it could not accomplish this goal by placing on the bookseller the procedural burden of examining every book in his store. To make a bookseller, criminally liable for all the books sold would necessarily "tend to restrict the books he sells to those he has inspected; and thus the State will have imposed a restriction upon the distribution of constitutionally protected as well as obscene literature . . . ."

Appellant compares its own situation to that of the bookseller in *Smith* and argues that the Order imposes an unconstitutional burden on a broadcaster's freedom of speech. The two situations are easily distinguishable.

Most obviously, a radio station can only broadcast for a finite period of twenty-four hours each day; at any one time a bookstore may contain thousands of hours' worth of readable material. Even if the Commission had ordered that stations pre-screen all materials broadcast, the burden would not be nearly so great as the burden imposed on the bookseller in *Smith*. As it is, broadcasters are not even required to pre-screen their maximum of twenty-four hours of daily programming. Broadcasters have specifically been told that they may gain "knowledge" of what they broadcast in other ways.

A more subtle but no less compelling answer to appellant's argument rests upon *why* knowledge of drug oriented music is required by the Commission. In *Smith*, knowledge was imputed to the purveyor in order that a criminal sanction might be imposed and the dissemination halted. Here the goal is to assure the broadcaster has adequate knowledge. . . .

We say that the licensee must have *knowledge* of what it is broadcasting; the precise *understanding* which may be required of the licensee is only that which is reasonable. No radio licensee faces any realistic possibility of a penalty for misinterpreting the lyrics it has chosen or permitted to be broadcast. If the lyrics are completely obscure, the station is not put on notice that it is in fact broadcasting material which would encourage drug abuse. If the lyrics are meaningless, incoherent, the same conclusion follows. The argument

12. 361 U.S. 147 (1959).

of the appellant licensee, that so many of these lyrics are obscure and ambiguous, really is a circumstance available to some degree in his defense for permitting their broadcast, at least until their meaning is clarified. Some lyrics or sounds are virtually unintelligible. To the extent they are completely meaningless gibberish and approach the equivalent of machinery operating or the din of traffic, they, of course, do not communicate with respect to drugs or anything else, and are not within the ambit of the Commission's order. Speech is an expression of sound or visual symbols which is intelligible to some other human beings. At some point along the scale of human intelligibility the sounds produced may slide over from characteristics of free speech, which should be protected, to those of noise pollution, which the Commission has ample authority to abate.[15]

We not only think appellant's argument invalid, we express our astonishment that the licensee would argue that before the broadcast it has no knowledge, and cannot be required to have any knowledge, of material it puts out over the airwaves. We can understand that the individual radio licensees would not be expected to know in advance the content or the quality of a network program, or a free flowing panel discussion of public issues, or other audience participation program, and certainly not a political broadcast. But with reference to the broadcast of that which is frequently termed "canned music," we think the Commission may require that the purveyors of this to the public make a reasonable effort to know what is in the "can." No producer of pork and beans is allowed to put out on a grocery shelf a can without knowing what is in it and standing back of both its content and quality. The Commission is not required to allow radio licensees, being freely granted the use of limited air channels, to spew out to the listening public canned music, whose content and quality before broadcast is totally unknown.

Supposedly a radio licensee is performing a public service—that is the raison d'etre of the license. If the licensee does not have specific knowledge of what it is broadcasting, how can it claim to be operating in the public interest? Far from constituting any threat to freedom of speech of the licensee, we conclude that for the Commission to have been less insistent on licensees discharging their obligations would have verged on an evasion of the Commission's own responsibilities.

By the expression of the above views we have no desire whatsoever to express a value judgment on different types of music, poetry, sound, instrumentation, etc., which may appeal to different classes of our most diverse public. "De gustibus non est disputandum." But what we are saying is that whatever the style, whatever the expression put out over the air by the radio station, for the licensee to claim that it has no responsibility to evaluate its product is for the radio

15. Cf. Noise Control Act of 1972, Pub.L. No. 92–574, 86 Stat. 1234 (1972).

station to abnegate completely what we had always considered its
responsibility as a licensee. All in all, and quite unintentionally, the
appellant-licensee in its free speech argument here has told us a
great deal about quality in this particular medium of our culture.

. . .

For the reasons given above, the action of the Federal Communications Commission is

Affirmed.

Notes and Questions

1. A motion for a rehearing en banc was denied over the objection of
Chief Judge Bazelon, who commented that

> . . . the Order restated its basic threat: "the broadcaster
> could jeopardize his license by failing to exercise licensee respon-
> sibility in this area." As we have recognized, "licensee responsi-
> bility" is a nebulous concept. It could be taken to mean—as the
> panel opinion takes it—only that "a broadcaster must 'know'
> what it is broadcasting." On the other hand, in light of the
> earlier Notice, and in light of the renewed warnings in the Order
> about the dangers of "drug-oriented" popular songs, broadcast-
> ers might have concluded that "responsibility" meant "prohibi-
> tion".

. . .

This case presents several other questions of considerable
significance: Is the popular song a constitutionally protected
form of speech? [23] Do the particular songs at which these
directives were aimed have a demonstrable connection with illegal activities? If so, is the proper remedy to "discourage or
eliminate" the playing of such songs? Can the FCC assert
regulatory authority over material that could not constitutionally
be regulated in the printed media? [25]

Clearly, the impact of the Commission's order is ripe for
judicial review. And, on that review, it would be well to heed
Lord Devlin's recent warning:

> If freedom of the press . . . [or freedom of speech]
> perishes, it will not be by sudden death. . . . It will be a
> long time dying from a debilitating disease caused by a

---

23. Popular songs might be considered mere entertainment, or even noise
pollution. Yale Broadcasting Co. v. FCC,
at 598, 599. On the other hand, historians and sociologists have noted that the
popular song has been an important medium of political, moral, and aesthetic
expression in American life. [ ]

25. See Brandywine-Main Line Radio,
Inc. v. FCC, 473 F.2d 16 (1972) (Chief
Judge Bazelon, dissenting) (application of

the Fairness Doctrine). Unlike the "Fairness Doctrine" cases, there can be no
assertion here that the chilling effect is
incidental to providing access to the media for viewpoints that would contribute
to a fuller debate on public issues. The
question is thus presented whether the
rationale of the "Fairness Doctrine", or
any other realities of the electronic media, warrant intrusion on broadcasters'
free speech rights in this case.

series of erosive measures, each of which, if examined singly, would have a good deal to be said for it.

2. The Supreme Court denied certiorari, 414 U.S. 914 (1973). Justice Brennan would have granted the writ and set the case for argument. Justice Douglas dissented along the lines sketched by Chief Judge Bazelon. He noted that the Commission majority apparently had intended to ban drug-related lyrics from the air and that at a Congressional hearing the Chairman testified that if a licensee were playing songs that the Commission thought promoted the use of "hard drugs," "I know what I would do, I would probably vote to take the license away." Even though drug lyrics might not cause great concern if banned, "next year it may apply to comedy programs, and the following year to news broadcasts." He concluded that

> The Government cannot, consistent with the First Amendment, require a broadcaster to censor its music any more than it can require a newspaper to censor the stories of its reporters. Under our system the Government is not to decide what messages, spoken or in music, are of the proper "social value" to reach the people.

3. Could Congress ban pro-drug broadcasts—whether of songs or of normal speech? Are your views here consistent with your views about Congressional power to ban cigarette commercials?

4. Could Congress ban pro-drug messages in the print media?

B. OBSCENITY AND INDECENCY

The subject of obscenity did not become a problem on radio and television until recently. In the earlier years of these media, the licensees apparently had no practical reason to want to test the limits of permissible communication and were unsure what the Commission might legally do to licensees who stepped over the line.

In the 1934 Act, § 326, the prohibition on censorship, also contained a passage forbidding the use of obscene or indecent speech in broadcasting. In 1948, that ban was removed from § 326 and added to the general criminal law in 18 U.S.C.A. § 1464:

> Whoever utters any obscene, indecent, or profane language by means of radio communication shall be fined not more than $10,000 or imprisoned not more than two years, or both.

Several other sections empower the Commission to impose sanctions for violation of § 1464.

In 1964, the Commission considered renewal of stations belonging to the Pacifica Foundation. Five programs had produced complaints: two poets reading their own works; one author reading from his novel; a recording of Edward Albee's "Zoo Story"; and a program "in which eight homosexuals discussed their attitudes and problems." All were late at night except one of the poetry readings.

The Commission indicated that it was "not concerned with individual programs" but with whether there had been a pattern of programming inconsistent with the public interest. Although it found nothing to bar renewal, the Commission discussed the five programs because it would be "useful" to the "industry and the public."

The Commission found three of the programs were well within the licensee's judgment under the public interest standard. The Commission recognized that provocative programming might offend some listeners. To rule such programs off the air, however, would mean that "only the wholly inoffensive, the bland, could gain access to the radio microphone or TV camera." The remedy for offended listeners was to turn off the program. The two poetry readings raised different questions. One did not measure up to the licensee's standards for presentation but it had not been carefully screened because it had come from a reputable source. The other reading, involving 28 poems, was broadcast at 7:15 p.m. because the station's editor admitted he had been lulled by the poet's "rather flat, monotonous voice" and did not catch unidentified "offensive words" in the 19th poem. The errors were isolated and thus caused no renewal problem. Pacifica Foundation, 36 F.C.C. 147, 1 R.R.2d 747 (1964). For a history of Pacifica's struggle in 1964, including the fact that no broadcaster came to its defense, see Barton, The Lingering Legacy of Pacifica: Broadcasters' Freedom of Silence, 53 Journ.Q. 429 (1976).

Another episode involved a taped interview on a noncommercial FM station with Jerry Garcia, leader of a musical group known as the Grateful Dead. Garcia apparently used "various patently offensive words as adjectives, introductory expletives, and as substitutes for 'et cetera.' " The opinion gave no examples. The Commission imposed a forfeiture of $100 for "indecency" and apparently hoped for a court test of its powers. Eastern Educational Radio (WUHY–FM), 24 F.C.C.2d 408, 18 R.R.2d 860 (1970). The licensee paid the fine and the case was over.

Next came charges of obscenity leveled at "topless radio," midday programs consisting of "call-in talk shows in which masters of ceremonies discuss intimate sexual topics with listeners, usually women." The format quickly became very popular. The Commission responded to complaints by ordering its staff to tape several of the shows and to present a condensed tape of some of the most offensive comments. The next day, Chairman Burch spoke to the National Association of Broadcasters condemning the format. Two weeks later the Commission issued a Notice of Apparent Liability proposing a forfeiture of $2,000 against one licensee. Sonderling Broadcasting Corp. (WGLD–FM), 27 R.R.2d 285 (F.C.C.1973). The most troublesome language was apparently:

> Female Listener: . . . of course I had a few hangups at first about—in regard to this, but you know what we did—I have a craving for peanut butter all that [sic] time so I used to spread

this on my husband's privates and after a while, I mean, I didn't even need the peanut butter anymore.

Announcer: (Laughs) Peanut butter, huh?

Listener: Right. Oh, we can try anything—you know—any, any of these women that have called and they have, you know, hangups about this, I mean they should try their favorite—you know like—uh. . . .

Announcer: Whipped cream, marshmallow . . ..

In addition, the host's conversation with a complaining listener was thought to be suffused with "leering innuendo." The Commission thought this program ran afoul of both the "indecency" and "obsceni- ty" standards of § 1464. On the other hand, the Commission dis- claimed any intention to ban the discussion of sex entirely:

> We are emphatically not saying that sex *per se* is a forbid- den subject on the broadcast medium. We are well aware that sex is a vital human relationship which has concerned humanity over the centuries, and that sex and obscenity are not the same thing. In this area as in others, we recognize the licensee's right to present provocative or unpopular programming which may offend some listeners, Pacifica Foundation, 36 FCC 147, 149 (1964). Second, we note that we are not dealing with works of dramatic or literary art as we were in *Pacifica*. We are rather confronted with the talk or interview show where clearly the interviewer can readily moderate his handling of the subject matter so as to conform to the basic statutory standards— standards which, as we point out, allow much leeway for provoc- ative material. . . . The standards here are strictly defined by the law: The broadcaster must eschew the "obscene or inde- cent."

Again the Commission sought a test: "we welcome and urge judicial consideration of our action." Commissioner Johnson dissented on several grounds, including the view that the Commission had no duty to act in these cases and should leave the matter to possible prosecu- tion by Justice Department. Sonderling denied liability but paid the fine. Two citizen groups asked the Commission to reconsider on the grounds that listeners' rights to hear such programs had been disregarded by the Commission's action. The Commission reaffirmed its action. 41 F.C.C.2d 777, 27 R.R.2d 1508 (1973). It indicated that it had based its order "on the pervasive and intrusive nature of broadcast radio, even if children were left completely out of the picture." It went on, however, to point out that children were in the audience in these afternoon programs and there was some evidence that the program was not intended solely for adults. "The obvious intent of this reference to children was to convey the conclusion that this material was unlawful, and that it was even more clearly unlawful when presented to an audience which included children."

The citizen groups appealed but lost. Illinois Citizens Committee for Broadcasting v. Federal Communications Commission, 515 F.2d 397 (D.C.Cir.1975). The court refused to allow the petitioners to make certain procedural arguments that it thought were open only to the licensee itself. On the merits:

> The excerpts cited by the Commission contain repeated and explicit descriptions of the techniques of oral sex. And these are presented, not for educational and scientific purposes, but in a context that was fairly described by the FCC as "titillating and pandering." The principles of Ginzburg v. United States, 383 U.S. 463 (1966) are applicable, for commercial exploitation of interests in titillation is the broadcaster's sole end. It is not a material difference that here the tone is set by the continuity provided by the announcer rather than, as in *Ginzburg*, by the presentation of the material in advertising and sale to solicit an audience. We cannot ignore what the Commission took into account—that the announcer's response to a complaint by an offended listener and his presentation of advertising for auto insurance are suffused with leering innuendo. Moreover, and significantly, "Femme Forum" is broadcast from 10 a.m. to 3 p.m. during daytime hours when the radio audience may include children—perhaps home from school for lunch, or because of staggered school hours or illness. Given this combination of factors, we do not think that the FCC's evaluation of this material infringes upon rights protected by the First Amendment.

> The FCC found Sonderling's broadcasts obscene . . . ..
>
> . . .

> Petitioners object that the Commission's determination was based on a brief condensation of offensive material and did not take into account the broadcast as a whole, as would seem to be required by certain elements of both the *Memoirs* and the *Miller* tests. The Commission's approach is not inappropriate in evaluating a broadcasting program that is episodic in nature—a cluster of individual and typically disconnected commentaries, rather than an integrated presentation. It is commonplace for members of the radio audience to listen only to short snatches of a broadcast, and programs like "Femme Forum" are designed to attract such listeners. . . .

> We conclude that, where a radio call-in show during daytime hours broadcasts explicit discussions of ultimate sexual acts in a titillating context, the Commission does not unconstitutionally infringe upon the public's right to listening alternatives when it determines that the broadcast is obscene.

The court explicitly did not rely upon the Commission's argument that it had latitude to hold things "indecent" that are not obscene.

A motion for rehearing en banc was denied over the lengthy dissent of Chief Judge Bazelon. He was much concerned about the ability of the Commission, by "raised eyebrow" and the Chairman's speech, to virtually end a very popular format. He saw this as "flagrant and illegal censorship." He also found four areas of error committed by the panel.

INTRODUCTION TO THE PACIFICA CASE

Two points are required to introduce the following case. The first involves the notion of "nuisance" in law. Activities that may be socially desirable are often called nuisances if located in the wrong place. This might include a factory that emits smoke in an amount that would be acceptable in a factory district, but is unacceptable in a residential district. The legal goal is to encourage the factory either to conform to the needs of its surroundings or to relocate to a factory area.

The second point involves a conflict within the Court about the legitimacy of regulations based on the content of the communication. In Police Department of Chicago v. Mosley, 408 U.S. 92 (1972), the Court invalidated an ordinance that barred picketing outside schools unless the picketing was related to a labor-management dispute concerning the school. "Once a forum is opened up to assembly or speaking by some groups, government may not prohibit others from assembling or speaking on the basis of what they intend to say."

In Young v. American Mini Theatres, Inc., 427 U.S. 50 (1976), Detroit adopted a zoning ordinance requiring that theatres that specialized in showing sexually explicit movies had to be separated from one another by a minimum distance. The Court upheld the ordinance 5–4, but there was no majority opinion. Justice Stevens, for the plurality of four, said that the *Mosley* statement must be kept in context. Even though the First Amendment did not permit "total suppression of erotic materials that have some arguably artistic value, it is manifest that society's interest in protecting this type of expression is of a wholly different, and lesser, magnitude than the interest in untrammeled political debate . . . . [F]ew of us would march our sons and daughters off to war to preserve the citizen's right to see 'Specified Sexual Activities' exhibited in the theaters of our choice."

The plurality then concluded that the record supported the city council's conclusions that unfortunate effects followed from the clustering of such enterprises in one area.

Justice Powell provided the crucial fifth vote on the ground that this case involved "an example of innovative land-use regulation, implicating First Amendment concerns only incidentally and to a limited extent." The ordinance did not "restrict in any significant way the viewing of these movies by those who desire to see them."

The four dissenters considered the decision "a drastic departure from established principles of First Amendment law." These principles require that regulations concerning the time, place and manner of communicating "be content-neutral except in the limited context of a captive or juvenile audience."

As we will see, this conflict reappears in *Pacifica*.

FEDERAL COMMUNICATIONS COMMISSION v. PACIFICA FOUNDATION

Supreme Court of the United States, 1978.
438 U.S. 726, 98 S.Ct. 3026, 57 L.Ed.2d 1073.

[George Carlin, a "satiric humorist," recorded a 12-minute monologue entitled "Filthy Words" before a live audience in a California theater. The theme was "the words you couldn't say on the public, ah, airwaves. . . ." Carlin then proposed a basic list: "The original seven words were shit, piss, fuck, cunt, cocksucker, motherfucker, and tits. Those are the ones that will curve your spine, grow hair on your hands and (laughter) maybe, even bring us, God help us, peace without honor (laughter) um, and a bourbon." Carlin then discussed "shit" and "fuck" at length, including the various phrases that use each word. The following passage gives some idea of the format:

> Now the word shit is okay for the man. At work you can say it like crazy. Mostly figuratively. Get that shit out of here, will ya? I don't want to see that shit anymore. I can't *cut* that shit, buddy. I've had that shit up to here. I think you're full of shit myself. (laughter) He don't know shit from Shinola. (laughter) You know that? (laughter) Always wondered how the Shinola people felt about that (laughter) Hi, I'm the new man from Shinola. (laughter) Hi, how are ya? Nice to see ya. (laughter) How are ya? (laughter) Boy, I don't know whether to shit or wind my watch. (laughter) Guess, I'll shit on my watch. (laughter) Oh, *the* shit is going to hit *de* fan. (laughter) Built like a brick shit-house. (laughter) Up, he's up shit's creek. (laughter) He's had it. (laughter) He hit me, I'm sorry. (laughter) Hot shit, holy shit, tough shit, eat shit. (laughter) Shit-eating grin. Uh, whoever thought of that was ill. (murmur laughter) He had a shit-eating grin! He had a what? (laughter) Shit on a stick. (laughter) Shit in a handbag. I always like that.

One Tuesday afternoon at 2:00 p.m., Pacifica's FM radio station in New York City played the monologue during a discussion about society's attitude toward language. The station warned that the monologue included language that might offend some listeners. A man who apparently did not hear the warning heard the broadcast while driving with his young son, and complained to the Commission. In response to an inquiry from the Commission, Pacifica responded that Carlin was a "significant social satirist" who "like Twain and Sahl before him, examines the language of ordinary people. . . ." Apparently, no one else complained about the broadcast.

The Commission ruled that Pacifica's action was subject to administrative sanction. Instead of imposing a formal sanction, it put the order in the file for possible use if subsequent complaints were received. The Commission asserted four reasons for treating broadcasting differently from other media: access by unsupervised children; since radio receivers are in the home, privacy interests are entitled to extra deference; unconsenting adults may tune in without a warning that offensive language is being used; and scarcity of spectrum space requires government to license in the public interest. Further facts are stated in the opinions.]

MR. JUSTICE STEVENS delivered the opinion of the Court (Parts I, II, III, and IV–C) and an opinion in which THE CHIEF JUSTICE and MR. JUSTICE REHNQUIST joined (Parts IV–A and IV–B).

This case requires that we decide whether the Federal Communications Commission has any power to regulate a radio broadcast that is indecent but not obscene.

. . .

. . . [T]he Commission found a power to regulate indecent broadcasting in two statutes: 18 U.S.C. § 1464, which forbids the use of "any obscene, indecent, or profane language by means of radio communications," and 47 U.S.C. § 303(g), which requires the Commission to "encourage the larger and more effective use of radio in the public interest."

The Commission characterized the language used in the Carlin monologue as "patently offensive," though not necessarily obscene, and expressed the opinion that it should be regulated by principles analogous to those found in the law of nuisance where the "law generally speaks to *channeling* behavior more than actually prohibiting it. . . . [T]he concept of 'indecent' is intimately connected with the exposure of children to language that describes, in terms patently offensive as measured by contemporary community standards for the broadcast medium, sexual or excretory activities and organs, at times of the day when there is a reasonable risk that children may be in the audience." 56 F.C.C.2d, at 98.[5]

. . . In summary, the Commission stated: "We therefore hold that the language as broadcast was indecent and prohibited by 18 U.S.C. 1464."

After the order issued, the Commission was asked to clarify its opinion by ruling that the broadcast of indecent words as part of a live newscast would not be prohibited. . . . The Commission noted

---

5. Thus, the Commission suggested, if an offensive broadcast had literary, artistic, political or scientific value, and were preceded by warnings, it might not be indecent in the late evening, but would be so during the day, when children are in the audience.

that its "declaratory order was issued in a specific factual context," and declined to comment on various hypothetical situations presented by the petition.[7] . . .

The United States Court of Appeals for the District of Columbia reversed, with each of the three judges on the panel writing separately. . . .

Having granted the Commission's petition for certiorari, 434 U.S. 1007, we must decide: (1) whether the scope of judicial review encompasses more than the Commission's determination that the monologue was indecent "as broadcast"; (2) whether the Commission's order was a form of censorship forbidden by § 326; (3) whether the broadcast was indecent within the meaning of § 1464; and (4) whether the order violates the First Amendment of the United States Constitution.

I

The general statements in the Commission's memorandum opinion do not change the character of its order. Its action was an adjudication. . . . The specific holding was carefully confined to the monologue "as broadcast."

. . . Accordingly, the focus of our review must be on the Commission's determination that the Carlin monologue was indecent as broadcast.

II

The relevant statutory questions are whether the Commission's action is forbidden "censorship" within the meaning of 47 U.S.C. § 326 and whether speech that concededly is not obscene may be restricted as "indecent" under the authority of 18 U.S.C. § 1464. The questions are not unrelated, for the two statutory provisions have a common origin. . . .

The prohibition against censorship unequivocally denies the Commission any power to edit proposed broadcasts in advance and to excise material considered inappropriate for the airwaves. The prohibition, however, has never been construed to deny the Commission the power to review the content of completed broadcasts in the performance of its regulatory duties.[9]

---

7. The Commission did, however, comment that:

" '[I]n some cases, public events likely to produce offensive speech are covered live, and there is no opportunity for journalistic editing.' Under these circumstances we believe that it would be inequitable for us to hold a licensee responsible for indecent language . . . .. We trust that under such circumstances a licensee will exercise

judgment, responsibility, and sensitivity to the community's needs, interests and tastes." [ ]

9. Zechariah Chafee, defending the Commission's authority to take into account program service in granting licenses, interpreted the restriction on "censorship" narrowly: "This means, I feel sure, the sort of censorship which went on in the seventeenth century in England—the deletion of specific items

During the period between the original enactment of the provision in 1927 and its re-enactment in the Communications Act of 1934, the courts and the Federal Radio Commission held that the section deprived the Commission of the power to subject "broadcasting matter to scrutiny prior to its release," but they concluded that the Commission's "undoubted right" to take note of past program content when considering a licensee's renewal application "is not censorship."

Not only did the Federal Radio Commission so construe the statute prior to 1934; its successor, the Federal Communications Commission, has consistently interpreted the provision in the same way ever since. [ ] And, until this case, the Court of Appeals for the District of Columbia has consistently agreed with this construction. . . .

Entirely apart from the fact that the subsequent review of program content is not the sort of censorship at which the statute was directed, its history makes it perfectly clear that it was not intended to limit the Commission's power to regulate the broadcast of obscene, indecent, or profane language. . . .

There is nothing in the legislative history to contradict this conclusion. . . .

We conclude, therefore, that § 326 does not limit the Commission's authority to impose sanctions on licensees who engage in obscene, indecent, or profane broadcasting.

III

The only other statutory question presented by this case is whether the afternoon broadcast of the "Filthy Words" monologue was indecent within the meaning of § 1464.[13] Even that question is narrowly confined by the arguments of the parties.

The Commission identified several words that referred to excretory or sexual activities or organs, stated that the repetitive, deliberate use of those words in an afternoon broadcast when children are in the audience was patently offensive, and held that the broadcast was indecent. Pacifica takes issue with the Commission's definition of indecency, but does not dispute the Commission's preliminary determination that each of the components of its definition was present. Specifically, Pacifica does not quarrel with the conclusion that this afternoon broadcast was patently offensive. Pacifica's claim that the

and dictation as to what should go into particular programs." 2 Z. Chafee, Government and Mass Communications 641 (1947).

13. In addition to § 1464, the Commission also relied on its power to regulate in the public interest under 47 U.S.C. § 303(g). We do not need to consider whether § 303 may have independent significance in a case such as this. The statutes authorizing civil penalties incorporate § 1464, a criminal statute. See 47 U.S.C. §§ 312(a)(6), 312(b)(2), and 503(b) (1)(E). But the validity of the civil sanctions is not linked to the validity of the criminal penalty. The legislative history of the provisions establishes their independence. . . .

broadcast was not indecent within the meaning of the statute rests entirely on the absence of prurient appeal.

The plain language of the statute does not support Pacifica's argument. The words "obscene, indecent, or profane" are written in the disjunctive, implying that each has a separate meaning. Prurient appeal is an element of the obscene, but the normal definition of "indecent" merely refers to nonconformance with accepted standards of morality.

Pacifica argues, however, that this Court has construed the term "indecent" in related statutes to mean "obscene" as that term was defined in Miller v. California, 413 U.S. 15. Pacifica relies most heavily on the construction this Court gave to 18 U.S.C. § 1461 in Hamling v. United States, 418 U.S. 87. See also United States v. Twelve 200-foot Reels of Film, 413 U.S. 123, 130 n. 7 (18 U.S.C. § 1462) (dicta). . . .

The reasons supporting *Hamling's* construction of § 1461 do not apply to § 1464. Although the history of the former revealed a primary concern with the prurient, the Commission has long interpreted § 1464 as encompassing more than the obscene. The former statute deals primarily with printed matter enclosed in sealed envelopes mailed from one individual to another; the latter deals with the content of public broadcasts. It is unrealistic to assume that Congress intended to impose precisely the same limitations on the dissemination of patently offensive matter by such different means.[17]

Because neither our prior decisions nor the language or history of § 1464 supports the conclusion that prurient appeal is an essential component of indecent language, we reject Pacifica's construction of the statute. When that construction is put to one side, there is no basis for disagreeing with the Commission's conclusion that indecent language was used in this broadcast.

IV

Pacifica makes two constitutional attacks on the Commission's order. First, it argues that the Commission's construction of the statutory language broadly encompasses so much constitutionally protected speech that reversal is required even if Pacifica's broadcast of the "Filthy Words" monologue is not itself protected by the First Amendment. Second, Pacifica argues that inasmuch as the recording

17. This conclusion is re-enforced by noting the different constitutional limits on Congress' power to regulate the two different subjects. Use of the postal power to regulate material that is not fraudulent or obscene raises "grave constitutional questions." Hannegan v. Esquire, Inc., 327 U.S. 146, 156. But it is well settled that the First Amendment has a special meaning in the broadcasting context. See, e.g., FCC v. National Citizens Committee for Broadcasting, 436 U.S. 775; Red Lion Broadcasting Co., Inc. v. FCC, 395 U.S. 367; Columbia Broadcasting System, Inc. v. Democratic National Committee, 412 U.S. 94. For this reason, the presumption that Congress never intends to exceed constitutional limits, which supported Hamling's narrow reading of § 1461, does not support a comparable reading of § 1464.

is not obscene, the Constitution forbids any abridgment of the right to broadcast it on the radio.

A

The first argument fails because our review is limited to the question whether the Commission has the authority to proscribe this particular broadcast. As the Commission itself emphasized, its order was "issued in a specific factual context." 59 F.C.C.2d, at 893. That approach is appropriate for courts as well as the Commission when regulation of indecency is at stake, for indecency is largely a function of context—it cannot be adequately judged in the abstract.

The approach is also consistent with Red Lion Broadcasting Co., Inc. v. FCC, 395 U.S. 367. . . .

It is true that the Commission's order may lead some broadcasters to censor themselves. At most, however, the Commission's definition of indecency will deter only the broadcasting of patently offensive references to excretory and sexual organs and activities.[18] While some of these references may be protected, they surely lie at the periphery of First Amendment concern. Cf. Bates v. State Bar, 433 U.S. 350, 380–381. Young v. American Mini Theatres, Inc., 427 U.S. 50, 61. The danger dismissed so summarily in *Red Lion*, in contrast, was that broadcasters would respond to the vagueness of the regulations by refusing to present programs dealing with important social and political controversies. Invalidating any rule on the basis of its hypothetical application to situations not before the Court is "strong medicine" to be applied "sparingly and only as a last resort." Broadrick v. Oklahoma, 413 U.S. 601, 613. We decline to administer that medicine to preserve the vigor of patently offensive sexual and excretory speech.

B

When the issue is narrowed to the facts of this case, the question is whether the First Amendment denies government any power to restrict the public broadcast of indecent language in any circumstances.[19] For if the government has any such power, this was an appropriate occasion for its exercise.

18. A requirement that indecent language be avoided will have its primary effect on the form, rather than the content, of serious communication. There are few, if any, thoughts that cannot be expressed by the use of less offensive language.

19. Pacifica's position would of course deprive the Commission of any power to regulate erotic telecasts unless they were obscene under Miller v. California, 413 U.S. 15. Anything that could be sold at a newsstand for private examination could be publicly displayed on television.

We are assured by Pacifica that the free play of market forces will discourage indecent programming. "Smut may," as Judge Leventhal put it, "drive itself from the market and confound Gresham," 556 F.2d at 35; the prosperity of those who traffic in pornographic literature and films would appear to justify his skepticism.

The words of the Carlin monologue are unquestionably "speech" within the meaning of the First Amendment. It is equally clear that the Commission's objections to the broadcast were based in part on its content. The order must therefore fall if, as Pacifica argues, the First Amendment prohibits all governmental regulation that depends on the content of speech. Our past cases demonstrate, however, that no such absolute rule is mandated by the Constitution.

The classic exposition of the proposition that both the content and the context of speech are critical elements of First Amendment analysis is Mr. Justice Holmes' statement for the Court in Schenck v. United States:

> "We admit that in many places and in ordinary times the defendants in saying all that was said in the circular would have been within their constitutional rights. But the character of every act depends upon the circumstances in which it is done. . . . The most stringent protection of free speech would not protect a man in falsely shouting fire in a theatre and causing a panic. It does not even protect a man from an injunction against uttering words that may have all the effect of force. . . . The question in every case is whether the words used are used in such circumstances and are of such a nature as to create a clear and present danger that they will bring about the substantive evils that Congress has a right to prevent." 249 U.S. 47, 52.

Other distinctions based on content have been approved in the years since *Schenck*. The government may forbid speech calculated to provoke a fight. See Chaplinsky v. New Hampshire, 315 U.S. 568. It may pay heed to the " 'commonsense differences' between commercial speech and other varieties." Bates v. State Bar, 433 U.S. 350, 381. It may treat libels against private citizens more severely than libels against public officials. See Gertz v. Robert Welch, Inc., 418 U.S. 323. Obscenity may be wholly prohibited. Miller v. California, 413 U.S. 15. And only two Terms ago we refused to hold that a "statutory classification is unconstitutional because it is based on the content of communication protected by the First Amendment." Young v. American Mini Theatres, 427 U.S. 50, 52.

The question in this case is whether a broadcast of patently offensive words dealing with sex and excretion may be regulated because of its content. Obscene materials have been denied the protection of the First Amendment because their content is so offensive to contemporary moral standards. Roth v. United States, 354 U.S. 476. But the fact that society may find speech offensive is not a sufficient reason for suppressing it. Indeed, if it is the speaker's opinion that gives offense, that consequence is a reason for according it constitutional protection. For it is a central tenet of the First Amendment that the government must remain neutral in the marketplace of ideas. If there were any reason to believe that the Commission's characterization of the Carlin monologue as offensive could be traced to its political content—or even to the fact that it satirized contemporary attitudes about four-letter words [22] —First Amendment protection might be required. But that is simply not this case. These words offend for the same reasons that obscenity offends.[23] Their place in the hierarchy of First Amendment values was aptly sketched by Mr. Justice Murphy when he said, "such utterances are no essential part of any exposition of ideas, and are of such slight social value as a step to truth that any benefit that may be derived from them is clearly outweighed by the social interest in order and morality." Chaplinsky v. New Hampshire, 315 U.S. 568, 572.

Although these words ordinarily lack literary, political, or scientific value, they are not entirely outside the protection of the First Amendment. Some uses of even the most offensive words are unquestionably protected. See, e.g., Hess v. Indiana, 414 U.S. 105. Indeed, we may assume, *arguendo*, that this monologue would be protected in other contexts. Nonetheless, the constitutional protection accorded to a communication containing such patently offensive sexual and excretory language need not be the same in every context. It is a characteristic of speech such as this that both its capacity to offend and its "social value," to use Mr. Justice Murphy's term, vary with the circumstances. Words that are commonplace in one setting are shocking in another. To paraphrase Mr. Justice Harlan, one occasion's lyric is another's vulgarity. Cf. Cohen v. California, 403 U.S. 15, 25.

In this case it is undisputed that the content of Pacifica's broadcast was "vulgar," "offensive," and "shocking." Because content of that character is not entitled to absolute constitutional protection under all circumstances, we must consider its context in order to determine whether the Commission's action was constitutionally permissible.

C

We have long recognized that each medium of expression presents special First Amendment problems. Joseph Burstyn, Inc. v. Wilson, 343 U.S. 495, 502–503. And of all forms of communication, it is broadcasting that has received the most limited First Amendment

---

22. The monologue does present a point of view; it attempts to show that the words it uses are "harmless" and that our attitudes toward them are "essentially silly." [ ] The Commission objects, not to this point of view, but to the way in which it is expressed. The belief that these words are harmless does not necessarily confer a First Amendment privilege to use them while proselytizing, just as the conviction that obscenity is harmless does not license one to communicate that conviction by the indiscriminate distribution of an obscene leaflet.

23. The Commission stated: "Obnoxious, gutter language describing these matters has the effect of debasing and brutalizing human beings by reducing them to their mere bodily functions . . . ." 56 F.C.C.2d, at 98. Our society has a tradition of performing certain bodily functions in private, and of severely limiting the public exposure or discussion of such matters. Verbal or physical acts exposing those intimacies are offensive irrespective of any message that may accompany the exposure.

protection. Thus, although other speakers cannot be licensed except under laws that carefully define and narrow official discretion, a broadcaster may be deprived of his license and his forum if the Commission decides that such an action would serve "the public interest, convenience, and necessity." Similarly, although the First Amendment protects newspaper publishers from being required to print the replies of those whom they criticize, Miami Herald Publishing Co. v. Tornillo, 418 U.S. 241, it affords no such protection to broadcasters; on the contrary, they must give free time to the victims of their criticism. Red Lion Broadcasting Co., Inc. v. FCC, 395 U.S. 367.

The reasons for these distinctions are complex, but two have relevance to the present case. First, the broadcast media have established a uniquely pervasive presence in the lives of all Americans. Patently offensive, indecent material presented over the airwaves confronts the citizen, not only in public, but also in the privacy of the home, where the individual's right to be let alone plainly outweighs the First Amendment rights of an intruder. Rowan v. Post Office Department, 397 U.S. 728. Because the broadcast audience is constantly tuning in and out, prior warnings cannot completely protect the listener or viewer from unexpected program content. To say that one may avoid further offense by turning off the radio when he hears indecent language is like saying that the remedy for an assault is to run away after the first blow. One may hang up on an indecent phone call, but that option does not give the caller a constitutional immunity or avoid a harm that has already taken place.[27]

Second, broadcasting is uniquely accessible to children, even those too young to read. Although Cohen's written message might have been incomprehensible to a first grader, Pacifica's broadcast could have enlarged a child's vocabulary in an instant. Other forms of offensive expression may be withheld from the young without restricting the expression at its source. Bookstores and motion picture theaters, for example, may be prohibited from making indecent material available to children. We held in Ginsberg v. New York, 390 U.S. 629, that the government's interest in the "well being of its youth" and in supporting "parents' claim to authority in their own household" justified the regulation of otherwise protected expression. Id., at 640 and 639.[28] The ease with which children may

---

27. Outside the home, the balance between the offensive speaker and the unwilling audience may sometimes tip in favor of the speaker, requiring the offended listener to turn away. See Erznoznik v. Jacksonville, 422 U.S. 205.

28. The Commission's action does not by any means reduce adults to hearing only what is fit for children. Cf. Butler v. Michigan, 352 U.S. 380, 383. Adults who feel the need may purchase tapes and records or go to theatres and nightclubs to hear these words. In fact, the Commission has not unequivocally closed even broadcasting to speech of this sort; whether broadcast audiences in the late evening contain so few children that playing this monologue would be permissible is an issue neither the Commission nor this Court has decided.

obtain access to broadcast material, coupled with the concerns recognized in *Ginsberg,* amply justify special treatment of indecent broadcasting.

It is appropriate, in conclusion, to emphasize the narrowness of our holding. This case does not involve a two-way radio conversation between a cab driver and a dispatcher, or a telecast of an Elizabethan comedy. We have not decided that an occasional expletive in either setting would justify any sanction or, indeed, that this broadcast would justify a criminal prosecution. The Commission's decision rested entirely on a nuisance rationale under which context is all-important. The concept requires consideration of a host of variables. The time of day was emphasized by the Commission. The content of the program in which the language is used will also affect the composition of the audience,[29] and differences between radio, television, and perhaps closed-circuit transmissions, may also be relevant. As Mr. Justice Sutherland wrote, a "nuisance may be merely a right thing in the wrong place—like a pig in the parlor instead of the barnyard." Euclid v. Ambler Realty Co., 272 U.S. 365, 388. We simply hold that when the Commission finds that a pig has entered the parlor, the exercise of its regulatory power does not depend on proof that the pig is obscene.

The judgment of the Court of Appeals is reversed.

Mr. Justice Powell, with whom Mr. Justice Blackmun joins, concurring.

I join Parts I, II, III, and IV(C) of Mr. Justice Stevens' opinion. The Court today reviews only the Commission's holding that Carlin's monologue was indecent "as broadcast" at two o'clock in the afternoon, and not the broad sweep of the Commission's opinion. . . .

I also agree with much that is said in Part IV of Mr. Justice Stevens' opinion, and with its conclusion that the Commission's holding in this case does not violate the First Amendment. Because I do not subscribe to all that is said in Part IV, however, I state my views separately.

I

It is conceded that the monologue at issue here is not obscene in the constitutional sense. See 56 F.C.C.2d 94, 98 (1975); Brief for Petitioner 18. Nor, in this context, does its language constitute "fighting words" within the meaning of Chaplinsky v. New Hampshire, 315 U.S. 568 (1942). Some of the words used have been held protected by the First Amendment in other cases and contexts. [ ] I do not think Carlin, consistently with the First Amendment, could be

---

29. Even a prime-time recitation of Chaucer's Miller's Tale would not be likely to command the attention of many children who are both old enough to understand and young enough to be ad-versely affected by passages such as, "And prively he caughte hire by the queynte." G. Chaucer, *The Miller's Tale* 1.3276 (c. 1386).

punished for delivering the same monologue to a live audience composed of adults who, knowing what to expect, chose to attend his performance. See Brown v. Oklahoma, 408 U.S. 914 (1972) (Powell, J., concurring in result). And I would assume that an adult could not constitutionally be prohibited from purchasing a recording or transcript of the monologue and playing or reading it in the privacy of his own home. Cf. Stanley v. Georgia, 394 U.S. 557 (1969).

But it also is true that the language employed is, to most people, vulgar and offensive. It was chosen specifically for this quality, and it was repeated over and over as a sort of verbal shock treatment. The Commission did not err in characterizing the narrow category of language used here as "patently offensive" to most people regardless of age.

The issue, however, is whether the Commission may impose civil sanctions on a licensee radio station for broadcasting the monologue at two o'clock in the afternoon. The Commission's primary concern was to prevent the broadcast from reaching the ears of unsupervised children who were likely to be in the audience at that hour. In essence, the Commission sought to "channel" the monologue to hours when the fewest unsupervised children would be exposed to it. See 56 F.C.C.2d at 98. In my view, this consideration provides strong support for the Commission's holding.

The Court has recognized society's right to "adopt more stringent controls on communicative materials available to youths than on those available to adults." Erznoznik v. City of Jacksonville, [   ]. This recognition stems in large part from the fact that "a child . . . is not possessed of that full capacity for individual choice which is the presupposition of First Amendment guarantees." Ginsberg v. New York, supra, at 649–650 (Stewart, J., concurring in result). Thus, children may not be able to protect themselves from speech which, although shocking to most adults, generally may be avoided by the unwilling through the exercise of choice. At the same time, such speech may have a deeper and more lasting negative effect on a child than an adult. For these reasons, society may prevent the general dissemination of such speech to children, leaving to parents the decision as to what speech of this kind their children shall hear and repeat:

> "[C]onstitutional interpretation has consistently recognized that the parents' claim to authority in their own household to direct the rearing of their children is basic in the structure of our society. 'It is cardinal with us that the custody, care and nurture of the child reside first in the parents, whose primary function and freedom include preparation for obligations the state can neither supply nor hinder.' Prince v. Massachusetts, [321 U.S. 158, 166 (1944)]. The legislature could properly conclude that parents and others, teachers for example, who have this primary responsibility for children's well-being are entitled to the support

of laws designed to aid discharge of that responsibility." Ginsberg v. New York, supra, at 639.

The Commission properly held that the speech from which society
may attempt to shield its children is not limited to that which appeals
to the youthful prurient interest. The language involved in this case
is as potentially degrading and harmful to children as representations
of many erotic acts.

In most instances, the dissemination of this kind of speech to
children may be limited without also limiting willing adults' access to
it. Sellers of printed and recorded matter and exhibitors of motion
pictures and live performances may be required to shut their doors to
children, but such a requirement has no effect on adults' access. See
Ginsberg v. New York, supra, at 634–635. The difficulty is that such
a physical separation of the audience cannot be accomplished in the
broadcast media. During most of the broadcast hours, both adults
and unsupervised children are likely to be in the broadcast audience,
and the broadcaster cannot reach willing adults without also reaching
children. This, as the Court emphasizes, is one of the distinctions
between the broadcast and other media to which we often have
adverted as justifying a different treatment of the broadcast media
for First Amendment purposes. [ ] In my view, the Commission
was entitled to give substantial weight to this difference in reaching
its decision in this case.

A second difference, not without relevance, is that broadcasting—unlike most other forms of communication—comes directly into
the home, the one place where people ordinarily have the right not to
be assaulted by uninvited and offensive sights and sounds. . . .
The Commission also was entitled to give this factor appropriate
weight in the circumstances of the instant case. This is not to say,
however, that the Commission has an unrestricted license to decide
what speech, protected in other media, may be banned from the
airwaves in order to protect unwilling adults from momentary exposure to it in their homes.[2] Making the sensitive judgments required
in these cases is not easy. But this responsibility has been reposed
initially in the Commission, and its judgment is entitled to respect.

II

As the foregoing demonstrates, my views are generally in accord
with what is said in Part IV(C) of Mr. Justice Stevens' opinion. I
therefore join that portion of his opinion. I do not join Part IV(B),
however, because I do not subscribe to the theory that the Justices of

2. It is true that the radio listener
quickly may tune out speech that is offensive to him. In addition, broadcasters
may preface potentially offensive programs with warnings. But such warnings do not help the unsuspecting listener who tunes in at the middle of the
program. In this respect, too, broadcasting appears to differ from books and
records, which may carry warnings on
their faces, and from motion pictures and
live performances, which may carry
warnings on their marquees.

this Court are free generally to decide on the basis of its content which speech protected by the First Amendment is most "valuable" and hence deserving of the most protection, and which is less "valuable" and hence deserving of less protection. Compare ante, at 15–19; Young v. American Mini Theatres, 427 U.S. 50, 63–73 (1976) (opinion of Stevens, J.), with id., at 73 n. 1 (Powell, J., concurring).[3] In my view, the result in this case does not turn on whether Carlin's monologue, viewed as a whole, or the words that comprise it, have more or less "value" than a candidate's campaign speech. This is a judgment for each person to make, not one for the judges to impose upon him.[4]

The result turns instead on the unique characteristics of the broadcast media, combined with society's right to protect its children from speech generally agreed to be inappropriate for their years, and with the interest of unwilling adults in not being assaulted by such offensive speech in their homes. Moreover, I doubt whether today's decision will prevent any adult who wishes to receive Carlin's message in Carlin's own words from doing so, and from making for himself a value judgment as to the merit of the message and words.

. . .

MR. JUSTICE BRENNAN, with whom MR. JUSTICE MARSHALL joins, dissenting.

I agree with Mr. Justice Stewart that, under Hamling v. United States, 418 U.S. 87 (1974), and United States v. 12 200-ft. Reels of Film, 413 U.S. 123 (1973), the word "indecent" in 18 U.S.C. § 1464 must be construed to prohibit only obscene speech. . . .

I

For the second time in two years, see Young v. American Mini Theatres, 427 U.S. 50 (1976), the Court refuses to embrace the notion, completely antithetical to basic First Amendment values, that the degree of protection the First Amendment affords protected speech varies with the social value ascribed to that speech by five Members of this Court. See opinion of Mr. Justice Powell . . .. Yet despite the Court's refusal to create a sliding scale of First Amendment protection calibrated to this Court's perception of the worth of a communication's content, and despite our unanimous agreement that the Carlin monologue is protected speech, a majority of the Court nevertheless finds that, on the facts of this case, the FCC is not constitutionally barred from imposing sanctions on Pacifica for its

3. The Court has, however, created a limited exception to this rule in order to bring commercial speech within the protection of the First Amendment. See Ohralik v. Ohio State Bar Association, 436 U.S. 447 (1978).

4. For much the same reason, I also do not join Part IV(A). I had not thought that the application *vel non* of overbreadth analysis should depend on the Court's judgment as to the value of the protected speech that might be deterred. . . .

airing of the Carlin monologue. This majority apparently believes that the FCC's disapproval of Pacifica's afternoon broadcast of Carlin's "Dirty Words" recording is a permissible time, place, and manner regulation. . . .

A

Without question, the privacy interests of an individual in his home are substantial and deserving of significant protection. In finding these interests sufficient to justify the content regulation of protected speech, however, the Court commits two errors. First, it misconceives the nature of the privacy interests involved where an individual voluntarily chooses to admit radio communications into his home. Second, it ignores the constitutionally protected interests of both those who wish to transmit and those who desire to receive broadcasts that many—including the FCC and this Court—might find offensive.

. . . I believe that an individual's actions in switching on and listening to communications transmitted over the public airways and directed to the public at-large do not implicate fundamental privacy interests, even when engaged in within the home. Instead, because the radio is undeniably a public medium, these actions are more properly viewed as a decision to take part, if only as a listener, in an ongoing public discourse. See Note, Filthy Words, the FCC, and the First Amendment: Regulating Broadcast Obscenity, 61 Va.L.Rev. 579, 618 (1975). Although an individual's decision to allow public radio communications into his home undoubtedly does not abrogate all of his privacy interests, the residual privacy interests he retains vis-á-vis the communication he voluntarily admits into his home are surely no greater than those of the people present in the corridor of the Los Angeles courthouse in *Cohen* who bore witness to the words "Fuck the Draft" emblazoned across Cohen's jacket. Their privacy interests were held insufficient to justify punishing Cohen for his offensive communication.

Even if an individual who voluntarily opens his home to radio communications retains privacy interests of sufficient moment to justify a ban on protected speech if those interests are "invaded in an essentially intolerable manner," Cohen v. California, supra, at 21, the very fact that those interests are threatened only by a radio broadcast precludes any intolerable invasion of privacy; for unlike other intrusive modes of communication, such as sound trucks, "[t]he radio can be turned off," Lehman v. City of Shaker Heights, 418 U.S. 298, 302 (1974)—and with a minimum of effort. . . . Whatever the minimal discomfort suffered by a listener who inadvertently tunes into a program he finds offensive during the brief interval before he can simply extend his arm and switch stations or flick the "off" button, it is surely worth the candle to preserve the broadcaster's right to send, and the right of those interested to receive, a message entitled to full First Amendment protection. . . .

The Court's balance, of necessity, fails to accord proper weight to the interests of listeners who wish to hear broadcasts the FCC deems offensive. It permits majoritarian tastes completely to preclude a protected message from entering the homes of a receptive, unoffended minority. No decision of this Court supports such a result. Where the individuals comprising the offended majority may freely choose to reject the material being offered, we have never found their privacy interests of such moment to warrant the suppression of speech on privacy grounds. . . .

B

Most parents will undoubtedly find understandable as well as commendable the Court's sympathy with the FCC's desire to prevent offensive broadcasts from reaching the ears of unsupervised children. Unfortunately, the facial appeal of this justification for radio censorship masks its constitutional insufficiency. . . .

Because the Carlin monologue is obviously not an erotic appeal to the prurient interests of children, the Court, for the first time, allows the government to prevent minors from gaining access to materials that are not obscene, and are therefore protected, as to them. It thus ignores our recent admonition that "[s]peech that is neither obscene as to youths nor subject to some other legitimate proscription cannot be suppressed solely to protect the young from ideas or images that a legislative body thinks unsuitable for them." [*Erznoznik*] [3] The Court's refusal to follow its own pronouncements is especially lamentable since it has the anomalous subsidiary effect, at least in the radio context at issue here, of making completely unavailable to adults material which may not constitutionally be kept even from children. . . .

In concluding that the presence of children in the listening audience provides an adequate basis for the FCC to impose sanctions for Pacifica's broadcast of the Carlin monologue, the opinions of my Brother Powell and my Brother Stevens both stress the time-honored right of a parent to raise his child as he sees fit—a right this Court

---

3. It may be that a narrowly drawn regulation prohibiting the use of offensive language on broadcasts directed specifically at younger children constitutes one of the "other legitimate proscription[s]" alluded to in *Erznoznik*. This is so both because of the difficulties inherent in adapting the *Miller* formulation to communications received by young children, and because such children are "not possessed of that full capacity for individual choice which is the presupposition of the First Amendment guarantees."

Ginsberg v. New York, 390 U.S. 629, 649–650 (1968) (Stewart, J., concurring). I doubt, as my Brother Stevens suggests, *ante*, at 17 n. 20, that such a limited regulation amounts to a regulation of speech based on its content, since, by hypothesis, the only persons at whom the regulated communication is directed are incapable of evaluating its content. To the extent that such a regulation is viewed as a regulation based on content, it marks the outermost limits to which content regulation is permissible.

has consistently been vigilant to protect. See Wisconsin v. Yoder, 406 U.S. 205 (1972); Pierce v. Society of Sisters, 268 U.S. 510 (1925). Yet this principle supports a result directly contrary to that reached by the Court. *Yoder* and *Pierce* hold that parents, *not* the government, have the right to make certain decisions regarding the upbringing of their children. As surprising as it may be to individual Members of this Court, some parents may actually find Mr. Carlin's unabashed attitude towards the seven "dirty words" healthy, and deem it desirable to expose their children to the manner in which Mr. Carlin defuses the taboo surrounding the words. Such parents may constitute a minority of the American public, but the absence of great numbers willing to exercise the right to raise their children in this fashion does not alter the right's nature or its existence. Only the Court's regrettable decision does that.[4]

C

As demonstrated above, neither of the factors relied on by both the opinion of my Brother Powell and the opinion of my Brother Stevens—the intrusive nature of radio and the presence of children in the listening audience—can, when taken on its own terms, support the FCC's disapproval of the Carlin monologue. These two asserted justifications are further plagued by a common failing: the lack of principled limits on their use as a basis for FCC censorship. No such limits come readily to mind, and neither of the opinions constituting the Court serve to clarify the extent to which the FCC may assert the privacy and children-in-the-audience rationales as justification for expunging from the airways protected communications the Commission finds offensive. . . .

. . . The opinions of both my Brother Powell and my Brother Stevens take the FCC at its word, and consequently do no more than permit the Commission to censor the afternoon broadcast of the "sort of verbal shock treatment," opinion of Mr. Justice Powell, involved here. To insure that the FCC's regulation of protected speech does not exceed these bounds, my Brother Powell is content to rely upon the judgment of the Commission while my Brother Stevens deems it prudent to rely on this Court's ability accurately to assess the worth of various kinds of speech.[6] For my own part, even accepting that

4. The opinions of my Brothers Powell and Stevens rightly refrain from relying on the notion of "spectrum scarcity" to support their result. As Chief Judge Bazelon noted below, "although scarcity has justified *increasing* the diversity of speakers and speech, it has never been held to justify censorship." 556 F.2d, at 29 (emphasis in original). See Red Lion Broadcasting Co. v. FCC, 395 U.S. 367, 396 (1969).

6. Although ultimately dependent upon the outcome of review in this Court,

the approach taken by my Brother Stevens would not appear to tolerate the FCC's suppression of any speech, such as political speech, falling within the core area of First Amendment concern. The same, however, cannot be said of the approach taken by my Brother Powell, which, on its face, permits the Commission to censor even political speech if it is sufficiently offensive to community standards. A result more contrary to rudimentary First Amendment principles is difficult to imagine.

this case is limited to its facts, I would place the responsibility and the right to weed worthless and offensive communications from the public airways where it belongs and where, until today, it resided: in a public free to choose those communications worthy of its attention from a marketplace unsullied by the censor's hand.

II

. . .

. . . The idea that the content of a message and its potential impact on any who might receive it can be divorced from the words that are the vehicle for its expression is transparently fallacious. A given word may have a unique capacity to capsule an idea, evoke an emotion, or conjure up an image. Indeed, for those of us who place an appropriately high value on our cherished First Amendment rights, the word "censor" is such a word. Mr. Justice Harlan, speaking for the Court, recognized the truism that a speaker's choice of words cannot surgically be separated from the ideas he desires to express when he warned that "we cannot indulge the facile assumption that one can forbid particular words without also running a substantial risk of suppressing ideas in the process." Cohen v. California, 403 U.S., at 26. Moreover, even if an alternative phrasing may communicate a speaker's abstract ideas as effectively as those words he is forbidden to use, it is doubtful that the sterilized message will convey the emotion that is an essential part of so many communications.

. . .

The Court apparently believes that the FCC's actions here can be analogized to the zoning ordinances upheld in Young v. American Mini Theatres, supra. For two reasons, it is wrong. First, the zoning ordinances found to pass constitutional muster in *Young* had valid goals other than the channeling of protected speech. [ ] No such goals are present here. Second, . . . the ordinances do not restrict the access of distributors or exhibitors to the market or impair the viewing public's access to the regulated material. [ ] Again, this is not the situation here. Both those desiring to receive Carlin's message over the radio and those wishing to send it to them are prevented from doing so by the Commission's actions. Although, as my Brethren point out, Carlin's message may be disseminated or received by other means, this is of little consolation to those broadcasters and listeners who, for a host of reasons, not least among them financial, do not have access to, or cannot take advantage of, these other means.

. . .

III

It is quite evident that I find the Court's attempt to unstitch the warp and woof of First Amendment law in an effort to reshape its fabric to cover the patently wrong result the Court reaches in this case dangerous as well as lamentable. Yet there runs throughout the opinions of my Brothers Powell and Stevens another vein I find equally disturbing: a depressing inability to appreciate that in our land of cultural pluralism, there are many who think, act, and talk differently from the Members of this Court, and who do not share their fragile sensibilities. It is only an acute ethnocentric myopia that enables the Court to approve the censorship of communications solely because of the words they contain.

. . . The words that the Court and the Commission find so unpalatable may be the stuff of everyday conversations in some, if not many, of the innumerable subcultures that comprise this Nation. Academic research indicates that this is indeed the case. [   ] As one researcher concluded, "[w]ords generally considered obscene like 'bullshit' and 'fuck' are considered neither obscene nor derogatory in the [black] vernacular except in particular contextual situations and when used with certain intonations." [   ] Cf. Keefe v. Geanakos, 418 F.2d 359, 361 (C.A.1, 1969) (finding the use of the word "motherfucker" commonplace among young radicals and protestors).

Today's decision will thus have its greatest impact on broadcasters desiring to reach, and listening audiences comprised of, persons who do not share the Court's view as to which words or expressions are acceptable and who, for a variety of reasons, including a conscious desire to flout majoritarian conventions, express themselves using words that may be regarded as offensive by those from different socio-economic backgrounds.[8] . . .

. . .

MR. JUSTICE STEWART, with whom MR. JUSTICE BRENNAN, MR. JUSTICE WHITE, and MR. JUSTICE MARSHALL join, dissenting.

. . .

The statute pursuant to which the Commission acted, 18 U.S.C. § 1464, makes it a federal offense to utter "any obscene, indecent, or profane language by means of radio communication." The Commission held, and the Court today agrees, that "indecent" is a broader concept than "obscene" as the latter term was defined in Miller v. California, 413 U.S. 15, because language can be "indecent" although it has social, political or artistic value and lacks prurient appeal. 56 F.C.C.2d, at 97–98. But this construction of § 1464, while perhaps plausible, is by no means compelled. To the contrary, I think that "indecent" should properly be read as meaning no more than "obscene." Since the Carlin monologue concededly was not "obscene," I believe that the Commission lacked statutory authority to ban it.

8. Under the approach taken by my Brother Powell, the availability of broadcasts *about* groups whose members comprise such audiences might also be affected. Both news broadcasts about activities involving these groups and public affairs broadcasts about their concerns are apt to contain interviews, statements, or remarks by group leaders and members which may contain offensive language to an extent my Brother Powell finds unacceptable.

Under this construction of the statute, it is unnecessary to address the difficult and important issue of the Commission's constitutional power to prohibit speech that would be constitutionally protected outside the context of electronic broadcasting.

. . .

Notes and Questions

1. There are now products available to control what programs can be seen on a television set. Using a weekly schedule, a parent can enter the day, time, channel number, and duration of time of each program the parent wishes a child to be able to see. If the set is turned to a channel that is not cleared for that day and time, no picture or sound will appear. A key permits changes to be made. If this were standard equipment on all television sets (and radios) might it meet some of the concerns in *Pacifica*?

2. Is the "risk" of tuning in an offensive program on radio or television any greater than the risk of encountering offensive language on a person's clothing on the streets, as in Cohen v. California, 403 U.S. 15 (1971)? Or offensive films visible from the street while being shown at an outdoor movie theatre, Erznoznik v. City of Jacksonville, 422 U.S. 205 (1975)? If averting your eyes is an adequate remedy in these cases why is turning off the radio or television set not adequate here? Is the fact that one may occur in the home relevant?

3. It is easier to warn viewers that an adult, or possibly offensive program, is being presented when television is involved. In some countries such programs carry a white dot in a corner of the picture so that a viewer can know the nature of the programming instantly. Would this solve our problems so far as television is concerned? Is there a similar technique that can be used for radio? Is it enough that certain stations become known as likely to present certain kinds of material offensive to some? What more could the licensee have done here to warn adult listeners? See Glasser and Jassem, Indecent Broadcasts and the Listener's Right of Privacy, 24 J. Broadcasting 285 (1980).

4. It has long been agreed that Congress has preempted the matter of obscenity on radio and television—both of which are within "radio communication." Thus, a state may not impose its movie censorship scheme on films shown on television.

5. In a clarification sought by the Radio Television News Directors Association (RTNDA), the Commission announced that its decision in the Pacifica case was not meant to impinge on the coverage of news events in which offensive speech is sometimes uttered without a chance for editing: "Under these circumstances we believe that it would be inequitable for us to hold a licensee responsible for indecent language." Pacifica Foundation, 59 F.C.C.2d 892, 36 R.R.2d 1008 (1976). What if there is time for editing the dialogue but to do so

would change the impact of the event?   Can this be handled by an announcer who says "At this point the speaker launched into a stream of obscenities"?

Vice President Nelson Rockefeller used a finger gesture generally considered "obscene" when replying in kind to a heckler during a campaign rally.   Most newspapers ran the photograph, but some did not.   Would the decision be different for television stations?   Are the considerations different for the 6 P.M. and the 11 P.M. news?   Does the fact that it was in the course of a live news event make a difference?

6.   Shortly after *Pacifica*, the Commission rejected a petition to deny renewal to a television station.   The petitioners had contended that the station had broadcast programs in which obscenities had been used, and also carried programs with unacceptable themes, such as a Masterpiece Theater episode that was said to approve of adultery. The Commission stated that its role in reviewing programs at renewal time "is and must be limited to determining whether the licensee's *overall* programming has served its service area, and not whether a particular program is 'appropriate' for broadcast."   Nor can the subjective views of groups of listeners be considered.

Turning to the relevance of *Pacifica*, the Commission stated that it "affords no general prerogative to intervene in any case where words similar or identical to those in *Pacifica* are broadcast over a licensed radio or television station.   We intend strictly to observe the narrowness of the *Pacifica* holding."   The FCC noted that in *Pacifica*, the Commission had stressed the "repetitive occurrence" of the words and that Justice Powell had stressed the same feature in his opinion.   "It was certainly not our intent . . . to inhibit coverage of diverse and controversial subjects by licensees, whether in news and public affairs or in dramatic or other programming contexts." WGBH Educational Foundation, 69 F.C.C.2d 1250, 43 R.R.2d 1436 (1978).

7.   Shortly after *Pacifica*, a primary election for governor was held in Georgia.   J.B. Stoner, a legally qualified candidate, speaking under § 315, made broadcast messages using the word "nigger."   Black groups asked the Commission to bar such language as indecent under the *Pacifica* principle.   The Broadcast Bureau rejected the request. First, it ruled that the word was not "language that describes in terms patently offensive by contemporary community standards for the broadcast medium, sexual or excretory activities and organs, at times of the day when there is reasonable risk that children may be in the audience," quoting the Commission's language in *Pacifica*.   Also, the Commission had already announced that "we intend strictly to observe the narrowness of the Pacifica holding."   Even if the Commission were to find the word obscene or indecent, under § 315 the candidate could not be prevented from using the word during his

"use" of the licensee's facilities. Julian Bond, 69 F.C.C.2d 943, 43 R.R.2d 1015 (Bd.Bur.1978).

8. During the 1980 Presidential campaign, one radio commercial began as follows: A man says "Bullshit!" After a woman says "What?", the man's voice replies: "Carter, Reagan, and Anderson. It's all bullshit! Bullshit!" Then the party's candidate says "Too bad people have to use such strong language, but isn't that what you think too? That's why we started an entirely new political party, the Citizens Party." The FCC, which received many complaints and inquiries, responded that the precedents were quite clear that no censorship was possible—at least unless a candidate created a clear and present danger of riot or violence.

The campaign director said that for six months the media had been covering only the three major candidates "despite the fact that they have little to say of substance about the problems of the nation." He observed that "It's a sad commentary on the media that we received more attention as a result of using that word than we've received in the last six months combined."

9. In 1983, *Hustler* magazine publisher Larry Flynt was reported to be intending to use clips from X-rated films in television ads supporting his presidential candidacy. This caused Senator Jeremiah Denton (R-Ala.) to introduce legislation to allow broadcasters to refuse to air pornographic political announcements despite the non-censorship provision of Section 315. Subsequently, the FCC indicated that they would not apply the no-censorship provision to obscene or indecent political announcements. The issue never arose as Flynt chose not to run.

10. Recently, there has been a strong push by some conservative groups to ban obscene or indecent programming from cable television. Some statutes and municipal ordinances have been passed banning all nudity on cable television. If such a statute is challenged on constitutional grounds, how should a court treat it? Should the reasoning of *Pacifica* be used to uphold the constitutionality of the statute or is the statute overbroad as *Erznoznik* would suggest? What characteristics of cable would you focus on in making a decision? See HBO v. Wilkinson, 531 F.Supp. 987 (D.Utah 1982) and Cruz v. Ferre, 571 F.Supp. 125 (S.D.Fla.1983). We will discuss cable in Chapter XVII.

C. SAFETY—VIOLENCE AND PANIC

Although the Surgeon General has issued reports on the relationship between violence and television, and other academic studies have addressed the same issue primarily in connection with children, the Commission has never attempted to regulate the area in any substantive way. It has been asked several times but each time has refused.

In 1972, for example, the Commission was asked to analogize the area to cigarette smoking because of the actions of the Surgeon

General in the two areas. George Corey, 37 F.C.C.2d 641, 25 R.R.2d 437 (1972). The complainant sought to have three Boston stations carry a public service notice at appropriate times: "Warning: Viewing of violent television programming by children can be hazardous to their mental health and well being." The Commission rejected the request on two grounds. First, it stated any action should come by rule making rather than moving against a few stations. Second, the Commission rejected the contention that the fairness doctrine was applicable to violent programming. The cigarette episode was discussed:

> However, it could not reasonably or logically be concluded that the mere viewing of a person smoking a cigarette during a movie being broadcast on television constitutes a discussion of a controversial issue of public importance thus raising a fairness doctrine obligation. Similarly, we cannot agree that the broadcast of violent episodes during entertainment programs necessarily constitutes the presentation of one side of a controversial issue of public importance. It is simply not an appropriate application of the fairness doctrine to say that an entertainment program—whether it be Shakespeare or an action-adventure show—raises a controversial issue if it contains a violent scene and has a significant audience of children. Were we to adopt your construction that the depiction of a violent scene is a discussion of one side of a controversial issue of public importance, the number of controversial issues presented on entertainment shows would be virtually endless (e.g., a scene with a high-powered car; or one showing a person taking an alcoholic drink or cigarette; depicting women in a soft, feminine or light romantic role). Finally, we note that there are marked differences in the conclusiveness of the hazard established in this area as against cigarette smoking. [ ]

> The real thrust of your complaint would appear to be not fairness in the discussion of controversial issues but the elimination of violent TV children's programming because of its effect on children. That issue is being considered particularly by appropriate Congressional committees and agencies such as HEW. [ ] It is a difficult, complex, and sensitive matter. But whatever its resolution, there is no basis for the action along the lines proposed by you.

In its Report on the Broadcast of Violent, Indecent, and Obscene Material, 51 F.C.C.2d 418, 32 R.R.2d 1367 (1975), the Commission explained to Congress that the violence area was unlike the obscenity area because of the totally different statutory framework involved. In the absence of any prohibitions on violence in programming, "industry self-regulation is preferable to the adoption of rigid governmental standards." The Commission took this position for two reasons. First, it feared the constitutional questions that would emerge from such an intrusion into program content. Second the judgments concerning the suitability of certain programming for children are "highly subjective." A speech by Chairman Wiley was quoted to the effect that slapstick comedy, an episode in Peter Pan when Captain Hook is eaten by a crocodile, and the poisoning of Snow White by the witch, all raise judgmental questions for which there is no objective standard.

One surge of interest has been concentrated on advertisers. A pilot study indicated that ten percent of those surveyed had considered not buying a product because it was advertised on a program they thought excessively violent. The president of a leading advertising agency announced that it counsels clients to consider the negative aspects of placing commercials in violent programs. Editor & Publisher, June 12, 1976 at 5. The FCC chairman also suggested that advertisers consider the commercial implications of such programs. See also Broadcasting, June 14, 1976 at 32, 42.

Mass Hysteria. Another substantive problem involves programs that frighten the listening public. At 11:00 p.m. on Oct. 30, 1974, a radio station in Rhode Island presented a contemporary version of the famous H.G. Wells' War of the Worlds, that had been presented on that same night in 1938. A meteorite was reported to have fallen in a sparsely populated community killing several people; later "black-eyed, V-shaped mouthed, glistening creatures dripping saliva" were reported to have emerged from what turned out to be a capsule, and other landings were reported. What steps would you expect the licensee to take before presenting such a program—or is it inappropriate to present such material at any time? Telephone calls from frightened, and later from angry, listeners flooded the station, police and other public service departments.

The licensee had taken several steps before the program to inform state public safety officials in the listening area of the station. The state police in turn sent notices to all their stations in the area alerting them to the program. Approximately once an hour from noon until 10:00 p.m. the licensee broadcast the following promotional announcement: "Tonight at 11:00 p.m., WPRO invites you to listen to a spoof of the 1930's a special Hallowe'en classic presentation. . . ." The last was made about an hour before the program. Three announcements were made during the program—after 47, 48, and 56 minutes. The reason for the timing was said to be that the first 30 to 35 minutes of the show involved what appeared to be a meteor crashing in a remote spot and the arrival of creatures was not reported until 30 minutes into the program.

The Commission told the licensee that it had not met its responsibility to operate in a manner consistent with the public interest. The warnings were inadequate because "it is a well known fact that the radio audience is constantly changing. The only way to assure adequately that the public would not be alarmed in this case would be an introductory statement repeated at frequent intervals throughout the program." One Commissioner dissented because intrusion into presentations of drama should be made with "utmost caution" and the licensee's precautions "were not in my opinion unreasonable." Capital Cities Communications, Inc., 54 F.C.C.2d 1035, 34 R.R.2d 1016 (1975).

Would the Commission's suggestions impinge on the dramatic effect sought by the licensee? Is that relevant? Can you think of other ways to meet the Commission's concern? Recall the greater ease of warning an unwilling audience about possibly offensive programs over television as opposed to radio. Is that distinction applicable here?

On April 1, 1980, a Boston television station's local news program was interrupted by a bulletin that a 635-foot mound in suburban Milton had just blown its top and erupted. The reporter indicated that the disaster was traceable to a chain reaction set off by the earlier eruption of Mt. St. Helens in Washington. After 98 seconds, the reporter held up a sign saying "April Fool."

"But by then it was too late. Local police and civil-defense officials were deluged with calls from more than a hundred frantic Milton residents trying to find out the best evacuation routes." Newsweek, April 14, 1980 at 35. The the executive producer of the program was fired.

D. CHILDREN'S PROGRAMMING—AND NAB CODES

Over the years, groups have expressed special concern about programs aimed at children. Some have been concerned primarily with commercials and others have been concerned about the content of the programs themselves. Still others have been concerned that there is too little children's programming. All of these concerns and conflicts became more heated in the late 1970's. As we consider each situation note the different approaches being considered. Sometimes it is prohibiting certain content; sometimes it involves mandatory programming; and sometimes it is conditional in the sense that if a broadcaster presents one kind of content it may be obligated to present other types of programs. Also note that occasionally the FCC invokes the aid of private groups, such as the National Association of Broadcasters (NAB) to alter a practice within the industry.

1. PROGRAM CONTENT

Most of the concern about the impact of television on children has stressed the use of violence and sexual innuendo. Although some groups have been concerned about these matters so far as adults are concerned, more seem concerned about their impact on children. Under Butler v. Michigan, 352 U.S. 380 (1957), it is unlawful for government to impose a complete ban on printed matter that is legally protected as to adults, simply to keep the material from children. Might that rule be different with television or radio? Does *Pacifica* suggest differences?

Several detailed studies of the impact of television on children are collected in 20 J. Broadcasting 1–68 (1976). See also, D. Cater and S. Strickland, TV Violence and the Child—The Evolution and Fate of the Surgeon General's Report, (1975).

The NAB is a private voluntary organization whose membership includes the three major networks, well over half the television stations in the country and some 3,000 radio broadcasters. The NAB promulgated codes and standards that members had to follow if they wished to retain membership. The codes addressed such matters as how many minutes of commercials were appropriate in an hour; what types of commercials should not be accepted; what material should not be shown on the screen; and how subjects, such as suicide or astrology or religion should be developed. We shall see examples from the NAB Code shortly.

A broadcaster that adhered to the code could display the NAB seal. The NAB maintained a staff that advised members about the propriety of their behavior under the codes.

In 1975, the result of the interaction of the network officials, the FCC chairman, and the NAB was the promulgation of the "family viewing policy" as an amendment to the NAB's Television Code. Under the policy, programs of a violent or sexually-oriented nature were wholly barred from the time slots before 9:00 p.m. (8:00 p.m. Central Time). This required moving some programs that had been popular in earlier prime-time slots and also involved decisions about which programs were affected in the first place. The entire story of the development and early enforcement of the family viewing policy is traced at length in G. Cowan, See No Evil: The Backstage Battle over Sex and Violence on Television (1979). See Writers Guild of America v. Federal Communications Commission, 609 F.2d 355 (9th Cir.1979); certiorari denied 449 U.S. 824 (1980).

2. Too Few Programs for Children

There has long been concern that too few programs are written expressly for children. Although the prime time access rule was motivated in part by hopes that this type of programming would result, the rule had no such effect. Following a petition in 1970 from Action for Children's Television (ACT) to require children's programming, the FCC spent much of the 1970's trying to decide how to react. In 1974, it issued a Policy Statement asking licensees to "make a meaningful effort" to increase overall programming for children; to air "a reasonable amount" of programming designed to educate and inform children, not simply to entertain them; to address the needs of both preschool and school-age children; and to air these programs on weekdays as well as weekends.

The Commission, in 1979, concluded that over a five-year period, the amount of children's programming per station had increased less than one hour per week (from 10.5 to 11.3 hours) and that this was totally accounted for by new programming from independent stations. Network affiliates had not increased their programming at all. No significant increase in education or informational programs was detected. Few licensees sought to develop age-specific programs for children. Finally, although only eight percent of children's television viewing occurs on weekends, almost half the programs for children are presented on weekends.

The staff concluded that "the small numbers of children and their limited appeal to advertisers, combined with the small number of outlets in most markets, create incentives for the commercial television system to neglect the specific needs of the child audience." Age-specific programming would be even less attractive to broadcasters because of the further splitting of an already small market.

In Children's Television Programming and Advertising Practices, 75 F.C.C.2d 138 (1979), the FCC announced a proposed rulemaking in which it listed five options. These were to rescind the 1974 Policy Statement and rely on program sources other than commercial broadcasting; to maintain or modify the policy statement; to institute mandatory programming requirements; to develop renewal guidelines; or to increase the number of video outlets.

The Commission completed the proceeding in late 1983. Mandatory children's programming obligations for television stations were rejected. The FCC found that the amount and variety of children's programming available was substantial and diverse. It noted that establishment of quotas might be impermissible content-based regulation and would create difficult definitional problems. Such quotas would also preclude the establishment of experimental children's services and efforts at specialization. Although no quotas were created, each licensee has the obligation to consider the needs of all significant elements of the community. A licensee at renewal time must demonstrate the attention devoted to the needs of children in its viewing audience, but may consider the alternative program sources available to children in their area. Children's Television Programming, 55 R.R.2d 199 (1984). On appeal, the D.C. Circuit affirmed the Commission's position that alternatives such as public broadcasting and cable could be considered in assessing the need for children's programming.

In addition, ACT and other groups are pursuing mandatory children's programming quotas in Congress. A House Bill (H.R. 4097, (1983)) would have required television stations to air an hour of educational programming for children per day five days a week. Broadcasting, Mar. 12, 1984 at 46.

An effort by citizen groups to deny license renewals to television stations that had no regularly scheduled children's programming failed in Washington Association for Television and Children v. Federal Communications Commission, 712 F.2d 677, 54 R.R.2d 293 (D.C.Cir.1983). The Commission's policy statement did not require regular scheduling and the Commission did not have to prefer a station that presented regularly scheduled cartoons to one that presented educational specials.

3. COMMERCIALS IN CHILDREN'S PROGRAMS

Efforts to eliminate all sponsorship of children's programs have been rejected by the Commission. The court of appeals affirmed on the ground that the FCC's refusal to adopt the ban "was a reasoned exercise of its broad discretion." The Commission had taken some steps, such as ordering a clear separation between programming and advertising on children's programs and this could not be held insufficient as a matter of law. Action for Children's Television v. Federal Communications Commission, 564 F.2d 458 (D.C.Cir.1977).

The Commission has also declined to require the networks to provide instructional programs to educate children about television advertising. The Commission was concerned about the impact of the First Amendment and § 326 on an order requiring programs with certain content. The issue was not so critical that, under the first part of the fairness doctrine, a licensee who ignored the issue would be acting unreasonably. Finally, since commercials being shown did not meaningfully discuss the issue, it did not come within the second part of the fairness doctrine. Council on Children, Media and Merchandising, 65 F.C.C.2d 421, 40 R.R.2d 1718 (1977).

The NAB Codes. As we have seen, indirect regulation of the content of broadcast programs was possible through the NAB Codes. The majority of television stations subscribed to the Codes. The adherence was even greater because of the membership of the three major networks. Since they abided by the Television Code, even affiliates that did not themselves belong would be carrying only material acceptable under the Code whenever they carried network programming.

In 1982, however, this all changed when a judge ruled that at least one provision of the NAB code violated the antitrust laws. As a result the NAB negotiated a consent decree with the Justice Department that prohibited the NAB from adopting any rule respecting the quantity, placement or format of advertising or other nonprogram material. In addition, although not as a requirement of the settlement, the NAB cancelled the advertising standards of the Television and Radio Codes and dissolved the Code Boards of Directors. Broadcasting and Government, June 1, 1983 at 150–151.

Chapter XVII

CABLE AND NEW TECHNOLOGIES

A. CABLE TELEVISION

---

1. DEVELOPMENT

Our discussion until this point has been addressed solely to broadcasting. Some programs reached the public through radios and others through television sets. We turn now to other forms of communication that do not necessarily involve broadcasting—though the end product does emerge through the television set. It is important to recognize at the outset that although broadcasting and the television set have been joined, new technology permits the television set to be used for communications that have not been broadcast. The most obvious example is the use of video cassette players and recorders, which permit the owner of a television set to buy a video cassette at a store and play it on his television set at home—all without any use of the spectrum. That activity much more closely resembles the showing of movies at home than anything else.

Cable television involves the transmission of electrical signals over wires to television sets in homes or elsewhere. The technique involves a studio, called the "head-end," and coaxial cables that physically connect the head-end with the television set of every user of the system. The cable is capable of carrying such a wide range of electrical signals that it can simultaneously carry signals sufficient for 55 or more television channels. (As the signals are carried along the cable they become weaker and must be amplified along the way.)

It is possible to transmit certain signals in scrambled form that require decoders, while others can be received by all users. It is also possible, as Warner Communications showed with QUBE in Columbus, Ohio, to run a system in which the users are able to send signals back to the head-end: voting on a question asked on a program, ordering merchandise, or telling a quarterback what plays to call in a semiprofessional football game.

The programming sent out from the head-end can come from many sources. The system owner might send out a variety of motion pictures he has bought or rented; he might send a camera crew out to cover the local high school football game; he might present live programs from his own studio; he might carry programs prepared by others specially for cable that he receives by wire or by satellite; or he might seek to transmit over his system the signals and programs broadcast by television stations. This last source of programming

643

raises serious questions of the relationship between cable and over-the-air television. So long as the cable system carries only programming from other sources, cable television is simply another competitor of broadcasting, along with movies, phonograph records, books and other communications sources. In fact, however, cable has been intimately involved with broadcasting since its inception—and that has produced substantial conflict.

Cable transmission was first used in the 1950's to provide television reception to remote locations that otherwise would have received none. For example, a community located in the mountains of West Virginia could construct an antenna on high ground to receive the signals of nearby television stations and transmit them through cable to households in the community. Such systems were called CATV for "community antenna television." Since cable was the only means of bringing television service to these remote areas, television broadcasters welcomed the additional viewers.

It was soon realized, however, that cable could do more than merely provide television service to remote areas. In 1961, a cable operator began serving San Diego, a city already served by three VHF network affiliates. The cable operator erected an antenna capable of picking up signals from Los Angeles, 100 miles away. In addition to the three networks received locally, cable offered four independent stations that served Los Angeles with sports, old motion pictures, and reruns of network shows. The San Diego experience demonstrated that the three channels offered by over-the-air signals were not enough to satisfy an ordinary audience and that viewers were willing to pay for more diversified programming through importation of distant signals. In effect, cable television service filled in the uneven pattern of FCC station allocation. Since cable offered a service alternative to that offered by local, over-the-air stations, television broadcasters began to view cable transmission as a competitive threat.

The spread of color television also provided a new impetus to cable development. VHF signals tend to bounce off large obstacles rather than bend around them. Hence a tall building can act like a weak transmitter, rebroadcasting the television signal at the same frequency as the station from which the signal originates. The result is interference, barely noticeable on a black-and-white set, but more pronounced on a color set. Cable provided the residents of large cities something that an over-the-air television signal could not—a high quality color picture. Hence, cable television invaded large cities, despite the presence of a full complement of VHF signals.

Finally, cable began to originate programming not available to viewers of network or independent television. Cable systems offered entertainment programming, sports events, and special programs designed to meet the interests of discrete groups. The discovery that viewers were willing to pay a few dollars more per month for programming not available on over-the-air television led to the development of pay cable service.

Pay cable involves the cable distribution of non-broadcast programming for which the subscriber is charged an additional program or channel fee beyond the regular monthly fee for the system's television signal reception service. The systems for distributing pay cable vary technically. The simplest method is to distribute the programming on one or more channels of a cable television system in garbled form. System subscribers who wish to receive the additional programming are supplied with a device that converts the programming transmission so that it can be understood. It is technically possible, but expensive, to use systems that permit a separate charge to be made for each program viewed. These either require the subscriber to purchase a ticket for each program in advance, which when inserted into a decoding device in the subscriber's home, provides access to the programming, or to utilize the return communications capacity of a cable system or a telephone connection to activate a central computer facility that releases the programming through the subscriber's decoding device and performs the billing functions. While the monthly fee currently predominates it is not yet clear which system fee will eventually become the industry norm.

The range of programming available via cable has grown greatly. In the New York area, for example, cable companies include more than ten services in the basic monthly fee, such as programming directed to racial and religious groups, all-news and all-sports channels, live coverage of the House of Representatives, children's programming, and "superstations" (discussed infra). For an extra monthly charge, subscribers may obtain an equal number of additional services, such as movie and entertainment channels, adult movies, and cultural programming.

In the late 1970's and early 1980's, new programming services were constantly beginning. More recently, a shakeout in the industry has started to take place. CBS shut down CBS Cable after its operation lost 30 million dollars in its first year. The RCA and Rockefeller Center entry, The Entertainment Channel, was discontinued after posting a 35 million dollar loss in nine months.

In 1983, Ted Turner agreed to pay ABC and Westinghouse 12.5 million dollars each to shut down Satellite News Channel, which was the main competitor to Turner's Cable News Network, and CNN Headline News. Group W and ABC promised not to compete in the cable news business for at least three years. Broadcasting, Oct. 17, 1983 at 27.

Thus, cable has provided a variety of services. It began as a way of bringing to a community programming that would have been available but for geographical barriers. Then, it imported programs from communities beyond the reach of normal reception. Later, it became a service for those who wished to improve reception of their local signals. These features have been combined with each other as well as with the origination of new programming on cable. Now it is possible to obtain the origination without any of the other features— and this origination may be local or part of a network that programs specially for cable subscribers.

By 1984, cable systems had been installed in 36.1 million (42.9 percent) of the nation's 84 million television homes. Systems varied in size from a few hundred homes to some in larger cities with hundreds of thousands of subscribers. Pay cable reached 25 million of these subscribers. The pay systems ranged from Home Box Office with 14.5 million subscribers to specialized services with only a few thousand subscribers.

2. FRANCHISING

Cable systems operate under franchise authority granted by a municipality, though state agencies also may grant permission to operate. See, e.g., Clear Television Cable Corp. v. Board of Public Utility Commissioners, 85 N.J. 30, 424 A.2d 1151 (1981). A franchise gives the cable operator access to city streets and other rights-of-way within a defined area for specific periods of time. Franchises usually are awarded after competitive bidding by several companies and are almost always exclusive. They specify services the system must provide, construction schedules and franchise fees. Many also specify fees the operators may charge subscribers, although much of this rate regulation has now been preempted by Congress and the FCC as we will discuss later in this Chapter.

For a while, the competition among cable operators for city franchises was incredibly intense. At the height of the franchising process operators were willing to promise almost anything to obtain a franchise. For example, in 1981, Denver attracted bids from three firms, one offering a 215-channel system including a 107-channel home network. The three offered basic home services for monthly fees ranging from nothing to $3.95.

Unfortunately, once they had obtained the franchises, some operators discovered that cable wasn't necessarily the goldmine they had anticipated. These operators are now asking cities to renegotiate the franchise agreements and eliminate some of the promised services, or selling the franchises to other operators. One company that found itself in that position, Warner Amex Cable Communications, is now building a 56-channel system in Milwaukee in lieu of the 108-channel system originally agreed upon. Broadcasting, Oct. 29, 1984 at 10.

In March 1985, the Ninth Circuit released a decision with far-reaching implications for the future of cable regulation. Preferred Communications had sued the City of Los Angeles claiming that requiring Preferred to go through a competitive franchising process violated its First Amendment rights. The District Court had dismissed the suit. On appeal the Court held that the competitive franchising process did, indeed, violate the First Amendment. "To the extent that . . . [the law] authorizes the government to protect its interest in regulating disruption of public resources through a system of permits or franchises . . . it passes muster . . . here. But we cannot agree with the suggestion in the legislative history that the provision 'grants to the franchising authority the discretion to determine the number of cable operators to be authorized to provide service in a particular geographic area.' A construction of such breadth would be invalid." Broadcasting, March 4, 1985 at 112. This case raises serious questions not only about the constitutionality of the franchising process, but also many provisions of the Cable Communications Policy Act of 1984, discussed later in this Chapter. As of March 11, 1985, the City of Los Angeles had not decided whether to seek a rehearing en banc or a petition for certiorari. Regardless of the City's decision, further legal proceedings on this issue are inevitable.

3. The FCC and Regulation of Cable Activities

When the first CATV systems emerged in the late 1950's, rural television stations became concerned about their local dominance. Their requests that the FCC assume jurisdiction over the activities of these new enterprises were rejected on the ground that the problem was trivial and no different from a request for protection against motion picture theaters or publishers who also compete with broadcasting.

In 1962, however, the FCC changed direction and began to deny cable systems permission to carry broadcast signals that might adversely affect local television. The Commission had two main concerns. First, it believed that if cable systems were allowed to import distant signals this would fragment the audience available to local stations, erode their revenue bases, affect their programming, and perhaps cause the stations to leave the air—to the public's detriment.

The second concern was that a cable system's use of retransmitted broadcast programming, for which the cable system had paid nothing, gave it an unfair competitive advantage over local television stations since the latter had to pay considerable sums to those who held the copyrights on particular programs.*

These two concerns—for fragmentation and program costs—led the FCC to embark on a series of regulations designed to keep cable systems subservient to over-the-air broadcasting. This attitude per-

---

* The copyright issue was sharpened when the Supreme Court held that cable retransmission of broadcast signals without consent did not constitute a "performance" within the 1909 Copyright Act and thus created no liability for copyright infringement. Fortnightly Corp. v. United Artists Television, 392 U.S. 390 (1968) and Teleprompter Corp. v. Columbia Broadcasting System, 415 U.S. 394 (1974).

sisted from the mid-1960's to the mid-1970's. Recall that this was the period of weak UHF stations, for whom audience fragmentation might well have been fatal.

Among the restrictions imposed during this period, the FCC barred cable systems from importing distant signals (those from outside the market area) into a top-100 market unless the cable system could prove that the importation would not hurt UHF development in that market. Although the regulation was challenged on the ground that the FCC had no statutory authority to issue it, the Supreme Court ruled that the regulation was "reasonably ancillary to the effective performance of [the FCC's] responsibilities for the regulation of television broadcasting." United States v. Southwestern Cable Co., 392 U.S. 157 (1968). In 1980, the FCC repealed all limits on the number of distant signals that a cable system could import.

Leapfrogging and Superstations. Another, called the anti-leapfrogging rule, provided that when it was permissible to import distant signals, the system had to select from among those nearest to the city in which the system was operating. The FCC deleted this rule in 1976. One result was the emergence of the so-called "superstation"—a VHF or UHF independent station that makes its programs available to cable systems throughout the country, via satellite transmission.

The most famous superstation is Ted Turner's Channel 17 in Atlanta, which has access to 200 live sporting events each year. By early 1985 the station was distributing its programs nationwide to 7,798 cable systems with 31.6 million subscribers. The satellite company charged the cable systems 10 cents per subscriber per month. The cable systems made the programs available as part of their basic monthly charge to attract subscribers.

Channel 17 prospered by increased charges for advertising on its programs that were now reaching up to 30 million more viewers than previously. As a result, Channel 17's local advertisers were replaced by those marketing national products when the superstation emerged. Program suppliers have increased charges to Channel 17 because the program is reaching a much larger audience than it did before and cable distribution may preclude sales to local stations in cities receiving the cable program.

Other independent local stations have begun similar ventures, but lag behind the Atlanta enterprise, which had a two-year headstart. Some, using wires instead of satellites, have become regional stations.

Exclusivity. To protect the local station when it was carrying network programs, the FCC promulgated exclusivity rules (formerly called non-duplication rules) to prevent cable from carrying an imported distant signal that was offering the same network program as the local network affiliate. First, the FCC required the cable system to black out the distant signal if the program was being broadcast on the same day as it was being presented by the local affiliate. Later, the FCC changed the rule to require black-out only if the two showings were at the same hour.

In the mid-1970's the Commission dropped the black-out requirement permitting the cable system to show the local station's signal (and its commercials) simultaneously on both the local channel and on the channel that normally carries the distant signal, even though the local station might suffer if the local audience stays with the distant station after the program is over. This protection survives.

Another regulation protecting local stations had provided that cable systems in large markets could not carry distant signals showing programs to which a local station had acquired exclusive future local rights. In 1980, the FCC repealed this restriction on the ground that viewers' interest in "time-diversity"—seeing programs when they wanted—was more compelling than the local station's interest in the exclusive programming. Deletion of the old rule would not reduce the supply of programs for television.

Must carry. One of the few regulations designed to protect broadcasters that still remains is the "must carry" rules. Cable systems are required to carry all local and "significantly viewed" broadcast signals. Though the must carry rules withstood previous legal challenges, Turner Broadcasting System (TBS) filed a new petition in 1981 asking the Commission for its repeal. TBS based its petition on the claim that the must carry rules inhibit rather than serve First Amendment interests and that it would be more efficient for local stations to be received off-the-air, not through cable systems. This would free up cable channels for services not available over the air. Broadcasters argued, however, that in many areas off the air reception is of a much lower quality than cable transmission. After three years, the FCC decided in early 1984 not to institute repeal proceedings. TBS has appealed. Oral argument was April 16, 1985.

Origination and Access. In the late 1960's the FCC began to require larger cable systems to originate a certain amount of programming from their own resources. This requirement was upheld, 5–4, by the Supreme Court in United States v. Midwest Video Corp., 406 U.S. 649 (1972), on the ground that the regulation was "reasonably ancillary" to the FCC's obligations to regulate over-the-air television. Since cable operators had become enmeshed with television broadcasting, the FCC could require them to engage in the functional equivalent of broadcasting. In 1974, however, after this victory, the FCC eliminated the origination requirement because it concluded that quality local programming could not be obtained by government mandate.

The access rules required new cable systems to allocate four of their 20 channels to public, educational, local government and leased access. The systems had to make equipment available for studio use by the public and could not control who might use the facilities or what they might say. Charges for use of the facilities were controlled. This time, a legal challenge succeeded. In F.C.C. v. Midwest Video Corp., 440 U.S. 689 (1979) (*Midwest II*), the Court, 6–3, held that the rules violated a provision of the 1934 Communications Act that "a person engaged in . . . broadcasting shall not . . . be deemed a common carrier" who must accept business from anyone who wished to patronize it. The Court considered the same limitation applicable to cable systems.

The mandatory access rules had also been challenged on First Amendment grounds. The Court chose not to address that issue, but it may soon reach the Court in Berkshire Cablevision of Rhode Island, Inc. v. Burke, 571 F.Supp. 976 (D.R.I.1983). At issue is a state PUC requirement that applicants for local franchises must set aside at least seven channels for public access. The judge likened cable more to broadcasting and subject to regulation than to newspapers. In the appeal of the Berkshire case, the First Circuit has asked the Rhode Island Supreme Court to determine whether the PUC had authority under state law to impose the access requirement. While a negative answer would eliminate the need to address the First Amendment question in this case, it will only be delaying the inevitable. As we will discuss later in this Chapter, Congress has recently authorized the imposition of access channel requirements.

As a result of all the FCC's recent actions cable systems are still subject to only three major restraints: (1) they must carry local broadcasters who want to be carried; (2) they must protect local broadcasters against simultaneous importation of distant stations carrying network programs that are being broadcast on local stations at the same time, and (3) they must not import a distant signal carrying a sporting event involving a local team playing at home if the game is not being telecast locally.

Copyright Problems. The removal of FCC restrictions has made the role of copyright law crucially important. In the 1976 copyright statute, in § 111, a complex compromise provides, in effect, that cablecasters need pay no royalties for programs on "local" (or "must carry") stations that they are required to carry. Cablecasters are permitted to carry the copyrighted programs of "distant" (or "may carry") stations without the owner's consent in return for the payment of a compulsory royalty fee. This fee is fixed by statute and depends on the size of the cable system and whether the distant station is commercial or educational.

The compulsory license and royalty provision has been under attack in Congress. The problem is that the 1976 Act did not contemplate the changes in FCC rules that have permitted the growth of superstations and increased carriage of distant signals. The result is that an increasing amount of cable programming is coming from distant sources, leaving the program suppliers with less control over geographical distribution of their products. Complaints are also being heard from major sports leagues because, for example, an Atlanta baseball game may be shown on a Boston area cable system at the same time another game is being played in Boston. In early 1985, the Atlanta Braves and New York Yankees agreed to pay the other major league teams a special annual fee based on the subscriber base of the superstations that carry their games. The New York Mets and Chicago Cubs, whose games are also carried by superstations, were expected to follow suit. Cablevision, Feb. 4, 1985 at 12.

Broadcasters argue that the compulsory license should be abolished and replaced by a negotiated agreement between the cable system and the originating broadcaster (who, under contract, would need the consent of the copyright owner). This need not lead to individual negotiations—the matter could be handled the way song writers grant licenses and collect royalties, through such groups as ASCAP and BMI that grant bulk licenses for a fee and then distribute the proceeds according to a formula.

A second controversy involves distribution of the royalties collected under the Act. The Copyright Royalty Tribunal, created for the purpose, must allocate the $15 million in cable royalties collected each year. Demands from the various claimants, such as program producers and syndicators, sports leagues, music groups, broadcast licensees themselves, and others, greatly exceed 100 percent. In September, 1980, the Tribunal allocated the 1978 revenues, giving 75 percent to program producers and syndicators, and 3.25 percent to commercial television broadcasters. This means that total copyright payments to all commercial television for programs carried during 1978 by cable systems amounted to $476,000.

As a result of the FCC's repeal of the distant signal rules, the Tribunal did raise the rates cable operators must pay for distant signals effective March 15, 1983. Large cable systems became liable for a compulsory license fee of 3.75% of their basic revenues for each distant signal added since June 24, 1981. This increase was upheld in National Cable Television Association v. Copyright Royalty Tribunal, 724 F.2d 176, 55 R.R.2d 387 (D.C.Cir.1983). In response, some cable operators dropped distant signals to reduce their copyright liability. Superstations were the major casualty.

Broadcasters maintain that cable's contribution to the fund is tiny when compared with the fact that commercial television broadcasters spend some 35 percent of their budgets on program acquisition. Cable operators claim the current fees, after the recent rate hikes, are already prohibitive. Meanwhile, the FCC has asserted that any economic problem for the broadcasters derives from the Copyright Act or the Tribunal's allocation—and relief must come from those sources.

4. State v. Federal Regulation

Cable, unlike broadcasting, is regulated by both federal and state government. As we discussed state and local jurisdiction was originally based primarily on the cable operator's use of the city streets and other rights of way. Federal jurisdiction grew out of the FCC's jurisdiction over broadcasting. Gradually a conflict arose over where the line between state and federal jurisdiction should be drawn.

The majority of cable operators preferred to restrict state and local jurisdiction as much as possible. They believed that some cities were making impossible demands in return for their franchises and imposing heavy burdens on the cable operators once the franchises were awarded. There were also serious fears that franchise renewal in cable would not carry the same renewal expectancy that is present in broadcasting (discussed in Chapter XIV).

At the same time the FCC was gradually asserting the right to preempt more and more state and local regulation. As these issues reached the courts, the Commission's position was generally being upheld. In mid-1984, the Commission received strong support for its asserted right to preempt in Capital Cities Cable, Inc. v. Crisp, 467 U.S. ___, 56 R.R. 263 (1984) even though ironically the FCC was not directly involved in the case.

The case centered on an Oklahoma statute banning the advertising of alcoholic beverages, except by the use of certain on-premises signs. In 1980, the state Attorney General concluded that retransmission of an out-of state commercial over cable television would violate the statute. Cable operators sued for declaratory and injunctive relief.

While the lower courts focused on whether the advertising in question was protected by the commercial speech doctrine as discussed in Chapter VIII, the Supreme Court chose to decide the case on federal preemption grounds. Noting that the FCC had already preempted "signal carriage, pay cable, leased channel regulations, technical standards, access, and several areas of franchisee responsibility," the Court concluded that "to the extent it has been invoked to control the distant broadcast and nonbroadcast signals imported by cable operators, the Oklahoma advertising ban plainly . . . trespasses into the exclusive domain of the FCC."

5. Cable Communications Policy Act of 1984

The FCC's increasingly aggressive policy of preemption had already led the National League of Cities (NLC) to pursue legislative relief. However, lengthy negotiations between NLC and the National Cable Television Association (NCTA) had not produced a compromise satisfactory to both constituencies. Perhaps given new impetus by Court decisions such as *Crisp,* a compromise bill was drafted and presented to Congress with the backing of both parties. In late 1984, this bill was enacted into law as the Cable Communications Policy Act of 1984.

The Act addresses many of the issues we have discussed in this chapter including jurisdiction, franchising, renewals, rate regulation and access channels. A brief summary of the major provisions follows.

Jurisdiction. The Communications Act of 1934 has been amended to specifically include "cable service to all persons engaged within the United States in providing such service, and to the facilities of cable operators which relate to such service, as provided in Title VI." 47 U.S.C. § 152. In addition, Title VI, Cable Communications has been added to the Communications Act of 1934. 47 U.S.C. §§ 601–639. Thus, the Commission no longer has to derive its jurisdiction over cable from its jurisdiction over broadcasting. Courts will no longer have to determine whether a Commission rule is reasonably ancillary to its jurisdiction over broadcasting.

Franchising. Franchising is still the province of state and local governments with only a few restrictions. Most important of these is the prohibition on regulating cable service as a common carrier. 47 U.S.C.A. 621.

Renewals. One of the great fears of cable operators was nonrenewal. Specific guidelines for franchise renewal are set out in great detail in § 626 of the Communications Act. 47 U.S.C. § 626. It appears to create a strong renewal expectancy. The full impact of this section will, of course, not be clear until it has been in effect for several years.

Rate Regulation. The new law only allows regulation of rates of basic cable service, and even that is only allowed in some circumstances. 47 U.S.C. § 623. This provision is viewed as a major victory for cable operators, who have long argued that rate regulation was unnecessary due to competition from other communication technologies. Opponents of the provision contended that cable is effectively a monopoly and thus, cable rates are not subject to adequate pressure from competition.

Access Channels. Arguably, access channels were the *quid pro quo* for the NLC's concessions on renewals and rate regulation. Section 611 provides that access channels for public, educational and governmental use can be required as part of a franchise proposal or a proposal for renewal. 47 U.S.C.A. 611. Furthermore, a federal requirement to set aside some channels for commercial use by persons unaffiliated with the operator is imposed on all systems with 36 or more activated channels. The number of channels that must be set aside varies according to the size of the system. 47 U.S.C. § 612.

Remember, however, that the constitutionality of this provision is still in question.

B. NEW COMMUNICATION TECHNOLOGIES

As we discussed earlier in this Chapter, at one time cable was seen as the ultimate communications technology. At the height of the franchising battles, operators were promising that cable would provide everything to everybody. Not only were those promises unfulfilled, but cable is no longer even the "new" technology. A proliferation of new delivery systems such as multi-point distribution service (MDS), direct broadcast satellites (DBS), and satellite master antenna television (SMATV) are fighting for their share of the communications marketplace.

As each of these services has developed, new regulatory questions have arisen. While a detailed examination of the regulatory framework for each of these services is beyond the scope of this book, we will briefly examine the nature of these services and provide an overview of the regulatory issues raised by their development.

1. THE NEW TECHNOLOGIES

Multipoint Distribution Service. MDS transmits microwave signals over super high frequencies within a range of about 25 miles. The signal is usually received by master antenna systems or other closed-circuit systems, which convert the signal and show it on a vacant VHF channel. In some urban areas in which cable is not available, MDS has been distributing HBO programming.

In 1983, the FCC reallocated 8 of the 28 instructional television fixed service (ITFS) microwave channels to MDS, making multichannel multipoint distribution service (MMDS) available. ITFS (MDS Reallocation), 54 R.R.2d 107 (1983). MMDS operators may also obtain extra channel capacity by leasing an ITFS operator's excess capacity. Utilizing these ITFS channels, an MMDS operator in Washington, D.C. is already providing four-channel service. Similar service is expected to be available in New York, San Francisco and Milwaukee by May, 1985. Broadcasting, Mar. 11, 1985.

Direct Broadcast Satellites. DBS is a system of broadcasting directly from studio to home via satellite. The technology involves the usual transmission to a satellite and the return to earth where the signal is collected by a receiving dish two or three feet in diameter that would be placed on the roof of the home of the subscriber.

The first DBS system began operating in November, 1983. United Satellite Communications Inc. (USCI) began five channel service to central Indiana. The consumer response was far less than envisioned and by 1985 USCI was struggling to stay in business. There is now some question whether DBS will ever be a viable service.

Satellite Master Antenna Television. SMATV involves setting up one or more earth stations on a large building or complex and distributing by wire or cable the various programming received. The distinction between SMATV and cable television is that no city streets or rights of way are used. This restriction prevents cities from subjecting SMATV operators to a franchising process. It also limits SMATV systems to large apartments and hotels where sufficient subscribers can be reached without crossing city streets.

Electronic Publishing. Electronic Publishing puts pages of information, both text and images, on television sets or other display tubes. Teletext is a one-way system with signals flowing only from the computer to the screen. It operates by sending a continuous cycle of information to home television screens during the regular vertical blanking interval of a television signal. A user chooses the "page" of information he wants from a published index, and instructs the receiver terminal to "grab" the page as it goes by. When the user is finished the page is released from the screen. Teletext can be delivered by either broadcasting or cable.

Another system, called "videotex," is a two-way system in which the computer holds a much larger data base and the user signals which information he wants to obtain. The selected pages are then transmitted to the user. This system requires telephone lines or cable.

Subsidiary Communications Authorizations. In 1983, the Commission authorized radio licensees to use their subcarriers for any purpose they wished. A subcarrier is a secondary transmission that can be "piggy-backed" on the primary signal. These subcarriers can only be heard through the use of special receivers. Under the limited authorization for subcarriers available prior to 1983, broadcasters have distributed such services as background music for stores and elevators. The new expanded authorization allows for such uses as entertainment programming, data transmission and paging. The Commission also increased the width of the FM baseband from 75 to 99 khz. This makes two rather than one subcarrier possible for each station.

2. REGULATORY OPTIONS

The FCC does not have complete freedom in developing regulatory frameworks for new technologies. Rather, the Commission must work within the context of the Communications Act. Originally, the Act provided two basic models for regulation. One, the "broadcast" model we have studied in Chapters XIII–XVI. The second is the "common-carrier" model to be discussed below. If a communications technology does not fit either of these models, the authority of the Commission to regulate it is questionable. This was a major issue in the regulation of cable. In *Midwest Video I,* the Commission's jurisdiction over cable was upheld as being ancillary to its jurisdiction over broadcasting. However, the exact limits of this jurisdiction were never clear, a problem that has apparently been solved by the Cable Communications Policy Act of 1984.

Common carriers are regulated under Title II of the Communications Act. The key element of common carrier regulation is that the "content is separated from the conduit." In other words, unlike broadcasters, common carriers have no editorial discretion. Instead, they must provide, in a non-discriminatory manner, the facilities for transmission of the customer's message. National Association of Regulatory Utility Commissioners v. Federal Communications Commission, 525 F.2d 630 (D.C.Cir.1976), certiorari denied 425 U.S. 992 (1976). Telephone and telegraph companies are examples of common carriers.

There are a number of other important distinctions between broadcasters and common carriers. The federal government has preempted state regulation of broadcasting. In contrast, common carriers are regulated on both the state and federal levels. Interstate service is regulated by the Federal Communications Commission, while intrastate service is regulated by state agencies.

Sometimes, however, the Commission will decide to preempt the states and regulate a service on a strictly federal basis, as it did in 1983 with SMATV. When the Commission decides to preempt state regulation it does not necessarily imply that the Commission will choose to regulate to the same extent. Instead, the FCC may choose to "preempt and forbear." This means that the Commission will eliminate the state regulations without substituting any of its own because the Commission believes as a matter of policy that no regulation is the proper regulation for that area.

The regulations most commonly subject to preemption are entry requirements and rate regulation. When a common carrier wishes to provide a service, it is usually required to demonstrate a need for the service. Some states require that, in addition to showing need, an applicant demonstrate that current carriers are either unable to or unwilling to provide the additional needed service. These requirements can effectively bar any new entrants into a given type of service. Such artificial entry barriers present a special problem when the Commission authorizes new technologies to offer services already provided by existing carriers. It was for this reason that in 1984 the Commission preempted entry requirements for SCAs. Amendment . . . of the Commission's Rules Concerning Use of the Subsidiary Communications Authorizations, ___ F.C.C.2d ___ (1984).

Because common carriers often enjoy either a natural or government-created monopoly, they are often subject to rate regulation by either the FCC or appropriate state agencies. Rate regulation is usually eliminated when there is a finding of sufficient effective competition in the services provided.

Traditionally, the Commission assigned services to the two regulatory models based on the method of transmission. Thus, all broadcasting was under the broadcast model while MDS was common carrier. This led to seemingly anomalous results. For example, an STV channel that leased its facilities to a movie service would be subject to different regulations than an MDS channel leasing its facilities to the same movie service. In fact, a third regulatory scheme would obtain when the same movie service was carried over cable. While many of these anomalies still exist, the Commission has started to take a new approach, imposing regulations based on the service provided as opposed to the method of transmission. In the case of SCAs and DBS the Commission left the initial choice of regulatory model up to the licensee. In other words, licensees could decide for themselves which regulatory model would be most appropriate for the type of service they wished to offer. That portion of the DBS ruling was struck down, however, on appeal. The court determined that DBS should be regulated under the broadcast model. National Association of Broadcasters v. Federal Communications Commission, 740 F.2d 1190 (D.C.Cir.1984).

Obviously, the flood of new communications technologies has presented the FCC with serious problems as it tries to fit them into the traditional regulatory models. Much of this area is in flux and it will undoubtedly be some time before the law can catch up with the technology. There is also now the question of the impact of *Preferred Communications* on other communications technologies besides cable. If nothing else the next few years should prove very interesting.

*

Appendix A

THE CONSTITUTION OF THE UNITED STATES OF AMERICA

We the People of the United States, in Order to form a more perfect Union, establish Justice, insure domestic Tranquility, provide for the common defence, promote the general Welfare, and secure the Blessings of Liberty to ourselves and our Posterity, do ordain and establish this Constitution for the United States of America.

ARTICLE I.

SECTION 1. All legislative Powers herein granted shall be vested in a Congress of the United States, which shall consist of a Senate and House of Representatives.

SECTION 2. The House of Representatives shall be composed of Members chosen every second Year by the People of the several States, and the Electors in each State shall have the Qualifications requisite for Electors of the most numerous Branch of the State Legislature.

No Person shall be a Representative who shall not have attained to the Age of twenty five Years, and been seven Years a Citizen of the United States, and who shall not, when elected, be an inhabitant of that State in which he shall be chosen.

Representatives and direct Taxes shall be apportioned among the several States which may be included within this Union, according to their respective Numbers, which shall be determined by adding to the whole Number of free Persons, including those bound to Service for a Term of Years, and excluding Indians not taxed, three fifths of all other Persons. The actual Enumeration shall be made within three Years after the first Meeting of the Congress of the United States, and within every subsequent Term of ten Years, in such Manner as they shall by Law direct. The Number of Representatives shall not exceed one for every thirty Thousand, but each State shall have at Least one Representative; and until such enumeration shall be made, the State of New Hampshire shall be entitled to chuse three, Massachusetts eight, Rhode Island and Providence Plantations one, Connecticut five, New York six, New Jersey four, Pennsylvania eight, Delaware one, Maryland six, Virginia ten, North Carolina five, South Carolina five, and Georgia three.

When vacancies happen in the Representation from any State, the Executive Authority thereof shall issue Writs of Election to fill such Vacancies.

The House of Representatives shall chuse their Speaker and other Officers; and shall have the sole Power of Impeachment.

SECTION 3. The Senate of the United States shall be composed of two Senators from each State, chosen by the Legislature thereof, for six Years; and each Senator shall have one Vote.

Immediately after they shall be assembled in Consequence of the first Election, they shall be divided as equally as may be into three Classes. The Seats of the Senators of the first Class shall be vacated at the Expiration of the second Year, of the second Class at the Expiration of the fourth Year, and of the third Class at the Expiration of the sixth Year, so that one third may be chosen every second Year; and if Vacancies happen by Resignation, or otherwise, during the Recess of the Legislature of any State, the Executive thereof may make temporary Appointments until the next Meeting of the Legislature, which shall then fill such Vacancies.

No Person shall be a Senator who shall not have attained to the Age of thirty Years, and been nine Years a Citizen of the United States, and who shall not, when elected, be an Inhabitant of that State for which he shall be chosen.

The Vice President of the United States shall be President of the Senate, but shall have no Vote, unless they be equally divided.

The Senate shall chuse their other Officers, and also a President pro tempore, in the Absence of the Vice President, or when he shall exercise the Office of President of the United States.

The Senate shall have the sole Power to try all Impeachments. When sitting for that Purpose, they shall be on Oath or Affirmation. When the President of the United States is tried the Chief Justice shall preside: And no Person shall be convicted without the Concurrence of two thirds of the Members present.

Judgment in Cases of Impeachment shall not extend further than to removal from Office, and disqualification to hold and enjoy any Office of honor, Trust, or Profit under the United States: but the Party convicted shall nevertheless be liable and subject to Indictment, Trial, Judgment, and Punishment, according to Law.

SECTION 4. The Times, Places and Manner of holding Elections for Senators and Representatives, shall be prescribed in each State by the Legislature thereof; but the Congress may at any time by Law make or alter such Regulations, except as to the Places of chusing Senators.

The Congress shall assemble at least once in every Year, and such Meeting shall be on the first Monday in December, unless they shall by Law appoint a different Day.

SECTION 5. Each House shall be the Judge of the Elections, Returns, and Qualifications of its own Members, and a Majority of each shall constitute a Quorum to do Business; but a smaller Number may adjourn from day to day, and may be authorized to compel the Attendance of absent Members, in such Manner, and under such Penalties as each House may provide.

Each House may determine the Rules of its Proceedings, punish its Members for disorderly Behaviour, and, with the Concurrence of two thirds, expel a Member.

Each House shall keep a Journal of its Proceedings, and from time to time publish the same, excepting such Parts as may in their Judgment require Secrecy; and the Yeas and Nays of the Members of either House on any question shall, at the Desire of one fifth of those Present, be entered on the Journal.

Neither House, during the Session of Congress, shall, without the Consent of the other, adjourn for more than three days, nor to any other Place than that in which the two Houses shall be sitting.

SECTION 6.   The Senators and Representatives shall receive a Compensation for their Services, to be ascertained by Law, and paid out of the Treasury of the United States.   They shall in all Cases, except Treason, Felony and Breach of the Peace, be privileged from Arrest during their Attendance at the Session of their respective Houses, and in going to and returning from the same; and for any Speech or Debate in either House, they shall not be questioned in any other Place.

No Senator or Representative shall, during the Time for which he was elected, be appointed to any civil Office under the Authority of the United States, which shall have been created, or the Emoluments whereof shall have been encreased during such time; and no Person holding any Office under the United States, shall be a Member of either House during his Continuance in Office.

SECTION 7.   All Bills for raising Revenue shall originate in the House of Representatives; but the Senate may propose or concur with amendments as on other Bills.

Every Bill which shall have passed the House of Representatives and the Senate, shall, before it becomes a Law, be presented to the President of the United States; If he approve he shall sign it, but if not he shall return it, with his Objections to that House in which it shall have originated, who shall enter the Objections at large on their Journal, and proceed to reconsider it.   If after such Reconsideration two thirds of that House shall agree to pass the Bill, it shall be sent, together with the Objections, to the other House, by which it shall likewise be reconsidered, and if approved by two thirds of that House, it shall become a Law.   But in all such Cases the Votes of both Houses shall be determined by Yeas and Nays, and the Names of the Persons voting for and against the Bill shall be entered on the Journal of each House respectively.   If any Bill shall not be returned by the President within ten Days (Sunday excepted) after it shall have been presented to him, the Same shall be a Law, in like Manner as if he had signed it, unless the Congress by their Adjournment prevent its Return, in which Case it shall not be a Law.

Every Order, Resolution, or Vote to which the Concurrence of the Senate and House of Representatives may be necessary (except on a question of Adjournment) shall be presented to the President of the United States; and before the Same shall take Effect, shall be approved by him, or being disapproved by him, shall be repassed by two thirds of the Senate and House of Representatives, according to the Rules and Limitations prescribed in the Case of a Bill.

SECTION 8. The Congress shall have Power To lay and collect Taxes, Duties, Imposts and Excises, to pay the Debts and provide for the common Defence and general Welfare of the United States; but all Duties, Imposts and Excises shall be uniform throughout the United States;

To borrow Money on the credit of the United States;

To regulate Commerce with foreign Nations, and among the several States, and with the Indian Tribes;

To establish an uniform Rule of Naturalization, and uniform Laws on the subject of Bankruptcies throughout the United States;

To coin Money, regulate the Value thereof, and of foreign Coin, and fix the Standard of Weights and Measures;

To provide for the Punishment of counterfeiting the Securities and current Coin of the United States;

To establish Post Offices and post Roads;

To promote the Progress of Science and useful Arts, by securing for limited Times to Authors and Inventors the exclusive Right to their respective Writings and Discoveries;

To constitute Tribunals inferior to the supreme Court;

To define and punish Piracies and Felonies committed on the high Seas, and Offences against the Law of Nations;

To declare War, grant Letters of Marque and Reprisal, and make Rules concerning Captures on Land and Water;

To raise and support Armies, but no Appropriation of Money to that Use shall be for a longer Term than two Years;

To provide and maintain a Navy;

To make Rules for the Government and Regulation of the land and naval Forces;

To provide for calling forth the Militia to execute the Laws of the Union, suppress Insurrections and repel Invasions;

To provide for organizing, arming, and disciplining, the Militia, and for governing such Part of them as may be employed in the Service of the United States, reserving to the States respectively, the

Appointment of the Officers, and the Authority of training the Militia according to the discipline prescribed by Congress;

To exercise exclusive Legislation in all Cases whatsoever, over such District (not exceeding ten Miles square) as may, by Cession of particular States, and the Acceptance of Congress, become the Seat of the Government of the United States, and to exercise like Authority over all Places purchased by the Consent of the Legislature of the State in which the Same shall be, for the Erection of Forts, Magazines, Arsenals, dock-Yards, and other needful Buildings;—And

To make all Laws which shall be necessary and proper for carrying into Execution the foregoing Powers, and all other Powers vested by this Constitution in the Government of the United States, or in any Department or Officer thereof.

SECTION 9. The Migration or Importation of such Persons as any of the States now existing shall think proper to admit, shall not be prohibited by the Congress prior to the Year one thousand eight hundred and eight, but a Tax or duty may be imposed on such Importation, not exceeding ten dollars for each Person.

The Privilege of the Writ of Habeas Corpus shall not be suspended, unless when in Cases of Rebellion or Invasion the public Safety may require it.

No Bill of Attainder or ex post facto Law shall be passed.

No Capitation, or other direct, Tax shall be laid, unless in Proportion to the Census or Enumeration herein before directed to be taken.

No Tax or Duty shall be laid on Articles exported from any State.

No Preference shall be given by any Regulation of Commerce or Revenue to the Ports of one State over those of another; nor shall Vessels bound to, or from, one State, be obliged to enter, clear, or pay Duties in another.

No Money shall be drawn from the Treasury, but in Consequence of Appropriations made by Law; and a regular Statement and Account of the Receipts and Expenditures of all public Money shall be published from time to time.

No Title of Nobility shall be granted by the United States: And no Person holding any Office of Profit or Trust under them, shall, without the Consent of the Congress, accept of any present, Emolument, Office, or Title, of any kind whatever, from any King, Prince or foreign State.

SECTION 10. No State shall enter into any Treaty, Alliance, or Confederation; grant Letters of Marque and Reprisal; coin Money; emit Bills of Credit; make any Thing but gold and silver Coin a Tender in Payment of Debts; pass any Bill of Attainder, ex post facto

Law, or Law impairing the Obligation of Contracts, or grant any Title of Nobility.

No State shall, without the Consent of the Congress, lay any Imposts or Duties on Imports or Exports, except what may be absolutely necessary for executing its inspection Laws: and the net Produce of all Duties and Imposts, laid by any State on Imports or Exports, shall be for the Use of the Treasury of the United States; and all such Laws shall be subject to the Revision and Controul of the Congress.

No State shall, without the Consent of Congress, lay any Duty of Tonnage, keep Troops, or Ships of War in time of Peace, enter into any Agreement or Compact with another State, or with a foreign Power, or engage in War, unless actually invaded, or in such imminent Danger as will not admit of delay.

ARTICLE II.

SECTION 1. The executive Power shall be vested in a President of the United States of America. He shall hold his Office during the Term of four Years, and, together with the Vice President, chosen for the same Term, be elected, as follows

Each State shall appoint, in such Manner as the Legislature thereof may direct, a Number of Electors, equal to the whole Number of Senators and Representatives to which the State may be entitled in the Congress: but no Senator or Representative, or Person holding an Office of Trust or Profit under the United States, shall be appointed an Elector.

The Electors shall meet in their respective States, and vote by Ballot for two Persons, of whom one at least shall not be an Inhabitant of the same State with themselves. And they shall make a List of all the Persons voted for, and of the Number of Votes for each; which List they shall sign and certify, and transmit sealed to the Seat of the Government of the United States, directed to the President of the Senate. The President of the Senate shall, in the Presence of the Senate and House of Representatives, open all the Certificates, and the Votes shall then be counted. The Person having the greatest Number of Votes shall be the President, if such Number be a Majority of the whole Number of Electors appointed; and if there be more than one who have such Majority, and have an equal Number of Votes, then the House of Representatives shall immediately chuse by Ballot one of them for President; and if no Person have a Majority, then from the five highest on the List the said House shall in like Manner chuse the President. But in chusing the President, the Votes shall be taken by States, the Representation from each State having one Vote; a quorum for this Purpose shall consist of a Member or Members from two thirds of the States, and a Majority of all the States shall be necessary to a Choice. In every Case, after the Choice of the President, the Person having the greatest Number of Votes of the Electors shall be the Vice President. But if there should remain two or more who have equal Votes, the Senate shall chuse from them by Ballot the Vice President.

The Congress may determine the Time of chusing the Electors, and the Day on which they shall give their Votes; which Day shall be the same throughout the United States.

No Person except a natural born Citizen, or a Citizen of the United States, at the time of the Adoption of this Constitution, shall be eligible to the Office of President; neither shall any Person be eligible to that Office who shall not have attained to the Age of thirty five Years, and been fourteen Years a Resident within the United States.

In Case of the Removal of the President from Office, or of his Death, Resignation, or Inability to discharge the Powers and Duties of the said Office, the Same shall devolve on the Vice President, and the Congress may by Law provide for the Case of Removal, Death, Resignation or Inability, both of the President and Vice President, declaring what Officer shall then act as President, and such Officer shall act accordingly, until the Disability be removed, or a President shall be elected.

The President shall, at stated Times, receive for his Services, a Compensation, which shall neither be encreased nor diminished during the Period for which he shall have been elected, and he shall not receive within that Period any other Emolument from the United States, or any of them.

Before he enter on the Execution of his Office, he shall take the following Oath or Affirmation:—"I do solemnly swear (or affirm) that I will faithfully execute the Office of President of the United States, and will to the best of my Ability, preserve, protect and defend the Constitution of the United States."

SECTION 2. The President shall be Commander in Chief of the Army and Navy of the United States, and of the Militia of the several States, when called into the actual Service of the United States; he may require the Opinion, in writing, of the principal Officer in each of the executive Departments, upon any Subject relating to the Duties of their respective Offices, and he shall have Power to grant Reprieves and Pardons for Offences against the United States, except in Cases of Impeachment.

He shall have Power, by and with the Advice and Consent of the Senate, to make Treaties, provided two thirds of the Senators present concur; and he shall nominate, and by and with the Advice and Consent of the Senate, shall appoint Ambassadors, other public Ministers and Consuls, Judges of the supreme Court, and all other Officers of the United States, whose Appointments are not herein otherwise provided for, and which shall be established by Law: but the Congress may by Law vest the Appointment of such inferior

Officers, as they think proper, in the President alone, in the Courts of Law, or in the Heads of Departments.

The President shall have Power to fill up all Vacancies that may happen during the Recess of the Senate, by granting Commissions which shall expire at the End of their next Session.

SECTION 3. He shall from time to time give to the Congress Information of the State of the Union, and recommend to their Consideration such Measures as he shall judge necessary and expedient; he may, on extraordinary Occasions, convene both Houses, or either of them, and in Case of Disagreement between them, with Respect to the Time of Adjournment, he may adjourn them to such Time as he shall think proper; he shall receive Ambassadors and other public Ministers; he shall take Care that the Laws be faithfully executed, and shall Commission all the Officers of the United States.

SECTION 4. The President, Vice President and all civil Officers of the United States, shall be removed from Office on Impeachment for, and Conviction of, Treason, Bribery, or other high Crimes and Misdemeanors.

ARTICLE III.

SECTION 1. The judicial Power of the United States, shall be vested in one supreme Court, and in such inferior Courts as the Congress may from time to time ordain and establish. The Judges, both of the supreme and inferior Courts, shall hold their Offices during good Behaviour, and shall, at stated Times, receive for their Services, a Compensation, which shall not be diminished during their Continuance in Office.

SECTION 2. The judicial Power shall extend to all Cases, in Law and Equity, arising under this Constitution, the Laws of the United States, and Treaties made, or which shall be made, under their Authority;—to all Cases affecting Ambassadors, other public Ministers and Consuls;—to all Cases of admiralty and maritime Jurisdiction;—to Controversies to which the United States shall be a Party;—to Controversies between two or more States;—between a State and Citizens of another State;—between Citizens of different States;—between Citizens of the same State claiming Lands under Grants of different States, and between a State, or the Citizens thereof, and foreign States, Citizens or Subjects.

In all Cases affecting Ambassadors, other public Ministers and Consuls, and those in which a State shall be Party, the supreme Court shall have original Jurisdiction. In all the other Cases before mentioned, the supreme Court shall have appellate Jurisdiction, both as to

Law and Fact, with such Exceptions, and under such Regulations as the Congress shall make.

The Trial of all Crimes, except in Cases of Impeachment, shall be by Jury; and such Trial shall be held in the State where the said Crimes shall have been committed; but when not committed within any State, the Trial shall be at such Place or Places as the Congress may by Law have directed.

SECTION 3. Treason against the United States, shall consist only in levying War against them, or in adhering to their Enemies, giving them Aid and Comfort. No Person shall be convicted of Treason unless on the Testimony of two Witnesses to the same overt Act, or on Confession in open Court.

The Congress shall have Power to declare the Punishment of Treason, but no Attainder of Treason shall work Corruption of Blood, or Forfeiture except during the Life of the Person attainted.

ARTICLE IV.

SECTION 1. Full Faith and Credit shall be given in each State to the public Acts, Records, and judicial Proceedings of every other State. And the Congress may by general Laws prescribe the Manner in which such Acts, Records and Proceedings shall be proved, and the Effect thereof.

SECTION 2. The Citizens of each State shall be entitled to all Privileges and Immunities of Citizens in the several States.

A Person charged in any State with Treason, Felony, or other Crime, who shall flee from Justice, and be found in another State, shall on Demand of the executive Authority of the State from which he fled, be delivered up, to be removed to the State having Jurisdiction of the Crime.

No Person held to Service or Labour in one State, under the Laws thereof, escaping into another, shall, in Consequence of any Law or Regulation therein, be discharged from such Service or Labour, but shall be delivered up on Claim of the Party to whom such Service or Labour may be due.

SECTION 3. New States may be admitted by the Congress into this Union; but no new State shall be formed or erected within the Jurisdiction of any other State; nor any State be formed by the Junction of two or more States, or Parts of States, without the Consent of the Legislatures of the States concerned as well as of the Congress.

The Congress shall have Power to dispose of and make all needful Rules and Regulations respecting the Territory or other Property belonging to the United States; and nothing in this Constitution shall be so construed as to Prejudice any Claims of the United States, or of any particular State.

SECTION 4. The United States shall guarantee to every State in this Union a Republican Form of Government, and shall protect each of them against Invasion; and on Application of the Legislature, or of the Executive (when the Legislature cannot be convened) against domestic Violence.

ARTICLE V.

The Congress, whenever two thirds of both Houses shall deem it necessary, shall propose Amendments to this Constitution, or, on the Application of the Legislature of two thirds of the several States, shall call a Convention for proposing Amendments, which, in either Case, shall be valid to all Intents and Purposes, as Part of this Constitution, when ratified by the Legislatures of three fourths of the several States, or by Conventions in three fourths thereof, as the one or the other Mode of Ratification may be proposed by the Congress; Provided that no Amendment which may be made prior to the Year One thousand eight hundred and eight shall in any Manner affect the first and fourth Clauses in the Ninth Section of the first Article; and that no State, without its Consent, shall be deprived of its equal Suffrage in the Senate.

ARTICLE VI.

All Debts contracted and Engagements entered into, before the Adoption of this Constitution, shall be as valid against the United States under this Constitution, as under the Confederation.

This Constitution, and the Laws of the United States which shall be made in Pursuance thereof; and all Treaties made, or which shall be made, under the Authority of the United States, shall be the supreme Law of the Land; and the Judges in every State shall be bound thereby, any Thing in the Constitution or Laws of any State to the Contrary notwithstanding.

The Senators and Representatives before mentioned, and the Members of the several State Legislatures, and all executive and judicial Officers, both of the United States and of the several States, shall be bound by Oath or Affirmation, to support this Constitution; but no religious Test shall ever be required as a Qualification to any Office or public Trust under the United States.

ARTICLE VII.

The Ratification of the Conventions of nine States, shall be sufficient for the establishment of this Constitution between the States so ratifying the Same.

. . .

ARTICLES IN ADDITION TO, AND AMENDMENTS OF, THE CONSTITUTION OF THE UNITED STATES OF AMERICA, PROPOSED BY CONGRESS, AND RATIFIED BY THE SEVERAL STATES, PURSUANT TO THE FIFTH ARTICLE OF THE ORIGINAL CONSTITUTION.

AMENDMENT I[1791]

Congress shall make no law respecting an establishment of religion, or prohibiting the free exercise thereof; or abridging the freedom of speech, or of the press; or the right of the people peaceably to assemble, and to petition the Government for a redress of grievances.

AMENDMENT II[1791]

A well regulated Militia, being necessary to the security of a free State, the right of the people to keep and bear Arms, shall not be infringed.

AMENDMENT III[1791]

No Soldier shall, in time of peace be quartered in any house, without the consent of the Owner, nor in time of war, but in a manner to be prescribed by law.

AMENDMENT IV[1791]

The right of the people to be secure in their persons, houses, papers, and effects, against unreasonable searches and seizures, shall not be violated, and no Warrants shall issue, but upon probable cause, supported by Oath or affirmation, and particularly describing the place to be searched, and the persons or things to be seized.

AMENDMENT V[1791]

No person shall be held to answer for a capital, or otherwise infamous crime, unless on a presentment or indictment of a Grand Jury, except in cases arising in the land or naval forces, or in the Militia, when in actual service in time of War or public danger; nor shall any person be subject for the same offence to be twice put in jeopardy of life or limb; nor shall be compelled in any criminal case to be a witness against himself, nor be deprived of life, liberty, or property, without due process of law; nor shall private property be taken for public use, without just compensation.

AMENDMENT VI[1791]

In all criminal prosecutions, the accused shall enjoy the right to a speedy and public trial, by an impartial jury of the State and district wherein the crime shall have been committed, which district shall have been previously ascertained by law, and to be informed of the nature and cause of the accusation; to be confronted with the witnesses against him; to have compulsory process for obtaining Witnesses in his favor, and to have the Assistance of Counsel for his defence.

AMENDMENT VII[1791]

In Suits at common law, where the value in controversy shall exceed twenty dollars, the right of trial by jury shall be preserved, and no fact tried by a jury be otherwise re-examined in any Court of the United States, than according to the rules of the common law.

AMENDMENT VIII[1791]

Excessive bail shall not be required, nor excessive fines imposed, nor cruel and unusual punishments inflicted.

AMENDMENT IX[1791]

The enumeration in the Constitution, of certain rights, shall not be construed to deny or disparage others retained by the people.

AMENDMENT X[1791]

The powers not delegated to the United States by the Constitution, nor prohibited by it to the States, are reserved to the States respectively, or to the people.

AMENDMENT XI[1798]

The Judicial power of the United States shall not be construed to extend to any suit in law or equity, commenced or prosecuted against one of the United States by Citizens of another State, or by Citizens or Subjects of any Foreign State.

AMENDMENT XII[1804]

The Electors shall meet in their respective states and vote by ballot for President and Vice-President, one of whom, at least, shall not be an inhabitant of the same state with themselves; they shall name in their ballots the person voted for as President, and in distinct ballots the person voted for as Vice-President, and they shall make distinct lists of all persons voted for as President, and of all persons voted for as Vice-President, and of the number of votes for each, which lists they shall sign and certify, and transmit sealed to the seat of the government of the United States, directed to the President of the Senate;—The President of the Senate shall, in the presence of the Senate and House of Representatives, open all the certificates and the votes shall then be counted;—The person having the greatest number of votes for President, shall be the President, if such number be a majority of the whole number of Electors appointed; and if no person have such majority, then from the persons having the highest numbers not exceeding three on the list of those voted for as President, the House of Representatives shall choose immediately, by ballot, the President. But in choosing the President, the votes shall be taken by states, the representation from each state having one vote; a quorum for this purpose shall consist of a member or members from two-thirds of the states, and a majority of all the states shall be necessary to a choice. And if the House of Representatives shall not choose a President whenever the right of choice shall devolve upon them, before the fourth day of March next following, then the Vice-President shall act as President, as in the case of the death or other constitutional disability of the President—The person having the greatest number of votes as Vice-President, shall be the Vice-President, if such number be a majority of the whole number of Electors appointed, and if no person have a majority, then from the two highest numbers on the list, the Senate shall choose the Vice-President; a quorum for the purpose shall consist of two-thirds of the whole number of Senators, and a majority of the whole number shall be necessary to a choice. But no person constitutionally ineligible to the office of President shall be eligible to that of Vice-President of the United States.

AMENDMENT XIII[1865]

SECTION 1. Neither slavery no involuntary servitude, except as a punishment for crime whereof the party shall have been duly convicted, shall exist within the United States, or any place subject to their jurisdiction.

SECTION 2. Congress shall have power to enforce this article by appropriate legislation.

AMENDMENT XIV[1868]

SECTION 1. All persons born or naturalized in the United States and subject to the jurisdiction thereof, are citizens of the United States and of the State wherein they reside. No State shall make or enforce any law which shall abridge the privileges or immunities of citizens of the United States; nor shall any State deprive any person of life, liberty, or property, without due process of law; nor deny to any person within its jurisdiction the equal protection of the laws.

SECTION 2. Representatives shall be apportioned among the several States according to their respective numbers, counting the whole number of persons in each State, excluding Indians not taxed. But when the right to vote at any election for the choice of electors for President and Vice President of the United States, Representatives in Congress, the Executive and Judicial officers of a State, or the members of the Legislature thereof, is denied to any of the male inhabitants of such State, being twenty-one years of age, and citizens of the United States, or in any way abridged, except for participation in rebellion, or other crime, the basis of representation therein shall be reduced in the proportion which the number of such male citizens shall bear to the whole number of male citizens twenty-one years of age in such State.

SECTION 3. No person shall be a Senator or Representative in Congress, or elector of President and Vice President, or hold any office, civil or military, under the United States, or under any State, who, having previously taken an oath, as a member of Congress, or as a member of any State legislature, or as an executive or judicial officer of any State, to support the Constitution of the United States, shall have engaged in insurrection or rebellion against the same, or given aid or comfort to the enemies thereof. But Congress may by a vote of two-thirds of each House, remove such disability.

SECTION 4. The validity of the public debt of the United States, authorized by law, including debts incurred for payment of pensions and bounties for services in suppressing insurrection or rebellion, shall not be questioned. But neither the United States nor any State shall assume or pay any debt or obligation incurred in aid of insurrection or rebellion against the United States, or any claim for the loss or emancipation of any slave; but all such debts, obligations and claims shall be held illegal and void.

SECTION 5. The Congress shall have power to enforce, by appropriate legislation, the provisions of this article.

AMENDMENT XV[1870]

SECTION 1. The right of citizens of the United States to vote shall not be denied or abridged by the United States or by any State on account of race, color, or previous condition of servitude.

SECTION 2. The Congress shall have power to enforce this article by appropriate legislation.

AMENDMENT XVI[1913]

The Congress shall have power to lay and collect taxes on incomes, from whatever source derived, without apportionment among the several States, and without regard to any census or enumeration.

AMENDMENT XVII[1913]

The Senate of the United States shall be composed of two Senators from each State, elected by the people thereof, for six years; and each Senator shall have one vote. The electors in each State shall have the qualifications requisite for electors of the most numerous branch of the State legislatures.

When vacancies happen in the representation of any State in the Senate, the executive authority of such State shall issue writs of election to fill such vacancies: *Provided,* That the legislature of any State may empower the executive thereof to make temporary appointments until the people fill the vacancies by election as the legislature may direct.

This amendment shall not be so construed as to affect the election or term of any Senator chosen before it becomes valid as part of the Constitution.

AMENDMENT XVIII[1919]

SECTION 1. After one year from the ratification of this article the manufacture, sale, or transportation of intoxicating liquors within, the importation thereof into, or the exportation thereof from the United States and all territory subject to the jurisdiction thereof for beverage purposes is hereby prohibited.

SECTION 2. The Congress and the several States shall have concurrent power to enforce this article by appropriate legislation.

SECTION 3. This article shall be inoperative unless it shall have been ratified as an amendment to the Constitution by the legislatures of the several States, as provided in the Constitution, within seven years from the date of the submission hereof to the States by the Congress.

AMENDMENT XIX[1920]

The right of citizens of the United States to vote shall not be denied or abridged by the United States or by any State on account of sex.

Congress shall have power to enforce this article by appropriate legislation.

AMENDMENT XX[1933]

SECTION 1. The terms of the President and Vice President shall end at noon on the 20th day of January, and the terms of Senators and Representatives at noon on the 3d day of January, of the years in which such terms would have ended if this article had not been ratified; and the terms of their successors shall then begin.

SECTION 2. The Congress shall assemble at least once in every year, and such meeting shall begin at noon on the 3d day of January, unless they shall by law appoint a different day.

SECTION 3. If, at the time fixed for the beginning of the term of the President, the President elect shall have died, the Vice President elect shall become President. If a President shall not have been chosen before the time fixed for the beginning of his term, or if the President elect shall have failed to qualify, then the Vice President elect shall act as President until a President shall have qualified; and the Congress may by law provide for the case wherein neither a President elect nor a Vice President elect shall have qualified, declaring who shall then act as President, or the manner in which one who is to act shall be selected, and such person shall act accordingly until a President or Vice President shall have qualified.

SECTION 4. The Congress may by law provide for the case of the death of any of the persons from whom the House of Representatives may choose a President whenever the right of choice shall have devolved upon them, and for the case of the death of any of the persons from whom the Senate may choose a Vice President whenever the right of choice shall have devolved upon them.

SECTION 5. Sections 1 and 2 shall take effect on the 15th day of October following the ratification of this article.

SECTION 6. This article shall be inoperative unless it shall have been ratified as an amendment to the Constitution by the legislatures of three-fourths of the several States within seven years from the date of its submission.

AMENDMENT XXI[1933]

SECTION 1. The eighteenth article of amendment to the Constitution of the United States is hereby repealed.

SECTION 2. The transportation or importation into any State, Territory, or possession of the United States for delivery or use therein of intoxicating liquors, in violation of the laws thereof, is hereby prohibited.

SECTION 3. This article shall be inoperative unless it shall have been ratified as an amendment to the Constitution by conventions in the several States, as provided in the Constitution, within seven years from the date of the submission hereof to the States by the Congress.

AMENDMENT XXII[1951]

SECTION 1. No person shall be elected to the office of the President more than twice, and no person who has held the office of President, or acted as President, for more than two years of a term to which some other person was elected President shall be elected to the office of the President more than once. But this Aritcle shall not apply to any person holding the office of President when this Article was proposed by the Congress, and shall not prevent any person who may be holding the office of President, or acting as President, during the term within which this Article becomes operative from holding the office of President or acting as President during the remainder of such term.

SECTION 2. This article shall be inoperative unless it shall have been ratified as an amendment to the Constitution by the legislatures of three-fourths of the several States within seven years from the date of its submission to the States by the Congress.

AMENDMENT XXIII[1961]

SECTION 1. The District constituting the seat of Government of the United States shall appoint in such manner as the Congress may direct:

A number of electors of President and Vice President equal to the whole number of Senators and Representatives in Congress to which the District would be entitled if it were a State, but in no event more than the least populous State; they shall be in addition to those appointed by the States, but they shall be considered, for the purposes of the election of President and Vice President, to be electors appointed by a State; and they shall meet in the District and perform such duties as provided by the twelfth article of amendment.

SECTION 2. The Congress shall have power to enforce this article by appropriate legislation.

AMENDMENT XXIV[1964]

SECTION 1. The right of citizens of the United States to vote in any primary or other election for President or Vice President, for electors for President or Vice President, or for Senator or Representative in Congress, shall not be denied or abridged by the United States or any State by reason of failure to pay any poll or other tax.

SECTION 2. The Congress shall have power to enforce this article by appropriate legislation.

AMENDMENT XXV[1967]

SECTION 1. In case of the removal of the President from office or of his death or resignation, the Vice President shall become President.

SECTION 2. Whenever there is a vacancy in the office of the Vice President, the President shall nominate a Vice President who shall take office upon confirmation by a majority vote of both Houses of Congress.

SECTION 3. Whenever the President transmits to the President pro tempore of the Senate and the Speaker of the House of Representatives his written declaration that he is unable to discharge the powers and duties of his office, and until he transmits to them a written declaration to the contrary, such powers and duties shall be discharged by the Vice President as Acting President.

SECTION 4. Whenever the Vice President and a majority of either the principal officers of the executive department or of such other body as Congress may by law provide, transmit to the President pro tempore of the Senate and the Speaker of the House of Representatives their written declaration that the President is unable to discharge the powers and duties of his office, the Vice President shall immediately assume the powers and duties of the office as Acting President.

Thereafter, when the President transmits to the President pro tempore of the Senate and the Speaker of the House of Representatives his written declaration that no inability exists, he shall resume the powers and duties of his office unless the Vice President and a majority of either the principal officers of the executive department or of such other body as Congress may by law provide, transmit within four days to the President pro tempore of the Senate and the Speaker of the House of Representatives their written declaration that the President is unable to discharge the powers and duties of his office. Thereupon Congress shall decide the issue, assembling within forty-eight hours for that purpose if not in session. If the Congress, within twenty-one days after receipt of the latter written declaration, or, if Congress is not in session, within twenty-one days after Congress is required to assemble, determines by two-thirds vote of both Houses that the President is unable to discharge the powers and duties of his office, the Vice President shall continue to discharge the same as Acting President; otherwise, the President shall resume the powers and duties of his office.

AMENDMENT XXVI[1971]

SECTION 1. The right of citizens of the United States, who are eighteen years of age or older, to vote shall not be denied or abridged by the United States or by any State on account of age.

SECTION 2. The Congress shall have power to enforce this article by appropriate legislation.

Appendix B

COMMUNICATIONS ACT OF 1934

48 Stat. 1064 (1934), as amended, 47 U.S.C.A. § 151 et seq.

TITLE I—GENERAL PROVISIONS

PURPOSES OF ACT; CREATION OF FEDERAL COMMUNICATIONS COMMISSION

Sec. 1. [47 U.S.C.A. § 151.]

For the purpose of regulating interstate and foreign commerce in communication by wire and radio so as to make available, so far as possible, to all the people of the United States a rapid, efficient, Nation-wide, and world-wide wire and radio communication service with adequate facilities at reasonable charges, for the purpose of the national defense, for the purpose of promoting safety of life and property through the use of wire and radio communication, and for the purpose of securing a more effective execution of this policy by centralizing authority heretofore granted by law to several agencies and by granting additional authority with respect to interstate and foreign commerce in wire and radio communication, there is hereby created a commission to be known as the "Federal Communications Commission," which shall be constituted as hereinafter provided, and which shall execute and enforce the provisions of this Act.

. . .

APPLICATION OF ACT

Sec. 2. [47 U.S.C.A. § 152.]

(a) The provisions of this Act shall apply to all interstate and foreign communication by wire or radio and all interstate and foreign transmission of energy by radio, which originates and/or is received within the United States, and to all persons engaged within the United States in such communication or such transmission of energy by radio, and to the licensing and regulating of all radio stations as hereinafter provided . . . .. The provisions of this Act shall apply with respect to cable service to all persons engaged within the United States in providing such service, and to the facilities of cable operators which relate to such service as provided in title VI.

. . .

677

TITLE III—PROVISIONS RELATING TO RADIO

LICENSE FOR RADIO COMMUNICATION OR TRANSMISSION OF ENERGY

Sec. 301. [47 U.S.C.A. § 301.]

It is the purpose of this Act, among other things, to maintain the control of the United States over all the channels of interstate and foreign radio transmission; and to provide for the use of such channels, but not the ownership thereof, by persons for limited periods of time, under licenses granted by Federal authority, and no such license shall be construed to create any right, beyond the terms, conditions, and periods of the license. No person shall use or operate any apparatus for the transmission of energy or communications or signals by radio (a) from one place in any Territory or possession of the United States or in the District of Columbia to another place in the same Territory, possession, or district; or (b) from any State, Territory, or possession of the United States, or from the District of Columbia to any other State, Territory, or possession of the United States; or (c) from any place in any State, Territory, or possession of the United States, or in the District of Columbia, to any place in any foreign country or to any vessel; or (d) within any State when the effects of such use extend beyond the borders of said State, or when interference is caused by such use or operation with the transmission of such energy, communications, or signals from within said State to any place beyond its borders, or from any place beyond its borders to any place within said State, or with the transmission or reception of such energy, communications, or signals from and/or to places beyond the borders of said State; or (e) upon any vessel or aircraft of the United States; or (f) upon any other mobile stations within the jurisdiction of the United States, except under and in accordance with this Act and with a license in that behalf granted under the provisions of this Act.

.   .   .

GENERAL POWERS OF THE COMMISSION

Sec. 303. [47 U.S.C.A. § 303.]

Except as otherwise provided in this Act, the Commission from time to time, as public convenience, interest, or necessity requires shall:

(a) Classify radio stations;

(b) Prescribe the nature of the service to be rendered by each class of licensed stations and each station within any class;

(c) Assign bands of frequencies to the various classes of stations, and assign frequencies for each individual station and determine the power which each station shall use and the time during which it may operate;

(d) Determine the location of classes of stations or individual stations;

(e) Regulate the kind of apparatus to be used with respect to its external effects and the purity and sharpness of the emissions from each station and from the apparatus therein;

(f) Make such regulations not inconsistent with law as it may deem necessary to prevent interference between stations and to carry out the provisions of this Act: *Provided, however,* That changes in the frequencies, authorized power, or in the times of operation of any station, shall not be made without the consent of the station licensee unless, after a public hearing, the Commission shall determine that such changes will promote public convenience or interest or will serve public necessity, or the provisions of this Act will be more fully complied with;

(g) Study new uses for radio, provide for experimental uses of frequencies, and generally encourage the larger and more effective use of radio in the public interest;

(h) Have authority to establish areas or zones to be served by any station;

(i) Have authority to make special regulations applicable to radio stations engaged in chain broadcasting;

(j) Have authority to make general rules and regulations requiring stations to keep such records of programs, transmissions of energy, communications, or signals as it may deem desirable;

. . .

(m)(1) Have authority to suspend the license of any operator upon proof sufficient to satisfy the Commission that the licensee—

(A) has violated any provision of any Act, treaty, or convention binding on the United States, which the Commission is authorized to administer, or any regulation made by the Commission under any such Act, treaty, or convention; or

. . .

(D) has transmitted superfluous radio communications or signals or communications containing profane or obscene words, language, or meaning. . . .

. . .

(r) Make such rules and regulations and prescribe such restrictions and conditions, not inconsistent with law, as may be necessary to carry out the provisions of this Act, or any international radio or wire communications treaty or convention, or regulations annexed thereto, including any treaty or convention insofar as it relates to the use of radio, to which the United States is or may hereafter become a party.

(s) Have authority to require that apparatus designed to receive television pictures broadcast simultaneously with sound be capable of adequately receiving all frequencies allocated by the Commission to television broadcasting when such apparatus is shipped in interstate commerce, or is imported from any foreign country into the United States, for sale or resale to the public.

. . .

ALLOCATION OF FACILITIES; TERM OF LICENSES

Sec. 307. [47 U.S.C.A. § 307.]

(a) The Commission, if public convenience, interest, or necessity will be served thereby, subject to the limitations of this Act, shall grant to any applicant therefor a station license provided for by this Act.

(b) In considering applications for licenses, and modifications and renewals thereof, when and insofar as there is demand for the same, the Commission shall make such distribution of licenses, frequencies, hours of operation, and of power among the several States and communities as to provide a fair, efficient, and equitable distribution of radio service to each of the same.

. . .

(d) No license granted for the operation of a television broadcasting station shall be for a term longer than five years . . . and any license granted may be revoked as hereinafter provided. Each license granted for the operation of a radio broadcasting station shall be for a term of not to exceed seven years. Upon the expiration of any license, upon application therefor, a renewal of such license may be granted from time to time for a term of not to exceed five years in the case of television broadcasting licenses, for a term of not to exceed seven years in the case of radio broadcasting station licenses, and for a term of not to exceed five years in the case of other licenses, if the Commission finds that public interest, convenience, and necessity would be served thereby. . . .

(e) No renewal of an existing station license in the broadcast or the common carrier services shall be granted more than thirty days prior to the expiration of the original license.

APPLICATIONS FOR LICENSES . . .

Sec. 308. [47 U.S.C.A. § 308.]

. . .

(b) All applications for station licenses, or modifications or renewals thereof, shall set forth such facts as the Commission by regulation may prescribe as to the citizenship, character, and financial, technical, and other qualifications of the applicant to operate the station; the ownership and location of the proposed station and of the stations, if any, with which it is proposed to communicate; the frequencies and the power desired to be used; the hours of the day or other periods of time during which it is proposed to operate the station; the purposes for which the station is to be used; and such other information as it may require. . . .

. . .

ACTION UPON APPLICATIONS; FORM OF AND CONDITIONS ATTACHED TO LICENSES

Sec. 309. [47 U.S.C.A. § 309.]

(a) Subject to the provisions of this section, the Commission shall determine, in the case of each application filed with it to which section 308 applies, whether the public interest, convenience, and necessity will be served by the granting of such application, and, if the Commission, upon examination of such application and upon consideration of such other matters as the Commission may officially notice, shall find that public interest, convenience, and necessity would be served by the granting thereof, it shall grant such application.

. . .

(d)(1) Any party in interest may file with the Commission a petition to deny any application . . . .

(2) If the Commission finds on the basis of the application, the pleadings filed, or other matters which it may officially notice that there are no substantial and material questions of fact and that a grant of the application would be consistent with subsection (a), it shall make the grant, deny the petition, and issue a concise statement of the reasons for denying the petition, which statement shall dispose of all substantial issues raised by the petition. If a substantial and material question of fact is presented or if the Commission for any reason is unable to find that grant of the application would be consistent with subsection (a), it shall proceed as provided in subsection (e).

(e) If, in the case of any application to which subsection (a) of this section applies, a substantial and material question of fact is presented or the Commission for any reason is unable to make the finding specified in such subsection, it shall formally designate the application for hearing on the ground or reasons then obtaining and shall forthwith notify the applicant and all other known parties in interest of such action and the grounds and reasons therefor, specifying with particularity the matters and things in issue but not including issues or requirements phrased generally. . . .

. . . .

(h) Such station licenses as the Commission may grant shall be in such general form as it may prescribe, but each license shall contain, in addition to other provisions, a statement of the following conditions to which such license shall be subject: (1) The station license shall not vest in the licensee any right to operate the station nor any right in the use of the frequencies designated in the license beyond the term thereof nor in any other manner than authorized therein; (2) neither the license nor the right granted thereunder shall be assigned or otherwise transferred in violation of this Act; (3) every license issued under this Act shall be subject in terms to the right of use or control conferred by section 606 of this Act.*

. . .

LIMITATION ON HOLDING AND TRANSFER OF LICENSES

Sec. 310. [47 U.S.C.A. § 310.]

(a) The station license required hereby shall not be granted to or held by any foreign government or representative thereof.

(b) No broadcast or common carrier . . . license shall be granted to or held by—

(1) Any alien or the representative of any alien;

(2) Any corporation organized under the laws of any foreign government;

. . .

(d) No construction permit or station license, or any rights thereunder, shall be transferred, assigned, or disposed of in any manner, voluntarily or involuntarily, directly or indirectly, or by transfer of control of any corporation holding such permit or license, to any person except upon application to the Commission and upon finding by the Commission that the public interest, convenience, and necessity will be served thereby. Any such application shall be disposed of as if the proposed transferee or assignee were making application under section 308 for the permit or license in question; but in acting thereon the Commission may not consider whether the public interest, convenience, and necessity might be served by the transfer, assignment, or disposal of the permit or license to a person other than the proposed transferee or assignee.

SPECIAL REQUIREMENTS WITH RESPECT TO CERTAIN APPLICATIONS IN THE BROADCASTING SERVICE

Sec. 311. [47 U.S.C.A. § 311.]

. . .

(c)(1) If there are pending before the Commission two or more applications for a permit for construction of a broadcasting station,

---

* [Section 606 grants substantial powers to the President to utilize communications facilities during wartime or a national emergency.]

only one of which can be granted, it shall be unlawful, without approval of the Commission, for the applicants or any of them to effectuate an agreement whereby one or more of such applicants withdraws his or their application or applications.

(2) The request for Commission approval in any such case shall be made in writing jointly by all the parties to the agreement. Such request shall contain or be accompanied by full information with respect to the agreement, set forth in such detail, form, and manner as the Commission shall by rule require.

(3) The Commission shall approve the agreement only if it determines (A) that the agreement is consistent with the public interest, convenience, or necessity; and (B) no party to the agreement filed its application for the purpose of reaching or carrying out such agreement. If the agreement does not contemplate a merger, but contemplates the making of any direct or indirect payment to any party thereto in consideration of his withdrawal of his application, the Commission may determine the agreement to be consistent with the public interest, convenience, or necessity only if the amount or value of such payment, as determined by the Commission, is not in excess of the aggregate amount determined by the Commission to have been legitimately and prudently expended and to be expended by such applicant in connection with preparing, filing, and advocating the granting of his application.

. . .

ADMINISTRATIVE SANCTIONS

Sec. 312. [47 U.S.C.A. § 312.]

(a) The Commission may revoke any station license or construction permit—

(1) for false statements knowingly made either in the application or in any statement of fact which may be required pursuant to section 308;

(2) because of conditions coming to the attention of the Commission which would warrant it in refusing to grant a license or permit on an original application;

(3) for willful or repeated failure to operate substantially as set forth in the license;

(4) for willful or repeated violation of, or willful or repeated failure to observe any provision of this Act or any rule or regulation of the Commission authorized by this Act or by a treaty ratified by the United States;

(5) for violation of or failure to observe any final cease and desist order issued by the Commission under this section;

(6) for violation of section 1304, 1343, or 1464 of title 18 of the United States Code; * or

(7) for willful or repeated failure to allow reasonable access to or to permit purchase of reasonable amounts of time for the use of a broadcasting station by a legally qualified candidate for Federal elective office on behalf of his candidacy.

(b) Where any person (1) has failed to operate substantially as set forth in a license, (2) has violated or failed to observe any of the provisions of this Act, or section 1304, 1343, or 1464 of title 18 of the United States Code, or (3) has violated or failed to observe any rule or regulation of the Commission authorized by this Act or by a treaty ratified by the United States, the Commission may order such person to cease and desist from such action.

(c) Before revoking a license or permit pursuant to subsection (a), or issuing a cease and desist order pursuant to subsection (b), the Commission shall serve upon the licensee, permittee, or person involved an order to show cause [at a hearing] why an order of revocation or a cease and desist order should not be issued. . . .

(d) In any case where a hearing is conducted pursuant to the provisions of this section, both the burden of proceeding with the introduction of evidence and the burden of proof shall be upon the Commission.

. . .

* [Relevant provisions read as follows:

§ 1304. Broadcasting lottery information

Whoever broadcasts by means of any radio station for which a license is required by any law of the United States, or whoever, operating any such station, knowingly permits the broadcasting of, any advertisement of or information concerning any lottery, gift enterprise, or similar scheme, offering prizes dependent in whole or in part upon lot or chance, or any list of the prizes drawn or awarded by means of any such lottery, gift enterprise, or scheme, whether said list contains any part or all of such prizes, shall be fined not more than $1,000 or imprisoned not more than one year, or both.

Each day's broadcasting shall constitute a separate offense.

§ 1343. Fraud by wire, radio, or television

Whoever, having devised or intending to devise any scheme or artifice to defraud, or for obtaining money or property by means of false or fraudulent pretenses, representations, or promises, transmits or causes to be transmitted by means of wire, radio, or television communication in interstate or foreign commerce, any writings, signs, signals, pictures, or sounds for the purpose of executing such scheme or artifice, shall be fined not more than $1,000 or imprisoned not more than five years, or both.

§ 1464. Broadcasting obscene language

Whoever utters any obscene, indecent, or profane language by means of radio communications shall be fined not more than $10,000 or imprisoned not more than two years, or both.

§ 1307. State-conducted lotteries

(a) The provisions of sections 1301, 1302, 1303, and 1304 shall not apply to an advertisement, list of prizes, or information concerning a lottery conducted by a State acting under the authority of State law—

(1) contained in a newspaper published in that State, or

(2) broadcast by a radio or television station licensed to a location in that State or an adjacent State which conducts such a lottery. . . .]

APPLICATION OF ANTITRUST LAWS; REFUSAL OF LICENSES AND PERMITS IN CERTAIN CASES

Sec. 313.   [47 U.S.C.A. § 313.]

(a) All laws of the United States relating to unlawful restraints and monopolies and to combinations, contracts, or agreements in restraint of trade are hereby declared to be applicable to the manufacture and sale of and to trade in radio apparatus and devices entering into or affecting interstate or foreign commerce and to interstate or foreign radio communications. Whenever in any suit, action, or proceeding, civil or criminal, brought under the provisions of any of said laws or in any proceedings brought to enforce or to review findings and orders of the Federal Trade Commission or other governmental agency in respect of any matters as to which said Commission or other governmental agency is by law authorized to act, any licensee shall be found guilty of the violation of the provisions of such laws or any of them, the court, in addition to the penalties imposed by said laws, may adjudge, order, and/or decree that the license of such licensee shall, as of the date the decree or judgment becomes finally effective or as of such other date as the said decree shall fix, be revoked and that all rights under such license shall thereupon cease: *Provided, however,* That such licensee shall have the same right of appeal or review, as is provided by law in respect of other decrees and judgments of said court.

(b) The Commission is hereby directed to refuse a station license and/or the permit hereinafter required for the construction of a station to any person (or to any person directly or indirectly controlled by such person) whose license has been revoked by a court under this section.

. . .

FACILITIES FOR CANDIDATES FOR PUBLIC OFFICE

Sec. 315.   [47 U.S.C.A. § 315.]

(a) If any licensee shall permit any person who is a legally qualified candidate for any public office to use a broadcasting station, he shall afford equal opportunities to all other such candidates for that office in the use of such broadcasting station: *Provided,* That such licensee shall have no power of censorship over the material broadcast under the provisions of this section. No obligation is imposed under this subsection upon any licensee to allow the use of its station by any such candidate. Appearance by a legally qualified candidate on any—

(1) Bona fide newscast,

(2) Bona fide news interview,

(3) Bona fide news documentary (if the appearance of the candidate is incidental to the presentation of the subject or subjects covered by the news documentary), or

(4) On-the-spot coverage of bona fide news events (included but not limited to political conventions and activities incidental thereto), shall not be deemed to be use of a broadcasting station within the meaning of this subsection. Nothing in the foregoing sentence shall be construed as relieving broadcasters, in connection with the presentation of newscasts, news interviews, news documentaries, and on-the-spot coverage of news events, from the obligation imposed upon them under this Act to operate in the public interest and to afford reasonable opportunity for the discussion of conflicting views on issues of public importance.

(b) The charges made for the use of any broadcast station by any person who is a legally qualified candidate for any public office in connection with his campaign for nomination for election, or election, to such office shall not exceed—

(1) During the 45 days preceding the date of a primary or primary runoff election and during the 60 days preceding the date of a general or special election in which such person is a candidate, the lowest unit charge of the station for the same class and amount of time for the same period; and

(2) At any other time, the charges made for comparable use of such station by other users thereof.

(c) For the purposes of this section:

(1) The term "broadcasting station" includes a community antenna television system.

(2) The terms "licensee" and "station licensee" when used with respect to a community antenna television system, mean the operator of such system.

(d) The Commission shall prescribe appropriate rules and regulations to carry out the provisions of this section.

MODIFICATION BY COMMISSION OF CONSTRUCTION PERMITS OR LICENSES

Sec. 316. [47 U.S.C.A. § 316.]

(a) Any station license or construction permit may be modified by the Commission either for a limited time or for the duration of the term thereof, if in the judgment of the Commission such action will promote the public interest, convenience, and necessity, or the provisions of this Act or of any treaty ratified by the United States will be more fully complied with. No such order of modification shall become final until the holder of the license or permit shall have been notified in writing of the proposed action and the grounds and reasons therefor, and shall have been given reasonable opportunity, in no event less than thirty days, to show cause by public hearing, if requested, why such order of modification should not issue . . . ..

(b) In any case where a hearing is conducted pursuant to the provisions of this section, both the burden of proceeding with the introduction of evidence and the burden of proof shall be upon the Commission.

ANNOUNCEMENT WITH RESPECT TO CERTAIN MATTER BROADCAST

Sec. 317. [47 U.S.C.A. § 317.]

(a)(1) All matter broadcast by any radio station for which any money, service or other valuable consideration is directly or indirectly paid, or promised to or charged or accepted by, the station so broadcasting, from any person, shall, at the time the same is so broadcast, be announced as paid for or furnished, as the case may be, by such person: *Provided,* That "service or other valuable consideration" shall not include any service or property furnished without charge or at a nominal charge for use on, or in connection with, a broadcast unless it is so furnished in consideration for an identification in a broadcast of any person, product, service, trademark, or brand name beyond an identification which is reasonably related to the use of such service or property on the broadcast.

. . .

FALSE DISTRESS SIGNALS; REBROADCASTING . . .

Sec. 325. [47 U.S.C.A. § 325.]

(a) No person within the jurisdiction of the United States shall knowingly utter or transmit, or cause to be uttered or transmitted, any false or fraudulent signal of distress, or communication relating thereto, nor shall any broadcasting station rebroadcast the program or any part thereof of another broadcasting station without the express authority of the originating station.

. . .

CENSORSHIP . . .

Sec. 326. [47 U.S.C.A. § 326.]

Nothing in this Act shall be understood or construed to give the Commission the power of censorship over the radio communications or signals transmitted by any radio station, and no regulation or condition shall be promulgated or fixed by the Commission which shall interfere with the right of free speech by means of radio communication.

PROHIBITION AGAINST SHIPMENT OF CERTAIN TELEVISION RECEIVERS

Sec. 330. [47 U.S.C.A. § 330.]

(a) No person shall ship in interstate commerce, or import from any foreign country into the United States, for sale or resale to the public, apparatus described in paragraph (s) of section 303 unless it complies with rules prescribed by the Commission pursuant to the authority granted by that paragraph: *Provided,* That this section shall not apply to carriers transporting such apparatus without trading in it.

. . .

TITLE V—PENAL PROVISIONS—FORFEITURES

FORFEITURES

Sec. 503. [47 U.S.C.A. § 503.]

. . .

(b)(1) Any person who is determined by the Commission, in accordance with paragraph (3) or (4) of this subsection, to have—

(A) willfully or repeatedly failed to comply substantially with the terms and conditions of any license, permit, certificate, or other instrument or authorization issued by the Commission;

(B) willfully or repeatedly failed to comply with any of the provisions of this Act or of any rule, regulation, or order issued by the Commission under this Act or under any treaty convention, or other agreement to which the United States is a party and which is binding upon the United States;

(C) violated any provision of section 317(c) or 509(a) of this Act; or

(D) violated any provision of sections 1304, 1343, or 1464 of Title 18, United States Code;

shall be liable to the United States for a forfeiture penalty. A forfeiture penalty under this subsection shall be in addition to any other penalty provided for by this Act; except that this subsection shall not apply to any conduct which is subject to forfeiture under . . . section 507 of this Act.

(2) The amount of any forfeiture penalty determined under this subsection shall not exceed $2,000 for each violation. Each day of a continuing violation shall constitute a separate offense, but the total forfeiture penalty which may be imposed under this subsection, for acts or omissions described in paragraph (1) of this subsection and set forth in the notice or the notice of apparent liability issued under this subsection, shall not exceed:

(A) $20,000, if the violator is (i) a common carrier subject to the provisions of this Act, (ii) a broadcast station licensee or permittee, or (iii) a cable television operator; or

(B) $5,000, in any case not covered by subparagraph (A).

The amount of such forfeiture penalty shall be assessed by the Commission, or its designee, by written notice. In determining the amount of such a forfeiture penalty, the Commission or its designee shall take into account the nature, circumstances, extent, and gravity of the prohibited acts committed and, with respect to the violator, the degree of culpability, any history of prior offenses, ability to pay, and such other matters as justice may require.

. . .

PROHIBITED PRACTICES IN CASES OF CONTESTS OF INTELLECTUAL KNOWLEDGE, INTELLECTUAL SKILL OR CHANCE

Sec. 509. [47 U.S.C.A. § 509.]

(a) It shall be unlawful for any person, with intent to deceive the listening or viewing public—

(1) To supply to any contestant in a purportedly bona fide contest of intellectual knowledge or intellectual skill any special and secret assistance whereby the outcome of such contest will be in whole or in part prearranged or predetermined.

(2) By means of persuasion, bribery, intimidation, or otherwise, to induce or cause any contestant in a purportedly bona fide contest of intellectual knowledge or intellectual skill to refrain in any manner from using or displaying his knowledge or skill in such contest, whereby the outcome thereof will be in whole or in part prearranged or predetermined.

. . .

TITLE VI—CABLE COMMUNICATIONS

PURPOSES

Sec. 601. [47 U.S.C.A. § 601.]

The purposes of this title are to

(1) establish a national policy concerning cable communications;

(2) establish franchise procedures and standards which encourage the growth and development of cable systems and which assure that cable systems are responsive to the needs and interests of the local community;

(3) establish guidelines for the exercise of Federal, State, and local authority with respect to the regulation of cable systems;

(4) assure and encourage that cable communications provide and are encouraged to provide the widest possible diversity of information sources and services to the public.

(5) establish an orderly process for franchise renewal which protects cable operators against unfair denials of renewal where the operator's past performance and proposal for future performance meet the standards established by this title; and

(6) promote competition in cable communications and minimize unnecessary regulation that would impose an undue economic burden on cable systems.

. . .

CABLE CHANNELS FOR PUBLIC, EDUCATIONAL OR GOVERNMENTAL USE

Sec. 611. [47 U.S.C.A. § 611.]

(a) A franchising authority may establish requirements in a franchise with respect to the designation or use of channel capacity for public, educational, or governmental use only to the extent provided in this section.

(b) A franchising authority may in its request for proposals require as part of a franchise, and may require as part of a cable operator's proposal for a franchise renewal, subject to section 626, that channel capacity be designated for public, educational, or governmental use, . . .

(c) A franchising authority may enforce any requirement in any franchise regarding the providing or use of such channel capacity. Such enforcement authority includes the authority to enforce any provisions of the franchise for services, facilities, or equipment proposed by the cable operator, which relate to public, educational, or governmental use of channel capacity, whether or not required by the franchising authority pursuant to subsection (b).

. . .

(e) Subject to section 624(d), a cable operator shall not exercise any editorial control over any public, educational, or governmental use of channel capacity provided pursuant to this section.

. . .

GENERAL FRANCHISE REQUIREMENTS

Sec. 621. [47 U.S.C.A. § 621.]

(a)(1) A franchising authority may award, in accordance with the provisions of this title, one or more franchises within its jurisdiction.

. . .

(3) In awarding a franchise or franchises, a franchising authority shall assure that access to cable service is not denied to any group of potential residential cable subscribers because of

the income of the residents of the local area in which such group resides.

. . .

(c) Any cable system shall not be subject to regulation as a common carrier or utility by reason of providing any cable service.

. . .

FRANCHISE FEES

Sec. 622.   [47 U.S.C.A. § 622.]

(a) Subject to the limitation of subsection (b), any cable operator may be required under the terms of any franchise to pay a franchise fee.

(b) For any 12-month period, the franchise fees paid by a cable operator with respect to any cable system shall not exceed 5 percent of such cable operator's gross revenues derived in such period from the operation of the cable system.

. . .

REGULATION OF RATES

Sec. 623.   [47 U.S.C.A. § 623.]

(a) Any Federal agency or State may not regulate the rates for the provision of cable service except to cable subscribers only to the extent provided under this section. Any franchising authority may regulate the rates for the provision of cable service or any other communications service provided over a cable system to cable subscribers, but only to the extent provided under this section.

(b)(1) Within 180 days after the date of the enactment of this title, the Commission shall prescribe and make effective regulations which authorize a franchising authority to regulate rates for the provision of basic cable service in circumstances in which a cable system is not subject to effective competition. Such regulations may apply to any franchise granted after the effective date of such regulations. Such regulations shall not apply to any rate while such rate is subject to the provisions of subsection (c).

(2) For purposes of rate regulation under this subsection, such regulations shall—

(A) define the circumstances in which a cable system is not subject to effective competition; and

(B) establish standards for such rate regulation.

. . .

(c) In the case of any cable system for which a franchise has been granted on or before the effective date of this title, until the end of the 2-year period beginning on such effective date, the franchising authority may, to the extent provided in a franchise—

(1) regulate the rates for the provision of basic cable service, including multiple tiers of basic cable service;

(2) require the provision of any service tier provided without charge (disregarding any installation or rental charge for equipment necessary for receipt of such tier); or

(3) regulate rates for the initial installation or the rental of one set of the minimum equipment which is necessary for the subscriber's receipt of basic cable service.

.   .   .

RENEWAL

Sec. 626.   [47 U.S.C.A. § 626.]

(a) During the 6-month period which begins with the 36th month before the franchise expiration, the franchising authority may on its own initiative, and shall at the request of the cable operator, commence proceedings which afford the public in the franchise area appropriate notice and participation for the purpose of—

(1) identifying the future cable-related community needs and interests; and

(2) reviewing the performance of the cable operator under the franchise during the then current franchise term.

(b)(1) Upon completion of a proceeding under subsection (a), a cable operator seeking renewal of a franchise may, on its own initiative or at the request of a franchising authority, submit a proposal for renewal.

(2) Subject to section 624, any such proposal shall contain such material as the franchising authority may require, including proposals for an upgrade of the cable system.

(3) The franchising authority may establish a date by which such proposals shall be submitted.

(c)(1) Upon submittal by a cable operator of a proposal to the franchising authority for the renewal of a franchise, the franchising authority shall provide prompt public notice of such proposal and, during the 4-month period which begins on the completion of any proceedings under subsection (a), renew the franchise or, issue a preliminary assessment that the franchise should not be renewed and, at the request of the operator or on its own initiative, commence an administrative proceeding after providing prompt public notice of such proceeding in accordance with paragraph (2) to consider whether—

(A) the cable operator has substantially complied with the material terms of the existing franchise and with applicable law;

(B) the quality of the operator's service including signal quality, response to consumer complaints, and billing practices, but without regard to the mix, quality, or level of cable services or other services provided over the system, has been reasonable in light of community needs;

(C) the operator has the financial, legal, and technical ability to provide the services, facilities, and equipment as set forth in the operator's proposal; and

(D) the operator's proposal is reasonable to meet the future cable-related community needs and interests, taking into account the cost of meeting such needs and interests.

. . .

(3) At the completion of a proceeding under this subsection, the franchising authority shall issue a written decision granting or denying the proposal for renewal based upon the record of such proceeding, and transmit a copy of such decision to the cable operator. Such decision shall state the reasons therefor.

(d) Any denial of a proposal for renewal shall be based on one or more adverse findings made with respect to the factors described in subparagraphs (A) through (D) of subsection (c)(1) . . ..

. . .

OBSCENE PROGRAMMING

Sec. 639. [47 U.S.C.A. § 639.]

Whoever transmits over any cable system any matter which is obscene or otherwise unprotected by the Constitution of the United States shall be fined not more than $10,000 or imprisoned not more than two years, or both.

Appendix C

CODE OF ETHICS

THE SOCIETY OF PROFESSIONAL JOURNALISTS, SIGMA DELTA CHI

(Adopted by the national convention, Nov. 16, 1973).

The Society of Professional Journalists, Sigma Delta Chi, believes the duty of journalists is to serve truth.

We believe the agencies of mass communication are carriers of public discussion and information, acting on their Constitutional mandate and freedom to learn and report their facts. *in doing*

We believe in public enlightenment as the forerunner of justice, *so are actually forerunner of justice* and in our Constitutional role to seek the truth as part of the public's right to know the truth.

We believe those responsibilities carry obligations that require journalists to perform with intelligence, objectivity, accuracy, and fairness.

To these ends, we declare acceptance of the standards of practice here set forth:

RESPONSIBILITY: The public's right to know of events of public importance and interest is the overriding mission of the mass media. The purpose of distributing news and enlightened opinion is to serve the general welfare. Journalists who use their professional status as representatives of the public for selfish or other unworthy motives violate a high trust.

FREEDOM OF THE PRESS: Freedom of the press is to be guarded as an inalienable right of people in a free society. It carries with it the freedom and the responsibility to discuss, question, and challenge actions and utterances of our government and of our public and private institutions. Journalists uphold the right to speak unpopular opinions and the privilege to agree with the majority.

ETHICS: Journalists must be free of obligations to any interest other than the public's right to know.

1. Gifts, favors, free travel, special treatment or privileges can compromise the integrity of journalists and their employers. Nothing of value should be accepted.

2. Secondary employment, political involvement, holding public office, and service in community organizations should be avoided if it compromises the integrity of the journalists and their employers. Journalists and their employers should conduct their personal lives in

694

a manner which protects them from conflict of interest, real or apparent. Their responsibilities to the public are paramount. That is the nature of their profession.

3. So-called news communications from private sources should not be published or broadcast without substantiation of their claims to news value.

4. Journalists will seek news that serves the public interest, despite the obstacles. They will make constant efforts to assure that the public's business is conducted in public and that public records are open to public inspection.

5. Journalists acknowledge the newsman's ethic of protecting confidential sources of information.

ACCURACY AND OBJECTIVITY: Good faith with the public is the foundation of all worthy journalism.

1. Truth is our ultimate goal.

2. Objectivity in reporting the news is another goal which serves as the mark of an experienced professional. It is a standard of performance toward which we strive. We honor those who achieve it.

3. There is no excuse for inaccuracies or lack of thoroughness.

4. Newspaper headlines should be fully warranted by the contents of the articles they accompany. Photographs and telecasts should give an accurate picture of an event and not highlight a minor incident out of context.

5. Sound practice makes clear distinction between news reports and expressions of opinion. News reports should be free of opinion or bias and represent all sides of an issue.

6. Partisanship in editorial comment which knowingly departs from the truth violates the spirit of American journalism.

7. Journalists recognize their responsibility for offering informed analysis, comment, and editorial opinion on public events and issues. They accept the obligation to present such material by individuals whose competence, experience, and judgment qualify them for it.

8. Special articles or presentations devoted to advocacy or the writer's own conclusions and interpretations should be labeled as such.

FAIR PLAY: Journalists at all times will show respect for the dignity, privacy, rights, and well-being of people encountered in the course of gathering and presenting the news.

1. The news media should not communicate unofficial charges affecting reputation or moral character without giving the accused a chance to reply.

2. The news media must guard against invading a person's right to privacy.

3. The media should not pander to morbid curiosity about details of vice and crime.

4. It is the duty of news media to make prompt and complete correction of their errors.

5. Journalists should be accountable to the public for their reports and the public should be encouraged to voice its grievances against the media. Open dialogue with our readers, viewers, and listeners should be fostered.

PLEDGE: Journalists should actively censure and try to prevent violations of these standards, and they should encourage their observance by all newspeople. Adherence to this code of ethics is intended to preserve the bond of mutual trust and respect between American journalists and the American people.

Appendix D
FEDERAL COMMUNICATIONS COMMISSION

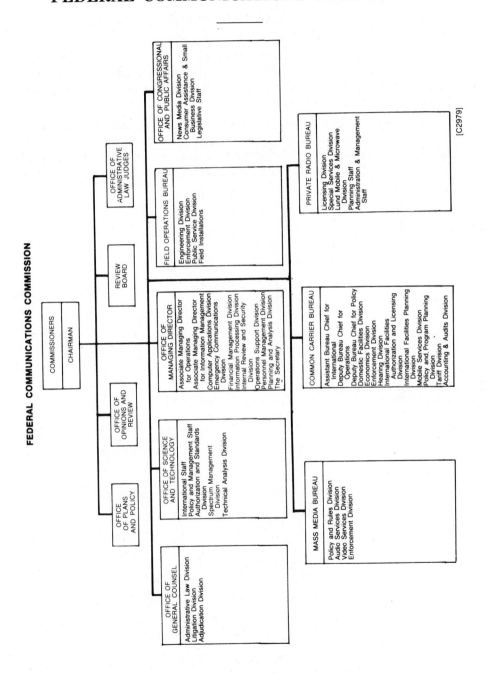

INDEX

†